JAPANESE THINGS

NOTE TO THE READER:

All the titles mentioned in the "books recommended" after
each article are published by the Charles E. Tuttle Company,
Inc., of Rutland, Vermont & Tokyo, Japan.

JAPANESE THINGS

Being Notes on Various Subjects
Connected with Japan

For the use of travelers and others

BY

BASIL HALL CHAMBERLAIN

CHARLES E. TUTTLE CO.: PUBLISHERS
Rutland, Vermont & Tokyo, Japan

Representatives
Continental Europe: BOXERBOOKS, INC., *Zurich*
British Isles: PRENTICE-HALL INTERNATIONAL, INC., *London*
Australasia: PAUL FLESCH & CO., PTY. LTD., *Melbourne*
Canada: M. G. HURTIG LTD., *Edmonton*

Published by the Charles E. Tuttle Company, Inc.
of Rutland, Vermont & Tokyo, Japan
with editorial offices at
Suido 1-chome, 2-6, Bunkyo-ku, Tokyo, Japan

Library of Congress Catalog Card No. 76-87791

International Standard Book No. 0-8048-0713-2

First Tuttle edition published 1971

0300-000216-4615
PRINTED IN JAPAN

Les longs ouvrages me font peur.
Loin d'épuiser une matière,
On n'en doit prendre que la fleur.

(La Fontaine.)

PUBLISHER'S FOREWORD

The publisher is proud to present a revised reprint of one of the stalwarts in the field of literature about Japan.

Japanese Things (originally entitled *Things Japanese*) was written by the late Prof. Basil Hall Chamberlain, a name revered among the Japanese as well as among present-day scholars who recognize the author's invaluable contribution to an understanding of this great and industrious nation which has leaped into the forefront of modern technological progress.

Prof. Chamberlain's book is as necessary today as it was at the turn of the century, for it acts as a healthy balance to this great progress—its articles pointing up the fabric, strength, and character of a nation which has been able to strike a happy balance between past and present.

Count Aisuke Kabayama in 1935 paid the author a high tribute when he said, "Professor Chamberlain, a foreigner, an Englishman, taught Japanese and Japan to the Japanese."

Chamberlain's contributions were many, including the first translation of the Japanese *Kojiki* and the first Japanese grammar ever written by a foreigner. A professor of Japanese and philology in the Imperial University of Tokyo, he introduced Japan to the West. This introduction, fortunately, is continued in the present work, a sizable outpouring of Japanalia as charming and impressive as the people written about. This book is a reprint of the fifth revised edition (1905) with a revised bibliography.

PREFACE

In the unlikely event of any one instituting a minute comparison between this edition and its predecessor, he would find minor alterations innumerable,—here a line erased, there a paragraph added, or again a figure changed, a statement qualified, a description or a list brought up to date. But to take it altogether, the book remains the same as heretofore. It would seem to have found favour in many quarters, to judge from the manner in which, years after its first appearance, newspapers and book-makers continue to quote wholesale from it without acknowledgment; and the title, which cost us much cogitation, and which we borrowed ultimately from the Spanish phrase *cosas de España,* has passed into general use, even coming to supply titles for similar works written about other lands in imitation of this one.

The article on *Archæology* contributed by Mr. W. G. Aston, C.M.G., to the second edition, and that on *Geology* by Prof. John Milne, F.R.S., remain untouched. Best thanks, once more, to these kind friends, as also to Mr. James Murdoch, Mr. H. V. Henson, Rev. Dr. D. C. Greene, and Abbé J. N. Guérin, who have supplied

information on points beyond the scope of our own
knowledge. To Mr. W. B. Mason and to Mr. W. D.
Cox we are under special obligations,—to the former for
constant advice and assistance during the progress of
the work, to the latter for revision of the proofs, a task
of a different order of difficulty in this country from what
it is at home with printers whose native language is
English. The greater part of the index has been compiled
by Mr. E. B. Clarke, of the First Higher School, Tōkyō.

MIYANOSHITA,
November, 1904.

NOTE ON THE PRONUNCIATION OF JAPANESE WORDS

Sound the vowels and diphthongs as in Italian, that is (approximately),

a *as in* "*father.*"	**u** *as in* "*bush.*"
e " " "*men.*"	**ai** " *the* "*y*" *of* "*my.*"
i " " "*police.*"	**ei** " " "*ay*" *of* "*may.*"
o " " "*for.*"	**au** " " "*ow*" *of* "*cow.*"

Distinguish long vowels from short, as in Latin; thus tori, "*bird,*" *but* tōri, "*street;*" zutsu, "[*one, etc.*] *at a time,*" *but* zutsū, "*headache.*"

Sound the consonants as in English, noting only that **g** *never has the* "*j*" *sound. At the beginning of a word it is pronounced as in* "*give;*" *in the middle it has the sound of English* **ng**. *Note, too, that* **z** *before* "*u*" *is pronounced as* **dz**, *thus* Kōzu (*kō-dzu*).

Consonants written double are distinctly pronounced double, as in Italian. Thus amma, "*a shampooer,*" *sounds quite different from* ama, "*a nun.*" (*Compare such English words as* "*oneness,*" "*shot-tower.*")

There is little if any tonic accent, all syllables, except such as have long quantity, being pronounced evenly and lightly, as in French. For instance, the word ama *given above sounds almost exactly like the French word* "*amas,*" *and would not be understood if pronounced like English* "*armour.*"

Sound the vowels and diphthongs as in Italian, thus is represented approximately.

INTRODUCTORY CHAPTER

To have lived through the transition stage of modern Japan makes a man feel preternaturally old; for here he is in modern times, with the air full of talk about bicycles and bacilli and "spheres of influence," and yet he can himself distinctly remember the Middle Ages. The dear old Samurai who first initiated the present writer into the mysteries of the Japanese language, wore a queue and two swords. This relic of feudalism now sleeps in Nirvana. His modern successor, fairly fluent in English, and dressed in a serviceable suit of dittos, might almost be a European, save for a certain obliqueness of the eyes and scantiness of beard. Old things pass away between a night and a morning. The Japanese boast that they have done in thirty or forty years what it took Europe half as many centuries to accomplish. Some even go further, and twit us Westerns with falling behind in the race. It is waste of time to go to Germany to study philosophy, said a Japanese savant recently returned from Berlin:—the lectures there are elementary, the subject is better taught at Tōkyō.

Thus does it come about that, having arrived in Japan in 1873, we ourselves feel well-nigh four hundred years old, and assume without more ado the two well-known privileges of old age—garrulity and an authoritative air. We are perpetually being asked questions about Japan. Here then are the answers, put into the shape of a dictionary, not of words but of things,—or shall we rather say a guide-book, less to places than to subjects ?—not an encyclopædia, mind you, not the vain attempt by one man to treat exhaustively of all things, but only sketches of many things. The old and the new will be found cheek by jowl. What will not be found is padding ; for padding is unpardonable in any book on Japan, where the material is so plentiful that the chief difficulty is to know what to omit.

In order to enable the reader to supply deficiencies and to form his own opinions, if haply he should be of so unusual a turn of mind as to desire so to do, we have, at the end of almost every article, indicated the names of trustworthy works bearing on the subject treated in that article. For the rest, this book explains itself. Any reader who detects errors or omissions in it will render the author an invaluable service by writing to him to point them out. As a little encouragement in this direction, we will ourselves lead the way by presuming to give each reader, especially each globe-trotting reader, a small piece of advice. We take it for granted, of course, that there are no Japanese listening, and the advice is this : whatever you do, don't expatiate, in the presence of Japanese of the new school, on those old, quaint, and beautiful things Japanese which rouse your most genuine admiration. Antiquated persons do doubtless exist here and there to whom Buddhist piety is precious ; others may still secretly cherish the swords bequeathed to them by their knightly forefathers ; quite a little coterie has taken up with art; and there are those who practise the tea ceremonies, arrange flowers according to the traditional esthetic rules, and even perform the mediæval lyric dramas. But all this is merely a backwater. Speaking generally, the educated Japanese have done with their past. They want to be somebody else and something else than what they have been and still partly are.

When Sir Edwin Arnold came to Tōkyō, he was entertained at a banquet by a distinguished company including officials, journalists, and professors, in fact, representative modern Japanese of the best class. In returning thanks for this hospitality, Sir Edwin made a speech in which he lauded Japan to the skies—and lauded it justly—as the nearest earthly approach to Paradise or to Lotus-land,—so fairy-like, said he, is its scenery, so exquisite its art, so much more lovely still that almost divine sweetness of disposition, that charm of demeanour, that politeness humble without servility and elaborate without affectation, which place Japan high above all other countries in nearly all those things that make life worth living. (We do not give his exact words, but we give the general drift.) —Now, do you think that the Japanese were satisfied with this meed of praise? Not a bit of it. Out comes an article next morning in the chief paper which had been represented at the banquet—an article acknowledging, indeed, the truth of Sir Edwin's description, but pointing out that it conveyed, not praise, but pitiless condemnation. Art forsooth, scenery, sweetness of disposition! cries this editor. Why did not Sir Edwin praise us for huge industrial enterprises, for commercial talent, for wealth, political sagacity, powerful armaments? Of course it is because he could not honestly do so. He has gauged us at our true value, and tells us in effect that we are only pretty weaklings.

Since Sir Edwin Arnold's time, doubtless, more than one war has been fought and won, and has proved to an astonished world and to the Japanese themselves that they are no weaklings, but extremely plucky, practical men. Since his time, too, Japan's sunny towns and even her green valleys have been darkened by the smoke of factory chimneys, and the flag of her merchant marine has been seen in every sea. Nevertheless, the feeling above alluded to persists, and to us it appears perfectly natural under the circumstances. For, after all, Japan must continue ever more and more to modernise herself if the basis of her new departure is to remain solid, if her swiftly growing ambition is to be gratified, and if her minister of finance is to be able to make both ends meet. Besides which, our European world of thought, of enterprise, of colossal scientific achievement, has been as much a wonder-world to the Japanese as Old Japan could ever be to us. There is this difference, however. Old Japan was to us a delicate little wonder-world of sylphs and fairies. Europe and America, with their railways, their telegraphs, their gigantic commerce, their gigantic armies and navies, their endless applied arts founded on chemistry and mathematics, were to the Japanese a wonder-world of irresistible genii and magicians. The Japanese have, it is true, evinced less appreciation of our literature. They esteem us whimsical for attaching so much importance as we do to poetry, to music, to religion, to speculative disquisitions. Our material greatness has completely dazzled them, as well it might. They know also well enough—for every Eastern nation knows it— that our Christian and humanitarian professions are really nothing but bunkum.* The history of India, of Egypt, of Turkey, is no secret to them. More familiar still, because fought out at their very gates, is the great and instructive case of the West versus China,—six or seven young tigers against one old cow. The Japanese would be blind indeed, did they not see that their best security for continued safety and success lies in the determination to be strong, and in the endeavour not to be too different from the rest of mankind; for the mob of Western nations will tolerate eccentricity of appearance no more than will a mob of roughs.

Indeed, scarcely any even among those who implore the Japanese to remain as they are, refrain, as a matter of fact, from urging them to make all sorts of changes. " Japanese dress for ladies is simply perfection," we hear one of these persons cry; " only don't you think that gloves might be added with advantage ? And then, too, ought not something to be done with the skirt to prevent it from opening in front, just for the sake of decency, you know ?" Says another, whose special vanity is Japanese music (there is considerable distinction about this taste, for it is a rare one)—says he—" Now please keep your music from perishing. Keep it just as it is, so curious to the archæologist, so beautiful, for all that the jeerers may say,

---

* It has pained the writer to find this sentence misinterpreted by some otherwise friendly critics of an earlier edition (the *Spectator*, for instance) into so shallow and arrogant an assertion as that " Christianity and humanitarianism are nothing but bunkum." (!) What is meant is simply what is said in the text, namely, that *our professions* are bunkum. No doubt, individuals may occasionally be found whose practice carries out their profession. But can an impartial student of history deny that, *as nations*, the Christian nations (so-called) flout their professions with their deeds ? Sometimes their hypocrisy is piquantly transparent, as when, to take a very modern instance, we find figuring prominently in the list of reasons officially alleged for the American annexation of Hawaii " the intimate part taken by citizens of the United States in there implanting the seeds of Christian civilisation." Could the most moral wolf desire any whiter wool for his sheep's clothing ?

There is only one small thing which I would advise you to do, and that is to harmonise it. Of course that would change its character a little. But no one would notice it, and the general effect would be improved." Yet another, an enthusiast for faience, wishes Japanese decorative methods to be retained, but to be applied to French forms, because no cup or plate made in Japan is so perfectly round as are the products of French kilns. A fourth delights in Japanese brocade, but suggests new breadths, in order to suit making up into European dresses. A fifth wants to keep Japanese painting exactly as it is, but with the trivial addition of perspective. A sixth—but a truce to the quoting of these self-confuting absurdities. Put into plain English, they mean, " Do so-and-so, only don't do it. Walk north, and at the same time take care to proceed in a southerly direction."

Meanwhile the Japanese go their own way. Who could expect that either their social conditions or their arts should remain unaltered when all the causes which produced the Old Japan of our dreams have vanished ? Feudalism has gone, isolation has gone, beliefs have been shattered, new idols have been set up, new and pressing needs have arisen. In the place of chivalry there is industrialism, in the place of a small class of aristocratic native connoisseurs there is a huge and hugely ignorant foreign public to satisfy. All the causes have changed, and yet it is expected that the effects will remain as heretofore !

No. Old Japan is dead, and the only decent thing to do with the corpse is to bury it. Then you can set up a monument over it, and, if you like, come and worship from time to time at the grave; for that would be quite " Japanesey." This unpretentious book is intended to be, as it were, the epitaph

recording the many and extraordinary virtues of the deceased,
—his virtues, but also his frailties. For, more careful of fact
than the generality of epitaphists, we have ventured to speak
out our whole mind on almost every subject, and to call things
by their right names, being persuaded that true appreciation is
always critical as well as kindly.

*　*　*　*　*　*　*　*

Yes, we repeat it, Old Japan is dead and gone, and Young
Japan reigns in its stead, as opposed in appearance and in aims
to its predecessor as history shows many a youthful prince to
have been to the late king, his father. The steam-whistle, the
newspaper, the voting-paper, the pillar-post at every street-
corner and even in remote villages, the clerk in shop or bank or
public office hastily summoned from our side to answer the ring
of the telephone bell, the railway replacing the palanquin, the
iron-clad replacing the war-junk,—these and a thousand other
startling changes testify that Japan is transported ten thousand miles away from her former moorings. She is transported out of her patriarchal calm into the tumult of Western competition,—a competition active right along the line, in diplomacy and war, in industries, in shipping, possibly even in
colonisation. Nevertheless, as Madcap Hal, when once seated
on the throne, showed plainly, despite all individual difference,
that the blood of prudent Henry IV ran in his veins, so is it
abundantly clear to those who have dived beneath the surface
of the modern Japanese upheaval that more of the past has
been retained than has been let go. It is not merely that the
revolution itself was an extremely slow growth, a gradual

movement taking a century and a half to mature.* It is that the national character persists intact, manifesting no change in essentials. Circumstances have deflected it into new channels, that is all. The arduous intellectual training of the Japanese gentry of former days—the committing to memory of the Confucian classics—fostered a mental habit at once docile, retentive, apt for detail. With these very same qualities their sons sit to-day at the feet of the science of the West. The devotion of the Samurai to his Daimyō and his clan was unsurpassed; for them, at any time, he would offer up his life, his all. This same loyal flame glows still at a white heat; only, the horizon having been widened by the removal of provincial barriers and the fall of petty feudal thrones, the one Emperor, the united nation have focussed all its rays into a single burning-point. The Japanese of former days, even when political combination for any purpose was penal, always moved in families, in clans, in wards of townsmen, in posses of peasants, in any corporate way rather than as individuals. The boycotts, the combines, the sudden fashions and gusts of feeling before which the whole nation bends like grass, manifest exactly the same trait in a novel guise. To take a more radical characteristic, the ingrained tendency of the national mind towards the imitation of foreign models does but repeat to-day, and on an equally large scale, its exploit of twelve centuries ago. At that early period it flung itself on Chinese civilisation as it has now flung itself on ours; and in both cases alike certain reservations have been made. The old national religion, for instance, was not abolished then, neither has it been abolished now, though in both cases full latitude has been

---

* See Article on HISTORY.

accorded by this nation of thoroughgoing latitudinarians to the alien religious and philosophical ideas.

Having absorbed all the manifestly useful elements of our culture, Young Japan's eager wish is to communicate them to her neighbours. To act as broker between West and East is her self-imposed mission. We cannot help thinking that Japan's precept and example will more rapidly leaven the Chinese lump with the leaven of Europeanism than Europe has been able to do in her own person,—and this for the simple reason that though Japan and her continental neighbours heartily despise each other, as the manner of neighbours is, they nevertheless understand each other in a way in which we can never hope to understand any of them. Europe's illusions about the Far East are truly crude. Who would dream of coupling together New-Englanders and Patagonians, simply because arbitrary custom has affixed the single name of " America " to the two widely separated regions which these two peoples inhabit ? Yet persons not otherwise undiscerning continue to class, not only the Chinese, but even the Japanese, with Arabs and Persians, on the ground that all are equally " Orientals," " Asiatics," though they dwell thousands of miles apart in space, and tens of thousands of miles apart in culture. Such is the power over us of words which we have ourselves coined. Then a further step is taken : on a basis of mere words a fantastic structure is raised of mere notions, among which the " Yellow Peril " has had most vogue of late. When a new power, or an old one in new shape, arises on soil which we have labelled " Western,"—for instance, Germany or Italy during the lifetime of men still living, the United States or Russia at an earlier date,—no one describes any special menace in such an event; it is recognised as one of the familiar processes of history. But let the word "Asia" be sounded, and at once a spectre is conjured up. In fact, we find ourselves back in that strange limbo of contradictions already noticed; for the very same folks blow hot and cold, raving about Japan's perfections at one moment, fearing her possible excesses at another.

It might be interesting to push these considerations further. But Japan herself is our theme, not Europe's fancies concerning her. We have merely alluded to these last in pursuance of our general plan, which is to indicate lines of thought for the reader himself to follow out. He will find leisure for such meditations as he speeds along in his jinrikisha, or else at some wayside resthouse among the blossom-strewn hills, while waiting for the dainty handmaiden to bring him his thimbleful of tea.

THINGS JAPANESE

Abacus. Learn to count on the abacus—the *soroban,* as the Japanese call it—and you will often be able to save a large percentage on your purchases. The abacus is that instrument, composed of beads sliding on wires fixed in a frame, with which many of us learnt the multiplication table in early childhood. In Japan it is used, not only by children, but by adults, who still mostly prefer it to our method of figuring with pen and paper. As for mental arithmetic, that does not exist in this archipelago. Tell any ordinary Japanese to add 5 and 7: he will flounder hopelessly, unless his familiar friend, the abacus, is at hand. And here we come round again to the practical advantage of being able to read off at sight a number figured on this instrument. You have been bargaining at a curio-shop, we will suppose. The shopman has got perplexed. He refers to his list, and then calculates on the instrument (which of course he takes for granted that you do not understand) the lowest price for which he can let you have the article in question. Then he raises his head, and, with a bland smile, assures you that the cost of it to himself was so and so, naming a price considerably larger than the real one. You have the better of him, if you can read his figuring of the sum. If you cannot, ten to one he has the better of you.

The principle of the abacus is this:—Each of the five beads in the broad lower division of the board represents one unit, and each solitary bead in the narrow upper division represents five units. Each vertical column is thus worth ten units. Furthermore, each vertical column represents units ten times greater than those in the column immediately to the right of it, exactly as in our own system of notation by means of Arabic numerals. Any sum in arithmetic can be done on the abacus, even to extracting of square and cube roots; and Dr. Knott, the chief English—or, to be quite correct, the chief Scotch—writer on the subject, is of opinion that Japanese methods excel ours in rapidity. Perhaps he is a little enthusiastic. One can scarcely help thinking so of an author who refers to a new Japanese method of long division as "almost fascinating." The Japanese, it seems, have not only a multiplication table, but a division table besides. We confess that we do not understand the division table, even with Dr. Knott's explanations. Indeed we will confess more: we have never learnt the abacus at all! If we recommend others to learn it, it is because we hope that, for their own sake, they will do as we tell them and not do as we do. Personally we have found one method of ciphering enough, and a great deal more than enough, to poison the happiness of one life-time.

The use of the abacus is not the only peculiarity of this nation in matters numerical. A more irritating one to the accurate European mind is their habit of "inclusive" reckoning. An example or two will best make this clear. You arrived in April, say. It is now June. According to the Japanese, you have been here three months—for the month of your arrival and the present month are both counted in. A child is born in December, 1901. By January, 1902, they currently talk of the child as being two years old, because it has lived through a *part* of two separate years. The thing may be exaggerated a degree further still, when, forgetting that the Japanese year formerly began some time in our February (as the Chinese year still does), they fail to make allowance for this in the case of births that took place in January or early February, previous to the reform of the calendar in 1873. In the case of a public man who died early in 1901, at the (real) age of 65, we noticed that all the obituaries were wrong by three years. They credited him with being 68; and of the various other dates mentioned, some were two years out, some three, according to the month to which they referred. The new-comer will therefore do well to treat Japanese statements regarding dates and ages with caution.

Books recommended. *The Japanese Abacus* by Takashi Kojima; *Advanced Abacus* by Takashi Kojima.

Abdication. The abdication of monarchs, which is exceptional in Europe, has for many ages been the rule in Japan. It came into vogue in the seventh century together with Buddhism, whose doctrines led men to retire from worldly cares and pleasures into solitude and contemplation. But it was made use of by unscrupulous ministers, who placed infant puppets on the throne, and caused them to abdicate on attaining to maturity. Thus it was a common thing during the Middle Ages for three Mikados to be alive at the same time, —a boy on the throne, his father or brother who had abdicated, and his grandfather or other relative who had abdicated also. From A.D. 987 to 991, there were as many as four Mikados all alive together:—Reizei Tennō, who had ascended the throne at the age of eighteen, and who abdicated at twenty; En-yū Tennō, emperor at eleven and abdicated at twenty-six; Kwazan Tennō, emperor at seventeen and abdicated at nineteen; and Ichijō Tennō, who had just ascended the throne as a little boy of seven. Under the Mikado Go-Nijō (A.D. 1302-8) there were actually *five* Mikados all alive together, namely Go-Nijō Tennō himself, made emperor at seventeen, and his four abdicated predecessors—Go-Fukakusa Tennō, emperor at four and abdicated at seventeen; Kameyama Tennō, emperor at eleven and abdicated at twenty-six; Go-Uda Tennō, emperor at eight and abdicated at twenty-one; and Fushimi Tennō, emperor at twenty-three and abdicated the same year. Sometimes it was arranged that the children of two rival branches of the Imperial family should succeed each other alternately. This it was, in part at least, which led to the civil war in the fourteenth century between what were known as "the Northern and Southern Courts;" for it was of course impossible that so extraordinary an arrangement should long be adhered to without producing violent dissensions.

After a time, it became so generally recognised that the monarch in name must not be monarch in fact, and *vice versâ*, that abdication, or rather deposition (for that is what it practically amounted to), was almost a *sine quâ non* of the inheritance of such scanty shreds of authority as imperious ministers still deigned to leave to their nominal lords and masters. When a Mikado abdicated, he was said to *ascend* to the rank of abdicated Mikado. It was no longer necessary, as at an earlier period, to sham asceticism. The abdicated Mikado surrounded himself with wives and a whole Court, and sometimes really helped to direct public affairs. Nor was abdication confined to sovereigns. Heads of noble houses abdicated too. In later times the middle and lower classes began to imitate their betters. Until the period of the late revolution, it was an almost universal custom for a man to become what is termed an *inkyo* after passing middle age. *Inkyo* means literally "dwelling in retirement." He who enters on this state gives over his property to his heirs, generally resigns all office, and lives on the bounty of his children, free to devote himself henceforth to pleasure or to study. Old age being so extraordinarily honoured in Japan, the *inkyo* has no reason to dread Lear's fate. He knows that he will always be dutifully tended by sons who are not waiting to find out "how the old man will cut up." The new government of Japan is endeavouring to put a stop to the practice of *inkyo*, as being barbarous because not European. But to the people at large it appears, on the contrary, barbarous that a man should go on toiling and striving, when past the time of life at which he is fitted to do good work.

Books recommended. *Japan: An Attempt at Interpretation* by Lafcadio Hearn; *A Japanese Miscellany* by Lafcadio Hearn.

Acupuncture. Acupuncture, one of the three great nostrums of the practitioners of the Far East (the other two being massage and the moxa), was brought over from China to Japan before the dawn of history. Dr. W. N. Whitney describes it as follows in his *Notes on the History of Medical Progress in Japan,* published in Vol. XII. Part IV. of the "Asiatic Transactions," p. 354:—

" As practised by the Japanese acupuncturists, the operation consists in perforating the skin and underlying tissues to a depth, as a rule, not exceeding one-half to three-quarters of an inch, with fine needles of gold, silver, or steel. The form and construction of these needles vary, but, generally speaking, they are several inches long, and of an average diameter of one forty-eighth of an inch. Each needle is usually fastened into a handle, which is spirally grooved from end to end.

" To perform the operation, the handle of the needle is held lightly between the thumb and first finger of the left hand, the point resting upon the spot to be punctured. A slight blow is then given upon the head of the instrument with a small mallet held in the right hand; and the needle is gently twisted until its point has penetrated to the desired depth, where it is left for a few seconds and then slowly withdrawn, and the skin in the vicinity of the puncture rubbed for a few moments. The number of perforations ranges from one to twenty, and they are usually made in the skin of the abdomen, although other portions of the body are not unfrequently punctured."

Adams (Will). Will Adams, the first Englishman that ever resided in Japan, was a native of Gillingham, near Chatham, in the county of Kent. Having followed the sea from his youth up, he took service, in the year 1598, as " Pilot Maior of a fleete of five sayle," which had been equipped by Dutch merchants for the purpose of trading to Spanish America. From " Perow" a portion of the storm-tossed fleet came on to " Iapon," arriving at a port in the province of Bungo, not far from " Langasacke " (Nagasaki), on the 19th April, 1600. From that time until his death in May 1620, Adams remained in an exile which, though gilded, was none the less bitterly deplored. The English pilot, brought first as a captive into the presence of Ieyasu, who was then on the point of becoming practically what Adams calls him, " Emperour " of Japan, had immediately been recognised by that shrewd judge of character as an able and an honest

man. That he and his nation were privately slandered to
Ieyasu by " the Iesuites and the Portingalls," who were at that
time the only other Europeans in the country, probably did him
more good than harm in the Japanese ruler's eyes. He was retained at the Japanese court, and employed as a shipbuilder,
and also as a kind of diplomatic agent when other English and
Dutch traders began to arrive. In fact, it was by his good
offices that the foundations were laid both of English trade in
Japan and also of the more permanent Dutch settlement. During his latter years, he for a time exchanged the Japanese
service for that of the English factory established by Captain
John Saris at " Firando " (Hirado) near Nagasaki; and he
made two voyages, one to the Luchu Islands and another to
Siam. His constantly reiterated desire to see his native land
again, and his wife and children, was to the last frustrated by
adverse circumstances. So far as the wife was concerned, he
partially comforted himself, sailor fashion, by taking another,
—a Japanese with whom he lived comfortably for many years
on the estate granted him by Ieyasu at Hemi, where their two
graves are shown to this day. Hemi, at that time a separate
village, has since become a suburb of the bustling modern
seaport, Yokosuka, and a railway station now occupies the site
of the old pilot's abode. Another adventurer, who visited him
there, describes Will Adams's place thus: " This Phebe* is a
Lordshipp geuen to Capt. Adames pr. the ould Emperour,† to
hym and his for eaver, and confermed to his sonne, called
Joseph. There is above 100 farms, or hows-holds, vppon it,
besides others vnder them, all which are his vassalls, and he
hath power of lyfe and death ouer them they being his slaues;
and he hauing as absolute authoritie ouer them as any tono (or
king) in Japan hath over his vassales." From further details
it would seem that he used his authority kindly, so that the
neighbours " reioiced (as it should seeme) of Captain Adames
retorne."

---

* Our author means Hemi.

† Iyeyasu was then dead.

Will Adams's letters have been published by the Hakluyt Society in their " Memorials of Japan " (*sic*), and republished in a cheaper form at Yokohama. They are well-worth reading, both for the lifelike silhouette of the writer which stands out from their quaintly spelt pages, and for the picture given by him of Japan as it then was, when the land swarmed with Catholic friars and Catholic converts, when no embargo had yet been laid on foreign commerce, and when the native energy of the Japanese people had not yet been numbed by two centuries and a half of bureaucracy and timid seclusion.

Adoption. It is strange, but true, that you may often go into a Japanese family and find half-a-dozen persons calling each other parent and child, brother and sister, uncle and nephew, and yet being really either no blood-relations at all, or else relations in quite different degrees from those conventionally assumed. Galton's books could never have been written in Japan; for though genealogies are carefully kept, they mean nothing, at least from a scientific point of view—so universal is the practice of adoption, from the top of society to the bottom. This it is which explains such apparent anomalies as a distinguished painter, potter, actor, or what not, almost always having a son distinguished in the same line:—he has simply adopted his best pupil. It also explains the fact of Japanese families not dying out.

So completely has adoption become part and parcel of the national life that Mr. Shigeno An-eki, the best Japanese authority on the subject, enumerates no less than ten different categories of adopted persons. Adoption is resorted to, not only to prevent the extinction of families and the consequent neglect of the spirits of the departed, but also in order to regulate the size of families. Thus, a man with too many children hands over one or more of them to some friend who has none. To adopt a person is also the simplest way to leave him money, it not being usual in Japan to nominate strangers as one's heirs. Formerly, too, it was sometimes a means of money-making, not to the adopted, but to the adopter. " It

was customary "—so writes the authority whom we quote below—" for the sons of the court-nobles, when they reached the
age of majority, to receive an income from the Government.
It often happened that when an officer had a son who was,
say, only two or three years old, he would adopt a lad who was
about fifteen (the age of majority), and then apply for a grant
of land or rice for him; after he had secured this, he would
make his own son the *yōshi* [adopted son] of the newly adopted youth, and thus, when the former came of age, the officer
was entitled to apply for another grant of land."—With this
may be compared the plan often followed by business people at
the present day. A merchant adopts his head clerk, in order
to give him a personal interest in the firm. The clerk then
adopts his patron's son, with the understanding that he himself is to retire in the latter's favour when the latter shall be
of a suitable age. If the clerk has a son, then perhaps that
son will be adopted by the patron's son. Thus a sort of alternate headship is kept up, the surname always remaining
the same.

For some time after the late revolution, adoption was a
favourite method of evading the conscription, as only-sons
were exempted from serving. Fond parents, anxious to assist
a favourite son to this exemption, would cause him to be
adopted by some childless friend. After a few years, it might
perhaps be possible to arrange for the lad's return to his
former family and resumption of his original surname.

Until quite recently the sole way in which a foreigner could
be naturalised was by getting a Japanese with a daughter to
adopt him, and then marrying the daughter. This may sound
like a joke, but it is not. It is a sober, legal fact, recognised
as such by the various judicial and consular authorities, and
acted on in several well-authenticated instances. Indeed, it
is still the easiest method to be pursued by those desirous of
naturalising themselves in this country.

We recommend, as a good occupation for a rainy day, the
endeavour to trace out the real relationships (in our European

sense of the word) of some of the reader's Japanese servants
or friends. Unless we are much mistaken, this will prove to
be a puzzle of the highest order of difficulty. (See also Article
on MARRIAGE.)

Books recommended. *Japan: An Attempt at Interpretation* by Lafcadio Hearn;
A Japanese Miscellany by Lafcadio Hearn.

Agriculture. Till recently the Japanese had neither manufactures nor foreign commerce, neither have they yet any flocks
of sheep and goats, and droves of geese, turkeys, or pigs. Even
cattle are comparatively scarce, and neither their flesh nor
their milk is in general use, beef being still regarded as a
luxury, and milk rather as a medicine than a food. The pas-
ture meadow and the farmyard are alike lacking. Here, far
more than in the West, agriculture in its narrower sense has
been all in all, forming the basis on which the whole social
fabric rests. Justly, therefore, in feudal times, did the
peasantry rank next to the Samurai or gentry, and before the
merchants and mechanics. Even under the new régime, more
than half the population is engaged in field labour, and nearly
half the national revenue flows from that source. There are
no large landed proprietors. As a rule, each farmer or peasant
tills his own field with the help of his sons and often his wife
and daughters; and the land is really his own, for the doctrine
that everything belongs absolutely to the Emperor is, of
course, only a convenient legal fiction. No wonder that he
works with a will.

In this land of mountains, barely twelve per cent. of the
entire surface can be cultivated, and even the cultivable portion is not highly fertile by nature. It is made so by subsoil
working, by minutely careful weeding, by manure judiciously
and laboriously applied, by terracing, and by an elaborate
method of irrigation. The whole agricultural system came
from China, and has altered little since the earliest ages.
The peasantry are the most conservative class in the nation,
and their implements still strangely primitive,—the plough in
common use, for instance, differing little from that of Egypt

in the time of the Pharaohs. The hoe is in great request. Spades of various shapes, harrows, and sickles are also used, together with an extremely rude type of flail and stamping trough; but Japanese rural economy knows nothing of wagons or wheelbarrows.

The Chinese and Japanese enumerate five cereals as the staples to which agricultural labour should be devoted. These are rice, barley, wheat, millet, and beans.* But rice ranks above all the rest,—equal in fact to all the others put together. These others are grown chiefly as winter crops, when the rice-fields have to lie fallow, or else in small patches, or on the higher ground, which want of water or a harsher climate renders unfit for the cultivation of the more important commodity.

The preparation of the rice-fields—" paddy-fields," as Europeans often call them—is extremely arduous, involving not only much hoeing, but the construction of perforated mud dams and a whole system of terracing, whereby water from a neighbouring stream is led gradually down from field to field; —for all high-class rice requires flooding, only an inferior sort being grown in the dry. Various manures are employed. The commonest is night-soil, whose daily conveyance all about the country apparently causes no distress to native noses. The seed is sown in small beds about the end of April, and it sprouts in five or six days. Early in June, the young shoots are plucked up and transplanted in rows. The generally lifeless fields may at that time be seen full of men and women standing knee-deep in the water and mud. Then comes the hot summer. What traveller in Japan will not recall, as the most characteristic feature of the summer landscape, those fields of vivid green, separated—chessboard-like—into squares which fill a gradually widening valley flanked by hills that rise abruptly, as if the whole had been cut out by the hand of man, as indeed it has through centuries of terracing ?

The rice-plant blossoms early in September, is reaped in October, and then hung up on short poles. Threshing is done

---

* The enumeration has differed slightly according to time and place.

either with the primitive flails above mentioned, or with a sort of large comb or heckle. Many Europeans believe that two rice crops are produced in the year. This occurs as a solitary exception in the province of Tosa, where the warming effect of the *Kuro-shio,* or Japanese Gulf Stream, makes itself felt with special energy. Elsewhere such a thing is rendered impossible by the length and severity of the winter.

Japanese rice is highly esteemed throughout the neighbouring countries, on account of its glutinous nature. The manner in which it is cooked makes it exceptionally palatable and nutritious, quite different from the Indian process, which leaves each grain separate and dry. Every one lives on it who can afford to do so; but as a rule, the peasantry cannot. Wheat, barley, and especially millet, are the real staples throughout the rural districts, rice being there treated as a luxury to be brought out only on high days and holidays, or to be resorted to in case of sickness. We once heard a beldame in a country village remark to another, with a grave shake of the head: " What ! do you mean to say that it has come to having to give her rice ? "—the unexpressed inference being that the patient's case must be alarming indeed, if the family had thought it necessary to resort to so expensive a dainty.

The market price of rice is quoted on 'change at so much per *hyō* (" bag ")*; but the retail vendors sell it at so many *shō* and *gō* per *yen* (Japanese dollar). In other words, in large transactions it is a fixed amount of the commodity itself that sells for a variable sum; in small purchases it is a fixed sum that is given for a variable amount of the commodity. The former method of calculation is familiar only to business men. But every pater and mater-familias takes a keen—not to say painful—interest in knowing whether rice is, say, 6 *shō* 1 *gō* per *yen*, or has advanced to 5 *shō* 9 *gō*. Four or five grades are habitually quoted, of which the extremes differ about 20 per cent. in price. Japanese rice is exported as a luxury to the neighbouring continent of Asia, which in return sends its

---

* See Article on WEIGHTS AND MEASURES.

poorer quality to be bought cheap by the Japanese lower classes. Hence the apparent anomaly that rice appears alike among Japanese imports and exports.

In the extreme south the sweet potato, which was introduced as late as A.D. 1698, now forms the chief food of the common people. Besides the cereals, vegetables of various sorts are raised, but are eaten chiefly pickled and in small quantities.

Some few of the principal agricultural industries, such as tea, camphor, and lacquer, will be found treated in separate articles.

Books recommended. *The New Far East* compiled by International Research Associates; *Meet Japan: A Modern Nation with a Memory* written under the auspices of Tsuneji Hibino.

Ainos. The Ainos, called by themselves *Ainu,* that is " men," are a very peculiar race, now inhabiting only the northern island of Yezo, but formerly widely spread all over the Japanese archipelago. The Japanese proper, arriving from the south-west, gradually pressed the Ainos back towards the east and north. It was only in the eighteenth century that they were completely subjugated. In retreating, the aborigines left the country strewn with place-names belonging to their own language. Such are, for instance, *Noto,* the name of the big promontory stretching out into the Sea of Japan (*nottu* means " promontory " in Aino), the *Tone-gawa,* or River Tone, near Tōkyō (*tanne* is Aino for " long "), and hundreds of others. So far as blood, however, is concerned, the Japanese have in the long run been little, if at all, affected by Aino influence. The simple reason is that the half-breeds, though numerous, die out in the second or third generation. The Ainos are the hairiest race in the world, their luxuriantly thick black beards and hirsute limbs giving them an appearance which contrasts strangely with the smoothness of their Japanese lords and masters. They are of sturdy build, and distinguished by a flattening of certain bones of the arm and leg (the *humerus* and *tibia*), which has been observed nowhere else except in the remains of some of the cave-men of Europe. The women tattoo moustaches on their upper lip, and geometrical patterns on their hands. Both sexes are of a mild and amiable disposition, but are terribly addicted to drunkenness. They are filthy in their persons, the practice of bathing being altogether unknown.*

The Ainos were till recently accustomed to live on the produce of the chase and the sea fisheries; but both these sources of subsistence have diminished since the settling of the island by the Japanese. Consequently they no longer hold up their heads as in former days, and notwithstanding the well-intentioned efforts of a paternal government, they seem doomed to disappear, though it is true that during the last twenty years their numbers have remained stationary at about 17,000. Their religion is a simple nature-worship. The sun, wind, ocean, bear, etc., are deified under the title of *Kamui,* "god," and whittled sticks are set up in their honour. The bear, though worshipped, is also sacrificed and eaten with solemnities that form the most original and picturesque feature of Aino life. Grace is said before meat. Mr. Batchelor quotes the following naive and touching form of words: "O thou Cereal Deity, we worship thee. Thou hast grown very well this year, and thy flavour will be sweet. Thou art good. The Goddess of Fire will be glad, and we shall rejoice greatly. O thou God! O thou divine Cereal! do thou nourish the people. I now partake of thee. I worship thee and give thee thanks." These poor people also treasure up numbers of charms or fetiches, such as feathers, snake-skins, the skulls of beasts or birds, etc., and their minds are saturated with a belief in various forms of magic and witchcraft.

Some of the Aino tales are quaint. Most of them embody

* Would-be investigators of Aino peculiarities should exercise scrupulous care in their choice of individuals for study, as almost every Aino village now includes a considerable percentage of half-breeds.

an attempt to account for some natural phenomenon. The following may serve as a specimen:—

WHY DOGS CANNOT SPEAK.

Formerly dogs could speak. Now they cannot. The reason is that a dog belonging to a certain man, a long time ago, inveigled his master into the forest under the pretext of showing him game, and there caused him to be devoured by a bear. Then the dog went home to his master's widow, and lied to her, saying: " My master has been killed by a bear. But when he was dying, he commanded me to tell you to marry me in his stead." The widow knew that the dog was lying. But he kept on urging her to marry him. So at last, in her grief and rage, she threw a handful of dust into his open mouth. This made him unable to speak any more, and therefore no dogs can speak even to this very day.

The Aino language is simple and harmonious. Its structure in great measure resembles that of Japanese; but there are some few fundamental divergences, such, for instance, as the possession of true personal pronouns and the formation of the passive voice by a prefix. The vocabulary, too, is quite distinct. The system of counting is extraordinarily cumbrous. Thus, if a man wants to say that he is thirty-nine years old, he must express himself thus: " I am nine, plus ten taken from two score." In Mr. Batchelor's translation of Matthew XII. 40, the phrase " forty days and forty nights " is thus rendered: *tokap rere ko tu hotne rere ko, kunne rere ko tu hotne rere ko,* that is, " day three days two score three days, black three days two score three days." Little wonder that the simpler Japanese numeration has come to supplant, in the mouths of many, this next to unmanageable system. In fact, the younger generation seems to be discarding the native language altogether in favour of Japanese. Hitherto the Aino have known nothing of the use of letters. Tales like the one we have quoted, and rude songs which are handed down orally from generation to generation, form their only literature.

Books recommended. *Folk Legends of Japan* by Richard M. Dorson; *Japan: An Attempt at Interpretation* by Lafcadio Hearn; *A Japanese Miscellany* by Lafcadio Hearn; *The Wonderful World of Netsuke: With One Hundred Masterpieces of Miniature Sculpture in Color* by Raymond Bushell.

Amusements. The favourite amusements of the Japanese are the ordinary theatre (*shibai*); the Nō theatre (but this is attended chiefly by the aristocracy); wrestling matches,— witnessing, not taking part in them; dinners enlivened by the performances of singing and dancing-girls; visits to temples, as much for purposes of pleasure as of devotion; picnics to places famous for their scenery, and especially to places noted for some particular blossom, such as the plum, cherry, or wistaria. The Japanese also divert themselves by composing verses in their own language and in Chinese, and by playing chess, checkers, and various games of the "Mother Goose" description, of which *sugoroku* is the chief. Ever since the early days of foreign intercourse they have likewise had certain kinds of cards, of which the *hana-garuta,* or "flower-cards," are the most popular kind,—so popular, indeed, and seductive that there is an official veto on playing the game for money. The cards are forty-eight in number, four for each month of the year, the months being distinguished by the flowers proper to them, and an extra value being attached to one out of each set of four, which is further distinguished by a bird or butterfly, and to a second which is inscribed with a line of poetry. Three people take part in the game, and there is a pool. The system of counting is rather complicated, but the ideas involved are graceful. There is another game of cards, in which stanzas from what are known as the "Hundred Poets" take the place of flowers. At this game no gambling is ever indulged in. It is rather an amusement for family parties, who at New Year time often sit up over it all night.

Some of the above diversions are shared in by the ladies; but take it altogether, their mode of life is much duller than that of their European sisters. Confucian ideas concerning the subjection of women still obtain to a great extent. Women are not, it is true, actually shut up, as in India; but it is considered that their true vocation is to sit at home. Hence visiting is much less practised in Japan than with us. It is further to be observed, to the credit of the Japanese, that amusement, though permitted, is never exalted by them to the rank of the great and serious business of life. In England— at least among the upper classes—a man's shooting, fishing, and golf, a girl's dances, garden-parties, and country-house visiting appear to be the centre round which all the family plans revolve. In Japan, in the contrary, amusements are merely picked up by the way, and are all the more appreciated.*

Some sixteen or seventeen years ago, it looked as if the state of things here sketched were about to undergo considerable modification. Poker, horse-racing, even shooting and lawn-tennis, had begun to find devotees among Japanese men, while the fair sex, abandoning their own charming costume for the corsets and furbelows of Europe, were seen boldly to join in the ball-room fray. True, as Netto wittily remarks in his *Papierschmetterlinge aus Japan,* " most of them showed by the expression of their faces that they were making a sacrifice on the altar of civilisation." Happily a reaction supervened, older customs and costumes were resumed, and on the now very rare occasions when Japanese ladies enter a ball-room, it is as spectators only, and in their infinitely more attractive native garb.

The sports of Japanese children include kite-flying, top-spinning, battledore and shuttlecock, making snow men, playing with dolls, etc., etc.,—in fact, most of our old nursery friends, but modified by the *genius loci.* The large, grotesquely coloured papier-mâché dogs given to babies, often by the kennelful,

---

* A critic of the first edition humorously suggested that, had the author been a merchant, he would have reversed this dictum, and have said that that which the Japanese merely picked up by the way was *business !*

owe their origin to some idea of the dog as a faithful protector, more especially against onslaughts by evil spirits. (See also Article on POLO.)

Books recommended. *The ABC's of Origami: Paper Folding for Children* by Claude Sarasas; *Chess Variations: Ancient, Regional, and Modern* by John Gollon; *A Chime of Windbells: A Year of Japanese Haiku in English Verse* translations with an essay by Harold Stewart; *The Game of Go* by Arthur Smith; *The Kabuki Handbook* by Aubrey S. Halford and Giovanna M. Halford.

Archæology. The remains of Japanese antiquity fall naturally into two classes, which it is in most cases easy to distinguish from each other. The first consists of objects connected with that early race of which only a small remnant now lingers in the Ainos of Yezo, but which at one time probably occupied all the Japanese islands. The second comprises the relics of the immigrants from the neighbouring continent of Asia, whose descendants constitute the bulk of the present Japanese nation.

To the former class belong various objects familiar to us in Europe, such as stone implements and weapons. Some of these are peculiar to Japan, though on the whole the resemblance to those found in more Western lands is very striking. Flint celts are perhaps the most common type; and it is curious to note that in Japan, as in the British Isles, the popular imagination has given them the name of "thunder-bolts." Stone clubs, plain or adorned with carvings, have been found in considerable numbers. One of these, described by the late Baron Kanda, measures five feet in length and nearly five inches in diameter, and must have been a truly formidable weapon when wielded by adequate hands. There are also stone swords, pestles, daggers, and a variety of miscellaneous objects, some of unknown use. The material of all these is polished stone. Chipped flints are not unknown, but occur chiefly in the form of arrow or spear-heads for which a high degree of workmanship was less necessary.

An interesting discovery was made in 1878 by Professor Morse near the Ōmori station of the Tōkyō-Yokohama railway. He found that the railway cutting at this place passed through mounds identical in character with the "kitchen-middens" of Denmark, which have attracted so much attention in Europe.

They contained shells in large quantities, fragments of broken bones, implements of stone and horn, and pottery of a special type, which differed from the ancient Japanese earthenware in being hand-made instead of turned on a wheel, and also in shape and ornamentation. Human bones were among those found, and Professor Morse considers the way in which they had been broken to be indicative of cannibalism.*

We know from history that the ancient Japanese were to some extent pit-dwellers; but no remains of such dwellings are now known to exist. In Yezo, however, and the adjacent islands, large numbers of pits which have been used as human habitations are still to be seen. They are rectangular in shape, measuring about twenty feet by fifteen feet, and having a depth of three or four feet. In these were planted posts, over which a roofing of thatch was placed. They were probably occupied chiefly as winter habitations. Professor Milne thinks that they were made by a race who inhabited Yezo and the northern parts of Japan before the Ainos, and who were driven northwards by the encroachments of the latter. The present inhabitants of the Kurile Islands he believes to be their modern representatives. Both they and the ancestors of the Ainos must have had a low type of civilisation. They had no iron or even copper or bronze implements and were probably entirely unacquainted with the art of agriculture.

The early history of the continental race which has peopled Japan is wrapped in obscurity. Whence and when they came, and what was the character of their civilisation at the period of their arrival, are questions to which only the vaguest answers can be given. The earliest notices of them, in Chinese literature, date from the first and second centuries of the Christian era. It would appear that the Japanese were then a much more advanced race than the Ainos ever became. They were agriculturists, not merely hunters and fishers, and were acquainted with the arts of weaving, brewing, and the building

---

* These mounds were cleared away several years ago; but others have been discovered at Tokyo, on the Yokohama " Bluff," and at numerous other places.

of junks. They had a sovereign who lived in a fortified palace of some architectural pretensions, and their laws and customs are described as strict. The earlier notices speak of their having arrow-heads of bone, but two centuries later iron arrow-heads are mentioned. It is uncertain whether the Japanese brought with them from their continental home the art of working in iron and other metals. It is possible that all the metallurgical knowledge of which we find them possessed at a later period was really derived from China, and in that case there must have been an interval during which they used stone implements; but of this we have no certain knowledge. There is little or no evidence of a bronze age in Japan.

The archæological remains of the ancient Japanese may be taken to date from a few centuries before the Christian era. The most remarkable of these are sepulchral monuments of their sovereigns and grandees, great numbers of which still exist everywhere except in the more northern part of the Main Island. They are most numerous in the Gokinai, *i.e.*, the five provinces near the ancient capitals of Nara and Kyōto. The plain of Kawachi, in particular, is one vast cemetery dotted over with huge tumuli.

These mounds vary in shape and character. The largest are those known as *misasagi*, the Japanese word for the tombs of emperors, empresses, and princes of the blood. In the most ancient times, say the Japanese antiquarians, the tombs of the Mikados were simple mounds. At some unknown period, however—perhaps a few centuries before the Christian era—a highly specialised form of tumulus came into use for this purpose, and continued for several hundreds of years without much change. It consists of two mounds—one conical, and the other of a triangular shape—merging into each other in this form ▱ , the whole being surrounded by a moat, and sometimes by two concentric moats with a narrow strip of land between. The interment took place in the conical part, the other probably serving as a platform on which were performed the rites in honour of the deceased. Seen from the side, the appearance is that of a saddle-hill, the conical part being slightly higher than the other. There are sometimes two smaller mounds at the base of the larger ones, filling up the angles where they meet. The slope of the tumulus is not regular, but is broken up by terraces, on which are placed in rows, at intervals of a few inches, curious cylinders coarsely made of baked clay shaped in a mould, and measuring from one to two feet in height and from six to fourteen inches in diameter. They are buried in the earth, their upper rims being just level with the surface. The number of these cylinders is enormous, amounting in the case of some of the larger *misasagi* to many thousands. Their object can scarcely yet be said to have been definitely ascertained. One purpose was no doubt to prevent the earth of the mounds from being washed away by rain; but the Japanese tradition which connects them with an ancient custom of burying alive a number of the servants of a deceased monarch in a ring around his grave, is probably founded in fact.

It is related that in the 28th year of the Emperor Suinin (2 B.C. of the popular chronology), his brother died. All his attendants were buried alive round the tumulus in a standing position. For many days they died not, but day and night wept and cried. The Mikado, hearing the sound of their weeping, was sad and sorry in his heart, and commanded all his ministers to devise some plan by which this custom, ancient though it was, should be discontinued for the future. Accordingly, when the Mikado himself died in A.D. 3, workers in clay were sent for to the province of Izumo and made images of men, horses, and various other things, which were set up around the grave instead of living beings. This precedent was followed in later times, and some of the figures still exist. The Ueno Museum in Tōkyō contains several specimens, and one (of a man) has been secured for the Gowland collection now in the British Museum. The cylinders above described are similar to these images in material and workmanship, and it is probable that they served as pedestals on which the images were placed, though in view of their immense number, this can hardly have been their only use.

The *misasagi* vary greatly in size. One in Kōzuke, measured by Sir Ernest Satow, was 36 feet in height, 372 feet long, and 284 feet broad. But this is a comparatively small one. That of the Emperor Ōjin near Nara measures 2,312 yards round the outer moat, and is some 60 feet in height. The Emperor Nintoku's tomb near Sakai is still larger, and there is a tumulus in Kawachi, known as the *Ō-tsuka*, or " Big Mound," on the flank of which a good-sized village has been built.

The *misasagi* are at present generally clothed with trees, and form a favourite nesting resort for the paddy-bird or white egret, and other birds. Of late years these interesting relics have been well-cared for by the Government, at least those which are recognised as Imperial tombs. They have been fenced round, and provided with honorary gateways. Embassies are despatched once or twice a year to worship at them. In former times, however, they were much neglected, and there is reason to fear that few have escaped desecration. A road has been run through the *misasagi* of the Emperor Yuryaku, and on other double mounds promising cabbage plantations have been seen growing.

In some, perhaps in most, cases the *misasagi* contains a large vault built of great unhewn stones without mortar. The walls of the vault converge gradually towards the top, which is then roofed in by enormous slabs of stone weighing many tons each. The entrance was by means of a long, low gallery, roofed with similar stones, and so constructed that its right wall is in a line with the right wall of the vault. During the later period of mound-building, the entrance to this gallery always faced south,—a practice which had its origin in the Chinese notion that the north is the most honourable quarter, and that the deceased should therefore occupy that position in relation to the worshippers. Sarcophagi of stone and pottery have been found in some of the *misasagi*.

Nobles and high officials were buried in simple conical mounds ten or fifteen feet high, containing a vault similar to those above described, but of smaller dimensions. An average specimen of a group of thirty or forty situated near the western shore of Lake Biwa, a few miles north of the town of Ōtsu, measured as follows:—

CHAMBER.

Length—from 11 feet 8 inches below to 10 feet above.

Breadth—from 6 feet 6 inches below to 4 feet at top.

Height—8 feet 9 inches.

GALLERY.

Breadth—2 feet 9 inches.

Height—4 feet.

Length—10 feet.

The roof of the chamber consisted in this instance of three large stones.

These tombs sometimes stand singly, but are more commonly found in groups of ten to forty or fifty. The lower slope of a hill, just where it touches the plain, is a favourite position for them. When the earth of these mounds has been washed away, so that the massive blocks of stone which form the roof protrude from the surface, they present a striking resemblance to the dolmens of Europe, and more especially to those megalithic monuments known in France as *allées couvertes*. The peasantry call them *iwa-ya*, or "rock-houses," and imagine that they were the dwellings of their remote ancestors, or that they were used as refuges from a fiery rain which fell in ancient times. They are little cared for by the Japanese, and in too many cases have been used as quarries for the building materials which they contain. Nearly all have been rifled at some period or other.

During the eighth century of the Christian era, this style of sepulture fell gradually into disuse under the influence of Buddhist ideas. In the eyes of a Buddhist, vast costly structures were not only a burden to the people, but were objectionable as tending to foster false notions of the real value of these mortal frames of ours. Many of the Mikados were earnest devotees of Buddhism. Beginning with Gemmyō Tennō in A.D. 715, a long series of them abdicated the throne in order to spend the remainder of their lives in pious seclusion. In several cases, by their express desire, no *misasagi* were erected over their remains, and some even directed that their bodies should be cremated and the ashes scattered to the winds.

It is remarkable that no inscriptions should be found in connection with the tombs of this period, although the Japanese became acquainted with Chinese writing early in the fifth century, if not sooner. The tombs have, however, yielded a large quantity of objects of antiquarian interest. Among these, pottery perhaps stands first. The clay cylinders, the figures of men and horses, and earthenware sarcophagi have been already noticed; but numerous vases, pots, dishes, and other utensils have also been found. They are usually turned on a wheel; but there is no trace of glaze or colouring, and they are of rather rude workmanship. The ornamentation is simpl⌐, consisting of wavy lines round the vessel,—similar to those seen round Egyptian water-bottles at the present day,—of circular grooves, or of parallel scorings, all made with a wooden comb or pointed stick when the clay was in a wet state. Many have "mat-markings," and the interior of the larger articles is usually adorned with a pattern known as the "Korean wheel." This consists of discs containing a number of concentric circles overlapping one another. They were produced by a wooden stamp one or two inches in diameter, and the object may have been to render the clay less liable to crack in baking. A stamp of this kind is actually used in Korea at the present time. Fragments of pottery with this mark may always be found in the vicinity of a Japanese dolmen. There are vases of a more pretentious character, having groups of rude figures round the upper part, and pedestals pierced with curious triangular openings. These were probably sacrificial vases. The Japanese pottery of this period is identical is shape, pattern, and material with the more ancient earthenware of Korea, from which country there is no doubt that the ceramic art of Japan was derived. Representative examples of it may be seen in the Gowland collection in the British Museum; the Ueno

Museum in Tōkyō is rich in fine specimens. Other antiquarian objects of this period are iron swords (straight and one-edged), iron spear-heads, articles of armour often adorned with gold and silver, mirrors of a mixed metal, horse-gear,—such as stirrups, bits, etc.,—ornaments, among which are thick rings of gold, silver, or bronze, besides glass beads, etc. All these are of good workmanship, and it is probable that some of the articles are of Chinese origin.

The *maga-tama,* or comma-shaped ornaments made of stone, probably belong to a very early period of Japanese history. They formed part, no doubt, of the necklaces of polished stone and clay beads which we know to have been worn by Japanese sovereigns and nobles in ancient times.

Books recommended. *A Correlated History of the Far East: China, Korea, Japan* by Maria Penkala; *History of Japanese Religion* by Masaharu Anesaki; *Japan: An Attempt at Interpretation* by Lafcadio Hearn; *Tales of Old Japan* by A. B. Mitford (Lord Redesdale).

Architecture.   The Japanese genius touches perfection in small things. No other nation ever understood half so well how to make a cup, a tray, even a kettle—a thing of beauty, how to transform a little knob of ivory into a microcosm of quaint humour, how to express a fugitive thought in half-a-dozen dashes of the pencil. The massive, the spacious, the grand, is less congenial to their mental attitude. Hence they achieve less success in architecture than in the other arts. The prospect of a Japanese city from a height is monotonous. Not a tower, not a dome, not a minaret, nothing aspiring heavenward, save in rare cases a painted pagoda half-hidden amidst the trees which it barely tops,—nothing but long, low lines of thatch and tiles, even the Buddhist temple roofs being but moderately raised above the rest, and even their curves being only quaint and graceful, nowise imposing. It was a true instinct that led Professor Morse to give to his charming monograph on Japanese architecture the title of *Japanese Homes*, the interest of Japanese buildings lying less in the buildings themselves than in the neat domestic ways of their denizens, and in the delightful little bits of ornamentation that meet one at every turn,—the elaborate metal fastenings, the carved friezes *(ramma)*, the screens both sliding and folding, the curiously ornamental tiles, the dainty gardens with their dwarfed trees. What is true of the dwelling-houses is true of the temples also. Nikkō and Shiba are glorious, not as architecture (in the sense in which we Europeans, the inheritors of the Parthenon, of the Doges' Palace, and of Salisbury Cathedral, understand the word architecture), but for the elaborate geometrical figures, the bright flowers and birds and fabulous beasts, with which the sculptor and painter of wood has so lavishly adorned them.

The ordinary Japanese house is a light frame-work structure, whose thatched, shingled, or tiled roof, very heavy in proportion, is supported on stones with slightly hollowed tops resting on the surface of the soil. There is no foundation, as that word is understood by our architects. The house stands *on* the ground, not partly *in* it. Singularity number two: there are no walls—at least no continuous walls. The side of the house, composed at night of wooden sliding doors called *amado,* is stowed away in boxes during the day-time. In summer, everything is thus open to the outside air. In winter, semi-transparent paper slides, called *shōji,* replace the wooden sliding doors during the day-time. The rooms are divided from each other by opaque paper screens, called *fusuma* or *karakami,* which run in grooves at the top and bottom. By taking out these sliding screens, several rooms can be turned into one. The floor of all the living-rooms is covered with thick mats, made of rushes and perfectly fitted together, so as to leave no interstices. As these mats are always of the same size,—six feet by three,—it is usual to compute the area of a room by the number of its mats. Thus you speak of a six mat room, a ten mat room, etc. In the dwellings of the middle classes, rooms of eight, of six, and of four and a half mats are those oftenest met with. The kitchen and passages are not matted, but have a wooden floor, which is kept brightly polished. But the passages are few in a Japanese house, each room opening as a rule into the others on either side.

When a house has a second storey, this generally covers but a portion of the ground floor. The steps leading up to it resemble a ladder rather than a staircase. The best rooms in a Japanese house are almost invariably at the back, where also is the garden; and they face south, so as to escape the northern blast in winter and to get the benefit of the breeze in summer, which then always blows from the south. They generally have a recess or alcove, ornamented with a painted or written scroll *(kakemono)* and a vase of flowers. Furniture is conspicuous by its absence. There are no tables, no chairs, no wash-hand-stands, no pianoforte,—none of all those thousand and one things which we cannot do without. The necessity for bedsteads is obviated by quilts, which are brought in at night and laid down wherever may happen to be most convenient. No mahogany dining-table is required in a family where each member is served separately on a little lacquer tray. Cupboards are, for the most part, openings in the wall, screened in by small paper slides,—not separate, movable entities. Whatever treasures the family may possess are mostly stowed in an adjacent building, known in the local English dialect as a "godown," that is, a fire-proof storehouse with walls of mud or clay.*

These details will probably suggest a very uncomfortable sum total; and Japanese houses *are* supremely uncomfortable to ninety-nine Europeans out of a hundred. Nothing to sit on, nothing but a brazier to warm oneself by, and yet abundant danger of fire, no solidity, no privacy, the deafening clatter twice daily of the opening and shutting of the outer wooden slides, draughts insidiously pouring in through innumerable

---

* "Godown" (pronounced *go-down*, not *god-own*) seems to be a Telugu or Tamil word, which passed first into Malay, and was adopted thence into Asiatic English. See that most delightful of dictionaries, Yule's *Hobson-Jobson*.

chinks and crannies, darkness whenever heavy rain makes it necessary to shut up one or more sides of the house,—to these and various other enormities Japanese houses must plead guilty. Two things, chiefly, may be said on the other side. First, these houses are cheap,—an essential point in a poor country. Secondly, the people who live in them do not share our European ideas with regard to comfort and discomfort. They do not miss fire-places or stoves, never having realised the possibility of such elaborate arrangements for heating. They do not mind draughts, having been inured to them from infancy. In fact an elderly diplomat, who, during his sojourn in a Japanese hotel, spent well-nigh his whole time in the vain endeavour to keep doors shut and chinks patched up, used to exclaim to us, " *Mais les Japonais* ADORENT *les courants d'air!* " Furthermore, the physicians who have studied Japanese dwelling-houses from the point of view of hygiene, give them a clean bill of health.

Leaving this portion of the subject, which is a matter of taste, not of argument, let us enquire into the origin of Japanese architecture, which is a matter of research. Its origin is twofold. The Japanese Buddhist temple comes from India, being a modification of the Indian original. The other Japanese styles are of native growth. Shintō temples, Imperial palaces, and commoners' dwelling-houses are alike developments of the simple hut of prehistoric times. Persons interested in archæological research may like to hear what Sir Ernest Satow has to say on the little-known subject of primeval Japanese architecture. He writes as follows* :—

" Japanese antiquarians tells us that in early times, before carpenter's tools had been invented, the dwellings of the people who inhabited these islands were constructed of young trees with the bark on, fastened together with ropes made of the rush *suge (Scirpus maritimus)*, or perhaps with the tough shoots of wistaria *(fuji)*, and thatched with the grass called *kaya*. In modern buildings the uprights of a house stand upon

---

* We quote from a paper entitled *The Shinto Temples of Ise*, printed in Vol. II. of the " Asiatic Transactions."

large stones laid on the surface of the earth; but this precaution against decay had not occurred to the ancients, who planted the uprights in holes dug in the ground.

" The ground plan of the hut was oblong, with four corner uprights, and one in the middle of each of the four sides, those in the sides which formed the ends being long enough to support the ridge-pole. Other trees were fastened horizontally from corner to corner, one set near the ground, one near the top, and one set on the top, the latter of which formed what we call the wall-plates. Two large rafters, whose upper ends crossed each other, were laid from the wall-plates to the heads of the taller uprights. The ridgepole rested in the fork formed by the upper ends of the rafters crossing each other. Horizontal poles were then laid along each slope of the roof, one pair being fastened close up to the exterior angles of the fork. The rafters were slender poles or bamboos passed over the ridge-pole and fastened down on each end to the wall-plates. Next followed the process of putting on the thatch. In order to keep this in its place two trees were laid along the top, resting in the forks, and across these two trees were placed short logs at equal distances, which, being fastened to the poles in the exterior angle of the forks by ropes passed through the thatch, bound the ridge of the roof firmly together.

" The walls and doors were constructed of rough matting. It is evident that some tool must have been used to cut the trees to the required length, and for this purpose a sharpened stone was probably employed. Such stone implements have been found imbedded in the earth in various parts of Japan in company with stone arrow-heads and clubs. Specimens of the ancient style of building may even yet be seen in remote parts of the country, not perhaps so much in the habitations of the peasantry, as in sheds erected to serve a temporary purpose.

" The architecture of the Shintō temples is derived from the primeval hut, with more or less modification in proportion to the influence of Buddhism in each particular case. Those of the purest style retain the thatched roof, others are covered

with the thick shingling called *hiwada-buki,* while others have
tiled and even coppered roofs. The projecting ends of the
rafters (called *chigi*) have been somewhat lengthened, and
carved more or less elaborately. At the new temple at Kudan-
zaka,* in Yedo, they are shown in the proper position, projecting from the inside of the shingling; but in the majority of
cases they merely consist of two pieces of wood in the form of
the letter X, which rest on the ridge of the roof like a pack-
saddle on a horse's back,—to make use of a Japanese writer's
comparison. The logs which kept the two trees laid on the
ridge in their place have taken the form of short cylindrical
pieces of timber tapering towards each extremity, which have
been compared by foreigners to cigars. In Japanese they are
called *katsuo-gi,* from their resemblance to the pieces of dried
bonito sold under the name of *katsuo-bushi.* The two trees
laid along the roof over the thatch are represented by a single
beam, called *muna-osae,* or ' roof-presser.' Planking has taken
the place of the mats with which the side of the building were
originally closed, and the entrance is closed by a pair of
folding doors turning, not on hinges, but on what are, I believe,
technically called ' journals.' The primeval hut had no floor-
ing; but we find that the shrine has a wooden floor raised some
feet above the ground, which arrangement necessitates a sort
of balcony all round, and a flight of steps up to the entrance.
The transformation is completed in some cases by the addition
of a quantity of ornamental metal-work in brass."

The same authority's account of the palaces of early days is
as follows:† " The palace of the Japanese sovereign was a
wooden hut, with its pillars planted in the ground, instead of
being erected upon broad flat stones as in modern buildings.
The whole frame(work, consisting of posts, beams, rafters, door-
posts, and window-frames, was tied together with cords made

---

* Commonly known as the *Shokonsha.* See Murray's *Handbook for Japan.* 7th edition,
p. 123.

† See an elaborate paper on *Ancient Japanese Rituals,* in Vol. XI. Part II. of the
" Asiatic Transactions."

by twisting the long fibrous stems of climbing plants, such as *Pueraria thunbergiana (kuzu)* and *Wistaria sinensis (fuji)*. The floor must have been low down, so that the occupants of the building, as they squatted or lay on their mats, were exposed to the stealthy attacks of venomous snakes, which were probably far more numerous in the earliest ages, when the country was for the most part uncultivated, than at the present day. . . . . . . There seems some reason to think that the *yuka,* here translated floor, was originally nothing but a couch which ran round the sides of the hut, the rest of the space being simply a mud-floor, and that the size of the couch was gradually increased until it occupied the whole interior. The rafters projected upward beyond the ridge-pole, crossing each other, as is seen in the roofs of modern Shintō temples, whether their architecture be in conformity with early traditions (in which case all the rafters are so crossed) or modified in accordance with more advanced principles of construction, and the crossed rafters retained only as ornaments at the two ends of the ridge. The roof was thatched, and perhaps had a gable at each end, with a hole to allow the smoke of the wood-fire to escape, so that it was possible for birds flying in and perching on the beams overhead, to defile the food, or the fire with which it was cooked."

To this description of Sir Ernest Satow's, it should be added that fences were in use, and that the wooden doors, sometimes fastened by means of hooks, resembled those with which we are familiar in Europe rather than the sliding, screen-like doors of modern Japan. The windows seem to have been mere holes. Rush-matting and rugs consisting of skins were occasionally brought in to sit upon, and we even hear once or twice of " silk rugs " being used for the same purpose by the noble and wealthy.

Since 1870, the Japanese have begun to exchange their own methods of building for what is locally termed "foreign style," doubtless, as a former resident* has wittily observed,

* Mr. E. G. Holtham, in his *Eight Years in Japan.*

because foreign to all known styles of architecture. This "foreign style" is indeed not one, but multiform. There is the rabbit-warren style, exemplified in the streets at the back of the Ginza in Tōkyō. There is the wooden shanty or bathing-machine style, of which the capital offers a wealth of examples. There is the cruet-stand style, so strikingly exemplified in the new Tōkyō Prefecture. The Brobdingnagian pigeon-house style is represented here and there both in wood and stone. Its chief feature is having no windows,—at least, none to speak of. After all, these things are Japan's misfortune, not her fault. She discovered Europe, architecturally speaking, at the wrong moment. We cannot with any grace blame a nation whom we have ourselves misled. If Japan's contemporary efforts in architecture are worse even than ours, it is chiefly because her people have less money to dispose of. Moreover, Nature herself confines them to the flat and the little:— three storeys are a dangerous experiment in this earthquake-shaken land.

Books recommended. *The Arts of Japan: An Illustrated History* by Hugo Munsterberg; *Cha-No-Yu: The Japanese Tea Ceremony* by A. L. Sadler; *The Folk Arts of Japan* by Hugo Munsterberg; *From Castle to Teahouse: Japanese Architecture of the Momoyama Period* by John B. Kirby, Jr.; *The Imperial Hotel: Frank Lloyd Wright & the Architecture of Unity* by Cary James; *The Japanese House: A Tradition for Contemporary Architecture* by Heinrich Engel.

Armour. Japanese armour might serve as a text for those authors who love to descant on the unchanging character of the East. Our own Middle Ages witnessed revolutions in the style of armour as complete as any that have taken place in the Paris fashions during the last three hundred years. In Japan, on the contrary, from the beginning of true feudalism in the twelfth century down to its extinction in 1871, there was scarcely any change. The older specimens are rather the better, rather the more complete; the newer are often rather heavier, owing to the use of a greater number of plates and scales; that is all. It is true that in quite old times Japanese armour was still imperfect. Cloth and the hides of animals seem to have been the materials then employed. But metal armour had already established itself in general use by the eighth century of our era. The weapons, too, then known were the same as a millennium later, with the exception of fire-arms, which began to creep in during the sixteenth century in the wake of intercourse with the early Portuguese adventurers.* Those who are interested in the subject, either theoretically or as purchasers of suits of armour brought to them by curio-vendors, will find a full description in the second part of Conder's *History of Japanese Costume,* printed in Vol. IX. Part III. of the "Asiatic Transactions." They can there read to their hearts' content about corselets, taces, greaves, mamelières, brassarts, and many other deep matters not known to the vulgar.

Book recommended. *The Armour Book in Honcho Gunki Ko by Hakuseki Arai.*

Army. For many centuries—say from A.D. 1200 to 1867— "soldier" and "gentleman" *(samurai)* were convertible terms. The Mikado and his Court, in their sacred retreat at Kyōto, were, it is true, removed by custom from all participation in martial deeds. At the other end of the scale, the peasantry were likewise excluded. But for the intermediate class—the gentry—to fight was not only a duty but a pleasure, in a state of society where the security of feudal possessions depended on the strong arm of the baron himself and of his trusty lieges. This was the order of things down to A.D. 1600. Thenceforward, though peace reigned for two and a half centuries under the vigorous administration of the Tokugawa Shōguns, all the military forms of an elder day were kept up. They were suddenly shivered into atoms at the beginning of the present Emperor's reign (A.D. 1868), when military advisers were called in from France, the continental system of universal conscription was introduced, and uniforms

---

* Compare Article entitled EUROPEANISATION.

of modern cut replaced the picturesque but cumbersome trappings of the old Japanese knight. The Japanese soldier's baptism of fire was in the suppression of the Satsuma rebellion in 1877. He won his spurs brilliantly in the China war of 1894–5, compelling the astonished admiration of all foreign experts. Specially thorough and satisfactory was the organisation of the commissariat department, which, in so rigorous a climate and so poor a country, bore the brunt of the undertaking. As the ill-led, unfed, and constitutionally unwarlike Chinamen mostly ran away, Japanese pluck scarcely met with full opportunity for showing itself. Nevertheless, the battle of Pingyang on the 15th September, 1894, the subsequent march through Manchuria, and the taking of Port Arthur in November of the same year, were notable exploits. More recently, in 1900, the Japanese contingent, by common consent, bore away the palm from the allied forces which relieved Peking :—they marched fastest, they fought best, they were most amendable to discipline, they behaved most humanely towards the conquered. While these pages pass through the press in the summer of 1904, the civilised warriors of Japan are again busy inscribing glorious deeds on the page of history, fighting for the first time against a European foe. It were probably no exaggeration to assert that Japan now disposes of the best army in the world, for its size. This fact —assuming it to be a fact—is the more remarkable, because the Japanese army is (if we may use the phrase) anonymous. No world-famed specialist—no Frederick, no Napoleon—constructed the splendid machine. It has been built up by men little heard of beyond a narrow circle,—a few French employés, afterwards supplemented by a few Germans and one or two Italians, and by natives possessed, so far as we know, of neither genius nor wide experience. Nevertheless, some good fairy has presided over all their acts. Of course it must be allowed that the material they have had to work upon is good,—a fair physique and a morale beyond all praise, the men, though small and nowise handsome, being sturdy and intelligently devoted, while the officers obey Milton's precept

"To scorn delights and live laborious days,"

not dancing attendance on " society," or dissipating time and energy on useless games. The intercourse between officers and men is frank and intimate,—a result of that seeming contradiction which we have discussed elsewhere,* the democratic spirit which has always permeated this paternally governed empire.

The published statistics of the forces are believed to be of little value at any time, because the authorities wisely keep precise details of the fighting strength and more particularly of the possibilities of mobilisation secret. Writing, as we do, during the progress of a war which strains all the nation's resources, it were even more idle than usual to attempt to gain any trustworthy information on such matters of high policy. When hostilities with Russia broke out, the army had for several years past been undergoing a process of expansion, to be completed—such was the generally accepted statement— in 1911; and persons supposed to be well-informed held that on the completion of all the contemplated changes, the following figures would be approximately correct, in any case not above the mark:—

Men with the colours (1st to 3rd year)	150,000
First Reserve (4th to 7th year)	150,000
Second Reserve (8th to 12th year)	150,000
Total	450,000

of whom between 8,000 and 9,000 officers, admitted partly by competition, partly after graduation at any of the middle schools. Exclusive of the Imperial Guard, there would be twelve divisions with headquarters at Tōkyō, Sendai, Nagoya, Ōsaka, Hiroshima, Kumamoto, Sapporo, Hirosaki, Kanazawa, Fukuchiyama, Marugame, and Kokura. Three brigades—say 7,500 men—are detached for service in Formosa. The cavalry has always been the weakest branch of the Japanese army, owing to the absence of good horses; neither does the build of the average Japanese tend to make him a graceful rider. As

---

* In the Articles on POLITENESS, NOBILITY, and EDUCATION.

at present fixed, there is one regiment (three squadrons) of cavalry per division,—eventual total, 39 squadrons,—besides two independent brigades (probably 12 additional squadrons) in process of formation, with headquarters at Tōkyō. The artillery (field) consists of six batteries per division and two independent artillery brigades (probably 12 additional batteries) in process of formation, with headquarters at Tōkyō. Both artillery and infantry are armed with new weapons,—the former with the " Arisaka " gun, of which large numbers have been made in France and Germany and some in Japan, the latter with what is called the " 30th year " rifle.* This weapon is a modification of the " Murata " rifle. Its chief distinctive feature is that five cartridges are loaded simultaneously in a clip.

The programme here briefly summarised includes the expenditure of vast sums on the construction of forts, barracks, and arsenals. Quantities of fire-arms, ordnance, and ammunition are manufactured at Tōkyō and Ōsaka. Japanese uniforms follow European models in all essentials, except for the use of straw sandals on active service instead of boots, which the men dislike.

In accordance with European precedents, the Emperor has assumed the supreme command. During the first China war, two of the Princes, his kinsmen, actually commanded in the field; others are now serving both with the army and with the navy. This steeping of the reigning family in militarism appeared quite revolutionary at the period when it was first decided on. As late as 1887, when Herr von Mohl, a high Prussian official, came over to help in the reorganisation of the Court on German lines, even a step apparently so natural as the appointment of aides-de-camp to His Imperial Majesty met with stout opposition. For the old Court life of Japan, its personnel, its ceremonial, and all its habits, were based on those of China, where, as is well-known, the soldiery have ever been regarded as a sort of pariah class,—desperadoes,

---

* So called from the 30th year of the Meiji period, that is, 1897 (see Article on TIME). Arisaka and Murata are the names of Japanese officers, who invented the weapons called after them. The Murata rifle, now superseded, dates from 1873.

ne'er-do-weels, ranking nowhere because leading a life deemed barbarous and degrading, fellows in fact whom it would be desecration to place near the person of the heaven-descended monarch. True, the Daimyōs and Samurai, with the Shōgun at their head, were, or had been, fighting men:—that was an element of contradiction in the structure of Japanese society, which did not exist in China. But though the Daimyōs and Samurai stood high in their own estimation and practically lorded it over the land, they never rose to social equality with the meanest hanger-on of the Mikado's Court; and if any of them obtained office there, it was in a civil capacity. How times have changed, and how swiftly !

To return from this digression, the men of the Japanese army, as already incidentally remarked, are raised by conscription. When the system was first introduced, numerous exceptions were allowed; but now the application of the law is stringent, no excuse other than physical unfitness being entertained. The limit of height is 5 Japanese ft., that is, about 4 ft. 11½ in. English; the age for entering is twenty. Every male between the ages of seventeen and forty belongs *ipso facto* to the " national army " *(Landsturm),* and is liable to be called out in case of emergency. This " national army " therefore includes, in addition to the untrained mass, that large body of men who have passed out of the Second Reserve fully trained.

The new-comer may smile to behold two or three Japanese soldiers strolling along hand in hand, as if they were Dresden shepherdesses. What would he say during a campaign to see private soldiers on the march, or even during a pause in actual battle, take fans out of their gaiters and fan themselves ? But after all, why not ? There is no effeminacy here, only common sense,—and coolness in both meanings of the term.

It is extraordinary into what minutiæ the Government has gone in its determination to foster the military spirit and raise the army to the highest point of perfection. Even books of war-songs have been officially composed and included in the course of instruction. The result, it must be confessed, has not been the production of poems of any very high order of merit. What cannot fail to elicit our admiration is the manner in which the company drill imposed on all government schools and adopted in most private schools as well, has been responded to by the scholars. Even little mites of boys bear the flag stoutly, march miles in the blazing sun, and altogether carry themselves so as to show that an enemy attempting to land on these shores must count, not only with every able-bodied man, but with every child throughout the empire.

Art. The beginnings of Japanese art, as of almost all things Japanese excepting cleanliness, can be traced to China through Korea. Even after Japanese art had started on its independent career, it refreshed its inspiration from time to time by a careful study and imitation of Chinese models; and Chinese masterpieces still occupy in the estimate of Japanese connoisseurs a place only hesitatingly allowed to the best native works. Even Chinese subjects preponderate in the classical schools of Japan. Speaking of the productions of the classical Japanese painters, Dr. Anderson says: " It may safely be asserted that not one in twenty of the productions of these painters, who to the present day are considered to represent the true genius of Japanese art, was inspired by the works of nature as seen in their own beautiful country." Whatever Indian, Persian, or Greek strain may be detected in Japan came through Korea and China in the wake of Buddhism, and is accordingly far less marked—if marked at all—in genuinely native Japanese paintings and carvings than in those archaic remains which, though often inaccurately spoken of as Japanese, were really the handiwork of Korean or Chinese artists or of their immediate pupils.

The most ancient painting now existing in Japan is a Buddhist mural decoration in the temple of Hōryūji near Nara, believed to date from A.D. 607 and to be the work of a Korean priest. For more than two centuries longer, art remained chiefly in Korean and Chinese priestly hands. The first native painter of eminence was Kose-no-Kanaoka, a Court noble who flourished from about A.D. 850 to 880, but scarcely any of whose works remain. That the art of painting, especially on screens, was assiduously cultivated at the Japanese Court during the ninth and tenth centuries, is proved by numerous references in literature. But it was not till about the year 1000 that the *Yamato Ryū* (lit. " Japanese School "), the first concerning which we have much positive knowledge, was established by an artist named Motomitsu. This school contained within itself the seed of most of the peculiarities that have characterised Japanese art ever since, with its neglect of perspective, its impossible mountains, its quaint dissection of roofless interiors, its spirited burlesques of solemn processions, wherein frogs, insects, or hobgoblins take the place of men. In the thirteenth century this school assumed the name of the *Tosa Ryū,* and confined itself thenceforward more and more to classical subjects. Its former humorous strain had been caught as early as the twelfth century by Toba Sōjō, a rollicking priest, who about A.D. 1160, distinguished himself by drawings coarse in both senses of the word, but full of verve and drollery. These are the so-called *Toba-e.* Toba Sōjō founded a school. To found a school was *de rigueur* in Old Japan, where originality was so little understood that it was supposed that any eminent man's descendants or pupils, to the twentieth generation, ought to be able to do the same sort of work as their ancestor had done. But none of the jovial abbot's followers are worthy of mention alongside of him.

The fifteenth century witnessed a powerful renaissance of Chinese influence, and was the most glorious period of Japanese painting. It is a strange coincidence that Italian painting should then also have been at its zenith. But it is apparently a coincidence only, there being no fact to warrant us in assuming any influence of the one on the other. The most famous names are those of the Buddhist priests Chō Densu and Jōsetsu. Chō Densu, the Fra Angelico of Japan, restricted himself to religious subjects, while Jōsetsu painted landscapes, figures, flowers, and birds. Both these great artists died early in the century. They were succeeded by Mitsunobu, the best painter of the Tosa School, and by Sesshū, Shūbun, and Kanō Masanobu, all of whom were founders of independent schools. The first Kanō's son, Kanō Motonobu, was more eminent than his father. He handed down the tradition to his own sons and grandsons, and the Kanō school continues to be, even at the present day, the chief stronghold of classicism in Japan. By " classicism " we mean partly a peculiar technique, partly an adherence to Chinese methods, models, and subjects, such as portraits of Chinese sages and delineations of Chinese land-scapes, which are represented, of course, not from nature but at second-hand.

The synthetic power, the quiet harmonious colouring, and the free vigorous touch of these Japanese " old masters " have justly excited the admiration of succeeding generations of their countrymen. But the circle of ideas within which the Sesshūs, the Shūbuns, the Kanōs, and the other classical Japanese painters move, is too narrow and peculiar for their pro-ductions to be ever likely to gain much hold on the esteem of Europe. European collectors—such men as Gonse, for instance—have been looked down on by certain enthusiasts in Japan for the preference which they evince for Hokusai and the modern Popular School *(Ukiyo-e Ryū)* generally. It is very bold of us to venture to express an opinion on such a matter; but we think that the instinct which led Gonse and others to Hokusai led them aright,—that Japanese art was itself led to Hokusai by a legitimate and most fortunate process of development, that it was led out of the close atmosphere of academical conventionality into the fresh air of heaven.

To say this is not necessarily to deny to the old masters superiority of another order. Chō Densu manifests a spiritual-ity, Sesshū a genius for idealising Chinese scenes, Kanō Tan-yū a power to evoke beauty out of a few chaotic blotches, all these and scores of their followers a certain aristocratic dis-tinction, to which the members of the Popular School can lay no claim. Grant the ideals of old Japan, grant Buddhism and Chinese conventions, and you must grant the claims of the worshippers of the old masters. But the world does not grant these things. Chinese history and conventions, even Buddhism itself, lie outside the main current of the world's development, whereas the motives and manner of the Popular School appeal to all times and places. Hence, the world being large and Japan being small, and influence on civilisation in general being more important than an isolated perfection incapable of transformation or assimilation, there can be little doubt that the Popular School will retain its exceptional place in European favour.

The beginning of the movement may be traced as far back as the end of the sixteenth century in the person of Iwasa Matahei, originally a pupil of the Tosa school and originator of the droll sketches known as *Ōtsu-e*. But a whole century elapsed before Hishigawa Moronobu began to devote himself to the illustration of books in colours and in popular realistic style. Then, towards the close of the eighteenth century, came Ōkyo, the founder of the style known as the *Shijō Ryū*, from the street in Kyōto where the master resided. Ōkyo made a genuine effort to copy nature, instead of only talking about doing so, as had been the habit of the older schools. His astonishingly correct representations of fowls and fishes, his pupil Sosen's portraitures of monkeys, and other striking triumphs of detail were the result. But none of the members of Ōkyo's school succeeded in disembarrassing themselves altogether from the immemorial conventionalities of their nation, when combining various details into a larger composition. Their naturalism, however, gave an immense impulse to the popularisation of art. A whole cloud of artisan-artists arose, —no longer the representatives of privileged ancient families, but commoners who drew pictures of the life around them to suit the genuine taste of the public of their own time and class. Art was released from its mediæval Chinese swaddling-clothes, and allowed to mix in the society of living men and women. And what a quaint, picturesque society it was,—that of the time, say, between 1750 and 1850,— the "Old Japan" which all now know and appreciate, because the works of the Artisan School have carried its fame round the world !

The king of the artisan workers was he whom we call Hokusai, though his real original name was Nakajima Tetsujirō, and his pseudonyms were legion. During the course of an unusually long life (1760–1849), this man, whose only possessions were his brush and his palette, poured forth a continuous stream of novel and vigorous creations in the form of illustrations to books and of separate coloured sheets,— illustrations and sheets which included, as Anderson justly says, "the whole range of Japanese art-motives, scenes of history, drama, and novel, incidents in the daily life of his own class, realisations of familiar objects of animal and vegetable life, wonderful suggestions of the scenery of his beloved Yedo and its surroundings, and a hundred other inspirations that would require a volume to describe." Contemporary workers in the art of colour-printing were Toyokuni, Kunisada, Shigenobu, Hiroshige, and others in plenty. Then, in 1853, four years after Hokusai's death, came Commodore Perry, the mere threat of whose cannon shivered the old civilisation of Japan into fragments. Japanese art perished. Kyōsai, who survived till 1889, was its last genuine representative in an uncongenial age. His favourite subjects had a certain grim appropriateness:—they were ghosts and skeletons. Charity compels us to draw a veil over the productions of many so-called painters, which, during the last two decades, have encumbered the shop-windows of Tōkyō and disfigured the walls of exhibitions got up in imitation of European usage. They seem to be manufactured by the gross. If not worth much, there are at least plenty of them. Meanwhile, here and there, a lover of the national traditions still goes on painting the old subjects nearly in the old way.

Japanese art is distinguished by directness, facility, and strength of line, a sort of bold dash due probably to the habit of writing and drawing from the elbow, not from the wrist. This, so to say, *calligraphic* quality is what gives a charm to the merest rough Japanese sketch. It has been well remarked

that if a Japanese artist's work be carried no further even than
the outlines, you will still have something worthy of being
hung on your wall or inserted in your album. Japanese art
disregards the laws of perspective and of light and shadow.
Though sometimes faultlessly accurate in natural details, it
scorns to be tied down to such accuracy as to an ever-binding
rule. Even in the same picture—say, one of a bird perched on
a tree—you may have the bird exact in every detail, the tree
a sort of conventional shorthand symbol. Or you may have a
bamboo which is perfection, but part of it blurred by an artificial atmosphere which no meteorological eccentricity could
place where the painter has placed it; or else two sea-coasts one
above another,—each beautiful and poetical, only how in the
world could they have got into such a relative position ? The
Japanese artist does not trouble his head about such matters.
He is, in his limited way, a poet, not a photographer. Our
painters of the impressionist school undertake less to paint
actual scenes than to render their own feelings in presence of
such scenes. The Japanese artist goes a step further: he paints
the feelings evoked by the *memory* of the scenes, the feelings
when one is between waking and dreaming. He is altogether
an idealist, and this at both ends of the scale, the beautiful and
the grotesque. Were he able to work on a large canvas, a
very great ideal art might have been the result. But in art,
as in literature, his nation seems lacking in the genius, the
breadth of view, necessary for making grand combinations. It
stops at the small, the pretty, the isolated, the vignette. Hence
the admirable adaptability of Japanese art to decorative purposes. In decoration, too, some of its more obvious defects
retire into the background. Who would look on the side of a
teapot for a rigid observance of perspective ? Still less in
miniature ivory carvings such as the *netsukes,* in the ornaments of sword-guards, the bas-reliefs on bronze vases, and
the patterns in pieces (and many of them are masterpieces)
of embroidery. As decoration for small surfaces, Japanese
art has already begun to conquer the world. In the days
before Japanese ideas became known to Europe, people there
used to consider it essential to have the patterns on plates,

cushions, and what not, arranged with geometrical accuracy. If on the right hand there was a Cupid looking to the left, then on the left hand there must be a Cupid of exactly the same size looking to the right, and the chief feature of the design was invariably in the exact centre. The Japanese artisan-artists have shown us that this mechanical symmetry does not make for beauty. They have taught us the charm of irregularity; and if the world owe them but this one lesson, Japan may yet be proud of what she has accomplished.

There exists, it is true, nowadays a small band of foreign enthusiasts, who deny that the art of Japan is thus limited in its scope, and decorative rather than representative. Having studied it with greater zeal and profit than they have studied European art, they go so far as to put Japanese art on a level with that of Greece and Italy. These enthusiasts have performed and are still performing a useful function. They are disseminating a knowledge of Japanese art abroad, disseminating it, too, in Japan itself, where it had been suffered to fall into neglect. But their cult of Japanese art partakes of the nature of a religious faith, and like other religionists, they are apt to be deficient in the sense of humour. They are much too much in earnest ever to smile about such serious matters. For instance, one ardent admirer of Japonism in art informs the public that the late painter Kyōsai "was perhaps the greatest limner of crows that Japan, nay the whole world, has produced." Does this not remind you of the artist in whose epitaph it was recorded that he was "the Raphael of cats?" The Japanese are undoubtedly Raphaels of fishes, and insects, and flowers, and bamboo-stems swaying in the breeze; and they have given us charming fragments of idealised scenery. But they have never succeeded in adequately transferring to canvas "the human form divine;" they have never made grand historical scenes live again before the eyes of posterity; they have never, like the early Italian masters, drawn away men's hearts from earth to heaven in an ecstasy of adoration. In a word, Japanese art, as Mr. Alfred East tersely said, when lecturing on the subject in Tōkyō, is "great in small things, but small in great things."

Some of the anecdotes about Japanese artistic notabilities ring curiously familiar to Western ears. Thus, there is the story of the painter Kanaoka, whose horses were so life-like that at night, quitting the screen which they adorned, they trotted off into a neighbouring garden and munched the shrubs, till some ingenious person hit on the plan of adding a rope to the picture in order to tether these lively steeds. The cats of another artist actually caught live rats, much to the relief of the priests inhabiting a temple infested by those vermin. In a third tale it was painted rats that started into life, and scampered off when the rector of the temple came to see what was the matter. We seem to hear an echo of the stories told of Zeuxis and Parrhasios.* It is, by the way, somewhat odd that horses and cats should have been selected by the anecdote-mongers; for it is precisely in the portraiture of quadrupeds that Japanese art fails most conspicuously to express anatomical truth. Did they tell us of painted carp or gold-fish swimming away, or of painted mantises biting, we should perhaps lend a more willing ear.

Japanese art-motives form a fascinating study, which the visitor to Japan and the stay-at-home collector may alike master little by little on every scroll, coloured print, picture-book, *netsuke,* swordhilt that he bargains for, even on penny fans and twopenny towels; for in the Japanese view of life the tritest articles of daily use should, if possible, rejoice the eye and feed the mind. Odds and ends are not combined merely because they will look pretty, as in the handiwork of our own modern decorators. The art-motives all have a rationale, either in actual reason,—as when the pine-tree and bamboo, as evergreens, appropriately symbolise long life, to which is added the plum-blossom for beauty, making a lucky triad;—or in idea, such as that which constantly associates the lion and peony, because the former is the king of beasts, the latter the king of flowers;—or else in history or legend, or in unalterable convention. Thus, the sparrow and the bamboo go together; the plum-blossom and the nightingale; the

---

* See Article on CARVING for similar anecdotes.

bamboo thicket and the tiger; the chrysanthemum and the butterfly; the snow, moon, and blossoms (highly convention-alised); the flute-playing lad on his bull Benkei and his great bronze bell the Gods of Luck each with his tame animal or other appropriate symbol, etc., etc.,—all with a reason. To mix any of these subjects together, as is done by foreign imitators, shocks the trained eye in exactly the same manner as a solecism in grammar shocks the ear. The plain black crow does not perch facing the sun merely for the sake of contrast, though, to be sure, the contrast cannot fail to strike:—he does so for the mythological reasons glanced at in our article on the Japanese FLAG. Similarly in a thousand other instances. European decorators pursued a like course in the Middle Ages, when, from the shape of the cathedral down to the smallest group of stone figures in a niche, everything possessed a sym-bolical signification, so that (as Ruskin has set forth at length) Amiens Cathedral is nothing less than the whole Bible in stone. The Japanese are still in that enviable stage, where decoration is organic. They have few mere "patterns." Unfortunately, any treatment of so vast a subject, to be satis-factory, would involve a history of the Japanese—and even of the Chinese—mind, its religious beliefs, the fairy-tales on which its youth has been fed, the places known to fame, the celebrated personages and picturesque events that have adorned the national annals.

(See also Articles on ARCHITECTURE, CARVING, CLOISONNE, METAL-WORK, MUSIC, PORCELAIN, and WOOD ENGRAVING.)

N.B.—A curious fact, to which we have never seen attention drawn, is that the Japanese language has no genuinely native word for "art." To translate the European term "fine art," there has been invented the compound *bi-jutsu*, by putting together the two Chinese characters 美 *bi*, "beautiful," and 術 *jutsu*, "craft," "device," "legerdemain:" and there are two or three other such compounds which make an approach to the meaning, but none that satisfactorily cover it. The Japanese language is similarly devoid of any satisfactory word for "nature." The nearest equivalents are *seishitsu*, "characteristic qualities;" *bambutsu*, "all things;" *tennen*, "spontaneously." This curious philological fact makes it difficult, with the best will and skill in the world, to reproduce most of our discussions on art and nature in a manner that shall be intelligible to those Japanese who know no European language.

The lack of a proper word for "art" is unquestionably a weakness in Japanese. Perhaps

the lack of a word for " nature " is a strength. For does not the word " nature " in our
Western tongues serve to conceal, and therefore encourage, confusion of ideas ? When we
talk, for instance, of being " inspired by nature," what precise sense can be attached to the
phrase ? Sometimes " nature "—especially with a big N—is a kind of deistic synonym or
euphemism for the Creator, who becomes " she " for the nonce. At other times it denotes His
creatures. Sometimes it is the universe minus man; sometimes it is man's impulses as opposed
to his conscious acts. Sometimes it sums up all that is reasonable and proper; sometimes, as in
theological parlance, the exact reverse. The word " nature " is a Proteus. It stands for
everything in general and nothing in particular,—impossible to define, and serving only as a
will-o'-the-wisp to mislead metaphysically minded persons.

Books recommended. *The Art and Technique of Sumi-e: Japanese Ink-Painting as
Taught by Ukai Uchiyama* by Kay Morrissey Thompson; *The Arts of Japan: An
Illustrated History* by Hugo Munsterberg; *Chats on Japanese Prints* by Arthur Davison
Ficke; *A Collection of Nagasaki Colour Prints and Paintings* by H. H. N. Mody;
A Copybook for Japanese Ink-Painting edited by Reiko Chiba; illustrated by Shutei
Ota; *The Folk-Arts of Japan* by Hugo Munsterberg; *The Hokusai Sketchbooks: Selec-
tions from the Manga* by James A. Michener; *The Ideals of the East with Special Refer-
ence to the Art of Japan* by Kakuzo Okakura; *Index of Japanese Painters* compiled by
the Society of Friends of Eastern Art; *Japanese Ink-Painting: Lessons in Suiboku
Technique* by Ryukyu Saito; *Japanese Painting: A Brief History* by Kenji Toda;
Japanese Prints: From the Early Masters to the Modern by James A. Michener; *Japanese
Woodblock Prints in Miniature: The Genre of Surimono* by Kurt Meissner; *Legend in
Japanese Art* by Henri L. Joly; *The Modern Japanese Print: An Appreciation* by
James A. Michener; *Netsuké* by F. M. Jonas; *Netsuke: A Guide for Collectors* by Mary
Louise O'Brien; photographs by Margaret Dhaemers; *The Netsuke Handbook of Ueda
Reikichi* adapted from the Japanese by Raymond Bushell; *Sumi-e: An Introduction
to Ink Painting* by Nanae Momiyama; *The Wonderful World of Netsuke: With One
Hundred Masterpieces of Miniature Sculpture in Color* by Raymond Bushell.

Asiatic Society of Japan. This society was founded in
1872, for " the collection of information and the investigation
of subjects relating to Japan or other Asiatic countries." The
two seats of the Society are Tōkyō and Yokohama. The
entrance fee is 5 *yen*, and the yearly fee likewise 5 *yen* to
residents, but 3 *yen* to non-residents. It is also optional to
residents to become life-members by paying the entrance fee
and a lump sum of 50 *yen*; similarly, to non-residents for the
entrance fee and 30 yen. Candidates are elected by the Council
of the Society. Persons desirous of membership should, therefore, apply to the Secretary or to some other member of the
Council. Members receive the *Transactions* of the *Asiatic
Society of Japan* free, from the date of their election, and have
the privilege of purchasing back numbers at half-price. These
are the *Asiatic Transactions,* so often referred to in the course
of the present work. Scarcely a subject connected with Japan
but may be found learnedly discussed in the pages of the

Asiatic Transactions. A *General Index* is in preparation; hitherto only that appended to Vol. XXIII has been available.

Besides the Asiatic Society, there is in Tōkyō a German Society, entitled *Deutsche Gesellschaft für Natur- und Völkerkunde Ostasiens,* the scope of whose labours is closely similar, and whose valuable *Mittheilungen,* or *German Asiatic Transactions,* as we have ventured to call them when quoting them, are strongly recommended to readers familiar with the German language. This Society was founded in 1873. The *Japan Society,* founded in London in 1892, has published many good papers, especially on subjects connected with art.

Aviation. The first Japanese to take up aviation were two officers trained abroad and who returned to Japan in 1911. Both the army and navy have their air squadrons. Civil aviation is at present controlled by the Communications Department. In July 1925 two Japanese built planes, fitted with Lorraine Dietrich engines and piloted by Japanese, flew from Japan to Moscow and thence on to Paris and London and back to Japan.

Bamboos. So extensive is the part played by the bamboo in Japanese domestic economy that the question is rather, what does it *not* do ? The larger species serve as poles for carrying heavy weights, drying clothes, punting boats, etc.; as flagstaffs, as water-pipes, recommended hereto by their valuable property of neither rusting like iron, nor yet rotting as wood is apt to do if the water be from a hot mineral spring. As carrying poles and when employed for the framework of houses, their combination of lightness with strength makes them peculiarly valuable, it being well-known to mechanicians that the hollow tube is of all forms that which best unites those two qualities. A small species of bamboo serves to make tobacco pipe-stems; one of intermediate size makes ornamental doors and palings, in which the varying height of the joints gives a natural pattern. Others, cut into thin strips, which are sometimes bound with silk, form window-blinds; and the tender sprouts of more than one species are even boiled and eaten as a vegetable. Penholders, broom-handles, walking-sticks, umbrella-handles and also the ribs of umbrellas, angling-rods, whips, ladders, yard-measures, bows and arrows, coolies' hats, submarine hedges for the collecting of oysters and of edible seaweed, hedges also round houses, embankments for rivers (large stones being placed for this purpose in bamboo crates), clapboarding, ornamental floors for verandahs and tea-rooms, travelling trunks, torches, chopsticks, spits, bird-cages, fish-traps, flutes, trumpets, picture-frames, cask hoops, even nails (for being non-conducters of heat and non-corrosible, bamboo nails do better for certain purposes than metal ones), ladles, tea-scoops, sieves, shutters, fans, even flower-vases, special apparatus of various sorts for use in the arts, toys and ornaments of innumerable kinds, are all manufactured out of bamboo. Nothing makes a better tube for keeping unmounted photographs from the damp than does a section of bamboo. The dried sheath of the culm of the young bamboo serves for wrapping up such things as rice sandwiches, meat, and cakes, which are apt to stain their receptacles; also for the manufacture of sandals and the soles of wooden clogs. The leaves of the bamboo grass (which is a sort of bamboo) provide a clean, cool surface on which to lay fish in a basket, the basket itself being often of bamboo split and twisted. Such twisted split bamboos also serve to make strong hawsers, which are employed to swing ferry-boats, and even for the construction of bridges in certain rural districts, as no other material is so cheap and so easy to handle. One kind at least can, by a process of boiling, be flattened out into trays which are much prized. Another species, which is non-hollow, is cut into seals. The above list could easily be extended. But it may suffice to show that Japanese life without the bamboo is almost as hard to picture to oneself as pastry without butter, landscape without light, or a Britisher without a grievance.

The numerous plants which common parlance lumps together under the general name of " bamboos " really form three distinct genera, known to botanists as *Bambusa, Arundinaria,* and *Phyllostachys,* each including many species. The number of species of bamboo found growing in Japan at the present day is stated by Prof. Matsumura, of the Tōkyō University and Botanical Gardens, at fifty, not including of course numerous varieties and sports. Thirty-nine are indigenous; the others have been introduced at various times from Korea, China, or the Luchu Islands, either for industrial use or as exotics for the adornment of rich men's gardens.* Such are the *hōchiku,* or square bamboo, and the *suwō-chiku* whose stem, when young, is of a bright red hue. To our own thinking, some of the commonest species are also the most graceful,—the *mōsō-dake* or "feathery bamboo," for instance, with its golden stem and overhanging plume-like fronds, clumps of which—though it, too, was introduced from China no earlier than A.D. 1738—are now among the most typical features of the Japanese landscape, and the *sasa,* or bamboo grass, that grows on hills and in country lanes, and whose leaves, bright green in spring, become edged with white as the year wanes, so that each comes to look like a little "cloud with a silver lining."

Most Europeans persist in regarding the bamboo as a delicate tropical plant, which would not stand our northern climate. We should like to show such persons the tall Japanese bamboos bending under the weight of the February snow, in parts of the country where the snowfall is measured, not in inches, but in feet. As a matter of fact, the bamboo in snowtime is a favourite Japanese art-motive.

By the Japanese themselves the bamboo is not regarded as a tree. In their eyes it forms a category apart, so that they speak of "trees *and* bamboos." Properly it belongs to the grasses:—it is just a giant grass, and nothing more. Its rate of growth is astonishing compared with that of most other

---

* In the opinion of Sir Ernest Satow, the number of indigenous species is much smaller than that stated by Prof. Matsumura. The question is a difficult one.

members of the vegetable kingdom, sometimes several feet in the course of four-and-twenty hours. Indeed, from every point of view the bamboo presents interesting subject-matter for observation, while practically it is one of nature's choicest gifts to man.

Bathing. Cleanliness is one of the few original items of Japanese civilisation. Almost all other Japanese institutions have their root in China, but not tubs. We read in the Japanese mythology that the god Izanagi, on returning from a visit to his dead wife in Hades, purified himself in the waters of a stream. Ceremonial purifications continue to form part of the Shintō ritual. But viewed generally, the cleanliness in which the Japanese excel the rest of mankind has nothing to do with godliness. They are clean for the personal satisfaction of being clean. Their hot baths—for they almost all bathe in very hot water of about 110° Fahrenheit—also help to keep them warm in winter. For though moderately hot water gives a chilly reaction, this is not the case when the water is extremely hot, neither is there then any fear of catching cold. There are over eleven hundred public baths in the city of Tōkyō, in which it is calculated that five hundred thousand persons bathe daily, the usual charge being 2½ *sen* (under three farthings of English money) for adults, 2 *sen* for children, and 1½ *sen* for infants in arms. In addition to this, every respectable private house has its own bath-room. Other cities and even villages are similarly provided. Generally, but not always, a barrier separates the sexes from each other. Where there are neither bathing establishments nor private bath-rooms, the people take their tubs out-of-doors, unless indeed a policeman, charged with carrying out the modern regulations, happen to be prowling about the neighbourhood; for cleanliness is more esteemed by the Japanese than our artificial Western prudery. As the editor of the *Japan Mail* has well said, the nude is seen in Japan, but is not looked at.

Some Europeans have tried to pick holes in the Japanese system, saying that the bathers put on their dirty clothes when they have dried themselves. True, the Japanese of the old school have nothing so perfect as our system of daily renovated linen. But as the bodies even of the men of the lowest class are constantly washed and scrubbed, it is hardly to be supposed that their garments, though perhaps dusty outside, can be very dirty within. A Japanese crowd is the sweetest in the world. The charm of the Japanese system of hot bathing is proved by the fact that almost all the foreigners resident in the country adopt it. There seems, too, to be something in the climate which renders hot baths healthier than cold. By persisting in the use of cold water one man gets rheumatism, a second gets fever, a third a never-ending continuance of colds and coughs. So nearly all end by coming round to the Japanese plan, the chief foreign contribution to its improvement being the use of a separate bath by each person. In a Japanese family the same bath does for all the members; and as man is the nobler sex, the gentlemen usually take it first, in the order of their age or dignity, the ladies afterwards, and then the younger children, the servants enjoying it last at a late hour of the evening, if they be not sent to a public bath-house instead. It must be understood that each bather first cleans himself outside the bath by ladling water over his body. Nowadays soap, too, is much used. The original national cleanser was the bran bag *(nuka-bukuro)*, made by sewing a handful of bran into a small piece of linen, which furnishes a deliciously soft washing material. Thus each one enters the bath already clean, to enjoy the luxury of a good boiling.

The national passion for bathing leads all classes to make extensive use of the hot mineral springs in which their volcano-studded land abounds. Sometimes they carry their enjoyment of this simple luxury to an almost incredible extreme. At Kawarayu, a tiny spa not far from Ikao in the province of Jōshū—one of those places, of which there are many in Japan, which look as if they were at the very end of the world, so steep are the mountains shutting them in on every side—the bathers stay in the water for a month on end, with a stone on their lap to prevent them from floating in their sleep. When we were there some years ago, the care-taker of the establishment, a hale old man of eighty, used to stay in the bath during the entire winter. To be sure, the water is, in this particular case, one or two degrees below blood-heat. Thus alone is so strange a life rendered possible. In another case, some of the inhabitants of a certain village famed for its hot springs excused themselves to the present writer for their dirtiness during the busy summer months: " For," said they, " we have only time to bathe twice a day." " How often, then, do you bathe in winter ? " " Oh! about four or five times daily. The children get into the bath whenever they feel cold."

Sea-bathing was not formerly much practised; but since 1885 the upper classes have taken to it, in imitation of European usage, and the coast is now dotted with bathing establishments under medical supervision. Ōiso, Ushibuse, Kamakura, and Dzushi are the favourite sea-side places of the gentry of Tōkyō.

Bibliography. The best, for European books on Japan, is Fr. von Wenckstern's *Bibliography of the Japanese Empire,* which, however, only goes as far as the year 1895. It includes a facsimile reprint of Léon Pagès' *Bibliographic Japonaise,* which had appeared a generation earlier. Though not a regular bibliography, Sir Ernest Satow's admirable article on *Japanese Literature* in the " American Cyclopædia " gives the titles of a considerable number of native Japanese books. The *Gunsho Ichiran,* published in 1801, ranks as the standard Japanese authority on the subject, but takes no notice of novels and other works of a popular nature. Samura's *Zusho Gedai* (revised edition, 1904) has a more extended scope.

Birthdays are not much observed in Japan, except that rice mixed with red beans is eaten on the auspicious day. All the little girls celebrate their yearly holiday on the 3rd March, and the little boys on the 5th May, as explained in the Article on CHILDREN. From another point of view, the 1st January may be considered the universal birthday; for the Japanese do not wait till the actual anniversary of birth has come round to call a person a year older, but date the addition to his age from the New Year, as already explained on page 12. The sixty-first birthday is the only one about which much fuss is made. This is because the old man or woman, having lived through one revolution of the sexagenary cycle, then begins a second round, which is in itself an extraordinary event; for the Japanese reckon youth to last from birth to the age of twenty, middle age from twenty to forty, and old age from forty to sixty. This last term corresponds to the Psalmists "three score and ten," as the natural limit of human existence.

Blackening the Teeth. This peculiar custom is at least as old as A.D. 920; but the reason for it is unknown. It was finally prohibited in the case of men in the year 1870 Even women have now abandoned it in Tōkyō Kyōto, and the circumjacent provinces; and to see it surviving as a means of feminine adornment (?), one must repair to certain remote rural districts,—the north-west coast, for instance, or the extreme north-east, where distance and poverty have acted as conservative forces. Every married woman in the land had her teeth blackened, until the present Empress set the example of discontinuing the practice. Fortunately, the efficacy of the preparation used wears out after a few days, so that the ladies of Japan experienced no difficulty in getting their mouths white again. Mr. A. B. Mitford, in his amusing *Tales of Old Japan,* gives the following recipe for tooth-blacking, as having been supplied to him by a fashionable Yedo druggist:—"Take three pints of water, and, having warmed it, add half a tea-cupful of wine.* Put into this mixture a quantity of red-hot iron; allow it to stand for five or six days, when there will be a scum on the top of the mixture, which should then be

---

* By "wine." must of course be meant Japanese *sake.*

poured into a small teacup and placed near a fire. When it is warm, powdered gall-nuts and iron filings should be added to it, and the whole should be warmed again. The liquid is then painted on to the teeth by means of a soft feather brush, with more powdered gall-nuts and iron, and, after several applications, the desired colour will be obtained."

Books on Japan.   Fr. von Wenckstern's *Bibliography of the Japanese Empire* contains a great many thousands of entries, from which it may be inferred that *not* to have written a book about Japan is fast becoming a title to distinction. The art of Japan, the history of Japan, the language, folk-lore, botany, even the earthquakes and the diseases of Japan—each of these, with many other subjects, has a little library to itself. Then there are the works of an encyclopedic character, and there are the books of travel. Some of the latter possess great value, as photographing Japanese manners for us at certain periods. Others are at the ordinary low level of globe-trotting literature, —twaddle enlivened by statistics at second-hand.

We give references at the end of most of the articles of this work to the chief authorities on each special subject. At the risk of offending innumerable writers, we now venture to pick out the following dozen works as probably the most generally useful that are accessible to English readers. Of course it is more than possible that some of the really best have escaped our notice or our memory. Anyhow, an imperfect list will perhaps be deemed better than none at all:—

1. " THE MIKADO'S EMPIRE," by the Rev. W. E. Griffis. This is the book best-calculated to give the general reader just the information that he requires, and to give it to him in a manner not too technical . The first volume is devoted to history, the second to the author's personal experiences and to Japanese life in modern days. The tenth edition brings the story down to 1903. More than one reader of cultivated taste has, indeed, complained of the author's tendency to " gush," and of the

occasional tawdriness of his style.* But these faults are on the surface, and do not touch the genuine value of the book.

2. Lafcadio Hearn's† "GLIMPSES OF UNFAMILIAR JAPAN," together with the succeeding volumes entitled "OUT OF THE EAST" and "KOKORO."‡ Never perhaps was scientific accuracy of detail married to such tender and exquisite brilliancy of style. In reading these profoundly original essays, we feel the truth of Richard Wagner's saying, that "*Alles Verständniss kommt uns nur durch die Liebe.*" Lafcadio Hearn understands contemporary Japan better, and makes *us* understand it better, than any other writer, because he loves it better. Japanese life, manners, thoughts, aspirations, the student class, the singing-girls, the politicians, the delightful country-folk of secluded hamlets who still bow down before ancestral gods, Japan's attitude in time of war, Buddhist funeral services chanted by priestly choirs in vestments gold-embroidered, not men only but ghosts and folk-lore fancies, the scenery of remote islands which Hearn alone among Europeans has ever trod,—not a single thing Japanese, in short, except perhaps the humorous side of native life, but these wonderful books shed on it the blended light of poetry and truth. Our only quarrel is with some of Lafcadio Hearn's judgments:—in righting the Japanese, he seems to us continually to wrong his own race. The objectionable character in his stories is too apt to be a European. However, Europe is well-able to take care of herself; and if this be the price demanded for so great a gift to literature and ethnologic science, we at least will pay it uncomplainingly.

3. "JAPANESE GIRLS AND WOMEN," by Miss A. M. Bacon. This modest volume and its sequel, A JAPANESE INTERIOR, give

---

* Thus the nose is spoken of as the "nasal ornament:" a volcano in a state of eruption is said to "ulcer its crater jaws:" laughing is called an "explosion of risibilities," etc., etc.

† Mr. Hearn's nationality having been sometimes questioned, we may mention that in 1896 he became a Japanese, assuming the new name of Koizumi Yakumo. Up till that time he had been a British subject, having been born in Corfu. Before settling in Japan in 1890, he had resided for many years in the United States, where his works have always been published.

‡ There are six or seven later volumes from the same gifted hand, displaying much of the same charm of style, but increasingly subjective in treatment.

in a short compass the best account that has yet been published of Japanese family life,—a sanctum into which all travellers would fain peep, but of which even most old residents know surprisingly little. The sobriety of Miss Bacon's judgments and the simplicity of her style contrast almost piquantly with Lafcadio Hearn's tropical luxuriance.

4. "Tales of Old Japan," by A. B. Mitford (Lord Redesdale), an old book, but always fresh. Love, revenge, the "happy despatch," adventure by land and sea, quaint fairytales, Buddhist sermons quainter still,—in a word, the whole picturesque life of Old Japan,—these are the things which Mr. Mitford gives us; and he gives them in a style that renders them doubly attractive.

5. "A History of Japanese Literature," by W. G. Aston. All that the outside world can ever hope to understand, or is ever likely to wish to learn, about Japanese poetry and prose is here compressed by the most accurate, and yet least pedantic, of scholars into the limits of a single octavo volume. This history of the Japanese mind during twelve centuries—for such in effect it is—shows how illusory are the common European notions of " the unchanging East;" for all, from 700 to 1900, were centuries of change, most were centuries of progress.

6. "The Soul of the Far East," by Percival Lowell. With a dazzling array of metaphysical epigrams, this distinguished Bostonian attacks the inner nature of the Japanese soul, whose hall-mark he discovers in " impersonality." Nothing on earth—or elsewhere—being too profound for an intellect so truly meteor-like in its brilliancy, Lowell, in his later work, Occult Japan, discovers to us Japanese possession, exorcism, and miracle-working, whose very existence had scarcely been suspected.

7. "Evolution of the Japanese," by Rev. Sidney L. Gulick. An elaborate and masterly study of the mental characteristics of the Japanese people, undertaken with special reference to that sweeping change in their institutions which the latter half of the nineteenth century inaugurated.

8. "A History of Japan during the Century of Early European Intercourse (1542–1651)," by J. Murdoch. Based on a critical study of the original documents in nine languages, this unique work describes in full detail not only civil wars, diplomatic intrigues, and the fortunes of Japan's greatest men, but also her first relations with the Portuguese, the Dutch, and other Western nations, and more especially the enthusiastic reception and subsequent persecution of the Catholic missionaries. Certain disorders of style alone mar the author's vivid picture of the most important century of Japanese history. A second volume is in preparation.

9. "The Capital of the Tycoon," by Sir Rutherford Alcock. Though published some forty years ago, and though as a narrative, it covers only the brief space of three years (1859–1862), this book is still delightful and profitable reading. In its pages we live with the fathers of the men who rule Japan to-day. True, these men may reject the application to their case of the proverb which says "like father, like son." But we foreign lookers-on, who perhaps after all see something of the game, must be permitted to hold a different opinion, and to believe that even in cases so exceptional as Japan's, the political and social questions of a country can only then be fairly comprehended when its past is constantly borne in mind. Sir Rutherford's book combines the light touch of the skilled diplomat and man of the world with the careful research of the genuine student.

10. "Japan and China," by Capt. F. Brinkley. This work in twelve handsome volumes, besides covering a multitude of other subjects, treats authoritatively of art—more especially ceramic art, to which an entire volume is devoted—and of the political history of the last fifty years. The large sections describing the manners and customs of the Japanese Court and people at various periods are also very interesting. But the seeker after information on Japan could dispense with the four volumes on China, which come as a sort of appendix to the eight volumes in which Japan, though a slenderer subject, is so much more fully dealt with.

11.   The " TRANSACTIONS OF THE ASIATIC SOCIETY OF JAPAN."
Almost every subject interesting to the student of Japanese
matters is treated of in the pages of these TRANSACTIONS, which
have, for more than thirty years past, been the favourite
vehicle of publication for the researches of Satow, Aston,
Gubbins, Blakiston, Pryer, Geerts, Batchelor, Troup, Wigmore,
Knox, Florenz, Greene, Lloyd, and other eminent scholars and
specialists. Of course the " ASIATIC TRANSACTIONS " are not
light reading; their appeal is to the serious student.

12.   " DESCRIPTIVE AND HISTORICAL CATALOGUE OF JAPANESE
AND CHINESE PAINTINGS IN THE BRITISH MUSEUM," by Wm.
Anderson. Such a little does injustice to what is really an
original and valuable book. Who would think of spending over
£1 sterling on a catalogue ? But this so-called catalogue is
really a mine of information on numberless Japanese matters.
To begin with, it gives a complete history of Japanese pictorial
art.   Then the author's painstaking research, with the
assistance of Sir Ernest Satow, into the " motives " of this
art—drawn, as they are, from the history of the country, from
its religions, its superstitions, its literature, its famous sites
—has shed a flood of light on these and many kindred subjects.
Not that the book is easy reading, or meant to be read at all
continuously. Still, the store of anecdotes which it contains
will interest every person, who, when confronted by a Japanese picture or other work of art, prefers knowing what it is
about to gaping at it ignorantly.

Where one has hundreds of books to choose from, such a
list as the above might of course be indefinitely extended.
Pearson's *Flights Inside and Outside Paradise* starts to our
recollection at once as the book of all others to help to while
away a rainy day at a tea-house. Miss Bird's (Mrs. Bishop's)
Unbeaten Tracks in Japan is a capital description of Japanese
travel in the " good old days " of a quarter of a century ago,
her account of the Ainos being specially valuable.   Rein's
Japan, with its sequel *The Industries of Japan,* is an
encyclopedic work now out of print and in some respects

antiquated, but which should nevertheless, if possible, be consulted by every serious student.* Black's *Young Japan* records the impressions of a well-informed resident during the years 1858–1879 with the vividness peculiar to memoirs jotted down from day to day, as the events they describe are unfolding themselves. Miss Scidmore's *Jinrikisha Days in Japan* will be found a genial companion, as also will Brownell's *Heart of Japan*. *Notes in Japan*, by Alfred Parsons, may be recommended. Knapp's *Feudal and Modern Japan* is bright and sympathetic. Dening's *Life of Hideyoshi* and *Japan in Days of Yore* give us refreshing peeps into a state of society less prosaic than our own. Inoue's *Sketches of Tōkyō Life* brim over with interest, while the various illustrated booklets printed on crape paper at Hasegawa's press form pretty souvenirs. Then, too, come the books in foreign languages, —such, for instance, as Humbert's *Le Japon et les Japonais,* Bousquet's *Le Japon de nos Jours,* Bellessort's *La Société Japonaise,* and Dumolard's *Le Japon Politique, Economique et Social.* Father Papinot's *Dictionnaire de l'Histoire et de la Géographic du Japon* is a useful compilation, to which no analogue exists in English. For Pierre Lotti's books the resident community has less respect than the public at home:— his inaccuracy and superficiality go against the grain. Nevertheless, the illustrations to his *Madame Chrysanthème* are very pretty, and the letter-press is worth skimming through, though the volume can in nowise be recommended either to misses or to missionaries. What has struck us as the liveliest and best of all popular books on Japan is in German. We mean Netto's *Papierschmetterlinge aus Japan,* with its delightful illustrations and its epigrammatic text. Nippold's descriptions and Junker von Lândegg's stories are much read. With more serious works, too, the Germans are naturally to the front. The *Mittheilungen* of the German Asiatic Society *(Deutsche Gesellschaft für Natur- und Völkerkunde Ostasiens)* are a mine of information on matters scientific, legal, etc., etc.

---

* We refer here to the authorised English translation, which was based on a careful revision of the original German text. This original, too, is now out of print; but a new edition of it is expected to appear shortly.

Not content with the reality of Japan as it is or as it was, some imaginative writers have founded novels on Japanese subjects. We thus have books such as *Arimas,* which is whimsical and clever, and a dozen others that somehow we have never been able to make up our mind to dip into. As for books of travel, there is literally no end to the making of them. Almost every possible space of time, from *Seven Weeks in Japan* to *Eight Years in Japan* and *Nine Years in Nipon,* has furnished the title for a volume. So have almost all the more piquant adjectives with the word "Japan" attached, as *The Real Japan, Heroic Japan, Ceremonial Japan, Agitated Japan, Le Japon Pittoresque, Le Japon Pratique,* etc., etc. There are *Expeditions to Japan, Sketches of Japan, Runs in Japan, Gleanings from Japan, Short Leave to Japan, Japan as we Saw it, Lotos-time in Japan, Journeys, Travels, Trips, Excursions, Impressions, Letters,* etc., etc., almost *ad infinitum;* " and apt alliteration's artful aid " has been borrowed for such titles as *A Jaunt in Japan, The Gist of Japan, Japanese Jingles,* and several others. *A Diplomatist's Wife in Japan,* by Mrs. Hugh Fraser, and other works from the same hand give a readable account of life in Tōkyō and at the usual summer holiday resorts, while Weston, in his *Japanese Alps,* leads us touring among the little-known peaks of the provinces of Etchū, Hida, and Shinano. Many excellent things, on the other hand, may be unearthed from the files of old newspapers. See, for instance, Rudyard Kipling's *Letters to the " Times," 1892,* which are the most graphic ever penned by a globe-trotter,—but then what a globe-trotter ! They have been republished in *From Sea to Sea.* Many general books of travel have chapters devoted to Japan. The liveliest is Miss Duncan's *Social Departure.* For though the author revels in Japan as " a many-tinted fairy-tale," the sense of humour which never deserts her prevents her enthusiasm from degenerating into mawkishness. Perhaps the most entertaining specimen of globe-trotting literature of another calibre is that much older book, Miss Margaretha Wepper's *North Star and Southern Cross.* We do not wish to make any statement which cannot be verified, and therefore we will *not* say that the author is as mad as a March hare. Her *idée fixe* seems to have been that every foreign man in Yokohama and " Jeddo " meditated an assault on her. As for the Japanese, she dismisses them as " disgusting creatures."*

More edifying, if less amusing, than such works are the numerous monographs on special subjects, particularly those on art. Such are Gonse's *L'Art Japonais*, Audsley and Bowes' various publications on *Keramic Art*, *Seals*, and *Enamels*, Franks's and Dresser's books, and above all, Anderson's *Pictorial Art of Japan*, which is a magnificent work, conceived in a critical spirit, written with competent knowledge, and beautifully illustrated. Conder's *Flowers of Japan* and *Japanese Gardens*, Piggott's *Music and Musical Instruments of Japan*, Leech's *Butterflies from Japan*, Gowland's *Dolmens and Burial Mounds in Japan*, and Munro's *Coins of Japan* may be confidently recommended as the best treatises on their respective subjects. Gubbins has translated the Japanese Civil Code, making his translation doubly useful by printing the original opposite to it on the same page. Lönholm, too, has done yeoman's service by rendering some of the codes into English, French, and German. *Japan's Volkswirthschaft und Staatshaushalt*, by K. Rathgen, ranks as the standard authority on Japanese financial and economic questions. Maurice

---

* Here is a portion of this authoress's description of Yokohama and its foreign residents:—
" It will be well understood that the life of the European in Japan is, after all, a wretched one. The senses and the animal appetite are abundantly provided for; but the mind, the heart, and the soul are left totally destitute. There are clubs, it is true, but at the time of my stay in Yokohama, they were mere gastronomical resorts. The pure-minded men of the island live at home, where they can enjoy just as much comfort as in the clubs, and are rarely seen in them, except when dramatic companies, comedians, whistlers, or such people visit this land. A few of the better Europeans visit the club to kill time.

" I had occasion to remark during my stay in Yokohama that the perennial monotony of the place, and the sensual life led there, have reduced many of them to a state bordering on imbecility. It was difficult to believe that the drivelling trash which they talked could have its origin in the head at all. The eyes of such men are dull, and they have a kind of idiotic stare. They see and hear only what directly attracts the stomach and senses. It is useless moralising further on this subject; but I cannot refrain from adding that the impression produced upon a healthy mind by this portentous abasement is very disheartening. Often when contemplating the superb scenery among which these depraved creatures live, I have involuntarily exclaimed in the words of the poet,
' Though every prospect pleases,
And only man is vile.' "

Courant has written learnedly on a variety of subjects in the
Journal Asiatique and elsewhere. Morse's *Japanese Homes* is
a delightful account, not only of Japanese architecture, but
of every detail of Japanese domestic life, even down to the
water-bucket and the kitchen tongs. The only drawback is the
author's set purpose of viewing everything through rose-
coloured spectacles, which makes those who would fain be
instructed feel that they are listening to a special pleader
rather than to a judge. Unfortunately for sober science, the
fascination exercised by Japan is so potent that a similar fault
impairs the value of several otherwise first-rate works. Ogawa's
albums of collotypes will delight every lover of the beautiful.
For coloured illustrations of scenery and the life of the people,
the traveller is recommended to the native book-shops and
print-stalls:—no foreign artist has succeeded in rendering
the peculiar Japanese colouring.

Among books of reference, may be mentioned Bramsen's
Chronological Tables, by which the exact equivalent of any
Japanese date can be ascertained; the *China Sea Directory,
Vol. IV;* the various *Memoirs of the Imperial University;* the
British Consular *Trade Reports;* the *Résumé Statistique de
l'Empire du Japon,* issued yearly; and the annual reports of
the various departments of the Imperial Government on such
matters as education, railways, posts, etc., etc. We advert to
these last, because not a few of them appear in English as
well as in the vernacular. Several Japanese educated abroad
have written books in European languages. The work of this
class that has made most noise of late years is a little volume
by Nitobe entitled *Bushido, the Soul of Japan,* which sets forth
in popular style the system of practical ethics that guided the
conduct of the Samurai of old. In somewhat amusing contrast
to the patriotic enthusiasm of this author, is the gloomy picture
of native family life drawn in Tamura's *Japanese Bride. How
I Became a Christian,* by Uchimura Kanzō, should interest a
large class of readers. Okakura's *Ideals of the East* might be

taken for Bostonian handiwork, but for the Japanese name on the title-page. We may also mention Nitobe's monograph on *The Intercourse between the United States and Japan,* Inagaki's *Japan and the Pacific,* Bunyiu Nanjio's *Catalogue of the Buddhist Tripîtaka,* and—though they have little relation to Japan—the so-called poems of Y. Noguchi, which have made a sensation (in California). Of works by early travellers, the copious *Letters of the Jesuit Missionaries,* the *Letters of the English Pilot Will Adams,* Kaempfer's *History of Japan,* and the elder Siebold's encyclopedic productions are the chief. But these are now mostly out of print, besides being out of date. Another excellent book, now difficult to obtain, is Hildreth's *Japan as it Was and Is,* in which the gist of what the various early travellers have left us concerning Japan is woven together into one continuous narrative, the exact text of the originals being adhered to as far as possible.

Botany. We have not the necessary space, even had we the necessary ability, to enter into a particular description of that rich and wonderful Japanese flora, which excites the imagination of the man of science as much as ever Japanese works of art in porcelain, bronze, and lacquer excited the imagination of the man of taste. We can only draw attention to a few striking facts and theoretical considerations, referring the reader for all details to Dr. Rein's masterly *résumé* of the subject, and to the works of Maximowicz, Savatier, Asa Gray, Sir Joseph Hooker, Itō Keisuke, and the other specialists whom Rein quotes.

The first impression made on any fairly observant person landing in Japan is the extraordinary variety of the vegetation. He sees the pine of the north flourishing by the side of the bamboo, or even of the tropical palmetto. A rice-field, as in India, stretches to his right; to his left will be a wheat or barley-field, reminding him of Europe; or else he is overshadowed by some giant camphor-laurel, the like of which grows only in Formosa. Equally unexpected juxtapositions occur wherever he travels throughout the archipelago. No wonder that the number of known species of trees and plants (exclusive of mosses and other low organisms) attains to the enormous figure of 2,728, distributed over 941 genera and 151 orders* while it is almost certain that further investigations will raise the figure considerably, the northern portion of the country having been as yet but imperfectly explored. Of forest-trees alone, Japan—or, to be strictly accurate, the Japanese region, which includes also Korea, Manchuria, and a portion of Northern China—possesses no less than 186 species divided among 66 genera, as against the 85 species in 33 genera of Europe. The Atlantic forest region of North America is nearly as rich as Japan, having 155 species in 66 genera. The Pacific forest region of North America is poorer even than Europe, having but 78 species in 31 genera. A further very curious fact is that North-Eastern America and Japan possess 65 genera in common. Evidently there must be some powerful underlying cause connecting phenomena at first sight so capricious. Dr. Rein lays great stress on the general similarity of climatic conditions obtaining in Eastern Asia and Eastern America, on the abundant rainfall of Japan, and on the convenient stepping-stones for vegetable immigrants formed by the Kurile Islands, Saghalien, Oki, Iki, the Luchuan archipelago, and other islands both to the west and south. May we not also accept Mr. Wallace's theory, as propounded in his charming book, *Island Life,* to the effect that the glacial epoch had great influence in bringing about the present state of things ? When the climate of the north temperate regions grew arctic, some of the trees and plants whose habitat was there must have perished, but others doubtless migrated in a southerly direction, where they could still find sufficient

---

* This is Maximowicz's estimate, made in the year 1884. Of the 2,728 species, 1,812 species belong to dicotyledons, 658 to monocotyledons, 44 to gymnosperms, and 214 to vascular cryptogams. During the last twenty years, various additions to and alterations in the list have been necessitated through the labours of botanists both native and foreign; but no later attempt than that of Maximowicz has been made to summarise the Japanese flora.

warmth to support their existence. In Europe, however, they were stopped—first by the barrier of the Alps, and then by the still more effectual barrier of the Mediterranean. On the Pacific slope of America, they mostly perished owing to the extreme narrowness of their habitat, which allowed of no free emigration in any direction. The conditions of Eastern America and of Eastern Asia were altogether different. Here were neither mountain ranges nor oceans to obstruct the southward march of the vegetation as it retreated before the ice; and when the ice had disappeared, all the heat-loving forms, safely preserved in the south, were able to return northward again, a considerable remnant of the richer vegetation of an earlier geological age being thus handed down to our own days in these two favoured regions.

A consideration to which little attention has hitherto been paid is the general identity of the Japanese flora with that of the adjacent coast of Asia. It is probable that when Korea shall have been thoroughly explored, not a few species now designated as *Japonica* will be found to be really continental forms. It is already known that some of the plants now most common in Japan have been introduced in historical times through human agency. Such are, to name but two, the tea-plant and the orange-tree. The introduction of the latter is mentioned by the Japanese poets of the eighth century. The tea-plant came in with Buddhism. We were ourselves, we believe, the first to point out, some twenty years ago, the help which philology can given to natural science in this field, by proving that plants and also animals now inhabiting Japan, but originally imported from China or Korea, may often be detected in the Japanese language by their slightly corrupted Chinese or Korean names.*

What we have for shortness' sake termed the Japanese region, is named by Rein "the north-eastern monsoon region," and is furthermore described by him as the "kingdom of

---

* See the "Asiatic Transactions," Vol. X. Supplement, p. 70 of the *Introduction to the Kojiki.*

magnolias, camellias, and aralias." It coincides very nearly in latitude with the region of the Mediterranean; but the character of the two is as different as can well be imagined. The Japanese region is the delight of the botanist. The Mediterranean region, with its severer forms and more sparing growth, better pleases the artist, who loves vegetation less for its own sake than as a setting for the works of man.

Books recommended. *A Japanese Miscellany* by Lafcadio Hearn; *Meet Japan: A Modern Nation with a Memory* written under the auspices of Tsuneji Hibino.

Bowing to the Emperor's Picture is a point of Japanese etiquette that has caused much heart-burning among foreigners and native Christian converts. The custom is no ancient one, dating back as it does only to 1891. It came in, like so much else, as a result of the modern recrudescence of imperialism, and is now observed in all schools and many public offices on certain occasions of annual recurrence. The ground whereon objection has been taken to it is that it savours of idolatry. But surely such an interpretation rests on confusion of thought. A human ruler is no Baal or Moloch. We have never heard of any one refusing to bow to the Japanese emperor, or any other emperor, when seen in the flesh. What harm, then, can there be in saluting his picture ? Moreover, if a prostration made before the living emperor does not amount to " worship," how in reason can one made before his picture be so construed ? This case and the case of the heathen idol are not parallel.

Bronze. See METAL-WORK.

Buddhism. Many writers, from St. Francis Xavier downwards, have drawn attention to the superficial resemblances between the Buddhistic and the Roman Catholic ceremonial,— the flowers on the altar, the candles, the incense, the shaven heads of the priests, the rosaries, the images, the processions. In point of dogma, a whole world of thought separates ·Bud-

dhism from every form of Christianity. Knowledge, enlightenment, is the condition of Buddhistic grace,—not faith. Self-
perfectionment is the means of salvation, not the vicarious
suffering of a Redeemer. Not eternal life is the end, and active
participation in unceasing praise and thanksgiving, but absorption into Nirvana (Jap. *Nehan*), practical annihilation. For
Buddhism teaches that existence is itself an evil, springing
from the double root of ignorance and the passions. In logical
conformity with this tenet, it ignores the existence of a supreme
God and Creator of worlds. There are, it is true, gods in the
cosmogony which Buddhism inherited from Brahminism; but
they are less important than the *Hotoke*, or Buddhas—men,
that is, who have toiled upward through successive stages of
existence to the calm of perfect holiness. In fact, philosophically speaking, two systems could hardly stand in more
glaring contrast, though it is true that in the lives of quiet,
pious folk not given to speculation or to the logical following
out of the faith that is in them, the practical result of both may
often coincide.

These few remarks are designed merely to point the reader
along the true path of enquiry. It does not, of course, fall
within the scope of a manual devoted to things Japanese to
analyse the doctrines and practices of the great and complicated Indian religion, which, commencing with the birth
of the Buddha Shaka Muni in the year 1027 B.C. (so say the
Chinese and Japanese Buddhists, but European scholars prefer
the date 653 B.C.), gradually became the main factor in the
religious life of all Eastern Asia.

Japan received Buddhism from Korea, whither it had spread
from China. The account which the native history books give
of the introduction of Buddhism into Japan is that a golden
image of Buddha and some scrolls of the sutras were presented to the Mikado Kimmei by the King of Hyakusai, one of
the Korean states, in A.D. 552. The Mikado inclined to the
acceptance of the new religion; but the majority of his council,
conservative Shintoists, persuaded him to reject the image
from his Court. The golden Buddha was accordingly conferred

upon one Soga-no-Iname, who turned his country-house into the first Buddhist temple existing on the soil of Japan. A pestilence, which shortly broke out, was attributed by the partisans of the old religion to this foreign innovation. The temple was razed to the ground; but such dire calamities followed on this act of sacrilege that it was soon allowed to be rebuilt. Buddhist monks and nuns then flocked over from Korea in ever-increasing numbers. Shōtoku Taishi, who was prince regent under the Empress Suiko from A.D. 593 to 621, himself attained almost to the rank of Buddhist saintship; and from that time forward the new religion became established as the chief religion of the land, though Shintō was never entirely suppressed. All education was for centuries in Buddhist hands, as was the care of the poor and sick; Buddhism introduced art, introduced medicine, moulded the folk-lore of the country, created its dramatic poetry, deeply influenced politics and every sphere of social and intellectual activity. In a word, Buddhism was the teacher under whose instruction the Japanese nation grew up. As a nation, they are now grossly forgetful of this fact. Ask an educated Japanese a question about Buddhism, and ten to one he will smile in your face,—a hundred to one that he knows nothing about the subject, and glories in his nescience.

Chinese and Korean Buddhism was already broken up into numerous sects and sub-sects when it reached Japan,—sects, too, all of which had come to differ very widely in their teaching from that of the purer, simpler Southern Buddhism of Ceylon and Siam. Japanese Buddhism follows what is termed the "Greater Vehicle" (Sanskrit *Mahâyâna*, Jap. *Daijō*), which contains many unwarranted accretions to the original teaching of the Buddha.* The most powerful sects now existing in Japan are the Tendai, Shingon, Jōdo, and Zen, which are of Chinese origin, the Shin (also called Ikkō or Monto), and the Nichiren or Hokke, both native Japanese sects dating

---

* This view of Southern Buddhism as the purer has the support of most European investigators. It is, however, not endorsed by Mr. Lloyd, quoted below as the first authority on Japanese Buddhism, who not unnaturally follows the lead of his Japanese instructors.

from the thirteenth century. The Nichiren sect is the most bigoted, the Shingon the most superstitious. The Monto has been compared to Protestantism, because it allows its priests to marry, and teaches the doctrine of justification by faith in Amida* alone. The Zen is the most interesting of all to the student of Japanese sociology, on account of its close connection with the cultivation of poetry and the arts.

The complicated metaphysics of Buddhism have awakened little interest in the Japanese nation. Another fact, curious but true, is that these people have never been at the trouble to translate the Buddhist canon into their own language. The priests use a Chinese version, the laity no version at all nowadays, though—to judge from allusions scattered up and down Japanese literature—they would seem to have been more given to searching the scriptures a few hundred years ago. The Buddhist religion was disestablished and disendowed during the years 1871–4, a step taken in consequence of the temporary ascendency of Shintō. More recently a faint struggle has been carried on by the Buddhist priesthood against rivals in comparison with whom Shintō is insignificant: we mean the two great streams of European thought,—Christianity and physical science. A few—a very few—men trained in European methods fight for the Buddhist cause. They do so, not as orthodox believers in any existing sect, but because they are convinced that the philosophical contents of Buddhism in general are supported by the doctrine of evolution, and that this religion needs therefore only to be regenerated on modern lines in order to find universal acceptance.

Books recommended. *The Book of Tea* by Kakuzo Okakura; *Bushido: The Soul of Japan* by Inazo Nitobe; *A First Zen Reader* compiled and translated by Trevor Pryce Leggett; *History of Japanese Religion* by Masaharu Anesaki; *The Ideals of the East with Special Reference to the Art of Japan* by Kakuzo Okakura; *Japan: An Attempt at Interpretation* by Lafcadio Hearn; *Japanese Youth Confronts Religion* by Fernando M. Basabe; *Religions in Japan* edited by William K. Bunce; *Zen Flesh, Zen Bones* compiled by Paul Reps.

---

* A deity dwelling in a lovely paradise to the west. Originally he was an abstraction, the ideal of boundless light.

Camphor. Japan's new colony of Formosa is the greatest camphor-producing district in the world, and Japan proper comes next, though the ruthless deforestation that has disgraced the present epoch bids fair to ruin this source of national income before the lapse of many more years. Unfortunately, camphor cannot, like lacquer or maple-sugar, be extracted by tapping. The tree must be felled and cut into chips, which are steamed in a vat, the vapour being made to carry off the fumes into a cooling apparatus, where condensation takes place and the camphor and camphor-oil are afterwards skimmed off. Cabinets made of camphor-wood are much esteemed, not only for the fine grain and silky sheen of the wood, but for its efficacy against the attacks of insects.

The camphor-laurel ranks among the stateliest of trees, frequently attaining to an enormous height and girth,—thirty, forty, and even fifty feet in circumference. Grand specimens may be seen at Atami, at Atsuta, and at Dazaifu,—all places on or near the ordinary lines of travel. Such giant trees are often worshipped by the simple country folk, who hang ropes of straw or paper round them in token of reverence.

Books recommended. Rein's *Industries of Japan*, pp. 143–150.—*Der Kampferbaum*, by Dr. E. Grasmann, in Part 56 of the "German Asiatic Transactions."

Capital Cities. If the Japanese annals may be trusted, Japan has had no less than sixty capitals. This is to be traced to the fact that in ancient days there was a superstitious dread of any place in which a person had died. The sons of a dead man built themselves a new house. Hence, too, the successor of a dead Mikado established a new capital. The provinces of Yamato, Yamashiro, Kawachi, and Settsu, which were the home and centre of the early Japanese monarchy, are dotted with places, now mere villages, sometimes indeed empty names, but once holding the proud position of capitals of the Empire.

In process of time, such perpetual changes proving incompatible with the needs of the more advanced civilisation introduced from China and Korea, a tendency to keep the Court settled in one place began to make itself felt. Nara in Yamato remained the capital for seven reigns, between A.D. 709 and 784. After further wanderings, the Court fixed itself at Kyōto in 794; and this city continued, with few interruptions, to be the residence of successive generations of Mikados till the year 1868, when it was abandoned in favour of Yedo (Tōkyō), which had been the capital of the Shōguns ever since the year 1590. Kyōto, however, still nominally retains the rank of a metropolis, as is indicated by its new name of 西京 *Saikyō*, or "western capital," in contradistinction to 東京 *Tōkyō*, the "eastern capital." The new name, however, is little used. The chief sights in and near Kyōto are the Mikado's palaces, the temples named Nishi Hongwanji, Chion-in, Kiyomizu-dera, Gion, Ginkakuji, Kinkakuji, Higashi Hongwanji, San-jū-san-gen-dō, and Inari-no-Jinja, Mount Hiei-zan, Lake Biwa, Arashi-yama famous for its cherry-blossoms and maple-leaves, and the rapids of the Katsura-gawa. Brocades and embroidery generally are the products for which Kyōto is chiefly noted. In the second rank come pottery, porcelain, cloisonné, and bronze.

Nara, whose charms have been sung by many a Japanese poet from the eighth century onwards, is distinguished by the almost English appearance of the park which surrounds the ancient Shintō temple of Kasuga, where tame deer crowd around the visitor to feed out of his hand. In Nara, likewise, stands the great Buddhist temple of Tōdaiji, with the colossal bronze image known as the *Daibutsu* or "Great Buddha," dating from A.D. 749.

Another of the old capitals, Kamakura, is distant only a few miles from Yokohama. It was never inhabited by the Mikados. It was the seat of the Shōguns from 1189 onwards, and of the so-called Regents of the Hōjō family during the troublous Middle Ages. Kamakura, taken by storm and burnt to the ground in 1455 and again in 1526, gradually lost its importance. Woods and rice-fields now stretch over the area that once afforded a home to more than a million inhabitants, and little remains to tell of its ancient splendour, save the great temple of Hachiman and the magnificent bronze image of Buddha, perhaps the grandest of all Japanese works of art.

The principal sights of Tōkyō are the Shiba temples, with the tombs of the Shōguns of the Tokugawa dynasty, near which is one of the best *Kwankōba* or Bazaars; the view over the city from the tower on Atago-yama; the Shintō temple named *Shōkonsha,* erected to the memory of the loyal troops slain in battle; the adjacent museum of military objects, called the *Yūshū-kwan;* Ueno Park, with tombs and temples similar to those of Shiba, and also an interesting museum; the popular Buddhist temple of Asakusa, to say nothing of such modern European buildings as the government offices, banks, hospitals, prisons, etc., which will have an interest for some persons. In addition to these, according to the time of year, there are the cherry-blossoms of Ueno, Shiba, and Mukōjima, the wistarias of Kameido, the irises of Horikiri, and the chrysanthemums of Dango-zaka. It is also worth while paying a visit to one of the theatres, of which the *Kabuki-za* and *Meiji-za* are the best, and to the wrestling-matches held at the temple of Ekō-in and elsewhere. But after all, the chief sight of Tōkyō to one fresh from home is Tōkyō itself,—the quaint little wooden houses, which brick structures in foreign style have only partially replaced, the open-air life of the people, the clatter of the clogs, the jinrikishas, the dainty children powdered and rouged for a holiday outing, the graceful native dress which Western fashions and fabrics have not succeeded in driving out, the indescribably grotesque combinations of this dress with billy-cock hats, Inverness capes, and crochet tippets. There are also the attractions of the shops, which make Mr. Percival Lowell truly observe that "To stroll down the *Broadway* of Tōkyō of an evening is a liberal education in every day art," for—as he adds—" whatever these people fashion, from the toy of an hour to the triumphs of all time, is touched by a taste unknown elsewhere." Mr. Lowell, as an artist in words, does not add what we, simple recorders of facts, are bound to do, that with so much to appeal to the eye, Tōkyō also has not a little that appeals to the nose.

Books recommended. *Enjoy Japan: A Personal and Highly Unofficial Guide* by Walt Sheldon; *Kyoto: A Contemplative Guide* by Gouverneur Mosher; *Meet Japan: A Modern Nation with a Memory* written under the auspices of Tsuneji Hibino; *Tokyo* by Erhard Hürsch.

Carving. The earliest specimens of Japanese carving—if we may so call objects more probably moulded by the hand—are the rude clay figures of men and horses occasionally found in the tumuli of Central and Eastern Japan (see Article on ARCHÆOLOGY). But the art made no progress till the advent of Buddhism in the sixth century. A stone image of the god Miroku was among the earliest gifts of the Court of Korea to that of Japan. Wooden images came also. The Japanese themselves soon learnt to carve in both materials. The colossal figure of Jizō, hewn in relief on a block of andesite on the way between Ashinoyu and Hakone, is a grand example. Like so many other celebrated Japanese works of unknown antiquity, it is referred by popular tradition to the Buddhist saint, Kōbō Daishi (ninth century), who is fabled to have finished it in a single night. The art of wood-carving has always been chiefly in Buddhist hands. The finest collection of early religious statues is that in the museum at Nara, brought together from various temples in the surrounding country.* Much later—seventeenth and eighteenth centuries—are the charming painted carvings of flowers and birds in the Nikkō temples and in those at Shiba and Ueno in Tōkyō.

---

* Whether some of the best of these statues are of native Japanese, or of Chinese or Korean workmanship, is a point still disputed among experts. On the one hand, it is alleged that nothing of equal merit has been discovered either in Korea or in China. On the other, there seems something strange in the fact of Japanese statuary being practically confined to the earlier ages, while all the rest of the fine arts went on improving until a culminating point was reached in the eighteenth century.

The old Japanese sculptors rarely attempted portraiture.
A good example is offered by the seated figure of Ieyasu in the
temple of Tōshōgu at Shiba. But in sculpture, even more than
in pictorial art, the strength of the Japanese talent lies rather
in decoration and in small things than in representation and
in great things. The *netsukes*—originally a kind of toggle for
the medicine-box or tobacco-pouch, carved out of wood or ivory
—are often marvels of minuteness, and alive with a keen sense
of humour and the grotesque. The Japanese weakness in
sculpture is no mere accident. It results from a whole mental
attitude, from the habit of looking at nature rather than at
man,—a habit itself rooted in that impersonality on which Mr.
Percival Lowell has laid so much stress as a Far-Eastern
characteristic.

Japan's most famous sculptor was Hidari Jingorō, born in
A.D. 1594. The two elephants and the sleeping cat in the
mortuary shrine of Ieyasu at Nikkō are among the best-known
productions of his chisel. He died in 1634, leaving a flourishing school and a reputation around which legend soon began
to busy itself. A horse which he had carved as an ex-voto used,
it is averred, to leave its wooden tablet at night, and go down
to the meadow to graze. On one occasion the artist, having
seen a frail beauty in the street, became so enamoured that
on getting home he set about carving her statue; and between
the folds of the statue's robe he placed a mirror, which the girl
had let drop and which he had picked up. Thereupon the
statue, Galatea-like, came to life, and the two lovers were made
supremely happy. Now for the characteristically Japanese
turn given to the tale. The times were stormy, and it fell
out that the life of the daughter of the artist's lord had to be
sacrificed. The artist instantly cut off this living statue's head
and sent it to the enemy, who were taken in by the ruse which
his loyalty had prompted. But a servant of his lord's, also
deceived, and believing that Hidari Jingorō had really killed
their lord's daughter, took his sword and cut off the sculptor's
right hand. Hence the name of Hidari Jingorō, that is, " left-

handed Jingorō." Probably Jingorō's left-handedness, which undoubtedly gave him his nickname of *Hidari,* also suggested the legend.

Since 1892, when the first bronze statue was set up in Tōkyō in front of the Shōkonsha temple, that ancient European method of commemorating departed and even living worth has gradually come into vogue. Not only so, but the friezes of public buildings now begin to be adorned with Cupids of a Japanese cast of countenance, slant-eyed Goddesses of Poetry and Agriculture, etc., etc. It is all very strange and—very ugly. Pity that the successful adopters of an alien civilisation should not have had the sense to stop short at such incongruous superficialities!

Books recommended. *The Arts of Japan: An Illustrated History* by Hugo Munsterberg; *The Folk Arts of Japan* by Hugo Munsterberg; *Masterpieces of Japanese Sculpture* by J. Edward Kidder, Jr.

Cats. As one of the first questions asked by every observant traveller landing at Yokohama refers to the tailless, or more properly short-tailed, Japanese cats, let it be known that the peculiarity is a natural one. The bones are all there, but not normally developed; hence the atrophied appearance of the tail. It is true, however, that the habit of seeing only tailless cats has engendered such a prejudice in their favour that, should a litter chance to be born with one long-tailed kitten, somebody will generally take upon himself to chop the tail off to a respectable shortness. The popular objection to long-tailed cats has doubtless been augmented by the snaky aspect of a normal cat's tail when waved from side to side, and by the superstition that there exist cats furnished with one or several long tails, and possessing the power of bewitching human beings after the manner of foxes and badgers (see Article on DEMONIACAL POSSESSION). Note, however, that the objection to long-tailed cats does not prevail throughout the country. It is confined to certain provinces. Another superstition calling for notice is the lucky character attributed by seafaring men to tortoise-shell tom-cats. The master of a junk will pay almost any price to obtain one, and thus secure immunity from shipwreck. In this case, it is probably the rarity of the animal that has given it its fictitious value; for though tortoise-shell cats exist in considerable numbers, they are—for some unexplained reason—almost all tabbies.

Among Europeans an irreverent person may sometimes be heard to describe an ugly, cross old woman as a cat. In Japan, the land of torpsy-turvydom, that nickname is colloquially applied to the youngest and most attractive,—the singing-girls. The reason is that singing girls bewitch men with their artful, sham coy ways, like the magic cats alluded to above. For a similar reason, fair women one degree lower still in the scale are called foxes, while the male buffoons or jesters, whose talents help to make the fun fast and furious at a spree, are termed badgers.

Cha-no-yu. See TEA CEREMONIES.

Characteristics. See JAPANESE PEOPLE.

Charms and Sacred Pictures are sold for a few farthings at hundreds of temples throughout the land. The custom seems to have originated with the Buddhists, who already on the continent of Asia and before the introduction of Shaka Muni's religion into Japan, had developed all the adjuncts of popular piety and superstition. But the Shintō priests have taken the custom up, not disdaining in these hard times to turn an honest penny wherever possible.

The commonest Japanese charms are scraps of paper with an inscription for the reversal of bad luck, the attainment of good luck, protection from the perils of the sea or of war, from fire, from sickness, and in child-bearing. Others are long strips inscribed with the name of some god, or a brief invocation, to which is occasionally added the picture of the supernatural being invoked,—the fox-god, for instance, or the holy crows of Kumano,* or the sacred dog of Mitsumine who is esteemed a powerful protector against robbers. This kind is to be seen pasted vertically on the outside of the houses of the poor in almost every province of the empire, while well-to-do families keep them inside the house, as part of the furniture of the domestic altar. To procure such charms is always one object

---

* See Murray's *Handbook for Japan*, 7th edition, page 390.

of the pilgrimages to sacred mountains and famous shrines, still so popular with those classes of society which are not yet fully imbued with European twentieth century notions. Coloured prints of the shrine visited are generally purchased at the same time, and treasured as mementoes of the pilgrimage. There is another very popular kind, which can be made at home, consisting of the imprint of a hand,—generally a child's hand. It is obtained by first wetting the hand with ink, and then applying it to a sheet of paper, and is believed to avert malign influences. Besides these paper charms, there exist several other sorts. At Ise, for example, sacred medals are for sale; but we suspect that these owe their origin to European influence. Another Ise charm, which is genuinely native, consists of fragments of the temples themselves; for when these temples are hewn down every twenty years in accordance with immemorial usage, preparatory to the erection of new ones, the wood is all chopped up into tiny splinters which are carried away by innumerable devotees. The food offered to the gods is also sold to pilgrims as a charm, both at Ise and elsewhere. Then, too, there are miniature editions of various sutras, microscopic images of the Gods of Luck carved out of rice-grains, facsimiles of Buddha's footprint on certain sacred stones, and in fine such a multifarious assortment of " objects of bigotry and virtue " that memory and space alike fail us in the attempt to enumerate them. One charm—generally a thin oblong slab of wood inscribed with the name of the great shrine of Narita— is constantly worn by members of the middle and lower classes in Tōkyō, being hung round the neck by a string next to the skin. It is supposed to protect the wearer against accidents. Women often wear it over their sash. Children habitually have a bright-coloured " charm-bag " hung at their side, as described in the Article on DRESS.

Chauvinism. Japan has not escaped, in these latter days, the wave of " jingo "* feeling that has swept round the world,

---

* Says a Monsieur Félix Martin, author of *Le Japon Vrai* (!): " Ce mot me semble avoir été emprunté par les Yankees au vocabulaire du Nippon: il ne serait autre que le nom de l'impératrice Jingo, femme vaillante et patriote, qui fit, au troisième siècle avant notre ère, la conquête de la Corée." (!!!)—For the bold female in question, see Article on HISTORY.

making the nations like each other less as they come to know each other better. For a few years, no doubt, "foreign" and "good" were synonymous terms; the Japanese sat at the feet of the Western Gamaliel, and treasured his slightest utterances as pearls of great price. This state of things passed away suddenly in 1887. The feeling now is, "Japan for the Japanese, and let it be a Japanese Japan." Foreign employés have been dismissed, and replaced by natives. In the Diet—it was in the Upper House, too—the metrical system of weights and measures has been opposed on the ground that the introduction of a foreign standard would be a blot on the national escutcheon. Only four or five years ago, the Tōkyō Chamber of Commerce resolved that the Roman nomenclature hitherto used on the silver and copper pieces should be dropped from the new coinage. Not only has the national costume come back again to a considerable extent, and interest in the native sports and the national antiquities been revived:—the peculiar feature of the present situation is that the Japanese are determined to beat us on our own ground and with our own weapons. Japan is to engross the trade of the Pacific, and to be the leader of Asia in modern warfare and diplomacy. According to some, she will remodel philosophy; for Europe is incurably superstitious, Japan essentially reasonable. Mr. Inagaki, a well-known publicist who has lived abroad and even published a book in English, has written essays to demonstrate Japan's special fitness for originating new and important views on international law. Meanwhile, the foreign missionaries are being abandoned as old-fashioned by their quondam converts. The Rev. Mr. Kozaki believes that Japan is the place where "the world-problem of Christianity is . . . . . . being gradually solved;" and numbers of leading Japanese Christians hold with Mr. Yokoi that Japanese Christianity must develop a superior theology of its own, to which European Christianity will in the future look for support. Politicians take the same line, *mutatis mutandis.* They point to the weary secular struggles, the bloody rebellions, through which the West has slowly won its way to constitutional government, whereas in Japan what has there been? A grateful and intelligent people accepting the free gift of self-government from a wise and benevolent Sovereign. Furthermore it has been discovered that courage, patriotism, and loyalty are specifically Japanese virtues, or that—at the least—Japanese courage, Japanese loyalty, and Japanese patriotism glow with an incomparably brighter radiance than the qualities called by those same names in inferior countries,—England, for instance, France, Germany, or America.

Dai Nihon Banzai ! "Long live Great Japan !" Japan is a young nation—at least a rejuvenated nation—and youth will be self-confident. The greybeards must not wish it otherwise.

Cherry-blossom. The Japanese cherry-tree (*Prunus pseudo-cerasus,* Lindley) is cultivated, not for its fruit, but for its blossom, which has long been to Japan what the rose is to Western nations. Poets have sung it for over a millennium past, and crowds still pour forth every year, as spring comes round, to the chief places where avenues of it seem to fill the air with clouds of the most delicate pink. Even patriotism has adopted it, in contradistinction to the plum-blossom, which is believed to be of Chinese origin—not, like the cherry-tree, a true native of Japan. The poet Motoori exclaims:

> *Shikishima no*
> *Yamato-gokoro wo*
> *Hito towaba,*
> *Asa-hi ni niou*
> *Yama-zakura-bana !*

which, being interpreted, signifies "If one should enquire of you concerning the spirit of a true Japanese, point to the wild-cherry-blossom shining in the sun."—Again a Japanese proverb saŷs: "The cherry is first among flowers, as the warrior is first among men."

The single blossom variety is generally at its best about the 7th April, coming out before the leaves; the clustering double variety follows a little later. The places best worth visiting in Tōkyō are Ueno Park, Shiba Park, the long avenue of Mukōjima, and, in the neighbouring country, Asuka-yama and Koganei. But the most famous spots for cherry-blossom in all Japan are Yoshino amid the mountains of Yamato, and Arashiyama near Kyōto.

The Japanese are fond of preserving cherry-blossoms in salt, and making a kind of tea out of them. The fragrance of this infusion is delicious, but its taste a bitter deception.

Chess. Japanese chess *(shōgi)* was introduced from China centuries ago; and though it has diverged to some extent from its prototype, the two games still have a feature in common distinguishing them from all other varieties. It is this. The rank on which the pawns are usually posted is occupied by only two pieces, called *p'ao* by the Chinese, and *hisha* and *kaku* by the Japanese. Also, on either side of the king are two pieces, called *ssŭ* in the Chinese, and *kin* in the Japanese game. These perform the duty imposed on the *ferz* or *visir* of the Persian *Shatranj,* which was the equivalent of the modern queen. Therefore, no queen or piece of similar attributes appears in either Chinese or Japanese chess. There are eighty-one squares on the Japanese board, and the game is played with twenty pieces on each side, distinguished, not by shape or colour, but by the ideographs upon them. Though the movements of the pieces resemble in most respects those followed in the European game, there are certain ramifications unknown to the latter. The most important of these are the employment of the pieces captured from the adversary to strengthen one's own game, and the comparative facility with which the minor pieces can attain to higher rank.

Chess is understood by all classes in Japan. The very coolies at the corners of the streets improvise out of almost anything around them materials with which to play, and thus while away the tedium of waiting for employment. But it is comparatively little patronised by the educated classes, who hold its rival *Go* in much higher esteem.

The following is a diagram of the board:—

Yari		Fu				Fu		Yari
Keima	Kaku	Fu				Fu	Hisha	Keima
Gin		Fu				Fu		Gin
Kin		Fu				Fu		Kin
Ō		Fu				Fu		Ō
Kin		Fu				Fu		Kin
Gin		Fu				Fu		Gin
Keima	Hisha	Fu				Fu	Kaku	Keima
Yari		Fu				Fu		Yari

Ō is the king, *keima* the knight, *hisha* the rook, and *kaku* the bishop,—or pieces having movements like them. *Fu* is the pawn. The movements of the *yari* also resemble those of the rook, but are confined to the single rank on which it stands. *Gin* (silver) and *kin* (gold) are not found in Western chess. *Gin* moves one square diagonally at a time, also one square forward. If removed from its original position, it can retreat one square diagonally only. The *kin*, besides having similar movements, has also the power of moving one square on each side of itself, but it cannot return diagonally. The *fu* advances one square forward, and captures as it moves. When any piece moves into the adversary's third row, it may become a *kin*, in the same way as queening is effected in our game. This is indicated by turning the piece over. Every piece so promoted

loses its original character, except the *hisha* and *kaku* to which
the movements of the *kin* are added. As already indicated, a
captured piece may be employed at any time for either attack
or defence. To checkmate with the *fu* is a thing vetoed—or at
least considered "bad form"—in this non-democratic game,
neither is stale-mate permissible in Japanese chess. You wait
until the adversary makes a move which admits of free action
on your part. The object of the game is, as with us, to
checkmate the king.

Books recommended. *Chess Variations: Ancient, Regional, and Modern* by John
Gollon; *Shogi: Japan's Game of Strategy* by Trevor Pryce Leggett.

Children. Japan has been called "a paradise of babies."
The babies are indeed generally so good as to help to make it
a paradise for adults. They are well-mannered from the cradle,
and the boys in particular are perfectly free from that gawky
shyness which makes many English boys, when in company,
such afflictions both to others and to themselves. Pity only
that a little later they are apt to deteriorate, the Japanese
young man being less attractive than his eight or ten-year-old
brother,—becoming self-conscious, self-important, sometimes
intrusive.

The late Mrs. Chaplin-Ayrton tried to explain the goodness
of Japanese children by a reference to the furnitureless condition of Japanese houses. There is nothing, she said, for them
to wish to break, nothing for them to be told not to touch. This
is ingenious. But may we not more simply attribute the pleasing fact partly to the less robust health of the Japanese, which
results in a scantier supply of animal spirits ? In any case,
children's pretty ways and children's games add much to the
picturesqueness of Japanese life. Nothing perhaps gives the
streets a more peculiar aspect than the quaint custom which
obtains among the lower classes of strapping the babies on to
the back of their slightly older brother and sisters, so that
the juvenile population seems to consist of a new species of
Siamese twins. On the 3rd March every doll-shop in Tōkyō,
Kyōto, and the other large cities is gaily decked with what are

called *O Hina Sama*,—tiny models both of people and of things, the whole Japanese Court in miniature. This is the great yearly holiday of all the little girls. The boys' holiday takes place on the 5th May, when the towns and villages are adorned with gigantic paper or cotton carps, floating in the air from poles, after the manner of flags. The idea is that as the carp swims up the river against the current, so will the sturdy boy, overcoming all obstacles, make his way in the world and rise to fame and fortune.

The unpleasant appearance of some Japanese children's heads is simply due to a form of eczema. The ailment is one by no means unknown in Europe, and is easily curable in a week. But as popular superstition invests these scabby heads with a health-giving influence in later life, no attempt is made to cure them. Probably shaving with dirty razors has something to do with the disease; for it generally ceases when shaving stops, and has noticeably diminished since the foreign custom of allowing children's hair to grow has begun to gain ground. The Japanese custom is to shave an infant's head on the seventh day after birth, only a tiny tuft on the nape of the neck being left. During the next five or six years, the mother may give rein to her fancy in the matter of shaving her little one's head. Hence the various styles which we see around us. Shaving is left off when a child goes to school, instead of, as among Europeans, generally commencing when he quits it. The Japanese lad's chin does not begin to sport a few hairs for several years later. Japanese infants are not weaned till they are two or three, sometimes not till they are five years old. This is doubtless one cause of the rapid ageing of the mothers.

European parents may feel at ease about their little ones' chance of health in this country. Medical authorities declare the mortality among children of European race in Japan to be exceptionally low.

Books recommended. *Children of the Sun* by William & Patricia Clark; drawings by Phyllis Brannen; *The Japanese Are Like That* by Ichiro Kawasaki.

Christianity in Japan. See Missions.

Clans. This is the usual English translation of the Japanese word *han* (藩) which may better be rendered " Daimiate," that is, the territory and personal followers of a Daimyō, or territorial noble in feudal Japan. The soldier-gentry of a Japanese Daimiate differed from the Highland clans in the fact that all the members did not claim a common origin or use the same surname; but they were equally bound to their lord by ties of love and implicit obedience, and to each other by a feeling of brotherhood. This feeling has survived the abolition of feudalism in 1871. Ever since that time, the members of the four great Daimiates of Satsuma, Chōshū, Tosa, and Hizen have practically " run " the government of Japan. Her greatest modern statesman, Itō, her best-known minister of foreign affairs, Inoue, and Yamagata, and Aoki, and Katsura are all Chōshū men, while such salient names as Ōyama, Matsukata, Yamamoto, and Kawamura, with more or less the whole navy, belong to Satsuma.

The student of Japanese politics who bears this fact in mind, will find many things become clear to him which before seemed complicated and illogical. Political questions are not necessarily questions of principle. They may simply be questions of personal or local interest. The present paramount influence of the four Daimiates of Satsuma, Chōshū, Tosa, and Hizen is partly an inheritance from olden times, partly the result of the share which they took in restoring the Mikado to his position as autocrat of the Empire in the revolution of 1868. The two strongest of the four are Satsuma and Chōshū, whence the term *Sat-Chō*, used to denote their combination; for in Japanese there is no vulgarity in cutting off the tails of words. On the contrary, to do so is considered an elegant imitation of the Chinese style, which is nothing if not terse. The Satsuma men are credited with courage, the Chōshū men with sagacity. The former are soldiers and sailors, men of dash and daring; the latter are diplomats and able administrators. Meanwhile, the aim of modern Parliamentarians is to pull down all that remains of the clan system, and to substitute party government in its stead. Their success is doubtless only a question of time.

Classes of Society. Japanese mankind was formerly divided into four classes,—the Samurai, or warrior-gentry (of whom the Daimyōs were the leaders), the peasantry, the artisans, and the tradespeople. Notice the place in which commerce stood, at the very bottom of the scale, below the very tillage of the soil. Traces of this contumely have survived modern changes; for men naturally become what the world holds them to be:— the hucksters or traders (we will not dignify them with the name of merchants) were a degraded class in Old Japan, and degraded their business morals remain, which is the principal cause of the difficulties experienced by European merchants in dealing with them.

After the revolution a change was made in the classification of society, and three orders are now established by law,—the nobility *(kwazoku)*, gentry *(shizoku)*, and common people *(heimin)*. The two former combined constitute five per cent., the common people ninety-five per cent., of the entire population. Some have used the word "caste" to denote these divisions; but the term is inappropriate, as there exists no impassable barrier between the different classes, nor yet anything approaching to Indian caste prejudice. The feeling only resembles that to which we are accustomed in England, if indeed it is as strong.

Japanese official regulations tolerate no subterfuges in matters of personal identity. Each citizen is required to nail up over his door a wooden ticket inscribed with his name and quality. Thus: "District of Azabu, Upper Timber Street, No. 8, a Commoner of the Prefecture of Shizuoka, So-and-So" (the surname followed by the personal name).

See also Article on ETA.

Climate. The exaggerated estimation in which the climate of Japan is held by many of those who have had no experience of it often prepares a bitter disappointment for visitors, who find a climate far wetter than that of England and subject to greater extremes of temperature. It should be added, on the other hand, that it also has more fine days,* and that the fine days which it has are incomparably finer and more inspiriting than the feeble, misty incertitudes that pass for fine weather among the natives of Great Britain.

The best season is the autumn. From the latter part of October to the end of the year, the sky is generally clear and the atmosphere still, while during a portion of that time (November), the forests display glorious tints of red and gold, surpassed only in Canada and the United States. During January, February, and March, snow occasionally falls, but it rarely lies longer than a day or two. The spring is trying, on account of the wet spells and the frequent high winds, which often seriously interfere with the enjoyment of the cherry, wistaria, peony, and other flowers, in which the Japanese take such pride. True, the rain is always pronounced exceptional. Never, it is alleged, was so wet a season known before, properly conducted years admitting of no rain but in June and the first week or two of July—the " rainy season " (nyūbai) duly provided for by the old Japanese calendar, in which not native only, but the foreign residents, exhibit a confidence which would be touching were it not tiresome. Statistics† show, however, that from April on to July inclusive nearly every other day is rainy, while in the months flanking them on either side—March and August—an average of more than one day in three is rainy. In September and October the average number of rainy days rises again to about one out of every two. The superstition concerning a special " rainy season " may be due to the trying combination of dark skies with the first heat of the year, making exercise wearisome when not impossible. So penetrating is then the damp that no care can succeed in keeping things from mildew. Boots, books, cigarettes, if put away

---

* Tokyo has 57.90 inches of yearly rainfall, as against 24.76 at Greenwich, but only 141.6 rainy days as against 166.1.

† See page 97.

		Jan.	Feb.	March	April	May	June	July	Aug.	Sept.	Oct.	Nov.	Dec.	Year
CENTRAL METEOROLOGICAL OBSERVATORY. 35° 41′ N. LAT. 139° 46′ E. LONG. HEIGHT 70 FEET. 25 YEARS, 1876–1900. (INCHES AND FAHRENHEIT DEGREES.)														
Mean Temperature		36.9	38.4	44.2	54.3	61.9	68.8	75.8	78.2	71.6	60.3	50.1	41.3	56.8
Mean Maximum Temp. ...		46.8	47.5	53.4	62.9	70.2	76.1	83.0	86.0	78.9	68.9	60.1	52.0	65.5
Mean Minimum Temp. ...		28.6	30.4	35.3	45.6	53.5	62.2	69.6	71.8	65.5	53.1	41.7	32.4	49.1
Absolute Maximum Temp.		97.9 14 July, 1891.												
Absolute Minimum Temp.		15.4 13 Jan., 1876.												
Mean Rainfall		2.14	3.03	4.32	5.04	5.91	6.52	5.01	4.37	8.12	7.07	4.35	2.02	57.90
Number of Rainy Days ...		7.2	9.1	12.4	14.8	13.3	14.4	14.1	11.8	16.2	13.1	9.0	6.3	141.6
Days with Snow		4.0	4.5	2.8	0.1	—	—	—	—	—	—	0.2	1.2	12.8
Mean Barometer (reduced to freezing point) ...		29.96	29.97	29.95	29.94	29.84	29.77	29.77	29.79	29.87	29.98	29.99	29.95	29.90
Mean Direction of Wind...		N22°W	N16°W	N8°W	N51°E	N44°E	S39°E	S20°E	S21°E	N47°E	N4°W	N14°W	N25°W	N1°W

The number of "rainy days" includes all days on which more than a tenth of a millimetre of rain fell, and also those on which any snow or hail fell. The "days with snow" are those on which snow fell, regardless of the question whether rain also did or did not fall. Few days are uninterruptedly snowy at Tōkyō,—perhaps only two or three in the year.

for a day, appear next morning covered with an incipient forest of whitish, greenish matter. No match-box can be got to strike; envelopes stick together without being wetted; gloves must be kept hermetically sealed in bottles, or they will come out a mass of spots. The second half of July and all August are hotter, but less damp, the rain then falling rather in occasional heavy storms which last from one to three days, and are followed by splendid weather. The heat generally vanishes suddenly about the second week in September, when the rain sets in with renewed energy and continues about a month. Such is the common order of things. But scientific observations stretching over a quarter of a century past prove that seasons differ very widely from each other.

One striking peculiarity of the Japanese climate is the constant prevalence of northerly winds in winter and of southerly winds in summer. Rooms facing south are therefore the best all the year round, escaping, as they do, the chill blasts of January and February, and profiting by every summer breeze. Another peculiarity is the lateness of all the seasons, as compared with Europe. The grass, for instance, which dies down during the cold, dry winter months, does not become really fit for tennis-playing before the middle of May. On the other hand, winter is robbed of the gloom of short afternoons by the transparent clearness of the sky down to the end of the year, and even throughout January whenever it is not actually raining of snowing. Travellers are recommended to choose the late autumn, especially if they purpose to content themselves with the beaten tracks of Kyōto, Tōkyō, Miyanoshita, Nikkō, etc., where the Europeanisation of hotels has brought stoves in its train; for stoveless Japanese tea-houses are wofully chilly places. April and May, notwithstanding a greater chance of wet weather, will be better for the wilds. There is then, too, neither cold nor heat to fear. Japanese heat, after all, is not tropical, and many will enjoy travelling throughout the summer months. Mountain climbing must in any case be reserved for that time of year, as the mountains are not " open " at other seasons,—that is to say, the huts on them are deserted, and the native guides mostly refuse to undertake any ascent.

The foregoing description of the Japanese climate applies to the Pacific seaboard of Central Japan, of which Tōkyō is fairly representative. But need we remind the reader that Japan is a large country? The northernmost Kuriles, now Japanese territory, touch Kamchatka. The most southern of the Luchu Isles is scarcely a degree from the tropic of Cancer, to say nothing of newly acquired Formosa. The climate at the extreme points of the empire, therefore, differs widely from that of temperate Central Japan. Speaking generally, the south-eastern slope of the great central range of the Main Island—the slope facing the Pacific Ocean and washed by the *Kuro-shio*,—Gulf-Stream of Eastern Asia—has a much more moderate climate than the north-western slope, which faces the Sea of Japan, with Siberia beyond. In Tōkyō, on the Pacific side, what little snow falls melts almost immediately. In the towns near the Sea of Japan it lies three or four feet deep for weeks, and drifts to a depth of fifteen to eighteen feet in the valleys. But the summer in these same towns is, like the Tōkyō summer, oppressively hot. That the Tōkyō rainfall more than doubles that of London has already been stated. But Tōkyō is by no means one of the wettest parts of the country; on the contrary, with the exception of the northern shore of the Inland Sea and the plain of Shinshū, it is among the driest. Many districts show double its rainfall, the Hida-Etchū mountains and the south-east coast of Kishū show treble.

Thunder-storms and sudden showers are rare in Japan, excepting in the mountain districts. Fogs, too, are rare south of Kinkwa-zan, about 38° 20′ North. From Kinkwa-zan right up the eastern coast of the Main Island, all along Eastern Yezo, the Kuriles, and up as far as Behring's Strait, thick fogs prevail during the calm summer months,—fogs which are relieved only by furious storms in autumn, and a wintry sea packed with ice. The average number of typhoons passing over Japan yearly is from four to five, of which Tōkyō receives one or two. The months liable to typhoons are (in a decreasing order of severity) September, August, October, and July. Typhoons have, it is true, been experienced as early as the end of March; but this is quite exceptional.

The climate of Japan is stated on the highest medical authority to be excellent for children, less for adults, the large amount of moisture rendering it depressing, especially to persons of a nervous temperament and to consumptive patients. Various causes, physical and social, contribute to make Japan a less healthy country for female residents of European race than for the men.

The table on page 97 gives the average of twenty-five years' observations [1876–1900], made at the Central Meteorological Observatory, Tōkyō.

Japan has been divided, for meteorological purposes, into ten districts, namely, I. Formosa and Luchu; II. the southern half of Kyūshū and Shikoku; III. the Inland Sea; IV. N. W. Kyūshū and the west coast of the Main Island up to the latitude of Kyōto; V. the Pacific coast from Ise to Tōkyō and the River Tonegawa; VI. the interior provinces to the north of the fifth district, from Hida on the west to Iwashiro on the east; VII. the N. W. coast from Wakasa to Ugo; VIII. the Pacific coast from the River Tonegawa to Sendai and Miyako; IX. the province of Rikuoku and the western half of the Island of Yezo; X. the eastern half of Yezo and the Kurile Island.

Book recommended. *The New Far East* compiled by International Research Associates.

Cloisonné. The art of cloisonné enamelling has been known in Japan since the sixteenth century and possibly earlier; but it has only been brought to perfection within the last thirty years. The few examples in the Nijō Palace at Kyōto (erected in 1601) are small and extremely rough. Mr. Namikawa, the great cloisonné-maker of Kyōto, will show visitors specimens that look antediluvian in roughness and simplicity, but date back no further than 1873.

Need it be explained that cloisonné is a species of mosaic, whose characteristic feature is a thin network of copper or brass soldered on to a foundation of solid metal, the interstices or cells of the network—the *cloisons,* as they are technically called—being then filled in with enamel paste of various colours, and the process completed by several bakings, rubbings, and polishings, until the surface becomes as smooth as it is hard ? Enamelling has also sometimes been applied in the same way to a porcelain and even to a wooden basis; but the best connoisseurs condemn this innovation as illegitimate, because unsuited to the nature of the material employed.

Kyōto, Tōkyō, and Nagoya are the three great centres of the enameller's art, and each has developed a special style. The difference between the Tōkyō and Kyōto styles consists in this, that whereas Namikawa at Kyōto makes no attempt to hide the metallic contours of his lovely floral and arabesque decorations, his namesake at Tōkyō prides himself on rendering the *cloisons* invisible, thus producing either pictures that might be mistaken for paintings on porcelain, or else monochromatic effects also similar to those observed in certain kinds of old Chinese porcelain. The Tōkyō school performs the greater *tour de force.* But persons of true artistic temperament, who recognise that each material has its natural limitations, to move gracefully within which beseems genius better than overstepping them, will surely prefer the productions of the Kyōto makers, whose cloisonné is honestly cloisonné, but cloisonné with a wealth of ornament, an accuracy of design, a harmony of colour, simply miraculous when one considers the character of the material employed and the risks to which it is subjected in the process of manufacture. These risks greatly enhance the price of cloisonné ware, especially of the large monochromatic pieces. The purchaser of a vase or plaque must pay not only for it, but for all the others that have been inevitably spoilt in the endeavour to produce one flawless piece.

The best Nagoya cloisonné differs from both the above. The great local artist, Kumeno, takes silver as the basis of his vases, and this is beaten up into the desired design, with specially fine effect in water and wave pieces. Wires are also used. The enamel put on is for the most part transparent, so that very delicate results are obtained by the silver shining through the glaze.

Book recommended. *Chinese and Japanese Cloisonné Enamels* by Harry M. Garner.

Confucianism. To describe in detail this Chinese system of philosophy, would be alien to the plan of the present work. Suffice it to say that Confucius (called by the Japanese *Kōshi*) abstained from all metaphysical flights and devotional ecstasies. He confined himself to practical details of morals and government, and took submission to parents and political rulers as the corner-stone of his system. The result is a set of moral truths—some would say truisms—of a very narrow scope, and of dry ceremonial observances, political rather than personal. This Confucian code of ethics has for ages satisfied the Far-Easterns of China, Korea, and Japan, but would not have been endured for a moment by the more eager, more speculative, more tender European mind.

The Confucian Classics consist of what are called, in the Japanese pronunciation, the *Shi-sho Go-kyō*, that is "the Four Books and the Five Canons." The Four Books are "The Great Learning," "The Doctrine of the Mean," "The Confucian Analects," and "The Saying of Mencius." Mencius, let it be noted, is by far the most attractive of the Chinese sages. He had an epigrammatic way about him and a certain sense of humour, which give to many of his utterances a strangely Western and modern ring. He was also the first democrat of the ancient East,—a democrat so outspoken as to have at one time suffered exclusion from the libraries of absolutistic Japan. The Five Canons consist of "The Book of Changes," "The Book of Poetry," "The Book of History," "The Canon of Rites," and "Spring and Autumn" (annals of the state of Lu by Confucius).

Originally introduced into Japan early in the Christian era, along with other products of Chinese civilisation, the Confucian philosophy lay dormant during the Middle Ages, the period of the supremacy of Buddhism. It awoke with a start in the early part of the seventeenth century, when Ieyasu, the great warrior, ruler, and patron of learning, caused the Confucian Classics to be printed in Japan for the first time. During the two hundred and fifty years that followed, the whole intellect of the country was moulded by Confucian ideas. Confucius himself had, it is true, laboured for the establishment of a centralised monarchy. But his main doctrine of unquestioning submission to rulers and parents fitted in perfectly with the feudal ideas of Old Japan; and the conviction of the paramount importance of such subordination lingers on as an element of stability, in spite of the recent social cataclysm which has involved Japanese Confucianism, properly so-called, in the ruin of all other Japanese institutions.

The most eminent Japanese names among the Confucianists are Itō Jinsai and his son, Itō Tōgai, at Kyōto; Arai Hakuseki, and Ogyū Sorai at Yedo. All four flourished about the end of the seventeenth and the beginning of the eighteenth century. They were merely expositors. No Japanese had the originality—it would have been hooted down as impious audacity—to develop the Confucian system further, to alter or amend it. There are not even any Japanese translations or commentaries worth reading. The Japanese have, for the most part, rested content with reprinting the text of the Classics themselves, and also the text of the principal Chinese commentators (especially that of Shushi, 朱子) pointed with diacritical marks to facilitate their perusal by Japanese students. The Chinese Classics thus edited formed the chief vehicle of every boy's education from the seventeenth century until the remodelling of the system of public instruction on European lines after the revolution of 1868. At present they have fallen into almost total neglect, though phrases and allusions borrowed from them still pass current in literature, and even to some extent in the language of every-day life.

Seidō, the great temple of Confucius in Tōkyō, is now utilised as an Educational Museum.

N.B.—A friendly German critic of the first edition of this work thought Confucius unfairly judged in the opening paragraph of the foregoing article. "Confucianism anticipated modern agnosticism, on the one hand," said he: "on the other—and this consideration deserves special weight—it has formed the basis of a social fabric far more lasting than any other that the world has seen. The endurance of the Papacy is often quoted in evidence of the truth of Roman Catholicism. What then, of Confucianism with its still higher antiquity?"

There is much force in this objection; and those who know China most intimately seem to agree in attributing her marvellous vitality and her power of assimilating barbarous tribes—both those she conquers and those that conquer her—to the fact that this great ethical system has infused its strength into the national life, and practically rules the country. We incline to agree with our critic as much as with ourselves. The best plan may perhaps be to present both sides of a question which is too complicated for any sweeping assertion about it to be wholly true.

Books recommended. *Bushido: The Soul of Japan* by Inazo Nitobe; *History of Japanese Religion* by Masaharu Anesaki; *The Ideals of the East with Special Reference to the Art of Japan* by Kakuzo Okakura; *Japan: An Attempt at Interpretation* by Lafcadio Hearn; *Religions in Japan* edited by William K. Bunce; *Shinto: The Kami Way* by Sokyo Ono in collaboration with William P. Woodard.

Conventions. Whether we or the Japanese be the more conventional, might furnish a nice point for argument; but in any case it is *their* conventions that strike *us*. They admire certain flowers,—the plum and cherry-blossom, the wistaria, the chrysanthemum, the insignificant "seven herbs of autumn," and have written poems about these and a few others for centuries; but new flowers, however beautiful, they will not admit at any rate into literature. They rave about the moon; the glories and pathos of sunset touch no chord within them. Their art bristles with conventions. So do their social habits, as when, in greeting a friend, they crave pardon for rudeness of which they were never guilty. The oddest conventional item of daily life, or rather death, is their habit of inventing a fictitious date for decease. Thus, all the world knows that such and such an admiral or general died on Monday morning. Nevertheless, he receives visits on the Tuesday, is promoted on the Wednesday, perhaps makes a railway journey on the Thursday, and at last, maybe, receives official permission to die on the Friday at precisely 7.45 p.m. This make-believe is inspired by the most practical motives. In former

days, when a Daimyō died away from home, he was considered
a deserter, and his estates were forfeited to the Crown. So,
in the event of his being assassinated out-of-doors, the fact
was hushed up; he was put into his palanquin, carried home,
and proclaimed to have died a natural death there, thus preserving the estate to his heirs. At the present day, higher
official rank brings with it a larger pension to the family.
It is, therefore, a gracious act on the part of Government
to permit the postponement of the date of death till after
certain honours shall have been conferred.

Cormorant-fishing. This strange method of fishing is mentioned in a poem found in the *Kojiki,* a work compiled in
A.D. 712, while the poem itself probably dates from a far
earlier age. The custom is kept up at the present day in
various districts of Japan, notably on the River Nagara, near
Gifu, in the province of Owari.

First catch your cormorant. "This," we are told by Mr.
G. E. Gregory, in Vol. X. Part I. of the "Asiatic Transactions,"—"this the people do by placing wooden images of
the birds in spots frequented by them, and covering the surrounding branches and twigs with bird-lime, on settling upon
which they stick fast. After having in this manner caught
one cormorant, they place it among the bushes, instead of
the image, and thus catch more." Mr. Gregory further says
that the fishermen take such care of the birds that they provide
them with mosquito-nets during the summer, in order to
minister to their comfort ! We cannot personally vouch for
such an extreme of solicitude, having seen (and alas! smelt)
the birds only during the cool off-season, which they idle away
in baskets in the fishermen's houses. Cormorant-fishing always
takes place at night and by torch-light. The method pursued
is thus described by the late Major-General Palmer, R.E.,
in a letter to the *Times,* dated 17th July, 1889:—" There are,
to begin with, four men in each of the seven boats, one of
whom, at the stern, has no duty but that of managing his craft.
In the bow stands the master, distinguished by the peculiar

hat of his rank, and handling no fewer than twelve trained
birds with the surpassing skill and coolness that have earned
for the sportsmen of Gifu their unrivalled pre-eminence. Amid-
ships is another fisher, of the second grade, who handles four
birds only. Between them is the fourth man, called *kako*,
from the bamboo striking instrument of that name, with which
he makes the clatter necessary for keeping the birds up to
their work; he also encourages them by shouts and cries, looks
after spare apparatus, etc., and is ready to give aid if required.
Each cormorant wears at the base of its neck a metal ring,*
drawn tight enough to prevent marketable fish from passing
below it, but at the same time loose enough—for it is never
removed—to admit the smaller prey, which serves as food.
Round the body is a cord, having attached to it at the middle
of the back a short strip of stiffish whalebone, by which the
great awkward bird may be conveniently lowered into the
water or lifted out when at work; and to this whalebone is
looped a thin rein of spruce fibre, twelve feet long, and so
far wanting in pliancy as to minimize the chance of entangle-
ment. When the fishing ground is reached, the master lowers
his twelve birds one by one into the stream and gathers their
reins into his left hand, manipulating the latter thereafter
with his right as occasion requires. No. 2 does the same with
his four birds; the *kako* starts in with his volleys of noise;
and forthwith the cormorants set to at their work in the
heartiest and jolliest way, diving and duckling with wonderful
swiftness as the astonished fish come flocking towards the
blaze of light. The master is now the busiest of men. He
must handle his twelve strings so deftly that, let the birds
dash hither and thither as they will, there shall be no
impediment or fouling. He must have his eyes everywhere and
his hands following his eyes. Specially must he watch for the
moment when any of his flock is gorged,—a fact generally
made known by the bird itself, which then swims about in a
foolish, helpless way, with its head and swollen neck erect.
Thereupon the master, shortening in on that bird, lifts it

---

* We believe that these rings are generally not of metal, but of bone or whalebone.

aboard, forces its bill open with his left hand, which still holds the rest of the lines, squeezes out the fish with his right, and starts the creature off on a fresh foray,—all this with such admirable dexterity and quickness that the eleven birds still bustling about have scarce time to get things into a tangle, and in another moment the whole team is again perfectly in hand.

" As for the cormorants, they are trained when quite young, being caught in winter with bird-lime on the coasts of the neighbouring Owari Gulf, at their first emigration southward from the summer haunts of the species on the northern sea-board of Japan. Once trained, they work well up to fifteen, often up to nineteen or twenty, years of age; and, though their keep in winter bears hardly on the masters, they are very precious and profitable hunters during the five months' season, and well deserve the great care that is lavished upon them. From four to eight good-sized fish for example, is the fair result of a single excursion for one bird, which corresponds with an average of about one hundred and fifty fish per cormorant per hour, or four hundred and fifty for the three hours occupied in drifting down the whole course. Every bird in a flock has and knows its number; and one of the funniest things about them is the quick-witted jealousy with which they invariably insist, by all that cormorant language and panto-mimic protest can do, on due observance of the recognized rights belonging to their individual numbers. No. 1. or ' Ichi,' is the *doyen* of the corps, the senior in years as well as rank. His colleagues, according to their age, come after him in numerical order. Ichi is the last to be put into the water and the first to be taken out, the first to be fed, and the last to enter the baskets in which, when work is over, the birds are carried from the boats to their domicile. Ichi, when aboard, has the post of honour at the eyes of the boat. He is a solemn, grizzled old fellow, with a pompous, *noli me tangere* air that is almost worthy of a Lord Mayor. The rest have places after him, in

succession of rank, alternately on either side of the gunwale.
If haply, the lawful order of precedence be at any time
violated—if, for instance, No. 5 be put into the water before
No. 6, or No. 4 be placed above No. 2—the rumpus that forthwith arises in that family is a sight to see and a sound to hear.

"But all this while we have been drifting down, with the
boats about us, to the lówer end of the course, and are again
abreast of Gifu, where the whole squadron is beached. As
each cormorant is now taken out of the water, the master can
tell by its weight whether it has secured enough supper while
engaged in the hunt; failing which, he makes the deficiency
good by feeding it with the inferior fish of the catch. At length
all are ranged in their due order, facing outwards, on the gunwale of each boat. And the sight of that array of great
ungainly sea-birds—shaking themselves, flapping their wings,
gawing, making their toilets, clearing their throats, looking
about them with a stare of stupid solemnity, and now and
then indulging in old-maidish tiffs with their neighbours—is
quite the strangest of its little class I have ever seen, except
perhaps the wonderful penguinry of the Falkland Islands,
whereat a certain French philosopher is said to have even
wept. Finally, the cormorants are sent off to bed, and we
ourselves follow suit."

Cremation. Cremation followed Buddhism into Japan about
A.D. 700, but never entirely superseded the older Shintō
custom of disposing of the dead by interment. Ludicrous as
it may appear, cremation was first discontinued in the case of
the Mikados on the representations of a fishmonger named
Hachibei, who clamoured for the interment of the Emperor
Go-Kōmei in 1644. On the 18th July, 1873, cremation was
totally prohibited by the Government, whose members seem
to have had some confused notion as to the practice being
un-European and therefore barbarous. Having discovered
that far from being un-European, cremation was the goal of
European reformers in such matters, they rescinded their
prohibition only twenty-two months later (23rd May, 1875).
There are now nine cremation grounds in Tōkyō. The charges

for cremation vary from 7 *yen* to 1½ *yen* for adults, and from 3 *yen* to 1 *yen* for children under six years of age. The good priest of whom we caused enquiry to be made on this point, said that poor folks often came begging to be let off more cheaply, but that in these hard times it was impossible to do so.

The system is quite simple, wood being the only fuel used. The corpse, enclosed in its wooden coffin, is thoroughly consumed in about three hours. Nothing remains but a few minute splinters of bone and the teeth, which latter are preserved and often sent to the great temple at Kōya-san. The ashes are placed in an urn and buried. We should add that on the 19th June, 1874, a law was passed against intramural interment, except in certain special cases. It is still prohibited, unless when the body has been cremated before burial.

Currency. A gold standard was adopted in 1897, and the coinage consists of gold, silver, nickel, and copper. The chief circulating medium, however, has generally been paper. The system is decimal, and the nomenclature as follows:—

1 *yen* (half-dollar)	= 100 *sen*.
1 *sen* (half-cent)	= 10 *rin*.
1 *rin*	= 10 *mō* (or *mon*).
1 *mō*	= 10 *shu*.
1 *shu*	= 10 *kotsu*.

Government and banking accounts do not take notice of any value smaller than the *rin;* but estimates by private tradesmen often descend to *mō* and *shu,* which are incredibly minute fractions of a farthing. No coins exist, however, to represent these Lilliputian sums. There are gold pieces of 20 *yen,* 10 *yen,* and 5 *yen;* silver pieces of 50 *sen* and under, nickel pieces of 5 *sen,* copper pieces for lesser values, and paper for various values great and small, from 1 *yen* upward. The paper notes now in use are redeemable in gold, and therefore stand at par. The large oblong brass pieces with holes in the middle, enabling them to be strung on a string, are called *tempō,* because coined during the period styled *Tempō* (A.D. 1830–1844). They are worth eight *rin,* but are now almost obsolete. The smaller round coins, also having holes in the middle, and commonly known to foreigners as "cash," are worth, some 10 *mō,* some 15, some 20. No coins of this kind are now issued. The style has been condemned by the modern Japanese, because not sanctioned by European precedent. But what is there to consult in such matters save convenience? And let him who has handled a thousand coppers thus strung, and attempted to handle a thousand loose ones, speak to the relative convenience of the two methods.

The Imperial mint is situated at Ōsaka. It was started under British auspices, but the last of the British employés left in 1889. The manufactory of paper money is at Tōkyō, being carried on at an institution called the *Insatsu Kyoku,* which well deserves a visit. Both the coins and the paper notes possess considerable artistic merit.

In Japan, as elsewhere, financiers have been engrossed by the monometallic and bimetallic controversy, the currency problem being not the least of those which the Government has had to solve. Forty years ago, when the country was still practically closed, little specie was in actual use, but there existed a banking system which sustained mercantile credit for the limited amount of internal business then transacted. Later, paper money was extensively employed, and at one time suffered great depreciation,—as much as sixty per cent. in the year 1881,—but was brought again to a par with silver by the issue of convertible silver notes, and so remained for over a decade. The industrial boom which followed the war with China in 1894–5, created a necessity for securing foreign capital to finance multitudinous undertakings which Japan herself had not the means to carry on unaided. Thereupon the Government, recognising the impossibility of borrowing in the Western money markets so long as Japan remained on a silver basis, passed a bill making the currency a gold one in the ratio of 32⅓ to 1, or say 2/0½ sterling per *yen.* The extreme difficulty of the situation could scarcely have been more strikingly exemplified than by the circumstance that, in the brief interval between Japan's decision to adopt a gold standard and the putting of that decision into effect, the relative value of the two metals had already again varied as much as five-eighths of a penny by the continued appreciation of gold. Far be it, however, from ignoramuses like ourselves to venture into the controversial quagmire.

Books recommended. *Meet Japan: A Modern Nation with a Memory* written under the auspices of Tsuneji Hibino; *The New Far East* compiled by International Research Associates.

Cycle. "Better fifty years of Europe than a cycle of Cathay." But it has been pointed out that there is, after all, little difference between the two terms of the comparison. The Chinese cycle, which the Japanese employ for historical purposes, has but sixty years (see Article on TIME).

Daimyō. The Daimyōs were the territorial lords or barons of feudal Japan. The word means literally "great name." Accordingly, during the Middle Ages, warrior chiefs of less degree, corresponding, as one might say, to our knights or baronets, were known by the correlative title *Shōmyō*, that is, "small name." But this latter fell into disuse. Perhaps it did not sound grand enough to be welcome to those who bore it. Under the Tokugawa dynasty, which ruled Japan from A.D. 1603 to 1867, the lowest Daimyōs owned land assessed at ten thousand bales of rice per annum, while the richest fief of all—that of Kaga—was worth over a million bales. The total number of the Daimyōs in modern times was about three hundred.

It should be borne in mind that the Daimyōs were not the only aristocracy in the land, though they were incomparably the richest and the most important. In the shadow of the Mikado's palace at Kyōto, poor but very proud of their descent from gods and emperors, and looking down on the feudal Daimyō aristocracy as on a mere set of military adventurers and *parvenus,* lived, or rather vegetated through centuries, the *Kuge,* the legitimist aristocracy of Japan. The revolution of 1868, in bringing about the fall of the Daimyōs, at last gave the *Kuge* their opportunity. With the restoration of the Mikado to absolute power, they too emerged from obscurity; and on the creation of a new system of ranks and titles in 1884, they were not forgotten. The old *Kuge* took rank as new princes, marquises, and counts, and what is more, they were granted pensions.

Books recommended. *A Daughter of the Samurai* by Etsu Inagaki Sugimoto; *Japan: An Attempt at Interpretation* by Lafcadio Hearn; *Tales of Old Japan* by A. B. Mitford (Lord Redesdale).

Dances. Our single word "dance" is represented by two in Japanese,—*mai* and *odori,* the former being a general name for the more ancient and, so to say, classical dances, the latter for such as are newer and more popular. But the line between the two classes is hard to draw, and both agree in consisting mainly of posturing. Europeans dance with their feet,—not to say their legs,—Japanese mainly with their arms. The dress, or rather undress, of a European *corps de ballet* would take away the breath of the least prudish Oriental.

One of the oldest Japanese dances is the *Kagura,* which may still be seen in a degenerate form at the yearly festival of almost any parish temple. It is of the nature of primitive theatricals,—half dance, half antic and buffoonery,—got up by the young men of the place, who appear in masks and great bundles of tawdry clothes, and twirl about and pursue each other to the incessant tomtoming of a drum and piping of a flute. Sometimes a rough platform is erected as a stage, sometimes the temple itself does duty for such. The original of the *Kagura* is said to have been the dance by means of which, soon after the beginning of the world, the Sun-Goddess was lured from a cavern into which she had retired, thus plunging all creation in darkness. The sacred dances at Nara and Ise belong to this category; but the *Ise Ondo,* some-

times mentioned by travellers, is a later profane invention,—
apparently an adaptation of the *Genroku Odori*, a dance that
may still occasionally be witnessed on the stage.

The *Bon Odori*, a popular dance which takes place on certain
days in summer all over provincial Japan, is believed to have
a Buddhist origin, though its meaning is far from clear. The
details vary from village to village; but the general feature
of this dance is a large circle or wheel of posturing peasants,
who revolve to the notes of the song sung and the flute and
drum played by a few of their number in the middle. Kyōto
and Tōkyō, being too civilised for such rustic exercises in
which all share, do their dancing by proxy. There, and in
the other large towns, the dancing-girls *(geisha)* form a class
apart. While one or more of the girls dance, others play the
shamisen and sing the story; for Japanese dances almost
always represent some story, they are not mere arabesques.
Herein the intimate connection that has always subsisted
between dancing and the drama finds its explanation, as will
be better understood by reference to the Article on the
THEATRE. The *Kappore* and the *Shishi-mai*, or Lion Dance,
are among those most often executed in the streets by strolling
performers.

The very newest of all forms of dancing in Japan is of course
that borrowed from Europe a few years ago. Its want of
dignity, together with certain disagreeable rumours to which
the unwonted meeting of the two sexes has given rise from
time to time, have caused the innovation to be looked at
askance by many who are otherwise favourable to European
manners and customs. A plain-spoken writer in an excellent
illustrated periodical entitled *Fūzoku Gwahō*, says that,
whereas his imagination had painted a civilised ball-room as
a vision of fairy-land, its reality reminded him of nothing so
much as lampreys wriggling up to the surface of the water,
and *(passez-lui le mot)* fleas hopping out of a bed.

Decorations. The heraldry of feudal Japan did not include
orders of knighthood, or decorations for military and other

service. Modern Japan imitated these things from Europe in the year 1875. There are now six orders of knighthood, namely, the Order of the Chrysanthemum, the Order of the Paulownia, the Order of the Rising Sun, the Order of the Sacred Treasure, the Order of the Crown, and the Order of the Golden Kite. The Order of the Crown is for ladies only. All the Orders are divided into various classes. The Grand Cordon of the Order of the Chrysanthemum is the highest honour which the Japanese Court can bestow. It is, therefore, rarely bestowed on any but royal personages. The Order of the Sacred Treasure is the distinction now most frequently conferred on foreign employés of the Government for long and meritorious service, the class given being usually the third, fourth, fifth, or sixth, according to circumstances— rarely the second. The holder of such a decoration, down to the third class inclusive, is, even though he be a civilian, granted a military funeral.

We next come to the War Medal, of which there is but one class, made of bronze obtained from captured guns. Conformably with the usage of European countries, it is given only for foreign service, not for service in civil war. Those who helped to put down the Satsuma rebellion did not gain it. After it rank the Civil Medals, distinguished by a red, a blue, and a green ribbon respectively. Then there is the Yellow Ribbon Medal, conferred on those who made proof of patriotism by subscribing to the Coast Defence Fund in 1887. It is divided into two classes, called respectively Gold and Silver. More recent still are the Commemorative Medal of 1889 distributed to those who were present at the proclamation of the Constitution on the 11th February of that year, and the medal struck in 1894 for those who assisted at the celebration of the Silver Wedding of Their Imperial Majesties. Of both these medals there are two classes,—gold for princes, silver for lesser folk.

The Order of the Kite, conferred for military merit only, is the newest of all the Japanese Decorations. It was established on the 11th February, 1890, in commemoration of Jimmu Tennō, the Romulus of Japan.

Demoniacal Possession. Chinese notions concerning the superhuman powers of the fox, and in a lesser degree of the badger and the dog, entered Japan during the early Middle Ages. One or two mentions of magic foxes occur in the *Uji Shūi,* a story-book of the eleventh century; and since that time the belief has spread and grown, till there is not an old woman in the land—or, for the matter of that, scarcely a man either—who has not some circumstantial fox story to relate as having happened to some one who is at least the acquaintance of an acquaintance. In 1889, a tale was widely circulated and believed of a fox having taken the shape of a railway train on the Tōkyō-Yokohama line. The phantom train seemed to be coming towards a real train which happened to be running in the opposite direction, but yet never got any nearer to it. The engine-driver of the real train, seeing all his signals to be useless, put on a tremendous speed. The result was that the phantom was at last caught up, when lo and behold! nothing but a crushed fox was found beneath the engine-wheels. Nor has the twentieth century witnessed any abatement in the popular belief. Fox stories—not necessarily vouched for, of course, but still deemed worthy of mention—are related in the same newspapers which chronicle sober facts and new scientific inventions. In fact, the name of such tales is legion. More curious and interesting is the power with which these demon foxes are credited of taking up their abode in human beings in a manner similar to the phenomena of possession by evil spirits, so often referred to in the New Testament. Dr. Baelz, of the Imperial University of Japan, who has had special opportunities for studying such cases in the hospital under his charge, has kindly communicated to us some remarks, of which the following is a *résumé:*—

" Possession by foxes *(Kitsune-tsuki)* is a form of nervous disorder or delusion, not uncommonly observed in Japan. Having entered a human being, sometimes through the breast, more often through the space between the finger-nails and the flesh, the fox lives a life of his own, apart from the proper self of the person who is harbouring him. There thus results a sort of double entity or double consciousness. The person possessed hears and understands everything that the fox inside says or thinks; and the two often engage in a loud and violent dispute, the fox speaking in a voice altogether different from that which is natural to the individual. The only difference between the cases of possession mentioned in the Bible and those observed in Japan is that here it is almost exclusively women that are attacked—mostly women of the lower classes. Among the predisposing conditions may be mentioned a weak intellect, a superstitious turn of mind, and such debilitating diseases as, for instance, typhoid fever. Possession never occurs except in such subjects as have heard of it already, and believe in the reality of its existence.

"The explanation of the disorder is not so far to seek as might be supposed. Possession is evidently related to hysteria and to the hypnotic phenomena which physiologists have recently studied with so much care, the cause of all alike being the fact that, whereas in healthy persons one half of the brain alone is actively engaged—in right-handed persons the left half of the brain, and in left-handed persons the right—leaving the other half to contribute only in a general manner to the function of thought, nervous excitement arouses this other half, and the two—one the organ of the usual self, the other the organ of the new pathologically affected self—are set over against each other. The rationale of possession is an auto-suggestion, an idea arising either with apparent spontaneity or else from the subject-matter of it being talked about by others in the patient's presence, and then overmastering her weak mind exactly as happens in hypnosis. In the same manner, the *idea* of the possibility of cure will often actually effect the cure. The cure-worker must be a person of strong mind and power of will, and must enjoy the patient's full confidence. For this reason the priests of the Nichiren sect, which is the most superstitious and bigoted of Japanese Buddhist sects, are the most successful expellers of foxes. Occasionally fits and screams accompany the exit of the fox. In all cases—even when the fox leaves quietly—great prostration remains for a day or two, and sometimes the patient is unconscious of what has happened.

"To mention but one among several cases, I was once called in to a girl with typhoid fever. She recovered; but during her convalescence, she heard the women around her talk of another woman who had a fox, and who would doubtless do her best to pass it on to some one else, in order to be rid of it. At that moment the girl experienced an extraordinary sensation. The fox had taken possession of her. All her efforts to get rid of him were vain. "He is coming! he is coming!" she would cry, as a fit of the fox drew near. "Oh! what shall I do? Here he is!" And then, in a strange, dry, cracked voice, the fox would speak, and mock his unfortunate hostess. Thus matters continued for three weeks, till a priest of the Nichiren sect was sent for. The priest upbraided the fox sternly. The fox (always, of course, speaking through the girl's mouth) argued on the other side. At last he said: "I am tired of her. I ask no better than to leave her. What will you give me for doing so?" The priest asked what he would take. The fox replied, naming certain cakes and other things, which, said he, must be placed before the altar of such and such a temple, at 4 p.m., on such a day. The girl was conscious of the words her lips were made to frame, but was powerless to say anything in her own person. When the day and hour arrived, the offerings bargained for were taken by her relations to the place indicated, and the fox quitted the girl at that very hour.

"A curious scene of a somewhat similar nature may occasionally be witnessed at Minobu, the romantically situated chief temple of the Nichiren sect, some two days' journey from Tōkyō into the interior. There the people sit praying for hours before the gigantic statues of the ferocious-looking gods called Ni-ō, which are fabled to have been carried thither from Kamakura in a single night on the back of the hero Asaina some six hundred years ago. The devotees sway their bodies backwards and forwards, and ceaselessly repeat the same invocation, "*Namu myōhō renge kyō! Namu myōhō renge kyō!*" At last, to some of the more nervous among them, wearied and excited as they are, the statues' eyes seem suddenly to start into life, and they themselves rise wildly, feeling a snake, or maybe a tiger, inside their body, this unclean animal being regarded as the physical incarnation of their sins. Then, with a cry, the snake or serpent goes out of them, and they themselves are left fainting on the ground."—

So far Dr. Baelz. His account may be supplemented by the remark that not only are there persons believed to be possessed by foxes *(kitsune-tsuki)*, but others believed to possess foxes *(kitsune-mochi)*, in other words, to be wizards or witches commanding unseen powers of evil which they can turn loose at will upon their enemies. The following extract from a Japanese newspaper (the *Nichi-Nichi Shimbun* of the 14th August, 1891) may serve to illustrate this point:—

"In the province of Izumo, more especially in the western portion, there exists a peculiar custom called fox-owning, which plays an important part in marriages and transfers of landed property. When a marriage is being arranged between persons residing several leagues apart and unacquainted with each other, enquiries into such points of family history as a possible taint of leprosy or phthisis are subordinated to the first grand question: is or is not the other party a fox-owner? To explain this term, we may say that fox-owning families are believed to have living with them a tribe of small, weazle-like foxes to the number of seventy-five, called human foxes, by whom they are escorted and protected wherever they go, and who watch over their fields and prevent outsiders from doing them any damage. Should, however, any damage be done either through malice or ignorance, the offender is at once possessed by the fox, who makes him blurt out his crime and some times even procures his death. So great is the popular fear of the fox-owners that any one marrying into a fox-owning family, or buying land from them, or failing to repay money borrowed from them, is considered to be a fox-owner too. The fox-owners are avoided as if they were snakes or lizards. Nevertheless, no one ever asks another point blank whether or not his family be a fox-owning family; for to do so might offend him, and the result to the enquirer might be a visitation in the form of possession by a fox. The subject is therefore never alluded to in the presence of a suspected party. All that is done is politely to avoid him.

" It should be noticed, moreover, that there are permanent fox-owners and temporary fox-owners. The permanent fox-owners silently search for families of a similar nature to marry into, and can never on any account intermarry with outsiders, whatever may be the inducement in the shape of wealth or beauty. Their situation closely resembles that of the pariahs and outcasts of former times. But even the strictest rules will sometimes be broken through by love which is a thing apart, and liaisons will be formed between fox-owners and outsiders. When such an irremediable misfortune takes place, parents will renounce even their well-beloved only son, and forbid him to cross their threshold for the rest of his life. Temporary fox-owners are those who have been expelled from the family for buying land from a permanent fox-owner. These circumstances conspire to give security to the fox-owners (whether such in truth or imagination, we are not in a position to say) ; for no one will harm them by so much as a hair's breadth. Therefore they are all well-to-do; some are even said to count among the most affluent families in the province. The very poorest people that have borrowed money from them will strain every nerve to raise money to repay the loan, because failure to do so would make others regard them as fox-owners and shun them. The result of all this is that a nervous malady resembling possession is much commoner in this province than elsewhere, and that Dr. Shimamura, assistant - professor at the Imperial University,* during his tour of inspection there this summer, has come across no less than thirty-one cases of it."

---

* Assistant, that is, to Dr. Baelz.

To this may be added that in the Oki Islands, off the coast of Izumo, the superstition is modified in such wise that dogs, not foxes, are the magic creatures. The human beings in league with them are termed *inu-gami-mochi,* that is, " dog-god owners." When the spirit of such a magic dog goes forth on an errand of mischief, its body remains behind, growing gradually weaker, and sometimes dying and falling to decay. When this happens, the spirit, on its return, takes up its abode in the body of the wizard, who thereupon becomes more powerful than ever. Our informant was a peasant from the Oki Islands,—the best authority on such a point, because himself a believer and with no thesis to prove.

Oddly enough, we ourselves once had to submit to exorcism at the hands of Shintō priests. It was in the summer of 1879, the great cholera year, and we were accused by the authorities of a certain village at which we desired to halt, of having brought the demon of cholera with us. For, true to human nature, each town, each village, at that sad season, always proclaimed itself spotless, while loudly accusing all its neighbours of harbouring the contagion. Accordingly, after much parley, which took place in the drenching rain, with night approaching and with the impossibility of finding another shelter for many miles, some Shintō priests were sent for. They arrived in their white vestments and curiously curved hats, and bearing branches of trees in their hands. They formed in two lines on either side of the way, and between them our little party of two Europeans and one Japanese servant had to walk. As we passed, the priests waved the dripping branches over our heads, and struck us on the back with naked swords. After that, we were sullenly accorded a lodging for the night. To the honour of the Japanese government, let it be added that when we returned to Tōkyō and reported the affair, the village authorities were at once deposed and another mayor and corporation set to reign in their stead. Perhaps we ought to apologise for thus obtruding our own personal adventures on the reader. We have only hesitatingly done so, because it seems to us that the exorcism of two Englishmen near the end of the nineteenth century is a little incident sufficiently strange to merit being put on record.

As for badgers, they are players of practical jokes rather than seriously wicked deceivers. One of their pranks is to assume the shape of the moon; but this they can only do when the real moon is also in the sky. Another common trick of theirs is to beat the tattoo on their stomach *(tanuki no hara-tsuzumi)*. In art they are generally represented thus diverting themselves, with an enormously protuberant abdomen for all the world like a drum.

Divination. Astrology, horoscopy, palmistry, physiognomy, foretelling the future by dreams,—all these forms of superstition are current in Japan; but the greatest favourite is divination by means of the Eight Diagrams of classical China. No careful observer can walk through the streets of any large city without noticing here and there a little stall where a fortune-teller sits with his divining rods in front of him, and small blocks inscribed with sets of horizontal lines, some whole, some cut in two. The manipulation of these paraphernalia embodies a highly complicated system of divination called *Eki,* literally "Changes," which is of immemorial antiquity. Confucius himself professed his inability to understand the matter thoroughly, and would fain have had fifty years added to his life for the purpose of plunging more deeply into its mysteries. The common fortune-tellers of to-day have no such qualms. Shuffling the divining rods, they glibly instruct their clients in all such thorny matters as the finding of lost articles, the propriety of removing to another quarter of the town, the advisability of adopting a child, lucky days for marriage or for undertaking a journey, occasionally—if those in power be not much maligned—even affairs of state. Mr. Takashima, one of the leading citizens of Yokohama, traces his wealth to his imprisonment when a lad; for in gaol a dog-eared copy of Confucius' venerable treatise on the Diagrams was his sole companion. He has not only realised a fortune by obedience to its precepts, but has published a voluminous commentary on the subject.

Few resident foreigners have any notion of the extent to which the Japanese with whom they come in contact are still under the influence of this order of ideas. We will give but one among several instances of which we have had personal cognizance. A favourite dog of the present writer's was lost in November, 1892, and all search, advertisement, and application to the police proved unavailing. Meanwhile, the servants and their friends privately had recourse to no less than three diviners, two of whom were priests. One of these foretold the dog's return in April, and another directed that an ancient ode containing the words, " If I hear that thou awaitest me, I will forthwith return," should be written on slips of paper and pasted upside down on the pillars of the house. It was the sight of these slips that drew our attention to the matter. The best of it is that the dog was found, and that, too, in *a* month of April, namely, April, 1896, after having been missing for three years and five months. How then attempt, with any good grace, to discredit the fortune-teller in the eyes of these simple folk ?

Books recommended. *A Japanese Miscellany* by Lafcadio Hearn; *Oriental Fortune Telling* by Jimmei Shimano; translated by Togo Taguchi; *Tales of Old Japan* by A. B. Mitford (Lord Redesdale).

Dress. It would take a folio volume elaborately illustrated to do justice to all the peculiarities of all the varieties of Japanese costume.

Speaking generally, it may be said that the men are dressed as follows. First comes a loin-cloth *(shita-obi)* of bleached muslin. Next to this a shirt *(juban)* or silk or cotton, to which is added in winter an under-jacket *(dōgi)* of like material. Outside comes the gown *(kimono)*, or in winter two wadded gowns *(shitagi* and *uwagi)*, kept in place by a narrow sash *(obi)*. On occasions of ceremony, there is worn further-more a sort of broad pair of trousers, or perhaps we should rather say a divided skirt, called *hakama*, and a stiff coat called *haori.* The *hakama* and *haori* are invariably of silk, and the *haori* is adorned with the wearer's crest in three places, sometimes in five. The head is mostly bare, but is sometimes covered by a very large straw hat, while on the feet is a kind of sock, named *tabi,* reaching only to the ankle, and having a separate compartment for the big toe. Of straw sandals there are two kinds, the movable *zōri* used for light work, and the *waraji* which are bound tightly round the feet with straw string and used for hard walking only. People of means wear only the *tabi* indoors, and a pair of wooden clogs, called *geta,* out-of-doors. The native costume of a Japanese gentleman is completed by a fan, a parasol, and in his belt a pipe and tobacco-pouch. Merchants also wear at their belt what is called a *yatate*—a kind of portable ink-stand with a pen inside. A cheap variety of the *kimono,* or gown, is the *yukata,* —a cotton dressing-gown, originally meant for going to the bath in, but now often worn indoors of an evening as a sort of *déshabille.*

Take it altogether, the Japanese gentleman's attire, and that of the ladies as well, is a highly elegant and sanitary one. The only disadvantage is that the flopping of the *kimono* hinders a free gait. Formerly the Japanese gentleman wore two swords, and his back hair was drawn forward in a queue over the carefully shaven middle of the skull; but both these fashions are obsolete. The wearing of swords in public was interdicted by law in 1876, and the whole gentry submitted without a blow.

Besides the loin-cloth, which is universal, the men of the lower classes, such as coolies and navvies, wear a sort of dark-coloured pinafore *(hara-gake)* over the bust, crossed with bands behind the back. They cover their legs with tight-fitting drawers *(momo-hiki)* and a sort of gaiters *(kyahan).* Their coat, called *shirushi-banten,* is marked on the back with a Chinese character or other sign to show by whom they are employed. But jinrikisha-men wear the *happi,* which is not thus marked,—that is, when they wear anything; for in the country districts and in the hot weather, the loin-cloth is often the sole garment of the common people, while the children disport themselves in a state of nature. It is not unusual to see a kerchief *(hachi-maki)* tied over the brow, to prevent the perspiration from running into the eyes. Travellers of the middle and lower classes are often to be distinguished by their *kimono* being lifted up and shoved into the sash behind, by a kind of silk drawers called *patchi,* by a sort of mitten or hand-protector called *tekkō,* and by a loose overcoat *(kappo).* The peasants wear a straw overcoat *(mino)* in rainy or snowy weather.

The Japanese costume for women is less different from that of the men than is the case with us. In many districts the peasant women wear trousers and rain-coats, like their husbands. This, coupled with the absence of beard in the men, often makes it difficult for a new-comer to distinguish the sexes. In the towns, the various elements of female dress are as follows. Beneath all, come two little aprons round the loins *(koshi-maki* and *suso-yoke),* then the shirt, and then the *kimono* or *kimonos* kept in place by a thin belt *(shita-jime).* Over this is bound the large sash *(obi),* which is the chief article of feminine adornment. In order to hold it up, a sort of panier or "improver" *(obi-age)* is placed underneath, while a handsome string *(obi-dome)* keeps it in position above. Japanese women bestow lavish care on the dressing of their hair. Their combs and hair-pins of tortoise-shell, coral, and other costly materials often represent many months of their husband's salaries. Fortunately all these things, and even dresses themselves, can be handed down from mother to daughter, as jewels and lace may be in European lands, Japanese ladies' fashions not changing quickly.

A Japanese lady's dress will often represent a value of 200 *yen,* without counting the ornaments for her hair, worth perhaps as much again. A woman of the smaller shop-keeping class may have on her, when she goes out holiday-making, some 40 or 50 *yen's* worth. A gentleman will rarely spend on his clothes as much as he lets his wife spend on hers. Perhaps he may not have on more than 60 *yen's* worth.

Thence, through a gradual decline in price, we come to the coolie's poor trappings, which may represent as little as 5 *yen*, or even 2 *yen*, as he stands.

Children's dress is more or less a repetition in miniature of that of their elders. Long swaddling-clothes are not in use. Young children, have, however, a bib. They wear a little cap on their heads, and at their side hangs a charm-bag *(kinchaku)*, made out of a bit of some bright-coloured damask, containing a charm *(mamori-fuda)* which is supposed to protect them from being run over, washed away, etc. There is also generally fastened somewhere about their little person a metal ticket *(maigo-fuda)*, having on one side a picture of the sign of the zodiac proper to the year of their birth, and on the other their name and address, as a precaution against their getting lost. Japanese girls do not, like ours, remain in a sort of chrysalis state till seventeen or eighteen years of age, and then "come out" in gorgeous attire. The tiniest tots are the most brilliantly dressed. Thenceforward there is a gradual decline the whole way down to old age, which final stage is marked by the severest simplicity. Many old ladies even cut their hair short. In any case, they never exhibit the slightest *coquetterie de vieillesse*.

Those having any acquaintance with Japan, either personal or by hearsay, will understand that, when, we say that the Japanese *wear* such and such things (in the present tense), we speak of the native costume, which is still in fairly common use, though unfortunately no longer in universal use. The undignified billy-cocks and pantaloons of the West are slowly but surely supplanting the picturesque, aristocratic-looking native garb,—a change for which the Government is mainly responsible, as it obliges almost all officials to wear European dress when on duty, and of course the inferior classes ape their betters. Nor have the women, though naturally more conservative, been altogether able to resist the radicalism of their time and country. In the year 1886, some evil counsellor induced the Court to order gowns from Paris—we beg pardon, from Berlin—likewise corsets, and those European shoes in

which a Japanese lady finds it so hard to walk without looking
as if she had taken just a little drop too much. Need it be
said that the Court speedily found imitators ? Indeed, as a
spur to the recalcitrant, a sort of notification was issued,
" recommending " the adoption of European costume by the
ladies of Japan. In vain the local European press cried out
against the barbarism, in vain every foreigner of taste
endeavoured privately to persuade his Japanese friends not
to let their wives make guys of themselves, in vain Mrs.
Cleveland and the ladies of America wrote publicly to point
out the dangers with which tight lacing, and European
fashions generally, threaten the health of those who adopt
them. The die was cast when, on the 1st November, 1886,
the Empress and her ladies appeared in their new German
dresses at a public entertainment. The Empress herself would
doubtless look charming in any garb. Would one could say
as much for all those with her and for those that followed
after ! The very highest society of Tōkyō contained, it is
true, from the beginning, a few—a very few—women of whose
dress Pierre Loti could say without flattery, *" toilette en
somme qui serait de mise à Paris et qui est vraiment bien
portée."* But the majority! No caricature could do justice
to the bad figures, the ill-fitting garments, the screeching
colours, that ran riot between 1886 and 1889. Since then
there has been a wave of reaction, in consequence of which
most ladies have happily returned to the national costume.
How charming it is to see a bevy of them thus dressed,—
dressed, mind you, not merely having clothes on,—such a
symphony of greys and browns and other delicate hues of
silk and brocade, the faultless costume being matched by the
coy, and at the same time perfectly natural and simple,
manners and musical voices of the wearers !

Duck-hunting with the help of decoys and a sort of large
hand-net, in grounds laid out for the purpose with ponds and
canals and high embankments and concealed alleys, is a sport
which was invented in Tōkyō some thirty years ago for the

amusement of members of the Imperial Family. Being thus modern in origin, and requiring an extensive park with large and quiet sheets of water for its pursuit, this sport has scarcely been taken up beyond the Imperial circle, except by one or two millionaire families who occasionally invite their friends to a battue. Catching ducks as one would catch butterflies must be good fun, and is said to require not a little skill.

Hawking, which was a favourite pursuit of the Japanese nobility in the Middle Ages, is still sometimes practised on the same occasions. In fact, the new sport of duck-hunting would seem to have developed out of the old one of hawking, while it was partly suggested by the fact that large numbers of ducks and other migratory water-fowl habitually come down from the north to spend the winter on the lagoons around Tōkyō and in the castle moats.

Earthquakes and Volcanoes. " Oh! how I wish I could feel an earthquake!" is generally among the first exclamations of the newly-landed European. "What a paltry sort of thing it is, considering the fuss people make about it !" is generally his remark on his *second* earthquake (for the *first* one he invariably sleeps through). But after the fifth or sixth he never wants to experience another; and his terror of earthquakes grows with length of residence in an earthquake-shaken land, such as Japan has been from time immemorial. Indeed, geologists tell us that much of Japan would never have existed but for the seismic and volcanic agency which has elevated whole districts above the ocean by means of repeated eruptions.

The cause of earthquakes remains obscure. The learned incline at present to the opinion that the causes may be many and various; but the general connection between earthquakes and volcanoes is not contested. The "faulting" which results from elevations and depressions of the earth's crust, the infiltration of water to great depths and the consequent generation of steam, the caving in of subterranean hollows—

hollows themselves produced in all probability by chemical
degradation—these and other causes have been appealed to as
the most probable. One highly remarkable fact is that volcanic
and earthquake-shaken regions are almost always adjacent
to areas of depression. The greatest area of depression in
the world is the Pacific basin; and accordingly round its
borders, from Kamchatka through the Kuriles to Japan, thence
through a line of small islands to the Philippines and to Java,
then eastward to New Zealand, and right up the western
coast of South America, is grouped the mightiest array of
volcanoes that the world contains. Another fact of interest
is the greater occurrence of earthquakes during the winter
months. This has been explained by Dr. Knott as the result
of " the annual periodicity of two well-known meteorological
phenomena—namely, snow accumulations over continental
areas, and barometric gradients."*

Japanese history is a concatenation of earthquake disasters,
exceeded only by those which have desolated South America.
But the Japanese people had perforce submitted to these
ravages, without attempting to investigate the causes of earthquakes scientifically. All they had done was to record anecdotes and superstitions connected with the subject, one of
the most popular of which latter (popular indeed in many
parts of the world besides Japan) is that earthquakes are due
to a large subterranean fish, which wriggles about whenever
it wakes up. Another notion commonly entertained, and embodied in the following doggerel verse, is that certain other
occurrences can be foreknown from the hour at which a shock
takes place :—

> *Ku wa yamai*
> *Go shichi ga ame ni*
> *Yotsu hideri*
> *Mutsu yatsu-doki wa*
> *Kaze to shiru-beshi*

---

* See his learned paper on the subject in Vol. IX. Part I. of the *Transactions of the
Seismological Society of Japan.*

Which may be Englished as follows:

> At twelve o'clock it means disease,
> At eight or four 'tis rain,
> At ten 'tis drought, while six and two
> Of wind are tokens plain.*

With the advent of the theoretically minded European, a new era was inaugurated. A society named the Seismological Society of Japan was started in the spring of 1880, chiefly through the efforts of Professor John Milne, F.R.S., who has ever since devoted all his energies to wrestling with the problems which earthquakes, earth oscillations, earth currents, and seismic and volcanic phenomena generally, supply in such perplexing quantity. The Japanese government, too, has lent a helping hand by the establishment of a chair of seismology in the Imperial University, and of several hundreds of observing stations all over the empire,—an empire, remember, dotted with no less than fifty-one active volcanoes, and experiencing about five hundred shocks yearly.

Can earthquakes be prevented ? If they cannot be prevented, can they at least be foretold ? Both these questions must unfortunately be answered in the negative. Still, certain practical results have been arrived at by Mr. Milne and his fellow-workers, which are by no means to be despised. It is now possible to make what is called a " seismic survey " of any given plot of ground, and to indicate which localities will be least liable to shocks. It has also been shown that the complete isolation of the foundations of a building from the surface of the soil obtains for the building comparative immunity from damage. The reason is that the surface shakes more than the adjacent lower layers of the soil, just as, if several billiard-balls be placed in a row, an impulse given to the first one will make only the last one fly off, while those in the middle remain nearly motionless. For the same reason,

---

* Those knowing a little Japanese will be puzzled at our rendering *ku* (9) by " twelve o'clock," *go* (5) by " eight," etc. The solution of the mystery will be found below in the Article entitled TIME.

it is dangerous to build near the edge of a cliff. To architects, again, various hints have been given, both from experience accumulated on the spot, and also from that of Manila and other earthquake-shaken localities. The passage from natural to artificial vibrations being obvious, Professor Milne has been led on to the invention of a machine which records, after the manner of a seismograph, the vibrations of railway trains. This machine keeps an automatic record of all the motions of a train, and serves to detect irregularities occurring at crossings and points, as also those due to want of ballast, defects in bridges, and so on.

Thus, imperfect as it still is, imperfect as the nature of the case may perhaps condemn it always to remain, the science of seismology has already borne practical fruit in effecting a saving of tens of thousands of dollars. To those who are interested in seismometers and seismographs, in earthquake maps and earthquake catalogues, in seismic surveys, in microseisms, earth tremors, earth pulsations, and generally in earth physics, we recommend a perusal of the *Transactions of the Seismological Society of Japan,* complete in sixteen volumes, of its continuation, the *Seismological Journal of Japan,* and of the volume entitled *Earthquakes,* by Professor Milne in the "International Scientific Series." Volume IX. Part II. of the *Seismological Transactions* is specially devoted to the volcanoes of Japan, and contains a mass of statistics, anecdotes, historical details, and illustrations,—each individual volcano, from the northernmost of the Kuriles down to Aso-san in Kyūshū, which has the largest crater in the world, being treated of in detail. The *Ansei Kembun Roku* and the *Ansei Kembun Shi* are capitally illustrated Japanese accounts of the great earthquake which wrecked Yedo in 1855. Lovers of the ghastly will search long before they find anything more to their taste than the delineations there given of men and women precipitated out of windows, cut in two by falling beams, bruised, smashed, imprisoned in cellars, overtaken by tidal waves, or worse still, burnt alive in one of the great fires caused by the sudden overturning of thousands of candles and braziers all over the city. Truly these are gruesome books.

Education. During the Middle Ages, education was in the hands of the Buddhist priesthood. The temples were the schools, the subject most insisted on was the Buddhist sutras. The accession of the Tokugawa dynasty to the Shōgunate (A.D. 1603–1867) brought with it a change. The educated classes turned Confucianist. Accordingly the Confucian Classics—the *Four Books* and the *Five Canons*—were installed in the place of honour, learnt by heart, expounded as carefully as in China itself. Besides the Chinese Classics, instruction was given in the native history and literature. Some few ardent students picked their way through Dutch books that had been begged, borrowed, or stolen from the Hollanders at Nagasaki, or bought, for their weight in gold, for the sake of the priceless treasures of medical and other scientific knowledge known to be concealed in them. But such devotees of European learning were forced to maintain the greatest secrecy, and were hampered by almost incredible difficulties; for the government of the day frowned on all things foreign, and more than one zealous student expiated by his death the crime of striving to increase knowledge.

With the revolution of 1868, the old system of education crumbled away. Indeed, even before 1868 the learning of foreign languages, especially English, had been tacitly connived at. A complete reform was initiated—a reform on Western lines—and it was carried out at first chiefly under American advice. The present Imperial University of Tōkyō is the representative and heir of several colleges established some thirty-five years ago,—a Language College, a Medical College, a College of Engineering. At the same time, primary instruction was being placed on a new basis, and specially promising lads were sent across the sea to imbibe Western learning at its source. When not allowed to go abroad, even well-born young men were happy to black the shoes of a foreign family, in the hope of being able to pick up foreign languages and foreign manners. Some of the more enterprising took French leave, and smuggled themselves on board homeward-bound ships. This was how—to mention but two well-known instances—the adventurous youths, Itō and Inoue, entered on the career which has led them at last to preside over the destinies of their country.

The Tōkyō University includes six faculties, namely, Law, Medicine, Engineering, Literature, Science, and Agriculture. The College of Medicine was till recently under German influence. The other colleges have had and still have professors of various nationalities, chiefly Japanese, Anglo-Saxon, and German. The students number 3,400. A second University was inaugurated at Kyōto in 1897, with the three faculties of Law, Medicine, and Science (including Engineering). Its courses are attended by over 640 students. Other important educational establishments started and maintained by the Government are two Higher Normal Schools for young men and one for young women, fifty-seven other Normal Schools, the Higher Commercial School, the Foreign Language School, the Technical School, the Nobles' School, the various Naval and Military Academies, the School of Navigation, the Fine Arts School, the Tōkyō Musical Academy, the Blind and Dumb School, the Agricultural College at Sapporo, and Six Higher Schools, of which one is in Tōkyō and five are in the provinces. Two other Higher Schools—one in Chōshū and one in Satsuma—derive their income from funds granted by the ex-Daimyōs of those provinces. To enter into further details would be beyond our scope. Something may be gleaned from the bare statement that the Japanese Government supports over 27,000 primary schools, which have a staff of 109,118 teachers and are attended by 5,135,400 scholars; and 258 middle schools, with 4,681 teachers and nearly 95,000 scholars, besides a large number of kindergartens. There are also numerous private colleges, great and small, of which the best-known are the Keiō Gijuku at Tōkyō, founded in 1868 by the celebrated free-thinker and writer Fukuzawa, and the Waseda College, also at Tōkyō, founded and still maintained by Count Ōkuma, an eminent politician, leader of the Progressist party. The scholastic establishments of the Protestant missionaries likewise fill a considerable place in public esteem.

Only a small percentage of Japanese students board at their respective schools. In Tōkyō alone there are (May, 1904) no less than 1,861 lodging-houses, which make their living by putting students up and feeding them cheaply. The system is not without its drawbacks, especially on the side of morals.

Female education is officially provided for by the Higher Normal School for Girls already referred to, by seventy-nine High Schools, the Peeresses' School, etc., etc. Of the many private institutions, the Industrial School for Girls is the largest. The University for Women, established at Tōkyō in 1901, granted 120 degrees in 1904. Nor, in even so slight a sketch as this, is it possible to omit reference to the numerous educational societies which, for a series of years past, have done good work throughout the country. The military drill, too, which figures in the curriculum of all government schools, deserves notice. It was made obligatory in 1886, and has produced excellent results both on the physique and the spirit of the scholars. Various European sports, though not insisted on, are encouraged. Baseball seems to be that to which the young fellows take most kindly. Even the girls are now made to pass through a course of gymnastics.

The leading idea of the Japanese Government, in all its educational improvements, is the desire to assimilate the national ways of thinking to those of European countries. How great a measure of success has already been attained, can be best gauged by comparing one of the surviving old-fashioned literati of the Tempō period (A.D. 1830–1844) with an intelligent young man of the new school, brought up at the Tōkyō University or at Mr. Fukuzawa's. The two seem to belong to different worlds. At the same time it is clear that no efforts, however arduous, can make the Europeanisation complete. In effect, what is the situation ? All the nations of the West have, broadly speaking, a common past, a common fund of ideas, from which everything that they have and everything that they are springs naturally as part of a correlated whole,—one Roman Empire in the background, one Christian religion at the centre, one gradual emancipation, first from feudalism and next from absolutism, worked out or now in process of being worked out together, one art, one music, one kind of idiom, even though the words expressing it vary from land to land. Japan stands beyond this pale, because her past has been lived through under conditions altogether different. China is her Greece and Rome. Her language is not Aryan, as even Russia's is. Allusions familiar from one end of Christendom to the other require a whole chapter of commentary to make them at all intelligible to a Japanese student, who often has not, even then, any words corresponding to those which it is sought to translate. So well is this fact understood by Japanese educators, that it has been customary for many years past to impart most of the higher branches of knowledge through the medium of the English tongue. This, however, is an enormous additional weight hung round the student's neck. For a Japanese to be taught through the medium of English, is infinitely harder than it would be for English lads to be taught through the medium of Latin, as Latin does not, after all, differ very widely in spirit from English. It is, so to say, English in other words. But between English and Japanese the gulf fixed is so wide and gaping that the student's mind must be for ever on the stretch. The simpler and more idiomatic the English, the more does it tax his powers of comprehension. It is difficult to see any way out of this dilemma. All the heartier, therefore, is the praise due to a body of educators who fight on so bravely, and on the whole so successfully.

As for the typical Japanese student, he belongs to that class of youth who are the schoolmaster's delight,—quiet, intelligent, deferential, studious almost to excess. His only marked fault is a tendency common to all subordinates in Japan,—a tendency to wish to steer the ship himself. "Please, Sir, we don't want to read American history any more. We want to read how balloons are made." Such is a specimen of the requests which every teacher in Japan must have had to listen to over and over again. Actual insubordination—unknown under the old regime—became very frequent, during the closing years of the nineteenth century, scarcely a trimester passing without the boys of some important school striking work on the plea of disapproval of their teachers' methods or management. Moreover, there sprang up a class of rowdy youths, called *sōshi* in Japanese,—juvenile agitators who, taking all politics to be their province, used to obtrude their views and their presence on ministers of state, and to waylay —bludgeon and knife in hand—those whose opinions on matters of public interest happened to differ from their own. These unhealthy symptoms, like others incidental to the childhood of the New Japan, seem now to have passed away without leaving any permanent ill effects.

Books recommended. *Meet Japan: A Modern Nation with a Memory* written under the auspices of Tsuneji Hibino; *The New Far East* compiled by International Research Associates.

EE—EE. These letters which, to the perplexity of European travellers, adorn the signboards of many forwarding agencies in modern Japan, stand for the English word "express."

Embroidery. The reader may ire of being told of each art in succession that it was imported into Japan from China via Korea by Buddhist missionaries. But when such is the fact, what can be done but state it ? The greatest early Japanese artist in embroidery of whom memory has been preserved was Chūjō Hime, a Buddhist nun of noble birth, who, according to the legend, was an incarnation of Kwannon, the Goddess of Mercy. After enduring relentless persecution at the hands of a cruel stepmother, she retired to the temple of Taema-dera in Yamato, where her grand embroidered picture, or *mandara* as it is called, of the Buddhist heaven with its many mansions, is still shown. The gods themselves are said to have aided her in this work.

The embroidery and brocade and painted silks of more modern days possess exquisite beauty. A comparatively recent invention is the *birōdo-yūzen*, in which ribbed velvet is used as the ground for pictures which are real works of art, the velvet being partly cut, partly dyed, partly painted. Pity only, as we could not help noticing on a recent visit to Kyōto, that the embroiderers tend more and more to drop the patterns of dragons and phenixes and flower-cars, etc., etc., which made their fame, and actually elect to work from photographs instead, thus degrading free art to the level of slavish imitation. They informed us that the globe-trotters prefer these less esthetic pieces with a real jinrikisha or a real street lamp-post to the formal, but oh! how beautiful, fancies of an earlier date. Doubtless new-comers have to be educated up to these things. However, being but a man, while some of our readers are sure to be ladies whose sharp eyes would soon detect mistakes, we must abstain from entering into any further details or disquisitions. We would only recommend all who can to visit the Kyōto embroidery and velvet-shops, and to take plenty of money in their purse. There may be two opinions about Japanese painting; there can be only one about Japanese embroidery.

Note in passing, as an instance of topsy-turvydom, that comparatively few Japanese embroiderers are women. All the best pieces are the work of men and boys.

Empress. The Salic law was only introduced into Japan with the brand-new Constitution of 1889. Before then, several empresses had sat on the 'throne, and one of them, the Empress Jingō—excuse the name, O English reader! it signifies " divine prowess "—ranks among the greatest heroic figures of early Japanese legend (see Article on HISTORY AND MYTHOLOGY). All Japanese empresses have been native-born. Doubtless the remoteness of Japan from other lands precluded the idea of foreign matrimonial alliances. The monarch's life-partner was habitually sought in the families of the native aristocracy, one consequence of which is that the Japanese

Imperial Family is absolutely native and national, not alien in blood, like the reigning houses of England, Russia, and many other European states.

The present Empress is of course Empress Consort. Her name is Haru-ko, correctly translated by Pierre Loti, in his *Japoneries d'Automne,* as " l'Impératrice Printemps." Wisely abstaining from even the shadow of interference in politics, this illustrious lady, daughter of a high noble of the Court of Kyōto, devotes her life to learning and to good works, hospitals in particular engrossing her attention. The Red Cross Hospital at Shibuya in Tōkyō, one of the most spacious—one might well say luxurious—hospitals in the East, was her creation, and the Charity Hospital at Shiba in Tōkyō also enjoys her munificent patronage.

English as she is Japped. English " as she is spoke and wrote " in Japan forms quite an enticing study. It meets one on landing, in such signboard inscriptions as

TAILOR NATiVE GOUNTRY.

DRAPER, MILLINER AND LADIES OUTFATTER.

*The Ribbons, the laces, the veils, the feelings.**

HAND PANTING POST CARDS

MANUFACTURED. BY CAKE & A. PIECE. OF. BREAD.†

EXTRACT OF FOWL *(over an egg-shop)*

PEST MILK.

Photographer Executed.

HEAD CUTTER. *(over a barber's shop)*

The European monkey jacket make for the Japanese.

WRITING FOR ANOTHER.‡

Specialist for the Decease of Children.

BEST PERFUMING WATER ANTI-FLEA.

DEALER OF.§

---

* Can the shopkeeper mean " frillings ? "

† On a baker's cart.

‡ Over a public letter-writer's. Owing to the difficulties of ideographic writing and a highly peculiar epistolary style, the public letter-writer continues to drive a brisk trade even among a population fairly well-educated.

§ Of *what,* does not appear.

and a hundred more. The thirsty soul, in particular, can
make himself merry, while he drinks, with such droll legends
on bottles as

FOGREN COUNTY WINES LITTLE SEAL.

Sᴛ. JUILEN *Bottled by* BORDEAUX.

Good wine, they say, needs no bush. Apparently, it is
equally independent of such aid as orthography can lend.

TRADE MARK

ル ー ビ ジ フ

FUJI BEER

The efficacy of this Beer is to
give the health and especially
the strength for Stomach.
The flovour is so sweet
and simple that not
injure for much
drink.

Many strange notices are stuck up, and advertisements
circulated. The following is the manner in which " Fragrant
Kōzan Wine " is recommended to public attention :—

If health be not steady, heart is not active. Were heart active, the
deeds may be done. Among the means to preserve health, the best
way is to take in Kozan wine which is sold by us, because it is to
assist digestion and increase blood. Those who want the steady health
should drink Kozan wine. This wine is agreeable even to the females
and children who can not drink any spirit because it is sweet. On
other words, this pleases mouth and therefore, it is very convenient
medicine for nourishing.

JAPAN INSTED OF COFFEE.*

More men is not got dropsg of the legs who us this coffee, which is contain nourish.

The following is the label usually to be found pasted on the handles of cheap Japanese fire-shovels:—

TRADE (K) MARK

Showvels Scoops and Spades which are exhibited of the above trade mark is very cheap in the pice and it is bonueniemt bor Use. There is no neceity exklain ally aeknorulebqe by thebll customers.

The following notice was stuck up a few years ago in one of the hotels at Kyōto:

NOTICE TO THE DEALERS.

On the dinning-time nobody shall be enter to the dinning-room, and drowing-room without the guests' allow. Any dealer shall be honestly his trade, of course the sold one shall be prepare to make up the safe package.

The reader may be curious to know who "the sold one" here referred to is. Might it not perhaps be the purchaser? No; at least that is not what the hotel-keeper wished to suggest. By translating back literally into Japanese idiom, we reach his meaning, which is that the merchant who sells the things must undertake furthermore to pack them securely.

NOTIES.

Our tooth is a very important organ for human life and conntenance as you know; therefore when it is attack by disease or injury, artificial tooth is also very useful.

I am engage to the Dentistry and I will make for your purpose.

---

* *I.e.,* "a Japanese substitute for coffee."

A lawyer desirous of attracting foreign clients ends up his business card by the cryptic announcement: *"I can manage the affairs without any affliction of an English."*

A *"Guide for Visitors to Atami"* informs us that the geyser there *was discovered by a priest named Man-gwan who made many improvements on the springs. Before that day, the springs boiled out in the sea, and was a suffering to aquatic families....If a people can not come to Atami is better to bathe in that water once or twice a day, and take good exercise in clean airs.* By "aquatic families," let it be noted, the writer means, not—as might perhaps be supposed—the fishermen, but the fishes. This Atami Guide-book is, however, quite eclipsed by *"A Guide on Hakone,"*—a perfect jewel, which sells on the spot for *"30 zonts."* Here is part of its description of the locality in question:—*Whenever we visit the place, the first pleasure to be longed, is the view of Fuji Mountain and its summit is covered with permanent undissolving snow, and its regular configuration hanging down the sky like an opened white fan, may be looked long at equal shape from several regions surrounding it. Every one who saw it ever has nothing but applause. It casts the shadow in a contrary direction on still glassy face of lake as I have just described. Buildings of Imperial Solitary Palace, scenery of Gongen, all are spontaneous pictures. Wind proper in quantity, suits to our boat to slip by sail, and moon-light shining on the sky shivers quartzy lustre over ripples of the lake. The cuckoo singing near by our hotel, plays on a harp, and the gulls flying about to and fro seek their food in the waves. All these panorama may be gathered only in this place.*—Nor are mere creature comforts less well-provided for in this paradise than esthetic pleasures. *Forty-five houses,* we read, *among whole machi are the hotels for cessation of travellers. Each of them has an untiring view of garden and an elegant prospect of landscape; hence many visitors are assembled at the summer days to attend their own health. Breads, fleshes of fowls and animals, and fresh fishes transporting on from Yoshihama and Fukuura satisfy the relish of people. The milk is distributed* to the hopers by the branch store in Hakone of Kōbokusha, the pasturage at Sengoku-hara. Streams of water issuing forth in the south-eastern valley of Hakone-machi, are used by whole inhabitants. Transparent and delicate liquid is constantly overflowing from the vat and its purity free from defilement so fully values on the applause of visitors as it is with the air.—This little work of thirty-three tiny pages has an " Analysis " in four Parts and thirty-two Sections, and the first edition had the Preface at the end.

English as she is Japped has even crossed the seas. The following notice adorns a laundry in Thursday Island:

We most cleanly and carefully wash our customers with cheap prices as under; Ladies—eight shillings per hundred; gentlemen seven shillings per hundred.

Letters offer some choice specimens. We select two epistolary gems, only changing the proper names. The first is from a young man, who entered into friendly relations with the family of a certain consul, in order to *perfect* his English.

Saga, August 18th.

Robert Fanshaw Esq.
    G. B. Consul.

Dear Sir,

    I am very glad to hear that you and your family are very well and I am also quite well as usual, but my grandfather's disease is very severe without changing as customary. I fear that it is a long time since I have pay a visit to you. I wish your pardon to get away my remote crime. We have only a few hot in Saga as well as summer is over, and we feel to be very cool in morning and evening. Sometimes we have an earthquake here at now, but the mens was afright no more.

    I grieves that a terrible accident took place in the school of military Saga. The story of it, a scholar had put to death some colleague with a greate stick on the floor and a doctor of anatomy dissected immediately with dead disciple, then all pupils of school were now to question its matter in the judgement seat; but do not it decide yet.

    Unequivocal matter would speak you of kind letter.

I am, &c.,

K. TANAKA.

The following is a letter sent in reply to one addressed by a foreign resident to the district office in Tōkyō, notifying the birth of a daughter:—

Mr. R. H. Saunders.

Dear Sir,

I am reiceved your letter of your beautiful baby birth, well; I understand the letter fact, but you must write with Japanese words, by Law calls. therefore I have translated Japanese for you. I hope you will write your name, age, yourself, with native words. the mark ( ) .... it s able to write.

Truly yours
M. Suzuki.

" China " having been set as a theme in a Tōkyō school, one student disposed summarily of the hereditary rivals of his race by remarking that

Chinese gentlemen adjourn their tales and clutches so long as they are able. The people are all liars.

Another young essayist was more diffuse, and let us hope got better marks:—

CHINA.

Here is an old man whose body is very large; he is about four thousand years of age and China is his name. His autobiography tells me that he was born in early times in Eastern Asia. He was a simple baby smiling with amiable face in the primitive cradle; and as a young man, he progressed hopefully. When he was full grown he accomplished many bright acts; he married a sweet lady who conceived the beautiful children of the arts and sciences. But by and bye he became old, lame, blind and decrepit.

I must feel sorry for the sad fate of an old teacher or neighbour of mine. Why his gleamy grew gloomy ? What compassion I feel for him !

There are many smokes of the opium but not holy blood of the cross.

THE CHARACTER OF THE ENGLISHMAN.

The England which occupied of the largest and greatest dominion which rarely can be. The Englishman works with a very powerful hands and the long legs and even the eminenced mind, his chin is so strong as decerved iron. He are not allowed it to escape if he did siezed something. Being spread his dominion is dreadfully extensive so that his countryman boastally say " the sun are never sets on our dominions." The Testamony of English said that he that lost the common sense, he never any benefit though he had gained the complete world. The English are cunning institutioned to establish a great empire of the Paradise. The Englishman always said to the another nation "give me your land and I will give you my Testimony." So it is not a robbed but exchanged as the Englishman always confide the object to be pure and the order to be holy and they reproach him if any them are killed to death with the contention of other man. (I shall continue the other time.)

The young essayist hits us rather hard—doesn't he ?—when he drags into the garish light of day our little foible for giving a " Testimony " in exchange for " the another nation's land."

A writer, who prefixes an English preface to an interesting " Collection of Registered Trade Marks," observes that *The society in niuteenth century is always going to be civiliged, and so all things are also improved.* The muse of course ranking among " civiliging " influences, a little volume has been published at Tōkyō with the object of inducting the Far-Eastern mind into the mysteries of English verse. It is entitled *New of Pom and Song the English and Japanese.* Occasionally Japanese youths themselves, like Silas Wegg, " drop into poetry."

THE MIDNIGHT WINDS.

At the midnight—my own darkness alone; none but God and myself!
A conscious slumber muffled the universe,
Palpitating on the lonely bed like a chilly sea in the misty dawn.
Be hunting (Oh) by the black boneless winds.
With the sewed eyes and the wild, weird, full-opened soul,
I'm reviewing the sheeted memories of past under an inky light;
Until—alas, the strange giant of winds inclosed about my breathless
    cabin :—
God made a night, a midnight for me alone !
Oh, our matchless God ! If the wizard rout
Flit in through the broken window for a lady-moon welcomed !
Ever a gentle violet upturns her eye :
Ever a radiant rose polish her thorns against.
I have such of none, but a withered, colorless soul !

The latter part of this poem is somewhat discursive; but the radiant rose polishing her thorns against a full stop is a genuine touch of genius. The following—so far as we apprehend its obscurities through the mist of poetic license—would appear to be a dithyramb in praise of woman, who is apostrophised as the cement of society, or, to use the youthful bard's own realistic expression, "social glue."

HER GLEE.

The purest flame, the hottest heat
  Is Woman's Power ever earth;
Which mighty black and pale down beat,
  And made the Eden, place of birth.

Of what? of what? can thou tell me?
  A birth of Noble, High, value—
The station He destined for thee—
  Of woman, Mother, Social Glue.

Let her be moved from earth, to try,
  What dark mist overhelms human Race !
Let Lady claim with all the cry:—
  " Can you still hold and hold your peace ? "

How sweet, how mirthful, gay is Name !
  What boon, thing, may exceed in kind ?
Would She be praised, entolled—not Shame :
  Tie Pale, of Both, to bound, to bind.

And now, Japanese readers, if haply any such favour this little book with their perusal, rise not in your wrath to indict us of treachery and unkindness. We mean nothing against the honour of Japan. But finding Tōkyō life dull on the whole, we solace ourselves by a little innocent laughter at an innocent foible whenever we can find one to laugh at. You yourselves could doubtless make up, on the subject of *Japanese as she is Englished,* an article which should be no less comical,—an article which should transcribe the first lispings in " globetrotterese," and the perhaps still funnier, because more pretentions, efforts of those of us who think themselves rather adepts in Japanese as spoken in the upper circles. For our own part, we can feel our heavy British accent dragging down to earth every light-winged syllable of Japanese as we pronounce it.

We laugh at ourselves for this. Why should be not laugh at you, when occasion offers ? There are only two styles of " English as she is Japped " which call, not for laughter, but for the severest blame. One of these occurs in books which are published under Japanese names as original matter, but are really made up of a cento of passages stolen from European writers. The alteration of a word here and there is naïvely supposed to effect concealment; but being almost always unskilfully done, it serves only to make the fraud more glaring. We ourselves have repeatedly been the *corpus vile* of such experiments. A second Japano-English style is exemplified in so-called educational works, such as *Conversations in English and Japanese for Merchant who the English Language,— English Letter Writer, for the Gentlemen who regard on the Commercial and an Official,—Englishand. Japanies. Names on Letteps,* and other productions whereby shameless scribblers make money out of unsophisticated students. And yet these curiosities of literature are too grotesque for at least the European reader to be long angry with them. One of the funniest is entitled *The Practical use of Conversation for Police Authorities.* After giving " Cordinal number," " Official Tittle," " Parts of the Body " such as " a gung,*" " a jow," " the mustacheo," diseases such as " a caucer," " blind," " a ginddness," " the megrim," " a throat wen," and other words useful to policemen, the compiler arrives at " Misseranious subjects," which take the form of conversations, some of them real masterpieces. Here is one between a representative of " the force " and an English blue-jacket :—

What countryman are you ?
I am a sailor belonged to the Golden-Eagle, the English man-of-war.
Why do you strike this Jinrikisha-man ?
He told me impolitely.
What does he told you impolitely ?
He insulted me saing loudly " the Sailor the Sailor " when I am passing here.

---

* The Japanese translation shows that " gum " is the word intended.

Do you striking this man for that ?

Yes.

But do not strike him for it is forbided.

I strike him no more.

*   *   *   *   *   *   *   *   *

The author teaches his policemen, not only to converse, but to moralise. Thus:

Japanese Police Force consists of nice young men.

But I regret that their attires are not perfectly neat.

When a constable come in conduct with a people he shall be polite and tender in his manner of speaking and movement.

If he will terrify or scold the people with enormous voice, he will become himself an object of fear for the people.

Civilized people is meek, but barbarous peoples is vain and haugty.

A cloud-like writing of Chinese character, and performance of the Chinese poem, or cross hung on the breast, would no more worthy, to pretend others to avail himself to be a great man.

Those Japanese who acquired a little of foreign language, think that they have the knowledge of foreign countries, as Chinese, English or French, there is nothing hard to success what they attempt.

They would imitate themselves to Cæsar, the ablest hero of Rome, who has been raised the army against his own country, crossing the river Rabicon.

A gleam of diffidence seems to cross the police mind when one policeman says to the other " You speak the English very well." and the other replies " You jest."

Esotericism. When an Englishman hears the word " esoteric," the first thing, probably, that comes into his head is Buddhism, the second the name of Mr. Sinnett or Mrs. Annie Besant. Matters stand somewhat differently in Japan. Not religion only, but every art, every pastime, here is or has been esoteric, —poetry, music, porcelain-making, fencing, football, even bone-setting, and cookery itself. Esotericism is not a unique mystery shrouding a special class of subjects. It is a general attitude of the mind at a certain stage, and a very natural attitude too, if one takes the trouble to look into it. Sensible men do not wear their hearts on their sleeves for daws to peck at. Why should an artist do so with his art? Why should he desecrate his art by initiating unworthy persons into its principles? Nor is it merely a question of advisability, or of delicacy and good taste. It is a question of possibility and impossibility. Only sympathetic pupils are fitted by nature to understand certain things; and certain things can only be taught by word of mouth, and when the spirit moves one. Moreover, there comes in the question of money. Esoteric teaching of the lower arts may be said to have performed, in old days, the function of our modern system of patents. The institution of guilds belonged to the same order of ideas.

Such are, it would seem, the chief headings of the subject, considered in the abstract. Fill them out, if you please, by further reflection and further research; and if you wish to talk to your Japanese friends about esotericism, remember the fascinating words *hiden,* " secret tradition; " *hijutsu,* " secret art; " and *okugi,* " inner mysteries," which play a notable part in Japanese history and literature.

Many are the stories told of the faithful constancy with which initiation into hidden mysteries has been sought. Early in the tenth century there lived a great musician, a nobleman named Hakuga-no-Sammi. But one Semi-Maru was a greater musician still. He dwelt in retirement, with no other companion but his lute, and there was a melody of which he alone had the secret. Hakuga—as he may be styled for shortness' sake—went every evening for three years to listen at Semi's gate, but in vain. At last, one autumn night, when the wind was soughing through the sedges, and the moon was half-hidden by a cloud, Hakuga heard the magic strains begin, and, when they ceased, he heard the player exclaim, " Alas! that there should be none to whom I might hand on this precious possession! " Thereupon Hakuga took courage. He entered the hermitage, prostrated himself, declared his name and rank, and humbly implored to be received by Semi as his disciple.

This Semi consented to, and gradually revealed to him all the innermost recesses of his art.—According to Mr. E. H. Parker, this story, like many another Japanese story, is but the echo of a far older Chinese tradition. But whether true or false, whether native or foreign, it is a favourite motive with Japanese painters.

Undoubtedly authentic, and very different in its tenor, is the tale of Katō Tamikichi, a manufacturer of porcelain at the beginning of the eighteenth century. His master, Tsugane Bunzaemon, who owned a kiln in the province of Owari, envied the skill of the Karatsu porcelain-makers in the use of blue and white, and was determined to penetrate their secret. Accordingly he succeeded in arranging a marriage between one of his pupils, Katō Tamikichi, and the daughter of the chief of the Karatsu people. Katō, thus taken into the family in so distant a province, was regarded as one of themselves and admitted into their fullest confidence. Things went on quietly for years, during which he became the father of several children. At last, one day, Katō expressed an earnest desire to revisit the scenes of his childhood and to enquire after his old master. Nothing doubting, the Karatsu people let him go. But when he reached Owari, he disclosed to his former master all that he had learnt at Karatsu, the consequence of which was that Owari porcelain was greatly improved, and obtained an immense sale in the neighbouring market of Ōsaka, the richest in the empire. When this came to the ears of the Karatsu people, they were so much enraged that they caused Katō's wife and children to be crucified. He himself died a raving lunatic.

Since the latter part of the Middle Ages, the general prevalence among the upper classes of luxury, idleness, and a superstitious veneration for the past, even in trivial matters, together with a love of mystery, produced the most puerile whims. For instance, a certain noble family at Kyōto kept to itself, with all the apparatus of esotericism, the interpretation of the names of three birds and of three trees mentioned in an ancient book of poetry called the *Kokinshū*. No sacrament could have been more jealously guarded from impious hands, or rather lips. But when the great scholar, Motoori, disdaining all mumbo-jumbo, brought the light of true philological criticism to bear on the texts in question, lo and behold! one of the mysterious birds proved to be none other than the familiar wagtail, the second remained difficult to fix accurately, and the third name was not that of any particular species, but merely a general expression signifying the myriad little birds that twitter in spring. The three mysterious trees were equally commonplace.

Foolish as the three bird secret was (and it was but one among a hundred such), it had the power to save the life of a brave general, Hosokawa Yūsai, who, being besieged in A.D. 1600 by a son of the famous ruler Hideyoshi, was on the point of seeing his garrison starved into a surrender. This came to the ears of the Mikado; and His Majesty, knowing that Hosokawa was not only a warrior, but a learned man, well-versed in the mysteries of the *Kokinshū*—three birds and all—and fearing that this inestimable store of erudition might perish with him and be lost to the world for ever, exerted his personal influence to such good effect that an edict was issued commanding the attacking army to retire.

Viewed from a critical standpoint, Chinese and Japanese esoterics well deserve thorough investigation by some competent hand. We ourselves do not think that much would be added thereby to the world's store of wisdom. But we do think that a flood of light would be shed upon some of the most curious nooks and crannies of the human mind.

Eta. The origin of the *Eta,* or Japanese pariahs, is altogether obscure. Some see in them the descendants of Korean captives, brought to Japan during the wars of the latter part of the sixteenth century. By others they are considered to be the illegitimate descendants of the celebrated generalissimo Yoritomo, who lived as far back as the twelfth century. Even the etymology of the name is a subject of dispute among the learned, some of whom believe it to be from the Chinese characters 穢多 *e-ta*, "defilement abundant," while others derive it from *e-tori* 餌取 "food-catchers," in allusion to the slaughtering of cattle and other animals, which, together with skinning such animals, digging criminals' graves, and similar degrading occupations, constituted their means of livelihood. We ourselves incline to date back the first gradual organisation of the *Eta* as a separate class to a very early period—say the seventh or eighth century—when the introduction of Buddhism had caused all those who were connected in any way with the taking of life to be looked on with horror and disdain. They lived apart, generally on the outskirts of towns or villages, and were governed by their own headmen; for the spirit of elaborate organisation pervading old Japanese society penetrated even to the dregs. There were three chiefs of the *Eta*, who resided at Yedo, Ōsaka, and Kyōto. Danzaemon, the Yedo chief, was privileged to wear two swords. Besides the *Eta* proper, there were the *Bantarō* or watchmen, and the *Kawara-mono* or vagrants, who travelled about as strolling players. Some trace to these the origin of the modern theatre.

The legal distinction between the *Eta* and other persons of the lower orders was abolished on the 12th October, 1871, at which time the official census gave 287,111 as the number of *Eta* properly so-called, and 982,800 as the total number of outcasts of all descriptions. Scorn of the *Eta* has naturally survived the abolition of their legal disabilities. It is a favourite theme of latter-day novelists, one of whom, Enchō, excellently adapted the plot of Wilkie Collins's *New Magdalen* to the Japanese life of our day, by substituting for the courtesan of the English original a girl who had degraded herself by marrying an *Eta*.

Books recommended. *Japan: An Attempt at Interpretation* by Lafcadio Hearn. *A Japanese Miscellany* by Lafcadio Hearn

Eurasians. Half-castes are often called Eurasians, from their being half-*Eur*opeans and half-Asiatics or *Asians*.

Eurasians usually resemble the Japanese mother rather than the European father, in accordance with the general physiological law whereby the fair parent gives way to the dark. The time that has elapsed since Japanese Eurasians began to be numerous is not long enough to inform us whether this mixed race will endure, or whether, as so often happens in such cases, it will die out in the third or fourth generation.

Europeanisation. The Europeanisation of Japan is universally spoken of as a sudden and recent metamorphosis, dating from the opening of the country during the life-time of men not yet old. But this implies a faulty and superficial reading of history. Europeanisation commenced over three hundred and fifty years ago, namely, in A.D. 1542, when three Portuguese adventurers discovered the Japanese island of Tane-ga-shima, and astonished the local princelet with the sight and sound of their arquebuses.

The Europeanisation of Japan has been a drama in three acts. First, the Hispano-Portuguese act, beginning in 1542 and ending with the religious persecution—the extermination rather—of 1617–38. This act offers a succession of stirring scenes. Scarcely even in our own day have changes more sudden been effected. To begin with, the art of war was revolutionised, as well for defence as attack. Japanese feudal barons had had their castles before then, no doubt. The exact construction of those early castles, stockades, or by whatever other name we might most fittingly denote such wood and plaster strongholds, is a curious question which must be left to Japanese antiquarians to decide. The first castle built in the style which now survives in some few perfect and numerous ruined examples, was that erected at Azuchi in the province of Ōmi by Oda Nobunaga, who lived from 1534 to 1582. His active career thus coincided with the first wave of European influence, the Portuguese having arrived when he was a child of eight years old, the earliest Catholic missionaries (1549) when he was a lad of fifteen. Nobunaga became the leading spirit among the warriors of his age; in fact, he may be said

to have dictated laws to the empire, and moreover he was a
declared patron of the Christians, though scarcely one of
whom they could be proud, as his hands were stained with
many crimes. It is related that when he had reared his famous
castle, " he placed the Christian God [*a crucifix?*] on the top
of the keep."* Significantly enough, the Japanese name for
a " castle keep," *tenshu*, is identical in sound with the translation of the name of " God " adopted by Japanese Catholics.
But whereas the latter is written with Chinese characters
having a perfectly clear and appropriate meaning, namely
天主 literally " Lord of Heaven," a " castle keep " is written
天守 " heavenly protection," a transcription not particularly
appropriate, which suggests the thought that it may have been
hit on merely as an expedient to distinguish the later from
the earlier acceptation of the term.† Once introduced, the new-
fashioned castle architecture spread rapidly throughout the
empire; for those were days of storm and stress. Christianity
spread too, some of the southern Daimyōs going so far in their
zeal as to prohibit the exercise of any other religion,—an act of
intolerance which was afterwards dearly expiated. At any
rate, the seed of religion then sown was never thoroughly

---

* According to another account, the first castle in the new style was that built by Matsunaga
Hisahide, which Nobunaga improved upon. As Hisahide was a contemporary of Nobunaga's and
likewise acquainted with some of the Jesuits, the result is much the same. At all events we may
infer that then, as now, the imported European ideas were translated into practice with feverish
haste.

† The etymology here given is that current among military men, and sanctioned by the
authority of the principal native Japanese dictionaries. Some recent Japanese investigators have
disputed its accuracy: They allege that, at that early stage of Japanese Christianity, the translation of " God " by the characters 天主 *(Tenshu)* had not yet been made, and they prefer
to seek a Buddhist origin for the word 天守 *(tenshu)*, " castle keep," suggesting that it may
come by aphæresis from 梵天主 *(Bontenshu)*, " Brahma's protection." To our mind, the
coincidence of the two words at such a date is a circumstance to shake which would require
weightier evidence than any yet adduced. In any case, the fact of Portuguese influence on
Japanese castle architecture is disputed by none, though some attribute less importance to it
than others. Details of plans, measurements, etc., were always kept secret as far as possible,
making the subject peculiarly difficult of investigation at this distance of time, more especially
in view of the strenuous endeavours of the government at Yedo to suppress all traditions of
former foreign intercourse, and of the strong nationalist feeling which ran in the same direction
for over two centuries.

eradicated. Christianity remained as a subterranean force, which rose to the surface again two or three centuries later, when some entire districts were found to be Christian (see Article on Missions). Spain and Portugal's minor contributions to the Europeanisation of Japan are no longer easy to trace, partly because persecution destroyed records, partly because the subject has never yet been thoroughly investigated. A knowledge of bread, with its name *pan,* certainly came thence. Capes (Jap. *kappa,* from Portuguese " capa ") and playing-cards (Jap. *karuta,* from Portuguese " carta ") may be mentioned among the loans whose names bewray them. Sponge-cake, whose Japanesse name *kasuteira* remains " Castille " scarcely disguised, is another humble but agreeable contribution from the same quarter ; mosquito-nets are another still more valuable. Before their introduction the fire of green wood, which is still used in some remote rural districts, was the only known method—a most disagreeable method as we can testify from personal experience—of driving away those insect pests. Doubtless a thorough sifting of Japanese customs, beliefs, and products would bring to light a number of interesting details.

In the second act of the drama of the Europeanisation of Japan, the scene is the islet of Deshima in Nagasaki harbour, the actors are Dutchmen. No religious zeal this time, nothing military, nothing heroic of any sort. Even scenes of screaming farce are brought before our eyes, when the deputation of Dutch traders convoyed to Yedo to offer their congratulations on the accession of each Shōgun, are set to amuse His Highness by singing songs, dancing, and pretending to be drunk. But such buffoonery was discontinued at the end of the seventeenth century. Some of the members of the Dutch factory were distinguished men. More than once, too, German scientific investigators, anxious for information concerning the secluded empire of Japan, enrolled themselves in the service of the factory, as a stepping-stone to the acquisition of such know-

ledge. Those Japanese who, despite official interdict, retained
a thirst for foreign learning, naturally sought the company of
such kindred spirits, and the results to Japan, though at first
meagre, were valuable and permanent.   The elements of
mathematics, geography, botany, and other sciences and of the
all-important art of medicine were obtained from this source.
So were various European products,—glass, velvet, woollen
fabrics, clocks, telescopes, etc.,—and it is to be presumed,
European business methods, at least in outline. Even scraps
of literature filtered through, for instance Esop's " Fables,"
which were translated as early as (about) 1670.   Precise
details are difficult to obtain, because of the censorship which
rigorously, though not quite successfully, repressed Dutch
studies except in one closely watched bureau of the administration at Yedo. But we know enough to be able to say positively
that during the two centuries from 1650 to 1850, the little
Dutch settlement at Nagasaki was constantly looked to by
eager minds as a fountain of intellectual light.

At last, but not quite suddenly even then,—for Commodore
Perry's famous expedition was preceded by others on a smaller
scale, both Russian and English,—a fresh impetus was given to
the Europeanisation of the country by its partial opening to
foreign trade and residence in 1859, and its complete opening
in 1899. This last, or Anglo-Saxon act of the drama—for in it
Anglo-Saxon influence has predominated—is still being played
out before our eyes. Once more the great art of war has
suffered a sea-change, and in every branch of intellectual and
social activity the pulse of a reinvigorated life runs quick.
Foreigners have often stood in amaze at Japan's ability to
swallow so many new ideas and institutions whole. They have
dubbed her superficial, and questioned the permanence of her
conversion to European methods. This is because they fail to
realise two things,—the innate strength of the Japanese
character, and the continuous process of schooling which has
enabled this particular race to face the new light without being

blinded. Another is thus added to the long list of instances proving that great historical changes never take place *per saltum*, and that those nations alone may be expected to put forth flowers and fruits in the future whose roots are twined solidly around the past. From the dawn of history to the present day, Japan, in her attitude towards foreign ideas—be they Chinese, mediæval Portuguese, old-fashioned Dutch, nineteenth century European—has shown herself consistently teachable. Periods marked chiefly by large importations from abroad have, it is true, alternated with periods chiefly devoted to the working up of that material into forms suitable to local needs. But neither process has ever been wholly discontinued, and the result—spread over fourteen centuries—has been a steady growth alike social, intellectual, and territorial, with but rare intervals of even apparent relapse. The superficiality attributed to her assimilation of imported civilisations exists only in the superficial knowledge of the would-be critics.

Fairy-tales. The Japanese have plenty of fairy-tales; but the greater number can be traced to a Chinese, and several of these again to a Buddhist, that is to an Indian, source. Among the most popular are *Urashima, Momotarō, The Battle of the Monkey and the Crab, The Tongue-Cut Sparrow, The Mouse's Wedding, The Old Man who Made the Trees to Blossom, The Crackling Mountain,* and *The Lucky Tea-Kettle.*

Though it is convenient to speak of these stories as " fairy-tales," fairies properly so-called do not appear in them. Instead of fairies, there are goblins and devils, together with foxes, cats, and badgers possessed of superhuman powers for working evil. We feel that we are in a fairy-land altogether foreign to that which gave Europe " Cinderella " and " Puss in Boots,"—no less foreign to that which produced the gorgeously complicated marvels of the " Arabian Nights."

Books recommended. *The Japanese Fairy Book* compiled by Yei Theodora Ozaki; *Old Tales of Japan* by Yuri Yasuda; illustrated by Yoshinobu Sakakura and Eiichi Mitsui; *Tales of Old Japan* by A. B. Mitford (Lord Redesdale).

Fans. Incidental mention of fans occurs in the oldest official annals of the country. Thus, under date A.D. 763, we read of Imperial permission being granted to a courtier to bring his staff and fan into the palace precincts, on the score of age and infirmity. Apparently fans were then tabooed by strict etiquette, which is remarkable, as they afterwards became an indispensable adjunct of Court dress for both sexes.

Fans are of two kinds,—two chief kinds, that is, for there is an immense number of minor varieties,—the round fan not capable of being shut *(uchiwa)*, and the folding fan *(ōgi* or *sensu)*. The fans of early days would seem to have been all of the non-folding type,—no wonder, seeing that the first natural fan was a palm-leaf. The Japanese pride themselves on being the inventors of the folding fan, which they assert to have been borrowed from them by the Chinese as late as the time of the Ming dynasty (1368–1644). A noble lady, widow of the youthful hero Atsumori,* is credited with the idea. At the temple of Miei-dō in Kyōto, whither she had retired to hide her grief under the garb of a nun, she cured the abbot of a fever by fanning him with a folding fan made of paper, over which she muttered incantations; and to the present day the priests of this temple are considered special adepts in the manufacture of fans, whence the name of Miei-dō adopted by many fan-shops all over the country.

Of the less common varieties of the fan, perhaps the strangest are the giant kinds carried at the festival of the Sun-Goddess in Ise and by the firemen of Kyōto, and especially the war-fans formerly used by military commanders to direct with and give force to their orders. Iron was the material usually employed, and the ornamentation consisted on one side of a red sun on a gold ground, on the other of a silver moon and stars on a black or dark blue ground. Ordinary fans are made of paper over split bamboo. Japanese fans excel in cheapness as in elegance, ten *sen* (2½d.) being the usual price for a plain folding fan,

---

* For an outline of Atsumori's touching story, see Murray's *Handbook to Japan*, 7th edit., pp. 78-9, under the heading *Kumagae Naozane*.

three or four *sen* for one of the non-folding kind. Fans are
used as bellows; they are even used as trays to hand things on.
A man of the lower class will often hold a partially opened
fan in front of his mouth when addressing a superior, so as to
obviate the possibility of his breath defiling the superior's
face; but to fan oneself vigorously in the presence of a
superior is not good manners.

To attempt a description of the quaint and poetical conceits
with which Japanese fan-makers adorn their wares, would be
to embark on a list of almost all the art-motives of the country;
for nearly all are made to contribute. The little picture is
often accompanied by a verse of poetry in black or gold letters,
or else there is only the poetry and no picture.

Fans have been extensively used as vehicles for advertisements; but the Japanese advertiser of the older school
generally disarmed criticism by the, so to say, apologetic
moderation with which he practised that most detestable of all
arts or rather artifices. In these latter days however, when
Europeanisation has corrupted everything, one has much to
suffer from while fanning oneself on a hot day. Art has surely
sounded its lowest depths when it comes to pourtraying a
lager-beer bottle on one side of a fan, and to providing a railway
time-table on the other.

Books recommended. *The Arts of Japan: An Illustrated History* by Hugo Munsterberg; *Legend in Japanese Art* by Henri L. Joly; *Painted Fans of Japan* by Reiko Chiba.

Fashionable Crazes. Japan stood still so long that she
has now to move quickly and often, to make up for lost time.
Every few years there is a new craze, over which the nation, or
at least that part of the nation which resides in Tōkyō, goes
wild for a season. 1873 was the rabbit year. There had been
none of these little rodents in Japan. Hence, when imported
as curiosities, they fetched incredible prices, as much as $1,000
being sometimes paid for a single specimen. Speculations in
$400 and $500 rabbits were of daily occurrence. In the following
year, 1874, the government put a capitation tax on rabbits, the
price fell in consequence from dollars to cents, and the luckless

rabbit-gamblers were ruined in a moment. 1874–5 were the cock-fighting years. In 1882–3, printing dictionaries and other works by subscription was the order of the day. Many of these literary enterprises turned out to be fraudulent, and had to be dealt with by the courts. About 1883 was also the great time for founding societies, learned and otherwise. Next came athletics in 1884–5. A rage for waltzing and for gigantic funerals marked 1886–7. During these years there was also, in official circles, an epidemic of what was locally known as "the German measles,"—a mania for imitating all things German, doubtless because "safer," more genuinely monarchical, than free Anglo-Saxondom. The following year took quite a new departure, setting mesmerism, table-turning, and planchette in fashion; and 1888 lifted wrestling from a vulgar pastime to a fashionable craze, in which the then prime minister, Count Kuroda, led the way. 1889 saw the sudden rise of joint-stock companies, together with a general revival of all native Japanese amusements, Japanese costume, anti-foreign agitation, etc. This was the great year of reaction. 1890 and following years,—railway speculation. 1893, the whole nation went mad over Colonel Fukushima's successful ride across Siberia; a perusal of the newspapers of the time can alone give any idea of the popular frenzy. 1896, stamp-collecting. 1898–1900, garden-parties. One of them lasted five days; others were held even in the snow, with bonfires lit in the vain hope of warming the shivering guests. Certain merchants of Yokohama, failing a real garden, went so far as to hold their garden-party (so-called) on board some lighters moored together and covered with an awning! Another craze of the closing years of the century was for busts and statues,—even silver statues of oneself. This last form of this particular craze reminds one of early mediæval times, when prominent princes and Buddhist saints (despite their assent to the doctrine that all phenomena are a mirage, and personality itself a delusion and a snare) seem to have devoted no inconsiderable portion of their leisure to painting and carving their own image. Sometimes, it is averred, the painting was the handiwork of a disciple, but the saint himself would then dot in the eyes. 1901, monster outings for children and workmen. One of the leading newspapers organised an excursion to Tōkyō for 120,000 operatives. But when this vast multitude neared the spot, only 5,000 were allowed by the police to proceed, and rioting ensued. A picnic of more manageable proportions was attended by 380 blind shampooers, who went out to see (?) the plum-blossoms at Sugita, and were made safe by means of a long rope, after the fashion of Alpine climbers. 1903, youths nourished on Schopenhauer and Nietsche took to practising "the denial of the will to live" by jumping into the great waterfall of Kegon at Nikkō. 1904, lantern processions to celebrate military successes.

Festivals. The holidays observed officially are:—

JAN. 1, 3, 5.—New Year.

JAN. 30.—Death of Kōmei Tennō, the late Mikado, A.D. 1867.

FEB. 11.—Accession of Jimmu Tennō, the first Mikado, 600 B.C.† Promulgation of the Constitution, A.D. 1889.

MARCH 20 (or 21).—Spring festival of the Imperial ancestors,—an adaptation of the Buddhist *Higan,* or Equinoctial festival of the dead, who are supposed to cross the ocean of existence and reach the other *(hi)* shore *(gan)*, that is, Nirvana.

APRIL 3.—Death of Jimmu Tennō.

SEPT. 23 (or 24). — Autumn festival of the Imperial ancestors.

OCT. 17.—Offering of first-fruits to the Shintō gods.

NOV. 3.—Birthday of the reigning Emperor.

NOV. 23.—The Emperor tastes the first-fruits offered to his ancestors.

The observance of most of these holidays is as modern as the flags that are flown and the salutes that are fired in their honour. The occasions of them may serve as a measure of the all-engrossing importance of the Imperial House since the revolution. There is another set of holidays of more ancient institution, which, though perhaps less observed year by year,

---

† This date is not to be accepted seriously; see Article on HISTORY.

still live on in the thoughts and usages of the people, and especially in their dinners, as the defeat of the Spanish Armada does in our English Michaelmas goose. The chief dates are as follows, and it is most convenient to begin the enumeration, *more Japonico*, at the end:—

DEC. 13.—This day is called *Koto-hajime,* that is, " the beginning of things," because such preparations for New Year as house-cleaning, decorating, and the pounding of rice for cakes *(mochi)* are then taken in hand. People eat *o koto-jiru* on this day,—a kind of stew whose ingredients are generally red beans, potatoes, mushrooms, sliced fish, and a root called *konnyaku.* Presents of money are made to servants by their masters at this time of year. Both the season in question and the present then given are termed *o scibo.*

DEC. 22.—The winter solstice *(tōji).* Doctors then worship the Chinese Esculapius.

JAN. 1–3.—Termed the *San-ga-nichi,* or " three days " of New Year, when the people eat a stew called *zōni.* In Tōkyō this stew consists of rice-cakes, and greens boiled in fish gravy. More fuss is made about the New Year in China and Japan than in any Western country. On the last night of the old year no one goes to bed, and bells are rung, and on New Year's morning the usual sweeping and dusting of rooms is preter-mitted, doubtless in order to avoid sweeping away good luck. Gateways are decorated at New Year time with pine-branches, straw ropes, oranges, and a lobster (the latter symbolising old age because of its crooked back), and presents are given called *o toshi-dama.*

JAN. 7.—This day is termed *Nana-kusa,* or the Seven Herbs, because in early times the Court and people used then to go out to pluck parsley and six other edible herbs,—a custom to which the poets make frequent allusion: Rice-gruel, or congee flavoured with greens, is the appropriate dish. (About the 9th January, the people resume their ordinary work).

JAN. 15–16.—The end of the New Year holidays. The 16th is the *(Hōkō-nin no Yabu-iri),* or Prentices' Holiday Home. Rice-gruel mixed with red beans is eaten.

JAN. 20.—*Kura-biraki,* that is, the day on which godowns are first opened. This is, however, more a name than a fact. *Zōni* is the dish of the day.

Setsubun is the name of a movable feast occurring sometimes late in January, sometimes early in February, on the eve of the first day of spring, Old Calendar. Beans are scattered about the house on the evening of this day in order to scare away demons, and of these beans each person present eats one more than the number of the years of his age.

N.B. *Azuki-meshi,* that is, rice mixed with red beans, is eaten on the 1st, 15th, and 28th of each month, these being the so-called *san-jitsu,* or "three days." On the 30th, people eat buckwheat vermicelli *(misoka-soba).*

The First Day of the Horse *(Hatsu-uma)* in FEBRUARY, consequently a movable feast. This day is sacred to the Fox-Goddess Inari. For the little that is known of this deity, see Murray's *Handbook to Japan,* 7th edit., pp. 49 and 336.

MARCH 3.—The Girls' Festival *(Jōmi no Sekku),* when every town is decked out with dolls. It is also called *Hina Matsuri,* that is, the Feast of Dolls. A sweet drink called *shiro-zake* is partaken of on this day.

MARCH 17.—This and the next six days are the already mentioned great Buddhist equinoctial festival of *Higan.* On the actual day of the equinox, the sun is believed to whirl round and round at sunset.

APRIL 8.—Buddha's Birthday. Images of the infant Buddha *(Tanjō-Shaka)* are set up in the temples for worshippers to pour liquorice tea *(ama-cha)* over with a ladle. This tea is then bought, and either partaken of at home in order to kill the worms that cause various internal diseases, or placed near the pillars of the house to prevent ants and other insects from entering.

MAY 5.—The Boys' Festival *(Tango no Sekku),* when such warlike toys as bows and arrows are sold, and gigantic paper fishes are flown from the houses, as explained on p. 93. Except New Year, this is of all Japanese festivals the one whose outward signs are most effective.

JUNE 22.—*Geshi,* or the summer solstice.

July 7.—*Tanabata*. The idea of this festival is most poetical. See last paragraph of the Article on Sun, Moon, and Stars.

July 13–16.—This is the great Buddhist festival of *Bon*, which is often termed by foreigners the Feast of Lanterns, but might better be rendered as All Souls' Day. The spirits of dead ancestors then visit the altar sacred to them in each household, and special offerings of food are made to them. The living restrict themselves to *maigre* dishes as far as possible. The ceremony of " opening the river " *(kawa-biraki)*, as it is called, generally takes place in Tōkyō about this time. The spectacle is a delightful one. Half the town goes out on the River Sumida in boats gaily decked with lanterns, while fireworks and music add to the gaiety of the evening. The rural population of most parts of the empire celebrate the festival by a dance known as *Bon-odori* (see p. 113). It is usual for masters to fee their servants at the *Bon* season. This should be done not later than the 13th.

July 16.—A second Prentices' Holiday.

The *Doyō no Iri,* or " First of the Dog-days," and the *Doyō Saburō,* or " Third Dog-day," are kept by the eating of peculiar cakes. The Third Dog-day is considered by the peasantry a turning-point in the life of the crops. Eels are eaten on any day of the Bull *(Doyō no Ushi)* that may occur during this period of greatest heat.

Sept. 9.—The *Chōyō no Sekku,* a holiday whose appropriate dish is rice mixed with chestnuts.

Sept. 20.—The autumn equinox.

Oct. 20.—The festival of *Ebisu-kō,* so called after one of the Gods of Luck, the only one of all the eight million deities to remain at large during October, which is called the " godless month " *(Kami-na-zuki),* because all the other gods then desert their proper shrines, and go off to the great temple of Izumo. The reason for Ebisu's not accompanying them is that, being deaf, he does not hear their summons. On this day tradesmen sell off their surplus stock, and give entertainments to their customers, correspondents, etc., as an amends—so it is half-jocularly said—for cheating them during the rest of the twelve-month. At present, when all such antique customs are falling into desuetude, the 20th October has come to be regarded rather as a day for what are called *konshinkwai*—social gatherings, that is, of the members of a guild, political coterie, learned society, and so forth.

NOVEMBER has several Shintō festivals. The most notable of these, held in honour of the Goddess of the Kitchen-range *(Hettsui no Kami)*, and termed *Fuigo Matsuri*, or the Feast of Bellows, takes place on the 8th. Fires are then also lighted in honour of Inari and other deities in the courts of Shintō temples,—the reason, so far as Inari is concerned, being the assistance rendered by that deity to the famous swordsmith Kokaji, for whom she blew the bellows while he was forging a sword for an ancient Mikado.

Nov. 15.—This is the day on which children who have reached the age of three are supposed to leave off having their heads shaved. It is accordingly called *Kami-oki*, that is, " hair-leaving," but corresponds to no actual reality, at least in modern times. The *Kazuki-zome*, or, " first veiling " of girls aged five, and the *Hakama-gi*, or " first trowsering " of boys aged five, formerly took place on the same day; but these also are now empty names.

DEC. 8.—The *Hari no Kuyō*, a festival at which women rest from the constant use of the needle by entertaining the other members of the household,—they, and not the men, directing matters for the nonce.

Thus ends the year. The adoption of the European calendar in 1873 tended to disorganise the old Japanese round of festivals; for with New Year coming five or six weeks earlier than formerly, the association of each holiday with a special season was destroyed. How go out and search for spring herbs on the 7th January, when winter weather is just beginning, instead of showing signs of drawing to an end?

Confronted with this difficulty, usage has vacillated. For the most part the old *date* has been retained, notwithstanding the change thus caused in the actual *day*. To take the instance just alluded to, the 7th of the 1st moon, which would formerly have fallen somewhere about the middle or end of February, is retained as the 7th January. In other cases the actual day is retained, irrespective of the date to which it may correspond in the new calendar; but this entails a fresh calculation every year, the old calendar having been lunar and irregular in several respects, not simply a fixed number of days behind ours, as, for instance, the Russian calendar is. A third plan has been to strike an average, making the date of each festival exactly one month later than formerly, though the actual day becomes about a fortnight earlier. Thus the festival of the 7th day of the 7th moon, Old Style, is in some places celebrated on the present 7th August, though really falling somewhere about the 20th August, if the calculation be properly worked out. Energetic holiday-makers will even celebrate the same festival twice,—first according to the new calendar and then according to the old, so as to be sure of keeping on good terms with the invisible powers that be. Altogether, there is great confusion and discrepancy of usage, each locality being a law unto itself.

The list given above does not of course pretend to be exhaustive. There are local as well as general festivals, and these local festivals have great importance in their special localities. Such are the *Gion* festival at Kyōto, and the *Sannō* and *Kanda* festivals at Tōkyō. *Gion* and *Sannō* take place in the middle of July, *Kanda* in mid-September. All three are distinguished by processions, of which the chief feature is a train of triumphal or rather mythological cars, called *dashi* by the Tōkyō people, *yama* or *hoko* by the people of Kyōto. These cars have recently been reduced in height, because they were found to interfere with the telegraph, telephone, and electric light wires that now spread their web over the great cities.

Books recommended. *The Five Sacred Festivals of Ancient Japan* by U. A. Casal; *Japanese Etiquette: An Introduction* by the World Fellowship Committee of the Tokyo Y.W.C.A.; *A Japanese Miscellany* by Lafcadio Hearn.

Filial Piety.[*] Filial piety is the virtue *par excellence* of the Far-Eastern world. From it springs loyalty[†] which is but the childlike obedience of a subject to the Emperor, who is regarded, in Chinese phrase, as "the father and mother of his people." On these two fundamental virtues the whole fabric of society is reared. Accordingly, one of the gravest dangers to Japan at the present time arises from the sudden importation of our less patriarchal Western ideas on these points. The traditional basis of morality is sapped.

There are no greater favourites with the people of Japan than the "Four-and-Twenty Paragons of Filial Piety" *(Ni-jū-shi Kō)*, whose quaint acts of virtue Chinese legend records. For instance, one of the Paragons had a cruel stepmother who who was very fond of fish. Never repining at her harsh treatment of him, he lay down naked on the frozen surface of a lake. The warmth of his body melted a hole in the ice, at which two carp came up to breathe. These he caught and set before his stepmother. Another Paragon, though of tender years and having a delicate skin, insisted on sleeping uncovered at night, in order that the mosquitoes should fasten on him alone, and allow his parents to slumber undisturbed. A third, who was very poor, determined to bury his own child alive, in order to have more food wherewith to support his aged mother, but was rewarded by Heaven with the discovery of a vessel filled with gold, on which the whole family, lived happily ever after. A fourth, who was of the female sex, enabled her father to escape, while she clung to the jaws of the tiger which was about to devour him. But the drollest of all is the story of Rōraishi. This Paragon, though seventy years old, used to dress in baby's clothes and sprawl about upon the floor. His object was piously to delude his parents, who were really over ninety years of age, into the idea that they could not be so very old after all, seeing that they had such a puerile son.

---

[*] In Japanese *ko*, or more popularly, *oya koko*.
[†] In Japanese *chu* or *chushin*.

Those readers who wish to learn all about the remaining
nineteen Paragons, should consult Anderson's *Catalogue of
Japanese and Chinese Paintings,* page 171, where also an
illustration of each is given. The Japanese have established
a set of " Four-and-Twenty Native Paragons " *(Honchō Ni-jū-
shi Kō)* of their own; but these are less popular.

The first question a European will probably ask on being
told of the lengths to which filial piety is carried in the Far-
East, is: how can the parents be so stony-hearted as to think
of allowing their children thus to sacrifice themselves ? But
such a consideration never occurs to a Chinese or Japanese
mind. That children should sacrifice themselves to their
parents is, in the Far-Eastern view of things, a principle as
indisputable as the duty of men to cede the best of everything
to women is with us. Far-Eastern parents accept their
children's sacrifices much as our women accept the front seat,
—with thanks perhaps, but as a matter of course. No text
in the Bible raises so much prejudice here against Christianity
as that which bids a man leave his father and mother, and
cleave unto his wife. " There! you see it," exclaims the anti-
Christian Japanese, pointing to the passage, " I always said
it was an immoral religion."

Fires were formerly so common in Japan's wood and paper
cities that the nickname of " Yedo Blossoms " was applied to
the flames which in winter almost nightly lit up the metropolis
with lurid lustre. So completely did this destructive agency
establish itself as a national institution that a whole vocabulary grew up to express every shade of meaning in matters
fiery. The Japanese language has special terms for an
incendiary fire, an accidental fire, fire starting from one's
own house, a fire caught from next door. a fire which one
shares with others, a fire which is burning to an end, the flame
of a fire, anything—for instance, a brazier—from which a fire
may arise, the side from which to attack a fire in order to
extinguish it, a visit of condolence after a fire, and so on.

We have not given half.* Were all records except the
linguistic record destroyed, one would still be able to divine
how terrible an enemy fire had been to Japanese antiquities.
Fire insurance, be it observed, was not among the words
connected with fire in Old Japan. It dates only from the new
regime, being Europe's contribution to the vocabulary. At
first the practice of insurance gained ground but slowly. It
may be matter for wonder that capitalists should have found
it worth their while to assume risks so heavy. Under the
circumstances, very high premiums are still charged; but
despite this drawback, the people seem now thoroughly to
appreciate the advantage of purchasing peace of mind even at
a heavy price, and for several years past companies have been
in operation all over the country to insure against fire and
other calamities.

To Ōoka, the Japanese Solomon, who was mayor and judge
of Yedo early in the eighteenth century, belongs the credit of
having organised the fire-brigades which formed so useful and
picturesque a feature of Yedo life. Since his day, fire engines
of European make have been brought into use. Moreover, the
number of conflagrations has been much diminished of late
years by the gradual introduction of stone and brick buildings
and of wider streets, and by stricter police control. Even,
therefore, granting the possible truth of the popular assertion
that in some parts of Tōkyō houses were only expected to
survive three years, that state of things happily belongs to
the past. Still, fire is an ever-dreaded foe. It is a foe at
whose entry into the city the carpenters, unless they are
greatly maligned, have frequently connived, because it brings
them work; and the peculiar dress and antics of the firemen
are things which no visitor to Japan should miss a chance of
seeing. Every year, on the 4th January, the firemen parade
the streets with their tall, light ladders, and give a gymnastic
performance gratis.

---

* Here are the Japanese originals of the above terms, for the benefit of the curious:
tsuke-bi, soso-bi, jikwa, morai-bi, ruisho, shita-bi, hinote, hinomoto, keshi-kushi, kwajimimai.
Fire insurance mentioned just below, is *kwasai-hoken.*

The most famous of all the many great Yedo fires was that
of 1657, when nearly half the city was destroyed and over
107,000 persons are said to have perished in the flames. The
government undertook the necessary gigantic interment, for
which the grounds of what is now known as the temple of
Ekō-in were selected, and priests from all the Buddhist sects
were called together to hold a seven days' service for the
benefit of the souls of the departed. Wrestling-matches are
now held in the same place,—a survival apparently of festivals
formerly religious, which consisted in bringing holy images
from the provinces to be worshipped awhile by the Yedo folk
and thus collect money for the temple, which could not rely
on the usual means of support, namely, gifts from the relations
of the dead, the fire of 1657 having been so destructive as to
sweep away whole families. The occurrence of every great fire
in Tōkyō is now wisely availed of in connection with a fixed
plan of city improvement, involving new thoroughfares and
the widening of old ones.

Fire-walking. Besides the superstitious notions already
mentioned in the Articles on DEMONIACAL POSSESSION and
DIVINATION, there are yet others which lead to acts of a most
surprising character,—to nothing less indeed than treading
barefoot over live coals, dashing boiling water about the
person, and climbing ladders of naked swords set edge upwards.
All these ancient rites (for they descend from a remote
antiquity) may still be witnessed in the heart of modern
Tōkyō, at least twice every year. The fire-walking usually
takes place in the courtyard of the little temple of Ontake at
the foot of the Kudan hill in April and September, and the
manner of its performance is as follows.*

Straw mats are placed upon the ground, and on them a layer
of sand. On the top of this the fuel is laid, originally pine-
wood, but now charcoal. The bed is about 1 foot deep, from
12 to 18 ft. long, and from 3 to 6 ft. wide. It should be square

---

* This account is condensed by permission from Mr. Percival Lowell's curious book,
Occult Japan.

to the points of the compass. Eight bamboos, with the fronds still on them, are stuck into the ground on the four sides of the charcoal bed, connected by a hempen rope, which is hung from frond to frond, about 5 ft. from the ground. From this hang forty-four of the sacred emblems called *gohei*,—strips of white paper cut into little angular bunches. Some of the attendants busily fan the flames with open fans strapped to the ends of long poles, while others pound the coals flat with staves. Then incantations are made,—incantations to the God of Water, who dwells in the moon, to descend and drive out the God of Fire. Prayers are offered up, and first one priest, then another begins slowly and solemnly to march round the charcoal bed, cabalistically twisting and flinging out his fingers the while. Soon all are engaged in this act of exorcism. On and on, round and round, do they march, each seemingly oblivious of the others, each gradually working himself up into a state akin to ecstasy. When this apparently interminable ceremony comes to an end, each priest takes a handful of salt from a large bowl, and strews it upon the living coal. Furthermore, a mat at either end of the bed of coals is spread with salt for those who are about to cross the fire to rub their feet on. The high priest salts his feet first, then steps boldly on to the surface of the burning floor, over which he strides with dignified gait. The attendant priests clad in white follow his example, and when all have gone over, all go over again.

The second part of the function, though less impressive, is more amusing; for now from among the crowd of bystanders all such as, to quote Mr. Lowell's phrase, have a mind to try their foot at it, imitate the priests and cross the hot crust. Men, women, and children, old and young, a whole family perhaps in due order of precedence, venture successfully along the line, though not a few show by their rapid skips towards the end that the trial is no mockery.

It should be added, for the sake of complete truthfulness, that the ordeal, when seen, is somehow less impressive than would probably be imagined from a written description. The space is narrow, the crowd motley and irreverent, and mostly

of the lower class,—loungers, dirty children with others on
their backs. The preliminary beating and pounding of the
fire-bed seems endless; the fanning of it drives smoke into one's
eyes and flakes on to one's clothes. The heat, too, is of course
unpleasant, and the actual fire-walking, when at length it does
begin, occupies but a few brief moments. Be it understood
that our object is nowise to deter any one from witnessing
what, after all, is a curious spectacle, but simply to warn
him that, like other genuine curios, it must be paid for. A
similar remark applies even more strongly to the "Ordeal by
Boiling Water." Far better read Mr. Lowell's account, which
is very graphic and entertaining, than devote hours to seeing
the rite itself, which is deadly dull, consisting, as it does, in
the dipping of bamboo fronds into boiling water, brandishing
them in the air, and letting the spray fall in a shower over
the performer's body, while prayers, incantations, and
gyrations are kept up *ad infinitum.*

*   *   *   *   *   *   *   *   *   *

The preceding article had just been written when, in
September, 1900, it being reported that no less than seven
foreigners had taken part in the "miracle," we wrote to one
of them, Prof. Percy Hillhouse, of the Imperial University,
Tōkyō, to request an account of the proceedings. That
gentleman's reply was as follows:—

"I went to the Imagawa Kōji temple on the 17th September,
with a secret desire to cross the glowing coals myself; but
though I saw all sorts and conditions of Japanese crossing, I
was unable to screw up my courage quite to the sticking point
until a number of Harvard graduates, who had carefully
examined the soles of those who had crossed, themselves
walked over. I at once took off my socks, and pushed my way
through the crowd to the end of the bed of charcoal. There
was a flattened heap of salt at the beginning of the path; and
after rubbing both feet well into this, I stepped across at a
sharp walking pace and got to the other end safely. Before
I started, a priest dusted me all over with a large mop of
gohei; and after I had crossed, the priest at the other end

made me stop and rub my feet in the pad of salt at the end of
the fiery path. No sooner was I safely over than I crossed
again with no evil result. As each foot touched the charcoal,
it only felt a comfortable warmth:—there was no *hot* sensation at all. I am certain that anybody could go over without
any unpleasant effects, if he stepped quickly enough and did
not scrape his feet in any way. One must step cleanly, so to
speak.

"H——, of the British Consulate in Yokohama, followed
me the first time, and later on a young lady from Yokohama
picked up her skirts and skipped over amid cheers from the
crowd. H—— said that he felt his feet a little sore after he
had come off. The first time I went, I did not feel the least
bad effect. The second time, some one in front having delayed
me a moment by stopping on the salt patch at the end, I felt
one foot slightly hot, and for about an hour afterwards a small
patch of skin at one side felt very slightly sore; but when I
examined my feet at night, I could see nothing, and the feeling
of soreness was gone.

"I am not physiologist enough to give any explanation as to
why we were not burnt. When a boy, I placed an iron kettle
of boiling water, just off the fire, on the palm of my hand, and
held it there for fifteen seconds or so, and it only felt slightly
warm. I think the explanation of that was that the soot on
the bottom was a good non-conductor, and that the moisture
of the hand, quickly evaporating, formed a layer of steam
which prevented actual contact of the metal and skin. The
Kudan 'miracle' may have a similar explanation. The surface
of the charcoal-bed was at least half-black, not red-hot, and the
damp salt may have provided the necessary moisture."

Fishing. Various queer methods of fishing are still
employed in the rural districts of Japan. In some of the
central provinces, baskets may be seen hung over a waterfall
to catch such fish as attempt to leap it. In certain other
places—for instance, at Numata on the Tonegawa—this
arrangement is modified by the construction of an inclined

bamboo platform, which produces an upward flow towards the
centre of the stream. Thither the fish are carried by the force
of the artificial current, as described in Murray's *Handbook.*
Then there is the well-known cormorant-fishing, of which
details are given on pp. 105–8 of the present work. The arrow-
shaped fish-traps lining the shores of Lake Biwa are a curiosity
calculated to strike any observant eye. So are the " fish out-
looks " that dot the coast of Izu. Each of these stands on
some lofty cliff overlooking the sea, where an experienced man
keeps watch, and blows a horn to the fishermen below to
draw in the large village net, whenever a school of albacore
has entered it. A sight fascinating on account of the great
dexterity involved, is that of the trout-fishers in some clear,
placid streams, who simply land their prey with hand-nets.
This may be witnessed on the waters of the Kitayama-gawa,
just below that loveliest of spots, Doro-Hatchō. To such
methods must be added the fish-spearing practised on many
points of the coast, and the whaling off Kishū and Shikoku,
the whales being sometimes actually caught in nets. The
flies used by Japanese anglers should also interest the
sportsman, being quite different from those employed by
European fishermen. To an English eye the native method
of fly-fishing will seem rude; but it is justified by its results.

Flag. The Japanese national flag *(Hi-no-Maru)* is a good
instance of Amiel's axiom that " nothing real is simple." The
sun upon a background,—why should not the idea have been
hit upon at once by the inhabitants of this " Land of the Rising
Sun ? " And yet, when we come to look into the matter, we
find this apparently obvious result to have been evolved from
a strangely complicated set of ideas, slowly changing through
the centuries.

It seems that, from time immemorial, the Chinese Court and
army had made use of banners adorned with figures founded
on astrological fancies,—the Sun with the Three-legged Crow

that inhabits it, the Moon with its Hare and Cassia-tree, the Red Bird representing the seven constellations of the southern quarter of the zodiac, the Dark Warrior (a Tortoise) embracing the seven northern constellations, the Azure Dragon embracing the seven eastern, the White Tiger embracing the seven western, and a seventh banner representing the Northern Bushel (Great Bear). The banners of the Sun and Moon assumed special importance, because the Sun was the Emperor's elder brother and the Moon his sister, for which reason he himself was, and still is, styled the Son of Heaven, —no mere metaphors these to the early Chinese mind, which implicitly believed that the Emperor's conduct could influence the course of the seasons.

The Japanese took over these things wholesale,—Imperial title, banners, mythological ideas, and all,—probably in the seventh century, for the official annals incidentally record their use in A.D. 700. In process of time most of the elements of this system were dropped, only the Sun and Moon Banners being retained as Imperial insignia, but without their fabulous inmates, though the Sun Crow and the Moon Hare still linger on in art. For such heathen fancies mediæval piety substituted effigies of the gods or an invocation to Buddha; but these, too, were dropped when Buddhist influence declined. Thus the sun (not originally a *rising* sun) alone remained; and when, in 1859, a national flag corresponding to those of Europe became necessary, the Sun Banner naturally stepped into the vacant place. A more elaborate design—the sixteen-petalled chrysanthemum, which is apparently only in another shape the sun with its rays—became fixed as the Imperial standard; for conformity to European usage prescribed such a distinction. The military flag with its sixteen rays is a modification of the same idea, the number sixteen itself being traceable to Chinese geomantic notions.

Book recommended. *Japanese Etiquette: An Introduction* by the World Fellowship Committee of the Tokyo Y.W.C.A.

Flowers. An enemy has said that Japanese flowers have no scent. The assertion is incorrect; witness the plum-blossom, the wild rose, and the many sweet-smelling lilies and orchids. But granting even—for the sake of argument, if for nothing more—that the fragrance of flowers greets one less often in Japan that at home, it must be allowed on the other side that the Japanese show a more genuine appreciation of flowers than we do. The whole population turns out several times in the year for no other purpose than to visit places which are noted for certain kinds of blossom. It is round these that the national holiday-makings of the most holiday-loving of nations revolve, and no visitor to Japan should fail to see one or other—all, if possible—of these charming flower festivals. The principal flowers cultivated in Tōkyō are:—the plum-blossom, which comes into flower about the end of January, and lasts on into March; the cherry-blossom, first half of April; the tree-peony, end of April or beginning of May; the azalea, early in May; the wistaria, ditto; the iris, early in June; the convolvulus, end of July and beginning of August; the lotus, early in August; the chrysanthemum, first three weeks of November; the maple (for such bright leaves are included under the general designation of flowers), all November.

The Japanese care but little for some flowers which to Europeans commend themselves as the fairest, and they make much of others which we should scarcely notice. All sorts of considerations come into play besides mere "look-see" (if we may for once be allowed the use of a convenient Pidjin-English term). The insignificant blossom of the straggling lespedeza shrub is a favourite, on account of ancient poetic fables touching the amours of the lespedeza, as a fair maiden, and of the stag her lover. The camellia is neglected, because it is considered unlucky. It is considered unlucky, because its red blossoms fall off whole in a way which reminds people—at least it reminds Japanese people—of decapitated heads. And so on in other cases. Of wild-flowers generally the Japanese take little account, which is strange; for the hills and valleys of their beautiful country bear them in profusion.

A very curious sight is to be seen at Lango-zaka in Tōkyō at the proper season. It consists of chrysanthemums worked into all sorts of shapes,—men and gods, boats, bridges, castles, etc., etc. Generally some historical or mythological scene is pourtrayed, or else some tableau from a popular drama. There, too, may be seen very fine natural chrysanthemums, though not quite so fine as the *élite* of Tōkyō society is admitted to gaze on once a year in the beautiful grounds of the old palace at Akasaka. The mere variety is amazing. There is not only every colour, but every shape. Some of the blossoms are immense,—larger across than a man's hand can stretch. Some are like large snowballs,—the petals all smooth, and curved in one on the top of the other. Others resemble the tousled head of a Scotch terrier. Some have long filaments stretched out like star-fish, and some, as if to counterbalance the giants, have their petals atrophied into mere drooping hairs. But the strangest thing of all is to see five or six kinds, of various colours and sizes, growing together on the same plant,—a nosegay with only one stem,—the result of judicious grafting. Of the *same* kind of blossoms, as many as thirteen hundred and twenty have been known to be produced on one plant! In other cases the triumph is just the opposite way:—the whole energies of a plan are made to concentrate on the production of a single blossom, a tawny, dishevelled monster, perhaps, called " Sleepy Head " (for each variety has some quaint name), or else the " Golden Dew," or the " White Dragon," or the " Fisher's Lantern "—a dark russet this—or the " Robe of Feathers," a richly clustering pink and white, or, loveliest of all, the " Starlit Night," a delicately fretted creature, looking like Iceland moss covered with hoar-frost. These results are obtained only by the accumulated toil of years, and especially by care, repeated many times daily, during the seven months that precede the period of blossoming. Such care is amply rewarded; for the chrysanthemum is a flower which will last several weeks if duly sheltered from the early frosts.

Much of the above, doubtless, will be no news to the professional European chrysanthemum-grower, who is accustomed nowadays to handle numerous splendid varieties of this beautiful flower. Let him remember, however, that the impulse towards chrysanthemum-growing, and even most of the actual varieties now shown, came from Japan scarcely more than twenty years ago.

Bouquet-making is not left in the Far-East, as it is in Europe, to individual caprice. Europeans are, in this respect, wild children of nature. The Chinese and Japanese have made an art of it, not to say a mystery demanding long and arduous study. Indeed, they invoke the aid of Confucianism itself, and arrange flowers philosophically, with due regard to the active and passive principles of nature, and in obedience to certain traditional rules which have been jealously handed down in the various flower-schools. It is well-worth the while of any intelligent enquirer to peruse Mr. Conder's beautifully illustrated work on this subject, though, to be sure, the whole gist of the matter may be given is half-a-dozen words:—a " floral composition " must consist of three sprays, the longest in the middle generally bent bow-like, a second half its length branching out on one side, and a third a quarter of its length, on the other. To obtain proper curvature, the stems are heated over a brazier, or else kept in position by means of wires and other artifices. Whatever may be thought of the so-called flower *philosophy,* the reader will at least have gained acquaintance with a graceful and intricate art, and with a curious chapter in the history of the human mind. Linear effect, and a certain balance or proportion achieved by means of studied irregularity, are the key-note and the dominant of Japanese floral compositions. The guiding principle is not harmony of colour.

An enthusiastic local critic, who is up to the ears in love with all things Japanese, opines that the Japanese linear arrangement of stems and leaves stands " at an unmeasurable height above the barbaric massing of colours that constitutes the whole of the corresponding art in the West." Such a verdict will scarcely find acceptance with those who esteem colour to be nature's most glorious gift to man, and the grouping of colours (unless we set above it the grouping of sounds in music) to be the most divine of human arts. Neither does sober enquiry into botanical fact produce any warrant for the hard-and-fast set of linear rules elaborated by a coterie of dilettanti in the fifteenth century, who had never looked at nature but when "to advantage dressed." Still, Japanese floral design offers a subject as attractive as it is original. If not, as its more zealous and intolerant sectaries claim, *the* way of treating flowers, it is *a* way, totally new way; and we are greatly mistaken if it and Japanese gardening do not soon make many European converts. The very flowerpots are delightful, with their velvety blue and white designs.

Books recommended. *Flower Arrangement Art of Japan* by Mary Cokely Wood; *Japanese Flower Arrangement: Classical and Modern* by Norman J. Sparnon; *Japanese Flower Arrangement: A Complete Primer* by Ellen G. Allen; *Japanese Flower Arrangement in a Nutshell* by Ellen Gordon Allen.

Food. Like most other nations, the Japanese take three meals a day,—one on rising in the morning, one at noon, and one at about sunset. Much the same sort of food is partaken of at all these meals, but breakfast is lighter than the other two. The staple is rice—which is replaced by barley, millet, or some other cheap grain in the poorer country districts—rice with fish and eggs, and minute portions of vegetables either fresh or pickled. Beans are in particular requisition.

Buddhism has left its impress here, as on everything in Japan. To Buddhism was due the abandonment of a meat diet, now over a thousand years ago. The permission to eat fish, though that too entailed the taking of life, which is contrary to strict Buddhist tenets, seems to have been a concession to human frailty. Pious frauds, moreover, came to the rescue. One may even now see the term "mountain whale" (*yama-kujira*) written up over certain eating-houses, which means that venison is there for sale. The logical process is this:—A whale is a fish. Fish may be eaten. Therefore, if you call venison "mountain whale," you may eat venison. Of course no actual prohibition against eating flesh, such as existed under the old regime, obtains now. But the custom of abstaining from it remains pretty general; and though beef and pork were introduced at the time of the late revolution, the fondness for them soon waned, as did that for bread which was the rage among the lowest class in 1890. The piles of loaves then displayed at every little cook-stall in Tōkyō, for the delectation of jinrikisha-men and other coolies, have vanished and been replaced by victuals of the orthodox Japanese type. Probably the poor quality of the bread, and the nasty way in which the meat was cooked, had much to do with this return to the ancestral diet.

Of beverages the chief are tea, which is taken without sugar or milk, and *sake,* an alcoholic liquor prepared from rice, whose taste has been not inaptly compared to that of weak sherry which has been kept in a beer-bottle. It is generally taken hot, and at the *beginning* of dinner. Only when the drinking-bout is over, is the rice brought in:—at a long dinner, one is apt never to reach it. When dining quietly in the home circle, the Japanese habitually drink tea only. Besides that drunk out of a cup, it is rather usual to have a little poured over the last bowlful of one's rice.

The following is a specimen of the bill of fare at a Japanese banquet. The reader must understand that everything is served in small portions, as each guest has a little table to himself, in front of which he squats on the floor:—

PRELIMINARY COURSE, served with *sake*:—*suimono,* that is, a kind of bean-curd soup; *kuchi-tori,* a relish, such as an omelette, or chestnuts boiled soft and sweet, or *kamaboko,* which is fish pounded and then rolled into little balls and baked; *sashimi,* minced raw fish; *hachi-zakana,* a fine large fish, either broiled with salt or boiled with soy; *uma-ni,* bits of fish or sometimes fowl, boiled with lotus-roots or potatoes in soy and in a sort of liqueur caller *mirin*; *su-no-mono,* sea-ears or sea-slugs served with vinegar; *chawan,* a thin fish soup with mushrooms, or else *chawan-mushi,* a thick custardy soup.

First Course (*Zembu*) :—*shiru,* soup, which may be made of bean-curd, of fish, of sea-weed, or of some other material; *o-hira,* boiled fish, either alone or floating in soup; *tsubo,* sea-weed or some other appetiser, boiled in a small deep bowl or cup; *namasu,* raw fish cut in slices, and served with vinegar and cold stewed vegetables; *aemono,* a sort of salad made with bean sauce or pounded sesamum seeds; *yakimono,* raw fish (although the name means "broiled") served in a bamboo basket, but generally only looked at and not eaten; *kō-no-mono,* pickled vegetables, such as egg-plant, cabbage-leaves, or the strong-smelling radish (*daikon*), which is as great a terror to the noses of most foreigners as European cheese is to the noses of most Japanese.

Second Course (*Ni no zen*) :—soup, raw fish (but only if none has been served in the first course). and rice.

Such banquets as the above are of course not given every day. At smaller dinners not more than half such a *menu* would be represented. Quiet, well-to-do people, living at home, may have a couple of dishes at each meal—a broiled fish perhaps, and some soup, or else an omelette, besides pickles to help the rice down with. The Oriental abstemiousness which figures so largely in travellers' tales, is no part of Japanese manners at all events. To make up for the comparative lightness and monotony of their food, the Japanese take plenty of it. It is the custom, too, to set food before a guest, at whatever time of day he calls. On such occasions *soba* is in request—a sort of buckwheat vermicelli, served with soy and the sweet liqueur called *mirin*; or else *shiruko,* that is, rice-cakes with a sauce made of red beans and sugar; or *sushi,* rice-cakes plastered over with fish or with seaweed on which vinegar has been sprinkled. Even when these things are not given—and among the Europeanised upper classes they are now mostly abandoned—tea and cakes are always set before every guest. Many of the Japanese cakes and sugar-plums are pleasant eating. They atone to some extent for the absence of puddings and for the poorness of Japanese fruit.*

Japanese dishes fail to satisfy European cravings. Imagine a diet without meat, without milk, without bread, without butter, without jam, without coffee, without salad or any sufficient quantity of nicely cooked vegetables, without puddings of any sort, without stewed fruit and with comparatively little fresh fruit,—the European vegetarian will find almost as much difficulty in making anything out of it as the ordinary meat-eater. If Dr. Johnson had ever partaken of such a dinner, he would surely have described the result as a feeling of satiety without satisfaction, and of repletion without sustenance. The food is clean, admirably free from grease, often pretty to look at. But try to live on it—no! The Japanese, doubtless, being to the manner born, prefer their own rice and other dishes for a continuance. At the same time, they by no means object to an occasional dinner in European style, and their appetite on such occasions is astonishing. Experts say that Japanese food, though poor in nitrogen and especially in fat, is rich in carbon, and amply sufficient to support life, provided the muscles be kept in action, but that it is indigestible and even deleterious to those who spend their time squatting on the mats at home.

---

* Since about 1893 or 1894, small quantities of excellent peaches and pears—presumably from American stock—have been raised at Kawasaki, near Yokohama, to supply foreigners' tables. None such are to be obtained in the country at large. The native *nashi*, though generally translated " pear," is quite a different fruit—round, wooden, and flavourless; the native peach is first-cousin to a brickbat. Of the apple, which only became common towards the close of the nineteenth century, a fairly palatable variety is grown. There are few cherries (despite the wealth of cherry-blossom), no raspberries, no currants, scarcely any gooseberries, no mulberries (although the land is dotted with mulberry-bushes to feed the silkworms), no tropical fruit of any sort. Figs are scarce and poor, grapes not abundant except in the single province of Koshu, strawberries neither good nor abundant, plums and apricots mediocre, the Japanese medlars (*biwa*) not to be compared with those of Southern Europe. The best fruits here are the orange, one or two kinds of melon, and—for those who like it—the persimmon, though it, too, shares in the woodenness and coarse flavour characteristic of Japanese fruits. Probably two causes have led to the result here noticed. The first is founded on the climate, the best-flavoured fruits being produced in dry climates, whereas in Japan the heat and wet come together, and make the fruit rot instead of mellowing. Thus European stock, which has improved in America and Australia, rapidly deteriorates in Japan. The second cause—itself partly dependent on the first—is that the national taste for fruit is unformed, fruit never having been here regarded as a regular article of diet, and circumstances having accustomed the Japanese to prefer that such fruit as they do take should be hard.

This would account for the healthy looks of the coolies, and for the too often dyspeptic and feeble bodily habit of the upper classes, who take little or no exercise. A foreigner forced by circumstances to rely on a Japanese diet should, say the doctors, devote his attention to beans, especially to the bean-soup called *miso*. Fortunately of this dish—and of this only—custom permits one to ask for a second helping (*o kawari*).

There is a circumstance connected with Japanese dinners that must strike every one who has seen a refectory where numbers of students, monks, soldiers, or other persons under discipline are fed,—the absence of clatter arising from the absence of knives, forks, and spoons. A hundred boys may be feeding themselves with the help of chopsticks, and yet you might almost hear a pin drop in the room. Another detail which will impress the spectator less favourably is the speed at which food is absorbed. In fact, some classes—the artisans in particular—seem to make a point of honour of devoting as little time as possible to their meals. To this unwholesome habit, and to the inordinate use of pickles and of green tea, may doubtless be attributed the fact that *hara ga itai* ("I have a stomach-ache") is one of their commonest phrases..

Most Japanese towns of any size now boast what is called a *seiyō-ryōri*, which, being interpreted, means a foreign restaurant. Unfortunately, third-rate Anglo-Saxon influence has had the upper hand here, with the result that the central idea of the Japano-European cuisine takes consistency in slabs of tough beefsteak anointed with mustard and spurious Worcestershire sauce. This culminating point is reached after several courses,—one of watery soup, another of fish fried in rancid butter, a third of chickens' drumsticks stewed also in rancid butter; and the feast not infrequently terminates with what a local cookery book terms a "sweat omelette."

Books recommended. *Japanese Cuisine: A Culinary Tour* by John D. Keys; *Japanese Food and Cooking* by Stuart Griffin; *Japanese Recipes* by Tatsuji Tada.

Foreign Employés in Japan. Though European influence, as we have elsewhere set forth, dates back as far as A.D. 1542, it became an overwhelming force only when the country had been opened in 1854, indeed, properly speaking, only in the sixties. From that time dates the appearance in this country of a new figure,—the foreign employé; and the foreign employé is the creator of New Japan. To the Japanese Government belongs the credit of conceiving the idea and admitting the necessity of the great change, furnishing the wherewithal, engaging the men, and profiting by their labours, resembling in this a wise patient who calls in the best available physician, and assists him by every means in his power. The foreign employé has been the physician, to whom belongs the credit of working the marvellous cure which we all see. One set of Englishmen—at first a single Englishman, the late Lieut. A. G. S. Hawes—took the navy in hand, and transformed junk manners and methods into those of a modern man-of-war. Another undertook the mint, with the result that Oriental confusion made way for a uniform coinage equal to any in the world. No less a feat than the reform of the entire educational system was chiefly the work of a handful of Americans. The resolute stand taken by a Frenchman led to the abolition of torture.* The same Frenchman began the codification of Japanese law, which Germans continued and completed. Germans for years directed the whole higher medical instruction of the country, and the larger steamers of the two principal steamship companies are still commanded by foreign captains of various nationalities. Again, consider the army which has

---

* This forward step was entirely due to the personal initiative of Monsieur Boissonade de Fontarabie. One day—it was on the 15th April, 1875—when busy with the preliminaries for the work of codification, he heard groans in an adjoining apartment, and asked what they meant. An evasive answer was returned; but he persisted, and finally burst into the room whence the groans issued, to find a man stretched on the torture-boards with layers of heavy stones piled on his legs. Returning to his Japanese colleagues, he plainly told them that such horrors and civilised law could not coexist, that torture must cease, or that he would resign. On the very next day he sent in a memorandum to the Minister of Justice, containing his resignation in the event of compliance being withheld. Some months elapsed, the translation of his memorandum was delayed, and many specious reasons were alleged by Japanese officialdom for the maintenance of a usage so ancient, which had moreover quite recently (25th August, 1874) been re-affirmed both in principle and in practice, provision having actually then been made afresh for monthly statistics on the subject! Nevertheless, Mr. Boissonade's unremitting efforts succeeded in interesting certain high officials in the cause, and torture was rendered illegal by a notification dated 10th June, 1876.

so recently astonished the world by the perfection of its organisation was Franco-German, and was drilled into the Japanese first by French, and then by German officers engaged for the purpose, and retained during a long series of years. The posts, the telegraphs, the railways, the trigonometrical survey, improved mining methods, prison reform, sanitary reform, cotton and paper mills, chemical laboratories, waterworks, and harbour works,—all are the creation of the foreign employés of the Japanese Government. By foreigners the first men-of-war were built, the first large public edifices erected, the first lessons given in rational finance. Nor must it be supposed that they have been mere supervisors. It has been a case of off coats, of actual manual work, of example as well as precept. Technical men have shown their Japanese employers how to do technical things, the name of *chef de bureau,* captain, foreman, or what not, being no doubt generally painted on a Japanese figure-head, but the real power behind each little throne being the foreign adviser or specialist.

It is hard to see how matters could have been otherwise, for it takes longer to get a Japanese educated abroad than to engage a foreigner ready made. Moreover, even when technically educated, the Japanese will, for linguistic and other reasons, have more difficulty in keeping up with the progress of rapidly developing arts and sciences, such as most European arts and sciences are. Similar causes have produced similar results in other parts of the world, though on a smaller scale—in Spanish America, for example. The only curious point is that, while Japanese progress has been so often and so rapturously expatiated upon, the agents of that progress have been almost uniformly overlooked. To mention but one example among many, Mr. Henry Norman, M.P., in his lively letters on Japan,* told the story of Japanese education under the fetching title of "A Nation at School"; but the impression left was that they had been their own

---

* Republished in book form as *The Real Japan.*

schoolmasters. In another letter on "Japan in Arms," he
discoursed concerning "the Japanese military re-organisers,"
the Yokosuka dockyard, and other matters, but omitted to
mention that the re-organisers were Frenchmen, and that the
Yokosuka dockyard also was a French creation. Similarly,
when treating of the development of the Japanese newspaper
press, he ignored the fact that it owed its origin to an
Englishman, which surely, to one whose object was reality,
should have seemed an item worth recording.

These letters, so full and apparently so frank, really so
deceptive, are, as we have said, but one instance among many
of the way in which popular writers on Japan travesty history
by ignoring the part which foreigners have played. The
reasons of this are not far to seek. A wonderful tale will
please folks at a distance all the better if made more
wonderful still. Japanese progress traced to its causes and
explained by reference to the means employed, is not nearly
such fascinating reading as when represented in the guise of
a fairy creation sprung from nothing, like Aladdin's palace.
Many good people enjoy nothing so much as unlimited sugar
and superlatives; and the Japanese have really done so much
that it seems scarcely stretching the truth to make out
that they have done the impossible. Then, too, they are such
pleasant hosts, whereas the foreign employés are not always
inclined to be hosts at all to the literary and journalistic
globe-trotter, who thirsts for facts and statistics, subject
always to the condition that he shall be free to bend the
statistics and facts to his own theories, and demonstrate to old
residents that their opinions are simply a mass of prejudice.
There is nothing picturesque in the foreign employé. With
his club, and his tennis-ground, and his brick house, and his
wife's piano, and the rest of the European entourage which
he strives to create around him in order sometimes to forget
his exile, he strikes a false note. The esthetic and literary
globe-trotter would fain revel in a tea-tray existence for the
nonce, because the very moment he tires of it, he can pack and

be off. The foreign employé cannot treat life so jauntily, for he has to make his living; and when a man is forced to live in Lotus-land, it is Lotus-land no longer. Hence an irreconcilable feud between the foreign employés in Japan and those literary gentlemen who paint Japan in the brilliant hues of their own imagination. For our part, we see no excuse—even from a literary point of view—for inaccuracy in this matter. Japan is surely fair enough, her people are attractive enough, her progress has been remarkable enough, for plenty of praise to remain, even when all just deductions are made and credit awarded to those who have helped her to her present position. Why exaggerate ? Japan can afford to borrow Cromwell's word, and say, " Paint me as I am ! "

(See also Article on EUROPEANISATION.)

Forfeits. The Japanese play various games of forfeits, which they call *ken*, sitting in a little circle and flinging out their fingers, after the manner of the Italian *mora*. The most popular kind of *ken* is the *kitsune ken*, or " fox forfeit," in which various positions of the fingers represent a fox, a man, and a gun. The man can use the gun, the gun can kill the fox, the fox can deceive the man; but the man cannot kill the fox without the gun, nor the fox use the gun against the man. This leads to a number of combinations. Another variety of the game of forfeits is the *tomo-se,* or " follow me," in which the beaten player has to walk round the room after the conqueror, with something on his back, as if he were the conquerors baggage coolie. The dance called by foreigners " John Kino " is a less reputable member of the same family of games.*

Formosa. The hazy geography of early times distinguished so imperfectly between Formosa and Luchu that it is often

---

* " John Kino " seems to be a corruption of *chon ki-na* or *choi ki-na,* " just come here! "

difficult to know which of the two is intended. Equally
obscure is the early history of the island. The Chinese would
seem to have discovered it at the beginning of the seventh
century, but the curtain falls again for over six hundred years.
From the beginning of trustworthy records, the spectacle
presented to us is that of a mountainous, forest-clad interior
inhabited by head-hunting savages of Malay race, and a flat
western seaboard overrun by buccaneers from various lands.
A peculiar tribe of Chinamen, called Hakka, permanently
settled this western coast during the fifteenth and sixteenth
centuries; but the Portuguese, the Dutch, and the Spaniards,
all of whom, about A.D. 1600, were striving together for
colonial supremacy, endeavoured with partial temporary
success to gain a foothold. The Japanese did likewise, both as
peaceable traders and as pirates. *Takasago*, one of their
names for Formosa, dates from that time, having been first
applied to a sandy stretch which was thought to resemble the
celebrated pine-clad beach of that name near the present town
of Kōbe. The other Japanese, or rather Chinese, appellation—
Taiwan ("terraced bay")—was at first confined to one of the
trading stations on the coast,—to which is not quite certain.
Our European name comes from the Portuguese navigators,
who, with somewhat exaggerated enthusiasm, called what
they saw of the place *Ylha Formosa*, that is, the "Beautiful
Island."

Dutch rule asserted itself as paramount over a large portion
of Formosa from 1624 to 1661, and to Dutch missionaries we
owe the first serious attempts at a study of the aborigines and
their multifarious dialects. Several young Formosans were
even sent to Holland to study theology, a circumstance which
gave rise to one of the most audacious literary frauds ever
perpetrated. A Frenchman, pretending to be a native convert,
published, under the pseudonym of George Psalmanazar,
"An Historical and Geographical Description of Formosa,"—
every line of which, including an elaborate grammar, an
alphabet, and a whole religious system, was pure invention, but
which deceived the learned world almost down to our own

day. The Dutch were ousted from Formosa by Koxinga (Koku-sen-ya), the son of a Chinese pirate by a Japanese mother. But his rule was short-lived, and the island passed in 1683 under the control of the Chinese Government, which retained it until its cession to Japan, in 1895, as one of the conditions of peace after the war between the two nations. The aborigines had already incidentally felt the force of Japanese arms in 1874, when an expedition was sent under General Saigō to chastise them for the murder of some ship-wrecked fishermen.

Formosa, as sufficiently indicated above, falls naturally into two unequal parts. To the west a narrow alluvial plain, richly cultivated by industrious Chinese living in towns and villages, slopes gently to the sea. Eastwards the country rises into mountain ranges covered with virgin forests of camphor laurel and other huge trees, beneath whose shade wild beasts and wild men fight for a subsistence. Mount Morrison, which stands almost exactly under the Tropic of Cancer, forms the culminating point of the island, and the highest peak of the whole Japanese empire, as it has an altitude of 14,350 ft., or 2,000 ft. more than Fuji. For this reason the Japanese have re-christened it *Nii-takayama*, that is, the " New Lofty Mountain." The cliffs of the east coast of Formosa are the highest and most precipitous in the world, towering in places sheer six thousand feet from the water's edge.

It is not for nothing that so many nations have striven for the overlordship of Formosa. Tea, camphor, sugar, fruits and vegetables of every kind, are produced in immense quantities, while coal and gold are known to abound, though the store of metals has as yet scarcely been touched. But there are several indispensable preliminaries to the exploitation of these riches by their present enlightened owners. The aborigines must be subjugated, and not only they, but armed bands of Chinese rendered desperate by real and fancied grievances. For several years things went wrong with the Japanese attempts to colonise their new dependency. A perpetual clamour rose

from the press of every shade of opinion and from public men
anent the waste, the corruption, the misgovernment, and
malpractices of every kind that were rampant. Foreigners told
exactly the same tale, adding details about the shameless lives
led by officials, and the insolence of the soldiery and imported
coolies, who, peasants for the most part at home, there got
brevet rank as representatives of the conquering race. On all
sides the cry was that a false start had been made, and that
an entirely new departure was needed, if this island—
"Beautiful," but unhappy—was ever to have rest. Since then
reform has been earnestly laboured for at Tōkyō, and considerable progress, both material and moral, has been made.
Roads have been pushed through the forests, lighthouses and
railways have been constructed, the Japanese school system
and the conscription law have been introduced. Evidently,
the official intention is that the incorporation of Formosa with
the Japanese empire shall be no mere form of words, but, so
far as may be, an actual assimilation of the conquered to the
conquerors.

*   *   *   *   *   *   *   *   *   *

It would not be possible at the present day, in however brief
a sketch of Formosa, to omit all reference to the Rev. Dr.
Mackay, recently deceased, the pioneer missionary, and author
of the first general account of the land and its people. Never,
in the wildest flight of imagination, could any layman have
guessed the nature of the evangelising method on which this
excellent man chiefly relied. It was—tooth-drawing ! ! !
"Toothache," writes he, "resulting from severe malaria and
"from beetle-nut chewing, cigar-smoking, and other filthy
"habits, is the abiding torment of tens of thousands of both
"Chinese and aborigines. . . . . Our usual custom in
"touring through the country is to take our stand in an open
"space, often on the stone steps of a temple, and, after
"singing a hymn or two, proceed to extract teeth, and then
"preach the message of the gospel. . . . . . I have myself,
"since 1873, extracted over twenty-one thousand, and the
"students and preachers have extracted nearly half that

" number. . . . . The priests and other enemies of the mission
" may persuade people that fever and other diseases have been
" cured, not by our medicines, but by the intervention of the
" gods; but the relief from toothache is too unmistakable,
" and because of this, tooth-extracting has been more than
" anything else effective in breaking down prejudice and
" opposition."

Book recommended. *Poo Poo Make Prant Glow* by Harvey E. Ward.

Forty-seven Rōnins.   Asano, Lord of Akō, while at Yedo in
attendance on the Shōgun, was entrusted with the carrying
out of one of the greatest state ceremonies of those times,—
nothing less than the reception and entertainment of an envoy
from the Mikado. Now Asano was not so well-versed in such
matters as in the duties of a warrior. Accordingly he took
counsel with another nobleman, named Kira, whose vast
knowledge of ceremonies and court etiquette was equalled only
by the meanness of his disposition. Resenting honest Asano's
neglect to fee him for the information which he had
grudgingly imparted, he twitted and jeered at him for a country
lout unworthy the name of Daimyō. At last, he actually
went so far as to order Asano to bend down and fasten up his
footgear for him. Asano, long-suffering though he was, could
not brook such an insult. Drawing his sword, he slashed the
insolent wretch in the face, and would have made an end of
him, had he not sought safety in flight. The palace—for this
scene took place within the precincts of the palace—was
of course soon in an uproar. Thus to degrade its majesty
by a private brawl, was a crime punishable with death and
confiscation. Asano was condemned to perform *harakiri* that
very evening, his castle was forfeited, his family declared
extinct, and all the members of his clan disbanded:—in
Japanese parlance they became Rōnins, literally " wave men,"
that is, wanderers, fellows without a lord and without a home.
This was in the month of April, 1701.

So far the first act. Act two is the vengeance. Ōishi
Kuranosuke, the senior retainer of the dead Daimyō, deter-
mines to revenge him, and consults with forty-six others of his
most trusty fellow-lieges as to the ways and means. All are
willing to lay down their lives in the attempt. The difficulty
is to elude the vigilance of the government. For mark one
curious point:—the vendetta, though imperatively prescribed
by custom, was forbidden by law, somewhat as duelling now
is in certain Western countries. Not to take vengeance on an
enemy involved social ostracism. On the other hand, to take
it involved capital punishment. But not to take it was an
idea which never entered the head of any chivalrous Japanese.

After-many secret consultations, it was determined among
the Rōnins that they should separate and dissemble. Several
of them took to plying trades. They became carpenters,
smiths, and merchants in various cities, by which means some
of their number gained acess to Kira's mansion, and learnt
many of the intricacies of its corridors and gardens. Ōishi
himself, the head of the faithful band, went to Kyōto, where
he plunged into a course of drunkenness and debauchery. He
even discarded his wife and children, and took a harlot to live
with him. Thus was their enemy, to whom full reports of all
these doings were brought by spies, lulled at last into complete
security. Then suddenly, on the night of the 30th January,
1703, during a violent snowstorm, the attack was made. The
Forty-seven Rōnins forced the gate of Kira's mansion, slew
his retainers, and dragged forth the high-born, but chicken-
hearted, wretch from an outhouse in which he had sought to
hide himself behind a lot of firewood and charcoal. Respectfully, as befits a mere gentleman when addressing a great
noble, the leader of the band requested Kira to perform
harakiri, thus giving him the chance of dying by his own hand
and so saving his honour. But Kira was afraid, and there was
nothing for it but to kill him like the scoundrel that he was.
That done, the little band formed in order, and marched (day
having now dawned) to the temple of Sengakuji at the other
end of the city. On their way thither, the people all flocked

out to praise their doughty deed, a great Daimyō whose palace
they passed sent out refreshments to them with messages of
sympathy, and at the temple they were received by the abbot
in person. There they laid on their lord's grave, which stood
in the temple-grounds, the head of the enemy by whom he had
been so grievously wronged. Then, came the official sentence,
condemning them all to commit *harakiri*. This they did
separately, in the mansions of the various Daimyōs to whose
care they had been entrusted for the last few days of their
lives, and they also were buried in the same temple grounds,
where their tombs can be seen to this day. The enthusiastic
admiration of a whole people during two centuries has been
the reward of their obedience to the ethical code of their time
and country.

Books recommended. *Bushido: The Soul of Japan* by Inazo Nitobe; *The Forty-seven
Ronin Story* by John Allyn; *Japan: An Attempt at Interpretation* by Lafcadio Hearn;
Tales of Old Japan by A. B. Mitford (Lord Redesdale).

Fuji. A fat and infuriated tourist has branded Fuji in print
as " that disgusting mass of humbug and ashes." The Japanese
poet Kada-no-Azuma-Maro was more diplomatic when he
simply said (we render his elegant verse into flat English
prose) : " The mountain which I found higher to climb than I
heard, than I had thought, than I had seen,—was Fuji's
peak."*

But such adverse, or at best cold, criticism is rare. Natives
and foreigners, artists and holiday-makers, alike fall down in
adoration before the wondrous mountain which stands utterly

* *Kikishi yori mo*
Omoishi yori mo
Mishi yori mo
Noborite takaki
Yama wa Fuji no ne.

alone in its union of grace with majesty. During the Middle
Ages, when Fuji's volcanic fires were more active than at
present, a commonplace of the poets was to liken the ardour
of their love to that which lit up the mountain-top with
flame. Another poet earlier still—he lived before the time of
King Alfred—sings as follows:

> There on the border, where the land of Kai*
> Doth touch the frontier of Suruga's land,
> A beauteous province stretched on either hand,
> See Fujiyama rear his head on high!
>
> The clouds of heaven in reverent wonder pause,
> Nor may the birds those giddy heights assay
> Where melt thy snows amid thy fires away,
> Or thy fierce fires lie quenched beneath thy snows.
>
> What name might fitly tell, what accents sing,
> Thine awful, godlike grandeur? 'Tis thy breast
> That holdeth Narusawa's flood at rest,
> Thy side whence Fujikawa's waters spring.
>
> Great Fujiyama, towering to the sky!
> A treasure art thou giv'n to mortal man,
> A God Protector watching o'er Japan:—
> On thee forever let me feast mine eye.

But enough of poetry. The surveyors tell us that Fuji is
12,365 feet high—an altitude easy to remember, if we take for
memoria technica the twelve months and the three hundred and
sixty-five days of the year.† The geologists inform us that Fuji
is a young volcano, to which fact may be ascribed the as yet
almost unbroken regularity of its shape. The beginning of
degradation is the hump on the south side, called Hōei-zan from
the name of the period when it was formed by the most recent
eruption of which history tells. This eruption lasted with
intervals from the 16th December, 1707, to the 22nd January,
1708. The geologists further assure us that Fuji had several
predecessors in the same vicinity,—Mounts Futago, Koma-ga-

---

take, and others in the Hakone district being volcanoes long since extinct. Futago, indeed, still has a crater which deserves a visit, so perfect is its shape and so thickly carpeted is it with moss and shrubs.

Philology is the science that can tell us least; for no consensus of opinion has yet been reached as to the origin of the name of *Fuji*—anciently *Fuzi* or *Fuzhi*. *Fuji-san*, the current popular name, simply means "Mount Fuji," *san* being Chinese for "mountain." *Fuji-no-yama*, the form preferred in poetry, means "the mountain of Fuji" in pure Japanese; and the Europeanised form *Fusiyama* is a corruption of this latter. But what is the etymology of *Fuji* itself? The Chinese characters give us no clue. Sometimes the name is written 不 二 "not two," that is, "unrivalled," "peerless"; sometimes 不 死 "not dying," "deathless;"—and with this latter transcription is connected a pretty legend about the elixir of life having been taken to the summit of the mountain in days of yore. Others write it 富 士 that is, "rich scholar," a more prosaic rendering, but no whit more trustworthy. Probably *Fuji* is not Japanese at all. It might be a corruption of *Huchi*, or *Fuchi*, the Aino name of the Goddess of Fire; for down to times almost historical the country round Fuji formed part of Aino-land, and all Eastern Japan is strewn with names of Aino origin. We, however, prefer the suggestion of Mr. Nagata Hōsei, the most learned of living Japanese authorities on Aino, who would derive *Fuji* from the Aino verb *push*, "to burst forth,"—an appellation which might have been appropriately given either to the mountain itself as a volcano, or more probably still to the chief river flowing down from it, the dangerous *Fujikawa;* for the general Aino practice is to leave even conspicuous mountains unnamed, but carefully to name all the rivers. The letter-changes from Aino *push* to classical *Fuzi* are according to Japanese rule, whereas the change from *Huchi* to *Fuzi* would be abnormal. The very circumstance, too, of the former etymology appealing less to the imagination is really in its favour.

A Japanese tradition ·(of which, however, there is no written notice earlier than A.D. 1652) affirms that Fuji arose from the earth in a single night some time about 300 B.C., while Lake Biwa near Kyōto sank simultaneously. May we not here have an echo of some early eruption, which resulted in the formation, not indeed of Lake Biwa distant a hundred and forty miles, but of one of the numerous small lakes at the foot of the mountain ?

The following miscellaneous items will perhaps interest some readers:—The Japanese are fond of comparing Fuji to an inverted fan.—Fuji is inhabited by a lovely goddess named *Ko-no-hana-saku-ya-hime,* which, being interpreted, means "the Princess who Makes the Blossoms of the Trees to Flower." She is also called Sengen or Asama, and numerous shrines are dedicated to her in many provinces.*—The peasants of the neighbouring country-side often speak of Fuji simply as *O Yama,* "the Honourable Mountain," or "the Mountain," instead of mentioning its proper name.—One of Hokusai's best picture-books is his *Fuji Hyakkei,* or "Hundred Views of Fuji," executed when he had reached the age of seventy-six. In it, the grand mountain stands depicted from every point of view and under every possible circumstance and a few impossible ones; for instance, the artist gives us Fuji in process of being ascended by a dragon. Copies of this book are common, but good ones are rather scarce.—According to a popular superstition, the ashes brought down during the day by the tread of pilgrims' feet re-ascend spontaneously at night. —The mountain is divided into ten stations, and formerly no woman was allowed to climb higher than the eighth. Lady Parkes was the first woman to tread the summit. This was in October, 1867.—Steam sufficiently hot to cook an egg still issues from several spots on the crater lip.—The Japanese have enriched their language by coining words for special aspects of their favourite mountain. Thus *kagami-Fuji,*

---

* May it be a misunderstood echo of this legend that has led some modern English writers to speak of Mount Fuji itself as "she," than which nothing can be less consonant with Japanese modes of thought ?

literally "mirror Fuji," means the reflection of Fuji in Lake Hakone. *Kage-Fuji,* or "shadow Fuji," denotes a beautiful phenomenon,—the gigantic shadow cast by the cone at sunrise on the sea of clouds and mist below. *Hidari Fuji,* "left-handed Fuji," is the name given to the mountain at the village of Nangō, for the reason that that is the only place on the Tōkaidō where, owing to a sharp twist in the road, Fuji appears on the left hand of the traveller bound from Tōkyō to Kyōto, instead of on his right.—From 12,000 to 18,000 persons ascend Fuji yearly, the majority being pilgrims.

The foregoing items are merely jotted down haphazard, as specimens of the lore connected with Japan's most famous volcano. To do justice to it geologically, botanically, historically, archæologically, would require a monograph at least as long as this volume.

Books recommended. *Down the Emperor's Road with Hiroshige* edited by Reiko Chiba; *Hiroshige's Tokaido in Prints and Poetry* edited by Reiko Chiba; *Hokusai's Views of Mt. Fuji* with poems by Easley Stephen Jones.

Fun. Serious ideas do for export. A nation's fun is for home consumption only:—it would evaporate before it could be conveyed across the border. For this reason, we must abandon the endeavour to give the foreign reader any full and particular account of the Japanese mind on its comic side. Perhaps the best plan would be to say what Japanese fun *isn't.* It certainly does not in the very faintest degree resemble French *esprit,* that child born of pure intellect and social refinement, and reared in the *salon* where conversation rises to the level of a fine art, where every word is a rapier, every touch light as air. Shall we compare it with the grim mixture which we Northerners call humour,—the grotesque suffused with the pathetic ? It may seem a little nearer akin to that. But no,—it lacks alike the hidden tear and the self-criticism of humour :—it has no irony, no side-lights. It is more like what we may picture to ourselves in the noisy revelling of the old Roman saturnalia,—the broad jest, the outrageous pun, the practical joke, the loud guffaw,

"Quips, and cranks, and wanton wiles,"

snatches of half-meaningless song, buffoonery, tomfoolery, high jinks of every sort, a very carnival of uproarious merriment. It is artless, it is thoroughly popular, in fact plebeian. Circumstances forced it to be so. The old Japanese nobility were nowise given to laughter. "Life is real, life is earnest," was their motto; and what a deadly dull life it must have been! To begin with, it was a society minus the fair sex. To admire the Court ladies' toilettes, to hang on their smiles, perhaps whisper some witty gallantry in a noble dame's ear, formed no part of a young Daimyō's order of the day at the Shōgun's Court. You can see him still on the stage; for the tradition remains, though the personage himself has vanished utterly. There he sits,—his straight back a perfect lesson of deportment, his countenance impassable, his few gestures stiff as the starch of his marvellous robes, his whole being hedged round with the prescriptions of an elaborate and rigid etiquette. Remember, too, that the government was a despotism which refused to be tempered even with epigram:—a single inappropriate jest might send you to languish in exile on one of the Seven Isles of Izu for the rest of your natural life. Spies swarmed everywhere; the walls—in these paper houses—almost literally had ears. The pleasures (so-called) of high life were ceremonies well-nigh as solemn as the actual ceremonial of government,—the stately *Nō*, or lyric drama, with its statuesque players also in starched robes and chanting in a dialect dead some centuries before, if indeed it ever had been living; or else the tea ceremonies, or the arrangement of flowers in obedience to the principles of philosophy, or the composition of verses after the model of the antique, or the viewing of scrolls painted according to ancient Chinese canons. The whole life in fact was swathed in formalism, like a mummy in its grave-clothes. The mere thought of it is enough to stifle mirth.*

---

* Though the Japanese are respecters of dignities, we have ourselves heard some who had had personal experience of life in a Daimyo's palace under the old regime, apply to it the popular verse. *Kiite gokuraku mite jigoku*, that is "Heav'n to hear tell about, but Hell to see."

Weighed down by this incubus at the top, the national spirits sought a vent in the lower strata of society. In the inimitable sketch-book of Hokusai, the bourgeois artist who threw all classical rules to the winds, we see the sort of people who really "had a good time" while their betters bored themselves to extinction, namely, the Japanese shopkeepers and artisans. We see their homely jokes, their drunken sprees, their occasional sly hits at superiors, as when, for example, a group of street Arabs is depicted making fun of some Confucian sage behind his back, or as when the stately Daimyō's procession becomes a procession of grass-hoppers bearing a mantis in a basket. The theatre, which no gentleman ever entered, was their happy hunting-ground, the pieces being written expressly to suit them, so that what flourished on the boards was, as may be supposed, not precisely a classic taste. The same in literature:—we must turn our backs on the books written for the upper class, and betake ourselves to vulgar company, if we want to be amused. Often, no doubt, the expressions are coarse. Nevertheless, let us give honour where honour is due. Though spades are called spades, we rarely, if ever, encounter any attractive refinement of wickedness.

It will have been gathered that most of the European forms of fun have Japanese parallels. Japanese puns, for instance, are not so very unlike our own, excepting one class which rests on the shapes of the Chinese written characters. Their comedies are of two kinds. The more modern ones are genuine comedies of manners; those handed down from the Middle Ages, and ranking as semi-classical because acted as interludes to the *Nō*, or lyric dramas, are of the nature of broad farce,— mere outline sketches of some little drollery, in which a leading part is generally played by the man-servant Tarōkaja, a sort of Japanese Leporello, and which always ends in a cut and run. Japanese comic poetry is mostly untranslatable. Fortunately their comic art speaks a dialect which all can more or less understand, though doubtless acquaintance with Japanese manners and customs, traditions, and superstitions will add much to an appreciation of the artists' verve.

And here we must leave—very inadequately treated—a subject of peculiar interest. To undertake the explanation of any Japanese puns or other jokes, would be a laborious business and cruel to the reader,—still more cruel to the jokes. We have thought, however, that some amusement might be derived from a perusal of the following specimen of the mediæval farce. The translation is literal.*

RIBS AND SKIN. (*HONE KAWA.*)

DRAMATIS PERSONÆ.

THE RECTOR OF A BUDDHIST TEMPLE.
HIS CURATE.   THREE OF THE PARISHIONERS.
SCENE.—THE TEMPLE.

Rector.—I am rector of this temple. I have to call my curate, to make a communication to him. Curate! are you there? are you there? Halloo!

Curate.—Here am I! What is your reason for being pleased to call me?

Rector.—My reason for calling you is just simply this:—I, unworthy priest that I am, am already stricken in years, and the duties of the temple service weigh heavily upon me. So do you please to understand that, from to-day, I resign this benefice in your favour.

Curate.—I feel deeply indebted to Your Reverence. But as I am still deficient in learning, and as, moreover, no time, however late, would seem too late to me, I beg of you to be so kind as to delay this change.

Rector.—Nothing could please me more than your most charming answer. But you must know that, though retiring from the rectorship, I do not intend to leave the temple. I shall simply take up my abode in the back apartment; so, if there should be any business of any kind, please to let me know.

Curate.—Well, if it must be so, I will act in accordance with your august desire.

Rector.—And mind (though it can scarcely be necessasy for me to say so) that you do everything in such a manner as to please the parishioners, and make the temple prosperous.

Curate.—Pray feel no uneasiness on that head! I will manage things in such a way as to please the parishioners right well.

---

* It was first published by us a quarter of a century ago, in the "Asiatic Transactions," and afterwards in a work entitled *The Classical Poetry of the Japanese*, which has long been out of print.

Rector.—Well, then, I retire without further delay. So, if there should be anything you want to ask, come and call me.

Curate.—Your commands are laid to heart.

Rector.—And if any parishioner should call, please to let me know.

Curate.—Your injunctions shall be kept in mind.—Ha! ha! this *is* delightful! To think of the joy of his ceding the benefice to me to-day, just as I was saying to myself, "*When* will the rector resign in my favour? when *will* he resign in my favour?" The parishioners, when they hear of it, are sure to be charmed; so I mean to manage in such a way as to give them all satisfaction.

* * * * * * * * *

First Parishioner.—I am a resident in this neighbourhood. I am on my way to a certain place on business; but as it has suddenly begun to threaten rain, I think I will look in at the parish temple, and borrow an umbrella. Ah! here I am. Hoy! admittance.

Curate.—Oh! there is some one hallooing at the gate! Who is that asking for admittance? Who is that hallooing?

First Par.—It is I.

Curate.—Oh! you are indeed welcome!

First Par.—It is long since I last had the honour of coming to enquire after you! but I trust that the worthy rector and yourself are still in the enjoyment of good health.

Curate.—Oh yes! we both continue well. But I must tell you that, moved by some impulse or other, my master has deigned to resign the benefice in my favour. So I pray that you will continue as heretofore to honour our temple with your visits.

First Par.—That is an auspicious event; and if I have not been already to offer my congratulations, it is because I was not apprised of it. Well! my present reason for calling is just simply this:—I am off to-day to a certain place; but as it has suddenly begun to threaten rain, I should feel much obliged if you would kindly condescend to lend me an umbrella.

Curate.—Certainly! Nothing easier! I will have the honour to lend it to you. Please wait here an instant.

First Par.—Oh! very many thanks.

Curate.—Here, then! I will have the honour to lend you this one.

First Par.—Oh! I owe you very many thanks.

Curate.—Please always tell me if there is anything of any kind that I can do for you.

First Par.—Certainly! I will call in your assistance. But now I will be off.

Curate.—Are you going?

First Par.—Yes. Good-bye!

Curate.—Good-bye !

First Par.—I am much indebted to you.

Curate.—Thanks for your visit.

First Par.—Ah ! well ! that is all right. I will hasten on.

* * * * * * * * *

Curate.—As he said I was to let him know if any of the parishioners came, I will go and tell him what has passed. Pray ! are you in ?

Rector.—Oh ! that is you !

Curate.—How dull Your Reverence must be feeling !

Rector.—No, I am not dull.

Curate.—Somebody has just been here.

Rector.—Did he come to worship, or was it that he had business with us ?

Curate.—He came to borrow an umbrella ; so I lent him one.

Rector.—Quite right of you to lend it. But tell me, which umbrella did you lend ?

Curate.—I lent the one that came new the other day.

Rector.—What a thoughtless fellow you are ! Would anybody ever dream of lending an umbrella like that one, which had not even been once used yet ? The case will present itself again. When you do not want to lend it, you can make an excuse.

Curate.—What would you say ?

Rector.—You should say : " The request with which you honour me is a slight one. But a day or two ago master went out with it, and encountering a gust of wind at a place where four roads meet, the ribs flew off on one side, and the skin* on another. So we have tied both skin and ribs by the middle, and hung them up to the ceiling. This being so, it would hardly be fit to answer your purpose." Something like that, something with an air of truth about it, is what you should say.

Curate.—Your injunctions shall be kept in mind, and I will make that answer another time.—Now I will be going.

Rector.—Are you off ?

Curate.—Yes.

Rector. } Good-bye ! good-bye !
Curate.

* * * * * * * * *

Curate.—What *can* this mean ? Let my master say what he likes, it *does* seem strange to refuse to lend a thing when you have it by you.

---

* The " cover " of an umbrella is called by the Japanese its *skin.* Similarly they speak of the skin of a tree, the skin of an apple, the skin of bread (its crust), etc. In fact, the outside of most things is termed their " skin."

Second Par.—I am a resident in this neighbourhood. As I am going on a long journey to-day, I mean to look in at the parish temple and borrow a horse.—I will go quickly. Ah! here I am! Hoy! admittance!

Curate.—There is some one hallooing at the gate again! Who is that asking for admittance? Who is that hallooing?

Second Par.—It is I.

Curate.—Oh! you are indeed most welcome!

Second Par.—My present reason for calling is just simply this:—I am off to-day on a long journey, and (though it is a bold request to make) I should feel much obliged if you would condescend to lend me a horse.

Curate.—Nothing could be slighter than the request with which you honour me. But a day or two ago my master went out with it, and encountering a gust of wind at a place where four roads meet, the ribs flew off on one side, and the skin on another. So we have tied both skin and ribs by the middle, and hung them up to the ceiling. This being so, it would hardly be fit to answer your purpose.

Second Par.—Why! it is a *horse* that I am asking for!

Curate.—Yes, certainly! a horse.

Second Par.—Oh well! then there is no help for it. I will be off.

Curate.—Are you going?

Secon Par.—Yes. Good-bye!

Curate.—Good-bye! Thanks for your visit.

* * * * * * * *

Second Par.—Well! I never! He says things that I cannot in the least make out.

* * * * * * * *

Curate.—I spoke as my master had instructed me; so doubtless he will be pleased. Pray! Are you in?

Rector.—Oh! that is you! Is it on business that you come?

Curate.—Somebody has just been here to borrow our horse.

Rector.—And you lent him, as he fortunately happened to be disengaged?

Curate.—Oh no! I did not lend it, but replied in the manner you had instructed me.

Rector.—What! I do not remember saying anything about the horse. What was it you answered?

Curate.—I said that you had been out with it a day or two ago, and that, encountering a gust of wind at a place where four roads meet, the ribs had flown off on one side, and the skin on the other, which being the case, it would hardly fit to answer his purpose.

Rector.—What *do* you mean? It was if they came to ask for an umbrella that I told you to reply like that! But would anybody ever dream of saying such a thing to a person who should come to borrow a horse ? Another time, when you do not want to lend it, you can make a fitting excuse.

Curate.—What would you say ?

Rector.—You shold say : " We lately turned him out to grass; and becoming frolicsome, he dislocated his thigh, and is lying down covered with straw in a corner of the stable. This being so, he will hardly be fit to answer your purpose." Something like that, something with an air of truth about it, is what you should say.

Curate.—Your injunctions shall be kept in mind, and I will profit by them next time.

Rector.—Be sure you do not say something stupid !

*   *   *   *   *   *   *   *   *

Curate.—What *can* this mean ? To say a thing because he tells me to say it, and then, forsooth, to get a scolding for it ! For all I am now my own master, I see no way out of these perplexities.

*   *   *   *   *   *   *   *   *

Third Parishioner.—I am a resident in this neighbourhood, and am on my way to the parish temple, where I have some business. Well, I will make haste. Ah ! here I am ! Hoy ! admittance !

Curate.—There is some one hallooing at the gate again ! Who is that hallooing ?

Third Par.—It is I.

Curate.—Oh ! a hearty welcome to you !

Third Par.—It is long since I last had the honour of coming to enquire after you. but I trust that the worthy rector and yourself are still in the enjoyment of good health.

Curate.—Oh yes ! we both continue well. But by the way, my master, moved by some impulse or other, has deigned to resign the benefice in my favour. So I pray that you will continue to honour our temple with your visits.

Third Par.—That is an auspicious event; and if I have not been already to offer my congratulations, it is because I was not appraised of it. To-morrow being a religious anniversary in my family, I should feel greatly obliged if our worthy rector and yourself would condescend to come to my house.

Curate.—For myself, I will come; but my master will scarcely be able to do so.

Third Par.—What ! has he any other business on hand ?

Curate.—No, he has no particular business on hand; but we lately turned him out to grass, and becoming frolicsome. he dislocated his thigh, and is lying down covered with straw in a corner of the stable. This being so, he will scarcely be able to come.

Thir Par.—Why! it is the rector that I am talking about!

Curate.—Yes, certainly! the rector.

Third Par.—Well! I am very sorry such a thing should have occurred. At any rate, do you, please, be so kind as to come.

Curate.—Most certainiy, I will come.

Third Par.—Now I will be off.

Curate.—Are you going?

Third Par.—Yes. Good-bye!

Curate.—Good-bye! Thanks for your visit.

* * * * * * * *

Third Par.—Well, I never! He says things that I cannot in the least make out.

* * * * * * * *

Curate.—This time, at all events, he will be pleased. Pray! are you in?

Rector.—Oh! that is you! Is it on business that you come?

Curate.—Somebody has just been here to ask both Your Reverence and myself to go to him to-morrow, when there is a religious anniversary in his family. So I said that I would go, but that you would scarcely be able to do so.

Rector.—What a pity! I should have liked to go, as I just happen to be at leisure to-morrow.

Curate.—Oh! but I said what you had instructed me to say.

Rector.—I do not remember. What was, it then, that you answered?

Curate.—I said that we had lately turned you out to grass, and that, becoming frolicsome, you had dislocated your thigh, and were lying down covered with straw in a corner of the stable, so that you would scarcely be able to go.

Rector.—You really and truly went and said that?

Curate.—Yes! really and truly.

Rector.—Well, I never! You *are* an idiot! Speak as I may, over and over again, nothing seems to be able to make you understand. It was if they came to borrow a *horse*, that I told you to make that answer! The end of all this is, that it will never do for you to become rector. Get along with you!

Curate.—Oh!

Rector.—Won't you get along? Won't you get along? Won't you get along?

Curate.—Oh dear! oh dear! oh dear! oh dear! oh dear! But, Reverend Sir, for all you are my master, it is an unheard-of shame for you to beat me thus. And for all you are the man you are, you cannot be said to have been without your frolics either,—that you cannot!

Rector.—When was I ever frolicsome ? If I ever was, out with it quick ! out with it quick !

Curate.—If I were to tell it, you would be put to shame.

Rector.—I am conscious of nothing that could put me to shame. If anything there be, out with it quick ! out with it quick !

Curate.—Well then, I'll tell it, I will.

Rector.—Out with it quick !

Curate.—Well, then ! the other day, pretty little Ichi, who lives outside the temple gate, was here.

Rector.—And what about Ichi, pray !

Curate.—Just listen, please ! Don't you call it a frolic to have beckoned to her, and then to have disappeared with her into one of the back rooms ?

Rector.—Insolent rascal, inventing things I never did, and bringing shame on your superior ! After this, by the God of War with his Bow and Arrows, I shall not let you escape me !

Curate.—For all you are my master, I do not intend to let myself get the worst of it.

Both.—Ah ! ah ! ah ! (Fighting.)

Curate.—Has the old fool learnt a lesson ? Oh ! oh ! I *am* glad ! I *am* glad ! I've beat ! I've beat !

Rector.—Deary, deary me ! where is he off to, after having put his master in such a plight ? Is there nobody there ? Catch him ! I won't let him escape ! I won't let him escape !

Funerals. Till recently all funerals were in the hands of the Buddhist hierarchy,—even the funerals of Shintō priests themselves ; but now the Shintoists are allowed to bury their own dead. The Shintō coffin resembles that used in Europe. The Buddhist coffin is small and square, and the corpse is fitted into it in a squatting posture with the head bent to the knees, —a custom which some derive from the devout habit of sitting rapt in religious meditation, while others discover in it a symbolical representation, in the last earthly scene, of the position of the unborn child in its mother's womb. Further outward and visible signs whereby to distinguish a Buddhist from a Shintō funeral, are, in the former, the bare shaven heads of the Buddhist priests and the dark blue coats of the coffin-bearers ; in the latter, the plain white garb of the coffin-bearers, the Shintō priests' non-shaven heads and curved gauze caps, and the flags and branches of trees borne in the procession. The use of large bouquets of flowers is common to both, and both religions have funeral services of great length and intricacy.

Vast sums of money are often lavished on funerals, more especially by the Imperial Family. When the Empress Dowager died, in 1897, no less than ¥700,000 were appropriated from the national treasury. Never, perhaps, was funeral pomp more elaborate than on this occasion, which, from first to last, occupied several weeks,—for the actual interment was only the last scene in an extraordinarily complicated set of observances. The procession was two miles in length, the final ceremony lasted over twenty-two hours, during all which time Imperial princes stood or walked almost barefoot in the snow without eating a morsel of food. An ox-wagon, with wheels purposely built so as to creak mournfully, bore the magnificent coffin in which the body lay preserved in vermilion. Three oxen drew it harnessed in single file—the leader jet-black, the next dun colour with black flecks, the third spotted white and black, with a white star on the forehead and four white stockings,—all this in accordance with ancient use. The actual grave-diggers were habited as birds with black wings, because for these, being devoid of reason, there could be no sacrilege in perching upon an Empress's tomb. All sound of music was hushed throughout the land for the space of a month, the schools were closed for a week, and thousands of criminals liberated. The Court itself suspended all festivities for a year. (See also Article on ARCHÆOLOGY.)

Books recommended. *A Daughter of the Samurai* by Etsu Inagaki Sugimoto; *Japan: An Attempt at Interpretation* by Lafcadio Hearn; *Japanese Etiquette: An Introduction* by the World Fellowship Committee of the Tokyo Y.W.C.A.; *Tales of Old Japan* by A. B. Mitford (Lord Redesdale).

Gardens. A garden without flowers may sound like a contradiction in terms. But it is a fact that many Japanese gardens are of that kind, the object which the Japanese land-scape-gardener sets before him being to produce something park-like,—to suggest some famous natural scene, in which flowers may or may not appear, according to the circumstances of the case. When they do, they are generally grouped together in beds or under shelter, and removed as soon as their season of bloom is over, more after the manner of a European flower-show. In this way are obtained horticultural triumphs, such as are described in the Article on FLOWERS. Triumphs of another kind are achieved by dwarfing. Thus you may see a pine-tree or a maple, sixty years old and perfect in every part, but not more than a foot high. Japanese gardeners are also very skilful in transplanting large trees. A judicious treatment of the accessory roots during a couple of years enables massive, aged trees to be removed from place to place, so that a Japanese *nouveau riche* can raise up anything—even an ancestral park—on whatever spot he fancies.

Japanese landscape-gardening is one of the fine arts. Ever since the middle of the fifteenth century, generations of artists have been busy perfecting it, elaborating and refining over and over again the principles handed down by their predecessors, until it has come to be considered a mystery as well as an art, and is furnished—not to say encumbered—with a vocabulary more complicated and recondite than any one who has not perused some of the native treatises on the subject can well imagine. There is a whole set of names for different sorts of garden lanterns, another for water-basins, another for fences (one authority enumerates nineteen kinds of screen fences alone), another—and this is a very important subject—for those large stones, which, according to Japanese ideas, constitute the skeleton of the whole composition.

Then, too, there are rules for every detail; and different schools of the art or science of gardening have rules diametrically opposed to each other. For instance, larger trees are planted and larger hills made by one school in the front portion of a garden, and smaller ones in the further portions, with the object of exaggerating the perspective and thus making the garden look bigger than it really is. Another school teaches the direct contrary. Suggestion is largely used, as when part of a small lake is so adroitly hidden as to give the idea of greater size in the part unseen, or as when a number of pebbles is made to represent a river-bed. Everything, in fact, has a reason,—generally an abstruse reason. Gardens are supposed to be capable of symbolising abstract ideas, such as peace, chastity, old age, etc. The following passage, from the authority quoted below, will show how the garden of a certain Buddhist abbot is made to convey the idea of the power of divine truth:—" This garden consists almost entirely of stones arranged in a fanciful and irregular manner in a small enclosure, the sentiment expressed depending for its value upon acquaintance with the following Buddhist legend, somewhat reminding us of the story of Saint Francis and the birds. A certain monk Daita, ascending a hillock and collecting stones, began to preach to them the secret precepts of Buddha, and so miraculous was the effect of the wondrous truths which he told that even the lifeless stones bowed in reverent assent. Thereupon the Saint placed them upon the ground around him, and consecrated them as the ' Nodding Stones.' "

What the Japanese call *hako-niwa* is a whole landscape-garden compressed into the microscopic limits of a single dish or flower-pot,—paths, bridges, mountains, stone lanterns, etc., all complete,—a fanciful little toy.

The roof ridge of a pasant's dwelling sometimes presents the aspect of a flower-garden; for when it is flat, it is apt to be overgrown with irises or red lilies. People disagree about the reason. Some say that the flowers are planted in order to avert pestilence, while others no less positively affirm the growth to be accidental. Others again assert that the object is to strengthen the thatch. We incline to this latter view. Bulbs do not fly through the air, neither is it likely that bulbs should be contained in the sods put on the top of *all* the houses in a village. We have noticed, furthermore, that in the absence of such sods, brackets of strong shingling are employed, so that it is safe to assume that the two are intended to serve the same purpose.

Books recommended. *Cha-No-Yu: The Japanese Tea Ceremony* by A. L. Sadler; *Japanese Gardens for Today* by David H. Engel; *Japanese Stone Gardens* by Kazuhiko Fukuda.

Geisha. See Singing-girls.

Geography. The boundaries of Japan have expanded greatly in the course of ages. The central and western portion of the Main Island, together with Shikoku, Kyūshū, and the lesser islands of Iki, Tsushima, Oki, Awaji, and perhaps Sado, formed the Japan of early historic days, say of the eighth century after Christ. At that time the Ainos, though already in full retreat northwards, still held the Main Island as far as the 38th or 39th parallel of latitude. They were soon driven across the Straits of Tsugaru into Yezo, which island was itself gradually conquered during the period extending from the twelfth to the seventeenth century. In the eighteenth century a portion of Saghalien was added to Japanese territory. But a discussion having arisen on this subject between Japan and Russia, the weaker of the two powers (for Japan was young and weak then) naturally went to the wall. Saghalien, with its valuable coal-fields and fisheries, was ceded to Russia by the treaty of St. Petersburg in 1875, and the barren, storm-swept Kurile Islands were obtained in exchange. Meanwhile, the Luchu and Bonin Islands had been added to the Japanese possessions, and in 1895 the valuable islands of Formosa was ceded by the vanquished Chinese. The empire, thus, in its present and furthest extent, stretches from Kamchatka on the north in about lat. 51°, to the extremity of Formosa on the south in lat. 22°, and from 120° to 156° of long. east of Greenwich.

Japan proper consists of three large islands, of which one, the largest or Main Island, distinguished as Hondo on some modern maps, has no name in popular use, while the other two are called respectively Shikoku and Kyūshū, together with the small islands of Sado, Oki, Tsushima, and a multitude of lesser ones still. The largest island is separated from the two next in size by the celebrated Inland Sea, for which latter also there is no generally current Japanese name. The area of the entire Japanese empire, excluding Formosa and the Pescadores, is between 146,000 and 147,000 square miles. Only twelve per cent. of this total area is cultivated, or even cultivable. By far the greater portion of it is covered with mountains, many of which are volcanoes either active or extinct. Fuji itself was in eruption as late as January, A.D. 1708. Of recently or constantly active volcanoes we may mention Asama, the two Shirane-sans, Nasu-yama, and Bandai-san in Eastern Japan, Vries Island (Ōshima) not far from the entrance to Yokohama harbour, Aso-san and Kirishima-yama in Kyūshū, and the beautifully shaped Koma-ga-take near Hakodate. Others, extinct or quiescent, are Ontake, Hakusan, Tateyama, Nantai-zan, Chōkai-zan, Iide-san, Ganju-san, and Iwaki-yama, all on the Main Island. Some are difficult to class, for instance, Sakura-jima in Kyūshū, whose smoke has long been reduced almost to nothing, and Onsen-ga-take in the same island, where all that remains active is a solfatara at its base. The grandest mountain mass in Japan is the Shinano-Hida range,—granite giants of from 8,000 to 10,000 ft. in height.

Owing to the narrowness of the country, most Japanese streams are rather torrents than rivers. The rivers best worth mentioning are the Kitakami, the Abukuma, the Tone, the Tenryū, and the Kiso, flowing into the Pacific Ocean, the Shinano-gawa flowing into the Sea of Japan, and the Ishikari in Yezo. Most of the smaller streams have no general name, but change their name every few miles on passing from village to village.

Lake Biwa near Kyōto is the largest lake, the next being Lake Iwashiro, on whose northern shore rises the ill-omened volcano, Bandai-san. The so-called lakes to the north-east of Tōkyō are but shallow lagoons formed by the retreating sea. The most important straits are the Strait of La Pérouse between Yezo and Saghalien, the Strait of Tsugaru between Yezo and the Main Island, the Kii Channel (Linschoten Strait) between the Main Island and eastern Shikoku, the Bungo Channel between western Shikoku and Kyūshū, and the Strait

of Shimonoseki between the south-western extremity of the
Main Island and Kyūshū. The most noteworthy gulfs or bays
are Volcano Bay in southern Yezo, Aomori Bay at the northern
extremity of the Main Island, Sendai Bay in the north-east,
the Gulfs of Tōkyō, Sagami, Suruga, Owari, and Kagoshima
facing south, and the Bay of Toyama between the peninsula
of Noto and the mainland.

Of peninsulas the chief are Noto, jutting out into the Sea
of Japan, and Kazusa-Bōshū and Izu. not far from Tōkyō
on the Pacific Ocean side. It is an interesting fact that both
Noto and Izu, words meaningless in Japanese—mere place-
names—can be traced back to terms still used by the Ainos to
designate the idea of a " promontory" or "peninsula."
Finally, even so rapid a sketch as this cannot pass over the
waterfalls of Nikkō, of Kami-ide near Fuji, of Nachi in Kishū,
of Todoroki in Shikoku, and of Yōrō. Still less must we forget
that mighty river in the sea—the Kuroshio, or " Black Brine "
—which, flowing norhtwards from the direction of Formosa
and the Philippine Islands, warms the southern and south-
eastern coasts of Japan much as the Gulf-stream warms the
coasts of western Europe. Very noteworthy, likewise, is the
Naruto Channel which separates the island of Shikoku and
Awaji, where the tide rushes with resistless force out of the
Inland Sea into the Pacific Ocean.

There are two current divisions of the soil of the empire—
an older and more popular one into provinces (kuni), of which
there are eighty-four in all, and a recent, purely administrative
one into prefectures (ken), of which there are forty-three,
exclusive of the three metropolitan districts (fu)—Tōkyō,
Kyōto, and Ōsaka—and of the islands of Yezo and Formosa.
Owing to the extensive use made of the Chinese language in
Japan, most of the provinces have two names,—one native
Japanese, the other Chinese. Thus, the provinces to the north
and west of Tōkyō marked Kōtsuke, Shinano, and Kai on our
map, are also called Jōshū, Shinshū, and Kōshū respectively,
the syllable shū (州) signifying " province " in Chinese. The
south-western province marked Nagato in the map bears the

alternative name of Chōshū, and forms part of the prefecture of Yamaguchi, which also includes the province of Suwō. To add to the perplexities of the foreign student, groups of provinces receive special names in popular and historical parlance. Such are, for instance, the *Go-Kinai,* or " Five Home Provinces," consisting of the Kyōto-Nara-Ōsaka district, the *Kwantō* which includes all the provinces of the East, the *San-yōdō* or " Sunny District," bordering the Inland Sea,, and the *San-indō,* or " Shady District," on the Sea of Japan. (See also Articles on CAPITAL, CITIES, POPULATION, FORMOSA, LUCHU, and YEZO.

Books recommended. *Enjoy Japan: A Personal and Highly Unofficial Guide* by Walt Sheldon; *The New Far East* compiled by International Research Associates; *The Tourist and the Real Japan* by Boye de Mente.

Geology. It is popularly supposed that Japan entirely consists, or almost entirely consists, of volcanic rocks. Such a supposition is true for the Kurile Islands, partially true for the northern half of the Main Island and for Kyūshū. But for the remainder of the country, that is, the southern half of the Main Island and Shikoku, the assumption is quite without support. The backbone of the country consists of primitive gneiss and schists. Amongst the latter, in Shikoku, there is an extremely interesting rock consisting largely of piedmontite. Overlying these amongst the Palæozoic rocks, we meet in many parts of Japan with slates and other rocks possibly of Cambrian or Silurian age. Trilobites have been discovered in Rikuzen. Carboniferous rocks are represented by mountain masses of *Fusulina* and other limestones. There is also amongst the Palæozoic group an interesting series of red slates containing *Radiolaria.*

Mesozoic rocks are represented by slates containing *Ammonites* and *Monotis,* evidently of Triassic age, rocks containing *Ammonites Bucklandi* of Liassic age, a series of beds rich in plants of Jurassic age, and beds of Cretaceous age containing *Trigonia* and many other fossils. The Cainozoic or Tertiary system forms a fringe round the coasts of many portions of the empire. It chiefly consists of stratified volcanic tuffs rich in coal, lignite, fossilised plants, and an invertebrate fauna. Diatomaceous earth exists at several places in Yezo. In the alluvium which covers all, the remains have been discovered of several species of elephant, which, according to Dr. Edmund Naumann, are of Indian origin. The most common eruptive rock is andesite. Such rocks as basalt, diorite, and tachyte are comparatively rare. Quartz porphyry, quartzless porphyry, and granite are largely developed.

The mineral most extensively worked in Japan is coal, large deposits of which exist in north-western Kyūshū and near Nagasaki in the south, and at Poronai and other places in Yezo at the northern extremity of the empire. Not only is the output sufficient to supply the wants of the country; foreign steamers largely use Japan coal, and considerable shipments are made all over the Far-East. The copper mines of Ashio near Nikkō, and of Besshi in Shikoku produce enormous quantities of copper, and the antimony production is among the most notable in the world. From the mine of Ichinokawa in Shikoku come the wonderful crystals of antimonite, which form such conspicuous objects in the mineralogical cabinets of Europe. There is a fair production of silver at Innai in the north and at Ikuno in Central Japan; but that of other metals is relatively small. The reports circulated from time to time of large discoveries of gold in Yezo have hitherto not been verified.

Globe-trotters have been described, once for all, by Mr. Netto in a passage of his *Papierschmetterlinge aus Japan*, of which the following is a faithful translation:—

" *Globe-trotter* is the technical designation of a genus which, like the phylloxera and the Colorado beetle, had scarcely received any notice till recent times, but whose importance justifies us in devoting a few lines to it. It may be subdivided, for the most part, into the following species:—

" 1. *Globe-trotter communis.* Sun-helmet, blue glasses, scant luggage, celluloid collars. His object is a maximum of travelling combined with a minimum of expense. He presents himself to you with some suspicious introduction or other, accepts with ill-dissembled glee your lukewarm invitation to him to stay, generally appears too late at meals, makes daily enquiries concerning jinrikisha fares, frequently invokes your help as interpreter to smooth over money difficulties between himself and the jinrikishamen, offers honest curio-dealers who have the *entré* to your house one-tenth of the price they ask, and loves to occupy your time, not indeed by gaining information from you about Japan (all that sort of thing he knows already much more thoroughly than you do), but by giving *you* information about India, China, and America, —places with which you are possibly as familiar as he. When the time of his departure approaches, you must provide him with introductions even for places which he has no present intention of visiting, but which he *might* visit. You will be kind enough, too, to have his purchases here packed up,—but, mind, very carefully. You will also see after freight and insurance, and despatch the boxes to the address in Europe which he leaves with you. Furthermore, you will no doubt not mind purchasing and seeing to the packing of a few sundries which he himself has not had time to look after.

" 2. *Globe-trotter scientificus.* Spectacles, microscope, a few dozen note-books, alcohol, arsenical acid, seines, butterfly-nets, other nets. He travels for special scientific purposes, mostly natural-historical (if zoological, then woe betide you!). You have to escort him on all sorts of visits to Japanese officials, in order to procure admittance for him to collections, museums, and libraries. You have to invite him to meet Japanese *savants* of various degrees, and to serve as interpreter on each such occasion. You have to institute researches concerning ancient Chinese books, to discover and engage the services of translators, draughtsmen, flayers and stuffers of specimens. Your spare room gradually develops into a museum of natural history, a fact which you can *smell* at the very threshold. In this case, too, the packing, passing through the custom-house, and despatching of the collections falls to your lot; and happy are you if the object arrive at home in a good state of preservation, and you have not to learn later on that such and such an oversight in packing has caused 'irreparable' losses. Certain it is that, for years after, you will be reminded from time to time of your inquisitive guest by letters wherein he requests you to give him the details of some scientific speciality whose domain is disagreeably distant from your own, or to procure for him some creature or other which is said to have been observed in Japan at some former period.

" 3. *Globe-trotter elegans.* Is provided with good introductions from his government, generally stops at a legation, is interested in shooting, and allows the various charms of the country to induce him to prolong his stay.

" 4. *Globe-trotter independens.* Travels in a stream-yacht, generally accompanied by his family. Chief goal of his journey: an audience of the Mikado.

" 5. *Globe-trotter princeps.* Princes or other dignitaries recognisable by their numerous suite, and who undertake the round journey (mostly on a man-of-war) either for political reasons or for purposes of self-instruction. This species is useful to the foreign residents, in so far as the receptions and fêtes given in their honour create an agreeable diversion. . . . . . .

" We might complete our collection by the description of a few other species, *e.g.*, the *Globe-trotter desperatus*, who expends his uttermost farthing on a ticket to Japan with the hope of making a fortune there, but who, finding no situation, has at last to be carted home by some cheap opportunity at the expense of his fellow-countrymen. Furthermore might be noticed the *Globe-trotter dolosus*, who travels under some high-sounding name and with a doubtful banking account, merely in order to put as great a distance as possible betwixt himself and the home police. Likewise the *Globe-trotter locustus,* the species that travels in swarms, perpetually dragged around the universe by Cook and the likes of Cook . . . . Last, but not least, just a word for the *Globe-trotter amabilis,* a species which is fortunately not wanting and which is always welcome. I mean the old friends and the new, whose memory lives fresh in the minds of our small community, connected as it is with the recollection of happy hours spent together. Their own hearts will tell them that not they, but others, are pointed at in the foregoing —perhaps partly too harsh—description."

Go, often with little appropriateness termed " checkers " by European writers, is the most popular of the indoor pastimes of the Japanese,—a very different affair from the simple game known to Europeans as *Goban* or *Gobang,* properly the name of the board on which *Go* is played. It is the great resource of most of the visitors to the hot springs and other health resorts, being often played from morning till night, save for the intervals devoted to eating and bathing. Clubs and professors of the art are found in all the larger cities, where, too, blind players may occasionally be met with. *Go* may with justice be considered more difficult than chess, its wider field affording more numerous ramifications. The game was introduced into Japan from China by Shimomichi-no-Mabi, commonly known as Kibi Daijin, who flourished during the reign of the Emperor Shōmu (A.D. 724–756). In the middle of the seventeenth century, a noted player, called Hon-im-bō, was summoned from Kyōto to entertain the Chinese ambassador then at the court of the Shōgun, from which time forward special *Go* players were always retained by the Shōguns of the Tokugawa dynasty.

Go is played on a square wooden board. Nineteen straight lines crossing each other at right angles make three hundred and sixty-one me, or crosses, at the points of intersection. These may be occupied by a hundred and eighty white and a hundred and eighty-one black stones (*ishi,* as they are termed in Japanese). The object of the game is to obtain possession of the largest portion of the board. This is done by securing such positions as can be most easily defended from the adversary's onslaughts. There are nine spots on the board, called *seimoku* supposed to represent the chief celestial bodies, while the white and black stones represent day and night, and the number of crosses the three hundred and sixty degrees of latitude, exclusive of the central one, which is called *taikyoku*, that is, the Primordial Principle of the Universe. There are likewise nine degrees—or classes as we should term them— of proficiency in the game, beginning with number one as the lowest, and ending with number nine as the highest point of excellence attainable.

In playing, if the combatants are equally matched, they take the white stones alternately; if unequal, the weaker always takes the black, and odds are also given by allowing him to occupy several or all of the nine spots or vantage points on the board,—that is, to place stones upon them at the outset. A description of how the game proceeds would be of little utility here, it being so complicated as to make the personal instruction of a teacher indispensable. Very few foreigners have succeeded in getting beyond a rudimentary knowledge of this interesting game. We know only of one, a German named Korschelt, who has taken out a diploma fo proficiency.

The easy Japanese game, called *Gobang,* which was introduced into England some years ago, is played on the *Go* board and with the go-ishi, or round black and white stones. The object of the game is to be the first is getting five stones in a row in any direction.

Books recommended. *The Game of Go* by Arthur Smith; *Stepping Stones to Go: A Game of Strategy* by Shigemi Kishikawa; *The Theory and Practice of Go* by O. Korschelt.

Government. In theory the Mikado—heaven-descended, absolute, infalliable—was always the head and fountain of all power. It belonged to him by a right divine, which none ever dreamt of disputing. The single and sufficient rule of life for subjects was implicit, unquestioning obedience, as to the mandates of a god. The comparatively democratic doctrines of the Chinese sages, according to whom " the people are the most important element in a nation, and the sovereign is the lightest," were ever viewed with horror by the Japanese, to whom the antiquity and the absolute power of their Imperial line are badges of perfection on which they never weary of descanting. A study of Japanese history shows, however, that the Mikado has rarely exercised much of his power in practice. Almost always has it been wielded in his name, often sorely against his will, by the members of some ambitious house, which has managed to possess itself of supreme influence over the affairs of state. Thus, the Fujiwara family soon after the civilisation of the country by Buddhism, then the Taira, the Minamoto, the Hōjō, and the Ashikaga during the Middle Ages, and the Tokugawa in modern times, held the reins of state in succession. Under these ruling families were numerous families of lesser though still high degree, the Daimyōs:—in other words, the polity was feudal. Even since the revolution of 1868, whose avowed object was to restore the Mikado to his pristine absolutism, it is allowed on all hands that at least a large share of the reality of power has lain with the two great clans of Satsuma and Chōshū, while the aim of the two clans next in influence—Tosa and Hizen— has been to put themselves in Satsuma and Chōshū's place. In 1889 there was granted a Constitution, which established a Diet consisting of two houses, and laid the foundation of a new order of things, a share in the government being thenceforth vested in the nobility and in those gentlemen and commoners whose property qualification entitles them to vote or to be voted for. Those possessing this privilege form a little over two per cent. of the total population. The members of the lower house—376 in all—receive each a yearly allowance of 2,000 *yen* (£200). A certain measure of popular control over local affairs was also granted in 1889.

The administration is at present divided into ten departments, namely, the Imperial Household, Foreign Affairs, the Interior, Finance, the Army, the Navy, Justice, Education, Agriculture and Commerce, and Communications (that is, Railways, Posts, Telegraphs, etc.), each presided over by a

minister of state. These, with the exception of the minister of
the Household Department, constitute the Cabinet. The
Cabinet is responsible only to the Emperor, by whom also
each minister is appointed and dismissed at will; for
government by party, according to the Anglo-Saxon plan, has
not yet succeeded in establishing itself. Besides the Cabinet,
there is a Privy Council, whose function is to tender advice.
The empire is divided into prefectures *(ken),*—each with a
governor,—which have, as in France, replaced the old
historical "provinces." There are three capital cities, Tōkyō,
Kyōto, and Ōsaka. An unusually large proportion of the
revenue is raised by land taxation. Viewed from an Anglo-
Saxon point of view, the Japanese are a much-governed people,
officials being numerous, their authority great, and all sorts of
things which with us are left to private enterprise being here
in the hands of government. But the contrast is less in this
respect between Japan and the nations of Continental Europe.
Administrative changes are frequent; corrupt practices often
come to light; political parties, too, form and dissolve and
form again around men rather than around measures. Still,
there is continuity, the aims of the government as a whole
running on in the same groove, despite changes of personnel.
The profound respect for the throne gives continuity. So does
the character of Marquis Itō, the ablest man in Japan, who
always takes the helm whenever the ship comes to some
dangerous shoal or current.

In any case, and whatever its shortcomings, the ruling
oligarchy has guided Japan with admirable skill and courage
through the perils of the last five-and-thirty years. The nation
may have—probably has—further administrative changes in
store for it. One things is certain:—these changes will all be
along that road leading westward, which the men of 1868 were
the first to open out. If it is true that the last fifteen years
have witnessed a cooling towards Europeanism, this has been
a matter of sentiment only, a return from cosmopolitanism to
nationalism in matters of minor importance, and has affected

nothing practical by so much as a hair's breadth. Inquisitive persons from home, who remember the Stuarts and the Legitimists and Don Carlos, sometimes ask whether there may not be a Japanese reaction in favour of feudalism. No! never,—not till the sun stops shining and water begins to flow uphill. (Compare ARTICLE ON CLANS.)

Books recommended. *A Brief Diplomatic History of Modern Japan* by Morinosuke Kajima; *The Emergence of Japan as a World Power, 1895–1925* by Morinosuke Kajima; *Hermann Roesler and the Making of the Meiji State* by Johannes Siemes; *Japan: An Attempt at Interpretation* by Lafcadio Hearn; *Modern Japan's Foreign Policy* by Morinosuke Kajima.

Harakiri. Need we say that *harakiri* was for centuries the favourite Japanese method of committing suicide ? There were two kinds of *harakiri*,—obligatory and voluntary. The former was a boon granted by government, who graciously permitted criminals of the Samurai class thus to destroy themselves instead of being handed over to the common executioner. Time and place were officially notified to the condemned, and officials were sent to witness the ceremony. This custom is extinct. Voluntary *harakiri* was practised by men in hopeless trouble, also out of loyalty to a dead superior, and in order to protest—when other protests might be unavailing—against the erroneous conduct of a living superior. Examples of this class still take place. That of a young man called Ōhara Takeyoshi, which occurred in 1891, is typical. He was a lieutenant in the Yezo militia, and ripped himself up in front of the graves of his ancestors at the temple of Saitokuji in Tōkyō. Following the routine customary in such cases, Lieutenant Ōhara left a paper setting forth the motives of his act, the only innovation being that this document was directed to be forwarded to the Tōkyō News Agency for

publication in all the newspapers. The writer, it seems, had
brooded for eleven years over the likelihood of Russian
encroachment, and feeling that his living words and efforts
were doomed to fruitlessness, resolved to try what his death
might effect. In this particular instance no immediate result
was obtained. Nevertheless Ōhara's self-sacrifice, its origin in
political considerations, and the expectation that an appeal
from the grave would move men's hearts more surely than
any arguments urged by a living voice,—all this was in
complete accord with Japanese ways of thinking. The
government had no sooner yielded to the pressure of France,
Russia, and Germany in 1895 by giving up the conquered
territory of Liao-tung, than forty military men committed
suicide in the ancient way. As we sit correcting these proofs
in June, 1904, news comes of many officers and men on board
a captured transport ripping themselves up rather than
surrender to the foe. Even women are found ready to kill
themselves for loyalty and duty, but the approved method in
their case is cutting the throat. Nowise strange, but admirable
according to Japanese ideas, was it that when, in 1895, the
tiding of Lieutenant Asada's death on the battle-field, were
brought to his young wife, she at once, and with her father's
consent, resolved to follow him. Having thoroughly cleansed
the house and arrayed herself in her costliest robes. she placed
her husband's portrait in the alcove, and prostrating herself
before it, cut her throat with a dagger that had been a wedding
gift.

The courage to take life—be it one's own or that of others—
ranks extraordinarily high in public esteem. It would appear
as if political assassination were at once forgiven, when the
desperado seals it with his own blood. Nishino Buntarō, the
Shintō fanatic who stabbed the Minister of Education,
Viscount Mori, on the day of the proclamation of the
Constitution in 1889, and who himself perished in the fray,
was worshipped almost as a god, his tomb was constantly
decked with flowers, incense was burnt before it, verses were
hung over it, pilgrimages made to it. The would-be assassin

of Count Ōkuma met with scarcely less glorification. At last, in 1891, the government actually felt itself constrained to issue an ordinance prohibiting costly funerals and other posthumous honours to deceased criminals.

Harakiri is not an aboriginal Japanese custom. It was evolved gradually during the Middle Ages. The cause of it is probably to be sought in the desire on the part of vanquished warriors to avoid the humiliation of falling into their enemies' hands alive. Thus the custom would come to be characteristic of the military class, in other words, of the feudal nobility and gentry; and from being a custom, it next developed into a privilege about A.D. 1500, as stated above.

Harakiri has sometimes been translated " the happy despatch," but the original Japanese is less euphemistic. It means " belly-cutting; " and that is what the operation actually consists in, neither more nor less. Or rather, no: there *is* more. In modern times, at least, people not having always succeeded in making away with themselves expeditiously by this method, it became usual for a friend— a " best man," as one might say—to stand behind the chief actor in the tragedy. When the latter thrust his dirk into himself, the friend at once chopped off his head.

It is an odd fact that the Japanese word harakiri, so well-known all over the world, is but little used by the Japanese themselves. The Japanese almost always prefer to employ the synonym *seppuku,* which they consider more elegant because it is derived from the Chinese. After all, they are not singular in this matter. Do not we ourselves say " abdomen," when what we mean is plain Saxon—well, we will not shock ears polite by mentioning the word again. Latinisms in English, " Chinesisms " in Japanese, cover a multitude of sins.

Suicide of a more commonplace type than *harakiri* has always been extremely common, especially what is termed *shinjū,* that is, suicide for love. Numberless are the tales of men who, being unable to wed the object of their passion,— generally some frail beauty,—have bound themselves tightly to her with a rope, and then precipitated themselves into the

water. But Japan is modernised even in this respect:—
instead of the rope and the watery grave, we hear now of
lovers taking doses of chloroform, or throwing themselves
under an approaching train. One can hardly take up a
newspaper without lighting on some such story.

Books recommended. *Bushido: The Soul of Japan* by Inazo Nitobe; *Hara-Kiri: Japanese Ritual Suicide* by Jack Seward; *Japan: An Attempt at Interpretation* by Lafcadio Hearn.

Heraldry. In Japan, as in Europe, feudalism produced the
"nobyl and gentyl sciaunce" of heraldry, though the absence
of such powerful stimuli as tournaments and the crusades
prevented Japanese heraldry from developing to the same high
degree of complexity as the heraldry of the West. Moreover,
the use of crests is not a privilege confined to persons of
quality:—even tradesmen may use them. Most of the great
Daimyōs possessed three crests or badges (*mon*), the lesser
Daimyōs had two, ordinary Samurai one. These served in
time of war to adorn the breast-plate, the helmet, and the flag.
In time of peace the crest was worn, as it still is by those
who retain the native garb, in five places on the upper garment,
namely, at the back of the neck, on each sleeve, and on each
breast. Various other articles were marked with it, such as
lanterns, travelling-cases (what modern curio-dealers call
"Daimyō boxes"), etc., etc. The Imperial family has two
crests,—the sixteen-petalled chrysanthemum *(kiku no go mon)*,
and the leaves and flowers of the paulownia *(kiri no go mon)*.
The crest of the Tokugawa dynasty of Shōguns was three
asarum leaves *(mitsu-aoi)*, whose points meet in the centre.
The bamboo, the rose, the peony, even the radish, have
furnished crests for noble families. Other favourite "motives"
are birds, butterflies, running water, fans, feathers, ladders,
bridle bits, Chinese characters, and geometrical designs. One
small Daimyō, named Aoki, had for his crest the summit of
Fuji, with its trifurcated peak issuing from the clouds. The
great Shimazu family of Satsuma has the cross within a circle.

Books recommended. *Bushido: The Soul of Japan* by Inazo Nitobe; *A Daughter of the Samurai* by Etsu Inagaki Sugimoto.

History and Mythology.   To the eye of the critical inves-tigator, Japanese history properly so-called opens only in the latter part of the fifth or the beginning of the sixth century after Christ, when the gradual spread of Chinese culture, filtering in through Korea, had sufficiently dispelled the gloom of original barbarism to allow of the keeping of records.

The whole question of the credibility of the early history of Japan has been carefully gone into during the last five-and-twenty years by Aston and others, with the result that the first date pronounced trustworthy is A.D. 461, and it is discovered that even the annals of the sixth century are to be received with caution. We ourselves have no doubt of the justice of this negative criticism, and can only stand in amaze at the simplicity of most European writers, who have accepted, without sifting them, the uncritical statements of the Japanese annalists.   One eminent German professor, the late Dr. Hoffmann, actually discusses the *hour* of Jimmu Tennō's accession in the year 660 B.C., which is much as if one should gravely compute in cubic inches the size of the pumpkin which Cinderella's fairy godmother turned into a coach and six. How comes it that profound erudition so often lacks the salt of humour and the guidance of common sense ?

Be this as it may, criticism is not at all a " Japanesey " thing; and as Japanese art and literature contain frequent allusions to the early history (so-called) of the country, the chief outlines of this history, as preserved in the works entitled *Kojiki* and *Nihongi,* both dating from the eighth century after Christ, may here be given.   We include the mythology under the same heading, for the reason that it is absolutely impossible to separate the two.   Why, indeed, attempt to do so, where both are equally fabulous ?

Before, then, the beginning of the world of men, there existed numerous generations of gods. The last of these " divine generations," as they are termed, were a brother and sister, named respectively Izanagi and Izanami, who, uniting in marriage, gave birth to the various islands of the Japanese archipelago and to a great number of additional gods and goddesses. The birth of the God of Fire caused Izanami's death, and the most striking episode of the whole Japanese mythology ensues, when her husband, Orpheus-like, visits her at the gate of the under-world to implore her to return to him. She would fain do so, and bids him wait while she takes counsel with the deities of the place. But he, impatient at her long tarrying breaks off one of the teeth of the comb in his hair, lights it and goes in, only to find her a hideous mass of putrefaction, in the midst of which are seated the eight Gods of Thunder. Eight, be it observed, is the mystic number of the Japanese, as six is the mystic number of the Ainos whom their ancestors drove out.

Returning to south-western Japan, Izanagi purifies himself by bathing in a stream, and as he does so, fresh deities are born from each article of clothing that he throws down on the riverbank, and from each part of his person. One of these deities was the Sun-Goddess Ama-terasu, who was born from his left eye, while the Moon-God sprang from his right eye, and the last born of all, Susa-no-o, whose name means " the Impetuous Male," was born from his nose. Between these three children their father divides the inheritance of the universe.

At this point the story loses its unity. The Moon-God is no more heard of, and the traditions concerning the Sun-Goddess diverge from those concerning the Impetuous Male Deity in a manner which is productive of inconsistencies in the rest of the mythology. The Sun-Goddess and the Impetuous Male Deity have a violent quarrel, and at last the latter breaks a hole in the roof of the hall in Heaven, where his sister is sitting at work with her " celestial weaving maidens," and through it lets fall " a heavenly piebald horse which he had flayed with a backward flaying." The consequences of this impious act were so disastrous that the Sun-Goddess withdrew for a season into a cave, from which the rest of the eight hundred myriad deities with difficulty allured her. The Impetuous Male Deity was thereupon banished, and the Sun-Goddess remained mistress of the field. Yet, strange to say, she thenceforward retires into the background, and the most bulky section of the mythology consists of stories concerning the Impetuous Male Deity and his descendants, who are represented as the monarchs of Japan, or rather of the province of Izumo. The Impetuous Male Deity himself, whom his father had charged with the dominion of the sea, never assumes that rule, but first has a curiously told amorous adventure and an encounter with an eight-forked serpent in Izumo, and afterwards reappears as the capricious and filthy deity of Hades, who, however, seems to retain some authority over the land of the living as he invests his descendant of the sixth generation with the sovereignty of Japan.

Of this latter personage a whole cycle of stories is told, all centring in the province of Izumo. We learn of his conversations with a hare and with a rat, of the prowess and cleverness which he displayed on the occasion of a visit to his ancestor in Hades, which is in this cycle of traditions a much less mysterious place than the Hades visited by Izanami, of his loves, of his triumph over his eighty brethren, of his reconciliation with his jealous consort, and of his numerous descendants. We hear too of a Lilliputian deity, who comes across the sea to request this monarch of Izumo to share the kingdom with him.

This last-mentioned legend repeats itself in the sequel. The Sun-Goddess resolves to bestow the sovereignty of Japan on a child of whom it is doubtful whether he were born of her or

of her brother, the Impetuous Male Deity. Three embassies
are sent from Heaven to Izumo to arrange matters; but it is
only a fourth that is successful, the final ambassadors
obtaining the submission of the monarch or deity of Izumo, who
surrenders his throne, and promises to serve the new dynasty
(apparently in the under-world) if a palace or temple be built
for him and he be appropriately worshipped. Thereupon the
child of the deity whom the Sun-Goddess had originally chosen
descends to earth,—not to Izumo in the north-west, as the
logical sequence of the story would lead one to expect,—but
to the peak of a mountain in the south-western island of
Kyūshū.

Here follows a quaint tale accounting for the odd
appearance of the *bêche-de-mer,* and another to account for
the shortness of the lives of mortals, after which we are told of
the birth under peculiar circumstances of the heaven-descended
deity's three sons. Two of these, Hoderi and Hoori, whose
names may be Englished as "Fire-Shine" and "Fire-Fade,"
are the heroes of a very curious legend, which includes an
elaborate account of a visit paid by the latter to the palace of
the God of Ocean, and of a curse or spell which gained for
him the victory over his elder brother, and enabled him to
dwell peacefully in his palace at Takachiho for the space of
five hundred and eighty years,—the first statement resembling
a date which the Japanese historians vouchsafe. Fire-Fade's
son married his own aunt, and was the father of four children,
one of whom, " treading on the crest of the waves, crossed over
to the Eternal Land," while a second "went into the sea-
plain," and the two others moved eastward, fighting with the
chiefs of Kibi and Yamato, having adventures with gods both
with and without tails, being assisted by a miraculous sword
and a gigantic crow, and naming the various places they passed
through after incidents in their own career. One of these
brothers was Kamu-Yamato-Iware-Biko, who (the other having
died before him) is accounted the first human emperor of
Japan—the first Mikado. The posthumous name of Jimmu
Tennō was given to him more than fourteen centuries after
the date which the historians assign for his decease.

Henceforth Yamato, which had scarcely been mentioned before, and the provinces adjacent to it, become the centre of the story, and Izumo again emerges into importance. A very indecent love-tale forms a bridge which unites the various fragments of the mythology; and the " Great Deity of Miwa," who is identified with the deposed monarch of Izumo, appears on the scene. Indeed, during the rest of the story, this " Great Deity of Miwa " and his colleague the " Small August Deity " (Sukuna-Mi-Kami), the deity Izasa-Wake, the three Water-Gods of Sumi, and the " Great Deity of Kazuraki " form, with the Sun-Goddess and with a certain divine sword preserved at the temple of Isonokami in Yamato, the only objects of worship specially named, the other gods and goddesses being no more heard of. This portion of the story is closed by an account of the troubles which inaugurated the reign of Jimmu's successor, Suisei Tennō, and then occurs a blank of (according to the accepted chronology) five hundred years, during which absolutely nothing is related excepting dreary genealogies, the place where each sovereign dwelt and where he was buried, and the age to which he lived, —this after the minute details which had been given concerning the previous gods or monarchs down to Suisei inclusive. It should likewise be noted that the average age of the first seventeen monarchs (counting Jimmu Tennō as the first) is nearly ninety-six years if we follow the *Kojiki,* and over a hundred if we follow the accepted chronology, which is based chiefly on the divergent statements contained in the *Nihongi.* The age of several of the monarchs exceeds a hundred and twenty years.

The above-mentioned lapse of a blank period of five centuries brings us to the reign of the emperor known to history by the name of Sujin Tennō, whose life of one hundred and sixty-eight years (one hundred and twenty according to the *Nihongi*) is supposed to have immediately preceded the Christian era. In this reign, the former monarch of Izumo or god of Miwa again appears and produces a pestilence, of the manner of staying which Sujin is warned in a dream.

In the folowing reign an elaborate legend, involving a
variety of circumstances as miraculous as any in the earlier
portion of the mythology, again centres in the necessity of
pacifying the great god of Izumo; and this, with details of
internecine strife in the Imperial family, of the sovereign's
amours, and of the importation of the orange from the
"Eternal Land" (Luchu?), brings us to the cycle of
traditions of which Yamato-take, a son of the Emperor Keikō,
is the hero. This prince, after assassinating one of his
brothers, accomplishes the task of subduing both western and
eastern Japan; and notwithstanding certain details
unacceptable to European taste, his story, taken as a whole,
is one of the most pleasing in Japanese legend. He performs
marvels of valour, disguises himself as a woman in order to
slay the brigands, is the possessor of a magic sword and fire-
striker, has a devoted wife who stills the fury of the sea by
sitting down upon its surface, has encounters with a deer and
with a boar who are really gods in disguise, and finally dies
on his way westward before he can reach his home in Yamato.
His death is followed by a highly mythological account of the
laying to rest of the white bird into which he ended by being
transformed.

The succeeding reign is a blank, and the next transports us
without a word of warning to quite another scene. The
sovereign's home is now in Kyūshū—the south-westernmost
island of the Japanese archipelago;—and four of the gods,
through the medium of the sovereign's consort, who is known
to posterity as the Empress Jingū, reveal the existence of the
land of Korea, of which, however, this is not the first mention
in the histories. The Mikado disbelieves the divine message,
and is punished with death for his incredulity. But the
empress, after a special consultation between her prime
minister and the gods, and the performance of various
religious ceremonies, marshals her fleet, and, with the
assistance of the fishes both great and small and of a
miraculous wave, reaches Shiragi (one of the ancient divisions
of Korea), and subdues it. She then returns to Japan, the
legend ending with a curiously naive tale of how she sat

a-fishing one day on a shoal in the River Ogawa in Kyūshū, with threads picked out of her skirt for lines. The date of the conquest of Korea, according to the orthodox chronology, is A.D. 200.

The next episode is the warrior-empress's voyage up to Yamato,—another joint in the story, by means of which the Yamato cycle of legends and the Kyūshū cycle are brought into apparent unity. The *Nihongi* has even improved upon this by making Jingō's husband dwell in Yamato at the beginning of his reign and only remove to Kyūshū later, so that if the less skilfully elaborated *Kojiki* had not been preserved, the tangled skein of the tradition would have been still more difficult to unravel. The empress's army defeats the troops raised by the native kings or princes, who are represented as her step-sons, and from that time forward the story runs on in a single channel, with Yamato as its scene of action.

China likewise is now first mentioned, books are said to have been brought over from the mainland, and we hear of the gradual introduction of various useful arts by Chinese and Korean immigrants. Even the annals of the reign of Jingō's son, Ōjin Tennō, however, during which this civilising impulse from abroad is said to have commenced, are not free from details as miraculous as any in the earlier portions of the history. The monarch himself is said to have lived a hundred and thirty years, while his successor lived eighty-three (according to the *Nihongi*, Ōjin lived a hundred and ten, and his successor Nintoku reigned eighty-seven years). It is not till the next reign that the miraculous ceases, a fact which significantly coincides with the time at which, says the *Nihongi,* "historiographers were first appointed to all the provinces to record words and events, and forward archives from all directions."

This brings us to the beginning of the fifth century of our era, just three centuries before the compilation of the annals that have come down to us, but only two centuries before the compilation of the first history of which mention has been preserved. From that time forward the story in the *Kojiki,* though not well told, gives us some very curious pictures, and reads as if it were trustworthy. It is tolerably full for a few reigns, after which it again dwindles into more genealogies, ending with the death of the Empress Suiko in A.D. 628. The Nihongi, on the contrary, supplies full details as far as A.D. 701, that is, to within nineteen years of the date of its compilation.

The reader who has followed this summary, or who will take the trouble to study the original Japanese texts for himself, will perceive that there is no break in the story—at least no chronological break—and no break between the fabulous and the real, unless it be in the fifth century of our era, or more than a thousand years later than the date usually assumed as the starting-point of authentic Japanese history. The only breaks are topographical, not chronological.

This fact of the continuity of the Japanese mythology and history has been fully recognised by the leading native commentators, whose opinions are those considered orthodox by modern Shintoists, and they draw from it the conclusion that everything in the standard national histories must be accepted as literal truth,—the supernatural equally with the natural. But the general habit of the more sceptical Japanese of the present day, that is to say, of ninety-nine out of every hundred of the educated, is to reject or rather to ignore the legends of the gods, while implicitly believing the legends of the emperors, from Jimmu Tennō, in 660 B.C., downwards. For so arbitrary a distinction there is not the shadow of justification.* The so-called history of Jimmu the first earthly Mikado, of Jingō the conqueror of Korea, of Yamato-take, and of the rest, stands or falls by exactly the same criterion as the legends of the creator and creatress Izanagi and Izanami.

---

* Since this article was first published, the Japanese government, obscurantist in nothing but the teaching of history, has produced convincing proof of the advisability of orthodoxy in matters historical by dismissing Prof. Kume from his chair at the University of Tokyo for no other offence than that of writing critically on the subject of the early Mikados. This step, taken in 1892, has duly served *pour encourager les autres*. Thus we find Mr. Haga, in his otherwise excellent little "Lectures on Japanese Literature" (國文學史十講), gravely informing his hearers that some of the odes preserved in the *Kojiki* and *Nihongi* were composed by the gods, some by Jimmu Tenno and other ancient Mikados, one *by a monkey!* The ridicule due to these absurdities must recoil on the government which imposes on highly educated men such humiliating restrictions.

Both sets of tales are told in the same books, in the same style, and with an almost equal amount of supernatural detail. The socalled historical part is as devoid as the other of all contemporary evidence. It is contradicted by the more trustworthy, because contemporary, Chinese and Korean records, and—to turn from negative to positive testimony— can be proved in some particulars to rest on actual forgery. For instance, the fictitious nature of the calendars employed to calculate the early dates for about thirteen centuries (from 660 B.C. onward) has not altogether escaped the notice even of the Japanese themselves, and has been clearly exposed for European readers by that careful investigator, the late Mr. William Bramsen, who says, when discussing them in the Introduction to his *Japanese Chronological Tables,* "It is hardly too severe to style this one of the greatest literary frauds ever perpetrated."

But a truce to this discussion. We have only entered into it because the subject, though perhaps dry, is at least new, and because one's patience is worn out by seeing book after book glibly quote the traditional dates of early Japanese history as if they were solid truth, instead of being the merest haphazard guesses and baseless imaginings of a later age. Arrived at A.D. 600, we stand on *terra firma,* and can afford to push on more quickly.

About that time occurred the greatest event of Japanese history, the conversion of the nation to Buddhism (approximately A.D. 552–621). So far as can be gathered from the accounts of the early Chinese travellers, Chinese civilisation had slowly—very slowly—been gaining ground in the archipelago ever since the third century after Christ. But when the Buddhist missionaries crossed the water, all Chinese institutions followed them and came in with a rush. Mathematical instruments and calendars were introduced; books began to be written (the earliest that has survived, and indeed nearly the earliest of all, is the already-mentioned *Kojiki,* dating from A.D. 712); the custom of abdicating the throne in order to spend old age in prayer was adopted,—

a custom which, more than anything else, led to the effacement of the Mikado's authority during the Middle Ages.

Sweeping changes in political arrangements began to be made in the year 645, and before the end of the eighth century, the government had been entirely remodelled on the Chinese centralised bureaucratic plan, with a regular system of ministers responsible to the sovereign, who, as "Son of Heaven," was theoretically absolute. In practice this absolutism lasted but a short time, because the entourage and mode of life of the Mikados were not such as to make of them able rulers. They passed their time surrounded only by women and priests, oscillating between indolence and debauchery, between poetastering and gorgeous temple services. This was the brilliant age of Japanese classical literature, which lived and moved and had its being in the atmosphere of an effeminate Court. The Fujiwara family engrossed the power of the state during this early epoch (A.D. 670–1050). While their sons held all the great posts of government, their daughters were married to puppet emperors.

The next change resulted from the impatience of the always manly and warlike provincial gentry at the sight of this sort of petticoat government. The great families of Taira and Minamoto arose, and struggled for and alternately held the reins of power during the second half of the eleventh and the whole of the twelfth century. Japan was now converted into a camp; her institutions were feudalised. The real master of the empire was he who, strongest with his sword and bow, and heading the most numerous host, could partition out the land among the chief barons, his retainers. By the final over-throw of the Taira family at the sea-fight of Dan-no-ura in A.D. 1185, Yoritomo, the chief of the Minamotos, rose to supreme power, and obtained from the Court at Kyōto the title of *Shōgun*, literally "Generalissimo," which had till then been applied in its proper meaning to those generals who were sent from time to time to subdue the Ainos or rebellious provincials, but which thenceforth took to itself a special sense, somewhat as the word *Imperator* (also meaning originally "general") did in Rome. The coincidence is striking. So is the contrast.

For, as Imperial Rome never ceased to be theoretically a republic, Japan contrariwise, though practically and indeed avowedly ruled by the Shōguns from A.D. 1190 to 1867, always retained the Mikado as theoretical head of the state, descendant of the Sun-Goddess, fountain of all honour. There never were two emperors, acknowledged as such, one spiritual and one secular, as has been so often asserted by European writers. There never was but one emperor,—an emperor powerless, it is true, seen only by the women who attended him, often a mere infant in arms, who was discarded on reaching adolescence for another infant in arms. Still, he was the theoretical head of the state, whose authority was only delegated to the Shōgun as, so to say, Mayor of the Palace.

By a curious parallelism of destiny, the Shōgunate itself more than once showed signs of fading away from substance into shadow. Yoritomo's descendants did not prove worthy of him and for more than a century (A.D. 1205–1333) the real authority was wielded by the so-called " Regents " of the Hōjō family, while their liege lords, the Shōguns, though holding a nominal court at Kamakura, were for all that period little better than empty names. So completely were the Hōjōs masters of the whole country that they actually had their deputy governors at Kyōto and in Kyūshū in the south-west, and thought nothing of banishing Mikados to distant islands. Their rule was made memorable by the repulse of the Mongol fleet sent by Kublai Khan with the purpose of adding Japan to his gigantic dominions. This was at the end of the thirteenth century, since which time Japan has never been attacked from without.

During the fourteenth century, even the dowager-like calm of the Court of Kyōto was broken by internecine strife. Two branches of the Imperial house, supported each by different feudal chiefs, disputed the crown. One was called the *Hokuchō*, or " Northern Court," the other the *Nanchō*, or " Southern Court." After lasting some sixty years, this contest terminated in A.D. 1392 by the triumph of the Northern dynasty, whose cause the powerful Ashikaga family had espoused. From 1338 down to the close of the sixteenth century, the Ashikagas ruled

Japan as Shōguns. Their Court was a centre of elegance, at which painting flourished, and the lyric drama, and the tea ceremonies, and the highly intricate arts of gardening and flower arrangement. But they allowed themselves to sink into effeminacy and sloth, as the Mikados had done before them; and political authority, after being for some time administered less by them than in their name, fell from them altogether in 1573, although the last representative of the line continued to bear the empty title of Shōgun till his death in 1597.

Meanwhile Japan had been discovered by the Portuguese (A.D. 1542) ; and the imprudent conduct of the Portuguese and Spanish friars (*bateren,* as they were called—a corruption of the word *padre*) made of the Christian religion an additional source of discord. Japan fell into utter anarchy. Each baron in his fastness was a law unto himself. Then, in the latter half of the sixteenth century, there arose successively three great men,—Oda Nobunaga, the Taikō Hideyoshi,* and Tokugawa Ieyasu. The first of these conceived the idea of centralising all the authority of the state in a single person; the second, Hideyoshi, who has been called the Napoleon of Japan, actually made himself master of the whole country, and added the invasion of Korea (A.D. 1592–1598) to his domestic triumphs as a preliminary step towards the conquest of China. Shortly after his death in 1598, Ieyasu, setting Hideyoshi's youthful son aside, stepped into the vacant place. An able general, unsurpassed as a diplomat and administrator, he first quelled all the turbulent barons, then bestowed a considerable portion of their lands on his own kinsmen and dependents, and either broke or balanced, by a judicious distribution of other fiefs over different provinces of the empire, the might of those greater feudal lords, such as Satsuma and Chōshū, whom it was impossible to put altogether out of the way. The Court of Kyōto was treated by him respectfully, and investiture as Shōgun for himself and his heirs duly obtained from the Mikado.

---

* *Taikō*(大閤), which means " great councillor," was the recognised title of a retired regent (*kwanpaku*); but being rarely applied to any except Hideyoshi, it has almost come to form part of his name in popular parlance.

In order further to break the might of the Daimyōs, Ieyasu compelled them to pass every alternate year at Yedo, which he had chosen for his capital in 1590, and to establish their wives and families permanently there as hostages. What Iyeyasu sketched out, the third Shōgun of his line, Iemitsu, perfected. From that time forward, " Old Japan," as we know it from the Dutch accounts, from art, from the stage, was crystallised for two hundred and fifty years,—the Old Japan of isolation (for Iemitsu shut the country up, to prevent complications with the Spaniards and Portuguese), the Old Japan of picturesque feudalism, of *harakiri*, of a society ranged in castes and officered by spies and censors, the Old Japan of an ever-increasing skill in lacquer and porcelain, of aristocratic punctilio, of supremely exquisite taste.

Unchangeable to the outward eye of contemporaries, Japan had not passed a hundred years under the Tokugawa regime before the seeds of the disease which finally killed that regime were sown. Strangely enough, the instrument of destruction was historical research. Ieyasu himself had been a great patron of literature. His grandson, the second Prince of Mito, inherited his taste. Under the auspices of this Japanese Mæcenas a school of literati arose, to whom the antiquities of their country were all in all,—Japanese poetry and romance, as against the Chinese Classics; the native religion, Shintō, as against the foreign religion, Buddhism; hence, by an inevitable extension, the ancient legitimate dynasty of the Mikados, as against the upstart Shōguns. Of course this political portion of the doctrine of the literary party was kept in the background at first; for those were not days when opposition to the existing government could be expressed or even hinted at without danger. Nevertheless it gradually grew in importance, so that, when Commodore Perry came with his big guns (A.D. 1853–4), he found a government already tottering to its fall, many who cared little for the Mikado's abstract rights caring a great deal for the chance of aggrandising their own families at the Shōgun's expense.

The Shōgun yielded to the demands of Perry and of the representatives of the other foreign powers—England, France,

Russia—who followed in Perry's train, and he consented to open Yokohama, Hakodate, and certain other ports to foreign trade and residence (1857–9). He even sent embassies to the United States and to Europe in 1860 and 1861. The knowledge of the outer-world possessed by the Court of Yedo, though not extensive, was sufficient to assure the Shōgun and his advisers that it were vain to refuse what the Western powers claimed. The Court of Kyōto had no means of acquiring even this modicum of worldly wisdom. According to its view, Japan, " the land of the gods," should never be polluted by outsiders, the ports should be closed again, and the " barbarians " expelled at all hazards.

What specially tended to complicate matters at this crisis was the independent action of certain Daimyōs. One of them, the Prince of Chōshū, acting, as is believed, under secret instructions from the Court of Kyōto, fired on ships belonging to France, Holland, and the United States,—this, too, at the very moment (1863) when the Shōgun's government, placed between foreign aggression and home tumult, as between hammer and anvil, was doing its utmost to effect by diplomacy the departure of the foreigners whom it had been driven to admit a few years before. The consequence of this act was what is called " the Shimonoseki Affair," namely, the bombardment of Shimonoseki, Chōshū's chief seaport, by the combined fleets of the powers that had been insulted, together with Great Britain which espoused their cause on the ground of the solidarity of all foreign interests in Japan. An indemnity of $3,000,000 was exacted,—a last blow, which broke the Shōgunate's back. The Shōgun Iemochi attempted to punish Chōshū for the humiliation which he had brought on Japan, but failed, was himself defeated by the latter's troops, and died. Hitotsu-bashi (also called Keiki), the last of his line, succeeded him. But the Court of Kyōto, prompted by the great Daimyōs of Chōshū and Satsuma, suddenly decided on the abolition of the Shōgunate. The Shōgun submitted to the decree, and those of his followers who did not were routed,— first at Fushimi near Kyōto (17th January, 1868), then at

Ueno in Yedo (4th July, 1868), then in Aizu (6th November, 1868), and lastly at Hakodate (27th June, 1869), where some of them had endeavoured to set up an independent republic.

The government of the country was reorganised during 1867–8, nominally on the basis of a pure absolutism, with the Mikado as sole wielder of all authority both legislative and executive. Thus the literary party had triumphed. All their dreams were realised. They were henceforth to have Japan for the Japanese. The Shōgunate, which had admitted the hated barbarians, was no more. Even their hope of supplanting Buddhism by the national religion, Shintō, was in great measure accomplished. They believed that not only European innovations, but everything—even Japanese—that was newer than A.D. 500, would be forever swept away. Things were to go back to what they had been in the primitive ages, when Japan was really " the land of the gods."

From this dream they were soon roughly wakened. The shrewd warriors of Satsuma and Chōshū, who had humoured the ignorance of the Court and the fads of the scholars only as long as their common enemy, the Shōgunate, remained in existence, now turned round, and declared in favour, not merely of foreign intercourse, but of the Europeanisation of their own country. History has never witnessed a more sudden *volte-face*. History has never witnessed a wiser one. We foreigners, being mere lookers-on, may no doubt sometimes regret the substitution of commonplace European ways for the glitter, the glamour of picturesque Orientalism. But can it be doubtful which of the two civilisations is the higher, both materially and intellectually ? And does not the whole experience of the last three hundred years go to prove that no Oriental state which retains distinctively Oriental institutions can hope to keep its territory free from Western aggression ? What of India ? What even of China ? And what was Commodore Perry's visit but a threat to the effect that if Japan chose to remain Oriental, she should not be allowed to remain her own mistress ? From the moment when the intelligent Samurai of the leading Daimiates realised that the

Europeanisation of the country was a question of life and death, they (for to this day the government has continued practically in their hands) have never ceased carrying on the work of reform and progress.

The first and greatest step was when the Daimyōs themselves came forward to surrender their estates and privileges,—when, in fact, the Japanese feudal system ended appropriately by committing *harakiri*. A centralised bureaucracy was set up on its ruins (1871). At the same time all social disabilities were removed, Buddhism was disestablished, an Imperial mint opened, and posts and telegraphs—followed next year by railways—were introduced. In 1873 vaccination, the European dress for officials were adopted, and the persecution of Christians was stopped. At the same time photography, meat eating, and other " Europeanisms " came pell-mell into vogue, not without official encouragement; and an edict was issued against wearing the queue. Steamship companies were established (1875–1885), torture was abolished, an immense financial reform was effected by the commutation of the Samurai's pensions (1876), a Bourse and Chamber of Commerce were inaugurated at Tōkyō (1878), new codes, inspired by the Code Napoleon, began to be published (1880), a Supreme Court of Justice was instituted (1883), and the English language was introduced into the curriculum of the common schools (1884). Most notable, next to 1873, were 1885–7, the years of the great " foreign fever," when Japanese society was literally submerged in a flood of European influence, such things as foreign dress for ladies, dancing, athletics, card-playing, etc., etc., coming in with a rush, while what is still remembered as the *Ō-jishin*, or " Great Earthquake," shook the political world. Then were administrative methods reformed, the hitherto excessive number of officials reduced, and new men, such as Itō and Inoue—names still the most famous in the land—assumed the highest posts.

Meantime, this energetic government had put down no less than three provincial risings,—the Higo Rebellion of 1876, the far more dangerous Satsuma Rebellion of 1877, headed by the ex-loyalist leader Saigō Takamori, who had taken umbrage at the ultra-European leanings of his colleagues, and the Saitama insurrection of 1884. Radical discontent, too, had been kept in check by stringent regulations concerning the press and public meetings, and by the " Peace Preservation Act " which banished numerous agitators and suspects from the capital; and foreign relations with the neighbouring Asiatic states had been conducted with vigour, the Formosan pirates having been chastised by an armed Japanese force in 1874, and Luchu annexed by diplomatic means in 1879. During these years of breathless activity, Europeanisation was sometimes pushed into finical details. For instance, our dreary Philistine institution of exhibitions was swallowed at a gulp,—yards of tape, cakes of soap, etc., all complete, and brand-new orders of knighthood (1875) and aristocracy (1884) were created,— sickly plants surely, which, in this age, may vegetate but cannot flourish. Such vagaries not unnaturally led many grave judges to shake their heads, especially abroad, where perhaps even to this day few thoroughly appreciate the fact that the Japanese of the old regime were no mere barbarians, but a community as highly cultured as it was intelligent,—a community moralised, humanised in the simple but wholesome school of the Chinese sages, knit together by the closest political and social bonds, and even to some slight extent penetrated by, or at least prepared for, European ideas by the Dutch influence emanating from Nagasaki, which was none the less real because it trickled underground.

But to return. The failure, in 1887, of long-protracted negotiations for treaty revision made of that year a turning-point in modern Japanese history. A strong reaction set in against foreigners and their ways, leading occasionally to murderous attacks on foreign residents and even to one on the present Czar of Russia, who happened, as Czarewitch, to be visiting Japan in 1891. Notwithstanding reaction, however, a long-promised Constitution, modelled to some extent on that of Prussia, was granted in 1889. Unfortunately it failed from the very beginning to work smoothly, and the average life of ministries has been only about twelve months. Summary suspension, following on violent altercations, has come to be looked forward to as the most likely fate of the yearly session. Meanwhile the gradual development of divers political parties in the state has helped to induce considerable exacerbation of feeling, and the spread of bribery and corruption has tended to lower the standard of public life. Besides the promulgation, from time to time, of the new codes (see Article on LAW), the most important administrative events of the last few years have been the promulgation of the Local Self-Government Act in 1888, the granting of bounties for navigation and ship-building in 1896, and the adoption of the gold standard in 1897. In international politics, the revision of the treaties with the various great powers calls for prominent notice. That with England was concluded first, in August, 1894; that with the United States a few months later. Great patriotic satisfaction was felt when, in 1899, these new treaties came into force, bringing all resident foreigners within the scope of Japanese law. At the same time the whole country was thrown open to them for trade and residence, a change which must more and more tend to Europeanise even the remoter rural districts. Moreover, despite what has just been said about the imperfect working of the constitutional machine, the nation is gradually developing a true political instinct. Though Oriental by geographical position and sturdily national in sentiment, it has become Western in its aims and methods.

War has been an all-important factor during the last decade, —all-important, because military successes have raised Japan to the rank of a great power. So long as her improvements were economc, administrative, scientific, and humanitarian merely, Europe looked on patronisingly, as at the college exercises of a clever, forward lad. But when this same lad showed himself to be a thorough man of war, Europe's tone began to change.

There have been three wars during the last ten years. The first, which took place in 1894–5, was waged against China to settle a long-standing dispute between the two empires about Korea. In it Japan demonstrated (what Europe should have discovered long ago) that the supposed political might of the Chinese empire was but a bubble waiting to be pricked. Within a year of the declaration of hostilities, China was forced to cede to Japan the peninsula of Liao-tung, besides paying a heavy indemnity. But European respect could not be gained all at once. Russia, which was then counted as irresistibly strong, wanted Liao-tung for herself; so she issued a summons to her humble follower France, and also to the Court of Berlin which was bound to that of St. Petersburg by ties of hereditary friendship. The three together forbade the cession of any territory on the Chinese mainland; and Japan, unprepared to face such a coalition, had to content herself with the island of Formosa. Her mortification was great, rejoicings over the victory gained were abandoned; particularly bitter was the disillusionment caused by Germany's having joined this unholy alliance,—Germany, whom official Japan had ever admired and striven to imitate, and whose hostile interference came as a bolt from the blue.*

The second military expedition of the present reign took place in 1900. When the world looked on aghast at the spectacle of a handful of foreigners in Peking defending themselves against overwhelming odds, the Japanese contingent of the allied army was the first to bring rescue.

One incidental result of such close contact with European diplomacy and with European soldiers was to diminish the respect of the Japanese for Europe. They discovered that their revered Western instructor in science and the practical arts was no better morally than themselves,—less good, indeed; that his unctuous phrases and laboured circumlocutions were a mere veil for vulgar greed. At the same time it began to be suspected that as soldiers, too, the Westerners might be no braver than the Japanese,—less brave perhaps. When

---

* The "true inwardness" of Germany's interference on behalf of the inviolability of Chinese territory was revealed two years later (1897) by her seizure of the neighbouring district of Kiao-chow.

therefore, in 1904, Russian aggression in Manchuria and Korea had become a standing menace to Japanese independence, and repeated protests proved unavailing, Japan silently and swiftly rushed on her gigantic foe, with the result, almost incredible to European self-sufficiency, that Russia's navy was practically annihilated in little more than two months. The conflict is still in progress on land. Whatever may be its final issue, one fact has deeply impressed all those who, by long residence among the Japanese and familiarity with their language, have been able to watch the attitude of all classes during the various wars and other changes here briefly sketched:—it is the fundamental sturdiness and healthiness of the national character. The assumed intellectual inferiority of Far-Eastern nations—at least of *this* Far-Eastern nation—to Europeans has been disproved. Disproved, likewise, is the supposed moral inferiority of " heathen " nations—at least of *this* " heathen " nation—to Christians. For no one fully cognisant of the events of the last forty years can allege that any Christian European nation could have shown itself readier to acknowledge its former errors, more teachable in all the arts of civilisation, franker and more moderate in diplomacy, more chivalrous and humane in war. If there be any " Yellow Peril," it must surely consist in Europe's own good qualities being surpassed by a higher grade of those same qualities in her new rivals. Such are the astonishing results of forty years of hard work on the part of a whole nation, which saw itself in a bad way, and resolutely determined to mend it.

* * * * * * * * * *

It is not possible to conclude this sketch of Japanese history with the usual formula, " Books recommended,"—for the reason that there are no general histories of Japan to recommend. The chapters devoted to history in the works of Griffis, Rein, David Murray, etc., hold, it is true, a respectable position as embodying the usual traditional account of the subject.

Brinkley, too, in his *Japan and China,* lets in welcome light on one highly important side of the subject, namely, manners and customs and the growth of various arts. But in the domain of history proper his loose method, his failure to quote original authorities, and above all his lack of the critical faculty render him an unsafe guide, except for the events of the last forty years whose gradual unfolding he has personally watched. Thus, a trustworthy history of Japan remains to be written,—a work which should do for every century what Mr. Aston has done for the earliest centuries only,* and Mr. Murdoch for the single century from 1542 to 1651. Here more than anywhere else is it necessary to listen at backdoors, to peep through conventional fences, and to sift native evidence by the light of foreign testimony. We should know next to nothing of what may be termed the Catholic episode of the sixteenth and seventeenth centuries, had we access to none but the official Japanese sources. How can we trust those same sources when they deal with times yet more remote ? There seems little doubt that the ruling powers at any given time manipulated both the more ancient records and the records of their own age, in order to suit their own private ends. Sometimes, indeed, the process may have been almost unconscious. The modern Japanese themselves are beginning to awake to these considerations, so far as the centuries immediately preceding their own are concerned. Dr. Shigeno An-eki, for instance, the greatest living authority on Japanese history, has undertaken to prove how certain historical episodes were " cooked " under the Tokugawa dynasty of Shōguns. But the process of " cooking " still persists, as may be seen by any critical pair of eyes that will take the trouble to examine contemporary official documents, and more especially the text-books published for use in the schools. Quite interesting is

---

* See his essay entitled *Early Japanese History,* printed in Vol. XVI. Part I. of the " Asiatic Transactions," and his elaborately annotated translation of the " *Nihongi,*" published by the Japan Society in 1896. The former approaches the subject chiefly from the Chinese, the latter from the Japanese, side. Murdoch's work is entitled *A History of Japan from A.D. 1542 down to the Present Time,* but only Vol. I., bringing the story down to 1651, has yet appeared. Compare our notice of this excellent work on p. 67.

the naiveté of the effort so to trim and pare the records of
the past as to make it appear that the spirit now ruling the
nation has been, to use a consecrated phrase. " unbroken for
ages eternal."

A little reflection will show that such manipulations of history
are likely to be the rule rather than the exception in Oriental
countries. The love of truth for truth's sake is not a general
human characteristic, but one of the exceptional traits of the
Modern European mind, developed slowly by many causes,
chiefly by those habits of accuracy which physical science does
so much to foster. The concern of ancient peoples and of
Oriental peoples has always been, not so much truth as
edification. Outside Europe and her colonies it is easy to
manipulate records, because such manipulation shocks no one
deeply, because the people are told nothing about the matter,
and because, even if they were told, they have neither the
means nor the inclination to be critical.

Meanwhile, in her attitude towards historical studies, as
in all else, Japan is undergoing a metamorphosis. Her literati
have been fired with the desire to emulate Europe the critical
and accurate, and government has laudably, if somewhat
spasmodically, encouraged their efforts, by occasionally
devoting a small yearly sum to the defrayal of expenses. An
enormous amount of historical material has been unearthed
from the archives of the ex-Daimyōs, from temple records, and
other miscellaneous sources, dealing not with state occurrences
only, but with trade, industry, literature, manners and customs,
everything in short that goes to make up the life of a nation.
This text, arranged chronologically with widely varied
illustrations, is slowly passing through the press, and is
expected to fill 300 volumes of 1,000 pages each, while
reproductions (some of them in facsimile) of over 100,000
documents will fill 200 volumes more of 600 pages each. 1915
has been announced as the probable date of completion. Such
is the *Dai Nihon Shiryō,* or " Materials for the History of
Great Japan," with its sequel the *Dai Nihon Kobunsho,* or

kakke patients, who, having been sent to the hills for change of air, have left a legacy of their disease to the inhabitants.

Kakemono. The _kakemono,_ or hanging scroll, is the form in which Japanese paintings are usually mounted. It takes the place of the framed picture of Europe; but the number of _kakemonos_ displayed in any single room is limited to one, a pair, or a set of three. Custom has moreover fixed on the _tokonoma,_ or alcove, as the only part of the room in which these scrolls shall be hung, and prescribes rigid rules for the dimensions and other details of the mounting.

The invention of this method of showing off pictures and preserving them—for when not displayed, the _kakemono_ is always tightly rolled up and stored away—goes back to very early Chinese days. Sometimes the _kakemono_ contains, instead of a picture, some valued specimen of calligraphy. For Far-Eastern painting is a sort of writing, and the writing a sort of painting, and calligraphic skill is no less esteemed than skill in the painter's art.

The _gaku_ is another Japanese method of mounting pictures, which more closely resembles the framed picture of Europe, but occupies quite a subsidiary place.

Books recommended. _Cha-No-Yu: The Japanese Tea Ceremony_ by A. L. Sadler; _Japanese Prints: From the Early Masters to the Modern_ by James A. Michener.

Lacquer. It is acknowledged by all connoisseurs that in the art of lacquer the Japanese far surpass their teachers, the Chinese. This may be partly because the lacquer-tree, though also apparently introduced from China, finds in Japan a more congenial climate; but we shall scarcely err in attributing the superiority chiefly to the finer esthetic instincts of the Japanese. So exactly did lacquer-work suit their taste and talent, that they were already producing triumphs in this

"Ancient Documents of Great Japan,"—works evidently destined to rank among those which are "more admired than read," but which perhaps some future Japanese historian, without "cooking," in the bad sense of the term, will judiciously boil down into something more palatable.

Books recommended. *Japan: An Attempt at Interpretation* by Lafcadio Hearn; *The Japanese Fairy Book* by Yei Theodora Ozaki.

Incense Parties. There is an elaborate ceremonial called *kiki-kō*, or "incense-sniffing," that has been a favourite ever since A.D. 1500, and still counts its votaries among esthetically minded persons. The gist of it is this:—The host produces, from among a score of different kinds of incense, five kinds, to each of which he affixes at pleasure a new name founded on some literary allusion, and each name receives a number The various kinds are then burnt in irregular order, sometimes in combinations of two or three kinds, and the guests have to write down the corresponding numbers on slips of paper by means of certain signs symbolical of the chapters in a celebrated classical romance called *Genji Mono-gatari*. He who guesses best wins a prize. When the nose gets jaded by much smelling, it is restored to normal discrimination by means of vinegar.

All this will sound to the foreign reader like an innocent, not to say insipid, little *jeu de société,* such as might suggest itself to a party of school-girls. But remember that Old Japan was in its childhood,—its second childhood. The art, the science, the mystery of incense sniffing was practised by priests, Daimyōs, and other reverend seigniors. The incense-burners and other utensils employed were rare works of art, the meetings were conducted with grave etiquette, serious treatises have been written on the subject,—in a word, incense-sniffing, coming next to the tea ceremonies in the estimation of men of taste, was a pastime at once erudite and aristocratic, and one which no Japanese would ever have thought of joking about. Nor need a European joke about it. Have we not rather cause for wonder, perplexity, almost awe, in the spectacle of a nation's intellect going off on such devious tracks

as this incense-sniffing and the still more intricate tea
ceremonies, and on bouquets arranged philosophically, and
gardens representing the cardinal virtues ? Such strict rules,
such grave faces, such endless terminologies, so much ado
about nothing !

This article, read together with the Articles on ESOTERICISM
and the TEA CEREMONIES and with portions of those on FLOWERS
and GARDENS, will afford a glimpse into a singular phase of
the Oriental character,—its proneness to dwell on subjects
simply because they are old and mysterious, its love of
elaborately conceived methods of killing time.

Books recommended. *The Book of Tea* by Kakuzo Okakura; *Cha-No-Yu: The
Japanese Tea Ceremony* by A. L. Sadler; *The Ideals of the East with Special Reference
to the Art of Japan* by Kakuzo Okakura; *Japan: An Attempt at Interpretation* by Lafcadio Hearn.

Indian Influence on Japan is a vast and somewhat obscure
subject, which the present writer does not feel himself fitted
to cope with:—he merely suggests it in the hope that some
better-equipped scholar will take it up and do it justice. In a
sense Japan may be said to owe everything to India; for from
India came Buddhism, and Buddhism brought civilisation,—
Chinese civilisation; but then China had been far more deeply
tinged with the Indian dye than is generally admitted even by
the Chinese themselves. The Japanese, while knowing, of
course? full well that Buddhism is Indian, not only habitually
underrate the influence of Buddhism in great matters; they
have no adequate notion of the way in which smaller details
of their lives and thoughts have been moulded by it. They do
not realise, for instance, that the elderly man or woman who
becomes, as they say, *inkyo,* that is, hands over the care of the
household to the next generation, and amuses him or herself
by going to the theatre or visiting friends,—they do not realise
that this cheery and eminently practical old individual is the
lineal representative of the deeply religious Brahman
householder, who, at a certain age,—his worldly duties
performed,—retired to the solitude of the forest, there to
ponder on the vanity of all phenomena, and attain to the

absorption of self in the world-soul through profound metaphysical meditation. Or take the complications treated of in our Article on NAMES:—the "true name," which is kept secret, is an Indian heritage. The fire-drill for producing the sacred fire at the great Shintō shrines of Ise and Izumo seems to be Indian; the elaboration of ancestor-worship seems to be Indian; all philological research in the Far-East is certainly of Indian origin, even to the arranging of the Japanese syllabaries in their familiar order. Not only can some of the current fairy-tales be traced to stories told in the Buddhist sutras, but so can some of the current fairy-tales be traced to stories told in the Buddhist sutras, but so can some of the legends of the Shintō religion, notwithstanding the claim confidently put forward, and too easily accepted by European writers, to the effect that everything Shintō is purely aboriginal. The very language has been tinctured, many learned words being of Indian derivation, and even a few common ones, such as *abata*, " pock-marks ; " *aka*, " water baled out of a boat ; " *baka*,* " fool ; " *dabi*, " cremation ; " *danna*, " master," originally " parishioner " (lit. " giver," that is, " contributor to a temple ") ; *hachi*, " bowl ; " *kawara*, " tile ; " *sendan* " sand-wood " (we English having borrowed the same Indian word for this Indian thing) ; *sora*, " the sky ; "—to say nothing of such words connected with religion as *garan*, " temple ; " *shamon*, " priest " English *shaman* is the same word) ; *kesa*, " vestment ; " *shari*, " relic," and numerous others. Indian of course is all Buddhist religious architecture and sculpture ; Indian is the use of tea now so characteristic of China and Japan ; India has dictated the national diet, fostering rice-culture and discrediting the use of flesh, which seems to have been a staple article of Japanese food in pre-Buddhistic days.

We jot down the above just as they occur to us. The idea suggested will bear elaboration, the steps of the process being

---

* Popularly derived from *ba*, "horse," and (shika), "stag," because of a story related of an ancient Chinese emperor who was such a ninny that, when told by his favourite that a stag was a horse, he actually believed him. But philologists do not accept this ingenious etymology.

in each case these:—first from India to China, second from China to Korea, third from Korea to Japan; or else from China to Japan direct, without Korean intervention, but this less often except in comparatively recent times.

Industrialism. About the year 1880, industrialism leapt into existence in this land which, under the old regime, had been divided between an exclusive aristocracy and a humble peasantry, both extremely simple in their tastes. Now almost every town has its sheaf of smoke-stacks, five thousand breaking the sky-line in Ōsaka and its suburbs alone. But why attempt to give statistics which a few weeks will turn into ancient history? Not a month passes without seeing new manufactories of cement, carpets, soap, glass, umbrellas, hats, matches, watches, bicycles, smelting-works, electrical works, steel foundries, machine-shops of every sort. Nor is everything left to private enterprise; government steps in with liberal bounties. The silk industry, once confined to certain narrow districts, is fast spreading over the entire centre and south. Formerly the Nakasendō was an old-world trail among the mountains. The last time we travelled along the new, finely graded carriage road, we were wakened every morning by the scream of the factory whistle. Journeying on and reaching the town of Kōfu, we found its silk filatures to be now its most noteworthy sight, troops of girls coming in at five every morning and working straight on till eight at night,—fifteen hours at a stretch!

The cloud of discontent that has darkened industrialism in the West already begins to obscure the Japanese sky. The " rights of labour " are asserting themselves. We hear of frequent strikes, than which nothing can be imagined further from the whole mental attitude of the working class of even seventeen years ago. For them, as for subjects generally, the watchword was, not rights, but duties. Now quite a new spirit is abroad. The spread of this spirit, the sudden rise in prices and consequently in wages since the China war of 1894–5, and the adoption of a gold standard have affected Japanese industrialism unfavourably. Neither has Japanese ambition been content with those fields of industrial activity, where natural adavntages counterbalanced the lack of experience, organisation, and capital. It is probably true also that Japanese labour and Far-Eastern labour generally is less cheap in the long run than appears at first sight; the result of the mechanic's daily toil has been found inferior in quality, and especially in quantity, to that of his Western rival. Doubtless, Japan is passing from the agricultural into the industrial stage, and she may look forward to a bright future, with China's huge market at her gates. Nevertheless, so far as our own mills and factories are concerned, we see little reason for alarm at the prospect of competition in this quarter.

Two or three of the characteristically Japanese industries, or rather arts—for arts they were—such as lacquer and wood-engraving, have been treated separately in this book. But to walk amidst the din of sledge-hammers and the smoke of factory chimneys is not to our taste, neither have we the talent to discourse of the two thousand three hundred odd Japanese banks, or of the brand-new insurance companies, or of the joint-stock companies which, after all, are not things Japanese, but things European recently transplanted.

Book recommended. *The New Far East* compiled by International Research Associates.

Japan. Our word "Japan," and the Japanese *Nihon* or Nippon, are alike corruptions of *Jih-pên,* the Chinese pronunciation of the characters 日本 literally "sun-origin," that is, "the place the sun comes from,"—a name given to Japan by the Chinese on account of the position of the archipelago to the east of their own country. Marco Polo's *Zipangu* and the poets' *Cipango* are from the same Chinese compound, with the addition of the word *kuo* (Jap. *koku*), 國 which means "country."

The name *Nihon* ("Japan") seems to have been first officially employed by the Japanese government in A.D. 670.

Before that time, the usual native designation of the country was *Yamato,* properly the name of one of the central provinces. *Yamato* and *Ō-mi-kuni,* that is, " the Great August Country," are the names still preferred in poetry and belles-lettres. Japan has other ancient names, some of which are of learned length and thundering sound, for instance, *Toyo-ashi-wara-no-chi-aki-no-naga-i-ho-aki-no-mizu-ho-no-kuni,* that is, " the-Luxuriant-Reed - Plains - the - Land - of - Fresh - Rice - Ears - of - a-Thousand-Autumns-of-Long-Five-Hundred-Autumns." But we shall not detain the reader with an enumeration of them. Any further curiosity on this head may be satisfied by consulting the pages of the *" Kojiki "* (see " Asiatic Transactions," Vol. X., Supplement).

Japanese People (Characteristics of the). Any account of the characteristics of a people must deal with two main points, namely, physical characteristics and mental characteristics. We will first say a few words about the physical characteristics, referring those who desire exhaustive information to Dr. Baelz's admirable monograph entitled *Die Körperlichen Eigenschaften der Japaner,* printed in Parts 28 and 32 of the " German Asiatic Transactions."

1. PHYSICAL CHARACTERISTICS. As stated in the Article entitled RACE, the Japanese are Mongols, that is, they are distinguished by a yellowish skin, straight black hair, scanty beard, almost total absence of hair on the arms, legs, and chest, broadish prominent cheek-bones, and more or less obliquely set eyes. These, with the other characteristics to be mentioned presently, are common both to the more slenderly built, oval-faced aristocracy, and to pudding-faced Gombei, the " Hodge " of Japanese Arcadia. Compared with people of European race, the average Japanese has a long body and short legs, a large skull with a tendency to prognathism (projecting jaws), a flat nose, coarse hair, scanty eye-lashes, puffy eyelids, a sallow complexion, and a low stature. The average stature of Japanese men is about the same as the average stature of

European women. The women are proportionately smaller. The lower classes are mostly strong, with well-developed arms, legs, and chests. The upper classes are too often weakly.

The above description will perhaps not be considered flattering. But it is not ours; it is the doctors'. Then, too, ideals of beauty differ from land to land. We Anglo-Saxons consider ourselves a handsome race. But what are we still, in the eyes of the majority of the Japanese people, but a set of big, red, hairy barbarians with green eyes ?

The Japanese women are, on the whole, better-looking than the men, and have, besides, pretty manners and charming voices.* Village beauties are rare, most girls of the lower class with any pretentions to good looks being, as it would seem, sent out to service at tea-houses in the towns, or else early obtaining husbands. Japanese children, with their dainty little ways and old-fashioned appearance, always insinuate themselves into the affections of foreign visitors. Old and young alike are remarkable for quietness of demeanor. The gesticulations of a southern European fill them with amazement, not to say contempt, and fidgeting of every kind is foreign to their nature.

The Japanese age earlier than we do. It has also been asserted they are less long-lived; but this is doubtful. If statistics may be trusted, the number of octogenarians, nonagenarians, and even centenarians is fairly high. In Japan, as in other countries, the number of very old women considerably exceeds that of the very old men. The diseases which make most havoc are consumption, disease of the digestive organs, and the peculiar affection called *kakke,* of which an account will be found in a separate article. The Japanese have less highly strung nerves than we Europeans.

---

* For a detailed analysis of the Japanese standard of female beauty, see Miss Bacon's *Japanese Girls and Women, pp.* 58—60, where also the true remark is made that foreigners long resident in Japan find their standard gradually change, " and see, to their own surprise, that their countrywomen look ungainly, fierce, aggressive, and awkward among the small, mild, shrinking, and graceful Japanese ladies."

Hence they endure pain more calmly, and meet death with comparative indifference.*

II. MENTAL CHARACTERISTICS. The tape-line, the weighing-machine, the craniometer, and the hospital returns give means of ascertaining a nation's physical characteristics ? which almost any one can apply and which none may dispute. Far different is it when we try to gauge the phenomena of mind. Does a new-comer venture on the task ? He is set down as a sciolist, a man without experience—the one thing declared needful. Does an old resident hold forth, expecting his experience to command attention ? The *Globe-trotter journalisticus* from London, or may be the cultured Bostonian literary critic, jumps upon him, tells him that living too long in one place has given him mental myopia, in other words has rendered his judgment prejudiced and worthless. The late Mr. Gifford Palgrave said, in the present writer's hearing, that an eight weeks' residence was the precise time qualifying an intelligent man to write about Japan. A briefer period (such was his ruling) was sure to produce superficiality, while a longer period induced a wrong mental focus. By a curious coincidence, eight weeks was the exact space of time during which that brilliant conversationalist and writer had been in Japan when he delivered himself of this oracle.

Again, are you in the Japanese service, and do you praise Japan ? Then you must be a sycophant. Do you find fault with it ? " Ah ! don't you know ? " it will be said, " when they renewed his engagement the other day, they cut his salary down $50 a month." Worse of all is it if you are a Yokohama merchant. Then you are informed flatly that you are an ignoramus, a " dollar-grinder," and that, as you never

---

* We have classed indifference to death among the *physical* characteristics, because none can doubt that a less sensitive nervous system must at least tend in that direction. It is possible, however, that opinions and beliefs have had some influence in the matter. Most Japanese are either agnostics looking forward to no hereafter, or they are Buddhists; and Buddhism is a tolerant, hopeful creed, promising rest at last to all, even though it may have to be purchased by the wicked at the price of numerous transmigrations. Christianity, on the other hand, with its terrible doctrine of final and hopeless perdition, may have steeped in a still more sombre hue the naturally excitable and self-questioning European mind. The Greeks and Romans appear to have faced death with an indifference to which few moderns can attain.

see any Japanese of the better class, but only coolies and hucksters, what you are pleased to call your opinion is a mere impertinence worth less than nothing.

All things considered, the would-be critic of Japanese mind, manners, and morals has a thankless task before him. The present writer feels that he cannot hope to escape being classed in some one or other of the above-named categories of pariahs not fit to have an opinion of their own. He has, therefore, decided to express none at all, but simply to quote the opinions of others. Perhaps he may thus avoid blame and unpleasantness. He has chosen the opinions impartially, or rather he has not chosen them, but taken them at random from his commonplace-book. He has not, it is true, thought fit to include all or any of the absurdities of the casual passer-by; —one French count, for instance, a stripling of twenty, who spent just three months in the country and then wrote a book about it, sums up his acquired wisdom in the tremendous assertion, " *Le japonais n'est pas intelligent.*" Of trash of this kind there is enough to fill many volumes. But who would care to wade through it ? The opinions which we quote will be seen to be in some cases judgments of the people, in others judgments of the country. But it is not practicable to separate one class from the other :—

" This nation is the delight of my soul." (St. Francis Xavier, middle of sixteenth century.)

" The people of this Iland of *Iapon* are good of nature, curteous aboue measure and valiant in warre: their justice is seuerely executed without any partialitie vpon transgressors of the law. They are gouerned in great ciuilitie. I meane, not a land better gouerned in the world by ciuill policie. The people be verie superstitious in their religion, and are of diuers opinions."—This last sentence does not fit the present day. No one now accuses the Japanese of superstitious religionism. Our author is again in touch with modern times when he speaks of " the peopell veri subject to thear gouernours and superiores." (Will Adams, early in the seventeenth century.)

" Bold,......heroic,......revengeful,......desirous of fame,
......very industrious and enured to hardships,......great
lovers of civility and good manners, and very nice in keeping
themselves, their cloaths and houses, clean and neat......As
to all sorts of handicrafts, either curious or useful, they are
wanting neither proper materials, nor industry and application, and so far is it, that they should have any occasion to
send for masters from abroad, that they rather exceed all
other nations in ingenuity and neatness of workmanship,
particularly in brass, gold, silver and copper......Now if we
proceed farther to consider the Japanese, with regard to
sciences and the embellishments of our mind, Philosophy
perhaps will be found wanting. The Japanese indeed are not
so far enemies to this Science, as to banish the Country those
who cultivate it, but they think it an amusement proper for
monasteries, where the monks leading an idle lazy life, have
little else to trouble their heads about. However, this relates
chiefly to the speculative part, for as to the moral part, they
hold it in great esteem, as being of a higher and divine origin
......I confess indeed, that they are wholly ignorant of
musick, so far as it is a science built upon certain precepts of
harmony. They likewise know nothing of mathematicks, more
especially of its deeper and speculative parts. No body ever
cultivated these sciences but we Europeans, nor did any other
nations endeavour to embellish the mind with the clear light
of mathematical and demonstrative reasoning......They
profess a great respect and veneration for their Gods, and
worship them in various ways: And I think I may affirm,
that in the practice of virtue, in purity of life, and outward
devotion, they far out-do the Christians: Careful for the
Salvation of their Souls, scrupulous to excess in the expiation
of their crimes, and extremely desirous of future happiness
......Their Laws and Constitutions are excellent, and
strictly observed, severe penalties being put upon the least
transgression of any." (ENGELBERT KAEMPFER, end of
seventeenth century.)

SIR RUTHERFORD ALCOCK, one of the most acute writers on
Japan, is also one of the most difficult to quote, as his whole

book, *The Capital of the Tycoon,* is one continued criticism of the Japan of his time (about 1860), and one would like to transcribe it all. Here are a couple of his witty sayings:

" (Japan) is a very paradise of babies."—" There is a mistake somewhere, and the result is that in one of the most beautiful and fertile countries in the whole world the flowers have no scent, the birds no song,* and the fruit and vegetables no flavour."

Sir Rutherford speaks, in his preface, of " the incorrigible tendency of the Japanese to withhold from foreigners or disguise the truth on all matters great and small." Yet he allows that they are " a nation of thirty millions of as industrious, kindly, and well-disposed people as any in the world."—Their art, too, rouses his admiration, though he makes a reservation to the effect that there are some departments in which they have failed to produce anything to be named in the same day with the masterpieces of the great artists of Europe. " Perhaps in nothing," says he, " are the Japanese to be more admired than for the wonderful genius they display in arriving at the greatest possible results with the simplest means, and the smallest possible expenditure of time and labour or material. The tools by which they produce their finest works are the simplest, and often the rudest that can be conceived. Wherever in the fields or the workshops nature supplies a force, the Japanese is sure to lay it under contribution, and make it do his work with the least expense to himself of time, money, and labour. To such a pitch of perfection is this carried, that it strikes every observer as one of the moral characteristics of the race, indicating no mean degree of intellectual capacity and cultivation."

" A brave, courteous, light-hearted, pleasure-loving people, sentimental rather than passionate, witty and humorous, of

---

* How often, we wonder, has this strange error been repeated ? We should like to take those who still credit it out upon the moors of almost any Japanese province in springtime, and let them listen to the carolling of the larks and the nightingales, or into the woods that re-echo with the note of the cuckoo and other songsters. As for Japanese flowers lacking scent, what of the fragrant plum-blossom, the cassia-tree, the lilies, jonquils, wild roses, and many more ?

nimble apprehension, but not profound; ingenious and inventive, but hardly capable of high intellectual achievement; of receptive minds endowed with a voracious appetite for knowledge; with a turn for neatness and elegance of expression, but seldom or never rising to sublimity."—But he adds, "The Japanese are never contented with simple borrowing. In art, political institutions, and even religion, they are in the habit of modifying extensively everything which they adopt from others, and impressing on it the stamp of the national mind." (W. G. ASTON, in *A History of Japanese Literature*.)

REV. C. MUNZINGER, who has striven with considerable success, in his work entitled *Die Japaner*, to cover the whole field of a criticism of the Japanese mind and of Japanese intellectual, social, and religious life, arrives at conclusions closely similar:—"Great talent, but little genius." "Martha rather than Mary,—busy, deft, practical, somewhat superficial withal, not deep, not given to introspection." "Extraordinarily perspicacious, not profoundly contemplative." "Highly ethical, not highly religious." "An intellectual life mechanical rather than organic." And Japonisation, that is, the method whereby native insufficiency is made good by loans from abroad, is "a radical process, in which little is bent and much is broken,......a process rather of accommodation than of assimilation." Nevertheless, and "with all his lack of originality, the Japanese is a strongly marked individuality, which refuses to rest permanently content with foreign importations in their foreign shape."

"The lack of originality of the Japanese is very striking after one has got over one's first dazzle at strange antipodal sights. Modification of foreign motif, modification always artistic, and at times delightfully ingenious, marks the extent of Japanese originality......A general incapacity for abstract ideas is another marked trait of the Japanese mind...... Lastly, the decorous demeanor of the whole nation betrays the lack of mental activity beneath. For it is not rules that make the character, but character that makes the rules. No energetic mind could be bound by so exquisitely exacting an etiquette." (PERCIVAL LOWELL, in *Occult Japan*.)

" We should say . . . . that the most striking quality of the Japanese is precocity, that the keenness of their perceptions is far in advance of the soundness of their judgments, that their minds, or rather the minds of their leading classes, are always on the rush, that they receive ideas and lay aside ideas much as acute youngsters do. . . . . The Japanese upper class strike us, in fact, as the undergraduates of the human family, clever, enjoying, and full of ' go,' but as yet immature. . . . . They love change for the sake of change, take up ideas because they are startling to their seniors or to their Government or to themselves, and suffer none of them to really dye their minds with any permanent colour. . . . . They are open to all teachings, which, however, go about one inch deep. They devise a constitution which does not work, except so far as it is sustained by the old fact of the Mikado's authority; they start a press which discusses everything in the spirit of an under-graduate's wine-party; they even adopt a new costume and live in constricting uniforms before the majority have given up the habit of living in a loin-cloth. . . . . [The Japanese] has an enormous respect for the words of ancient philosophers and European writers, will quote them, as our countrymen quote proverbs, as if they ended discussion; but he does not all the while absorb this wisdom, and will pass from believing in, say, St. Augustine, to believing in, say, Mr. Grant Allen at a bound, and with no sense that he is exhibiting volatility of intellect." (From an article in the SPECTATOR of the 5th December, 1896, founded on numerous appreciations forwarded by a twenty years' resident.)

PIERRE LOTI, in his *Madame Chrysanthème* and *Japoneries d'Automne*, emphasises over and over again one particular aspect of Japanese life—its smallness, its quaintness, its comicality. Here are just a few samples of the adjectives which he sows broadcast over his pages, almost exhausting the resources of the French language in that direction: *petit*, *bizarre, disparate, hétérogène, invraisemblable, mignon, bariolé, extravagant, inimaginable, frêle, monstrueux, grotesque, mièvre, exotique, lilliputien, minuscule, maniéré,* etc., etc. The houses are all *maisonnettes;* each garden is, not a *jardin,* but a *jardinet,* each meal a *dînette,* each inscription a *griffonnage.* The Kōbe-Kyōto railway is *un drôle de petit chemin de fer, qui n'a pas l'air sérieux, qui fait l'effet d'une chose pour rire, comme toutes les choses japonaises.*—Doubless there is an element of truth in all this. Query: is it the whole truth? Pierre Loti's final and sweeping condemnation of Japan, as he was preparing to set sail, is as follows: " *Je le trouve petit, vieillot, à bout de sève; j'ai conscience de son antiquité antédiluvienne; de sa momification de tant de siècles, qui va bientôt finir dans le grotesque et la bouffonnerie pitoyable, au contact des nouveautés d'occident.*"—Such criticism, published sixteen years ago, reads oddly nowadays. Instead of Japan being at fault, it was her French detractor whose self-centred, unsympathetic attitude rendered him unfit for the comprehension of a highly complex subject.

MR. WALTER DENING, whose acquaintance with modern Japanese literature and with the men who produce it is probably unrivalled, writes as follows:

"It is well-known that one of the most marked characteristics of the Japanese mind is its lack of interest in metaphysical, psychological, and .ethical controversy of all kinds. It is seldom you can get them to pay sufficient attention to such questions to admit of their understanding even their main outlines." And again:—

" Neither their past history nor their prevailing tastes show any tendency to idealism. They are lovers of the practical and the real: neither the fancies of Goethe nor the reveries of Hegel are to their liking. Our poetry and our philosophy and the mind that appreciates them are alike the result of a network of subtle influences to which the Japanese are comparative strangers. It is maintained by some, and we think justly, that the lack of idealism in the Japanese mind renders the

life of even the most cultivated a mechanical, humdrum affair
when compared with that of Westerns. The Japanese cannot
understand why our controversialists should wax so fervent
over psychological, ethical, religious, and philosophical
questions, failing to perceive that this fervency is the result
of the intense interest taken in such subjects. The charms
that the cultured Western mind finds in the world of fancy
and romance, in questions themselves, irrespective of their
practical bearings, is for the most part unintelligible to the
Japanese."

DR. BUSSE, in his elaborate essay on the Japanese ethical
literature of the present day, complains of the want of
thoroughness, of insight, and of original thought which inclines
the leaders of Japanese opinion to a superficial eclecticism.
They attack problems, says he, with a light heart, because not
appreciating their true difficulty.

A careful and fair-minded writer says, speaking of the
danger run by Japan from European aggression during the
first years of renewed intercourse: " She was saved by the
possession of a remarkable combination of national
characteristics,—the powers of observation, of appreciation,
and of imitation. In a word, her sensitiveness to her
environment and her readiness to respond to it proved to be
her salvation." He also repeatedly asserts the Japanese to be
" an emotional people." The whole trend of his argument
however, goes to minimise racial divergences and special
aptitudes or failings. " The differences," he writes, " which
separate the Oriental from the Occidental mind are
infinitesimal as compared with the likenesses which unite
them." (REV. S. L. GULICK, in *Evolution of the Japanese.*)

In discussing their Japanese neighbours, the foreign
residents frequently advert to the matter-of-fact way of
looking at things which characterises all the nations that
have come under Chinese influence. The EDITOR of the
" JAPAN MAIL " has drawn an acute distinction between the
matter-of-fact Japanese and the *practical* European,

instancing the calculations of a pamphleteer anent a projected line of railway, the probable yearly profits of which were worked out to decimals of a cent ! The matter-of-fact Japanese calculator simply transferred to his pamphlet the figures that came out on his abacus. The practical (because also theoretical) European knows that such apparent exactness is illusory. We have ourselves often seen, when travelling through various provinces of Japan, the distances along roads (in one instance across a wide strait of the sea) given, not only down to feet, but down to *inches !*

Here are two or three shorter dicta on the land and its people :—

" The land of disappointments." (An OLD RESIDENT in the Japanese service.)

" They impress me as the ugliest and the most pleasing people I have ever seen, as well as the neatest and most ingenious." (MRS. BISHOP, in *Unbeaten Tracks in Japan*.)

" The land of gentle manners and fantastic arts." (SIR EDWIN ARNOLD.) The same author says of the Japanese: " They have the nature rather of birds or butterflies than of ordinary human beings. . . . . They will not and cannot take life *au grand sérieux*." (!!)

People are fond of drawing comparisons between the Chinese and the Japanese. Almost all seem agreed that the Japanese are much the pleasanter race to live with,—clean, kindly, artistic. On the other hand, the Chinese are universally allowed to be far more trustworthy. " I know," says SIR EWEN CAMERON, late Manager of the Hongkong and Shanghai Bank in Shanghai, " of no people in the world I would sooner trust than the Chinese merchant or banker. . . . . For the last twenty-five years the bank has been doing a very large business with Chinese in Shanghai, amounting, I should say, to hundreds of millions of taels, and we have never met with a defaulting Chinaman." Or listen (we cull at random one more testimony from among a hundred) to MR. J. HOWARD GWYTHER, chairman of the Chartered Bank of India, Australia, and

China. Speaking in 1900 at the half-yearly general meeting of the bank in London, that gentleman said: " I take this opportunity of stating that the bank has had very extensive dealings with Chinese traders, and has always found them reliable and honest. By their integrity and solvency they have shown a bright example to other mercantile communities." MR. T. R. JERNIGAN, ex-Consul-General of the United States at Shanghai, expresses himself in almost identical terms in his work entitled *China's Business Methods and Policy*, published in 1904.—Woefully different from this is the tale told by the European bankers and merchants in Japan. They complain, it is true, not so much of actual, wilful dishonesty—though of that, too, they affirm there is plenty—as of pettiness, constant shilly-shallying, unbusinesslikeness almost passing belief. Hence the wide divergence between the impressions of the holiday-making tourist, and the opinions formed by the commercial communities at the open ports. Japan, the globe-trotter's paradise, is also the grave of the merchant's hopes. Another deep-seated difference between the Chinese and the Japanese is that the former have race pride, the latter national vanity. The Chinese care nothing for China as a political unit, an abstraction, an ideal to die for if need be; but they are nevertheless inalienably wedded to every detail of their ancestral civilisation. The Japanese, though they have twice, at intervals of a millennium, thrown everything national overboard, are intense nationalists in the abstract. In fact, patriotism may be said to be their sole remaining ideal. No Chinaman but glories in the outward badges of his race; no Japanese but would be delighted to pass for a European in order to beat Europeans on their own ground. The Japanese, too, are brave almost beyond the limits of practicality. The Chinese, eminently practical folks, follow the doctrine that

> He who fights and runs away,
> May live to fight another day.

The characteristic in which the Chinese and Japanese most agree (and other Far-Eastern peoples—the Koreans for example—agree in it also) is materialism. That is where the false note is struck, which, when long residence has produced familiarity, jars on European nerves and prevents true intellectual sympathy.

One more quotation only. It is from the Rev. G. M. Meacham, a missionary of many years' standing, and epitomises what hundreds of residents have thought and said :—

" A few months do not suffice to give a correct understanding of the situation, though the visitor should enjoy the kind attention and guidance of high officials. There are perhaps no people under heaven who know better the happy art of entertaining their guests, and none perhaps who succeed better in preoccupying them with their views. Indeed, the universal experience of those who remain long enough in this country to see beneath the surface is that first impressions are very deceitful."

To sum up: the average judgment formed by those who have lived some time among the Japanese, seems to resolve itself into three principal items on the credit side, which are cleanliness, kindliness, and a refined artistic taste, and three items on the debit side, namely, vanity, unbusinesslike habits, and an incapacity for appreciating abstract ideas.

As for the imitativeness which strikes all observers, we hesitate to which side of the account to pass it. Most persons seem to blame it as a symptom of intellectual inferiority :— they term it lack of originality. By some we have heard it commended as a proof of practical wisdom in a world where most ideas of any value have been ventilated already. Whether it be good or bad, one cannot but marvel at seeing into what finicky details imitation is carried. This will strike even a new-comer, but it impresses itself on an old hand with ever-increasing force. We remember, for example, that some years ago the question was gravely debated as to whether the custom of " April fool " should or should not be introduced into Japan ! That particular suggestion happens to have been rejected; but the fact of its being mooted at all may serve to instance the extraordinary lengths to which the passion for adopting things foreign has been pushed.

So far this little symposium on the mental characteristics of the Japanese. Any one who thinks it not full enough or not representative enough, is earnestly requested to supplement it, either from his personal experience or from his reading. For our own part, we cannot but feel surprise at the way in which, like sheep jumping over a fence, one writer after another has enlarged on certain traits as characteristic of the Japanese nation, which history shows to be characteristic merely of the stage through which the nation is now passing. Their modern favour of loyalty is a good case in point:—Europe manifested exactly the same symptom on her emergence from feudalism.

Just one consideration more:—how do *our* characteristics strike the Japanese ? From hints dropped by several of the educated, and from the still more interesting, because frankly naive, remarks made by Japanese servants whom the present writer has taken with him to Europe at different times, he thinks he may state that the travelled Japanese consider our three most prominent characteristics to be dirt, laziness, and superstition. As to the comparative dirtiness, there can be no doubt in any unprejudiced mind. You yourself, honoured Madam, of course take your tub regularly every morning. But are you so sure that your butler, your coachman, even your lady's maid, as regularly take theirs ? Again, what is a stranger who hails from a land of fifteen working hours daily and of well-nigh three hundred and sixty-five working days yearly, to conclude from the habits of European artisans and servants, from post-offices closed on Sundays either totally or during portions of the day, etc., etc. ? With regard to superstition, that is a matter of individual opinion. Of our poetry, our music, our metaphysics, our interest in all manner of things scattered over the two worlds of sense and thought, the Japanese visitor to Western lands can naturally notice little and appreciate less. Neither our pictures nor our cathedrals touch any chord in his heart. On the other hand, all our materially useful inventions are already shared by his countrymen, who work them—if not quite as well—at any rate more cheaply than we do, and in ways more suitable to their peculiar needs. For all these and yet other reasons,

Europe and America make a far less favourable impression on the Japanese visitor than seems to be generally expected. Be he statesman or be he valet, he is apt to return to his native land more patriotic than he left it. (See also Article on WOMAN.)

Books recommended. *The Art of Being Japanese* by Bob Dunham; *A Daughter of the Samurai* by Etsu Inagaki Sugimoto; *It's Better with Your Shoes Off* by Anne Cleveland; *Japan: An Attempt at Interpretation* by Lafcadio Hearn; *Japan Unmasked* by Ichiro Kawasaki; *The Japanese Are Like That* by Ichiro Kawasaki; *A Japanese Miscellany* by Lafcadio Hearn; *To Live in Japan* by Mary Lee O'Neal & Virginia Woodruff.

Jinrikisha. The origin of the jinrikisha is, to use a grandiloquent phrase, shrouded in obscurity. One native account attributes the spark of invention to a paralytic old gentleman of Kyōto, who, some time before 1868, finding his palanquin uncomfortable, took to a little cart instead. According to another version, one Akiha Daisuke, of Tōkyō, was the inventor, about 1870; but the first official application to be allowed to manufacture jinrikishas was made about the same time by a man called Takayama Kōsaku. The usual foreign version is that an American named Goble, half-cobbler and half-missionary, was the person to suggest the idea of a modified perambulator somewhere about 1867; and this has the support of Mr. Black, the author of *Young Japan*. In any case, the invention, once made, found wide-spread favour. There are now over 33,000 jinrikishas and 31,600 jinrikisha-men in Tōkyō alone;† and the ports of China, the Malay peninsula, and India, as well as Japan, owe to the jinrikisha a fruitful source of employment for their teeming coolie population and of comfort for the well-to-do residents.

The compound word *jinrikisha* (人力車) means literally "man-power-vehicle," that is, a vehicle pulled by a man, or, as the late Mr. Baber wittily suggested, a "pull-man-car." Some have imagined *sha* to be a corruption of the English

---

† At the beginning of the century (1901), the number was still larger, viz. 41,000 jinrikishas and 43,000 jinrikisha-men. Since then electric trams have been introduced, whose low fares (3 *sen*, that is 3 farthings all over the city) have entailed a partial disuse of other conveyances.

" car." This is quite erroneous. *Sha* is a good old Chinese word. The poor word *jinrikisha* itself suffers many things at the hands of Japanese and foreigners alike. The Japanese generally cut off its tail and call it *jinriki,* or else they translate the Chinese syllable *sha* into their own language, and call it *kuruma.* The English cut off its head and maltreat the vowels, pronouncing it *rickshaw.* One English dictionary actually gives it as *jennyrickshaw !*

An ordinary working jinrikisha costs a little over 30 *yen,* and will last three years if repaired a couple of times yearly. Handsome private jinrikishas may come to 45 or even 50 *yen.* The total cost of the outfit of a jinrikisha-man—coat, drawers, hat, and lantern all complete—is estimated at from 2½ to 5 *yen.* The usual fare is from 15 to 25 *sen* per *ri* (2½ miles English). Many men work on their own account, their one jinrikisha being their stock in trade. These are they that loiter about the street corners, waiting for a job. Others board with, and work for, a master, or—as the more patriarchal Japanese phrase has it—a " parent " *(oya-kata),* this master owing, it may be, ten or twenty jinrikishas, and reckoning with his men twice monthly. In the large cities, a man may earn as much as 30 *yen* a month by this humble occupation, that is, more than the salary of many a small official of several years' standing, and with a far greater share of excitement, amusement, and independence. No wonder that fresh batches of lads from the country continually pour in to replace those whom consumption and heart-disease—the result of cold and over-exertion—only too swiftly remove from the busy scene. Jinrikishas are now largely exported to Shanghai and other places.

The heroes of the jinrikisha world are two men called Mukōbata and Kitaga, who, in May, 1891, saved the life of the then Czarewitch (the present Czar) from an assassin's sword, and were forthwith almost smothered under the rewards and honours that poured down upon them, alike from their own sovereign and from the Russian Court. One of them unites virtue to good fortune; the other has given himself over to riotous living.

Kaempfer. If Marco Polo was the first to bring the existence
of such a country as Japan to the knowledge of Europeans, and
Mendez Pinto the first to tread its shores, Engelbert Kaempfer
(1651–1716) may truly be called its scientific discoverer. A
native of Lemgow in Westphalia, he travelled while a youth in
northern Germany, Holland, and Poland. At the age of thirty-
two he joined the Swedish diplomatic service as secretary of
legation, in which capacity he proceeded through Russia and
Tartary to the Court of Ispahan. Eager for a sight of yet
more distant lands, he then entered the service of the Dutch
East India Company in the capacity of surgeon, sailed from
Ormuz to Batavia in 1688, and thence via Siam to Japan,
where he arrived in the month of September, 1690. At that
time, the Dutch were the only European nation permitted to
trade with Japan, and even they were confined to Deshima,
—a part of Nagasaki,—where jealous care was taken by the
authorities to keep them in ignorance of all Japanese matters.
A yearly journey to Yedo to make obeisance before the Shōgun
was the only change in their monotonous existence.

Kaempfer remained in Japan but two years and two months.
Yet, in this short period and under these disadvantageous
circumstances, he compiled a work which for the first time
gave the world fairly accurate information concerning the
history, geography, religious beliefs, manners and customs, and
natural productions of the mysterious island empire.
Returning to Europe in 1694, Kaempfer settled first at Leyden
and then in his native town, where he employed himself in
writing his two celebrated works, the *History of Japan* and the
Amœnitates Exoticæ, in practising as a physician, and in
quarrelling with the odious wife whose bad temper is said to
have aggravated the fits of colic which ended in his death.

The *History of Japan* appeared, strange to say, first in an
English translation in 1727–8; then in Latin (1728), Dutch
(1729), and French (1729). All these were translated from the
English version. Lastly, in 1777, came a German edition,—not
exactly the German original, because Kaempfer's style was so

terribly dry and involved as to make the booksellers fear that it would disgust even the German public, long-suffering as the German public is in that respect. The diction was accordingly modernised and touched up. Hence Kaempfer's work has never appeared in Kaempfer's words. Copies of all the editions are now rare, and command high prices.

Kago. The generic meaning of *kago* is "basket;" but the word is applied specifically to one particular kind made of split bamboos, having a light roof atop and sometimes a strip of cotton stuff on one side to ward off the sun's rays, and swung on a pole which two men—one in front and one behind —bear on their shoulders. This is the country *kago,* still the general means of conveyance in mountainous districts, where jinrikishas are not practicable, sometimes even where they are. The person carried squats much in the same way as the Japanese are accustomed to sit, except that the posture is semi-recumbent. He does not experience any difficulty in (so to say) abolishing his legs. The *kago* has been variously modified as to details at different times and places. The old norimono of the towns, so often mentioned by travellers of an early date in their descriptions of Daimyōs' processions, was but a glorified *kago.* Being larger and more stately, it might perhaps be termed a palanquin. The specimens preserved (for instance at the Ueno Museum in Tōkyō) show the extent to which luxury was carried in this conveyance, where the bamboo structure of its rustice prototype was exchanged for costly lacquer, where carefully fitted slides having jalousies bound with silk kept out the profane gaze of passers-by, and finely wrought metal fastenings at every available point proclaimed in heraldic language the occupant's aristocratic birth.

We are not aware at what period the *kago* was introduced. But it must have been comparatively late, as in mediæval days exalted personages escaping from the pursuit of their enemies are recorded to have done so pick-a-back on the shoulders of some sturdy henchman. Old pictures show us the Emperor Go-Daigo fleeing in this guise somewhere about the year 1333.

At that period the only known vehicles seem still to have been those lumbering bullock-carts so often pourtrayed in art, which had for centuries served the Japanese nobility in their pleasure parties round the old capital, Kyōto. But probably it was only round the capital that roads on which they could be used existed, nor were they in any case applicable to occasions demanding speed and secrecy.

Kakke is the same disease as that known in India and the Malay peninsula under the name of *beri-beri,* and may be defined in popular language as a sort of paralysis, as it is characterised by loss of motive power and by numbness, especially in the extremities. It is often accompanied by dropsy. All these symptoms are due to a degeneration of the nerves, which is the main anatomical feature of the complaint. In severe cases it affects the heart, and may then become rapidly fatal, though the usual course of the disease extends over several months, and mostly ends in recovery. But he who has had one attack may expect another after an interval of a year or two. Some persons have had as many as ten or even twenty attacks, all setting in with the warm weather and disappearing in the autumn. *Kakke* attacks with special frequency and virulence young and otherwise healthy men,— women much less often, scarcely ever indeed except during pregnancy and after childbirth. Children of both sexes enjoy almost absolute immunity. The disease springs, in the opinion of some medical authorities, not from actual malaria, as was formerly imagined, but from a climatic influence resembling malaria. Others have sought its origin in the national diet,— some in rice, some in fish. In favour of this latter view is to be set the consideration that the peasantry, who often cannot afford either rice or fish, and have to eat barley or millet instead, suffer much less than the townsfolk, and the further fact that an extraordinary improvement in this respect has been observed in the health of the Japanese navy ever since Dr. Takagi, late Surgeon-General, introduced a meat and bread diet for the seamen.* Dr. Scriba, Emeritus Professor of Surgery at the Imperial University of Tōkyō, traverses both these opinions.† According to him, it is the crowding together of men in spaces imperfectly ventilated, especially when these spaces are covered with mats which are rarely taken up or renewed, that favours the development of the germs of the malady. The change of diet has had no direct influence in ridding the navy of *kakke*. What has done so is the increased attention paid of recent years to cleanliness and ventilation, combined with the general open-air life of the seamen. He compares the suppression of *kakke* in the navy to the suppression of hyæmia, erysipelas, etc., in hospitals since the introduction of hygienic and antiseptic precautions. This opinion gains weight from the notorious fact of the influence of crowding in propagating the disease, and from its comparative frequency in low alluvial situations.

Whether *kakke* is indigenous or imported, is a question that cannot yet be answered; but the latter alternative seems the more probable, as the first mention of it occurs only two hundred years ago. Then, and till about fifty years ago, it was confined to a few ports on the Pacific coast of Japan and to some large cities in constant communication with those ports, such as Kyōto; and in all these localities, barracks, schools, and prisons were the places most affected. The construction of railways, steamers, and carriage roads has converted *kakke* from a local into a national scourge. Restricting itself no longer to low-lying situations, it has invaded almost the entire country, the visitation being in some cases mysterious, in others clearly traceable to the residence of

---

* In 1883 the ratio of *kakke* patients was 231 per mil. of the entire naval force, and 49 of the cases ended in death. In 1898 the ratio had sunk to 0.87 per mil., and there was but a single death; in other words, the disease had been practically stamped out. The daily rations of the Japanese seaman, as revised, consist of ½ lb. of bread, 2/5 lb. of meat, 2/3 lb. of rice, and 5/16 lb. of vegetables, besides small quantities of fresh fish, tinned meat and fish, various cereals, beans, tea, sugar, and soy. It is claimed that under this system, not only has *kakke* ceased to be a scourge, but the average weight of the men has increased.

† In a private communication to the present writer.

branch of art at an epoch when England was still rent by the barbarous struggles of the Heptarchy. The highest perfection was, however, not reached at once. The end of the fifteenth century may be said to have been the dawn of the classic age, which, culminating about the year 1700, lasted on through the whole eighteenth century and the first half of the nineteenth.

Appreciation of lacquer is a taste which has to be acquired, but which, when acquired, grows upon one, and places the best lacquer in the category of almost sacred things. To show a really fine piece casually to a new-comer, or to send it home as a gift to one of the uncultivated natives of Europe or America, is, as the Japanese proverb says, "like giving guineas to a cat." He will take it up for an instant, just glance at it, say "What a pretty little thing!" and put it down again, imagining it to be worth at most a couple of dollars. Not improbably it cost a hundred, and was the outcome of years of patient toil and marvellous art.

The material employed is the sap which exudes from the lacquer-tree (*Rhus vernicifera*) when incised. This tapping for lacquer, as it may perhaps be called, affords a means of livelihood to a special class of men, who, on the approach of mild weather in April, spread all over the northern provinces of the empire, where the best lacquer-trees grow, and continue their operations on into the autumn. The age of the tree, the season when the tree is tapped, and the treatment to which the sap is afterwards subjected—as, for instance, by being mixed with iron filings, turpentine, or charred wood—produce widely different kinds of lacquer, which are accordingly appropriated to different uses. Every species of lacquer turns black on exposure to the light; and it is a fact, mysterious but undoubtedly authentic, that lacquer dries most quickly in a damp atmosphere. The damper the atmosphere and the darker the room, so much the more quickly will the lacquer harden.

Many kinds of material admit of being lacquered. On metal, in particular, very pleasing results have been obtained.

But the favourite material is wood, and the best kinds of wood for the purpose are the *hinoki* (*Chamæcyparis obtusa*) and kiri (*Paulownia imperialis*). The woods of the *Cryptomeria japonica* (*sugi*) and *Planera japonica* (*keyaki*) are those best adopted to general purposes, such as common bowls, trays, etc. The Japanese constantly employ lacquer utensils to hold boiling soups, alcoholic drinks, and even burning cigar-ash. But so strong is the substance that it suffers little if any damage from such apparently rough treatment.

The process of lacquering is complicated and tedious. To begin with, the surface of the wood is covered with triturated hemp and glue, and then the first coating of lacquer is applied, only to be itself covered with the very finest hempen cloth. Numerous coatings of various qualities of lacquer are laid on this foundation. A careful drying intervenes between each coating, and a partial rubbing off with a whetstone follows each drying. A power formed of calcined deer's horn serves in most cases to give the final polish. But all this process, of which we have merely indicated the bare outlines, is itself but preparatory if the object is to produce one of those beautiful gold-lacquered boxes which the word "lacquer" generally calls up in the mind of the European collector. In this case, writes one of the authorities quoted below:

" A thin species of paper, prepared with sizing made of glue and alum, is used. On this paper the design required to be transmitted to the lacquered article is drawn. On the reverse of this paper, the outline is lightly traced in lacquer— previously roasted over live charcoal to prevent its drying— with a very fine brush made of rat's hair. This paper is then laid on the article to be lacquered, and is rubbed with a spatula made of *hinoki* or whalebone, where the lacquer has been applied, and on removing the paper the design is observed lightly traced in lacquer.

" To make it perfectly plain, this is rubbed over very lightly with a piece of cotton wool, charged with finely powdered whetstone, or tin; this brings the pattern out white. From one tracing, upwards of twenty impressions can be taken off, and when that is no longer possible, from the lacquer having become used up, it only requires a fresh tracing over the same paper to reproduce the design *ad infinitum*. This tracing does not dry, owing to the lacquer used for the purpose having been roasted, as previously mentioned, and can be wiped off at any time.

"The pattern thus traced out is then filled in with ground-work lacquer, with a brush made of hare's hair, great care being taken not to touch or paint out the original tracing line. This is then powdered over with fine gold dust, silver dust, or tin dust, according to the quality of the ware. This dust is applied with a piece of cotton wool, charged with the material to be used, and the article is then gently dusted with a very soft brush made from the long winter coat of a white horse, to remove any loose metal dust that might adhere to the article, and to slightly smoothen the surface. If the article under manufacture is large, only a small portion is done at a time, and it is at once enclosed in an air-tight press, so as to prevent any dust or outside matter adhering to the freshly lacquered surface. At the proper time, when the lacquer has sufficiently hardened, the article is taken out, and the part over which the gold dust has been sprinkled receives a coat of transparent varnish *(suki-urushi)*, laid on with a hare's hair brush, and a further portion is prepared with a coating of gold dust, as on the previous day : the article is again closed up in the air-tight damp press as before, till dry. When the portion which has received the second coat of lacquer over the gold dust is quite hard, it is rubbed smooth with a piece of hard charcoal made from camellia wood or *hōnoki*, until the whole is level with the surrounding parts. Then it is rubbed with the finger and some finely powdered whetstone and deer's horn, with the smallest quantity of oil, till it attains a fine polish. If upon this surface any further work takes place, such as the veining of leaves, or the painting of stamens, etc., of flowers, these are traced in lacquer and covered with gold dust, and when dry the final polish is given with the finger and powdered deer's horn."

Such is the most usual process, which is suitably modified in the case of raised gold lacquer and other varieties. It should be added that much of the so-called gold or silver lacquer is really manufactured with the aid of bronze and tin, especially at the present time, when cheapness and quantity are insisted on by a foreign public whose taste is imperfectly educated. Nevertheless, specimens worthy of the best age still continue to be produced. Competent critics assert that Shibata Zeshin, who died as lately as 1891, was probably as great as any lacquer artist that ever existed, and that others no less skilled are still living to-day.—The lacquer poison, of which so much has been said by travellers, is never fatal, though it is extremely painful in some cases. Blood to the head, swelling, violent itching and burning, occasionally small festering boils, are the symptoms. Lacquer in any stage, except when perfectly dry, is capable of producing it. The lacquer tappers always use gloves as a protection.

Only one item more. If you possess any specimens of good lacquer, be careful to dust them with a fine old silk cloth. A common duster will scratch them. Some of the best collections in Europe have been ruined by rough treatment.

Books recommended. *The Arts of Japan: An Illustrated History* by Hugo Munsterberg; *The Folk Arts of Japan* by Hugo Munsterberg; *Inro & Other Miniature Forms of Japanese Lacquer Art* by Melvin & Betty Jahss; *The Wonderful World of Netsuke With One Hundred Masterpieces of Miniature Sculpture in Color* by Raymond Bushell.

Language. Excepting the twin sister tongue spoken in the Luchu Islands, the Japanese language owns no kindred, and its classification under any of the recognised linguistic families remains doubtful. In structure, though not to any appreciable extent in vocabulary, it closely resembles Korean; and both it and Korean may possibly be related to Mongol and to Manchu, and might therefore lay claim to be included in the so-called "Altaïc" group. In any case, Japanese is what philologists term an agglutinative tongue, that is to say, it builds up its words and grammatical forms by means of suffixes loosely soldered to the root or stem, which is invariable. Though not originally related to Chinese, Japanese has adopted an enormous number of Chinese words, such words having naturally followed Chinese civilisation into the archipelago. Even at the present day, the Japanese language has recourse to Chinese for terms to indicate all such new things and ideas as "telegram," "bicycle," "photograph," "democracy," "natural selection," "limited liability," etc., etc., much as we ourselves have recourse to Latin and Greek. Hence a curious result :—the Europeanisation of Japanese institutions has made the language far more humbly tributary to China to-day than it ever was while Confucianism reigned supreme in the land.

The fundamental rule of Japanese syntax is that qualifying words precede the word they qualify. Thus the adjective or genitive precedes the noun which it defines, the adverb precedes the verb, and explanatory or dependent clauses precede the principal clause. The object likewise precedes the verb. The predicative verb or adjective of each clause is placed at the end of that clause, the predicative verb or adjective of the main clause rounding off the entire sentence, which is often, even in familiar conversation, extremely long and complicated. The following is an example of Japanese construction :—

Kono goro ni itarimashite, Bukkyō
This period at having-arrived, Buddhism
to mōsu mono wa, tada katō-
that (they)say thing as-for, merely low-
jimmin no shinjiru tokoro to nat-
class-people's believing place that having-
te, chūtō ijō de
become, middle-class thence-upwards in
wa sono dōri wo wakimae-teru
as-for, its reason(accus.) discerning-are
hito ga sukunaku; shūmon to
people(nom.) being-few, religion that
ieba, sōshiki no toki bakari ni
if-one-says, funeral-rite's time only in
mochiiru koto no yō ni omoimasu.
employ thing's manner in (they)think.

"At the present day, Buddhism has sunk into being the belief of the lower classes only. Few persons in the middle and upper classes understand its *raison d'être*, most of them fancying that religion is a thing which comes into play only at funeral services."

This one example may suffice to show how widely divergent (compared with Europe) are the channels in which Japanese thought flows. Nor is it merely that the idioms differ, but that the same circumstances do not draw from Japanese speakers remarks similar to those which they would draw from European speakers. In accidence also the disparity is remarkable. Japanese nouns have no gender or number, Japanese adjectives no degrees of comparison, Japanese verbs no person. On the other hand, the verbs have peculiar complications of their own. They have a negative voice, and forms to indicate causation and potentiality. There is also an elaborate system of honorifics, which to some extent replaces the use of person in the verb and makes good the general omission of personal pronouns.

The Japanese vocabulary, though extraordinarily rich and constantly growing, is honourably deficient in terms of abuse. It affords aboslutely no means of cursing and swearing. Another negative quality is the habitual avoidance of personification,—a characteristic so deep-seated and all-pervading as to interfere even with the use of neuter nouns in combination with transitive verbs. Thus, this language rejects such expressions as " the *heat makes* me feel languid," " *despair drove* him to commit suicide," " *science warns* us against overcrowding," " *quarrels degrade* those who engage in them," etc., etc. One must say, " being hot, I feel languid," " having lost hope, he killed himself," " on considering, we find that the fact of people's crowding together is unhealthy," and so on,—the idea being adequately rendered no doubt, but at the expense of verve and picturesqueness. Nor can any one fully realise how picturesque our European languages are, how saturated with metaphor and lit up with fancy, until he has familiarised himself with one of the tamer tongues of the Far East. Poetry naturally suffers more than prose from this defect of the language. No Japanese Wordsworth could venture on such metaphorical lines as

> " If *thought and Love desert us*, from that day
> Let us break off all *commerce with the Muse* :
> With *Thought and Love companions* of our way—
> Whate'er *the senses take or may refuse*,—
> The *mind's internal heaven shall shed her dews*
> *Of inspiration* on the humble lay."

In fact, most metaphors and allegories are incapable of so much as intelligible explanation to Far-Eastern minds.

Japanese—with its peculiar grammar, its uncertain affinities, its ancient literature—is a language worthy of more attention than it has yet received. We say " language; " but " languages " would be more strictly correct, the modern colloquial speech having diverged from the old classical tongue almost to the same extent as Italian has diverged from Latin. The Japanese still employ in their books, and even in correspondence and advertisements, a style which is partly classical and partly artificial. This is what is termed the " Written Language." The student therefore finds himself confronted with a double task. Add to this the necessity of committing to memory two syllabaries, one of which has many variant forms, and at least two or three thousand Chinese ideographs in forms standard and cursive,—ideographs, too, most of which are susceptible of three or four different readings according to circumstances,—add further that all these kinds of written symbols are apt to be encountered pellmell on the same page, and the task of mastering Japanese becomes almost Herculean. Fortunately the pronounciation is easy, and there is no difficulty in acquiring a smattering that will greatly enhance the pleasure and comfort of those who reside or travel in the country. Another grain of comfort, in the midst of all Japanese linguistic complications, may be extracted from the fact that local dialects have but little importance. It is not as in China, where, if you speak Pekingese you are incomprehensible at Canton, and if you speak Cantonese you are incomprehensible at Amoy or at Shanghai. Here the one standard language will carry you right through the country. No doubt the peasantry of different districts have local modes of pronunciation and expression; but the trouble thus caused is no greater than what may be experienced at home in England. From the philologist's standpoint, the most interesting dialects are those of the extreme South and West, which preserve archaic forms. The speech of the more recently settled North is for the most part a mere patois, an omnium-gatherum produced by the concourse of immigrants from other provinces. (See also Articles on LITERATURE and WRITING.)

Books recommended. *Basic Japanese Conversation Dictionary* by Samuel E. Martin; *Easy Japanese: A Direct Approach to Immediate Conversation* by Samuel E. Martin; *Essential Japanese: An Introduction to the Standard Colloquial Language* by Samuel E. Martin; *A Guide to Reading & Writing Japanese: The 1,850 Basic Characters & the Kana Syllabaries* edited by Florence Sakade; *Japanese-English Lingograms* by Guy J. Marenghi; *A Japanese Reader: Graded Lessons in the Modern Language* by Roy Andrew Miller; *Let's Study Japanese* by Jun Maeda; *The Missionary Language Handbook for Japan* compiled and edited by Kenny Joseph & Russell Stellwagon; *The Modern Reader's Japanese-English Character Dictionary: Revised Edition* by Andrew N. Nelson; *Read Japanese Today* by Len Walsh.

Law.[*] Dutifully obedient to authority and not naturally litigious, the Japanese are nevertheless becoming a nation of lawyers. Few branches of study are more popular than law with the young men of the present generation. Besides being often a stepping-stone to office, it seems to have for them a sort of abstract and theoretical interest; for (and more's the pity) Japanese law has at no time been the genuine outcome of the national life, as English law, for instance, is the outcome of English national life,—a historical development fitting itself to the needs of the nation as a well-made glove fits the hand. Twelve hundred years ago Japan borrowed Chinese law wholesale. She has borrowed French and German law (that is to say, practically, Roman law) wholesale in our own day. It is hard to see what else she could have done; for she would never have been admitted into the so-called comity of civilised nations unless equipped with a legal system commanding those nations' approval, and those nations approve no legal system

[*] Ignorant as we are of law, this article must be considered as proceeding from our informant, Mr. Masujima. All that we have done has been to put into shape and abridge the information which he kindly supplied.

save such as they are accustomed to themselves. True, there was a party almost from the beginning which said: "Japan for the Japanese. Our laws must suit our people. They must not be mere handles for obtaining political recognition. Wait to codify until the national courts, interpreting national needs, shall have evolved precedents of their own. French and German codes are alien things, mechanically superimposed on our Japanese ways of thought and modes of life, which are not in touch with foreign civilisations and the laws that have sprung from them." But this national party lost the day. Possibly, in time to come, modifications dictated by national needs may creep in. It is noticeable that (perhaps as a result of the healthy reaction of the last sixteen or seventeen years) the Civil Code, the most recently published of all, does to a not inconsiderable extent take into account the existing fabric of Japanese society,—a fabric differing widely in many essential points from that of the West; for in Japan the family is the social unit, not, as with us, the individual.

The new codes resulting from the legislative activity of the present reign are: (1) the Criminal Code and the Code of Criminal Procedure, drafted by Monsieur Boissonade de Fontarabie on the basis of the Code Napoleon, with modifications suggested by the old Japanese Criminal Law; these were published in 1880, and came into force in 1882; the Code of Criminal Procedure was, however, revised in 1890,* in order that it might be uniform with the Code of Civil Procedure, according to the provisions of (2) the Law of the Organisation of Judicial Courts, promulgated in the month of February, 1890, and put into force on the 1st November of the same year; (3) the Code of Civil Procedure which went into effect at once, and the Civil Code and the Commercial Code which were put into force in 1898. Though not actually

---

* In 1901, a radical revision of the Criminal Code was proposed. But such opposition was raised by members of the legal profession that the bill had to be put off to the next session of the Diet, when a further bill for the revision of the Code of Criminal Procedure is expected to be submitted.

entitled codes, we may also include; (4) the Constitution, with
its attendant laws regarding the Imperial House, the Diet, and
Finance; (5) the Laws for the Exercise of Local Self-
Government; and (6) divers statutes on miscellaneous subjects.

Crimes, as classified in the Criminal Code, are of three kinds,
namely: (1) crimes against the state or the Imperial Family,
and in violation of the public credit, policy, peace, health, etc.;
(2) crimes against persons and property; (3) police offences.
There is furthermore a subdivision of (1) and (2) into major
and minor crimes.

The punishments for major crimes are: (1) death by
hanging; (2) deportation with or without hard labour, for life
or for a term of years; (3) imprisonment with or without hard
labour, for life or for a term of years. The punishments for
minor crimes include confinement with or without hard labour,
and fines. The punishments for police offences are detention
for from one to ten days without hard labour, and fines varying
from 5 *sen* to 2 *yen*. The court which tries persons accused
of major crimes consists of three judges, that for minor crimes
of one judge or three according to the gravity of the charge,
and that for police offences of one *juge de paix*.* An appeal is
allowed in the case of both major and of minor crimes for a
trial of facts. Capital punishments are carried out in the
presence of a procurator. They are now extremely rare.
Criminals condemned to deportation are generally sent to the
island of Yezo, where they sometimes work in the mines. The
ordinary prisons are situated in various parts of the empire,
and number one hundred and thirty-two.

A person who has suffered injury from crime lodges his
complaint at a police office or with the procurator of any court
having jurisdiction over the crime in question. Policemen can
arrest an offender whose crime was commited in their presence,
or which the complainant avers to have actually seen
committed. In all other cases they can arrest by warrant

---

* The system being French, it seems advisable to retain the French terms in cases where there
is no exact, or no generally current, English equivalent.

only. Bail is allowed at the discretion of the judge, but only after reference to the procurator who has taken up the case. Accused persons are often kept in prison for a considerable time before trial, and no lawyer is allowed to be present at the preliminary examination, which also is often long delayed. The law promulgated in February, 1890, relative to the organisation of judicial courts, embodied the usage developed since the establishment of the courts in 1872, but it introduced at the same time certain changes borrowed rather from German than from French sources.

The history and nature of modern Japanese legal institutions are, very briefly, as follows. Down to 1872, the Judicial Department had united in itself the functions of chief law-court and chief executive office for the transaction of judicial business throughout the land, the same staff of officials serving for both purposes. In that year, however, a separation took place. Judges, procurators, a judicial police for the arrest of prisoners, *avoués, avocats,* and notaries were established, as also separate judicial courts and a law school. The pattern copied was French. Since that time numerous changes have taken place. At present the courts are divided into local courts (presided over by *juges de paix*), district or provincial courts, courts of appeal, and a supreme court *(cour de cassation),* all of which have jurisdiction both in criminal and civil suits. Each of these courts has branch offices established to accommodate suitors, regard being had to population and to the area of jurisdiction. The local courts have jurisdiction over police offences and such minor crimes as the procurators may deem it proper to punish with a lighter kind of punishment adjudged by one of those courts; the district courts have jurisdiction over crimes, besides acting as courts of preliminary investigation; the appeal courts hear new trials; the supreme courts hears criminal appeals on matters of law. Crimes of whatever sort, except police offences, are as a rule subjected to preliminary examination before actual trial. When, however, the charge is perfectly clear of doubt, the procurators ask for an immediate trial in the case of minor crimes. The

conducting of criminal cases, from the very beginning down
to the execution of the criminal, if he be condemned to suffer
death, rests with the procurator, who unites in his own person
the functions of public prosecutor and of grand jury.

The present judiciary consists almost entirely of graduates
of the Law College of the Imperial University and of the
private law colleges, of which there are six in Tōkyō and eight
altogether in the empire. About a thousand young men
graduate yearly. Lawyers are bound to pass a certain
examination before being admitted to practise at the bar; but
it is of a very theoretical nature. The new law concerning the
constitution of courts requires candidates for judgeships to
pass two competitive examinations, unless they are graduates
of the University, in which case they need only pass the second
of the two, after having served as probationary judges for a
term of three years. Judges are appointed for life; but the
salaries are so miserably poor (from 600 to 4,000 *yen,* or £60
to £400 per annum !) that many of the ablest judges soon resign
in order to become practising barristers, the bench thus, as
has been sarcastically remarked, serving merely as a half-way
house to the practise of the law. Things have indeed come to
such a pass that in the spring of 1901 a number of the judges
and public procurators actually went out on strike ! The
president of the supreme court receives 5,500 *yen* (£550), and
is of *shinnin* rank.* The chief procurator receives 5,000 *yen*
(£500), and is of *chokunin* rank.

The system of trial, as well in civil as in criminal cases, is
inquisitorial. It was so in Old Japan, and is so in France,
whence the greater part of modern Japanese law has been
derived. Formerly no convictions were made except on
confession by the prisoner. Hence an abundant use of torture,
now happily abolished,† and a tendency, even in civil cases,
to find against the defendant, although the *theory* is that the

---

* All officials are classified into four ranks, *shinnin, chokunin, sonin,* and *hannin.* The *shinnin* are the highest of all, receiving their nomination from the Emperor himself.

† See page 182, footnote.

defendant must be presumed to be in the right until actually proved the contrary. In this characteristic, Japan does but conform to her Continental models, and indeed to the universal usage of mankind with the solitary exception of the English. The judge conducts the trial alone. All questions by counsel must be put through him. Counsel do not so much defend their clients as represent them. Their statement or admissions stand for those of their clients, strange as such a thing will sound to English ears. Another peculiarity—at least according to English notions, though we believe that something similar exists in France—is that husband and wife, parent and child, master and servant, cannot witness against each other. At the same time, they are not entirely excluded from the examination. The Code of Criminal Procedure draws a fine distinction, excluding them as witnesses, but admitting them as "referees,"—we can think of no better equivalent for the difficult Japanese term *sankōnin* (参考人). A "referee" is a witness and yet not an authoritative witness, a quasi-witness, if one might so phrase it, who is not called upon to be sworn. The idea is, of course, that persons thus related are likely to be prejudiced in each other's favour, and that their testimony should accordingly be allowed little weight in comparison with that of others more probably impartial. Witnesses are sworn, though not exactly in the European manner. The oath is rather a solemn asseveration, and is entirely unconnected with any religious sanctions. It is in the form of a written document, to which the person sworn affixes his seal, or, failing that, his signature. The proceedings at a trial are all committed to writing, but not always in the actual words used, as Japanese custom is averse to the employment of the colloquial for literary purposes. The general plan is, therefore, to translate the gist of the questions and answers into the book style.

Needless to say that the above is the merest shadowy outline of a vast subject. Transformed, revolutionised as it has been, Japanese law nevertheless retains not a few curious features of its own, which would interest both the legal specialist and the student of history and sociology. In some cases of comparatively little importance, the customary law of an earlier date is still followed, though variously modified by the application, more or less tentative, of European principles of jurisprudence.

Books recommended. *Hermann Roesler and the Making of the Meiji State* by Johannes Siemes; *Japan's Modern Century* edited by Edmund Skrzypczak; *The Japanese Legal Advisor: Crimes and Punishments* by George M. Koshi.

Literature. We hear of one or two Japanese books as having been composed in the seventh century of the Christian era, shortly after the spread of a knowledge of the Chinese ideographs in Japan had rendered a written literature possible. The earliest work, however, that has come down to us is the *Kojiki,* or "Record of Ancient Matters," dating from the year 712. This has sometimes been called the Bible of the Japanese, because it contains the mythology and earliest history of the nation; but it gives no moral or religious precepts. It was followed in A.D. 720 by the *Nihongi,* or "Chronicles of Japan," a more pretentious work written in Chinese, the Latin of that age and country. In about A.D. 760 came the *Man-yōshū,* or "Collection of a Myriad Leaves." It is an anthology of the most ancient poems of the language, and is invaluable as a repertory of facts and allusions interesting to the philologist, the archæologist, and the historian. Its poetical merit is also rated very high by the orthodox native critics, who are unacquainted with any literature but their own, unless it be the Chinese. From that time forward the literary stream has never ceased. It has flowed in a double channel,—that of books in the native language, and that of books written in Classical Chinese. Chinese has been generally preferred for grave subjects,—law, for instance, and history; Japanese for poetry, romance, and other branches of *belles-lettres*. Sir Ernest Satow, following the native authorities, classifies Japanese literature under sixteen heads, which are:

I. STANDARD HISTORIES. Besides the *Kojiki* and *Nihongi* already mentioned, the most important standard history is the *Dai Nihonshi*. This huge work in one hundred volumes was compiled at the end of the seventeenth century by a whole company of Japanese and Chinese men of learning, under the general superintendence of the second Prince of Mito, who was a munificent patron of literature.

II. MISCELLANEOUS HISTORICAL WORKS, that is, histories written by private persons and therefore devoid of official sanction. Such are the *Mitsu Kagami,* the *Gempei Seisuiki,* the *Heike Mono-gatari,* the *Taiheiki,* and a host of others, concluding with the *Nihon Gwaishi,* which, a few years ago, was in every educated person's hands, and which, by its fanatically Imperialist sentiments, contributed in no small measure to bring about the fall of the Shōgunate.—All Japanese histories are written in a style which repels the European reader. They are, for the most part, annals rather than histories properly so-called. Sir Ernest Satow's translation of the first five books of the *Nihon Gwaishi* should be glanced through by any one who doubts this assertion. He will find it almost impossible to bring himself to believe that a book so intolerably dry could ever have fired a whole nation with enthusiasm. That it did so is one of the curiosities of literature.

III. LAWS. The *Ryō no Gige* and the *Engi-shiki* are the works in this division which are most often quoted.

IV. BIOGRAPHY.

V. POETRY. (See special Article on this subject.)

VI. CLASSICAL ROMANCES. This is the most curious department of standard Japanese literature, lifting, as it does, the curtain from the long-forgotten life of the Japanese Court of the tenth and eleventh century of our era. The lords and ladies of those days step out before us with all the frivolity, but also with all the elegance, of their narrow aristocratic existence, which was bounded by the horizon of the old capital, Kyōto. We have their poetastering, their amorous intrigues of course, their interminable moon-gazings and performances on the flute, even minute descriptions of their dresses and of the parties they gave,—one among various witnesses to the fact that many of these books were written by women. The earliest story commonly classed among the romances is more properly a fairy-tale; for it deals with the adventures of a maiden who was exiled from the moon to this our workaday world. It is entitled *Taketori Mono-gatari,* or the "Bamboo-cutter's Romance," because the maiden was discovered in a section of bamboo, where she lay sparkling like gold. To mention but three or more out of a hundred, there are the *Utsubo Mono-gatari* and the *Ise Mono-gatari,* both attributed to the tenth century, the *Sumiyoshi Mono-gatari,* of uncertain date, and the *Konjaku Mono-gatari,* with its sequel the *Uji Shūi,* which are collections of shorter tales. The most celebrated of all, is the voluminous *Genji Mono-gatari,* which dates from the year 1004.

VII. MISCELLANIES. These books are a sort of *olla podrida* of the thoughts of their authors, jotted down without any attempt at classification, but with a great deal of literary chiselling. The two miscellanies most to be recommended are the *Makura no Sōshi,* by a Court lady named Sei Shōnagon who flourished in the eleventh century, and the *Tsurezure-Gusa* by a Buddhist monk who died in the year 1350.

VIII. DIARIES. Of these, the *Hōjōki* is probably the one which the student will find most interesting. Like the *Tsurezure-Gusa,* it is the work of a Buddhist monk. The author describes the calamities of his times, and expatiates on the superiority of life in a hermit's cell to that which he had previously led amidst worldly vanities. It dates from about the year 1200. The *Murasaki Shikibu Niki,** which is the diary

---

* This word is commonly pronounced *nikki,* but *niki* is more ancient and correct.

of the most celebrated of Japanese authoresses, is remarkable as being probably the hardest book to construe in the Japanese language.

IX. TRAVELS. Under this heading, the bibliographers class many works which might more advantageously be counted among the DIARIES, as not only are they diaries in fact, but are so entitled by their authors. The easiest and most attractive of the Japanese classics is to be found in this division. It is entitled the *Tosa Niki,* that is, " Diary of [a Voyage Home from] Tosa," by the poet Tsurayuki, who had been governor of that remote province. It dates from the year 935. Travels are the least voluminous department of Japanese literature. How should it accord with the fitness of things in this stay-at-home country to have a Sir John Maundeville or a Captain Cook ?

X. DRAMAS. Thesre are treated of in the Article on the THEATRE.

XI. DICTIONARIES AND WORKS ON PHILOLOGY. The best native dictionaries of Classical Japanese are the *Wakun no Shiori* and the *Gagen Shūran;* but both are unfortunately fragmentary. The recently published *Genkai,* or " Sea of Words," and the *Kotoba no Izumi,* or " Fountain of Words " aim at greater completeness. The fullest native grammar is the *Kotaba no Chikamichi,* by Minamoto-no-Shigetane. The chief writers of the old school on general philological subjects are Mabuchi (died 1769), Motoori (died 1801), and Hirata (died 1843). In Motoori's works the classical Japanese language reached its acme of perfection. Specially remarkable are, among his greater undertakings, the standard commentary on the *Kojiki,* entitled *Kojiki Den,* and, among his lighter essays, the *Tama-Gatsuma* containing jottings on all sorts of subjects, philological and otherwise.

XII. TOPOGRAPHY. The more popular publications of this class, dating roughly from the middle of the nineteenth century, are really the best, though they are less esteemed by the Japanese literati than are other works bearing the stamp of greater antiquity. These popular topographical works are illustrated guide-books to the various provinces of the empire, and are known under the collective name of *Meisho Zue*. Though by various authors, they are all constructed on a uniform plan, somewhat resembling that of our county histories, though more discursive and better adapted to the practical needs of travellers.

XIII. LITERATURE OF THE SHINTO RELIGION. Chief works: the *Kojiki Den,* already mentioned under another heading—for it is one of the corner-stones of Japanese literature—and Hirata's still only half-published *magnum opus,* entitled *Koshi Den.* This latter is remarkable for its extraordinary elaborateness and for the vast erudition of its author. Unfortunately Hirata was very bigoted as well as very learned. Consequently the reader must be always on his guard, so as to distinguish how much really belongs to Shintō and how much to Hirata himself; for Hirata never scrupled to garble a sacred text, if he could thereby support his own views as to what the sacred writers *ought* to mean. Extremely interesting to the specialist are the ancient Shintō rituals termed *Norito,* round which a mass of modern commentary has gathered. A noteworthy peculiarity of this section of Japanese literature is the attempt made by its authors to use pure Japanese only, without any admixture of the Chinese element.

XIV. BUDDHIST LITERATURE. This division comprises singularly few works of merit, Buddhism having found an uncongenial soil in the Japanese mind. Certain sets of hymns *(wasan)* are, it is true, favourites with the lower class of devotees; but we do not know of any Japanese Buddhist book that occupies, either in literature or popularity, a place at all comparable to that taken among ourselves by the " Imitation of Christ," the English " Prayer-Book," or the " Pilgrim's Progress." Shintō, though immeasurably inferior to Buddhism as a religion, must be admitted to have carried off from its rival all the literary laurels on Japanese soil. Besides the Buddhists proper, there is a school of moralists calling themselves *Shingakusha,* founded partly on Buddhism, partly on Confucianism, partly on utilitarian commonsense. Some of their *Dowa,* or "Moral Discourses," which date from the first half of the nineteenth century, offer a certain interest. But the best things in this line are two small collection of moral aphorisms entitled *Jitsu-go Kyō,* or "Teaching of the Words of Truth," and *Dōji Kyō,* or "Teaching for Children."

XV. MODERN FICTION. Japan's greatest modern novelist, in the opinion of the Japanese themselves, is Bakin (1767–1848), the most widely popular of whose two hundred and ninety works is the *Hak-ken Den,* or "Tale of Eight Dogs," itself consisting of no less than a hundred and six volumes. Though Japanese volumes are smaller than ours, the *Hak-ken Den* is a gigantic production. Other universally popular novels of the earlier part of the nineteenth century are the *Ukiyo-buro,* by Samba, and the *Hiza Kurige,* by an author who writes under the name of Jippensha Ikku. In our opinion this latter is, with some of the lyric dramas *(Nō no Utai),* the cleverest outcome of the Japanese pen. In it are related with a Rabelaisian coarseness, but also with a Rabelaisian verve and humour, the adventures of two men called Yajirobei and Kidahachi as they travel along the Tōkaidō from Yedo to Kyōto. The impecunious heroes walk most of the way, whence the title of *Hiza Kurige,* which may be roughly rendered "Shanks' Mare." The author of this work occupies in literature a place akin to that which Hokusai occupies in art. Warmly appreciated by the common people, who have no preconceived theories to live up to, both Hokusai and Jippensha Ikku are admitted but grudgingly by the local dispensers of fame to a place in the national Walhalla. They must look abroad for the appreciation of critics taking a wider view of the proper functions of literature and art. Gravity, severe classicism, conformity to established rules and methods, —such qualities still constitute the canon of orthodox Japanese literary judgment. Many Japanese novels are of the historical kind. The most interesting of these is the

I-ro-ha, Bunko, by one Tamenaga Shunsui, which, with its sequel, the *Yuki no Akebono,* gives the lives of each of the celebrated Forty-seven Rōnins. The *Ōoka Meiyo Seidan* is another book of this class, much to be recommended to the student for its interest and its easy style. It purports to be an authenic account of numbers of *causes célèbres* tried by Ōoka, the Japanese Solomon, who flourished early in the eighteenth century.

XVI. MISCELLANEOUS LITERATURE, including cyclopædias, works on industries, sciences, arts, and inventions, works on Confucianism, works on Japanese and Chinese antiquities, and on a hundred other subjects. Under this heading, the popular moral treatises of Kaibara Ekken and Arai Hakuseki, Confucianists of the seventeenth century, call for particular notice, partly because their ideas are those that long moulded Japanese society, partly because the easy, flowing style of these books specially fits them for the student's use.

To the foregoing enumeration, borrowed from Sir Ernest Satow, one item more can now be added, namely:—

XVII. EUROPEANISED LITERATURE. The opening of the country was the death-blow to Japanese literature proper. True, thousands of books and pamphlets still pour annually from the press—more, probably, than at any previous time. But the greater number are either translations of European works, or else works conveying European ideas. From " Mrs. Caudle " up to Captain Mahan, nothing is amissing. It is but natural and right that this should be so. Immense civilising effects in every department of intellectual activity have been produced by the contemporary school of Europeanised authors, with Fukuzawa, Katō, and a dozen other eminent men leading the van. But of course their translations, adaptations, and imitations can interest Western readers, who are in possession of the originals, far less than do the books written under the old order; besides which, by the very nature of the case, most of their handiwork is provisional only. Some of these days, when the life-time of competent scholars shall have been given to the task, Shakespeare and Victor Hugo may possibly be rendered into Japanese not much more unsatisfactorily than we render Homer into English. In their present hastily donned Japanese dress, they send a cold shiver down one's back.

No department but has yielded to the new influence. Even Japanese novel-writers nowadays draw their inspiration from abroad. The first European novel to be translated was (of all books in the world!) Bulwer Lytton's "Ernest Maltravers," which appeared in 1879, under the title of *Kwaryū Shunwa,* literally, "A Spring Story of Flowers and Willows." The most successful perhaps in recent years, among publications of this class, has been the version of "Little Lord Fauntleroy."* Paraphrase is frequently resorted to:—a plot is borrowed, and the proper names which occur in it are slightly Japonised, as *Shimizu* for Smith, *O Risa* for Eliza, and details altered to suit Japanese social conditions. The first original novel of Japanese life composed in imitation of the European style was the *Shosei Katagi,* by Tsubouchi Yūzō. (1886), who seems to have put into it his own experiences as a student. Sometimes a more ambitious kind of historical romance is attempted. We would willingly wager ten thousand to one that not a single reader of these pages could ever guess the hero of a work which for several years enjoyed such popularity that its author, Yano Fumio, was able to take a trip to Europe and to build himself a fine house with the proceeds. The hero is— Epaminondas! The work in question, entitled *Kei-koku Bidan,* takes the whole field of Theban politics for its subject-matter. That not a few of the allusions might be transferred without much difficulty to contemporary Japanese politics, was doubtless one reàson for the immense sale which it had. Another successful novel, the *Kajin no Kigū,* has its opening scene laid in the Capitol at Washington, where one of the characters—a Japanese—reads aloud to his companion the Declaration of Independence. The Carlists, the wicked

---

* When Mrs. Iwamoto, the accomplished translator of this novel, died, copies of her works, of all the Tokyo newspapers published on the day of her funeral, and of recent magazines and other books were buried with her, every care being taken to guard against decay, and thus preserve intact for future ages specimens of the literary activity of the present reign.

English who robbed Egypt of her native prince Arabi Pasha, etc., etc., all appear in kaleidoscopic variety in the pages of this work, which by a curious contradiction, is written in the most classical Chinese style. Sometimes the future is peered into, after the example of Lytton and the author of " The Battle of Dorking." In 1895, while Japan was busy beating China, and had convinced herself that she could beat the world, one of the Tōkyō papers achieved a success by the publication of a serial novel entitled *Asahi-Zakura,* by a feuilletonist called Murai Gensai. The heroines of this book were two Red Cross nurses, and the story was that of the coming defeat of England by Japan, who, after annexing Hongkong, India, Malta, and Gibraltar, sends her fleet up the Thames to raze the fortresses there and to exact from the cowering Britishers an enormous indemnity.

The favourite novelists of the present day are Rohan, a subjective, introspective writer, and Tokutomi Roka, whose *Omoi-de no Ki* and *Hototogisu* may be particularly recommended to the foreign student for their good colloquial style. Aeba Kōson's short stories, collected under the title of *Muratake,* are also much read. So are the works of the realist Kōyō Sanjin, who died in 1903. The European influence in most such modern prose-writers affects not only the choice and treatment of the subject-matter, but the very style and grammar. Even when perusing an original production, one might often take it for a translation, so saturated is it apt to be with " Europeanisms." An effort was made a few years ago to Europeanise even poetry, by the introduction of rhyme and by other innovations; but the genius of the language proving essentially unsuitable, the attempt failed. After all, if poetry is to be started on a new flight, the first prerequisite would be an original poet, and that is precisely what was and still is lacking. Sasaki Nobutsuna may be mentioned as the most attractive of contemporary writers of verse. Though he adheres to the old thirty-one syllable form,—is, in fact, thoroughly Japanese and a conservator of the past,—still he has contrived to infuse some measure of new vigour into the volume of his selected best pieces entitled *Omoi-gusa,* published in 1903.

Among more serious and influential modern productions may be mentioned *The Opening of Japan,*[1] by Shimada Saburō; *The History of Two Thousand Five Hundred Years,*[2] by Takekoshi Yosaburō; *The History of the Tokugawa Shōguns,*[3] by Naitō Chisō; *The Decline and Fall of Feudalism,*[4] by Fukuchi Genichiro; *The Japan of the Future,*[5] by Tokutomi Iichirō, and the same author's *Life and Opinions of Yoshida Shōin;*[6] *A Treatise on the Constitution,*[7] by Ono Azusa; the Constitution itself, with Marquis Itō's Commentary (see p. 219); Nakamura's excellent translation of Smiles' *Self-Help,*[8] together with such more recent scholastic works as Mikami and Takatsu's *History of Japanese Literature,*[9] two great dictionaries, namely, Ōtsuki's *Sea of Words,*[10] and Ochiai's *Fountain of Words,*[11] Takahashi Gorō's excellent Japanese-English dictionary,[12] Taguchi's encyclopædia entitled *A Dictionary of Japanese Society,*[13] Tsubouchi Yūzō's *History of English Literature,*[14] and Kuroiwa's work on monism entitled *A Treaties on Heaven and Man.*[15] But the work which undoubtedly did more than any other single factor to mould Japan into its present shape was *The Condition of Western Countries*[16] by Fukuzawa—a book now thirty years old. The reception accorded to the same author's "Hundred Essays,"[17] published in 1897, showed his popularity to be as fresh as ever; and his *Autobiography,*[18] which appeared in 1899, has since then passed through thirty-four editions, and is, in the present writer's opinion, one of the most interesting books in the Japanese language. The fact that it is written in colloquial should facilitate its perusal by foreign students.

(1) *Kaikoku Shimatsu.*
(2) *Ni-sen Go-hyaku Nen Shi.*
(3) *Tokugawa Ju-go-dai Shi.*
(4) *Bakufu Suibo Ron.*
(5) *Shorai no Nihon.*
(6) *Yoshida Shoin.*
(7) *Kokken Hanron.*
(8) *Saikoku Risshi Hen.*
(9) *Nihon Bungaku Shi.*
(10) *Genkai.*
(11) *Kotoba no Izumi.*
(12) *I-ro-ha Jiten.*
(13) *Nihon Shakwai Jii.*
(14) *Eibun-gaku Shi.*
(15) *Ten-jin Ron.*
(16) *Seiyo Jijo.*
(17) *Fukuo Hyaku-wa.*
(18) *Fukuo Jiden.*

And now it may be asked: What is the value of this Japanese literature—so ancient, so voluminous, locked up in so recondite a written character? We repeat what we have already said of the "Collection of a Myriad Leaves,"—that it is invaluable to the philologist, the archæologist, the historian, the student of curious manners which have disappeared or are fast disappearing. We may add that there are some clever and many pretty things in it. The *Tosa Niki*, for instance, is charming—charming in its simplicity, its good taste, its love of scenery and of children. The *Makura no Sōshi* teems with touches of wit and delicate satire. Several of the lyric dramas are remarkable poems in their way. Some of the Lilliputian odes in the "Songs Ancient and Modern" sparkle like dew-drops in the sun; and of Bashō's still tinier poems—the wee seventeen syllable mites—many are flashes of delicate fancy, atoms of perfect naturalistic description, specks of humour, truth, or wisdom. For Jippensha Ikku, the Rabelais of Japan, we have already expressed our warm admiration. Not a few of the writers of the present reign would, if born under other skies, have taken a respectable rank among European literature. On the other hand, much of that which the Japanese themselves prize most highly in their literature seems intolerably flat and insipid to the European taste. The romances—most of them—are every bit as dull as the histories, though in another way:—the histories are too curt, the romances too long-winded. If the authoress of the *Genji Mono-gatari,* though lauded to the skies by her compatriots, has been branded by Georges Bousquet as *cette ennuyeuse Scudéry japonaise,* she surely richly deserves it.*
And what shall we say of Bakin, on whom her mantle fell in modern times,—Bakin and his *Hakken Den,* which every Japanese has read and re-read till he knows it almost by

---

* Sir Ernest Satow's judgment of the Genji Mono-gatari agrees with ours. "The plot," writes he, "is devoid of interest, and it is only of value as making a stage in the development of the language." Fairness, however, requires that the very different estimate of this work formed by Mr. Aston, the accomplished historian of Japanese literature, should be here cited. He writes as follows:—

"I do not profess to have read more than a small part of this portentously long romance, but judging from a study of a few books of it, the above condemnations appear to me underserved. The ornate style to which these adverse critics object consists chiefly in the

heart? "How inimitable!" cries the enraptured Japanese reader, "how truly excellent!" "Excellent, yes!" the European retorts, "excellent to send one to sleep, with its interminable accounts of the impossible adventures of eight knights, who personify the eight cardinal virtues through the labyrinth of a hundred and six volumes!"

Sum total: what Japanese literature most lacks is genius. It lacks thought, logical grasp, depth, breadth, and many-sidedness. It is too timorous, too narrow to compass great things. Perhaps the Court atmosphere and predominantly feminine influence in which it was nursed for the first few centuries of its existence stifled it, or else the fault may have lain with the Chinese formalism in which it grew up. But we suspect that there was some original sin of weakness as well. Otherwise the clash of India and China with old mythological Japan, of Buddhism with Shintō, of imperialism with feudalism, and of all with Catholicism in the sixteenth century and with Dutch ideas a little later, would have produced more important results. If Japan has given us no

honorific terminations of the verbs, as natural to a courtly dialect as the gorgeous but cumbrous costumes and the elaborate ceremonial of the palace. There is no superabundance of descriptive adjectives or anything to correspond to our word-painting. The want of interest complained of seems to me to proceed from a misunderstanding of the writer's object. She was not bent on producing a highly wrought plot or sensational story. Her object was to interest and amuse her readers by a picture of real life, and of the sentiments and doings of actual men and women. There is no exaggeration in the *Genji*, no superfine morality, and none of the fine writing that abounds in modern Japanese fiction. What Murasaki-no-Shikibu did for Japanese literature was to add to it a new kind of composition, viz., the novel, or epic, of real life as it has been called. She was the Richardson of Japan, and her genius resembled his in many ways. She delighted specially in delineating types of womanhood. Indeed, the whole work may be regarded as a series of pictures of this kind, drawn with minute care, and from a full knowledge of her subject-matter. She does not deal in broad strokes of the pen. Her method is to produce graphic and realistic effects by numerous touches of detail. This is, however, incompatible with simplicity of style. Her sentences are long and somewhat complicated, and this with the antique language and the difference of manners and customs constitutes a very serious difficulty to the student. The *Genji* is not an easy book either to us or to the author's modern fellow-countrymen. The labour of mastering its meaning is probably one reason why it is not more appreciated. As a picture of a long past state of society, there is nothing in the contemporary European literature which can for a moment be compared with it. It contains a host of personages from Mikados down to the lowest court attendants, to elucidate whose genealogy the standard *Kogetsusho* edition has devoted a whole volume. Its scene is laid sometimes in Kyoto, but also changes to Hiyeizan, Suma, and other places in the neighbourhood. A whole calendar of court ceremonies might be compiled from it. If we remember that it was written long before Chaucer, Dante, and Boccaccio shone on the horizon of European literature, it will appear a truly remarkable performance." (This quotation is made, not from the *History of Japanese Literature* itself, but from a preliminary essay entitled *The Classical Literature of Japan*, read before the Japan Society, London, in June, 1898.)

music, so also has she given us no immortal verse, neither do her authors atone for lack of substance by any special beaut.es of form. But Japanese literature has occasional graces, and is full of incidental scientific interest. The intrepid searcher for facts and " curios " will, therefore, be rewarded if he has the courage to devote to it the study of many years. A certain writer has said that " it should be left to a few missionaries to plod their way through the wilderness of the Chinese language to the deserts of Chinese literature." Such a sweeping condemnation is unjust in the case of Chinese. It would be unjust in that of Japanese also, even with all deductions made.

Books recommended. *Botchan* by Soseki Natsume; translated by Umeji Sasaki; *The Counterfeiter and Other Stories* by Yasushi Inoue; translated, with an introduction, by Leon Picon; *Five Women Who Loved Love* by Saikaku Ihara; translated by William Theodore de Bary; *Geisha in Rivalry* by Kafu Nagai; translated by Kurt Meissner; *The Golden Country* by Shusaku Endo; translated by Francis Mathy, s.j.; *The Gossamer Years: The Diary of a Noblewoman of Heian Japan* translated by Edward Seidensticker; *Harp of Burma* by Michio Takeyama; translated by Howard Hibbett; *The Hunting Gun* by Yasushi Inoue; translated by Sadamichi Yokoö and Sanford Goldstein; *The Japanese Fairy Book* by Yei Theodora Ozaki; *The Life of an Amorous Man* by Saikaku Ihara; translated by Kengi Hamada; *The Love of Izayoi & Seishin: A Kabuki Play* by Kawatake Mokuami; translated by Frank T. Motofuji; *The Magical Carpenter of Japan* by Rokujiuyen; translated by Frederick Victor Dickins; *Modern Japanese Stories: An Anthology* edited by Ivan Morris, with translations by Edward Seidensticker, George Saito, Geoffrey Sargent, Ivan Morris; *This Outcast Generation* by Taijun Takeda; translated by Yusaburo Shibuya and Sanford Goldstein; *Renaissance in Japan: A Cultural Survey of the Seventeenth Century* by Kenneth P. Kirkwood; *Season of Violence and Other Stories* by Shintaro Ishihara; translated by John G. Mills, Toshie Takahama & Ken Tremayne; *Silence* by Shusaku Endo; translated by William Johnston; *Shanks' Mare: Being a Translation of the Tokaido Volumes of "Hizakurige,"* Japan's Great Comic Novel of Travel & Ribaldry by Ikku Jippensha; translated by Thomas Satchell; *This Scheming World* by Saikaku Ihara; translated by Masanori Takatsuka & David C. Stubbs; *The Wild Geese* by Ogai Mori; translated by Sanford Goldstein and Kingo Ochiai.

Little Spring. *Ko-haru,* or " the Little Spring," is the Japanese name for the Indian Summer,—those beauteous weeks in November and December, when the burden and heat of the year are over, when the sky is constantly blue and the atmosphere golden, and the maple-trees (to borrow a favourite expression of the Japanese poets) put on their damask robes.

Living used to be extremely cheap in Japan. It is so no longer. The general voice of grumblers among the residents proclaims that it nowadays costs as much to live here in exile as at home in Europe, with the additional drawback that you get less for your money, except it be comparative ease of mind in the matter of servants. Grumblers among the tourists give vent to complaints of similar tenour. Travelling in Japan, they allege, is as expensive as in America, and infinitely less

comfortable. To our mind the question, so far as travellers
are concerned, really reduces itself to this:—are you willing to
forego some of your home conveniences, are you willing to
spend money, in order to study a unique civilisation in one of
its most interesting phases? If not, if your object in coming
abroad is to find or make everything exactly the same as at
home, then you have miscalculated.

Statistics published towards the end of 1900 showed the
average prices of the forty principal staples of Japanese
production to have advanced forty-two per cent. between the
years 1896 and 1899 alone. This extraordinarily rapid rise
was ascribed by the then Minister of Finance to inflation
consequent on the successful war against China in 1894–5.
Doubtless that was one cause. Side issues branching out from
it may be discovered in the doubling of the personnel of the
army which was then commenced, and which, while taking
away hands from production, added idle mouths. Furthermore the emigration of artisans and coolies to Formosa
contributed to a rise of wages in Japan proper, and may
have affected prices in other ways; for so potent a cause
cannot have remained without far-reaching results. Be this
as it may, and without attempting to treat the question
exhaustively, but merely mentioning a few items at haphazard,
we note that the price of land in Tōkyō trebled during the last
four or five years of the nineteenth century, that house rent
has trebled during the last thirty years (for the very poor it
has quintupled), that the average price of labour has trebled,
that hotel charges have trebled, washing has nearly doubled,
jinrikisha hire has quadrupled, and that it costs three times
as much to build a house now as it did then. University
students, who formerly got along on 11 *yen* a month, can
scarcely now manage under 20 *yen*. The price of a box for
the ten days' wrestling matches at Ekō-in, Tōkyō, rose from
40 to 54 *yen* for the best places, and from 38 to 45 *yen* for the
next best in the single year between January, 1900, and
January, 1901. The published accounts of a Tōkyō lady's
household testify to the following rise in prices between the
years 1877 and 1900 :—

Public bath	7 *rin**	2½ *sen*
Potatoes (per quart)	3½ *sen*	8 *sen*
Charcoal (per bag)	18 *sen*	28 *sen*
Radishes (per bundle)	4½ *sen*	7½ *sen*
Paper (per quire)	1$\frac{7}{10}$*sen*	3 *sen*
do. (best)	11 *sen*	25 *sen*
Pickled greens (per barrel)	41 *sen*	75 *sen*
Indoor sandals (per pair)	5 *sen*	7 *sen*
Lamp oil (vegetable)	3 *sen*	5$\frac{4}{10}$*sen*
Best soy (per barrel)	1 *yen* 12½ *sen*	2 *yen* 80 *sen*
Firewood (per 50 bundles)	1 *yen* 50 *sen*	2 *yen* 80 *sen*
Maidservant per month	1 *yen*	Over 2 *yen*
Carpenter (per diem)	25 *sen*	80 *sen*

The only household requisites that had become cheaper, according to the same authority, during the quarter century were

Lamp chimneys	12 *sen*	5 *sen*
Petroleum (per tin)	2 *yen* 40 *sen*	1 *yen* 70 *sen*

owing, doubtless, to the discovery of native petroleum fields, and to the fact that glass is now manufactured at Tōkyō instead of being imported, as formerly, from abroad.

All the above statements as to prices are endorsed by another notable housewife whom we have consulted, and who points out that a further considerable rise has taken place even between 1900 and 1904 in certain articles,—soy, for instance, which now stands as high as 3 *yen* 75 *sen* per barrel, charcoal which is 50 *sen* as against 28, maidservants' wages which now range between 3 and 5 *yen* monthly, and carpenters' pay which is 1 *yen* a day. In others, the rise is very slight:— thus, vegetable oil costs 6 *sen* in 1904 as against 5$\frac{4}{10}$ *sen* in 1900. The same lady contributes the following comparative list for the last twenty-nine years:—

---

* For this and the other values mentioned, see p. 109.

	(1875)		(1904)	
Ladies' hairdressing	5	*sen*	10	*sen*
„ clogs*	80	*sen*	3 yen 80	*sen*
Kitchen maids' ditto	5	*sen*	22	*sen*
Eggs	from 5 *rin* to 1½	*sen*	3 to 3½	*sen*
Chickens (per lb.)	6	*sen*	33	*sen*
Sake (good)	25	*sen*	70	*sen*
Sugar (per lb.)	8	*sen*	16	*sen*
Mats *(tatami)*	65	*sen*	3	*yen*
Matting *(goza,* 6 ft. piece)	16	*sen*	50	*sen*

A quarter of a century ago, the native traveller who sat down to rest awhile and sip a cup of tea at a wayside teahouse, bestowed, on departing, what was called a *tempō sen*, that is, 8 *rin* of modern money, or less than an English farthing. He now gives 5 *sen*, and if well-dressed, 10 *sen*, that is, two-pence half-penny, or twelve and a half times as much as formerly.

If the whole subject were to be discussed in detail, it would be proper to draw attention to the fact that previous to 1897 the standard currency of Japan was silver, which had steadily depreciated in value during a long term of years as compared with gold. To state the case more fully still, however, it would be proper to draw attention to the further fact that, as the Japanese public had practically never known gold, the depreciation of silver as measured by foreigners in gold had for them no actuality. Moreover, prices have risen continuously and rapidly even since the introduction of the gold standard, as exemplified in some of the items above quoted. Standards and bi- and monometallisms have, therefore, little to do with the case. Prices have risen absolutely, and they go on rising daily, quite irrespective, too, of any increased demands on comfort by the people at large. True, all classes now display a somewhat greater inclination towards expensive habits than of old. But the change has been

---

* Part of this extraordinary rise is accounted for by the fact that the present article is a better and more luxurious one.

slow and comparatively slight,—nowise equal in magnitude to the political change, nor yet equal to that general rush for luxury which has revolutionised the whole life and manners of the agricultural and artisan classes in England during the last two generations. Speaking generally and subject to certain reservations of detail, the Japanese peasant or artisan of to-day lives as he always lived,—inhabits the same sort of wood and paper house, eats the same light food, wears the same garments, goes about his daily avocations and his occasional amusements in the same manner.

The constantly increasing price of living weighs heavily on persons having small incomes or fixed salaries,—very heavily, for instance, on all the lower officials. If, nevertheless, the shops lack not customers, and the theatres, though expensive, are always crowded, the reason lies in the rapid development of a class hitherto unknown,—an upper middle class of contractors, speculators, bankers, mine-owners, railway magnates. At its head stand such *nouveaux riches* as the Iwasakis, the Shibusawas, the Ōkuras, the Furukawas, for whom the feudal society of Old Japan would have had no place.

Logic in the Far East works by laws differing appreciably from those which the Western mind acknowledges. We have quoted in another part of this volume the recent decision of a learned judge, who ruled that a firm which had imitated the registered label of a brand of mineral water need not be restrained from so doing, because, as it was winter time, few persons would be drinking water, and the proprietor of the label did not therefore stand to lose much by the theft. We must allow a quantum of sense in this decision:—it is not altogether unreasonable. At the same time, the sense is not that to which our Western reason would lead us. Four or five years ago, the postmen of a certain district complained of getting no promotion after long and faithful service. Their claim was found just and was acceded to, each man being granted one step upwards. At the same time, however, the salary of each grade was reduced to what that of the grade next below it had hitherto been, so that in reality the men gained nothing. In such circumstances, Europeans would have protested that insult had been added to injury; but it is not recorded that the Japanese concerned evinced any discontent. About the same time, an old-established hotel in one of the largest cities of the empire was burnt down. With us, permission to rebuild would have been granted at once (supposing any permission to be necessary):—the fact that the proprietor had carried on business successfully during a long term of years, would have been deemed the best of all reasons for encouraging him to continue. Not so in Japan. The municipality held that he had made plenty of money already, and that the other hotels in the place, which had found in him a dangerous competitor, should be given a chance. Permission was, therefore, refused for more than a twelvemonth, and when at last granted, it was accompanied with vexatious conditions. Here again we see the action of reason of a certain kind, and also a jealous regard of a certain kind for the rights of others; but the eye with which this regard and this reason view the matter appears to a European to squint. What would he say to the report published in 1899 by the directors of a certain brewery company in the neighbourhood of Yokohama, wherein an item of 5,000 *yen* for advertising was entered as an *asset?*(!) These clever folks were but looking ahead; their prophetic soul viewed as an already accomplished fact the increase to their business which such advertising would produce, and they passed the 5,000 *yen* to the credit side accordingly. On another occasion, the manager of a Japanese insurance company applied to an English expert for advice on the state of the firm, which ssemed to be not wholly satisfactory. When the expert looked into the accounts, he discovered a deficit of 700,000 *yen,* which of course he advised the company to publish, adding that the best way to make it good would be to write it off from the reserve fund. A grateful acknowledgment was received; but—

so the reply ran—the Englishman's advice could not be taken,
"because, according to government regulations, all insurance
companies were obliged to hold a reserve of 500,000 *yen*." The
accounts were therefore "cooked," and not for eighteen months
more were the facts made public, when to conceal them was no
longer possible. From a Japanese point of view, there was
nothing specially grotesque or dishonest in this course; for
is not literal obedience to official regulations the first duty of
every loyal subject?

It is especially in business transactions at the open ports
that the European mind and Japanese logic are brought into
contact, whence frequently friction and mutual misunderstanding. Certain aspects of the mental attitude in question
recur, however, so constantly that the resident European
merchants have learnt how to deal with them. The peculiarity
most often cited is the refusal of Japanese tradesmen to make
a reduction on a quantity. We Europeans of course argue
thus:—" I, the buyer, am giving a large order; the seller will
in any case make a considerable profit on this single
transaction, comparatively quickly and with comparatively
slight trouble; therefore he can afford to lower his price. If
a dozen goes at the rate of so much, the gross must go at so
much less." Nothing appears to us more obvious:—it is a
cardinal principle of our trade. But the Japanese dealer
views the matter differently. " If," says he, " Messrs. Smith
and Co., instead of ordering only one bale of silk, order a
hundred, that shows that they are badly in want of it, and
must be able to pay a good price. Furthermore, if I sell all
I have to them, I shall have none left for other customers,
which may prove very inconvenient. Their expecting me to
reduce my figure is another instance of that unreasonableness
on the part of the redhaired foreigner, of which I and my
countrymen have already witnessed so many proofs." Hence
of course a dead-lock, but for the fact, already noted, that
many European merchants engaged in the Far-Eastern trade
have by this time learnt this peculiarity, and protect them-

selves against it by such devices as splitting up their orders and giving them in different names.

The subject is an extremely curious one. Sometimes, after a recurrence of astounding instances, one is apt to exclaim that Japanese logic is the very antipodes of European logic, that it is like London and New Zealand,—when the sun shines on the one, 'tis night-time in the other, and *vice versa*. Were it really so, action would be easy enough:—one would simply have to go by the "rule of contraries." But no; that will not do either. The contradiction is only occasional, it only manifests itself sporadically and along certain,—or uncertain —lines; it is more like a fold in a garment, a crease which you know not where to expect; and the result is that the oldest resident—for all that his hair has grown grey in the land of the bamboo and the jinrikisha—may still, to the end of the chapter, be pulled up sharp, and forced to exclaim that all his experience does not yet suffice to probe the depths of the mental disposition of this fascinating, but enigmatical race.

Race, yes, that is it. The word slipped accidentally from our pen; but racial difference is doubtless the explanation of the phenomenon under discussion,—an explanation which, it is true, explains nothing, a key not possible practically to fit into the lock, but nevertheless an index of the truth. Why so? Because "Man" is an exploded fiction. Instead of "Man" in the abstract, anthropology shows us races of men, each with an intellectual constitution differing slightly from other races. That each race should object to the others, should fail to enter into the ways and thoughts of the others, is but one aspect of the assertion of its own individuality. But here a distinction is called for. Europeans dislike the Chinaman or the "Nigger" instinctively, but they are not perplexed by him, because they dismiss him summarily as "a queer creature." His pigtail or his black skin accounts for his funny ways. They would be surprised if he did think as they think. It is when different races have come to dress alike, to use the same sort of phraseology, have closely similar institutions, and in fact stand on the same general plane of civilisation, that a painful shock is caused whenever the fundamental contradiction happens to break through the surface. Many of us have experienced somewhat of the same feeling at home, in the case of persons having foreign blood in their veins. They may speak English like natives, and be imbued with English notions. Yet suddenly they will go off, as it were, at a tangent, showing that, though with us, they are not of us. We thought they were our cousins, and we make the unwelcome discovery that they are strangers after all.

Long-tailed Fowls. Few things Japanese are more curious and beautiful than the long-tailed cock, which a century of artificial selection has produced from common barndoor fowls at the village of Shinowara near Kōchi in the island of Shikoku. They are of various hues, some being pure white. The tail-feathers, which are from 15 to 24 in number and are never moulted, measure from 7 or 8 to 11 ft. in length, and proceed from quills considerably stouter than those of ordinary fowls. The present writer has measured one specimen 13½ ft. long; and as great a length as 18 ft. is said to have been attained. The body-feathers, which hang down on either side of the back above the tail grow to a length of 4 ft., adding greatly to the ornamental appearance of the bird.

As it is essential to the preservation of the tail-feathers that they be allowed to hang free, these cocks are kept in high narrow cages, quite dark except close to the top; for light at the bottom would attract them. When the tail-feathers become too long and touch ground in the cage, a bamboo is put a little way back, so as to form an arch and thus increase the distance. The bird sits all day on a flat perch three inches wide, and is only taken out once in two days, and allowed to walk about for half-an-hour or so, a man holding up its tail all the while to prevent it from getting torn or soiled. Once or twice a month it is carefully washed with warm water, and is then as carefully dried on some high place,—the roof or wherever may

be most convenient—a man holding the tail till it is quite dry.
The birds are fed on unhulled rice and greens. They must be
given plenty of water. When one of the long-tailed cocks is
to be moved from place to place, it is put in a long narrow box
similar to those in which the Japanese keep *kakemono* (hanging
scrolls), the birds body being laid at full length, the tail
twisted round as little as may be. The dimensions of the box
are about 6 inches square, and 4 ft. 6 in. long. There is a
grating for air at one end only, and a division to guard the
feathers.

The hen of course is as nothing by the side of these splendid
cocks. Yet even she is a handsome bird, with tail-feathers
longer than those of any ordinary hen,—sometimes as much
as 8 inches. The hens lay in spring and autumn, one bird
producing 30 eggs yearly, which are hatched by other hens.
One, or at most two, hens are allowed to each breeding cock.
The latter's tail-feathers are cut, to allow of his walking about
freely. Thus does he pay with his beauty for the privilege of
liberty ,and of living a little longer than his long-tailed, captive,
and celibate brethren. It is satisfactory, however, to know that
even they are fairly hardy, bearing both heat and cold well,
and sometimes living to the age of nine. They are almost
as tame as dogs, and will nestle most affectionately on their
master's arm when taken out of their dark travelling-box into
the light of day.

Lotus. The so-called lotus of this country is really a species
of water-lily, the *Nelumbium,* which inhabits shallow ponds,
wherefore the Japanese Buddhists compare a virtuous man
dwelling in this wicked world to a lotus-flower growing out of
the mud. Sir Monier Williams says that "Its constant use
as an emblem seems to result from the wheel-like form of the
flower,—the petals taking the place of spokes, and thus
typifying the doctrine of perpetual cycles of existence." In
any case, the connection between the lotus and Buddhism

is very close. Buddha is figured standing on a lotus, gold and silver paper lotuses are carried at funerals, tombstones are often set on an inverted lotus-flower of stone as their base, lotus-beds often surround shrines built on islets. Owing to this association with the idea of death the lotus is a flower apart, not sharing in the popularity of the cherry-blossom, the iris, and the chrysanthemum. But this sentimental objection does not exclude its pips and roots from being used as a common article of diet.

Stately and yet tender is the beauty of the lotus-blossom early on a summer's morning—for its petals close before the overpowering heat of the August noonday—while the great bluish-green leaves, studded with water-drops, continue to reflect the sky.

Luchu. Luchu—pronounced *Dūchū* by the natives and *Ryūkyū* by the Japanese—is, in its widest acceptation, the general name of several groups of islands which stretch nearly the whole way between the Southernmost outlying islets of the Japanese archipelago and the North-Eastern extremity of Formosa. But it is usually restricted in practice to the central group, the chief members of which are Amami-Ōshima and Okinawa. This group is of coral formation, and lies between 127° and 130° long. east of Greenwich, and between 26° and 28° 30′ of North lat. To this position it owes a mild climate, marred only by the extreme violence of occasional typhoons during the summer months. The soil is so fertile as to produce two crops of rice yearly.

In race and language the Luchuans are closely allied to the Japanese, but for many centuries the two peoples seem not to have communicated with each other. The veil lifts in A.D. 1187 with the accession of King Shunten, said to have been a son of Tametomo, the famous Japanese archer. It is recorded that the Luchuans first sent an ambassador with presents to the Shōgun of Japan in the year 1451, that they discontinued such presents or tribute at the beginning of the seventeenth century, and were chastised for this neglect by the then Prince of

Satsuma. Luchu continued to be a sub-fief of Satsuma, but with a ruler bearing the title of King, until the time of the Japanese revolution of 1868. Meanwhile the Luchuans, who had obtained their civilisation from China, also paid tribute to the Chinese Court, and received investiture for their kinglets from Peking. The little kingdom thus faced two ways, so that trouble was bound to ensue. An embassy was sent to Tōkyō in 1878, to endeavour to arrange matters in such wise that the double protectorate might be maintained,—China being, as the envoys said, honoured by the Luchuans as their father, and Japan as their mother. But the Japanese Government refused to admit this claim. The Luchuan king was brought captive to Tōkyō in 1879, and the archipelago was organised into a Japanese prefecture under the title of Okinawa-Ken. This change, though intensely disagreeable to the little insular Court and aristocracy, who forfeited most of their privileges, is believed to have been beneficial to the people at large.

The Luchuans—even the men—are distinguished in appearance by a top-knot of hair, through which they pass a large pin or skewer of gold, silver, or copper, according to their rank. Formerly corpses, instead of being interred at once, were left to decay either in a provisional grave or in a stream of water, and it was only after three years that the last funeral rites were performed. This custom has happily fallen into disuse. The capital of Luchu is Shuri, whose port is Nafa, called Okinawa by the Japanese. The chief products are rice and sugar, the latter of which is the main staple of commerce. The area of the islands has been roughly estimated at 1,000 square miles; and the population is 453,000. The Luchus may easily be reached from Kōbe via the Inland Sea and Kagoshima. The steamer first visits the island of Amami-Ōshima, and then proceeds to Nafa, where it stops three days. The round trip from Kōbe and back takes seventeen days.

Books recommended. *Customs and Culture of Okinawa* compiled by Gladys Zabilka; *Okinawa: A People and Their Gods* by James C. Robinson; *Okinawa: The History of an Island People* by George H. Kerr; *Okinawa at Work: Selected Tours of Industrial Establishments* by Isamu Fuchaku and Mitsugu Miyagi.

Luck (Gods of). The Seven Gods of Luck *(Shichi Fukujin)*
are: Fukurokuju, distinguished by a preternaturally long
head, and attended by a crane, a deer, or a tortoise;
Daikoku, who stands upon a pair of rice-bales and is
accompanied by a rat; Ebisu, bearing a fish; Hotei, with an
enormous naked abdomen, a bag on his back and a fan in his
hand; Bishamon, clad in armour, and bearing a spear and a toy
pagoda; Benten, distinguished by being the only female in the
assemblage and having it in her power to confer, not only
victory and riches, but eloquence and wisdom; the serpent or
dragon is her creature of predilection; lastly, Jurōjin, a sort
of repetition of Fukurokuju.

The Seven Gods of Luck have been swept together from
many incongruous sources—Japanese Shintoism, Chinese
Taoism, Indian Buddhism and Brahmanism. Their union in
one group is the result of nothing more recondite than popular
ignorance and confusion of ideas, and can be traced no further
back than the commencement of the 17th century. The reader
will find in Anderson's *Catalogue of Japanese and Chinese
Paintings in the British Museum* (pp. 27–46), a full discussion
of the origin and attributes of these divinities, and will be
surprised to discover how slender is the basis on which their
modern popularity has been reared.

Connected with the Gods of Luck is the *Takara-bune,* or
Treasure Ship," which is supposed to sail into port on New
Year's Eve, with the Gods of Luck as passengers and, as cargo,
the *takara-mono,* or " treasures " of popular lore, which are
enumerated by Anderson as follows:—the hat of invisibility,
the lucky rain-coat, the sacred key, the inexhaustible purse,
the precious jewel, the clove, the scrolls, the hammer, the
weight *(fundō),* and the *shippō,*—a flat object apparently
representing a coin. Pictures of this " Treasure Ship " are
hawked about the streets at New Year time, and every person
who puts one into the little drawer of his wooden pillow on
the night of the 2nd January, is believed to ensure a lucky
dream. At the side of the picture is printed a stanza of poetry
so arranged that the syllables, when read backwards, give the
same text as when read forwards.

Maps. Much the best maps of Japan are those now in course of publication by the Geological Office of the Imperial Department of Agriculture and Commerce. There are three series,—geological proper, agronomical, and topographical, these last being specially recommended for all ordinary purposes, and obtainable of Messrs. Kelly and Walsh at Yokohama. The Yokohama section is particularly useful, including, as it does, many of the localities most frequently visited by pleasure-seekers, such as Kamakura, Enoshima, Miyanoshita, etc. There are two editions of this valuable set of maps,—one on the scale of 1 in 200,000, the other of 1 in 400,000. Unfortunately, neither set has yet been pushed to completion. A complete map on the scale of 1 in 400,000 was, however, issued in 1900.

The *Fujimi Jū-san-Shū*, or "Thirteen Provinces round Fuji-yama," is the best of the old-fashioned Japanese maps. The distances are given in figures on the roads, and the green mountains rise as in a picture. The father of Japanese cartography was Inō Chūkei (born A.D. 1744), of whose life and labours Dr. Knott has given a short account in Vol. XVI. Part II. of the "Asiatic Transactions." The only reward he earned from the government of that day was to be cast into a dungeon.

Marriage. In everything relating to marriage, the difference between East and West is still very strongly marked. Marriage among the Japanese is less of a personal and more of a family affair than it is in Western lands. Religion has no say in the matter, and the law regards it from a different point of view. An Englishman chooses his wife himself; but the English law, though perfectly neutral during this initial stage of the proceedings, steps in as soon as the knot is tide, and imperiously forbids its severance except in case of gross misconduct by one of the parties. Japanese marriages, on the contrary, are arranged by the two families, and the step is less solemn and not irrevocable, Japanese law remaining as neutral at the end as at the beginning. For though marriage is a legal

contract while it lasts, it may, like other contracts, be
terminated by the joint request and consent of the contracting
parties.

The way things are managed is this. When their child—
whether boy or girl—has reached a marriageable age, the duty
of the parents is to secure a suitable partner. Custom, however,
rules that the conduct of the affair must be entrusted to a
middleman *(nakōdo)*—some discreet married friend, who not
only negotiates the marriage, but remains through life a sort
of godfather to the young couple, a referee to whom disputes
and even arrangements for divorce may be submitted for
arbitration. Having fixed on an eligible *parti,* the middleman
arranges for what is termed the *mi-ai,* literally, the "mutual
seeing,"—a meeting at which the lovers (if persons unknown
to each other may be so styled) are allowed to see, sometimes
even to speak to each other, and thus estimate each other's
merits. In strict etiquette, the interview should take place
either at the middleman's own residence, or at some other
private house designated by the parents on both sides. But
among the middle and lower classes, a picnic, a party to the
theatre, or a visit to a temple often serves the purpose. If the
man objects to the girl or the girl to the man after the "mutual
seeing," there is an end of the matter, in theory at least. But
in practice the young people are in their parents' hands, to do
as their parents may ordain. The girl, in particular, is a
nobody in the matter. It is not for girls to have opinions.

If both parties are satisfied with what they have seen of each
other, gifts consisting of clothes, or of money to purchase
clothes, and of certain kinds of fish and edible seaweed, are
exchanged between them. This exchange of presents is called
yuinō. It corresponds to betrothal, and is binding—if not in
actual law, at any rate in custom. The presents once
exchanged, neither party can draw back. A lucky day is then
chosen for the wedding. When it comes, the bride, dressed all
in white, the colour of mourning—to signify that she dies to
her own family, and that she will never leave her husband's
house but as a corpse—is borne away at nightfall to her new

home, escorted by the middleman and his wife. The parental house is swept out on her departure, and in former days a bonfire was lighted at the gate,—ceremonies indicative of the purification necessary after the removal of a dead body.

The wedding, which takes place immediately on the bride's arrival at the house of her husband's parents, is of the nature of a dinner-party. The distinguishing feature of it is what is termed the *san-san ku-do,* that is, literally, " three three, nine times," because both the bridegroom and the bride drink three times out of each of three wine-cups of different sizes, making nine times in all,—or rather they do not drink, but only lift the cup to their lips. Another essential part of the ceremony is the changing of garments. The bride, on reaching her new home, changes her white dress for one given to her by her husband. But immediately after the ceremonial drinking-bout, and while the guests are still assembled at the feast, she reties and puts on a coloured dress brought with her from her parents' house. The bridegroom changes his dress at the same time in another apartment.* At the conclusion of the feast, the newly married couple are led into the bridal chamber by the middleman and his wife, whereupon they pledge each other in nine more cups of wine. It is significant that the husband, as lord and master, now drinks first. At the earlier stage of the proceedings the bride drank first, in her quality of guest. This ends the wedding ceremony.

A few days late—strictly speaking it should be on the third day—a visit is paid by the couple to the bride's parents. This is termed her *sato-gaeri,* or " return home." On this occasion, she wears a dress presented to her by her husband or his family. Meantime the necessary notice has been given to the authorities, which is the only legal form to be observed. It consists in a request to the district office by the head of the family to which the girl formerly belonged, that her registration may be transferred to the office within whose

---

* Some men are now married in European evening dress, in which case no change takes place.

jurisdiction her husband, or the head of her husband's family, if the husband himself be not a householder, has his domicile. An official intimation of the transfer follows this request, and all is then in order.

The above is the usual form of marriage. In some cases, however, the bridegroom is adopted into the bride's family, instead of the bride into the bridegroom's. This takes place mostly when a parent has only a daughter or daughters, but no son. In order to preserve the family intact—due regard being had to the circumstance that no female can be its legal head—it is then necessary to adopt a son-in-law, who, literally becoming a son in the eyes of the law, drops his own surname and takes that of his wife. None but poor men are generally willing to place themselves in such a false position.

Amongst the lower classes, ceremonies and considerations of all kinds are often honoured only in the breach, many of the so-called marriages of plebeians being mere cohabitation founded on mutual convenience. This accounts for the " boy " and the cook—to their foreign master's increasing astonishment—being found to bring home a new wife almost as often as they bring home a new saucepan. Such laxity would never be tolerated in well-bred circles.

When it is added that a Japanese bride has no bridesmaids, that the young couple go off on no honeymoon, that a Japanese wife is not only supposed to obey her husband, but actually does so, that the husband, if well enough off, probably has a concubine besides and makes no secret of it, and that the mother-in-law, with us a terror to the man, is not only a terror but a daily and hourly cross to the girl—for in nine cases out of ten, the girl has to live with her husband's family and be at the beck and call of his relations—when due consideration is given to all these circumstances, it will be seen that marriage in Japan is a vastly different thing, socially as well as legally, from marriage in Anglo-Saxon countries. The reader will be still more firmly persuaded of this truth, if he will take the trouble to glance at the Article on Woman.

He will see that in this part of the world it is a case, not of *place aux dames,* but *place aux messieurs.**

The men, having everything their own way, naturally marry young. Speaking broadly, there are no bachelors in Japan. For an exactly contrary reason, there are no old maids. The girls are married off without being consulted, and they accept their fate as a matter of course, because their mothers and grandmothers, ever since the beginning of the world, accepted a like fate before them. One love marriage we have heard of, —one in thirty years. But then both the young people had been brought up in America. Accordingly they took the reins into their own hands, to the great scandal of all their friends and relations.

It would be interesting, were it possible, to ascertain statistically the effect on morality of early marriage as practised in this part of the world. Our impression is that the good results anticipated from such a system by certain European reformers do not show themselves here in fact. Not that wider intercourse with the people bears out the casual observer's harsh judgment on the standard of Japanese female morality. Japanese ladies are every whit as chaste as their Western sisters. But so far as we have been able to observe, the only effect of early marriage on the men is to change the date of their wild-oats sowing, making it come after wedlock instead of before. Divorce is common. During the earlier part of the period covered by statistics, the proportion of divorces to marriage was nearly as 1 to 3; but since 1901 matters have improved, and the figures are now about 1 to 5.

---

* May the writer be permitted here to record a little experience of his own ? In his *Introduction to the Kojiki,* he had drawn attention to the inferior place held by women in ancient as in modern Japan. Some years afterwards, six of the chief literati of the old school did him the honour to translate this *Introduction* into Japanese, with a running commentary. They patted him on the back for many things; but when they reached the observation anent the subjection of women, their wrath exploded. " The subordination of women to men," so runs this commentary, " is an extremely correct custom. To think the contrary is to harbour European prejudice......For the man to take precedence over the woman, is the grand law of heaven and earth. To ignore this, and to talk of the contrary as barbarous, is absurd."——It does not fall to every one's lot to be anathematised by half-a-dozen Japanese literary popes——and that, too, merely for taking the part of the ladies!

The immense majority of cases occur among the lower classes. The upper classes rarely resort to divorce. Why, indeed, should a man take the trouble to get separated from an uncongenial wife, when *any* wife occupies too inferior a position to be able to make herself a serious nuisance, and when society has no objection to his keeping any number of mistresses?

The student of anthropology may like to know that neither ancient nor modern Japanese custom shows any trace of exogamy,—a fact the more remarkable when one considers the immense influence exerted on Japan by China, where it has been forbidden from time immemorial for a man to marry a girl bearing the same surname as his own.

Books recommended. *A Daughter of the Samurai* by Etsu Inagaki Sugimoto; *Japanese Etiquette: An Introduction* by the World Fellowship Committee of the Tokyo Y.W.C.A.; *A Japanese Miscellany* by Lafcadio Hearn.

Maru. It is often asked: What does the word *Maru* mean in the names of ships—as *Tōkyō Maru, Sagami Maru, Hiryū Maru,* etc.? The answer is that the origin of the term is obscure. *Maru* means " round; " but how came ships by so inappropriate a name?

The first thing to note is that in former times ships had not the monopoly of the name. Swords, musical instruments of various kinds, pieces of armour, dogs, hawks, and the concentric sections of castles, were called *Maru* also. The probability is that two distinct words—*maru* and *maro*—have flowed into one, and so got confused. To name the concentric sections of a castle *maru*, "round," was but natural. The word *maro*, on the other hand, is an archaic term of endearment. Hence its use in such ancient proper names as *Tamura-Maro,* a great general who subdued the Ainos; *Abe-no-Nakamaro,* an eminent scholar of the eighth century; *Okina-maro,* a favourite dog of the Emperor Ichijō, and so on. The warrior's pet sword, the sportsman's favourite dog or hawk, the oarsman's boat, would naturally come to be distinguished by the same half-personal name, much as the English sailor or engineer calls his ship or locomotive " she." When the ancient word *maro* ceased to be understood, it would easily slide into the more familiar *maru,* by the alteration of the final vowel, *o* and *u* being particularly apt to interchange in Japanese.

Observe that *Maru* is applied to merchant vessels only. Men-of-war take *Kan* instead, as *Maya Kan, Asama Kan. Kan* was originally a Chinese word meaning " war-vessel." It is now pronounced *lan* in China itself, and is no longer there used in the same sense.

Massage has for centuries played an important role in Japanese medicine,—it, acupuncture, and the moxa being universally credited with more than all the many virtues which Beecham, among ourselves, claims for his pills, and " Mother Seigel " for her syrup. The shampooers, popularly known as *amma san,* also occupy a conspicuous place in Japanese social life. Immemorial custom limits the profession to the blind, who thus support their families, instead of, as is mostly the case in Western countries, being a burden to them. Such sums are they enabled to accumulate, that they often turn money-lenders as well and are correspondingly hated.

Till about the year 1870, all the shampooers in Japan formed one immense guild under two provosts, one of whom lived at Yedo, the other at Kyōto. This guild possessed various legal privileges, and admittance to it took place on the passing of certain tests and the payment of fees. It was divided into several grades, the rise from grade to grade being conditioned by new tests and higher fees. For the highest grade to which any ordinary blind mortal could aspire—the grade next under that of provost—a fee of $1,000 was exacted. This organisation is now fast falling into decay; but the melancholy whistle of the blind shampooer, as he slowly gropes his way along the street at night, staff in hand, is still one of the characteristic sounds of every Japanese town.

Massage is much to be recommended to tired pedestrians and to persons suffering from lumbago, rheumatism, and other pains and aches. The old-fashioned Japanese shampooers, however, make the mistake of shampooing down instead of shampooing up. A portion of the good done is thus neutralised, one object of scientific massage being to help back towards the centre the blood which is lingering in the superficial veins. This fact is now beginning to be known and acted on in Japan, —one of the fruits of German medical tuition.

Metal-work. Bronze was introduced into Japan from China via Korea, and the Japanese still call it "the Chinese metal" *(Kara kane)*. But it is the metal in which Japanese art was already winning its brightest laurels over a thousand years ago. The chief forms are the mirror, the temple bell, the gong, the vase (originally intended for the adornment of Buddhist altars), the lantern, and the colossal representation of divine personages. The temple bells at Ōsaka, Kyōtō, and Nara count among the largest in the world; but the grandest example of Japanese bronze-casting is the *Dai-butsu* (literally, "great Buddha") at Kamakura, which dates from the thirteenth century. He who has time should visit this *Dai-butsu* repeatedly; for, like Niagara, like St. Peter's, and several other of the greatest works of nature and of art, it fails to produce its full effect on a first or even on a second visit; but the impression it produces grows on the beholder each time that he gazes afresh at the calm, intellectual, passionless face, which seems to concentrate in itself the whole philosophy of Buddhism,—the triumph of mind over sense, of eternity over fleeting time, of the enduring majesty of Nirvana over the trivial prattle, the transitory agitations of mundane existence.

Armour is another use to which metal (iron and steel) was put from the very earliest ages. The best examples of iron and steel armour date from the thirteenth and fourteenth centuries. The best swords date from the same time. The ornamental sword-hilts, guards, etc., date only from the sixteenth century onwards. The eighteenth and nineteenth centuries were the most fruitful epoch for the production of small bronze objects, whose chief *raison d'être* is ornament, such, as clasps, paper-weights, small figures of animals mouthpieces for pipes, and vases intended for dwelling-rooms, —not for Buddhist altars, as in earlier days. Damascening, or inlaying on metal, has been carried to great perfection, notably of late years, when designs in various metals and alloys on a basis of bronze or iron have been made to reproduce whole landscapes with the minuteness of a painting. Contemporary artists in silver are obtaining delightful results. Hitherto the gold and silver work of the Japanese had been less remarkable than their bronzes. In enamel—especially in what is known as cloisonné—they are beyond all praise. (See also Articles on ARMOUR, CLOISONNE, MIRRORS, and SWORDS).

Books recommended. *The Armour Book in Honcho Gunki Ko* by Hakuseki Arai; *The Arts of Japan: An Illustrated History* by Hugo Munsterberg; *The Folk Arts of Japan* by Hugo Munsterberg; *History of Japanese Religion* by Masaharu Anesaki; *Legend in Japanese Art* by Henri L. Joly.

Mikado. Though this is the name by which the whole outer world knows the sovereign of Japan, it is not that now used in Japan itself, except in poetry and on great occasions. The Japanese have got into the habit of calling their sovereign by such alien Chinese titles as *Tenshi*, "the Son of Heaven;" *Ten-ō*, or *Tennō*, "the Heavenly Emperor;" *Shujō*, "the Supreme Master." His designation in the official translations of modern public documents into English is "Emperor." It will be a pity if this entirely supersedes, in literary and colloquial European usage, the traditional title of "Mikado," which is at once ancient, sonorous, and distinctively Japanese.

The etymology of the word *Mikado* is not quite clear. Some —and theirs is the current opinion—trace it to *mi*, "august," and *kado,* a " gate," reminding one of the " Sublime Porte " of Turkey. Sir Ernest Satow prefers to derive it from *mika,* an archaic word for " great," and *to,* " a place." In either case the word is one indicative of the highest respect, as it is but natural that the name used by the Japanese of old to designate their heaven-descended sovereign should be. The word *Mikado* is often employed to denote the monarch's Court as well as the monarch himself, Japanese idiom lending itself to such double usage for a single word.

The antiquity of the Imperial family of Japan is unparalleled. The Japanese themselves claim that, after endless ages passed in higher spheres, it began its earthly career with the first human monarch, Jimmu Tennō, in the year 660 before Christ. From this, historical criticism bids us subtract more than a millennium, as Japanese history does not become a record of solid facts till the fifth or sixth century *after* Christ. It should also be pointed out that the succession has by no means followed those stringent rules which Europe considers necessary for legitimacy. Many Mikados, even down to quite recent times, have been the sons of concubines; others have been merely adopted from some related branch. Still, all deductions made, the family as such stands forth proudly as the oldest in the world. We know positively that it has reigned ever since the dawn of history in this archipelago, and that even then it was considered of immemorial age. The fact is peculiarly striking, if we reflect upon the usually brief life of Oriental dynasties. Little wonder, therefore, all things considered, if a religious reverence for the Imperial line is as axiomatic in Japan, as completely removed beyond all doubt or controversy, as is the doctrine of the equal rights and duties of all men in the democratic societies of the West.

The present Mikado was born on the 3rd November, 1852, and succeeded to the throne in 1867. His name is Mutsuhito; but this name is scarcely ever mentioned, and is probably not even known to the great majority of the nation. In Japan the Emperor is simply the Emperor,—not a personality, an almost familiar individuality, as King Edward, for instance, and Kaiser Wilhelm are to us. Such a question as " Is the Mikado popular? " which we have sometimes been asked in England, shows the questioner to be ten thousand miles from an appreciation of the attitude of men's minds in Japan, or indeed in any Far-eastern land,—an attitude entirely reverential and distant, as to a god. Future generations of Japanese will probably know the present monarch as *Meiji Tennō,* the word *Tennō,* as already explained, signifying " Henvenly Emperor," and *Meiji* being the chronological designation of the years comprised in his reign. The reign itself will doubtless stand out in Japanese history as prominently as those witnessed Japan's first great revolution, —her conversion to Buddhism and Chinese civilisation.

A point of etiquette which foreigners should bear in mind, is that neither the Emperor himself nor any member of the Imperial Family must ever be *looked down on.* Should an Imperial procession pass by, do not stand at an upper window or on any commanding height. The occasional infraction of this rule has given great offence, and produced disagreeable results.

Books recommended. *A Daughter of the Samurai* by Etsu Inagaki Sugimoto; *Hermann Roesler and the Making of the Meiji State* by Johannes Siemes; *Japan: An Attempt at Interpretation* by Lafcadio Hearn; *Japan's Modern Century* edited by Edmund Skrzypczak.

Mineral Springs. Japan, the land of volcanoes and earth-quakes, is naturally rich in mineral springs: and the Japanese, with their passion for bathing, make the fullest use of them. The most noted of the many hundreds of Japanese spas are:— for sulphur baths, Kusatsu, Ashinoyu, Yumoto near Nikkō, Nasu, Shiobara, and Unzen near Nagasaki; for iron baths, Ikao, Arima, and Beppu; for salt baths, Atami and Isobe. Miyanoshita, one of those best-known to foreigners, has only traces of salt and soda. Its waters may therefore be used without medical advice, simply for pleasure's sake. There are powerful iron and sulphur springs at Ōjigoku (lit. " big hell "), some four miles beyond Miyanoshita. The crater of

Shirane-san in the province of Kōtsuke has a pool so rich in hydrochloric acid ($2\frac{1}{2}$ per cent. according to Dr. Divers, F.R.S.), that it may be administered as an excellent lemonade in the treatment of stomach and other affections. But speaking generally, sulphur, iron sulphate, and salt are everywhere the chief minerals found in the Japanese springs. Excepting the Hirano water used for Seltzer, very few contain carbonic acid gas. Few are cold; few are efficacious, like Vichy and Karlsbad, in diseases of the stomach and liver. On the other hand, the Kusatsu waters probably stand alone in the world by reason of their double character, consisting, as they do, of cold corrosively acid water and nearly boiling sulphur water. Little short of miraculous are the cures which, by virtue of their temperature and their mineral acids, sulphur, and arsenic, they are capable of working, when mixed, upon syphilitic persons and on those afflicted with the severer forms of rheumatism. The Japanese have a proverb to the effect that love is the only grave distemper against which Kusatsu can effect nothing.

In many cases a spring is famous in its own neighbourhood only. But it then almost invariably gains in one way what it loses in another. The good country folk for twenty miles around consider it a panacea for all the ills to which flesh is heir. It is impossible to picture to oneself anything more grotesquely dissimilar to an Ems or a Homburg than one of these tiny spas, perched—say—amidst the mountains of Shinshū or or Etchū, and visited only by Japanese of the most old-fashioned type and limited means—where, instead of a table d'hôte, each guest is served in his own poor room with a bowl of rice or maybe millet, a scrap of salted egg-plant, and perhaps, on high days and holidays, a small broiled fish. Even this is luxury compared with the state of things existing in some remote districts, where the peasant invalids come bringing their own rice and bedding with them on pack-horses, and pay only five cents a day for lodging, for the use of the mineral spring, and a titbit or two at each meal to help the rice down.

In opposition to all European sanitary ideas, the mineral springs of Japan are used at very high temperatures. Invalids enter baths of from 110° to 115° Fahrenheit, and their healthy friends go in with them for the sake of killing time agreeably. At Kusatsu the temperature of the baths is higher still. It ranges from 120° to 130° Fahrenheit; and as the first effect of the waters is to bring out sores all over the body, even if there were none before, the sufferings of those condemned to " make a cure " may be imagined. So excruciating is the agony that experience has dictated a peculiar device for meeting it:—the bathers are subjected to military discipline. The squad of unfortunates approaches the bath to the sound of the trumpet, they wet their scalps and foreheads at another trumpet blast, in order to prevent a rush of blood to the head, and so on throughout the performance, notice being given to them of the passing of the minutes while they sit boiling, with a view to keeping up their courage by the knowledge that the ordeal will soon be over. The whole life at Kusatsu is so strange that he whose stomach is not easily upset by nasty sights would do well to go and inspect it. To squeamish persons we say most emphatically, " Keep away ! "

Mirrors. Old-fashioned Japanese mirrors are circular, and are made of metal,—generally of bronze coated on the front with an amalgam of tin and quicksilver beautifully polished. The back is adorned in relief with flowers, birds, or Chinese characters, and there is a handle on one side, the general appearance being that of a sort of handsome metal fan.

An extraordinary peculiarity characterises some of these Japanese mirrors: sunlight reflected from their *face* displays a luminous image of the design on their *back !* So strange a phenomenon has naturally attractead the attention of men of science. After much speculation, it has been clearly proved by Professors Ayrton and Perry to arise from the fact that the curvature of the face of the mirror over the plain part of the back is greater than over the design. The mirror is cast flat, and then rendered convex before polishing, by being so strongly scratched with an iron tool as to cause a buckling of the metal into a convex form, which convexity is afterwards increased by rubbing in mercury repeatedly. The effect of both these processes is greater on the thinner parts of the mirror than on the parts over the raised design. Hence the unequal convexity, which gives the reflection of the design from the face of the mirror.

Books recommended. *The Arts of Japan: An Illustrated History* by Hugo Munsterberg; *The Folk Arts of Japan* by Hugo Munsterberg.

Missions. (I. ROMAN CATHOLIC.) When the first Portuguese reached Japan in 1542, one Anjirō, a native of Kagoshima in Satsuma, who had many sins on his conscience, heard through them of the fame of Francis Xavier, "the Apostle of the Indies," and started for Malacca in quest of this wonderful soul-doctor. After missing Xavier once (he being then in the Moluccas), Anjirō ultimately met him at Malacca in 1547. The reports of Japan brought to Xavier by this Japanese and by certain Portuguese merchants aroused in his breast a desire to evangelise the island empire. Accordingly Anjirō, who already knew something of the Portuguese language, was sent for further instruction to the Jesuit College at Goa, where he and his servant, together with a third Japanese, received baptism. In April, 1549, Xavier, accompanied by these three and by two compatriots of his own,—one of whom was a monk,—left Goa for Japan. The party reached Kagoshima in August of the same year, and during Xavier's twelve months' stay in that province about 150 natives were baptised. The total result of his twenty-six months' sojourn in Japan was nearly 1,000 converts. In the winter of 1550–1 he made an extremely arduous journey to Kyōto, the capital; but it proved fruitless from a religious point of view. His long stay at Yamaguchi in Western Japan (1551) produced 600 baptisms. At Hirado there were about 200.

The seed thus sown grew apace. Thirty years later, in 1582, the "Annual Letter" sent from Japan to the Jesuit headquarters at Rome puts the number of converts in the empire at 150,000, more or less. This certainly was a wonderful harvest, especially when the paucity of the reapers is taken into consideration. In this year of 1582 there were, indeed, as many as 75 members of the Company of Jesus in the country, some 30 of whom were Japanese. But down to 1577 there had never been more than eighteen, and down to 1563 no more than nine. Of the 150,000 converts, about 25,000 were in Central Japan, 10,000 in the province of Bungo (North-Eastern Kyūshū), and the remainder in certain maritime fiefs in Kyūshū,—Ōmura, Arima, Amakusa, and the Gotō Islands. The method of conversion adopted in these fiefs was simple. The local princelets were eager for the Portuguese trade, and the merchants loyally co-operated with the Jesuit missionaries. The plan pursued by these last was to convert the rulers, and then get them to proscribe all non-Christian cults within their domains. In some cases, only a single day's notice was granted for those who would not adopt the foreign religion to quit their ancestral homes, the images of Buddha were hacked to pieces, and the native temples given over to the flames. In Central Japan, where there was no foreign trade, the conversions seem often to have been the result of honest conviction; but the *modus operandi* was the same. Hence the fact, inexplicable at first sight, that of 24,000 converts in the neighbourhood of Kyōto, no less than 18,000 were upon one small fief. Kyōto itself never contained more than 300 believers.

The celebrated ruler Nobunaga (see p. 234) treated the Christians with marked favour. On his death in 1582, Hideyoshi, a greater ruler still, assumed the direction of affairs. He, too, befriended the missionaries during the first five years of his sway; consequently, his sudden suppression of Christianity in 1587 came like a bolt from the blue. The account given of this circumstance by Froez, a leading Jesuit, is as follows:—One of Hideyoshi's Court physicians, a bigoted

Buddhist, " had noticed that the Fathers were devoting most
" of their efforts to the conversion of men of noble birth; and,
" believing that their pretext of saving souls was merely a
" device for the conquest of Japan, he had done his best to rouse
" Hideyoshi's suspicions." The latter " had at first merely
" laughed at him; " but " when he arrived in Kyūshū against
" the King of Satsuma, and noted that many lords with their
" vassals had become Christians, and that the same were bound
" to each other in great concord and exceedingly devoted to
" the Fathers, he began to recall what " Toquun had already
" filled his ears with, and to understand (although in this
" he was auguring falsely) that the propagation of the faith
" would be prejudicial to the safety of the Empire. And this
" is the true cause of the aversion he now declares."
Nevertheless, the persecution foreshadowed by this change of
sentiment on the ruler's part was delayed ten years. Despite
his suspicions of the missionaries' ulterior aims, Hideyoshi
clung to the present advantages which accrued to his realm
from the Portuguese trade, and he temporarily shut his eyes
to the presence of 130 or 140 Jesuits on Japanese soil.

Meantime, mischief had been brewing in another quarter.
A Papal Bull, promulgated in 1585, had given the Jesuits a
monopoly of missionary work in Japan, and the terms of the
Concordat entered into between Spain and Portugal in 1580
on the occasion of the union of the two crowns confined the
Japan trade to members of the latter nation. However, in
the year 1593, the intrigues of a Japanese adventurer anxious
for trade with the Philippine Islands, then a Spanish
possession, led to the despatch from Manila of four Spanish
Franciscan monks, not indeed as missionaries but as
ambassadors. They were permitted to proceed to Kyōto, on
the express condition of engaging in no proselytising work;
but this pledge they violated in the most flagrant manner.
Hideyoshi's attention was called to their doings in October,
1596, by an incident which has remained famous. A Spanish
galleon, called the " San Felipe," had been stranded on the
Japanese coast, and her cargo, including 600,000 crowns in

silver, had been confiscated. In the absence of the captain, the pilot endeavoured to overawe the local Japanese authorities. He produced a map of the world, and pointed out the vast extent of the Spanish monarch's dominions. On being asked how it was that so many countries had been subjected to a single ruler, he replied: " Our kings begin by sending into " the countries they wish to conquer priests who induce the " people to embrace our religion; and when these have made " considerable progress, troops are despatched who combine " with the new Christians, and then our kings have not much " trouble in accomplishing the rest.* " This speech was reported to Hideyoshi, whose fury knew no bounds. The immediate outcome was that six Spanish Franciscans, together with seventeen of their native converts and three Japanese Jesuits, were crucified at Nagasaki on the 5th February, 1597.

To this first outbreak of persecution there succeeded a respite of several years, traceable partly to the civil wars and other distractions that accompanied the establishment of the Shogunate in the family of Tokugawa Ieyasu. This powerful ruler suppressed Christianity for political reasons in 1614, ordering the deportation of all the foreign ecclesiastics. But 47 contrived to remain behind at Nagasaki and elsewhere, and the others quickly returned. Meantime, some of the native Christian lords had been seeking to establish relations abroad, the most noted of these efforts being the despatch of envoys from the Kyūshū Princes to the Pope in 1582, and that of Date, Lord of Sendai, to the King of Spain and the Pope in 1613. When Ieyasu finally triumphed over all his political enemies, wih some of whom the Catholics had been associated, a duel to the death began between the Japanese authorities who were resolved to maintain the political integrity of the Empire which they believed to be menaced, and the foreign

---

* Though not to be taken literally, there was doubtless a foundation of fact for the statement thus imprudently blurted out:—the rulers of Spain and Portugal, as we know full well from their proceedings in other quarters of the globe, were anything but single-minded in their dealings with native races. History repeats itself; for the conduct of Europe towards China in our own day exhibits precisely the same medley of genuine piety on the part of the missionaries, and shameless aggression on the part of the countries which send them out.

priests equally resolved to discharge what they held to be their duty to God. This contest lasted for nearly thirty years, the missionaries displaying intrepid devotion, and many of the converts a remarkable constancy. At its most flourishing period (before the persecution of 1597), Christianity in Japan numbered 300,000 converts. One Japanese record tells us that no fewer than 200,000 persons were " punished " for the crime of Christianity. " Punished," however, evidently cannot mean " executed; " for the Jesuit Father Cardim's list of martyrs gives only between 1,400 and 1,500 victims. It is plain, from the missionary records themselves, that the Japanese authorities were far from eager to proceed to extremities. Even at the last moment those converts who consented to abandon their belief were spared, and such few ecclesiastics as apostatised were granted a decent maintenance. But the heroic persistence of the great majority forced the government's hand, and (once the suppression of Christianity had been decided on in principle) left them no choice in the matter. Two irreconcilable ideals were at stake; each side was fighting for what it held most sacred. Hence the application and the endurance on Japanese soil of tortures no less fiendish than those with which Spanish and Portuguese rulers had extinguished heresy in their own dominions. The Japanese government emerged victorious from this deadly duel; but its victory was achieved only by the cessation of intercourse with the outside world, and the all but total isolation of the Empire.

Nevertheless, the Church of Japan was not forgotten. The Jesuit Father Sidotti and others, nothing daunted, disembarked on the Japanese coast at intervals during the eighteenth century, but were at once cast into prison. In 1846 the Pope nominated a bishop and several missionaries, who took up their station in the neighbouring Luchu Islands, and entered Japan on the signing of the treaties of 1858. These men had the joy, in 1865, to discover several Christian communities round about Nagasaki, surviving the ruin of the church of their forefathers over two centuries before. They had preserved certain prayers, the rite of baptism, and a few books. But if these Christian communities survived, the persecuting spirit survived also. In 1867–70, all those Christians—and they numbered over four thousand—who refused to forswear the faith, were torn from their native villages and distributed over various provinces of the empire, where they were kept as prisoners by the respective Daimyōs. After some years of exile, they were at length set at liberty in 1873. The Church of Japan, thus restored, is now slowly but surely developing, thanks to the toleration enjoyed under the Imperial Government.

The Church was governed from 1846 to 1877 by a single bishop, from 1877 to 1888 by two bishops, from 1888 to 1891 by three, and since 1891 by an archbishop (assisted by a bishop coadjutor) and three bishops, whose respective residences are at Tōkyō, Ōsaka, Nagasaki, and Sendai. The Catholic population of the empire amounted, in 1903, to 58,000 souls, as against 44,300 in 1891. They are grouped in some 360 stations or congregations, spread more or less all over the country, but most thickly in the island of Kyūshū. The clergy consists—besides the archibishop and bishops—of 129 European missionaries and 32 Japanese priests. The missionaries are all seculars belonging to the *Société des Mission Etrangères de Paris*.* There are also 70 European teachers, of whom 18 Cistercian friars devoted to agriculture in the island of Yezo, and 197 nuns (of whom 145 are European and 52 Japanese) engaged in teaching. The missionaries are assisted by 280 male catechists, besides 265 women employed as catechists and in nursing the sick. The Catholic educational establishments include three seminaries for native priests, where 60 students are now pursuing their course, and 58 other schools and orphanages, with an attendance of about 6,000 pupils. There exist furthermore two lepers' homes, where 147 lepers are cared for, and several small hospitals.

---

* The summary here given does not include the island of Formosa, where there are old-established missions in the hands of Spanish Dominican friars.

II. ANGLICAN. The Church of England, in conjunction with the Episcopal Churches of America and Canada, has missions collectively designed by the title of *Nihon Sei Kōkwai*, or the Church of Japan. The origin of this church goes back to the year 1859, when two American clergymen settled in Nagasaki. The missions in Tōkyō, both American and English, were started at the same time, in 1873. There are now six bishops—two American and four English,—some 64 foreign and 50 Japanese priests and deacons, and 87 foreign lay workers of both sexes, besides a large body of Japanese catechists and school-teachers, and over 11,000 baptised persons on the roll. The increase in numbers has been steady during the past few years, as has also the amount contributed from native sources for self-support. The affairs of the Church are managed by a synod consisting of the bishops and of delegates from the clergy and laity, both foreign and Japanese. These delegates are themselves elected at the local synods, which are presided over by their respective bishops, and held annually in the various jurisdictions of North and South Tōkyō, Kyōto, Ōsaka, Kyūshū, and Hokkaidō, into which the whole country has now been divided. The general synod meets once in three years. The aim of the Church is to be in communion with, but not in subjection to, the Churches of England and America, —in fact, to occupy in Japan much the same position as the Anglican Church occupies in the United States. The Japanese Prayer Book is based, with necessary modifications, on those of the Anglican and American Churches.

III. PROTESTANT. In 1859, shortly after the arrival of the earliest Anglican missionaries, representatives of the American Presbyterian and Dutch Reformed Churches landed in Japan, and the Protestant missions have ever since continued to be chiefly in American hands. The first baptism took place in 1864, the first native church was organised at Yokohama in 1872, and the first church building was consecrated in 1875. In 1872 the work of Biblical translation, till then hindered by want of sufficient familiarity with the language, was vigorously undertaken. It should be added that the existence of several Chinese versions, which all educated Japanese could read, rendered the necessity for a version in the vernacular less urgent than would have been the case in other lands. A complete version of the New Testament was published in 1880, of the Old Testament in 1887.* Meanwhile the opposition of the government to Christianity faded away, and the number of converts increased,—slowly at first, for in 1872 no more than ten persons had been baptised, but afterwards by leaps and bounds. Besides actual evangelising work, much general school work has been engaged in. The venerable Dr. Hepburn and others have also combined the art of healing bodies with that of curing souls. The educational efforts of the missionaries have met with amazing success, even allowing for an interval of disappointment during the last decade of the nineteenth century, consequent on the spread of chauvinistic feeling and the difficulty of conforming to school standards insisted on by a non-Christian Government. Obstructions of this nature have now been removed, the higher departments of certain Christian colleges (including at least one theological school) having even received formal official recognition, and been accorded equal rank in the national educational system with those government colleges that represent the grade immediately below the Imperial Universities. Thus their scholars share in the much-prized privilege of postponement of the call to military service until the completion of eight years of school life.

The leading Protestant denominations having missions in Japan may be classified under four heads, which we notice in the order of their local importance:—

The *Presbyterians*, representing seven religious societies, number 55 male and 53 female missionaries,† whose labours

---

* Unfortunately the Japanese language, intricate and impersonal, is singularly ill-fitted to reproduce the rugged sublimity of Hebrew thought. Chinese lends itself somewhat better to the task.

† If the wives of married missionaries be included in the enumeration, the number of female missionaries in this and the other Protestant mission will be considerably increased.

are aided by those of 38 ordained and 112 unordained Japanese fellow-workers,—the whole force being distributed over 74 organised churches, besides many out-stations. In 1903 (the last year for which statistics are available), the total membership numbered over 12,400, and contributed during that year a sum of 34,800 *yen*. They suported 3 boarding-schools for boys and 11 for girls, together with 10 day-schools, the aggregate number of scholars being 2,289. The various Presbyterian bodies—American and Scotch—amalgamated in the year 1877 into a single church, which is now known as the *Nihon Kirisuto Kyōkwai*, or Church of Christ in Japan, and which, no longer insisting on such standards of doctrine as the Canons of the Synod of Dort, the Westminster Confession of Faith, the Shorter Catechism, or the Heidelberg Catechism, confines itself to a much simpler "Confession of Faith," consisting mainly of the Apostles Creed.

The *Congregational* or *Kumi-ai* Churches are associated exclusively with one body,—the mission of the American Board of Commissioners for Foreign Missions. In 1903 there were 23 male and 25 female workers on the staff, besides 48 ordained and 41 unordained Japanese. There are 106 organised churches, 38 of which are self-supporting, and over 11,400 members, who in 1903 contributed 41,800 *yen*. The Dōshisha College at Kyōto—by far the largest Christian institution in Japan—is under the control of this mission.

The *Methodists,* representing six American societies and one Canadian, consist of 59 male and 71 female missionaries, 126 ordained and 101 unordained Japanese fellow-workers, 139 organised churches, and over 9,600 members, who in 1903 contributed 36,600 *yen*. The Methodists have 18 boarding-schools and 19 day-schools, with a total of 4,761 scholars. To them belongs the Aoyama Gakuin, the most important Christian College in Tōkyō.

The *Baptists* represent four American societies, and number 36 male and 24 female missionaries, with 28 ordained and 45 unordained Japanese workers in 55 organised churches, with a membership of over 3,361, who in 1903 contributed 5,681 *yen*. The two leading Baptist bodies support a theological seminary with 18 students, one academy for boys, five boarding-schools for girls, with a total of 302 students, and eight day-schools with 588 pupils.

The *Salvation Army,* which invaded Japan in 1895, has now 15 corps here with 51 officers. Ten thousand copies of the *Toki no Koe* (the Japanese edition of the "War-Cry") are published fortnightly. The Army has deserved well of Japan by the stout fight which it has made and still makes to rescue girls from the thraldom of licensed immorality.

Besides the above, must be mentioned the *Society of Friends;* furthermore, the American and London *Religious Tract Societies,* which have joint headquarters at Tōkyō, and the *Young Men's Christian Association of Japan,* etc., the total number of missions represented being twenty-eight.

Numerous as are the Protestant bodies labouring on Japanese soil, and widely as some of them differ in doctrine, fairness requires it to be stated that they rarely, if ever, have made Japan the scene of sectarian strife. The tendency has been rather to minimise differences,—a tendency exemplified in the amalgamation of the various Presbyterian churches and of the various Episcopal churches, the proposed amalgamation of the Methodist churches, and the cementing influence of the Young Men's Christian Association work and of the General Conferences of all denominations held from time to time. At one period, orthodoxy and union were menaced by the advent of the so-called "Liberal Churches,"—the *Unitarians* and *Universalists* (1889–90),—who for a brief season seemed likely to obtain a hold over the Japanese mind. But the Unitarian mission is now extinct, and the Universalists have little or no following. The *German Evangelical Mission,* while numbering few actual converts, claims (with what justice we have no means of estimating) to have exerted a strong influence upon the thought of the Christian community, and even upon others outside the Christian pale.

IV. The ORTHODOX RUSSIAN CHURCH, presided over by Bishop Nicolaï, and served by 37 native priests and deacons, has had a mission in Japan ever since the year 1861. It claims a total following of over 27,000. The Russian cathedral, which was opened for worship in 1891, is the only ecclesiastical edifice in Tōkyō with any pretensions to splendour. From the eminence on which it stands, it seems to dominate the whole city.

V. GENERAL CONSIDERATIONS. To those who can look back forty, or even only thirty years, the varying fortunes through which Christianity has passed in Japan are most striking, indeed wellnigh incredible. As late as 1870, it was perilous for a Japanese to confess Jesus. Later on, such confession became rather fashionable than otherwise. Then it was hard for a missionary to obtain a native teacher. Now there are hundreds of ordained and unordained native preachers and teachers of Christianity. The old proclamation, which, since A.D. 1638, had prohibited the religion of Jesus as " an evil sect," was still posted on the notice-boards of the public thoroughfares in 1873. The government now openly tolerates the building of churches and the performance of Christian funeral rites, in accordance with Article XXVIII of the new Constitution, which decrees that " Japanese subjects shall, within limits not prejudicial to peace and order, and not antagonstic to their duties as subjects, enjoy freedom of religious belief." Such were the strides made during the decade from 1878 to 1888 as to suggest the notion that in future the danger might be, no longer from persecution, but from worldly-minded favour. Some of the leaders of Japanese thought, while professing themselves personally indifferent to all religions, used then cold-bloodedly to advocate the adoption of Christianity as a school of morals and music, and as likely to be advantageous in political negotiations with the powers of the West! To make all Japan Christian by edict some fine morning, might not have been on the programme of the Japanese statesmen of the hour; but that something of the kind should happen before the end of the century, appeared far less unlikely than many things that have actually happened in this land of realised improbabilities. But 1888 witnessed a reaction in every department of Japanese life and thought. Angry with Europe for the recent failure of treaty revision, the leading classes then turned their backs on all such European things as appeared to them non-essential,—not on the electric light of course, or on banking, or surgery, or anything of evident material utility, but on European dress, European cookery, European amusements, European ideals. Christianity, being alien and non-utilitarian, has come in for its share of this cold wave. While the population grows rapidly, the number of the converts grows slowly. This spirit, too, has changed, their regard for the missionaries has cooled, they desire to walk alone. Not only so:—they wish to Japonise Christianity itself, in essence as well as in outward form, and seem inclined to throw overboard even that minimum of dogma on which the Protestant missionaries feel bound to insist. Evidently a modern Bossuet would find in Japan materials for a new chapter on the *Variations of Protestantism* within the space of a single generation.

Prophesying is no safe occupation nowadays. Nevertheless, we hazard a guess to the effect that in the future the Protestants of Japan will be occupied with questions of morals and practice—the temperance question, for instance, and Sunday observance—rather than with subtle doctrinal theories, the Japanese mind being too essentially unspeculative for the fine distinctions of the theologians to have any charm for it, much less for it to seek to split new hairs for itself. The failure of Buddhist metaphysical abstractions to take any hold of the national sympathies, is a finger-post in history pointing to what may be expected in the future. People will never greatly excite themselves about beliefs that sit lightly on them; and Japanese religious beliefs have always sat lightly. Has not the whole attitude of the Far-Eastern mind with regard to the supernatural been aptly described as one of "politeness towards possibilities?" Doubtless this natural disinclination to a spiritual religion on the part of the Chinese and Japanese is aided and abetted by special local causes. There may be a measure of truth in the assertion often made in religious circles that missionary enterprise is impeded by the openly immoral lives of many of the (so-called) Christian residents. We feel absolutely certain of another thing, namely, that missionary enterprise is impeded by the openly immoral politics of the (so-called) Christian nations. When Protestant England grabs at Hongkong, Weihaiwei, and Thibet, while " Holy " Russia grabs at sundry other provinces of a country which has never done either of the aggressors any harm; when France and Germany, anti-clerical at home, eagerly avail themselves of each bespattered priest or battered mission-house to exact some commercial advantage or snatch some strip of territory abroad, what is the Far-Eastern to think ? He thinks, precisely as we ourselves should think, *mutatis mutandis;* he thinks, and thinks rightly, that our professions of religion are a mere cloak for vulgar greed. The Japanese perhaps, being strong enough to protect themselves, might be deemed likely to feel this consideration less than other Orientals. They do feel it, however, as expressions of opinion in their press testify from time to time. They feel that physical compulsion and spiritual influence cannot be successfully yoked together, that what has come to be known as the " gospel and gunboat policy " is a contradiction in terms, and that if the missionaries are ever to assert themselves as an apostolic force, they must, like the apostles, dissociate their personal status from all reliance on alien intervention. The naturalisation of the missionaries in the land of their labours, their complete subjection to native law, and rejection of all diplomatic interference on their behalf, would at once enormously increase their influence. But doubtless such a step would be viewed with disfavour by home politicians, to whose mind the sole advantage of missionary enterprise is that it may open markets and pave the way for annexation.

Books recommended. *A Collection of Nagasaki Colour Prints and Paintings* by N. H. N. Mody; *The Complete Journal of Townsend Harris* edited by Mario Emilio Cosenza; *Japan's Modern Century* edited by Edmund Skrzypczak; *The Missionary Language Handbook for Japan* compiled and edited by Kenny Joseph & Russell Stellwagon; *Silence* by Shusaku Endo; translated by William Johnston.

Moral Maxims. Few Japanese books are more likely to please the foreign student than two small volumes of practical ethics, entitled respectively *Jitsu-go Kyō*, or "Teaching of the Words of Truth," and *Dōji Kyō*, or "Teaching of the Young." They are ascribed to Buddhist abbots of the ninth century; but the doctrine of both has a Confucian no less than a Buddhistic flavour, and many of the maxims are transcribed bodily from Chinese sources. Both collections were for many ages as familiar to the youth of Japan as the Sermon on the Mount is to us. The following may serve as specimens:—

"Treasures that are laid up in a garner decay: treasures that are laid up in the mind decay not.

"Though thou shouldst heap up a thousand pieces of gold: they would not be so precious as one day of study.

"If thou, being poor, enter into the abode of the wealthy: remember that his riches are more fleeting than the flower nipped by the hoar-frost.

"If thou be born in the poor man's hovel, but have wisdom: then shalt thou be like the lotus-flower growing out of the mud.

"Thy father and thy mother are like heaven and earth: thy teacher and thy lord are like the sun and moon.

---

* Properly *Niishima* or *Niijima*; but the awkward transliteration of former days has been usually retained for this particular name.

" Other kinsfolk may be likened unto the rushes: husbands and wives are but useless stones.*

" He that loveth iniquity beckoneth to misfortune: it is, as it were, the echo answering to the voice.

" He that practiseth righteousness receiveth a blessing: it cometh as surely as the shadow followeth the man.

" Be reverent when thou goest past a grave: alight from thine horse when thou goest past a Shintō shrine.

" When thou art near a Buddhist temple or pagoda, thou shalt not commit any unclean act: when thou readest the sacred writings, thou shalt do nothing unseemly.

" Human ears are listening at the wall: speak no calumny, even in secret.

" Human eyes look down from the heavens: commit no wrong, however hidden.

" When a hasty word hath once been spoken: a team of four horses may pursue, but cannot bring it back.

" The flaw in a mace of white jade may be ground away: but the flaw of an evil word cannot be ground away.

" Calamity and prosperity have no gate: they are there only whither men invite them.

" From the evils sent by Heaven there is deliverance: from the evils we bring upon ourselves there is no escape.

" The gods punish fools, not to slay but to chasten them: the teacher smiteth his disciple, not from hatred but to make him better.

" Though the sins committed by the wise man be great, he shall not fall into hell: though the sins committed by the fool be small, he shall surely fall into hell.

" Life, with birth and death, is not enduring: and ye should haste to yearn after Nirvana.

" The body, with its passions, is not pure: and ye should swiftly search after intelligence.

---

* According to the Confucian ethical code, which the Japanese adopted, a man's parents, his teacher, and his lord claim his lifelong service, his wife standing on an immeasurably lower plane.

"Above all things, men must practise charity: it is by alms-giving that wisdom is fed.

"Less than all things, men must grudge money; it is by riches that wisdom is hindered."

Mourning. The Japanese, like other nations under Chinese influence, are very strict on the subject of mourning. Formerly three mourning codes *(Bukki Ryō)* prevailed simultaneously. Of these one was for Shintō priests, another for the Kyōto nobility, and yet another for the Daimyō and Samurai. The last alone has survived, and its prescriptions are still followed by old-fashioned persons. Mourning, be it remarked, consists of two things—the wearing of mourning garments, and abstinence from animal food. This premised, the following table is self-explanatory:—

	Garments.	Food.
Great-great-grandparents*	30 days	10 days
Great-grandparents*	90 „	20 „
Grandparents*	150 „	30 „
Real parents	13 months	50 „
Adopted parents	13 „	50 „
Step-parents	30 days	10 „
Father's legitimate wife†	30 „	10 „
Divorced mother	150 „	30 „
(Woman's) parents-in-law	50 „	20 „
Uncle and aunt*	90 „	20 „
Husband	13 months	50 „
Wife	90 days	20 „
Brothers and sisters*	90 „	20 „
Half-brothers and sisters	30 „	10 „
Eldest son	90 „	20 „

* On the paternal side. The inferior status of women in the East causes a considerable reduction to be made in the period of mourning for corresponding relatives on the maternal side. A maternal grandfather, for instance, is only mourned for during 90 days. a maternal uncle during 30 days.

† A man's legitimate wife is considered the "legal mother" of any children he may have by a concubine. Such children mourn their "legal mother's" death during the period indicated in the text.

	Garments.	Food.
Other children	30 days	10 days
Eldest son's eldest son	30 „	10 „
Other grandchildren	10 „	3 „
Adopted son	30 „	10 „
Nephews and nieces	7 „	3 „
First cousins	7 „	3 „

Infants under three months are not mourned for, and the
period of mourning for children is greatly reduced if they
are under seven years of age.

Whenever a death occurs in the family of an official, he
must at once report it to the Department to which he is
attached. The theory is that he should remain at home during
the whole of the proper period of mourning. But as this
would cause inconvenience in practice, he is always absolved
from the operation of the rule, and ordered to " attend office
though in mourning." When any member of the Imperial
family dies, a notification is issued prohibiting all sound of
music throughout the land for the space of three days, and
even for a longer period if the deceased personage stood very
near the throne.

Periodical visits to the grave of the deceased—*haka-mairi*,
as they are termed—form an essential part of the Japanese
system of mourning. The days prescribed by custom for these
visits are the seventh day after decease, the fouteenth, twenty-
first, thirty-fifth, forty-ninth, and hundredth; then the first
anniversary, the third anniversary, the seventh, thirteenth,
seventeenth, twenty-third, twenty-seventh, thirty-third, thirty-
seventh, fiftieth, and hundredth. On the more important of
these occasions Buddhist services are performed, for instance,
on the first and third anniversaries. By some, especially
among the poorer classes, the whole of this extensive
programme proves to be impossible of fulfilment, and even in
the upper class not a few are now found who sensibly imitate
Europe by moderating the outward symbols of grief; but the
seventh and thirty-fifth days and the first and third
anniversaries are never neglected. The observance of the

anniversaries of several members of a family is sometimes lumped together when the dates nearly coincide, provided always that none of the honoured dead be kept waiting beyond his due time. All these numbers are calculated according to the old Japanese " inclusive " system or reckoning, so that the so-called third anniversary is really the second, etc. (see p. 12). White is the colour of mourning—not black as in Western lands.

Moxa. " Moxa " is one of the few Japanese words that have found their way into the English language. It is properly *mogusa*, a contraction of *moe-kusa*, that is " the burning herb,"—a name given, on account of its use, to the plant which we call " mugwort." It is employed as a cautery, fragments of it being rolled into a tiny cone, and then applied to the body and set fire to.

In the old Chinese and Japanese system of medicine, burning with the moxa was considered a panacea for almost every human ill. It was prescribed for fainting fits, nose-bleeding, rheumatism, and a hundred other ailments. A woman unable to bear the pangs of child-birth was to be relieved by having three places burnt with it on the little toe of her right foot. In addition to this, the moxa was used as a punishment for chlidren, many being burnt—generally on the back—when more than usually naughty. This practice, which is not yet obsolete, accounts for some at least of the cicatrices on the naked backs and legs of jinrikisha-men and other coolies. There is a well-known story of a child, who, having committed arson, and rendered himself thereby liable, under the former severe law of the realm, to be burnt alive, was dragged out with impressive pomp to the place of execution, but let off at the last moment with an unusually severe application of the moxa.

Music. Music, if that beautiful word must be allowed to fall so low as to denote the strummings and squealings of Orientals, is supposed to have existed in Japan ever since mythological times. But Japanese music as at present known

—its lutes, flutes, drums, and fiddles of various sorts—came over from China, like most other things good and bad, in the train of Buddhism. The *koto,* a sort of lyre which is the most highly esteemed of modern instruments, was gradually evolved from earlier Chinese models, and perfected in the first half of the seventeenth century by Yatsuhashi, who has been styled the father of modern Japanese music. The *samisen,** or "three strings," now the favourite instrument of the singing-girls and of the lower classes generally, seems to have been introduced from Manila as recently as the year 1700.

The perfection of Japanese classical music may be heard at Tōkyō from the Band of Court Musicians attached to the Bureau of Rites. Having said that it may be heard, we hasten to add that it cannot be heard often by ordinary mortals. The easiest way to get a hearing of it is to attend one of the concerts given by the Musical Society of Japan (an association founded in 1886 for the cultivation alike of Japanese and European music), at which the Court Musicians occasionally perform. A more curious ceremony still is the performance by these same musicians, at certain Shintō festivals, of a *silent* concert. Both stringed and wind instruments are used in this concert; but it is held that the sanctity of the occasion would be profaned, were any sound to fall on unworthy ears. Therefore, though all the motions of playing are gone through, no strains are actually emitted! This is but one among many instances of the strange vagaries of the Japanese musical art, and of the extreme esoteric mystery in which the families hereditarily entrusted with the handing down of that art enshroud their knowledge.†

---

* More often pronounced *shamisen;* but *samisen* is considered correct.

† The existence of these " silent concerts " was set in doubt by a critic of the first edition of this work. Never having heard, or rather seen, any ourselves, we describe them on the authority of Mr. Isawa, who, in a private communication on the subject, reminds us that such esoteric mysteries would not willingly be alluded to by their old-fashioned possessors, least of all in reply to the scientific enquiries of a foreigner, and that the very explanations given— supposing any to be given—would probably be couched in ambiguous language. We may add that some mystery is made about certain tunes for such common instruments as the *koto* and *samisen,* only those persons being allowed to play them who have studied and paid money to receive diplomas.

The chanting of the Buddhist liturgy, also, at certain temple services is considered classical. This chanting has been held by some to resemble the Ambrosian and early Gregorian tones; but local colouring is sufficiently provided for, inasmuch as each performer utters the strain in the key that best suits the pitch of his own voice. For this classical music there exists a notation,—a notation which is extremely complicated. There is none for the more popular instruments,—for the *samisen* and *kokyū*,—while that which exists for the *koto* is kept as an esoteric secret by the heads of the profession, the teachers of the teachers. An attempt to popularise it was made about the middle of the eighteenth century; but the teachers, deeming their authority threatened, successfully opposed the innovation, much as codification is opposed by English lawyers.

It may seem odd that so fundamental a question as the nature of the Japanese scale should still be a matter of debate. Yet so it is. According to Dr. Müller, one of the earliest and most interesting writers on the subject, this scale consists, properly speaking, of five notes of the harmonic scale, the fourth and seventh being omitted, because, as there are five recognised colours, five planets, five elements, five viscera, and so on, there *must* also be five notes in music,—a method of reasoning which is only too familiar to students of Chinese and Japanese literature and which was not unknown to our own ancestors. Mr. Piggott believes the normal Japanese scale to agree with that of modern Europe, though he allows the prevalently pentatonic character of most of the tunes actually composed. But Drs. Knott and DuBois by no means agree with him, and Dr. Divers twits Mr. Piggott with setting aside the peculiarities that distinguish the Japanese from the European system, instead of accounting for them. The late Mr. Ellis's opinion on the subject will be found in his paper mentioned below. But Mr. Isawa, the greatest Japanese authority on music, says, in a private communication addressed to us, that Mr. Ellis was misled on some important points by his having given too much weight to the performances of an ignorant woman at the "Japanese Village" in London. As well, says Mr. Isawa, take a jinrikisha-man for referee on questions of grammar and diction, as such a woman for an authority on a matter so delicate as musical intervals. According to Mr. Isawa, the second, fourth, and sixth in the classical music of Japan are identical with the same intervals of the modern European scale, but the third (major third) is sharper, and the seventh flatter. The popular or *samisen* scale is different. Like the scale of mediæval Europe—we still quote Mr. Isawa—it has for its chief peculiarity a semitone above the tonic, which is one among various reasons for believing the *samisen,* together with its scale, to have found its way here from the Spaniards at Manila, and not from Luchu according to the current Japanese opinion. Mr. R. Dittrich, the latest investigator, diverges from all his predecessors, and establishes three separate scales, which are properly pentatonic, but sometimes made heptatonic through the addition of two auxiliary notes. These generally omitted notes are to our ears the most important of all, namely the third and the sixth.

Be the scale what it may, the effect of Japanese music is, not to soothe, but to exasperate beyond all endurance the European breast. Miss Bacon, in her charming book entitled *Japanese Girls and Women,* demurely remarks: "It seems to me quite fortunate that the musical art is not more generally practised." That is what every one thinks, though most Europeans of the sterner sex would use considerably stronger expressions to relieve their feelings on the matter. Japanese music employs only common time. Harmony it has none. It knows nothing of our distinction of modes, and therefore, as a writer on the subject has pointed out, it lacks alike the vigour and majesty of the major mode, the plaintive tenderness of the minor, and the marvellous effects of light and shade which arise from the alternations of the two. Perhaps this is the reason why the Japanese themselves are so indifferent to the subject. One never hears a party of Japanese talking seriously about music; musical questions

are never discussed in the newspapers; no one goes to a
temple service

"Not for the doctrine, but the music there;"

a Japanese Bayreuth is unthinkable. Men on the spree
send for singing-girls chiefly in order to ogle and chaff
them, and to help along the entertainment by a little
noise. To ask the name of the composer of any tune the girls
are singing, is a thing that would never enter their heads.
Still, of course pathology is as legitimate a study as
physiology. Those, therefore, who wish to investigate more
minutely the ways and means whereby injury is inflicted on
sensitive ears should consult the authorities enumerated
below, especially Mr. Piggott's book, where will be found
capital illustrations of Japanese musical instruments, together
with specimens of tunes transcribed into the European
notation, so far—for that is one of the points in dispute—as
such transcription is possible.

Dislikes are apt to be mutual. Of all the elements of
Europeanisation, European music is the one for which the
Japanese have been slowest to evince any taste. Bands do
now, it is true, sometimes parade the streets—alas! In fact,
an English bandmaster was engaged by one of the departments
of the government as far back as the early seventies, and his
successor, a German, harmonised the national anthem which
was considered a necessary item of Japan's new outfit;—for,
as each modern nation of Europe possesses a national anthem,
it followed logically that Japan could not remain without one.
Fifteen or twenty years later, a Miss Kōda was sent to
Germany to study the violin, and returned as an admirable
executant. Her younger sister following her example, was
placed under Jaochim's personal care.* Other efforts were
made, an academy of music was founded at Tōkyō, and
towards the close of the nineteenth century passed under the
direction of Prof. A. Junker, who, in the brief space of five or

---

* This Koda family is a distinguished one, one brother being the eminent novelist who
writes under the pseudonym Rohan, while the other, Lieut. Gunji, of the Imperial Japanese
Navy, has made a name for himself by his adventurous life in the Kurile Islands.

six years, has done marvels, evolving a pleasing chorus of some eighty singers out of a chaos of disagreeable, nasal voices, producing too a respectable orchestra of forty executants and two hundred and fifty pupils who possess a considerable amount of theoretical knowledge. First some of the Imperial Princesses, now also the Empress herself and the Crown Princess have taken the matter up, and the pupils of the academy, aided by foreign amateurs, occasionally give concerts at which over a thousand persons attend. It is to be presumed that most do so out of curiosity, and some bring infants who accompany the performance with their squalls. Still a beginning has been made, and we know that sometimes a little leaven leaveneth the whole lump. May this happen here before another century elapses, and then may all the *samisen, kotos,* and other native instruments of music be turned into firewood to warm the poor, when—if at no previous period of their existence—they will subserve a purpose indisputably useful!

Books recommended. *Folk Songs of Japanese Children* by Donald Paul Berger; *A Japanese Miscellany* by Lafcadio Hearn; *Japanese Music and Musical Instruments* by William P. Malm; *Nagauta: The Heart of Kabuki Music* by William P. Malm.

Mythology. See HISTORY.

Names. The Japanese have more than one kind of surname, more than one kind of Christian (or should we say heathen ?) name, besides nicknames, pseudonyms, and even posthumous names. The subject is a labyrinth. We merely sketch out the following as a clue to guide the student in threading his way through it. He will find, then, that there are:—

1. The *kabane* or *sei,* a very ancient and aristocratic sort of family name, but now so widely diffused as to include several surnames in the narrower sense of the word. The grand old names of *Minamoto, Fujiwara, Tachibana,* are *kabane.*

2. The *uji* or *myōji,* our surname, and dating like it only from mediæval times. Most names of this class were originally nothing more than the names of the localities in which the families bearing them resided, as *Yama-moto,* "foot of the mountain;" *Ta-naka,* "among the rice-fields;" *Matsu-mura,* "pine-tree village." Down to about 1870, surnames were borne only by persons of gentle birth, common folks being allowed but No. 3, much as in Europe during the middle ages.

3. The *zokumyō* or *tsūshō,* literally, "common name." It corresponds pretty closely to our Christian name. Very often such names end in *tarō* for an eldest son, in *jirō* for a second, in *saburō* for a third, and son down to *jūrō* for a tenth son, as *Gentarō Tsunajirō,* etc.; or else these distinctive terminations are used alone without any prefix. They mean respectively "big male," "second male," "third male," and so on. Other *zokumyō,* end in *emon, suke, nojō, bei,*—words formerly serving to designate certain official posts, but now quite obsolete in their original acceptation.

4. The *nanori* or *jitsumyō,* that is, "true names," also corresponding to our Christian name. Examples of it are *Masashige, Yoshisada, Tamotsu, Takashi.* Until recently, the *jitsumyō* had a certain importance attached to it and a mystery enshrouding it. It was used only on solemn occasions, especially in combination with the *kabane,* as *Fujiwara no Yoritsugu* (*no*="of"). Since the revolution of 1868, there has been a tendency to let No. 1 retreat into the background, to make No. 2 equivalent to the European surname, and to assimilate Nos. 3 and 4, both being employed indiscriminately as equivalents of the

European Christian name. If a man keeps No. 3, he drops No. 4, and *vice versâ*.

5. The *yōmyō*, or " infant name." Formerly all boys had a temporary name of this sort, which was only dropped, and the *jitsumyō* assumed, at the age of fifteen. Thus the child might have been *Tarō* or *Kikunosuke*, while the young man became Hajime or *Tamotsu*. The classes of names next to be mentioned, though all existing in full force, are less important than the preceding classes.

6. The *azana*, translated " nickname," for want of a better equivalent. Such are *Mokei, Bunrin, Sotan, Shisei*. Chinese scholars specially affect these, which are not vulgar, like our nicknames, but on the contrary, highly elegant.

7. The *gō*. " Pseudonym" is the nearest English equivalent, but almost every Japanese of a literary or artistic bent has one. Indeed he may have several. Some of the Japanese names most familiar to foreign ears are merely such pseudonyms assumed and dropped at will, for instance, *Hokusai* (who had half-a-dozen others), *Ōkyo*, and *Bakin*. Authors and painters are in the habit of giving fanciful names to their residences, and then they themselves are called after their residences, a *Bashō-an* (" banana hermitage "), *Suzunoya-no-Aruji* (" master of the house with a bell "). Such names often end in *dōjin, sanjin, koji, okina*, that is, " hermit," " mountaineer," " retired scholar," " aged man."

8. The *haimyō* and *gagō*. These are but varieties of the *gō*, adopted by comic poets and by painters.

9. The *geimyō*, " artistic name," adopted by singing and dancing-girls, actors, story-tellers, and other professional entertainers of the public. Thus, *Ichikawa Danjūrō* was not the real name, but only the hereditary " artistic name," of the most celebrated of modern Japanese actors. To his friends in private life, he was Mr. Horikoshi Shū (Horikoshi being the *myōji*, No. 2; Shū the *jitsumyō*, No. 4).

10. The *okuri-na*, or posthumous honorific appellation of exalted personages. These are the names by which all the Mikados are known to history,—names which they never bore during their lifetime. *Jimmu Tennō* and *Jingō Kōgō* are examples.

11. The *hōmyō* or *kaimyō,* a posthumous appellation chosen by the Buddhist priests for each believer immediately after death, and inscribed on the funeral tablet. Such names end in *in, koji, shinji, shinnyo, dōji,* etc., according to the age, sex, rank, and sect of the deceased.

It is characteristic of Japanese ways that the native friend who assisted in the above classification never thought of mentioning women's names *(yobi-na),* which we will call No. 12. These are generally taken from some flower or other natural object, or else from some virtue or from something associated with good luck, and are preceded by the word, *O,* "honourable." Thus we find *O Kiku,* "Chrysanthemum;" *O Take,* "Bamboo;" *O Gin,* "Silver;" *O Haru,* "Springtime," *O Kō,* "Filial Piety," *O Mitsu,* "Abundance," etc., etc. But if the name has more than two syllables, the honorific prefix is omitted, as *Kaoru,* "Fragment." Of late years it has become fashionable among the upper classes to drop the prefix *O,* "honourable" and to use the suffix *ko,* literally "child," instead, thus *Take-ko, Mitsu-ko.*

It was formerly the custom for a man to alter his name at any crisis of his career. Even now, adoption and various other causes, frequently entail such changes. The card is brought in to you of a Mr. Abō, of whom you have never heard:—the man himself walks into the room, when lo and behold! it is your old friend Hayashi. A teacher in mid-term suddenly loses track of a student named Suzuki, and has to pick it up as best he may in an apparent new-comer called Mitsuhashi. Not human beings only, but places exhibit this fickleness. Hundreds of place-names have been altered during the present reign, to the dire confusion of geographical and historical studies. The change of Yedo to Tōkyō is only the best-known of these. The idea, which is an old Chinese one, is to emphasise by the adoption of a new name some new departure in the fortunes of a city, village, mountain, school, etc. It is as if we should have changed the name of London and other places at the Reformation, or of Eton when the new Latin grammar was introduced. Bureaucratic readjustments have acted extensively in the same direction, hamlets, for instance, being grouped together and receiving a general name, which may be either totally new or else that of one or other member of the group. In the former case, one is entirely at sea; in the latter, one is confused between the larger and the smaller entity.

Another peculiarity is what may be termed the transmission of names. A teacher, for instance, hands on his own pseudonym to a favourite pupil, in order to help to start him in popular favour. In this manner a bit of faience may be signed "Kenzan," and yet not be by the original potter Kenzan at all. In many cases only a part of the name is given or adopted. The Shōguns of the Tokugawa dynasty offer a good example of this remarkable custom. The name of the founder of the house being *Ieyasu*, his successors styled themselves *Iemitsu*, *Ietsuna*, *Ienobu*, and so on.

Now were we, or were we not, right in the statement with which we set out, that Japanese names are a labyrinth?

Naturalisation. See third paragraph of page 18.

Navy. * The Japanese have from early days been a seafaring race:—they proved this by their repeated piratical attacks on the seaboard of Korea and China, which became so disastrous that the timid Chinese government for a time let a belt of land along the coast lie waste as a protection. But of a navy properly so called during the Middle Ages, little is known. Both the central government and the Daimyōs possessed war-ships which were worked, like the galleys of the Mediterranean, partly with sails and partly with oars; and although the outward form differed from that of the galley, the internal arrangements were the same. These ships played an important part in the domestic feuds of the times. The national annals tell of their presence at the famous battle of Dan-no-ura in A.D. 1185 between the partisans of the great houses of Taira and Minamoto, and again in the still more famous expedition to Korea under Hideyoshi at the end of the sixteenth century. This ancient navy, however, disappeared without leaving any traditions.

The foundation of the modern Japanese navy dates from the last days of the Shōgunate, when a few young men were sent to Holland for instruction in seamanship, and the services of a small party of British naval officers and men, under the leadership of Commander Tracey, R. N., were obtained through the instrumentality of Sir Harry Parkes, then British minister at Yedo. Ths was in September, 1867. Five months later, the revolution which drove the Shōgun from his throne broke out, and the Naval Mission, as it was termed, was withdrawn, first to Yokohama, then home to England. During the troublous times that ensued, some of the greater Daimyōs devoted all their energies to military matters. One of them, the Prince of Hizen, eager to possess a navy of his own, engaged Lieutenant Hawes, of the Royal Marines, as gunnery instructor on board a vessel named the *Ryūjō Kan;* and this officer, who had an unusual talent for organisation, and who occupied himself, both on board the *Ryūjō Kan* and later on in other positions, with many matters besides gunnery and the training of marines, may be considered the real father of the Japanese navy. In the year 1873, when all storms were over and the Mikado had long been restored to absolute power, the British government lent the services of a second Naval Mission, headed by Commander Douglas, R. N., and consisting of thirty officers and men. A Naval College was built in Tōkyō, and instruction in all the necessary branches was seriously commenced, young officers and seamen being drafted off from time to time to the various ships, so as to constitute, as it were, a leaven by which a practical knowledge of naval matters should be spread. The drill was formed on the model of the English Naval Gunnery School, and the excellence of the system can be traced down to the present day. The second Naval Mission left Japan after six years' service. The Naval College was later on removed to Etajima in the Inland Sea, an Academy for senior officers was established at Tōkyō, and gunnery and torpedo schools were also organised. In addition to ordinary training-ships, a standing squadron is kept afloat, which goes out every year for long cruises and squadron exercises. A suitable law of conscription, based largely on the volunteer system, is in force.

As regards dockyards, there are four "first-class naval stations," each of which is provided with ship-building plant. The oldest is that at Yokosuka near Yokohama, which was built by French naval architects some forty years ago, and has since been greatly extended; but the most important is Kure on the Inland Sea, which, in addition to a well-equipped dockyard and a magnificent harbour, possesses a fine arsenal for the manufacture of large-calibre modern breach-loading steel guns, and also of large-calibre steel shell. Sasebo in Kyūshū ranks as the third naval station, with three dry docks. The fourth is Maizuru on the Sea of Japan, completed in 1901. A fifth is to be established at Muroran in Yezo. Most of the ships and guns are, however, still imported from abroad.

When the war with China broke out in 1894, the navy was already well-prepared to take its share in the fray, because, though numerically weaker than the Chinese fleet, it was superior in seamanship and in discipline. The advance, alike in morale and in *matériel,* was so constant, so solid, that, when preparing the last edition of this book in 1901, we ventured to express ourselves as follows:—

"We are no sailor, and the opinion of an amateur on naval "matters is notoriously worthless. Nevertheless, we cannot "refrain from repeating in other words what we have already "said of the Japanese army. We cannot help expressing our "admiration of and belief in the Japanese navy also, and of "Japan altogether as a military power. Though it may not "be for us to judge of the technical excellencies of ships and "guns and docks, it is perhaps given to an old resident who "has travelled widely, and read a good deal, and mixed much "with all classes, to appreciate the existence of those qualities "of intellect and *morale* which go to make up a good fighting

" man whether on land or sea. To our thinking, any foreign
" power that should venture to attack Japan in her own
" waters, would be strangely ill-advised."

Need we say how brilliantly this prophecy has been realised
in the great war with Russia now (1904) being fought out
before the eyes of an astonished world ? In less than two
months from its inception, the Japanese established their
superiority in the handling of modern vessels, in gunnery, in
tactics, in everything that makes for efficiency. Now, after six
months, little remains of their opponents' fleet but disabled
hulks, while the exploits of Admiral Tōgō, and his brave
subordinates will live on in the memory of future generations.*

Newspapers. The founder of Japanese journalism was an
Englishman, Mr. John Black, one of the earliest foreign
residents of Yokohama. Before his time there no doubt
existed street-criers *(yomi-uri),* who hawked small sheets
roughly struck off from wooden blocks whenever some horrid
murder or other interesting event took place. The *Kwaigai
Shimbun* of 1864–5, published by " Joseph Heco,"‡ was a step
in advance. Then, in 1871, appeared a small quasi-journalistic
venture, entitled the *Shimbun Zasshi,* believed to be inspired
by Kido, a then prominent politician. But Mr. Black's *Nisshin
Shinjishi,* started in 1872, was the first newspaper worthy of
the name,—the first to give leading articles and to comment
seriously on political affairs. The seed once sown, Japanese
journalism grew apace. There are now 781 newspapers and
magazines published in the empire, of which 209 in Tōkyō
alone. The most important newspapers appearing in the
capital are the *Kwampō,* or " Official Gazette;" the *Kokumin,*
semi-official; the *Nihon,* conservative and anti-foreign; the

---

* We refrain from all naval statistics, which the far-reaching results of the war would
render useless in a few weeks. Readers are referred to the blue-books and other official reports
which are sure to be issued from time to time.

‡ A native of the province of Harima, on the Inland Sea, who was cast away in a junk
in the year 1850, rescued, and carried to America, where he lived for some years, returning
as interpreter when Japan was opened. He died in 1897. The story of his checkered career
is told in *The Narrative of a Japanese.*

Yomi-uri and the *Mainichi,* progressionist; the *Jiji Shimpō,*
independent; the *Nichi Nichi,* generally regarded as an organ
of Baron Itō; the *Chūgwai Shōgyō Shimpō,* commercial. The
Asahi, the *Miyako,* the *Chūō,* and the *Hōchi* enjoy great
popularity, as does also the *Yorozu Chōhō,* whose exaggerations
and violent personalities amuse all readers except such as are
the objects of them. No one is safe nowadays from black-mail.
The largest circulation (200,000 copies) is claimed by the
Yorozu Chōhō, the *Ōsaka Asahi* coming next·with 150,000.
Some few papers have an English column. The *Japan Times*
is published entirely in English. Among the magazines, the
Taiyō is perhaps that which enjoys the greatest vogue with
general readers all over the country; pure literature is
represented by the *Teikoku Bungaku* and two or three others;
red-hot chauvinism by the *Nihon-jin;* Christianity by the
Rikugō Zasshi and several others, and satire and humour by
the *Maru-Maru Chimbun,* or Japanese "Punch," while
medicine,   chemistry,   anthropology,   philology,   political
economy, and other sciences all have their organs, some of
them conducted with great ability and a closeness to European
models which is almost startling. The names of Shimada,
Tokutomi, Kuga, and Asaina may be mentioned among those
of the leading Tōkyō journalists.

Newspapers, like books, are published in what is called
the "Written Language,"—a literary dialect considerably
removed from the colloquial both in grammar and in
vocabulary, the simple plan of writing as one speaks not
having yet approved itself to the taste of any Far-Eastern
nation. But though the style of Japanese newspapers is not
popular, their prices are. Most of the larger journals charge
only two *sen*—about a halfpenny—for a single copy, and from
thirty-five to fifty *sen* per month; the smaller journals, one
and a half *sen* for a single copy, and twenty or thirty *sen* per
month. Several have rough illustrations. Most now have
feuilletons devoted to the publication of novels in serial form.
Extras are issued whenever any notable event occurs. During
a change of ministry, for instance, and especially in war time,

the cry of "*Gōgwai! Gōgwai!*" ("Extra! Extra!") becomes the commonest of all street sounds.

The Japanese press-laws, therefore extremely rigorous, were at length softened in 1897 and again in 1900. The Ministers of the Army and Navy, it is true, retain the power of prohibiting the sale or distribution of any issue of a newspaper that has disclosed military secrets, and a similar power is vested in the Minister of Foreign Affairs to suppress the publication of anything tending to embroil Japan with other governments. Perseverance in the publication of such forbidden items, insults to the dignity of the Imperial family, attacks on existing institutions, and breaches of the public peace and morality render the offending journal liable to a criminal prosecution, which may end in total suppression and the confiscation of the plant used. Furthermore, fines ranging from 5 to 500 *yen,* and imprisonment for terms varying from one month to two years are provided for. All newspapers have to put up a certain sum as surety for good behaviour. This varies according to localities; at Tōkyō it is 1,000 *yen.*

Even the present state of things will appear stringent enough to home readers. But let us be just. The thoughtful enquirer will surely always lay most stress, not on the point at which any given institution has arrived, but on the direction in which it is tending. Now the marked tendency of all existing Japanese institutions is towards greater liberality. The restrictions which still hamper the full liberty of the press in Japan are not, historically speaking, retrograde measures, that is, they do not come after better things in the past. Under the old feudal regime, not only did liberty of speech not exist in fact; the right to some measure of it was not so much as recognised in theory, nor would the men who made the revolution of 1868 have dallied with the idea for a moment in their then frame of mind. They would have shuddered at it as sacrilege. The idea has entered Japan more recently, in the wake of English and American text-books for schools and of Anglo-Saxon ideas generally.

Imprisonment for press offences is still common. So openly
has it come to be reckoned among the probable incidents of
a journalistic career that most papers employ what is called
"a prison editor," that is, a man who, though nominally
editor-in-chief, has little or nothing to do but go to prison
when the paper gets into trouble. The real editor, meanwhile,
remains an uncrowned king, figuring on the books simply as a
contributor. In fact, the traditional Japanese fondness for
dual offices has cropped up again in modern guise. Formerly
there was an Emperor *de jure* and an Emperor *de facto*, there
were nominal Daimyōs and the Daimyōs' right-hand men with
whom lay all the actual power. Now there are real editors
and dummy "prison editors." But much practice has made
ready writers. Recourse to allegory, *double entente*, and
other ingenious devices for conveying "more than meets the
ear," generally suffices to keep Japanese journalists on the
safe side of the law. Taking one thing with another, it seems
surprising that any man of ability should be tempted to
enter the journalistic profession in Japan. The highest
remuneration given barely exceeds £120 a year; but only some
half-dozen individuals in the empire succeed in climbing to
that giddy height. From £30 to £50 a year is the usual pay.

The foreign press at the "Open Ports" is principally in
English hands. The newspapers there published are rendered
more interesting than the majority of colonial journals by the
constant and striking changes in Japanese politics and social
life that have to be chronicled. Think what a paradise for
the journalist must a country be where the administrative
organisation has been recast a dozen times in less than
three dozen years, and everything else revolves in similar
kaleidoscopic fashion! But this paradise has its drawbacks.
Fancy-free till the year 1899, the foreign press in Japan saw
itself thenceforward subjected, as a consequence of the
abandonment of treaty privileges, to the same disabilities as
are imposed on native printed speech. This reactionary step
had been eagerly awaited by the Japanese newspaper men,
who, though crying out for more liberty themselves, chuckled

at the prospect of seeing their foreign brethren become their companions in misfortune. This is but human nature:—
"*Nous avons tous assez de force pour supporter les maux d' autrui.*"

In the case of one important branch of modern journalism, the Japanese government has struck a blow whose result may be world-wide. When hostilities with Russia broke out in the spring of 1904, foreign newspaper men immediately flocked to Tōkyō, eager for the fray. They were politely received, they were dined, they were wined, they were taken about the Inland Sea in a yacht, and continually received assurances to the effect that they would be allowed to start for the front to-morrow or, at the latest, next week or next month. But the to-morrow was so long of coming that most of the correspondents, weary of this endless waiting, returned home angrier and possibly wiser men, though not in martial experience. Some few, who were actually granted a peep of the seat of war, found that their telegrams to the home papers were so greatly delayed in transit through Korea as to be rendered useless. Evidently, the Japanese government considers war correspondence little better than a roundabout means of assisting the enemy to a knowledge of one's own military movements. The experience of other nations, from Franco-Prussian days down to England's big bungle in South Africa, was there to instruct them; and they elected to safeguard their own troops at the risk of arousing the hostility of the foreign press, whose enormous outlay to procure war news had thus been made of none effect.

Nō. See THEATRE.

Nobility. The Japanese nobility may be called very old or very new, according to the way one looks at it. In its present form, it dates from the 7th July, 1884, when the Chinese titles of *kō, kō,* * *haku, shi,* and *dan,* corresponding respectively to our duke (or prince), marquis, count, viscount, and baron,

---

* The two *ko's,* though chancing to sound alike, are different words written with different Chinese characters. The first is 公 (Chinese *kung*), the second is 侯 (Chinese *hou*).

were bestowed by Imperial edict on a number of distinguished persons. But there had been an aristocracy before. Properly speaking, there had been two,—the *Kuge* who were descended from the younger sons of ancient Mikados, and the Daimyōs who were the feudal lords lifted to title and wealth by the sword and by the favour of the Shōguns. When feudalism fell, the Daimyōs lost their territorial titles, and were amalgamated with the *Kuge* under the designation of *Kwazoku,* or "flowery families," which is still the current name for noblemen generally, irrespective of what their particular grade may be. These aristocrats by birth formed the nucleus of the new nobility of 1884, among the five grades of which they were distributed according to their historical and other claims to distinction. To them has gradually been added a number of new men, eminent for their talents or for services rendered to the government. The successful termination of the first China war naturally witnessed a large batch of new creations. The members of the nobility receive pensions from the civil list. They are also placed under special restrictions. For instance, they may not marry without official permission. On the other hand, the new Constitution grants to a certain number of them the privilege of sitting in the upper house of the Imperial Diet.

A total absence of snobbishness towards the nobility is a commendable feature of the Japanese character. They do not, like us Britishers and Yankees, "dearly love a lord,"— follow him about, imitate him, snap at him with kodaks, egg on their daughters to snap him up in a manner still more daring. They simply do not care. In their eyes, "a man's a man for a' that." Very often they do not so much as know whether the man has a title or not, and except in print rarely make use of it, but mention, for instance, Count Ōkuma, as *Ōkuma San,* "Monsieur Ōkuma," as the French, too, would often say. In fact—now we come to think of it—this absence of snobbish feeling should not be specially counted to the Japanese as righteousness. Most nations resemble them in not having it. The taint of snobbery is so peculiarly Anglo-

Saxon that we doubt whether any language but English even has a word for it.

Numerical Categories. Number has long exercised a peculiar fascination over the Far-Eastern mind. European languages, no doubt, have such expressions as "the Four Cardinal Virtues" and "the Seven Deadly Sins;" but it is no part of our mental disposition to divide up and parcel out almost all things visible and invisible into numerical categories fixed by unchanging custom, as is the case among the nations from India eastward. The Chinese speak of their "Three Religions," of "the Three Forms of Obedience," "the Four Classics," "the Five Duties," "the Eight Diagrams," "the Four-and-Twenty Paragons of Filial Piety," whole pages of their books of reference being devoted to lists of expressions of this kind. The Japanese have followed suit. They have adopted most of the Chinese numerical categories, and have invented new ones of their own. Here are ten of the commonest (ten being the Japanese dozen), chosen from among many scores:—

THE THREE VIEWS (三景), namely, Matsushima near Sendai in the North, Miyajima in the Inland Sea, and Ama-no-Hashidate of the Sea of Japan. These are considered the three most beautiful places in the empire.

THE THREE CAPITALS AND FIVE PORTS (三府五港). The former are Tōkyō, Kyōto, and Ōsaka; the latter are Yokohama, Kōbe, Nagasaki, Niigata, and Hakodate.

THE FIVE FESTIVALS (五節句). They are the 7th January, the 3rd March, the 5th May, the 7th July, and the 9th September. (See Article on FESTIVALS.)

"THE SEVEN HERBS OF AUTUMN" (秋の七草), sung by Japanese poets from very early times:—

> *Hagi* ga hana,
> *Obana, Kuzu*-hana,
> *Nadeshiko* no
> Hana, *ominaeshi*,

Mata *Fuji-bakama,*
Asa-gao no hana.*

The *hagi* is the lespedeza. The *obana* is identified with the flowering eulalia *(susuki),* a beautiful tall grass which sways in the wind and seems to beckon to the wanderer over pathless moors. The *kuzu* is the pueraria, which bears masses of purple blossom. The *nadeshiko* is the wild pink; the *ominaeshi,* a tiny yellow flower, the patrinia. The *fuji-bakama,* with small pink and white flowers, is the eupatorium. The *asa-gao,* in modern usage, is the convolvulus; but this is said to be an imported plant, and the *asa-gao* of early days was probably either the platycodon grandiflorum or else an althea.

[There are also Seven Herbs of Spring (春の七草); but these are of a more homely nature,—parsley, chickweed, etc.— and are made into a sort of thick soup, which is eaten on the seventh day of the first moon, with a view to warding off all diseases during the coming year.]

" The Eight Views " (八景). Following an old Chinese precedent, almost every picturesque neighbourhood in Japan has its eight views. The best-known are " the Eight Views of Lake Biwa " *(Ōmi Hakkei),* which are enumerated as follows :—the autumn moon seen from Ishiyama, the evening snow on Hirayama, the sunset at Seta, the evening bell of Miidera, the boats sailing back from Yabase, the bright sky with a breeze at Awazu, rain by night at Karasaki, and the wild geese alighting at Katata. Pretty and thoroughly Oriental ideas,—are they not ?

" The Eight Great Islands " (大八洲), namely, the eight largest islands of the Japanese archipelago; hence, in poetical parlance, Japan itself.

" The One-and-Twenty Great Anthologies " (二十一代 集). These are the standard collections of Japanese classical

---

* This list in verse of the flowers in question is by Yamanoe-no-Okura a poet of the first half of the eighth century.

poetry, brought together by Imperial command during the middle ages,—the first in A.D. 905, the last circa 1440.

"THE THREE-AND THIRTY PLACES" (三十三所) sacred to Kwannon, the Goddess of Mercy.

"THE SIX-AND-THIRTY POETICAL GENIUSES" (三十六歌仙). A full list of their names is given in Andersons' *Catalogue of Japanese and Chinese Paintings,* p. 145.

"THE FIFTY-THREE STAGES" (五十三次) on the Tōkaidō. Though the railway has done away with the old Tōkaidō journey by road, these fifty-three stages will always remain familiar to lovers of Japanese painting in the colour-prints of Hokusai, Hiroshige, and other old-time artists.

Painting. See ART.

Paper. The Japanese use paper for a score of purposes to which we in the West have never thought of putting it, one reason being that their process of manufacture leaves uncut the long fibres of the bark from which the paper is made, and consequently renders it much tougher than ours. Fans, screens, and lanterns, sometimes even clothes, are made of paper. A sheet of nice, soft paper does duty for a pocket-handkerchief. Paper replaces glass windows, and even to a certain extent the walls which with us separate room from room. Japanese housemaids do their dusting with little brooms made of strips of paper; and dabs of soft paper serve, instead of lint, to arrest bleeding. Oil-paper is used for making umbrellas, rain-coats, tobacco-pouches, and air-cushions, as well as for protecting parcels from the wet in a manner of which no European paper is capable. Paper torn into strips and twisted takes the place of string in a hundred minor domestic uses. We have even seen the traces of a harness mended with it, though we are bound to say that the result, with a restive horse, was not altogether satisfactory. Then, too, there is the so-called leather paper, which is used for boxes and more recently for dados and hangings, and the crape paper now familiar abroad as a material for doilies and illustrated booklets. Japanese writing-paper, properly so called, lends itself admirably to the native brush, but not to our pointed pens, which stick and splutter in its porous fibre. But a factory at Tōkyō now turns out large quantities of note-paper sufficiently sized and glazed for European use, and remarkable for its untearable quality. Correspondents should, however, abstain from committing to this medium any communication delicate in its nature and liable to be pried into by indiscreet eyes; for the envelopes can be opened with perfect ease, and shut again without any evidence remaining of their having been tampered with. Other machine-made paper similar to that of Europe is also now manufactured for the printing of books and newspapers. This has the advantage of being able to receive an impression on both sides, whereas Japanese paper, owing to its porosity, admits of being printed on one side only.

Several plants and trees contribute their bark to the manufacture of Japanese paper. The paper mulberry *(Broussonetia papyrifera)* is the most important of these; but the one most easily recognised by the unlearned is the *Edgeworthia papyrifera,* which has the peculiarity that its branches always divide into three at every articulation, whence the Japanese name of *mitsu-mata,* or " the three forks."

Parkes (Sir Harry). Born at Birchill's Hall, near Walsall, Staffordshire, in 1828, Sir Harry Parkes was left an orphan at the age of five, and came out to Canton, when still a lad, to be under the charge of his kinsman, the Rev. Charles Gutzlaff, a missionary and consular interpreter well-known for his writings on Chinese subjects. Sir Harry thus acquired at an early age that intimate knowledge of the Chinese language and of the Oriental character, which helped to make of him England's most trusty and able servant in the Far East for a period of forty-three years, that is, until his death as British Minister to the Court of Peking, in 1885. Beginning as what would now be termed a student interpreter on the staff of Sir Henry Pottinger during the first China War of 1842, he occupied in turn most of the Chinese consular posts, notably that of Canton, where he was appointed Commissioner during the occupation of the city by the British troops. He was also instrumental in negotiating a treaty with Siam. But the most striking episode of his life was his capture by the Chinese during the war of 1860, when, together with a few companions, he was sent by Lord Elgin under a flag of truce to sign a convention of peace with Prince Tsai, the Chinese Emperor's nephew, but was treacherously seized, cast into a dungeon, and put to the torture. Most of the party fell victims to Chinese barbarity; but Sir Harry's unflinching resolution triumphed equally over torture and over diplomatic wiles, and he was eventually set free. In 1865 he was appointed Minister Plenipotentiary and Envoy Extraordinary to the Court of Yedo, which post he continued to hold till 1883, when he was promoted to Peking. His career in Japan coincided with the most stirring years of modern Japanese history. He even helped to mould that history. When, at the beginning of the civil war of 1868, all his diplomatic colleagues were inclined to support the Shōgun, Sir Harry, better informed than they as to the historical rights of the Mikado and the growing national feeling in favour of supporting those rights, threw the whole weight of British influence into the loyal side against the rebels;—not only so, but he carried his reluctant colleagues with him.

Sir Harry was always a staunch supporter of his country's commercial interests, and a believer in the "gunboat policy" of his master, Lord Palmerston. His outspoken threats earned for him the dread and dislike of the Japanese during his sojourn in Japan. But no sooner had he quitted Tōkyō, than they began to acknowledge that his high-handed policy

had been founded in reason. The respect felt for his talents
was pithily expressed by a high Japanese official, who said to
a friend of the present writer: "Sir Harry Parkes was the
only foreigner in Japan whom we could not twist round our
little finger." But courage, talent, and patriotism were not
Sir Harry's only titles to lasting fame. We like him better
still as a practical philanthropist labouring for the good,
not merely of his own people, but of aliens. He it was who
persuaded the Japanese to adopt vaccination, with the result
that whereas the percentage of pockpitted persons was
enormous only a quarter of a century ago, such disfigurement
is now scarcely more common than at home. Lock-hospitals
were another of his creations, as was also the elaborate
lighthouse system which has so greatly lessened the chance
of shipwreck on this dangerous coast. We cull but two or
three items out of a score,—enough perhaps, though, to
indicate the difference between this truly great man and the
scurvy pack who used to yelp at his heels.

Even now, some twenty years after his disappearance from
the Japanese political scene, the British residents in Japan—
and not they alone, but the "old hands" of all nationalities
—continue to hold his memory dear. How often, under every
one of his successors, have we not heard the exclamation,
"Oh! for an hour of Sir Harry Parkes!" But we incline
to think that the comparisons made by local people are
sometimes tinged with injustice, and that these critics fail to
realise that the deterioration of which they persistently
complain results partly from circumstances beyond the reach
of any personality to control. Rapid transit, and especially
telegraphy, have revolutionised diplomacy since about 1880,
or rather they have killed it. There may, it is true, still be
one great diplomat at headquarters, as minister for foreign
affairs; but under existing conditions, he will

> "Bear, like the Turk, no brother near the throne."

The title of "Plenipotentiary," with which the diplomat
accredited to a foreign court continues to be nominally
decorated, has become simple irony in days when the force of

events has reduced him to the position of a clerk, whose work it is to translate cypher telegrams which make of himself a mere cypher. The field is no longer open for original thought and daring action; there is no longer any responsibility to take, for every point must be referred home. Only the outward show survives,—the grand house, the elaborate dinners to *les chers collègues,* the congratulatory visits on various august occasions, perhaps an occasional chance of snatching some snippet of a "concession" for railway iron, or what not, for his nationals. But that is all, and Sir Harry Parkes himself, if brought to life again, could scarcely do more. What has happened in Japan has happened simultaneously all over the world. In time, we suppose, the fate which has overtaken so many other venerable institutions will overtake the diplomatic career:—it will die a natural death, drop out of modern life, because no longer suited to modern conditions.

Books recommended. *Foreigners in Mikadoland* by Harold S. Williams; *Shades of the Past: or Indiscreet Tales of Japan* by Harold S. Williams; *Tales of the Foreign Settlements in Japan* by Harold S. Williams.

Perry (Commodore). Matthew Calbraith Perry, Commodore in the United States Navy, was born at Newport, Rhode Island, in the year 1794, and died at New York in 1858. In the naval circles of his day, Perry's name was well-known as that of an upright and energetic officer; but his title to lasting fame rests on his having been the man who opened Japan to the world. Various attempts, American and others, had been previously made in order to attain an end so desirable on commercial grounds, so necessary for the protection of shipwrecked mariners. Liberalism, too, was then in the air. Unrestricted international intercourse was at that time regarded by all Christian nations as an indisputable right, a sacred duty. Americans could with some good grace, or at least without breach of logic, insist on the door of Eastern Asia being flung open to them; for they had not yet begun to barricade themselves behind a Chinese wall of exclusiveness.

In July, 1853, Commodore Perry's fleet anchored off Uraga, a port at the entrance of Yedo Bay. Setting aside all the obstacles which Japanese astuteness sought to place in his way, Perry delivered to the representatives of the Shōgun the letter of President Fillimore demanding the establishment of international relations. Then he steamed away to Luchu and China. Next spring he returned for an answer. The answer took the shape of Japan's first foreign treaty, which was signed at Kanagawa on the 31st March, 1854. By this treaty the ports of Shimoda and Hakodate were opened to American trade, and good treatment promised to shipwrecked American mariners. Such were the first-fruits of the triumph over Japan's stubborn refusal to recognise the existence of the outside world. Treaties with the other nations of Christendom, and a revolution which, after plunging Japan into confusion and bloodshed, has regenerated on Western lines all her institutions, ideas, and aims,—this, which it takes so few words to say, but which implies so much, is the result of what Perry was instrumental in doing. Many things precious to the lover of art and antiquity perished in the process. For Old Japan was like an oyster:—to open it was to kill it.

Perry being thus a hero, fancy and myth have already begun to gather round his name. Patriotic writers have discoursed on " the moral grandeur of his peaceful triumph," and have even gone so far as to try to get people to believe that the Japanese actually enjoyed knuckling under to him. The erection in 1901, amid international rejoicings, of a memorial on the spot where the Commodore landed, will assist the mythopœic process, if memory lets slip the circumstance that this memorial was proposed, not by the Japanese, but by an American survivor of Perry's expedition, and that the Japanese government's share in the matter was but a courteous following of American official lead. Perry's was a peaceful triumph only in a catachrestical sense, analogous to that of Napoleon's maxim that "Providence is on the side of the big battalions." To speak plainly, Perry triumphed by frightening the weak, ignorant, utterly unprepared, and insufficiently armed Japanese out of their senses. If he did not use his cannon, it was only because his preparations for using them and his threats of using them were too evidently genuine to be safely disregarded by those who lay at his mercy. His own *Narrative* is explicit on this point. Nor shall we, at least, blame him. Perry was a naval officer, and he acted with the vigour of a naval officer, carrying out the orders of his superiors, and at the same time bringing to bear on the situation the tact of a born diplomatist. The event shows that the "gunboat policy," so often decried by amiable but misinformed persons, is really and truly a policy well-suited to certain times and places,— to circumstances in which any other method of action is liable to be interpreted as a sign of weakness. Might *is* right in many cases. The "gunboat policy" is the only one which is understood by a semi-civilised Oriental power, such as Japan then was and remained for several years after. We therefore give Perry all honour. As for the sentimental gloss which has been laid over his actions, few will probably be found to pay any heed to it.

Books recommended. *Foreigners in Mikadoland* by Harold S. Williams; *Shades of the Past: or Indiscreet Tales of Japan* by Harold S. Williams; *Tales of the Foreign Settlements in Japan* by Harold S. Williams.

Philosophy.   The Japanese have never had a philosophy of their own. Formerly they bowed down before the shrine of Confucius or of Wang Yang Ming.* They now bow down before the shrine of Herbert Spencer or of Nietsche. Their philosophers (so-called) have been mere expositors of imported ideas. The names of the principal old-fashioned ones will be found on page 103. In our own day, a new light arose in the person of Fukuzawa Yukichi, the "Sage of Mita," thus called from the district of Tōkyō in which he latterly resided. So wide-spread is the influence exercised by this remarkable man that no account of Japan, however brief, would be complete without some reference to his life and opinions.

Born in 1835 and dying in 1901, Fukuzawa's youth coincided with the period of ferment inaugurated by the

---

* *O-yo-mei*, in the Japanese pronunciation.   His chief Japanese expositor was Nakae Toju (1605–78), commonly known as " the Sage of Omi."

first contact with foreigners, his mature age with the settlement of all the institutions that go to make up modern Japan. He was a Samurai from one of the southern provinces, poor, and left an orphan at an early age. But he made his way first to Ōsaka, where Dutch was taught in semi-privacy under plea of the study of medicine, then in 1858 to Yedo. One of the most striking pages in his striking *Autobiography* is where he tells of his disappointment on discovering, by a visit to the then infant settlement of Yokohama, that the language current among the merchants was not Dutch, but English. Nothing daunted, he tackled the new task. At that period, anti-foreign feeling still ran high: all persons who showed any leaning towards alien ways were *ipso facto* suspects liable to personal violence. Nevertheless, translations of various foreign works and documents had gradually become a necessity of the times. Fukuzawa undertook them, and made himself so useful that he was attached to the staff of the first embassy which was sent abroad in 1860. But on returning to his native shores, he thenceforth steadily declined all connection with officialdom, and resumed—never more to drop it—the self-imposed task of enlightening his countrymen, detaching them from Orientalism, Europeanising them, or, it might be better said, Americanising them,—for America was ever his cynosure among Western lands. The democracy which he had found there, the simple family life, and also, it must be owned, the common-sense empiricism, the "Franklinism" (if one may so style it) of America exactly suited his keen, practical, but somewhat pedestrian intellect. The strong devotional bent of Anglo-Saxondom struck no sympathetic chord in his heart. He always regarded religion as mere leading-strings for the ignorant. Spencer's agnostic philosophy attracted him on its negative side; but almost his whole activity displayed itself in a utilitarian direction,—in teaching his countrymen how to construct electric batteries, how to found cannon, how to study such practical sciences as geography and elementary physics, to acquire such knowledge concerning foreign

institutions as could be put to use in money-making, to lead
decent, self-respecting lives, to discard foolish old customs,
to diffuse well-being throughout the nation by levelling ranks,
—he himself giving the example, for he dropped his Samurai
privileges, and became a mere commoner, and, as already
noticed, uniformly rejected all official preferments and
emoluments. He it was who first introduced into Japan the
practice of lecturing and public speaking, for which several
of his most progressive contemporaries had declared the
Japanese language unfit. He it was who led the way in
fitting the language better still to bear its new responsibilities
by coining equivalents for English technical terms. Besides
composing, compiling, translating, paraphrasing, and
abridging a whole library of books and editing a popular
newspaper, Fukuzawa occupied himself with the foundation
and supervision of a school, which became famous throughout
the land under the name of Keiō Gijiku,— a school in both
senses of the word, as an educational institution and as a
centre of intellectual and social influence. On this school
his mind impressed itself so powerfully during a period of
over thirty years, his revolutionary views and methods so
closely suited the needs of a rising generation which had
broken with its entire past, the numbers who flocked to learn
of him were consequently so great and so easily moulded, that
it is no exaggeration to call Fukuzawa the intellectual father
of more than half the men who now direct the affairs of the
country. Therein lies the importance of his life-work; for
though locally lauded as a thinker, Fukuzawa was far more
of a worker. Like the French encyclopædists, he laboured
for universal enlightenment and for social reform. His
" philosophy " was not original, and amounted at best to
little more than an amiable optimism of a utilitarian cast.
But such as it was, the leading minds among his countrymen
have adopted it.

Fukuzawa's success as an author was phenomenal. His
separate works, as usually enumerated, amount to 50, making
105 volumes, of which, between 1860 and 1893, no less than
3,500,000 copies, or 7,490,000 volumes, had been issued from

the press.   But some of his best-known productions are
omitted from this count, because posterior to the year 1893.
Such are the *Autogiography** already cited, of which
seventeen editions have already appeared, the *Hundred
Essays*,† of which there have been no less than thirty-four
editions, and three or four others.   Indeed, so voluminous
were his writings that he early found it advantageous to keep
a printing-office for his own use.   Two causes united to bring
about this result.   One was the (to a Japanese public) novelty
and interest of the subjects treated; the other was an
exceptionally lucid style.   Fukuzawa tells us himself, in the
Introduction to his collected works, that his constant
endeavour had been to write so clearly that "not only every
uneducated tradesman or peasant should understand him
perfectly, but that even a servant-girl fresh from the country,
chancing to hear a passage read aloud by some one on the
other side of a screen, should carry away a good general notion
of the sense."   And he adds that he had been in the habit of
submitting his writings to the test of comprehension by a
neighbouring poor woman and her children, and of simplifying
every expression at which they stumbled.   Little wonder that
an author so truly democratic should have achieved an
unequalled popularity.

        *   *   *   *   *   *   *   *   *

Perhaps the reader may object that these pages, though
labelled "Philosophy," have little or nothing about philosophy
in them.   We would remind him that we set out by hinting
that, although the word "philosophy" may be found in
Japanese dictionaries, the thing itself is scarcely Japanese.
If we ask him, therefore, to put up with a makeshift, that is
no more than what the Japanese themselves have habitually
done.

Pidgin-Japanese.   In China, where the native language is
very difficult to pick up, and the natives themselves have a

---

* *Fukuo   Jiden.*
† *Fukuo   Hyaku-wa.*

decided talent for learning foreign tongues, the speech of the most numerous body of foreigners—the English—has come to be the medium of intercourse. It is not pure English, but English in that modified form known as "Pidgin-English." * In Japan, where the conditions are reversed, we have "Pidgin-Japanese" as the *patois* in which new-comers soon learn to make known their wants to coolies and tea-house girls, and which serves even as the vehicle for grave commercial transactions at the open ports. A Yokohama resident of old days, Mr. Hoffman Atkinson, made up a most entertaining little book on this subject, entitling it *Exercises in the Yokohama Dialect;* but its humour cannot be fully appreciated except by those to whom real Japanese is familiar.

In the dialect under consideration, a "lawyer" is called *consul-bobbery-shto,* a "dentist" is *ha-daikusan* (literally "tooth carpenter"), a "lighthouse" is *fune-haiken-sarampan-nai-rosoku,* a "marine insurance surveyor" is *sarampan-fune-haiken-danna-san,* and so on.

Pilgrimages. The reputation of most Japanese shrines is bounded by a somewhat narrow horizon. The Yedo folk—the Eastern Japanese—make pilgrimages to Narita, and up Fuji and Ōyama. Devout natives of the central provinces round Kyōto repair to the great monastery of Kōya-san, or perform what is termed the "tour of the holy places of Yamato" (*Yamato-meguri*), including such celebrated temples as Miwa, Hase, and Tōnomine; and they also constitute the majority of the pilgrims to the shrine of the Sun-Goddess in Ise. The religious centre of Shikoku is a place called Kompira or Kotohira; in the North that rank belongs to the sacred island of Kinkwa-zan, while the Inland Sea has another sacred and most lovely island—Miyajima—where none are ever allowed either to be born or to be buried, and where the tame deer, protected by a gentle piety, come and feed out of the stranger's hand. But some of the greatest shrines have branches in other

---

* "Pidgin" is believed to be a corruption of the word "business."

provinces. Kompira has a branch in most Japanese cities; the great Kyōto temple of the fox-deity Inari has a branch in almost every village. Again there are shrines whose very nature is multiple. Such, for instance, are the Thirty-three Holy Places of Kwannon, the Goddess of Mercy.

Pilgrimages are generally of a social nature. There exist innumerable pious associations called *kō* or *kōjū*, whose members contribute each a cent or two a month, and then, when the proper time of year comes round, a certain number of persons are chosen by lot to represent the rest at the shrine of their devotion, all expenses being defrayed out of the common fund. When these representatives form a considerable band, one of them, who has made the pilgrimage before, acts as leader and cicerone, recounting to his gaping audience the legend of each minor shrine that is passed on the way, and otherwise assisting and controlling the brethren. The inns to be put up at on the road are mostly fixed by custom, a flag or wooden board inscribed with the name of the pilgrim association being hung up over the entrance. Inns are proud to display many such authentic signs of constant patronage, and visitors to Japan will often notice establishments whose whole front is thus adorned. As a general rule, the pilgrims wear no special garb; but those bound for Fuji, Ontake, or other high mountains, may be distinguished by their white clothes and very broad and sloping straw hats. While making the ascent, they often ring a bell and chant an invocation which, being interpreted, signifies, " May our six senses be pure, and the weather on the honourable mountain be fair."*

The Japanese, as has been often remarked, take their religion lightly. Ise and other favourite goals of piety are equally noted for the distractions which they provide of an evening. Nor is much enquiry made into the doctrines held at any special shrine. Kompira was Buddhist and is now

---

* *Rokkon Shojo, O Yama Kaisei.* The six senses, according to the Buddhists, are the eyes, ears, nose, tongue, body, and heart. The pilgrims repeat the invocation, for the most part, without understanding it, as most of the words are Chinese.

Shintō, having been made so by order of government during the present reign. But the pilgrims flock there all the same, the sanctity of the name of the shrine overbalancing any lapses in the theology of the priests. Nor need this be matter for wonderment, seeing that the pilgrim ranks are recruited almost exclusively from the peasant and artisan classes, whose members scarcely realise that Buddhism and Shintō are two separate cults, and are prepared to pay equal respect to all the superhuman powers that be. When tradesmen of any standing join a pilgrim association, they mostly do so in order to extend their business connection, and to see new places cheaply and sociably.

People who remember the " good old times," assert that pilgrimages are on the wane. Probably this is true. The influence of religion has been weakened by the infiltration of Western ideas of " progress " and material civilisation. Then, too, taxation weighs far more heavily than of yore, so that there is less money to spend on non-essentials. Still many thousands of persons, mostly pilgrims, annually ascend Fuji; over 8,000 pilgrims went up Nantai-zan this summer, and the concourse of worshippers at the temple of Ikegami near Tōkyo is so great that on the last annual festival for which we have statistics, over 51,000 persons passed through the wicket at the suburban railway station, where the daily average is only some 2,000. Many, doubtless, were mere holiday-makers, and the scene in the grounds was that of a great holiday-making. The happy crowds trot off to amuse themselves, and just do a little bit of praying incidentally,—give a tap at the gong, and fling a copper into the box,—so as to be sure of being on the right side. They are ten thousand miles away from Benares, and from Mecca, and from the Scotch Kirk.

The holy objects which Japanese pilgrims go out for to see and to bow down before, belong exactly to the same category as the holy objects of Christian devotion, modified only by local colouring. Minute fragments of the cremated body of a Buddha (these are called *shari*), footprints of a

Buddha, images and pictures by famous ancient saints, such as the Abbot Kōbō Daishi and Prince Shōtoku Taishi, whose activity in this direction was phenomenal if legend can at all be trusted,—holy swords, holy garments, wells that never run dry, statues so lifelike that when struck by an impious hand, blood has been known to flow from the wound,—these things and things like these are what will be brought to the notice of the traveller curious to pry into the arcana of Japanese piety.

Pipes.　The diminutive pipes of modern Japan are but one among the innumerable instances of the tendency of Japanese taste towards small things.　To judge from the old pictures that have been preserved, the first Japanese pipes must have been as large as walking-sticks, whereas those now used give a man but three whiffs.　After the third whiff, the wee pellet of ignited tobacco becomes a fiery ball, loose, and ready to leap from the pipe at a breath; and wherever it falls, it pierces holes like a red-hot shot.　But the expert Japanese smoker rarely thus disgraces himself.　He at once empties the contents of the mouthpiece into a section of bamboo (*hai-fuki*) which is kept for the purpose, somewhat after the fashion of a spittoon.　Not so the foreigner ambitious of Japonising himself.　*He* begins his new smoking career by burning small round holes in everything near him,—the mats, the cushions, and especially his own clothes.

The pipe may be made either of metal only, or of bamboo with metal at either end,—the bowl and the mouthpiece.　The metal commonly employed is brass, but silver is more fashionable; and as massive silver would be inconveniently heavy, the plan followed is to engrave and inlay it elaborately, thereby both lightening the article and beautifying it.　A really fine pipe may cost as much as thirty *yen,* and will be handed down as an heirloom.　A friend of the present writer has collected over a hundred sorts, ranging from such artistic triumphs down to the five *sen* pipe of the navvy or the navvy's wife,—for in smoking, if in nothing else, Japanese manners sanction complete equality between the sexes.

Around the pipe as an evolutionary centre, a whole intricate and elegant little world of smoking furniture and smoking etiquette has come into existence. There is the *tabako-ire,* or tobacco-pouch,—as far removed in its dainty beauty from the cheap gutta-percha atrocities of Europe as a butterfly is from a blunderbuss,—the *netsuke,* or carved button, used to attach the pouch to the owner's girdle, and above all the *tabako-bon,* or smoking-box, which contains a brazier and other implements. In aristocratic houses the smoking-box is sometimes lacquered, and the brazier is of plated or solid silver. A specially light and graceful kind is that invented for use in theatres, and arranged so as to be easily carried in the hand. The smoker before whom, on a winter's day, is placed—let us say—a handsome bronze brazier to warm his hands and light his pipe at, must not empty the pipe into it by knocking the metal head upon the rim. He must insert the leather flap of his tobacco-pouch between the pipe head and the brazier, so as to prevent the tapping of the former from making a dent in the bronze. The introduction of European costume among the upper classes has entailed certain modifications in the smoking paraphernalia. The tobacco-pouch has been reshaped so as to accommodate itself to a breast or side-pocket, and the little pipe itself has been shortened so as to be enclosed in the pouch, much as a pencil is enclosed in a pocket-book. The old plan was for the pipe to be carried at the girdle in a case of its own. These innovations have happily not, as in so many other cases, been attended with loss of beauty. On the contrary, charmingly designed articles have sprung into existence, and are all the more interesting for their novelty.

To clean a Japanese pipe is an art in itself. One plan is to heat the pipe head in the charcoal of the brazier, and then blow out the refuse; but this method corrodes the metal of a fine pipe. Such must be cleaned by means of a twist (*koyori*) of fine, tough paper, which is passed up the stem and pulled out through the head, the operation being repeated until all the nicotine has been removed. An industry worth mentioning in this connection is that of workmen who replace worn-out bamboo pipe-stems by new ones of any desired length. The stems are now often beautifully speckled in imitation of tortoise-shell, porcupine quills, and other things.

Must it be revealed, in conclusion, that in vulgar circles the pipe, besides its legitimate use, occasionally serves as a domestic rod ? The child, or possibly the daughter-in-law, who has given cause for anger to that redoubtable empress, the *Obāsan*, or "Granny," before whom the whole household trembles, may receive a severe blow from the metal-tipped pipe, or even a whole volley of blows, after which the old lady resumes her smoke. (See also Article on TOBACCO.)

Poetry. Japanese prosody, though exceptionally simple, has interest in the eyes of specialists, because it is one of the few indisputably original productions of the Japanese mind. There is no rhyme, no weighing of syllables, as in China and other lands further to the west. All syllables count alike. The rule is that lines of 5 syllables and 7 syllables must alternate. Besides this, there must be an additional line of 7 syllables at the end. That is all. " Stanzas," " cantos," etc., are things entirely unknown. Thus, Japanese poems assume the following shape:—5, 7, 5, 7, 5, 7,......7. Some poems may run into as many as fifty or a hundred lines, say, a page or two of this book. Such are styled *Naga-uta*, literally " long poems," though they would be deemed short in other literatures. But the overwhelming majority are tiny odes (*Tanka*) of no more than five lines each, of the shape 5, 7, 5, 7, 7, making but thirty-one syllables all told. The first three lines of such an ode, is called the *kami no ku*, or " upper hemistich ; " the second is the *shimo no ku*, or " lower hemistich." A slight pause is always made between the two in reciting. Thus:

(5)	*Hototogisu*
(7)	*Nakitsuru kata wo*
(5)	*Nagamureba—*
(7)	*Tada ari-ake no*
(7)	*Tsuki zo nokoreru**

that is, literally rendered,

" When I gaze towards the place where the cuckoo has been singing, nought remains but the moon in the early dawn."— Such is the narrow circle within which the poets of Japan have elected to move.

The favourite subjects of the Japanese muse are the flowers, the birds, the snow, the moon, the falling leaves in autumn, the mist on the mountains,—in fact, the outward aspect of nature,—love of course, and the shortness of human life. Many of our Western commonplaces are conspicuously absent: no Japanese poet has expatiated on the beauties of sunset or starlight, or has penned sonnets to his mistress's eyebrows, or even so much as alluded to her eyes; much less would he be so improper as to hint at kissing her. Japanese poetry has commonplaces of its own, however; and rules from which there is no appeal prescribe the manner in which each subject is to be treated. One rule of general application in the odes forbids the employment of Chinese words,—a circumstance which narrowly limits the range of thought and expression, seeing that more than half the words in the language, and nearly all those denoting abstractions and delicate shades of meaning, are of Chinese origin.

Many Japanese odes are mere exclamations,—words outlining a picture for the imagination, not making any assertion for the logical intellect. Take, for instance, the following, written by an anonymous poet a thousand years ago:

---

* Some critic, very learned in everything but Japanese, will perhaps say that the first and fifth, and the second and fourth lines of this little poem do rhyme together, after all. We would remind him that rhyme is the intentional likeness of sound, not an accidental likeness, and that such accidental concurrences are not to be prevented in a language which, like Japanese, has but six finals, namely, the five vowels, *a, e, i, o, u,* and the consonant *n.* No rhyme is perceived in any such cases by the Japanese themselves, nor is it easy at first to get them to appreciate our European rhymes, or even to hear them.

Shira-kumo ni
  Hane uchi-kawashi
Tobu kari no—
  Kazu sae miyuru
  Aki no yo no tsuki !

that is,

" The moon on an autumn night making visible the very
number of the wild-geese that fly past with wings intercrossed
in the white clouds."—Such a manner of expression may seem
strange at first, but its charm grows upon one.

With the doubtful exception of the *Nō*, or classical dramas,
all the genuine poetry of Japan is lyrical. The Japanese have
also burlesque or comic stanzas. Even their serious poetry
admits of a curious species of pun, named " pivot," in which
the first part of the sentence has no logical end, the second
part no logical beginning; and also of " pillow-words,"—
terms which, often devoid of meaning themselves, serve as
props for other significant words to rest on, somewhat after
the fashion of the stock epithets in Homer. Acrostics,
anagrams, and palindromes are well-known to the Japanese,
all such conceits having come in early in the Middle Ages.
The introduction of the poetical tournaments known as
Uta-awase, which originated in China about A.D. 760, may
be traced to the end of the ninth century. It was then that
the custom grew up of setting themes on which thirty-one
syllable odes were written to order on the spot,—a custom
which has lasted ever since, and has done more than ought
else to conventionalise Japanese poetry alike in subject-matter
and in treatment, and to degrade it into a mere exercise of
ingenuity. The poets of an elder day had given expression
to the genuine feelings evoked from time to time by their
individual experience. Henceforth this was rarely to be the
case. The narrow bounds of the thirty-one syllable form
contributed towards the same undesirable end. It contributed doubly,—on the one hand by enabling almost anybody
to say *something* in verse, on the other by making it well-nigh
impossible for even the truest poet to say anything of value.

But the limit of the little was not yet reached. A favourite game at these tournaments, called *Renga,* wherein one person composes the second hemistich of a verse and another person has to provide it with a first hemistich, seems to date from the eleventh century. Out of this, at a later date, by the dropping of the second hemistich, grew the *Haikai* or *Hokku,* an ultra-Lilliputian class of poem having but seventeen syllables (5, 7, 5). Here are a couple of specimens:

Rakkwa eda ni *Kaeru to mireba* *Kochō kana!**	"What I saw as a fallen blossom returning to the branch, lo! it was a butterfly."
Yūdachi ya *Chie sama-zama no* *Kaburi-mono*	"A shower, and head-gear variously ingenious."

this latter a vignette of the scattering caused by an unexpected shower, when one, maybe, will hold up a fan, another don a kerchief, etc., to get as little wet as possible.—Millions of these tiny dashes of colour or humour have been considered worthy of preservation. In fact, the votaries of the *Hokku* claim, not without justice, that though but half the length of the classic ode, it is wider in scope, as no theme however unconventional is excluded by its rules, neither does it lay half the dictionary under a ban.

The nearest European parallel to the Japanese poems of thirty-one or seventeen syllables is the epigram, using that term in its earlier sense. Or we might say of the seventeen-syllable poems in particular, that they correspond to such prominent half-stanzas as

> "The linnet born within the cage,
> That never knew the summer woods,"

or

> "And Autumn laying here and there
> A fiery finger on the leaves,"

which, in the hands of our poets, are evolved as parts of members of a complex organic whole, but would in Japanese

---

* This lin may seem to have but four syllables. There are, however, five in writing, and even to a Japanese ear in pronunciation, as the long syllable *cho* counts double.

literature each stand alone as an independent composition. Naturally the brevity needed to put *any* statement into so narrow a compass soon led to an elliptical and enigmatic style, which continually crosses the border-line of obscurity.

The twin stars of early Japanese poetry are Hitomaro and Akahito, both of whom loved and sang during the opening years of the eighth century. Perhaps the most illustrious next to them—illustrious not only in verse, but in prose—is Tsurayuki, a great noble of about the year 930, after which time the decline of Japanese poetry set in. There are many other well-known poets, and also poetesses. But the Japanese consider poetry more as the production of an epoch than of an individual. They do not, as a rule, publish separately the works of any single author, as we publish Chaucer, Spenser, and the rest. They publish anthologies of all the poetical works of an era. The *Man-yōshū*, or "Collection of a Myriad Leaves," was the first of these anthologies, and is therefore the most highly prized. It was compiled in the eighth century. The moderns have devoted a whole mountain of commentary to the elucidation of its obscurities. The *Kokinshū*, or "Songs Ancient and Modern," collected by Tsurayuki and including many of his own compositions, dates from the tenth century, a period whose style has remained the model which every later poet has striven to imitate. Other collections—all made by Imperial order—followed in the eleventh, twelfth, thirteenth, fourteenth, and fifteenth centuries. These, together with the "Songs Ancient and Modern," are known under the general name of the "Anthologies of the One-and-Twenty Reigns" (*Ni-jū-ichi Dai Shū*). A much shorter collection, the *Hyaku-nin Is-shu,* or "Hundred Odes by a Hundred Poets," brought together by Teika Kyō, a nobleman of the thirteenth century, has long enjoyed exceptional favour with the public at large,—so much so that every one having a tincture of education knows it by heart; but the native critics justly refuse to endorse this superficial popular verdict. The acknowledged king of the seventeen-syllable style is Bashō, who flourished at the end of the seventeenth century, and left ten principal followers, the so-called "Ten Wits," who flourished early in the eighteenth, and in their turn left imitators innumerable down to the present day.

Previous to the changes wrought by the revolution of 1868, it was considered one of the essential accomplishments of a Japanese gentleman to be able to write verses. This was not so difficult as might be imagined; for nothing was less honoured than originality. On the contrary, the old ideas had to be expressed in the old words, over and over again, plagiarism being accounted no crime, but rather a proof of wide reading and a retentive memory. Japanese gentlemen also composed Chinese verses, much as our schoolboys compose Latin verses. A good deal of all this still goes on. Numbers of persons, both men and women, make their living as teachers of the poetic art. Meetings are held, diplomas conferred, and time spent in elegant exercises, around which, as is the Japanese wont, a whole forest of technical terms has grown up. There lies before us the programme for 1904 of one of these teachers, an accomplished lady, whose poetry days are the first Sunday of each month. July and August are vacation time. The themes set for the other months, printed on neat little slips of paper and circulated among her friends and patronesses, are as follows, and may serve as specimens of a score of others:—

January.	Snow in the Capital. The Pleasures of Seclusion.
February.	A Traveller Listening to the Nightingale. Plum-blossoms in the Snow.
March.	A Moor in Spring. A Mountain Hut in Spring.
April.	Cherry-blossoms on a Dark Night. A Wistaria Blossoming on a Ruin.
May.	Rice-fields in Summer. A Prospect of Villages and Green Trees.
June.	Taking the Air at Eve. Clouds on the Mountains.

September. The Moon upon the Waters. Coolness after Rain.

October. A River in Autumn. Wild-geese Traversing the Clouds.

November. The Deer at Eve. Maple-leaves Stained by the First Hoarfrost.

December. Winter Flowers. Distant Mountains Seen through the Leafless Trees.

It will be noticed that the themes are in most cases appropriate to the month to which they are allotted,—a consideration made clearer still by reference to Japanese literary conventions. For instance, an uncultured European may suppose that the moon belongs equally to every season. He is wrong: the moon is the special property of autumn, and the still more private and particular property of September. You ask, why ? That only shows your want of education. Educated persons accept all such literary dicta without question. European notions may be all very well in such matters as railways, and drainage, and steam-boilers, and things of that sort; but when it comes to poetry, the Japanese cry halt, for this is sacred ground. There are, no doubt, some heretics in these latter days:—one programme shown to us proposes such themes as " A Torpedo-boat," " The Yearly House-cleaning," " Lucifer Matches." (!) A few men have even endeavoured to lead Japanese poetry into completely new paths,—to introduce rhyme, with stanzas formed on the English model, etc.; but such innovators have scant following. —To return to orthodoxy. The Palace itself, conservative in most things non-political, offers to the nation an example of fidelity to the national traditions in matters relating to poetry. The Imperial family has its teachers of the art. The Emperor's passion for poetry is such that he devotes a portion of every evening to the writing of verse, and during the nine years from 1893 to 1901 composed no fewer than 27,000 odes in the thirty-one syllable style. Once a year too, in January, a theme is set, on which the Emperor, the Empress, and other exalted personages compose each a thirty-one syllable ode, and the whole nation is invited to compete, with the result that many thousands of verses are sent in, written on thick paper of a certain size prescribed by custom.* In January, 1904, the theme was "A Pine-tree on a Rock." In January, 1903, it was "The Plum-tree at New Year." In other years it was "Patriotic Congratulations," "Pine-trees Reflected in the Water," and so on, the general custom being to insinuate some delicate compliment to the reigning house, even when the theme may make that a feat involving some difficult twisting.

All that has been written above refers to the poetry of the educated. As for the common people, they have songs of their own, which conform as far as possible to classical models, but are much mixed with colloquialisms, and are accordingly despised by all well-bred persons. The ditties sung by singing-girls to the twanging of the guitar belong to this class. Perhaps we should also mention the *Wasan,* or Buddhist hymns, which, sharing in the general contempt poured by the modern Japanese spirit on all things Buddhistic, yet retain considerable influence over the uninstructed classes. The Rev. Arthur Lloyd, who has made a special study of this recondite subject, informs us that not a few of the hymns composed by a famous abbot of the fifteenth century, named Rennyo Shōnin, will bear comparison with the productions of Christian hymn-writers. Many others are simply versified paraphrases of sutras.

One poor little category, standing apart on the lowest plane, is mnemonic verse. Its use suggested itself early; for there still exists a booklet of such, intended to teach the Chinese characters, which goes back to the ninth century of the Christian era. Quite recently a whole shower of these charitable endeavours to prompt dull youth has fallen on the Tōkyō bookshops. There lies before us a little volume enumerating in orthodox fives and sevens all the thoroughfares and sights of the metropolis; two others give the stations on

---

* The number in the last year for which we have statistics was 12,357.

various lines of railway; a fourth—quite a triumph of doggerel —serves to impress on recalcitrant memories the names of the ships forming the Imperial Japanese navy, together with the speed and tonnage of each. One feels almost sorry, on glancing over it, that so much industry should not rather have been devoted to something more generally useful

Books recommended. *A Chime of Windbells: An Anthology of Japanese Haiku* with verse translations and an essay by Harold Stewart; *Haiku in English* by Harold G. Henderson; *Hiroshige's Tokaido in Prints and Poetry* edited by Reiko Chiba; *Hokusai's Views of Mt. Fuji* with poems by Easley Stephen Jones; *The Japanese Haiku* by Ken Yasuda; *A Net of Fireflies: Japanese Haiku and Haiku Paintings* with verse translations and an essay by Harold Stewart; *Renaissance in Japan: A Cultural Survey of the Seventeenth Century* by Kenneth P. Kirkwood.

Politeness is universally allowed to be a distinguishing Japanese trait. Personal intercourse with this people for more than thirty years has convinced the present writer that it is *la politesse qui vient du cœur,*—something deeper than mere bows and smiles,—that it is rooted in genuine kindliness, especially among the lower classes.

The politeness of the Japanese being thus a fact disputed by none,—least of all by the writer of these miniature essays, —there may be some interest in noting a few items on the negative side; for in some exceptional particulars this most courteous nation does offend glaringly against the canons of courtesy, as understood in the West. Japanese will dog your footsteps in the streets. They will contradict you flat. They will answer in English when you have addressed them in their own lanaguage. They will catechise you about your plans: "Whither are you going? Whence do you come? What is your business? Are you married? If not, how extremely odd of you!" If you turn them off, they will interrogate your servant, and that to your very face. At other times, seeing that you speak Japanese, they will wag their heads and smile condescendingly, and admit to each other that you are really quite intelligent,—much as we might do in presence of the learned pig or an ape of somewhat unusual attainments. But the most fundamental and all-pervading breach of courtesy (from the European standpoint) is displayed in the way servants and other inferiors behave towards their superiors. You tell a jinrikisha-man to set you down, that you may walk

a hill. You probably have to do so four times before he obeys:
—he assumes that you surely cannot mean it. You order your
cook to buy mutton. He goes straightway and invests in beef:
—he knows beef to be cheaper, and thinks to spare your pocket.
Disobedience, in fact, is the rule,—not disobedience from malice
prepense, but from an ineradicable assumption on the
subordinate's part that he can do better for his master than
his master can do for himself. Sometimes this is true; for
the native servant knows native ways better than his foreign
master can ever hope to do. Sometimes it is true, because the
native retainer has sharper wits than his native lord. "Dull
as a Daimyō," was almost a proverb in old feudal days. But
in any case, what a novel state of things does this open out
to the minds of us Europeans, to whom obedience is the first
rule of courtesy, abstention from inquisitiveness the second!
The visitor to Japan is advised to accommodate himself, once
for all, to local conditions in this as in other matters. He
cannot possibly change them, and he will spare himself much
loss of temper, and at the same time will preserve his dignity
in Japanese eyes, by frankly accepting the situation. He
should read over, in this connection, what we have already
mentioned on pages 134–5 and 356 concerning the comparative
social equality of all ranks and stations in this country. He
will then begin to realise a truth which the existence of an
almost absolute government and of an elaborate code of
manners at first tends to conceal, namely, that the Japanese
and Far-Easterns generally are at bottom more democratic
than Anglo-Saxons on either side of the Atlantic. They are
more polite, yes, on the whole; and we, for our part, admire
the way in which they manage to unite independence with
courtesy. But their courtesy does not go the length of
discarding their methods in favour of those of a social superior,
neither does it go the length of leaving him his freedom,
neither does it take into consideration that abstract multiple
being whom we call "the public," nor again does it specially

display itself towards women. This may be one reason, among several, why ladies are apt to view Japan less favourably than do travellers of the male sex.

The habit which Japanese subordinates have of thinking for themselves, and more particularly of esteeming themselves ever so much smarter than their employers, leads to various small mishaps. While we are penning these pages, an instance occurs, which may be quoted because typical of a thousand. A friend staying with us in the country (we will call him Smith Senior for short) had sent a registered letter to his son, Smith Junior, in Tōkyō. Does the postman deliver it ? Not he:—he does nothing so commonplace. Instead of delivering it, he unfolds his great mind and thinks. He remembers that various letters for Smith Senior have recently passed through his hands re-directed to the country:—*ergo* this particular letter must be re-directed to the country, and so to Smith Senior it returns after many days. The consequence is that Smith Junior is kept waiting for his monthly allowance, probably in no very filial frame of mind. This sort of thing it is that has given rise to a bitter remark current among the foreign residents. "The Japanese," they aver, "never think; and when they do, they think wrong."

Polo. The game of polo, which is believed by the best European authorities to have originated in Persia, was introduced into Japan from China in the sixth or seventh century after Christ. It is known here by the Chinese name *of da-kyū* 打 毬 literally, "striking balls." A Japanese poet of the early part of the eighth century mentions polo as being then a favourite pastime at Court. It still remains essentially aristocratic, as a game played on horseback and entailing considerable apparatus and expense can scarcely fail to do.

The Japanese polo club, or rather racket, weighs a trifle under 2 ounces. It has a tapering bamboo handle some 3ft. 6in. in length, and of about $\frac{1}{2}$ in. diameter at the thick end. To the thin end is spliced, with silk or cotton cord, a flat piece of split bamboo ½in. in width, bent round so as almost to form a frame, and kept in position by a piece of double cord fastened from its extremity to the handle just above the splicing. Across this frame a light net of silk or cotton cord is stretched sufficiently loosely to avoid elasticity, but not loosely enough to present any " catch " in slinging the ball. The interior of this scoop or net measures 4 in. by 2½ in. The balls are of four kinds,—plain white, plain red, banded red, and banded white. They measure 1½ in. in diameter, weigh about 1¼ ounce, and are formed of small pebbles wrapped in rice straw or bamboo fibre, and coated with several layers of thin paper fastened up with rice paste.

The correct number of players is fourteen—seven a side—but the game is sometimes played with a greater and often with a less number. Each side wears a distinctive badge—white and some colour. The players with white badges play with white balls, those with coloured badges play with red balls.

The court is a rectangular enclosure railed in by a stout bamboo post and rail fence about 4 ft. high, except at one end, where a boarded fence or screen about 8 ft. high replaces the post and rail. In the centre of this screen is a circular hole about 1 ft. 6 in. in diameter, behind which is fixed a netted bag rather longer than an ordinary landing-net. This is the goal. *Eighteen ft. from this goal screen, another post and rail about 3 ft. 6 in. high are fixed as a barrier right across the enclosure. Three ft. nearer the goal, a balk-line formed by a bamboo embedded in the earth is fixed parallel to the barrier and goal fence. At the other end (entrance end), another barrier forms a small enclosure for attendants with balls and rackets. Close to this end are openings in the side post and rails, allowing the players ingress and egress. The space thus railed in measures 180 ft. from barrier to barrier, 60 ft. from side to side.

---

* This distance is somewhat variable, being occasionally reduced to as little as 15 ft. The diameter of goal is then reduced with the distance from 1 ft. 6 in. to 1 ft. 2 in.

The players having entered the enclosure on horseback, each provides himself with a ball of similar colour to the badge worn by his side, the ball being carried balanced in the net of the racket. Each side then forms in single file at the entrance end of the enclosure, so that the two files are parallel both to the borders of the enclosure and to one another. The border of the enclosure which each side occupies is denoted by a flag and string of balls of the colour proper to that side, placed right and left of the goal. Each horseman faces goal, but also slightly turns his horse inwards, so as to face somewhat towards his corresponding opponent also. Each player then raises his racket, with the ball balanced on the net, to a horizontal position across his chest, breast high—the club being held in the right hand—and thus awaits the word to start. This being given, both sides canter *en masse* to the "goal barrier," and endeavour to sling their balls through the "goal hole," at the same time obstructing foes and protecting friends as far as possible. The object of the players, on both sides, during this first stage of the game, is to score seven balls of their respective colours as soon as possible. Should a player inadvertently put a ball of the opponents' colour into goal, it scores for them, and against his own side. The duration of each game being limited to half-an-hour, scoring is of more importance during the first stage than obstructing. Consequently the play is chiefly confined to shooting at goal. If, however, one side gains a long lead at starting, it is usual for the other side to station a "goal keeper," in front of the goal to impede the shooting of the successful side. At the entrance end of the court, behind the barrier, are piles of balls of both colours. It is usual for a player of each side to supply his allies with ammunition, by slinging up balls of their colour towards the goal. For during the first stage of the game the number of balls in play is practically unlimited, those only being out of play which fall outside the enclosure, or remain between the balk-line and goal screen. It is not "good form" to sling the opponents' balls out of the enclosure, but it is so to return them towards the entrance end.

The fragile nature of the rackets necessitates gentle play, and reduces hitting or striking to a minimum. It is not allowable to handle the ball, or to carry it in any other way than in the racket net. The score is kept by means of two strings of seven balls each, of the respective colours of the two sides. These strings of balls are hung outside the screen on either side of goal. When a ball is put into goal, a ball of the same colour is taken off its string. Thus the number of balls remaining on each string denotes, not the number of balls already scored by each side, but the number which still remains to be scored to complete the tale of seven. The scoring of a ball is further announced by two blows upon a drum for one side, upon a gong for the other.

When one side has scored seven balls, it enters the second and final stage of the game. Drum or gong, as the case may be, loudly announces the fact by repeated strokes. The side's hitherto slanting flagstaff is raised to a vertical position, its scoring string stands empty. A banded ball of its colour is thrown into the enclosure from the entrance barrier by an attendant, and is scrambled for by both sides. This is the only ball of the colour now in play. Should it be forced out of play, it is immediately replaced by a similar banded ball thrown into the enclosure in the same manner, and so on. Should it be slung into goal, the game is over, the side of that colour winning the game. In like manner, should the other side score their seventh ball before the opponents score their banded ball, they too are heralded into the second stage of the game, with flag, gong, or drum, and empty scoring string. They, too, have a banded ball of their colour thrown into court, the only one of that colour then in play, also replaced by a similar ball in the event of its being forced out of play. The two sides are in that case again equal, and whichever side scores its banded ball first wins the game. (Until the unsuccessful side scores its seventh ball, however, it still remains in the first stage of the game, and can play with an unlimited number of balls.) The winning stroke is announced by loud beating of the gong or drum, and by waving of the

flag which distinguishes the winning side. The winners ride
out of the enclosure in single file, while the losers dismount
and follow on foot, leading their horses,—a picturesque
conclusion to a noble and manly game. Should neither side
score its banded ball within a given time (half-an-hour usually)
from the commencement of play, the game is drawn.

The following minor points deserve notice:—

The importance of the banded ball is always denoted by a
change in the whole character of the game. " Goal keepers "
are stationed near the goal to defend it. Players are told off
to endeavour to obtain and keep possession of the opponents'
banded ball. Dodging, slinging from a distance, passing,
dribbling, and empounding all add an animation and
excitement to the last stage of the game which are somewhat
wanting in the first.

Picking up the ball is an art easily acquired; not so the
wrist motion necessary to retain the ball in the racket net.
This must be the result either of practice or of natural sleight
of hand.

The game is sometimes played with three balls instead of
seven, either in order to shorten it, or when there is not the
full complement of players.

*   *   *   *   *   *   *   *   *   *

Other games played on horseback are the *Samurai Odori,* or
Warriors' Dance, which may perhaps be best described as a
giant quadrille in armour, and the *Inu Ou Mono,* or Dog Chase,
a cruel though not exactly bloody sport, the gist of which
is shooting at dogs with blunt arrows. Both are now
extremely rare.

Population.   The latest census gives the population of Japan
proper, exclusive of Formosa, at 45,426,651, of whom 22,928,043
men, and 22,498,649 women. These figures refer to the 31st
December, 1901. A comparison with those for each year from
1892 onwards, when the total was only 41,089,940 shows an
average annual increase of 1.09 per cent. The great cities also

show a constant growth. Tōkyō, which in 1894 had 1,368,000 inhabitants, numbered 1,440,000 at the last census; the corresponding figures for Ōsaka, the second largest and commercially the most important city in the empire, are respectively 506,000 and 821,000; those for Kyōto 343,000 and 353,000. The next in population after these are Nagoya with 244,000, Kobe with 215,000, Yokohama with 193,000, Hiroshima with 122,000, and Nagasaki with 107,000; and there are now twenty-one cities of over 50,000 inhabitants, sixty-one more having over 20,000.

While Japan remained closed, plague and famine helped from time to time to keep the population down. World-wide intercourse now completely obviates any recurrence of famine, and scientific hygiene restricts epidemic diseases within narrow limits. But emigration has stepped in as a new depopulating agency. Yezo, an empty and barbarous waste, which hardly counted as part of Japan proper till about 1870, has to be filled up; Formosa, since its annexation in 1895, requires at least officials and soldiers; Hawaii, lying so near at hand, and with a native population too idle to perform much work in the sugar-plantations, has for several years past offered a tempting field to Japanese labour; Hongkong, Singapore, even the American and Australian Pacific ports attract numbers of young men of slightly higher class, who go off to seek their fortune as clerks, shopboys, hair-dressers, domestic servants, etc.; and the mere knowledge that emigration is practised by Europeans has been a factor favouring it in the minds of several of the leaders of this most imitative nation.

Notwithstanding all this, it is plain to every observer that emigration does not genuinely suit the Japanese bent. Yezo itself, rich though it be, and despite some colonies officially planted, does not get filled up. Thousands, it is true, cross over there every season for the fisheries and fortune-hunting generally; but with the approach of winter, they fly home to the Main Island. The same thing happens with the emigrants to Hawaii. They are but contract labourers taken over for a time in batches, managed for corporately, and all returning home as soon as their little pile is made. Climate may have something to do with it. The Japanese, unlike the Chinese, do not habituate themselves readily either to heat or cold. Their method of house-building, which they carry with them unaltered, is singularly ill-suited to a cold climate, neither is it well-suited to a hot and damp one as, for instance, that of Formosa. They long for Japanese food, for the Japanese hot springs, for such Japanese social pleasures as go with the twanging of the *samisen,* for the thousand and one little amenities and facilities of Japanese life. Officials sent even to the provinces of Japan proper eat their hearts out yearning for Tōkyō, which is to them all that Paris ever was to the typical Frenchman. How much worse must they find their exile, when set down on some distant shore!

A sore point with those Japanese who favour genuine emigration is the discovery, made for them by statistics, that the class by which, of all others, they would least wish their country to be represented abroad is that which emigrates most,—at any rate to the China ports and as far south as Singapore. The subject is a delicate one; but we shall be understood if we say that, at more than one census, it has been found that the young female Japanese residents in such ports outnumber the males. Strenuous efforts are made to prevent emigration of this particular kind; but the cunning with which they are evaded is often remarkable. Another particular calling for improvement is the behaviour of Japanese emigrants towards less civilised races. Every one who has seen them in Formosa, and especially in Korea, tells of supercilious and often brutal conduct. They have imitated the white man in everything, even in his ill-treatment of what he contemptuously terms "natives." Hence the bitter hatred with which the Japanese are regarded throughout Korea, where, of all countries in the world, it would have been expedient to court popularity, and endeavour thus to efface the recollection of old-time wrongs.

Porcelain and Pottery. At the end of the sixteenth century after Christ, the Korean polity and civilisation were ruthlessly overthrown by Japanese invaders. The Korean art of porcelain-making then crossed the water. All Japan's chief potteries date from that time, her teachers being Korean captives. What had gone before was but preparatory,—such things, we mean, as the coarse clay vessels attributed to the eighth century saint, Gyōgi Bosatsu, the black and chocolate-coloured tea-jars of Seto, which date from the thirteenth century, and Shonzui's imitations of Chinese blue porcelain, which date from the first half of the sixteenth century. These early efforts may greatly interest the antiquary; and the association of some of them with the celebrated " tea ceremonies" *(cha-no-yu)* gives them a *succès d'estime* in the eyes of native collectors. But they are not art properly so called. Japanese ceramic art dates, roughly speaking, from the year 1600. It reached its zenith, also roughly speaking, between the years 1750 and 1830. The " Old Satsuma " crackled ware, of which European collections contain (query: do they ?) such numerous specimens, possesses therefore no fabulous antiquity; the only thing often fabulous about it is its genuineness. The real golden age of *Satsuma* faience was the half-century from 1800 to 1850.

The other principal centres of the Japanese ceramic art are the province of *Hizen,* noted for the enamelled porcelain made at *Arita*—the " Old Japan " of European collectors—besides other varieties; *Kaga,* which, after a long and checkered history, is now known chiefly for the *Kutani* porcelain richly decorated in red and gold; and the *Kyōto,* whose *Raku* faience has long been associated with the tea ceremonies. Kyōto is also the home of the *Awata* faience originated by the celebrated artist Ninsei about A.D. 1650, and of other varieties known by the names of *Kiyomizu, Gojō-zaka, Iwakura-yaki,* etc. The potteries of Kyōto are those within most easy reach of the traveller, and a visit to them should on no account be omitted. Then there is *Owari,* which produces many varieties of porcelain and certain descriptions of faience and stoneware. Though here named last, the Owari potteries would seem to be the most ancient of all; and the village of Seto in this province has given its name to pottery and porcelain in general, such objects being familiarly spoken of by the Japanese as *seto-mono,* that is, " Seto things," much as we use the word " china."

Japan boasts many other famous ceramic wares. Such are the various kinds of *Bizen* ware, of which the most original are humorous figures, of gods, birds, lions, and other creatures; the thin, mostly unglazed *Banko* ware, whose manufacturers at the present day display great ingenuity in giving quaint fanciful shapes to tea-pots and other small articles; the *Awaji* faience, consisting chiefly of small monochromatic pieces with a bright yellow or green glaze; the *Sōma* pottery, to be recognised by the picture of a running horse; the egg-shell cups of *Mino;* and the *Takatori, Izumo,* and *Yatsushiro* wares, the last of which—especially in its more ancient specimens—is very highly prized.

The qualities of sobriety and " distinction," which are so noticeable in the other branches of Japanese art, have not failed to impress themselves on the ceramics of this esthetic land. Some of the early Arita porcelain was, it is true, manufactured to the order of Dutch traders at Nagasaki, and bears the marks of this extraneous influence in the gaudy overcrowding of its decoration. For this fault Wagenaar and other chiefs of the Dutch factory are responsible, not the Japanese whom they employed. A British matron possessed of the necessary funds may dictate as she pleases to a Paris *modiste;* but the result is not necessarily a perfect index of Parisian taste. The typical Japanese ceramists were no hired workmen, no mere sordid manufacturers, but artists, and not only artists, but clansmen faithful to their feudal chief. By him they were fed; for him and for the love of their art they worked. Pieces were made for special occasions,—for presents, say, from their lord to the Shōgun at Yedo, or for the trousseau of their lord's daughter. Time was no object. There was no public of mediocre taste to cater for. Nothing was made, as the vulgar phrase is, for the million. The art was perfectly and essentially aristocratic. Hence the distinction of, for instance, the early Satsuma ware, the delicacy of its drawing, the subdued harmony of its colouring. It is a mere piece of amiable optimism to suppose it possible that such a tradition can be kept up in the days which have produced that frightful, but aptly descriptive, term, " art *manufacture.*" The same thing is true, generally speaking, of Japanese art in all its branches. The painter ,the lacquerer, the worker in metal, —all had in view the personal requirements of a small and highly cultivated class of nobles. Money-making was never their aim, nor were their minds distracted by the knowledge of the existence of numerous styles besides their own.

It need scarcely be added that public " collections," whether of porcelain or of other art-objects, were entirely foreign to the spirit and usage of Old Japan. They date back only a few decades, and owe their origin to European influence. The Ueno Museum at Tōkyō and the Museum at Nara are perhaps the best in the country. But we believe that the finest collections of Japanese porcelain and pottery are to be seen abroad, that brought together by Professor E. S. Morse and now belonging to the Museum of Fine of Arts at Boston, Massachusetts, being the most complete and therefore the most instructive in the world. (See also Article on ARCHÆOLOGY.)

Books recommended. *The Arts of Japan: An Illustrated History* by Hugo Munsterberg; *Cha-No-Yu: The Japanese Tea Ceremony* by A. L. Sadler; *The Ceramic Art of Japan: A Handbook for Collectors* by Hugo Munsterberg; *The Folk Arts of Japan* by Hugo Munsterberg.

Posts. When Ieyasu, in A.D. 1603, brought Japan to a state of peace which lasted for two hundred and fifty years, a rude postal system spontaneously sprang up in the shape of private agencies, called *hikyaku-ya,* which undertook, for a low charge, but also at a low rate of speed, to transmit private correspondence from place to place both by land and sea. The official despatches of the Shōgunate were all sent by special government couriers, under the control of postmasters *(ekiteishi)* at the various post-towns. Couriers belonging to the different clans carried the despatches of their respective Daimyōs to and from the seat of government at Yedo.

The first approximation to a modern postal system was that introduced early in 1871, chiefly through the efforts of Mr. (now Baron) Maejima, following American models. A government postal service was then established along the Tōkaidō between Tōkyō, Kyōto, and Ōsaka, and extended in 1872 to the whole country, with the exception of certain parts of Yezo. The 1 *sen* 6 *rin*, 8 *sen, and* 16 *sen* stamps of those early days have become extremely rare. Concurrently with the Imperial Japanese post-office, American postal agencies continued to exist at the Treaty Ports until the end of 1873, and French and English agencies until 1879, when Japan was admitted into the International Postal Union, with full management of all her postal affairs. Japanese letter-postage soon became the cheapest in the world, because originally based on a silver standard which naturally shared in the universal depreciation of that metal. Inland letters went for 2 *sen*, that is, about a halfpenny, post-cards for half that sum. In 1899 these rates were raised fifty per cent, so that domestic letters now cost 3 *sen* (for ½oz.), post-cards 1½ *sen*. Foreign postage to all countries included in the Postal Union is 10 *sen* (two-pence halfpenny, though originally intended to be equivalent to fivepence). There is an excellent system of postal savings-banks, and money orders and parcel-post are largely made use of. In the last year for which statistics are available (1903), the number of domestic letters carried was 213,956,000, of post-cards 488,890,000, and of parcels 10,413,000, while the miscellaneous items amounted to 199,845,000. The total of foreign items (letters, post-cards, etc.) was 13,808,000. The deal-letter office in Japan has very light work, as it is the commendable national habit for correspondents to put their own name and address on the back of the envelope.

During the early years of its independent career, the Japanese post-office won golden opinions. Of late it has fallen somewhat in public esteem. The reason of the deterioration may probably be found in the want of continuity in the executive, and in the fact that the Ministry of Communications, to which the post-office belongs, has come to be treated as a political prize, which is bestowed, not on a competent specialist, but on some politician whose temporary support it is thought desirable to secure.

Besides the early stamps mentioned above, those issued in 1895 to commemorate the Emperor's Silver Wedding, and those issued in 1896 to commemorate the China war will have special interest for collectors. Of both these issues, only the values 2 *sen* and 5 *sen* exist. The War Commemoration stamps are also noteworthy, because one set of each value bears the image of the late Prince Arisugawa, Commander-in-Chief, and another set that of Prince Kita-Shirakawa, who died fighting in Formosa. A peculiar feeling of awe has hitherto prevented the Emperor's effigy from being thus used, and some conservative persons objected at the time even to the issue bearing the effigies of the Imperial Princes. The latest special issue was a pink 3 *sen* stamp commemorative of the Wedding of the Crown Prince in May, 1900. On it is represented a box of rice-cakes *(mochi),* such as are partaken of by Imperial personages on the first three evenings of wedded life, while below, in a smaller box, are some chopsticks with which to convey them to the mouth. Picture postcards came into vogue about the beginning of the century; some of them take up in a charming manner the art motives of "Old Japan." Others follow the vulgarest European precedents.

Praying-wheel. This instrument of devotion, so popular in Thibetan Buddhism, is comparatively rare in Japan, and is used in a slightly different manner, no prayers being written on it. Its *raison d'être,* so far as the Japanese are concerned, must be sought in the doctrine of *ingwa,* according to which everything in this life is the outcome of actions performed in a previous state of existence. For example, a man goes blind: this results from some crime committed by him in his last avatar. He repents in this life, and his next life will be a happier one; or he does not repent, and he will then go from bad to worse in successive rebirths. In other words, the doctrine is that of evolution applied to ethics. This perpetual succession of cause and effect resembles the turning of a wheel. So the believer turns the praying-wheel, which thus becomes a symbol of human fate, with an entreaty to the compassionate god Jizō* to let the misfortune roll by, the pious desire be accomplished, the evil disposition amended as swiftly as possible. Only the Tendai and Shingon sects of Buddhists use the praying-wheel—*goshō-guruma* as they call it—whence its comparative rarity in Japan. Visitors to Tōkyō will find three outside a small shrine dedicated to the god Fudō close to the large temple of Asakusa. They are mounted on low posts not unlike pillar post-boxes.

The wheel which figures so frequently in Buddhist architectural design is not the praying-wheel, but the so-called *hōrin* (Sanskrit *dharmachakra*), or " Wheel of the Law," a symbol of the doctrine of transmigration. Neither must the praying-wheel be confounded with the " revolving libraries " *(tenrinzō* or *rinzō)*, sometimes met with in the grounds of Buddhist temples. These " revolving libraries " mostly contain complete or nearly complete sets of the Buddhist scriptures; and he who causes the library to revolve, lays up for himself as much merit as if he had read through the entire canon.

Printing reached Japan from China in the wake of Buddhism; but it came somewhat later than the other arts. The earliest example of block-printing in Japan dates from A.D. 770, when the Empress Shōtoku caused a million Buddhist charms to be printed on small slips of paper, for distribution among all the temples in the land. Some of these ancient slips are still in existence. The first notice of printed books occurs in the tenth century, and the oldest specimen extant belongs to a date falling somewhere between 1198 and 1211.

---

* See Introduction to Murray's *Handbook for Japan* (Article " Gods and Goddesses ") for an account of this popular deity.

For about six hundred years after the introduction of printing, Buddhist works—and those but few in number—seem to have been the only ones that issued from the press. The *Confucian Analects* were first reprinted in Japan in 1364, from which time down to the end of the sixteenth century Japanese editions of various standard Chinese works, both in poetry and prose, were published from time to time. But the impulse to a more vigorous production was given by the conquest of Korea at the end of the sixteenth century, and by the Shōgun Ieyasu's liberal patronage of learning at the beginning of the seventeenth. The Japanese learnt from the vanquished Koreans the use of movable types. These, however, went out of fashion again before the middle of the seventeenth century, the enormous number of types necessary for the printing of the Chinese written character making the method practically inconvenient.

The first genuinely Japanese production to appear in print was the *Nihongi*, or rather the first two books of the *Nihongi*, in A.D. 1599. This work, which contains the native mythology and early history, had been composed as far back as A.D. 720. The collection of ancient poems entitled *Man-yōshū* (see p. 378), dating from the middle of the eighth century, was also first printed about the same time. From that period onward, the work of putting into print the old manuscript stores of Japanese literature went on apace, while a new literature of commentaries, histories, poems, popular novels, guide-books, etc., kept the block-cutters constantly employed. The same period saw the introduction of pictorial wood engraving.

Since about 1870, the Japanese have adopted European methods of type-founding. The result is that movable types have again come to the fore, though without causing block-printing to be entirely abandoned. All the newspapers are printed with movable types. A Japanese movable type printing-office would be a strange sight to a European printer. Provision has to be made for, not 26 characters, but 6,100, which is approximately the number of Chinese ideographs in every-day use; and of each character there must of course be

different sizes—pica, long primer, brevier, and so on. Needless
to say that so vast a number of characters cannot possibly
fit into one small case within reach of a single man's hand
and eye. They are ranged round a large room on trays, in
the order of their " radicals; " and youths, supplied each with
a page of the " copy " to be set up, walk about from tray to
tray, picking out the characters required, which they put in
a box and then take to the compositor. As these youths,
more japonico, keep droning out all the while in a sort of
chant the text on which they are busy, the effect to the ear
is as peculiar as is to the eye the sight of the perpetual motion
of this troop of youths coming and going from case to case.

We have used the word " radicals " in the above description.
For the sake of those who are unfamiliar with Chinese writing,
it must be explained that the Chinese characters are put
together, not alphabetically, but by the combination of certain
simpler forms, of which the principal are termed " radicals."
Thus 木 is the radical for " tree " or " wood." under which
are grouped 梅 " plum-tree," 揚 " willow," 板 " a board," etc.,
etc. The radical for " water "is 水, abbreviated in compounds
to 氵; and under it accordingly come 池 " a pond," 油 " oil,"
酒 " wine," 游 " to swim," and hundreds of other words
having, in one way or another, to do with fluidity. Of course
Japanese printing-offices also have to make provision for the
native syllabic characters, the so-called *Kana*. But as there
are only between two and three hundred forms of these, and
as they are generally used only for terminations and particles,
they are comparatively unimportant.

The 6,100 Chinese characters in common use are cast in
metal, according to one of the European processes. When a
rare character occurs in an author's manuscript, it is cut in
wood for the occasion. To keep types on hand for all the
seventy or eighty thousand characters of the Chinese language,
would entail an expense too heavy for even the largest printing-
office to bear, and would require too much room. (Compare
Article on WOOD ENGRAVING.)

Proverbs. Here are a few Japanese proverbs* :—

Proof rather than argument.

Dumplings rather than blossoms.

Breeding rather than birth.

A mended lid to a cracked pot. *(An assemblage of incapables; for instance, a drunken husband and a silly wife.)*

A cheap purchase is money lost.

A bee stinging a weeping face. *(One misfortune on the top of another.)*

Cows herd with cows, horses with horses. *(Birds of a feather flock together.)*

Not to know is to be a Buddha. *(Ignorance is bliss.)*

A man's heart and an autumn sky (are alike fickle). *The exact converse of the famous " Souvent femme varie."*

Hate the priest, and you will hate his very hood.

Never trust a woman, even if she has borne you seven children.

The acolyte at the gate reads scriptures which he has never learnt.

Excessive tenderness turns to hundred-fold hatred.

To lose is to win.

Ten men, ten minds. *(Literally, " ten men, ten bellies," the mental faculties being, according to popular belief, located in the abdomen.)*

---

* Some persons may like to see the Japanese originals of these proverbs, which are given in the same order as that of the English renderings above:

> *Ron yori shōko.*
> *Hana yori dango.*
> *Uji yori sodachi.*
> *Ware-nabe ni toji-buta.*
> *Yasu-mono-kai no zeni ushinai.*
> *Naki-tsura wo hachi ga sasu.*

When folly passes by, reason draws back.

The drunkard belies not his true character. *(In vino veritas.)*

A physician breaking the rules of health. *(To preach and not to practise.)*

Amateur tactics cause grave wounds. *(A little learning is a dangerous thing.)*

Lazyboots working on a holiday. *(Useless show in lieu of quiet perseverance in good.)*

Pug-dogs. The *chin,* or Japanese pug, is a delicate, timid little creature generally black and white, weighing no more than a small cat, and having goggle eyes that stick out like glass marbles. If, at birth, the nose is not considered sufficiently snub, it is pressed in with the finger. Doubtless this process, by stopping up some passage, induces the habit of constant sneezing with which many of these animals are afflicted:—" She looks like a pug sneezing," is a common phrase to denote one particular kind of ugly face. Owing to their extreme delicacy, the greatest care is needed in their management. Formerly, in Daimyōs' mansions, the pet pugs were under the care of special women, and were never allowed to set foot out-of-doors. Nevertheless, one—so the true story goes—could not be kept from following its lord's procession, and was therefore taken up into his august palanquin and brought to the capital, which example of fidelity coming to the Sovereign's ears, the little creature was granted

---

Ushi wa ushi-zure, uma wa uma-zure,
Shiranu ga Hotoke.
Otoko no kokoro to aki no sora.
Bōzu ga nikukereba, kesa made nikui.
Shichi-nin no ko wo nasu to mo, onna ni kokoro wo yurusu na.
Monzen no kozō narawanu kyō wo yomu.
Kawaisa amatte, nikusa ga hyaku-bai.
Makeru ga kachi.
Jū-nin to-hara.
Muri ga tōreba, dōri hikkomu.
Nama-yoi honshō tagawazu.
Isha no fu-yōjō.
Nama-byōhō ōkizu no moto,
Namake-mono no sekku-bataraki.

official rank. A very light diet is essential:—rice with a trifle of grated dried bonito just to give it a flavour, but no other fish or meat. Eggs, too, are good, and bread and milk or biscuits, but not too much of anything. Contrary to the practice mentioned above, the dealers recommend a modicum of exercise. With care, a *chin* may live to the age of fourteen or fifteen.

The origin of the *chin* is obscure, though the probability is in favour of its descent from the Chinese pug, perhaps via Luchu, seeing that the breed can be traced southwards to Satsuma. Such differences as now exist would have arisen from crossing with other small dogs to which breeders frequently resort, because the race is too delicate to propagate itself for many generations unless reinforced from some sturdier stock. Purchasers are therefore apt to be confronted with a dilemma:—either the animal offered to them is pure bred, but sickly; or it is healthy, but not a good specimen. Beware of "legginess." Perfect specimens are undoubtedly very captivating, and one or two of them form charming ornaments to a lady's boudoir. They can be taught tricks, a favourite one being *o mawari*, that is, turning round and round. The price (1904) varies from about 60 to 80 *yen*.

The Japanese do not look on pugs as dogs. They speak of "dogs *and* pugs" *(inu ya chin)*, as if the latter formed a distinct species.

Race. There has been much strife among the learned on this question: to which race do the Japanese belong? Not scientific considerations only, but religious and other prejudices have been imported into the discussion. One pious member of the Scotch Kirk derives the Japanese from the Lost Tribes of Israel. An enthusiastic German professor, on the other hand, Dr. Wernich, takes up the cudgels to defend so charming a nation against "the reproach of Mongolism,"—whatever that may be. The two greatest authorities on the subject, Baelz and Rein, say, purely and simply, that the Japanese are Mongols. We incline to follow Baelz in his hypothesis of two chief streams

of immigration, both coming from Korea, and both gradually
spreading eastward and northward. The first of these
immigrations would have supplied the round or so-called
"pudding-faced" type, common among the lower classes. The
second would have supplied the aristocratic type, with its more
oval outline, thinner nose, more slanting eyes, and smaller
mouth,—the type to which Japanese actors endeavour to
conform when representing noblemen and heroes. Be it
remarked that both these types are Mongol. Both have the
yellowish skin, the straight hair, the scanty beard, the broadish
skull, the more or less oblique eyes, and the high cheek-bones,
which characterise all well-established branches of the Mongol
race. It is certain that *some* Mongols have come over and
settled in Japan, namely Koreans and Chinamen at various
epochs of authentic Japanese history.

A grave difficulty in the way of all pat theories on the
subject of the origin of the Japanese is the sharp line of
demarcation between the Japanese language and the languages
of the neighbouring continent. The Japanese grammatical
system, it is true, shows remarkable similarity to Korean;
but such connection as Mr. Aston has endeavoured to make
out between the two vocabularies is scant and shadowy.
Something will be gained if we throw back to an indefinitely
early period the immigration of that element of the nation
whose language came to be adopted by all classes,—that is,
as we presume, the pudding-faced element, the peasantry which
forms the substratum of the whole, and which, as Dr. Florenz
and Dr. Simmons have made clear, remained in a state of
serfdom till comparatively recent times.

On this hypothesis Jimmu Tennō, the "first earthly emperor,"
and his followers would have been this early people's
conquerors, or one set of its conquerors,—the latest and most
renowned, whose legendary deeds, blended with those of other
invading bands in Izumo, and with echoes of the doings of
native—or perhaps also foreign—dynasties in Yamato, were
worked up, under the influence of Chinese ideas, into that
fantastic compound know as "early Japanese history." The

solidarity of the Luchuan language with Japanese is an element of the problem that has to be taken into account. Either the little archipelago must have been occupied by the language-giving race before the foreign conquest, or else it must have been occupied by the conquering race after the latter had adopted the language. Two other considerations may be worth adding. One is that Japanese history is solely the history of the ruling caste; the other, that from the very earliest glimmerings of that history, the student can trace a steady backward gaze at Korea as the one country beyond seas with which, from time to time, intercourse had existed.

Many guesses have been hazarded concerning possible Malay immigrations from the South, by sea or via the Luchu Islands. But there is no certain information, there are not even any legendary traces, of such immigrations. The Ainos, who are not Mongols, are indeed joint occupiers of the soil of Japan with the Japanese, and intermarrying has gone on between the two peoples, and goes on still. It has, however, been pretty well proved that this mixed breed becomes unfruitful in the third or fourth generation,—a fact which explains the rare traces of Aino blood even in the population of the extreme north of the island. The two races are as distinct as the whites and the reds in North America.

Railways. Strategical, no less than business, considerations have been taken into account by the Japanese government in constructing its lines of railway. The great aim was to connect the two capitals, Tōkyō and Kyōto. As a first step, work was begun on the eighteen miles separating Tōkyō from Yokohama as long ago as the year 1870, with the assistance of English engineers; and the line was opened in 1872. Kōbe and Ōsaka were then connected, and other short pieces followed, the intercapital trunk line being delayed by various causes. Japan is not naturally suited to railway construction: the country is too mountainous; the streams—mere beds of sand to-day—are to-morrow, after a heavy rain, wild surging rivers that sweep away bridges and embankments. For these reasons, the idea of carrying the Tōkyō-Kyōto railway along the Nakasendō, or backbone of the country, which would have been far better in time of war, as being removed from the possibility of an attack from the seaside, fell through, the engineering difficulties proving insuperable. The only alternative was to follow the Tōkaidō, the great highway of Eastern Japan, which skirts the coast along the narrow strip of flat country intervening between the foot of the hills and the Pacific Ocean. This work was completed, and the thousandth mile of railway opened, in the summer of 1889. The total mileage had increased to 4,237 at the end of March, 1903. The most difficult line constructed was that opened for traffic in 1893, between Yokohama and Karuizawa, on the way from Tōkyō to Naoetsu. It leads over a steep mountain pass called the Usuitōge, and the inclination is 1 in 15 for a length of five miles, three miles of which are in tunnels all cut through rock. The train is taken up the pass by " Abt " engines, which have a cogwheel working on a rack-rail laid between the ordinary rails.

Japanese railway enterprise, although started by the government, is now far from being exclusively in official hands. Companies, on the contrary, are numerous, some private, others more or less under government shelter and patronage. The most important is the *Nippon Tetsudō Kwaisha* (" Japan Railway Company "), which owns the main line running north to Aomori. Next to it come the Kyūshū Railway, and the Sanyō Railway which owns the main line running along the the northern shore of the Inland Sea. The total mileage of the various private lines aggregates nearly three-quarters of the whole given above.

Reduced to its simplest expression, the Japanese railway system practically consists of one long trunk line from Aomori in the extreme north to Shimonoseki in the south-west, together with two large branches connecting each capital with the fruitful provinces of the west coast, minor branches to various points in the two metropolitan districts, and local lines in the islands of Kyūshū, Shikoku, and Yezo.

Notwithstanding the natural obstacles to be overcome and the destructive climate, the Japanese lines of railways have been cheaply built, because labour is cheap; and they already pay fairly well. In round numbers, the cost to government since 1872 of construction and equipment has been 125,000,000 *yen*. The profits on the railways, both government and private, have increased steadily year by year. The net profit to government for the financial year ending the 31st March, 1903, was 9,270,000 *yen*. The total number of passengers carried during the same period of twelve months over the government lines was 31,897,000; the total freight was 3,200,000 tons. On the private lines the passengers numbered 78,121,000, and the total freight was 12,987,000 tons. The proportion of the receipts per cent on the government lines was as follows:—passenger receipts, 66.54 per cent; goods 31.83; miscellaneous, 1.63. The low proportion of goods receipts, which will surprise persons whose experience has been gained in England, India, or the United States, is easily explained by geographical conditions, Japan's immense coast-line and the lofty mountain-ranges that cut up the greater portion of the surface being reasons that dictate, and must continue to dictate, a preference for water-carriage over carriage by rail. The most formidable obstacle in the way of Japanese railway enterprise is that conflicting interests and local intrigues are apt to render the law of expropriation for public benefit little more than a dead letter. The extension of the Inland Sea Line (*Sanyō Tetsudō*) was long impeded by this cause, as capitalists could not afford to buy land at the preposterous price demanded by the owners. Perhaps, after all, an instinct of self-preservation sometimes guides these obstructionists. Experience on the Tōkaidō, on the " Pilgrim Line " to Ise, on the way to Nikkō, everywhere in fact, has shown conclusively that though some

of the larger cities profit by the railways, and though the
empire as a whole profits, their approach has sounded the
death-knell of the smaller country towns. In old walking and
jinrikisha days, every little town and village along the chief
highways was bustling and prosperous. Now their shops are
empty, their merry inns deserted; for their former customers
are whirled past them without stopping.

We have alluded to the trouble caused by the capricious
nature of Japanese rivers. Japan is perhaps the only country
in the world where a railway may be obliged to go under a
river instead of over it. In the district between Kōbe and
Ōsaka and also near Lake Biwa, almost all the rivers tend
to raise their beds above the level of the surrounding fields,
owing to the masses of sand and pebbles continually carried
down by their rapid current. The river-bed thus stands
athwart the flat strip of country between the mountain and
the sea as a sort of wall or dyke, and the only thing to do
is to take the line underneath it by a tunnel, when the wall
is of sufficient height to give headway for the train. Every
now and then one of these river-banks bursts, the whole
country-side is flooded, and the railway department of course
put to heavy expense. Apart from such exceptional cases, the
recurrence of torrential rains, typhoons, and earthquakes causes
havoc which almost every year throws the system into
temporary disorder.

The Japanese railways are narrow gauge,—three feet six
inches. The rates are extremely low. One may travel first
class in Japan more cheaply than third class in an English
parliamentary train. Nevertheless the percentage of first and
even second-class passengers is small, the two together only
forming seven per cent. of the entire number carried. The check
system for luggage is in force. Sleeping and dining-cars
(European food) have recently been introduced on some of
the longer lines. On the others—in the absence of refreshment-
rooms—neat little boxes of native food, and drinks of various
kinds, are hawked about at the principal stations.

Despite such conveniences, a railway journey in this country is apt to be anything but a joy. Owing to some cause not yet explained, the Japanese who, when abiding in their own native ways, are the very pink of neatness, become slipshod, not to say dirty, when introduced to certain conditions of European life. On stepping into even a first-class car, one as often as not has to pick one's way among orange-peel, spilt tea, cigar ends, beer-bottles overturned. The travellers are wallowing semi-recumbent along the seats, in untidy habiliments and dishabiliments. We have even seen a man—he was a military officer, and his dutiful spouse assisted him—change all his clothes in the car, though to be sure he availed himself of a friendly tunnel for the more adventurous portion of the enterprise. On another recent occasion, being ourselves somewhat short-sighted, we could not at first make out the nature of the occupation of an old gentleman who had just finished a good lunch. Closer scrutiny showed that he held his artificial teeth in his hand, and was busy picking and wiping them! Then, too, there is inordinate crowding, and whole batches of second-class passengers are, on the slightest provocation, transferred to the first. In fact, the whole thing is queer and unpleasant, unless of course the traveller be a philosopher to whom every novel experience supplies welcome material for meditation. Such a philosopher will perhaps enquire the reason of the stripe of white paint across the windows of the third-class cars on certain lines. It is a precautionary measure adopted for the safety of country bumpkins; for it has happened that some of these, lacking personal experience of glass, have mistaken it for air, and gashed themselves horribly in the attempt to shove their heads through what, in their innocence, they supposed to be that non-resisting medium.

The nomenclature of many Japanese railways is peculiar. The *Ō-U* line, for instance, is so called because it runs through the northern provinces of Rikuzen, Rikuchū, and Rikuoku, which together anciently bore the name of *Ōshū,* and the provinces of *Uzen* and *Ugo*. Thus the first syllable of each of these words is taken. The *Ban-Tan* line, connecting the provinces of Harima and Tajima, receives its name from the fact that the first of the two Chinese characters employed to write the word Harima is pronounced *Ban* in other contexts, while the first character of Tajima is properly *Tan*, though not so pronounced in this particular instance. Perhaps this may make the European tyro's head swim, but to the Japanese it appears perfectly plain and simple.

Japan has now its "Bradshaw," under the title of *Ryokō Annai,* published monthly. The rapid swelling of this useful periodical from half-a-dozen pages to two fat little volumes is a striking index of Japan's material progress.

Religion.† Undevotional by temperament,* the Japanese have nevertheless accorded a measure of hospitality to the two greatest religions of the world—Buddhism and Christianity. Their own unassisted efforts in the direction of religion are summed up in archaic Shintō. Modern Shintō has been profoundly influenced by Buddhism and Confucianism.

---

† See Appendix.

* Thus, for instance, wrote the late Mr. Fukuzawa, Japan's most representative thinker and educationalist: "It goes without saying that the maintenance of peace and security in society requires a religion. For this purpose any religion will do. I lack a religious nature, and have never believed in any religion. I am thus open to the charge that I am advising others to be religious, when I am not so. Yet my conscience does not permit me to clothe myself with religion, when I have it not at heart. * * * * Of religions, there are several kinds,—Buddhism, Christianity, and what not. Yet, from my standpoint, there is no more difference between these than between green tea and black tea. It makes little difference whether you drink one or the other. The point is to let those who have never drunk tea partake of it and know its taste. Just so with religion. Religionists are like tea-merchants. They are busy selling their own kind of religion. As for the method of procedure in this matter, it is not good policy for one to disparage the stock of others in order to praise his own. What he ought to do is to see that his stock is well-selected and his prices cheap, etc., etc." (We quote from the translation given in the "Japan Herald" for the 9th September, 1897.)—Similar utterances from the mouths of leading men might be quoted by the score. Characteristic, too, is it that whereas one of the first subjects on which the average European seeks information is the nature of Japanese religious belief, no Japanese with whom we have come in contact has ever questioned us regarding Western religion. The subject apparently interests none except those few who become converts.

On more than one occasion we have heard a Japanese asked by a European traveller what his religion was,—whether Buddhist or Shintō,—and have been amused at his look of blank perplexity. He could not, for the life of him, make out what the enquirer was driving at. It is the established custom to present infants at the Shintō family temple one month after birth. It is equally customary to be buried by the Buddhist parish priest. The inhabitants of each district contribute to the festivals of both religions alike, without being aware of any inconsistency. They do not draw the hard and fast distinctions with which we are familiar.

Lest such laxity and the use of the epithet " undevotional," which we have employed above, should mislead the reader, he must remember that devotion and ethics, theology and conduct, are separate things. Because the Japanese seem irreligious, we would be no means be understood to accuse them of being specially immoral. Even the word " irreligious " will be considered by some of those who know them best scarcely to suit the case. The family shrine in every household, the numerous temples, the multitudes who still make pilgrimages, —all these things will be appealed to as proofs that the masses are believers, whatever the intellectual classes may say. In any case, Japanese irreligion differs favourably from the utterly blank irreligion that is flaunted in the modern West. Though they pray little and make light of supernatural dogma, the religion of the family—filial piety—binds them down in truly sacred bonds. The most materialistic Japanese would shrink with horror from neglect of his father's grave, and of the rites prescribed by usage for the anniversaries of a father's or other near kinsman's death. Though unmindful of any future for himself, he nevertheless,. by a happy inconsistency, acts as if the dead needed his care. This state of things is not confined to Japan, but characterises the whole Far East, the whole Chinese world. Furthermore—for we have no pet theory to prove, but are inclined rather to view contradiction as of the very essence of the facts of life—it may be alleged, and alleged truly, that the Japanese sometimes contribute large sums and make considerable sacrifices for pious ends. For example, no less than 1,200,000 *yen* were subscribed in six provinces alone for the benefit of the Nishi Hongwanji temple at Kyōto during the year 1900. On other occasions, not only has money been forthcoming in abundance for the rearing of temples of the favourite Monto sect, but men have given their own manual labour to the task, as something more personal than mere silver and gold. They have even cut off their queues, and the women have cut off their tresses, wherewith to make hawsers to lift into place the timbers of the sacred edifice. We imagine, however, that such zealots belonged almost exclusively to the peasant and artisan classes. The subject is a difficult one. These (perhaps inconsistent) remarks are thrown out merely by way of suggestion, in order to restrain Europeans from judging too summarily of conditions alien to the whole trend of their own experience.

* * * * * * * * * *

It has oft ⟨ been alleged of late that patriotism and loyalty to the sacred, heaven-descended Mikado amount to a religion in Japan. If we are to accept this statement, one important qualification must be made, which is that the fervour of patriotism and loyalty to the throne, which we see to-day at a white heat, is no legacy from a hoary antiquity, but a quite recent development,—one of the many indirect results of the Europeanisation of Japanese institutions, as already hinted on page 8. It is no ingrained racial characteristic; it is a phase, comparable in some ways to the Puritan fervour which blazed up in England two or three centuries ago, and for a season moulded everything to its own temper. Like the stern enthusiasm of Cromwell's Ironsides, like the fiery zeal of the French revolutionary hosts, like all partly moral, partly political enthusiasms, it arms its votaries, and in fact the whole nation, with well-nigh irresistible might for the time being. It is a highly interesting phenomenon,—admirable in the fearless self-abnegation which it inspires, grotesque in the misrepresentations of history and even of patent contemporary facts on which it partly rests, vastly important in the concrete results which it achieves. New Japan could never have risen and expanded as she has done without some ideal to beckon her onwards; and this Imperialistic ideal was the only one within reach. It has been the lever that has raised her from Oriental impotence to her present rank among the great powers of the world. Whether it should be called a religion is a mere question of how we may choose to define that word. To the present writer, the term "ideal" seems less open to misconstruction.

(See also Articles on BUDDHISM, HISTORY AND MYTHOLOGY, MISSIONS, and SHINTŌ.)

Roads. Several of the chief highways of Japan are extremely ancient. Such are some of the roads near Kyōto, and the Nakasendō running the whole way from Kyōto to Eastern Japan. The most celebrated road of more recent origin, though itself far from modern, is the Tōkaidō, along which the Daimyōs of the western provinces used to travel with their splendid retinues to the Shōgun's court at Yedo. The Ōshū Kaidō leading north, and the Reiheishi Kaidō leading to Nikkō, are other great historic roads. Many roads in Japan are lined with tall cryptomerias and other trees. Shortly after the introduction of telegraphy into the country, the Japanese began to hew down these monumental trees in their zeal for what they believed to be civilisation. The telegraph-poles would, they thought, show to much better advantage without such old-fashioned companions. A howl from the foreign press of Yokohama fortunately brought the official Goths to their senses, and after the Tōkaidō had been partially denuded, the remaining avenues were spared.

In too many of the newly built roads, though the engineering selection may be good, the execution is bad. Roads are made of clay and dirt only. They run over artificial embankments supported by mud foundations, there is no sufficient provision

made for carrying off water, and the gradient of the hillside
along which the road itself is carried is left much too steep.
Holes, ruts, and landslips often attended with loss of life,
are the result. There is no idea of macadamising. As for
mending, that is done by cart-loads of stones or earth, which
effectually supply travellers with dust during the dry weather
and a slough of despond whenever it rains. Sometimes twigs
of trees and even old cast-off straw sandals are utilised as
materials for road-mending. In Tōkyō itself, the capital of
the empire, the roads are a scandal. Down to the present day
they continue to be there made with block-stone foundations,
on which are poured layers of round pebbles and earth or
fine sand. The cruel labour entailed on jinrikisha-men by such
a system may be imagined. Something, no doubt, should be
put to the account of the loose volcanic soil of the great Tōkyō
plain and of Eastern Japan generally, which does not lend
itself easily to good road-building. It is in the province of
Ise, in some of the larger islands of the Inland Sea, and along
the shores of Lake Biwa, where nature provides first-rate
material in the shape of disintegrated granite, that the best
highways are to be found.

During the years 1880–90, an immense amount of money
was spent in opening up mountain districts by means of new
roads, bridges, and viaducts. But as the development of the
railway system almost simultaneously drew traffic away to
other parts, and as the roads themselves were not calculated
to withstand the rigour of the climate, and, above all, were not
really needed by the scanty peasant population, many have
disappeared leaving not a trace behind, while in other cases
the narrow but permanent ancient track is preferred, because
shorter. The once noted road over the Harinoki Pass and
that from Aizu to Shiobara may be adduced as instances.

Rowing. A discussion was carried on some years ago in the
local press concerning the respective merits of the Japanese
and European styles of rowing. The *pros* and *cons* are as
follows :—

PRO.

" The Japanese method of rowing is entirely different from ours. We row with our oars at right angles to the side of the boat, while we are seated. The Japanese oars are almost parallel to the side of the boat, and they row standing with their faces to the side. The movement is different also. We lift our oars from the water after each stroke. The Japanese oar is always submerged, and the oarsman moves it backward and forward with a sculling motion. There is an oar also at the stern of the boat, as well as on the sides. In our style of rowing, we exert our force only from the waist up, and at every stroke must exert motion out of the water with our oar to secure another hold on the water. The Japanese bring into action all their muscles from the feet up; and as there is no removal of the oar from the water, there is no loss of the power they exert." *

CONTRA.

" Putting the Japanese and foreign methods of rowing into comparison, full credit is due to the Japanese method of rowing (or *yuloing†*), for its affording the most complete bodily exercise. As Professor Bell says, every muscle from the feet up comes into action. Another instance where *yuloing* comes in practically and usefully is in passing narrow passages, when a Japanese boat *(sampan)* can continue to be propelled forward, while the crew of a gig would probably have to shift oars. Its superiority or advantage over the foreign way of rowing, in any other direction, I, however, venture to question.

Speed.—Taking a pilot *sampan* as an example with six good sailors, a speed at the rate of 4 to 4½ knots an hour can be obtained, while a well-manned six-oared gig can do 5½ to 6 knots without much trouble. Besides, the latter can easily keep up that speed for an hour or more, while 4½ knots *yuloing*

---

* Quoted from Dr. Bell, as reported in the " *Yorozu Choho* " newspaper, Tokyo, 17th February, 1899.

† From the Chinese 搖 艣 the Chinese and Japanese method of rowing being identical, owing to the Japanese having borrowed from China, as usual.

for that length of time would hardly be possible, because the exertion in *yuloing* is very much greater than in rowing, and this for the very reason that the *yulo* being always submerged, every movement is an exertion, and swinging oar through the air after each stroke gives the oarsman a rest. Rowing on fixed seats means work for the arms and the back, which little affects the lungs; *yuloing* is as fatiguing as rowing on sliding seats. The heavier and more clumsy build of a Japanese boat does not account for this difference in speed.

"*Stability of the boat.*—In smooth water one man *yuloing* creates a most disagreeable, wobbling, side-way motion for passengers. A *sampan* manned on both sides goes more steadily, but yet there is not the perfect steadiness of a gig. In rough water it occurs to the most skilful of Japanese oarsmen that the *yulo* shifts off the pin; and putting it into position again is not always easy in a rough sea, especially as yulos are long, and necessarily made of strong and heavy wood. A good gig-oarsman will never lose his oar, and if it by mischance should jump out of the rowlock, it is easily fetched in again. Moreover, it stands to reason that men sitting down in a boat will balance a boat better than men standing up, as is the case in *yuloing*.

"*Resistance to wind.*—It is needless to point out that men sitting offer less resistance than men standing in a boat." *

                *   *   *   *   *   *   *   *   *   *

So far the discussion on Japanese rowing. In the north, among the Ainos, may be seen a style of rowing quaint indeed. The boatman uses his two oars, not together, but alternately; or if there be more than one rower, those on the right pull while those on the left raise their oars, and *vice versâ,* so that the boat goes sidling along like a sailing-craft perpetually tacking. It is hardly conceivable how so absurd a method can have maintained itself in use, as it apparently has from time immemorial.

---

* Quoted from the "Japan Herald," February, 1899.

Sake. No appropriate European name exists for this favourite intoxicant. Both "rice-beer" and "rice-brandy," by which the word has sometimes been translated, give a false idea of the thing. *Sake* is obtained from fermented rice by a complicated process, which can only be carried out during the winter, and it contains from eleven to fourteen per cent. of alcohol. Curiously enough, European heads seem to be affected by it much less easily than the Japanese themselves are; but it is unwise to indulge in *sake* and wine at the same repast. A very strong variety called *shōchū,* which is distilled from the dregs, contains from twenty to fifty per cent of alcohol. Another kind, called *mirin,* is more of a liqueur.

Salutations. The only native Japanese salutation is the bow, which often amounts to a prostration wherein the forehead touches the ground. Hand-shaking was unknown till a few years ago, and is little practised even now,—a proof of Japanese good sense, especially in hot weather. As for kissing, that is tabooed as utterly immodest and revolting.

Samurai. In the early Middle Ages—say, before the twelfth century—the soldiers of the Mikado's palace were said to *samurau,* that is, " be on guard " there. But when feudalism came in, the word *Samurai* was taken to denote the entire warrior class. " Warriors," " the military class," " the gentry," are perhaps the best English renderings of the word; for it was of the essence of Old Japan that all gentlemen must be soldiers, and all soldiers gentlemen.

The training, the occupations, the code of honour, the whole mental atmosphere of the Samurai exhibited a striking similarity to those of our own nobility and gentry during the Middle Ages. With them, as with us, obedience unquestioning and enthusiastic was yielded to feudal superiors, to monarchs ruling by right divine,—obedience even unto death. With them, as with us, it was birth and breeding that counted, not money. The Samurai's word was his bond, and he was taught to be gentle as well as brave. Doubtless, some well-marked shades of local colour distinguished Japanese chivalry from that of the West. The practice of suicide *(harakiri)* as part of the code of honour, where our own ancestors had the duel, at once occurs to the mind as a special feature. Even more so does the absence of gallantry towards the fair sex. No Japanese Ariosto would have dreamt of beginning his epic of chivalry with the words.

> Le donne, i cavalier, l'arme, gli amori,
> Le cortesie, l'audaci imprese io canto.

" God and the ladies! " was the motto of the European knight. But neither God nor the ladies inspired any enthusiasm in the Samurai's breast. Still, it is impossible not to see that, despite varying details, the same general trend of conditions produced kindred results on the two opposite sides of the globe. It is to be observed, too, that in Japan as in Europe the living reality of the earlier chivalry faded at last, under a centralised absolutism, into pageant and etiquette, though in the East as in the West a strong tinge of chivalrous feeling has survived in the upper class even to the present day.

The Japanese craze for altering names was exemplified in 1878, by the change of the historical and genuinely native word *Samurai* to that of *Shizoku,* a Chinese term of precisely the same meaning. Under this new designation, the Samurai still continue to exist, as one of the three classes into which Japanese society is divided.

In the feudal times, which lasted till A.D. 1871, the Samurai lived in his Daimyō's castle, attended his Daimyō on all occasions, and received from him rations for himself and his family,—rations which were calculated in so many *koku,* that is, bags of rice, annually. One of the early measures of the new Imperial administration was to commute these incomes for a lump sum, to be paid in government bonds. Optional at first, in 1873, the commutation was rendered obligatory by a second edict published in 1876. Since that time, many of the Samurai—unaccustomed as they had been to business and to the duty of working for their livelihood—have fallen into great misery. The more clever and ambitious, on the other hand, practically constitute the governing class of the country at the present day, their former lords and masters, the Daimyōs, having lagged behind in the race, and there being still a sufficient remnant of aristocratic spirit to render the rise of a plebeian to any position of importance a matter of considerable difficulty.

Books recommended. *Bushido: The Soul of Japan* by Inazo Nitobe; *Japan: An Attempt at Interpretation* by Lafcadio Hearn; *The Samurai Sword: A Handbook* by John M. Yumoto; *Tales of Old Japan* by A. B. Mitford (Lord Redesdale).

Sculpture. See CARVING.

Shimo-bashira. The peculiar phenomenon known by this name, which means literally "frost-pillars," has provoked some curiosity among the resident learned. These frost-pillars are first seen after a bright cold night in early winter, and always in damp, friable soil, the fine uppermost layer of which is borne upwards on their surface, so that one may fail to notice them until, in walking, the foot crushes down two or three inches —sometimes even five or six inches—into what had looked like firm ground; but often they cling to the high sides of shady lanes. Examined singly, they present the appearance of tiny hexagonal columns, or rather tubes, of ice; but they generally occur in clumps or bundles half melted together, and the longer ones sometimes curl over like shavings. Sometimes joints can be perceived in them, and at each joint a minute particle of earth. The late Dr. Gottfried Wagener explained the phenomenon as follows:—" When the surface of damp soil, in which the water is divided into slender canals, cools at night by radiation, the water at the exits of the canals hardens into ice. This ice then assists the hardening of the adjacent particles of water, which also congeal before the soil itself has fallen to freezing-point, and before therefore the water can freeze fast to the particles of earth. The ice then extends in the direction of least resistance, that is, upwards. In this manner, one molecule of ice after another pushes its way out of the slender canals,—a process which also explains the thread-like structure of the frost-pillars. These push up with them, in their growth, the minute particles of earth which lie between their extremities, and which also are cooled by radiation and stick to the ice. They form a crust which itself protects the underlying soil against further radiation. This accounts for the fact that the soil on which the frost-pillars stand, far from being frozen, is so soft and wet that a thin cane may easily be stuck deep into it. That the ice needles really grow from below and force their way up out of the soil, is proved by the circumstance that in shady places, where they are not melted during the day and can therefore continue to grow for several nights in succession, several sharply defined thin layers of earthy particles may be distinguished in the pillars. Frost-pillars are also formed under a thin covering of snow, when the upper surface of this latter melts during the day-time. The water then penetrates into the lower layer of snow, and thence into the soil. The thin snow-covering freezes during the night, and the hardening process, as above described, proceeds on into the canals below ground."

So far as our experience goes, frost-pillars, as here described, are unknown in Europe. An English gentleman long resident in Virginia tells us, however, that they occur there, going by the local name of " frost-flowers."

Shintō, which means literally " the Way of the Gods," is the name given to the mythology and vague ancestor and nature-worship which preceded the introduction of Buddhism into Japan, and which continues to exist in a modified form. Referring the reader to the Article on HISTORY AND MYTHOLOGY for a sketch of the Shintō pantheon, we would here draw attention to the fact that Shintō, so often spoken of as a religion, is hardly entitled to that name even in the opinion of those who, acting as its official mouthpieces to-day, desire to maintain it as a patriotic institution. It has no set of dogmas, no sacred book, no moral code. The absence of a moral code is accounted for, in the writings of native commentators, by the innate perfection of Japanese humanity, which obviates the necessity for such outward props. It is only outcasts, like the Chinese and Western nations, whose natural depravity renders the occasional appearance of sages and reformers necessary; and even with this assistance, all foreign nations continue to wallow in a mire of ignorance, guilt, and disobedience towards the heaven-descended, *de jure* monarch of the universe—the Mikado of Japan.

It is necessary, however, to distinguish three periods in the evolution of Shintō. During the first of these—roughly speaking, down to A.D. 550—the Japanese had no notion of religion as a separate institution. To pay homage to the gods, that is, to the departed ancestors of the Imperial family, and to the manes of other great men, was a usage springing from the same mental soil as that which produced passive obedience to, and worship of, the living Mikado. Besides this, there were prayers to the wind-gods, to the god of fire, to the god of pestilence, to the goddess of food, and to deities presiding over the saucepan, the cauldron, the gate, and the kitchen. There were also purifications for wrong-doing, as there were for bodily defilement, such, for instance, as contact with a corpse. The purifying element was water. But there was not even a shadowy idea of any code of ethics or any systematisation of the simple notions of the people concerning things unseen. There was neither heaven nor hell, —only a kind of neutral-tinted Hades. Some of the gods were good, some were bad; nor was the line between men and gods

at all clearly drawn. There was, however, a rude sort of
priesthood, each priest being charged with the service of some
particular local god, but not with preaching to the people.
One of the virgin daughters of the Mikado always dwelt at
the ancient shrine of Ise, keeping watch over the mirror,
the sword, and the jewel, which he had inherited from his
ancestress, Ama-terasu, Goddess of the Sun. Shintō may be
said, in this its first phase, to have been a set of ceremonies
as much political as religious. Whether and how far, even
at that remote period, unacknowledged spiritual influences
emanating from China had made themselves felt, is a curious
question. The coincidence of a few myths, together with other
scattered indications, seem to point in that direction. The
Chinese tincture of the version of the mythology and legendary
history preserved in the *Nihongi* is obvious to the least critical
reader, and shows that, in the eighth century at any rate, the
idea of endeavouring to preserve the national traditions free
from foreign influence was not present to the Japanese mind.

By the introduction of Buddhism in the middle of the sixth
century after Christ, the second period of the existence of
Shintō was inaugurated, and further growth in the direction
of a religion was stopped. The metaphysics of Buddhism were
far too profound, its ritual far too gorgeous, its moral code
far too exalted, for the puny fabric of Shintō to offer any
effective resistance. All that there was of religious feeling
in the nation went over to the enemy. The Buddhist priesthood
diplomatically received the native Shintō gods in their
pantheon as avatars of ancient Buddhas, for which reason
many of the Shintō ceremonies connected with the Court were
kept up, although Buddhist ceremonies took the first place
even in the thoughts of the converted descendants of the sun.
The Shintō rituals *(norito,)* previously handed down by word
of mouth, were then first put into written shape. The term
" Shintō " itself was also introduced, in order to distinguish
the old native way of thinking from the new doctrine imported
from India; for down to that time, no one had hit on the
notion of including the various fragmentary legends and local

usages under one general designation. But viewing the matter broadly, we may say that the second period of Shintō, which lasted from about A.D. 550 to 1700, was one of darkness and decrepitude. The various petty sects into which it then split up, owed what little vitality they possessed to fragments of cabalistic lore filched from the baser sort of Buddhism and from Taoism. Their priests practised the arts of divination and sorcery. Only at Court and at a few great shrines, such as those of Ise and Izumo, was a knowledge of Shintō in its native simplicity maintained; and even here it is doubtful whether changes did not creep in with the lapse of ages. Most of the Shintō temples throughout the country were served by Buddhist priests, who introduced the architectural ornaments and the ceremonial of their own religion. Thus was formed *Ryōbu Shintō,*—a mixed religion founded on a compromise between the old creed and the new,—and hence partly (for other causes have contributed to produce the same effect) the tolerant ideas on theological subjects of most Japanese of the middle and lower classes, who will worship indifferently at the shrines of either faith.

The third period in the history of Shintō began about the year 1700, and continues down to the present day. It has been termed the period of the " revival of pure Shintō." During the seventeenth and eighteenth centuries, under the peaceful government of the Tokugawa dynasty of Shōguns, the literati of Japan turned their eyes backward on their country's past. Old manuscripts were disinterred, old histories and old poems were put into print, the old language was studied and imitated. Soon the movement became religious and political,—above all, patriotic, not to say chauvinistic. The Shōgunate was frowned on, because it had supplanted the autocracy of the heaven-descended Mikados. Buddhism and Confucianism were sneered at, because of their foreign origin. Shintō gained by all this. The great scholars Mabuchi (1697–1769), Motoori (1730–1801), and Hirata (1776–1843), devoted themselves to a religious propaganda,—if that can be called a religion which sets out from the principle that the only two things needful are to follow one's natural impulses and to obey the Mikado. This order of ideas triumphed for a moment in the revolution of 1868. Buddhism was disestablished and disendowed, and Shintō was installed as the only state religion, the Council for Spiritual Affairs being given equal rank with the Council of State, which latter controlled things temporal. At the same time thousands of temples, formerly Buddhist or *Ryōbu-Shintō*, were, as the phrase went, " purified," that is, stripped of their Buddhist ornaments, and handed over to Shintō keeping. But as Shintō had no root in itself,—being a thing too empty and jejune to influence the hearts of men,—Buddhism soon rallied. The Council for Spiritual Affairs was reduced to the rank of a department, the department to a bureau, the bureau to a sub-bureau. The whole thing is now a mere shadow, though Shintō is still in so far the official cult that certain temples are maintained out of public moneys, and that the attendance of certain officials is required from time to time at ceremonies of a semi-religious, semi-courtly nature. Hard pressed to establish their *raison d'être* and retain a little popularity, the priests have taken to selling cheap prints of religious subjects, after the fashion of their Buddhist rivals. Some private scholars, too—Dr. Inoue Tetsujirō, for example—have recently attempted to infuse new life into Shintō by decking it out in ethical and theological plumes borrowed from abroad. One of these visionaries, a Mr. Sakamoto, has urged the establishment of an association which should inculcate, under new Shintō names, the seven cardinal virtues *(Confucian)*, the doctrine of cause and effect *(Buddhist,)* and that of a trinity in unity *(Christian)*. But of course such cut flowers, having no vital sap left in them, wither at once. A larger measure of success has attended the establishment of two new quasi-Shintō sects, the Tenri-kyō and Remmon-kyō, which, while claiming to represent the genuine national cult, mingle therewith shreds of superstition borrowed from various sources, and (if they are not greatly belied) an abundant measure of licentiousness. The founders of both these sects were ignorant peasant women.

The lover of Japanese art will bear the Shintō revivalists ill-will for the ridiculous "purification" which has destroyed countless gems of Buddhist architecture and ornament,—not for the sake of a grand moral ideal, as with the Puritans of Europe, but for an ideal immeasurably inferior to Buddhism itself. On the other hand, the literary style of their writings outshines anything produced by the Buddhists; and their energy in rescuing the old Japanese classic authors from neglect is worthy of all praise.

The Shintō temple *(yashiro* or *jinja)* preserves in a slightly elaborated form the type of the primeval Japanese hut, differing in this from the Buddhist temple *(tera)*, which is of Chinese and more remotely of Indian origin. Details of the names and uses of the various temple buildings, together with other matters, will be found in the Introduction to Murray's *Handbook for Japan.* It may suffice briefly to indicate here a means of distinguishing from each other the temples of the two religions. The outward and visible signs of Shintō are,— first, a wand from which depend strips of white paper cut into little angular bunches *(gohei)*, intended to represent the offerings of cloth which were anciently tied to branches of the sacred cleyera tree at festival time; secondly, a peculiar gateway called *torii.* Another difference is that the Shintō temple is thatched, whereas the Buddhist temple is tiled. Furthermore, the Shintō temple is plain and empty, while the Buddhist is highly decorated and filled with religious properties. (See also Articles on ARCHITECTURE and on TORII.)

Books recommended. *History of Japanese Religion* by Masaharu Anesaki; *The Ideals of the East with Special Reference to the Art of Japan* by Kakuzo Okakura; *Japan: An Attempt at Interpretation* by Lafcadio Hearn; *Religions in Japan* edited by William K. Bunce; *Shinto: The Kami Way* by Sokyo Ono in collaboration with William P. Woodard.

Shipping. The shipping industry is one of the most important in Japan, holding now, as it would seem to have done from time immemorial, a prominent place in the commerce of the country. The reason for this is not far to seek, being found in Japan's insular position, her extensive sea-board, and her mountainous interior. The Japanese take kindly to a seafaring life. During the Middle Ages, they were distinguished among Oriental nations for their spirit of maritime enterprise. Korea, China, Formosa, even the distant Philippine Islands, Cambodia, and Siam saw the Japanese appear on their coasts, now as peaceful traders, now as buccaneers. The story of one of these buccaneers, named Yamada Nagamasa, *alias* Tenjiku Hachibei, who ended by marrying a Siamese princess and becoming viceroy of the country, reads more like a chapter from the " Arabian Nights " than like sober reality. It is evident, too, that the Japanese of the early part of the seventeenth century were determined not to be left behind in the art of shipbuilding. The English master-mariner Will Adams, who came to Japan in the year 1600, built ships for Ieyasu, the then Shōgun, one of which made voyages to Manila and even to Mexico. Suddenly all was changed. Alarmed beyond measure at the progress of Catholicism, and fearing that in Japan, as elsewhere, the Spanish monk would be followed by the Spanish soldier of fortune, Iemitsu, the third Shōgun of the Tokugawa dynasty, issued an edict in the year 1636, whereby all foreign priests were expelled from the empire, foreign merchants were restricted to the two south-western ports of Nagasaki and Hirado, and all Japanese subjects were forbidden under pain of death to leave Japan. Drastic measures were resorted to in order to enforce the terms of this edict, all vessels of European build and even all large vessels of native build were ordered to be destroyed, only small junks sufficient for coasting purposes being allowed to be retained. This is the style of junk still seen at the present day in Japanese waters. It is distinguished by a single square sail, which is so awkward as to render the vessel difficult to handle except when running before the wind. Japan's shipping enterprise was crippled for over two centuries, though the number of coasting junks no doubt remained large; for the character of the country made communication by water indispensable.

When the feudal government fell like a card palace, the restrictions on shipbuilding fell with it. The new Imperial government took a laudable interest in the development of a mercantile marine of foreign build. Among other measures adopted with this end in view, a regulation prohibiting the construction of junks of over five hundred *koku** burthen may be cited as one of the most efficacious. Nor was everything left to official initiative. Iwasaki Yatarō, the celebrated millionaire, started steamers of his own somewhere about 1870; and the company which he worked with the aid of judiciously selected European directors and agents, European captains, and European engineers, soon rose, under the name of the Mitsubishi† Mail Steamship Company, to be the most important commercial undertaking in the empire. It even influenced politics; for to the facilities which the Mitsubishi afforded for carrying troops at the time of the Satsuma rebellion, was due in no small measure the triumph of the Imperialists in that their hour of need. Later on, another company, named the *Kyōdō Un-yu Kwaisha,* was formed to run against the Mitsubishi. But the rivalry between the two proving ruinous, they were amlgamated in 1885, under the name of the *Nippon Yūsen Kwaisha,* or Japan Mail Steamship Company. This company now ranks as one of the principal steamship companies of the world, and not only trades between the various parts of the coast, but maintains regular services between Japan and Europe, Australia, British India, America,

---

* Article 3 of the " Regulations and Rules for the Measures of Vessels' Capacity," published in 1888 by the Mercantile Marine Bureau of the Imperial Department of Communications, fixes the capacity of the *koku,* in vessels of Japanese build, as equivalent to 10 cubic feet. Whether this was the precise value of the maritime *koku* in earlier times, we cannot say.

† From *mitsu,* " three " and *hishi,* " the water caltrop," hence " lozenge," the leaves of the caltrop being approximately lozenge-shaped, and three lozenges having been chosen as the company's crest.

China, Siberia, and the Philippines. The *Ōsaka Shōsen Kwaisha* is another important private company, owning a large fleet of vessels engaged in the domestic carrying trade and running to Korea, Formosa, and up the Yangtse. The *Tōyō Kisen Kwaisha* is a third, which runs steamers to San Francisco and Hongkong. A score of smaller companies and numerous privately owned vessels render the means of travel and transit everywhere easy.

Iwasaki's keen enterprising spirit, seconded by government assistance, greatly contributed to develop the country. Places formerly dependent on the casual services of junks found themselves supplied with regular shipping facilities, or were at least able to command tonnage at short notice. Methods, too, rapidly improved. The happy-go-lucky way of conducting the loading of a junk, which could afford to wait an indefinite period for a cargo, necessarily yielded to prompt shipment at the time stipulated. The China war of 1894–5 gave a great impetus to shipping. Many private steamers were engaged as transports, and others bought to supply their place. Then followed laws for the encouragement of navigation and shipbuilding, also the granting of liberal subsidies, with the result that Japanese steamers—as indicated above—now compete with the foreign carriers on the chief lines to and from Japan. The outlay has been considerable for a country which is not rich; yet it may be regarded as a sound investment, because calculated to pay in the long run. It has already succeeded in ousting foreign competition from certain fields, from the Formosa coast, for instance, where British shipping, so late as 1896, amounted to over 86 per cent of the whole steam tonnage entered from abroad, but where the *Ōsaka Shōsen Kwaisha* now reigns supreme. Great attention, too, has been devoted to the construction of repairing and building-yards and of dry docks.

So far the domestic trade. Japan is no less well-supplied with foreign tonnage, thanks partly to the sudden and enormous increase in the number of tourists visiting these shores. The P. and O. Company, the Messageries Maritimes, and the Norddeutscher Lloyd all run steamers regularly throughout the year to Europe, to say nothing of several regular cargo lines and numerous " tramp " steamers. Across the Pacific Ocean, communication is kept up by the Occidental and Oriental Company and the Pacific Mail running to San Francisco, by the Canadian Pacific Company, whose destination is Vancouver, and by lines to Seattle, Tacoma, and Portland.

Shogun. The title of *Shōgun,* which means literally "generalissimo," and which was destined to play such a momentous part in Japanese history, seems to have been first used in A.D. 813, when one Watamaro was appointed *Sei-i Tai-Shōgun,* that is, " Barbarian-subduing Generalissimo," to wage war against the Ainos in the north of the empire. The title was employed afterwards in similar cases from time to time. But Yoritomo, at the end of the twelfth century, was the first of those generalissimos to make himself also, so to say, Mayor of the Palace, and in effect ruler of the land. From that time forward, various dynasties of Shōguns succeeded each other throughout the Middle Ages and down to our own days. The greatest of these families were the Ashikaga (A.D. 1336–1570) and the Tokugawa (A.D. 1603–1867). A concatenation of circumstances, partly political, partly religious, partly literary, led to the abolition of the Shōgunate in the year 1868. The Mikado then stepped forth again, to govern as well as reign, after an eclipse of well-nigh seven hundred years.

It has already been stated on page 236 that the name of the last of the Shōguns was Hitotsu-bashi. For him to have committed *harakiri* when the crash came (which was what many of his retainers expected) would have formed a dignified and memorable end to the Japanese feudal system. He prferred to live. After spending many yars in retirement in a provincial town, he removed to the capital; and still later, when he was admitted to some function at the Imperial Court, his appearance there scarcely evoked an expression of surprise. To readers brought up in Europe, with its Carlists, its Bourbons, in old days its Stuarts, at all times its irreconcilables of various names and degrees, it would seem but natural that a party favouring the restoration of the Shōgunate should linger on to embarass the new regime. This is not the case. Far-Eastern minds view these matters differently. Being matter-of-fact by nature, they accept the logic of events more easily and more absolutely than we do. In this part of the world, a lost cause does not simply fall:— it ceases to exist.

The practice of most modern writers on Japanese subjects —foreigners as well as natives—is to treat the Shōguns as usurpers. But surely this is a highly unphilosophical way of reading history. It is not even formally correct, seeing that the Shōguns obtained investiture from the Court of Kyōtō as regularly as ministers of state have obtained their commissions in later times. We cannot undertake here to go into the causes that produced Japanese feudalism, with the Shōguns at its head. But if seven centuries of possession do not constitute a legal title, how many of the governments at present existing in the world are legitimate ? And what test is there, or can there be, of the legitimacy of any government except the general acquiescence of the governed ?

Books recommended. *Bushido: The Soul of Japan* by Inazo Nitobe; *Japan: An Attempt at Interpretation* by Lafcadio Hearn; *Renaissance in Japan: A Cultural Survey of the Seventeenth Century* by Kenneth P. Kirkwood.

Shooting. No one is advised to come to Japan for sport, Deer and even bears do, no doubt, exist in the northern island of Yezo; pheasants, snipe, quail, wild-duck, teal, hares, and other small game in the Main Island, but not in sufficient numbers to wander so far afield for, seeing that Europe and America offer superior attractions. Shooting licenses may be obtained at the prefectural office *(kenchō)* of the various open ports, and at the *Tōkyō Fu,* or city office, in Tōkyō. The fee varies according to the income of the applicant, but practically all foreigners likely to require licenses come under the 20 *yen* clause.* The shooting season, speaking generally, lasts from the 15th October to the 15th April. These dates will seem late to English sportsmen; but it must be remembered that the seasons begin later in Japan than in England,—spring as well as autumn.

Siebold. Philipp Franz, Freiherr von Siebold (A.D. 1796–1866), author of many books, both in Latin and German, on the zoology, botany, language, and bibliography of Japan and the neighbouring lands, and best known by the magnificently illustrated folio work entitled *Nippon, Archiv zur Beschreibung von Japan,*† which is in itself an encyclopædia of the information concerning Japan which existed in his day, came of an old Bavarian family. Like Kaempfer a century and a half before him, he judged, and judged rightly, that the service of the Dutch East India Company was the royal road to a knowledge of the then mysterious empire of Japan. Appointed leader of a scientific mission fitted out at Batavia, he landed at Deshima, the Dutch portion of Nagasaki, in the month of August, 1823. By force of character, by urbanity of manner, by skill as a physician, even by a system of bribery which fell in with the customs of the country, and which surely, under the circumstances, no sensible man of the world will condemn, he obtained an extraordinary hold over the Japanese, suspicious and intractable as they then were. Having, in 1826, accompanied to Yedo the Dutch embassy which went once every four years to pay its respects to the Shōgun, Siebold made great friends with the Court astronomer, Takahashi by name, and received from him a map of the country which in those days it was high treason to put into the hands of any foreigner. When two years later, the affair leaked out, Takahashi was cast into a dungeon where he died, Siebold's house was searched, his servants were arrested and tortured, and he himself had to appear on his knees before the Governor

---

* Raised temporarily to 30 *yen* during the continuance of the war.

† A second abridged edition was published by his sons a few years ago.

of Nagasaki to answer for his share in the crime. He adroitly
contrived to save his chief treasures, including the map so
precious to geographical science, but he was banished from the
country, and sailed for Batavia on the 2nd January, 1830.
His persecuted pupils, sheltered by some of the leading
Daimyōs, did not a little to further the cause of European
learning in Japan.*

Arriving in Holland, Siebold was created a baron and a
colonel in the army by the king of that country, and spent the
next twenty-nine years in writing his numerous works and
arranging his scientific collections in the museums of Leyden,
Munich, and Würzburg. More permanent even in their results
than these learned labours was his activity in the field of
practical botany. To him our western gardens owe the
Japanese lilies, peonies, aralias, chrysanthemums, and scores
of other interesting and beautiful plants with which they
are now adorned.

Meanwhile, Commodore Perry's expedition had burst open
Japan. Siebold, in his old age, returned as a semi-official
ambassador to the country which he had quitted in disgrace
so many years before. This mission was not altogether
successful. The times were for war, not for the peaceful
negotiations of a man of science. Siebold's proper field was
not politics, but learning. It was therefore perhaps no loss
to his reputation that a second semi-political expedition to
Japan, which Napoleon III. had thought of entrusting to him,
was never carried out. Judged by his scientific works and
their practical results, Siebold is the greatest of the many
great Germans who have contributed so much to the world's
knowledge of Japan,—Kaempfer in the seventeenth century
and Rein in our own day being the other most illustrious
names. If small people may be allowed to criticise giants, we
would here note that the only weakness discoverable in the

---

* A somewhat different account of this incident was printed in previous editions of the
present work, on the authority of an obituary article by Gerhard Schirnhofer. The present
more trustworty version was obtained from J. Murdoch, the critical historian of modern
Japan, who has collated the original authorities.

early German school of investigators, as represented by Kaempfer, Thunberg, Siebold, and even Rein, is a certain insufficiency of the critical faculty in questions of history and language. Surely it is not enough to get at the Japanese sources. The Japanese sources must themselves be subjected to rigorous scrutiny. It was reserved for the English school, represented by Satow and Aston, to do this,—to explore the language with scientific exactness, and to prove, step by step, that the so-called history, which Kaempfer and his followers had taken on trust, was a mass of old wives' fables. More recently, however, Riess, Florenz, and others have gained for German scholarship bright laurels in this field also.

Books recommended. *A Collection of Nagasaki Colour Prints and Paintings* by N. H. N. Mody; *The Complete Journal of Townsend Harris* edited by Mario Emilio Cosenza; *Foreigners in Mikadoland* by Harold S. Williams; *Renaissance in Japan: A Cultural Survey of the Seventeenth Century* by Kenneth P. Kirkwood.

Silk. The silkworm was still a rare novelty at the dawn of Japanese history,—just imported, as it would seem, from Korea. The first mention of it is in the annals of the reign of the Emperor Nintoku, who is supposed to have died in A.D. 399. Up till then, the materials used for clothing had been hempen cloth and the bark of the paper-mulberry, coloured by being rubbed with madder and other tinctorial plants. The testimony of Japanese tradition to the foreign origin of silk, and its absence here in earlier ages, go to support the results of modern research to the effect that neither the true silkworm nor the mulberry-tree on whose leaves it feeds ever occurs wild in this archipelago. Striking change indeed! Silk has, for at least thirteen hundred years, helped to dress the Japanese upper classes, male as well as female, and has come to form the chief mainstay of the national prosperity.

The Japanese silkworm moth is the *Bombyx mori,* L.; its mulberry-tree the "white mulberry,"—*Morus alba,* L. Insect and tree have alike developed several varieties under cultivation. As a rule the trees are pollarded, and Japanese thrift takes advantage of the space between the stumps to grow small crops of useful vegetables. The branches are generally carried home for stripping. The Japanese silkworm manifests some marked peculiarities at different stages of its life-history. The eggs have extremely fragile shells, for which reason the moths are made to deposit them on cardboard; the worms are sluggish in their habits, and the cocoons smaller and lighter than those of Italy and the Levant, though the silk is but little inferior in quality. Some indeed, from certain filatures in the province of Shinano, is superior on account of its brilliantly white colour. Careless reeling, with consequent irregularity, is the weak point. In many parts of the country, primitive methods of working survive unchanged; in others, foreign machinery has been introduced.

Besides the true silkworm, there is another species called *yama-mayu,* which feeds on the oak-leaf, and produces cocoons of great strength and beauty. Yet another—a wild one, called *sukari,* whose food is the leaf of the chestnut tree—has less value.

The central and northern provinces of the Main Island have from time immemorial been dotted with silk-producing districts. Nothing is so remarkable in the recent industrial development of Japan as the manner in which these districts have spread, until scarcely a rural commune remains without its mulberry plantations. Statistics confirm what any observant eye can notice. During the last twenty years the area planted with mulberry-trees has increased about 200 per cent, and as much as 88,000,000 *yen* worth of silk has been sent oversea in a single year. What the domestic consumption is, we cannot say; but it must be enormous. Think of the dresses, the sashes, the quilts, the wrappers for gifts, the brocades, the silk crape, the rolls of silk for painting or writing on, and the thousand other uses to which this most beautiful of all fabrics is put.

Silk is exported in various forms,—in its raw state, reeled as filatures, re-reels, and hanks, as cocoons, and waste-silk; manufactured, chiefly in the form of piece-goods and handkerchiefs. For some years there was also a large export of silkworms' eggs. Continental Europe and the United States are Japan's chief customers for raw and waste silk. Her manufactured silk finds a market all over the world.

Singing-girls. The charms of the Japanese singing-girl, or *geisha,* as the Japanese term her, have been dwelt on so often that we gladly leave them to her more ardent admirers. Deprived of her, Japanese social gatherings would lose much of their vivacity and pleasing unconstraint, and many a match, interesting to the gossips, would never be made; for quite a number of prominent men have shown their partiality for the fair warblers in the most practical of ways, namely, by marrying them. The singing-girl's talk, more even than her songs, helps her to such occasional good fortune; for she alone, of all classes of her countrywomen, has divined something of the art of conversation. Or the antecedents of the marriage may have been on this wise. A poor student becomes enamoured. His friends, hearing of what they deem evil courses, stop supplies. The singing-girl supports her lover, who thereupon passes brilliant examinations, and obtains an official post. They are married, and he rises to be one of the leading men in the empire, while she of course is a great lady, with her carriage and her weekly reception days. Such is the outline of more than one modern Japanese romance in real life.

Of late years the field of the singing-girl's operations has been limited by the fact that in official circles, the European banquet, with its familiar *salmis* and *aspics* and its intolerable after-dinner speeches, has well-nigh supplanted the native feast. Waiters in swallow-tails replace the damsels of the guitar and the wine-cup. The training of a singing-girl, which includes lessons in the art of dancing, often begins when she is seven years old. She is then practically engaged for a number of years, the career once entered on being difficult to quit, unless good fortune brings some wealthy lover able and willing to buy her out. There is a capitation tax of four *yen* per month on the actual singing-girls, and of half that sum on the little 'prentices. Such, at least, are the present rates in Tōkyō. They vary in the provinces.

Book recommended. *The Geisha Story: With Doll-and-Flower Arrangements* by Billie T. Chandler.

Societies. The Japanese of our day have taken kindly to societies and associations of all sorts. They doubtless feel that their nation has to make up now for the long abstinence from such coöperative activity which was enforced during the Tokugawa regime, when it was penal for more than five persons to club together for any purpose.

The six most influential societies at present are the Military ·Virtues Society, with over 982,000 members; the Red Cross Association, under the immediate patronage of the Empress, with a membership of over 930,000; the Ladies' Patriotic Society, with over 140,000; the Agricultural Society, with over 9,000; the Associated Temperance Unions, with some 9,000; and the Sanitary Society, with nearly 7,000. These, and not a few of those next to be mentioned, have branches in the provinces, and most of them publish transactions. The Educational Society, the Geographical Society, the Oriental Society, the Economical Society, the Philosophical, Engineering, Electrical, Medical, Historical, and Philological Societies, and the *Gakushi Kwai-in*, an association with aims kindred to those of the Educational Society, have done excellent work. We have, furthermore, a Society of Arts, Judicial, Anthropological, and various other scientific and literary Societies, a Colonisation Society, a number of Young Men's Christian Associations and Women's Temperance Societies, an Association of Buddhist Young Men, and others of various hues and complexions, not to mention political clubs, of which the number is very great and continually changing.

Some of the Japanese societies have eccentric rules. Thus, there is one called the Mustache Society, whose members consist of amateur singers,—of the male sex only, for no one without a mustache is eligible. The object of the Growlers' Society is

to ventilate discontent and emphasise every public grievance.
The Dotards' Society, on the contrary, is a clique of antiquated
wits and *passées* beauties who have prudently determined to
make the best even of old age, and to have a good time up to
the very end. The Pock-mark Society, we believe, still exists,
though vaccination has sadly thinned its ranks. The Society
for the Abolition of Present-giving has (thank Heaven!) come
to grief. In no country of the world do *les petits cadeaux
qui entretiennent l'amitié* play a more charming part than in
Japan. Japan is becoming prosaic fast enough in all
conscience. Why ruthlessly pull up by the roots the few graces
that remain ?

Society in Japan is almost purely official. There is nothing
here corresponding to the English " county families," whose
members may or may not accept office, but who, if they do so,
add a lustre to it, far from its adding any to them. Neither
is there any class superior by birth or by intellect, as in
France or in America, which stands scornfully aloof and
would deem it derogatory to take any part in the vulgar
scramble for office. The Court is in Japan the sole and actual
fountain of honour; fallen causes have in this land no partisans.
Even money is comparatively little esteemed. There are few
millionaires, and it so happens that the half-dozen men who
have amassed large fortunes in business during the last twenty
or thirty years are, for the most part, either indifferent to
society or little qualified to shine in it. The Court (or whoever
it is that acts in the name of the Court) has raised up a new
bureaucracy on the ruins of the old feudalism,—a bureaucracy
composed partly of men of good birth, partly of men of good
brains sharpened by the best attainable training, that is, in
the proper and original sense of the word, an aristocracy
which is the state, which is society, and precludes the existence
of any rival. Even the outward aspect of the country bears
testimony to these peculiar social conditions. " Where are
the country houses ? " we have sometimes been asked. There

are none, for the good reason that there is no one to live in them. Peasants live in the country, officials naturally live in the town, where their offices are. To go and bury themselves in the country, is an idea that never occurs to them. How should it ? They do not walk, they are not sportsmen. As for any ties binding the rich to their lowly neighbours, that feudal or semi-feudal view of things has passed away. At the most, the high official and his family may go for a week or a fortnight to some mineral spring resort or to the seaside; but they are not really happy till they get back to town.

It would be interesting to follow out in detail the far-reaching results of a constitution of society differing so widely from that to which Anglo-Saxons—whether of the Kingdom, the States, or the Commonwealth—are accustomed. One is that Japanese society is dull, because it is not continuous:—at least the non-continuity greatly aggravates that dullness which is rooted in the unfitness of Japanese ladies for social life, in our sense of the word. These sweet, retiring little creatures, who perform uncomplainingly all the duties of the home, lack influence over the men, and have (so far at least) acquired none of the arts of social leadership. What they might learn of such matters is subject to frequent interruption; for when a man is out of office, he is eclipsed utterly, and society sees him and his wife no more, as all invitations are issued according to official lists, and his own means of entertaining are conditioned by the drawing of his official salary. If you are not in office, those who are have no need of you, no room for you.

Curiously enough, even travellers are sometimes affected by this state of things. If we have heard one, we have heard a score of complaints somewhat to the following effect:—" Why! when the so-and-so's (mentioning some minister maybe, or consul-general, or head of commission and his wife) were in Europe, they dined with us over and over again, I helped Mme. so-and-so to choose her things, etc., etc.; and yet when I called

upon them in Tōkyō, they seemed to be always out or
something, and they never asked us to anything, and we are
so disappointed, because what we should have enjoyed, of all
things, would have been to see a nice Japanese home,—see
how they live,—and it seems so odd, too, after all we did for
them. Of course, we got an invitation to the Imperial Garden
Party and to the Birthday Ball; but that is different." These,
or something like these, are the expressions of disappointment
which we have heard drop from the lips of not a few intelligent
ladies visiting Japan, nor have we always found it easy to
make them appreciate the situation. If the Japanese couple
in question are removed, temporarily or permanently, from
official life, they are almost certainly in reduced circumstances.
When they were in Europe, they dressed *à l'européenne*, lived
altogether *à l'européenne*. Now they can do so no longer;
not improbably they do not even care to do so, but when in
office, found the having to do so rather a constraint. They
went to see you in London as great folks; you come to see
them at Tōkyō when they have shrivelled into small folks.
They feel a delicacy about asking you to their house, for fear
you should be uncomfortable squatting on the floor,—for fear,
too, lest you should inwardly make comparisons unfavourable
to them or their country. Our Anglo-Saxon idea is to let the
foreign visitor take pot-luck with the home circle. Well-bred
Japanese are more formal, official life having helped to make
them so. If they cannot make ready for you a kid, they would
rather say "not at home." The result is unpleasing; yet
there is no intentional breach of hospitality. How hospitable
this nation can be, has been demonstrated over and over again
by the reception accorded to notabilities political, literary, and
journalistic. But there, once more, it is officialdom that has
stepped in, money has been granted by one of the public
departments, action has been directed from headquarters. In
fact, officialdom is an overwhelming element in Japanese
society, it is the dominant element: without official assistance,
nothing can be done. Anglo-Saxons will be apt to judge such
want of individualism a source of weakness. But Japan's

marvellous rise, the position she has won for herself in a single generation of officially directed effort, supplies an incontestable proof to the contrary. She has succeeded, as Prussia succeeded, through centralisation; her five-and-forty millions move as one man.

The functions—we hesitate to call them entertainments, so little entertaining are they—incident to Japanese society as at present constituted, are of two kinds. First, dinners in native style for men only, often served by singing-girls, meetings of political or scientific associations, club gatherings, and the like;—these do offer a modicum of fun and interest, and much *sans-géne,* but lack that refinement which the presence of ladies would confer. The other category includes dinners in European style, where, if foreigners are present, the language difficulty, combined with the paucity of mutually interesting topics of conversation, doubles and trebles that gloom of dullness which the absence of social talent and of the habit of society spreads in deep layers over the whole surface of Tōkyō life. Besides dinners, there are balls at which the Japanese have now—after an ineffectual attempt—practically ceased to dance, and garden parties consisting either of men alone(!) or of men and women. Some well-advised hosts supply an actual performance on such occasions,—jugglers, day fireworks, the *Nō* dance, or a public story-teller (see Article so entitled). Occasionally, too, nowadays there is a band; but in the lack of all talent for music, it were better dispensed with. The foreign residents of Tōkyō—or rather the members of the diplomatic body—entertain each other a great deal. In fact, more dinners are given there during the winter than in many a European capital; for, in the absence of European theatres, concerts, galleries, lectures, and intellectual interests generally, what remains but the " pleasures of the table ? " Needless to say, however, that this charmed circle is fast closed to travellers, unless they happen to be personally intimate with one of its members.

It will be judged from the above that social functions are not what any well-advised person will cross these seas to seek.

Even so fascinating a country as Japan cannot provide everything. The charm here is in the street life of the lower classes, the kindliness of the simple country folk, the delicate art adorning each common object of every-day life, the parks of cherry-blossom that break the monotony of the cities, the trim chrysanthemum gardens, above all the enchanting scenery, —those giant cedars that overshadow moss-grown shrines, those volcanic cones of ineffably graceful logarithmic curve, those torrents to be crossed warily on stepping-stones or on "hanging bridges" stretched like a spider's thread and trembling at every step, and the breezy uplands carpeted with wild flowers and re-echoing with the carolling of nightingales and larks, and the summer hills around which the vapours twirl in grey semi-diaphanous garlands, and the valleys of mingled scarlet maple and deepest green, whose pinnacled rock-walls zigzag the sky with their sharply serrated line. Surely the catalogue of Japan's perfections is sufficiently long and goodly. But when your cultured soul begins to sigh for the delights of the drawing-room and the concert-hall, you had better invest in a ticket home.

Story-tellers. Though the Japanese are a nation of readers, they love also to listen to the tales of the professional story-teller, who is quite an artist in his way. The lower sort of story-teller may be seen seated at the street-corner, with a circle of gaping coolies round him. The higher class form guilds who own special houses of entertainment called *yose*, and may also be engaged by the hour to amuse private parties. Some story-telling is rather in the nature of a penny reading. The man sits with an open book before him and expounds it, —the story of the Forty-seven Rōnins perhaps, or the Chinese novel of the "Three Kingdoms" *(Sangoku Shi)*, or an account of the Satsuma rebellion, or of the old wars of the Taira and Minamoto families in the Middle Ages;—and when he comes to some particularly good point, he emphasises it by a rap with his fan or with a little slab of wood kept by him for the purpose. Such a reading is called *gundan* if the subject be war; otherwise it is *kōshaku,* which means literally a "disquisition." The *hanashi-ka* or story-teller proper, deals in love-tales, anecdotes, and imaginary incidents.

The entertainment offered at a *yose* is generally mixed. There will be war-stories, love-tales, recitations to the accompaniment of the banjo, the same programme being mostly adhered to for a fortnight, and a change being made on the 1st and 16th of the month. As the number of such houses in every large city is considerable, hearers may nevertheless find something new every night to listen to, and the higher class of story-tellers themselves may realise what for Japan is a very fair income. For they drive about from one house of entertainment to another, stopping only a quarter of an hour or so at each,—just time to tell one story and earn a dollar or two by it.

Many foreign students of the Japanese language have found the *yose* their best school; but only two have hitherto thought of going there, not as listeners, but as performers. One is an Englishman named Black, whose command of Japanese is so perfect, and whose plots borrowed from the stores of European fiction prove such agreeable novelties, that the Tōkyō story-tellers have admitted him to their guild. The other—also an Englishman, of the name of John Pale—is said to sing Japanese songs as well as any native.

Sun, Moon, and Stars. In the early Japanese mythology the sun is ruled over by a goddess, the glorious Ama-terasu, or "Heaven-Shiner," from whom is descended the Imperial family of Japan. The moon belongs to her brother, the rough and violent god Susa-no-o. According to the later Japanese poets, there grows in the moon a cassia-tree *(katsura),* whose reddening leaves cause its brighter refulgence in autumn. They also tell us of a great city in the moon *(tsuki no miyako),*

and the mythmakers have brought down a maiden from the moon to do penance on earth amid various picturesque scenes. But the genuinely popular imagination of the present day allows only of a hare in the moon, which keeps pounding away at rice in a mortar to make into cakes. The idea of the hare was borrowed from China; but the rice-cakes seem to be native, and to have their origin in a pun,—the same word *mochi* happening to have the two acceptations of "rice-cake" and "full moon." The sun is supposed to be inhabited by a three-legged crow,—also a Chinese notion. Hence the expression *kin-u gyoku-to*, "the golden crow and the jewelled hare," is a periphrasis for the sun and moon.

Far more important than the sun to esthetic persons is the moon. Of all subjects, this is the one on which Japanese poets and romance-writers most constantly dwell, one of them emphatically asserting that "all griefs can be assuaged by gazing at the moon." People still worship the crescent, each time it is first seen; but the greatest nights of the lunar year are the 26th of the 7th moon, the 15th of the 8th moon, and the 13th of the 9th moon, Old Calendar, which roughly correspond to dates some five or six weeks later according to our calendar, and thus include the three moons of the autumn trimester. On the 26th night of the 7th moon, people in Tōkyō visit the tea-houses at Atagoyama or those on the sea-shore of Takanawa, and sit up till a very late, or rather early, hour to see the moon rise over the water, drinking *sake* the while, and composing verses appropriate to the sentimental character of the scene. The 15th night of the 8th moon, which is no other than our harvest-moon at the full, is celebrated by an offering of beans and dumplings and of bouquets of eulalia-grass and lespedeza blossom. This moon is termed the "bean moon." The 14th night of the 9th moon sees offerings of the same bouquets, of dumplings, and of chestnuts. It is termed the "chestnut moon."

The stars are much less admired and written about in Japan than in Europe. No Japanese bard has ever apostrophised them as " the poetry of heaven." The only fable worth mentioning here in connection with the stars is that which inspires the festival named *Tanabata*. This fable, which is of Chinese origin, relates the loves of a Herdsman and a Weaving-girl. The Herdsman is a star in Aquila, the Weaver is the star Vega. They dwell on opposite sides of the " Celestial River," or Milky Way, and may never meet but on the 7th night of the 7th moon, a night held sacred to them, strips of paper with poetic effusions in their honour being stuck on stems of bamboo grass and set up in various places. According to one version of the legend, the Weaving-girl was so constantly kept employed in making garments for the offspring of the Emperor of Heaven—in other words, God—that she had no leisure to attend to the adornment of her person. At last, however, God, taking compassion on her loneliness, gave her in marriage to the Herdsman who dwelt on the opposite bank of the river. Hereupon the woman began to grow remiss in her work. God, in his anger, then made her recross the river, at the same time forbidding her husband to visit her oftener than once a year. Another version represents the pair as mortals, who were wedded at the early ages of fifteen and twelve, and who died at the ages of a hundred and three and ninety-nine respectively. After death, their spirits flew up to the sky, where the Supreme Deity bathed daily in the Celestial River. No mortals might pollute it by their touch, except on the 7th day of the 7th moon, when the Deity, instead of bathing, went to listen to the chanting of the Buddhist scriptures.

Supernatural Creatures of divers semi-human and animal shapes are still spoken of by the common people with a sort of half-belief, and retain an assured place in art. The *Tennin,* or Buddhist angels, are neither of the male sex, nor white-clad, nor winged:—they are females, apparently of a certain age, who float in mid-air, robed in long, gay-coloured garments resembling swadding-clothes, and who often play on flutes and lutes and other musical instruments. More popular than these—in fact, most popular of all supernatural beings—are the *Tengu,* a class of goblins or gnomes that haunt the mountains and woodlands, and play many pranks. They have an affinity to birds; for they are winged and beaked, sometimes clawed.* But often the beak becomes a large and enormously long human nose, and the whole creature is conceived as human, nothing bird-like remaining but the fan of feathers with which it fans itself. It is often dressed in leaves, and wears on its head a tiny cap. Several fine temples are still dedicated to these goblins, that of Dōryō Sama near Miyanoshita being specially beautiful. Then there are the *Sennin,* or "mountain genii,"—men in shape, but immortal. They are stately, not grotesque and elfish like the other class just mentioned. The *Shōjō* are red-haired sea monsters, given to drinking enormous quantities of liquor. The "Three-eyed Friar" and the "Single-eyed Acolyte" (his single eye glares in mid-forehead) must be uncanny persons to meet in the gloaming, nor less so the "White Woman" who wanders about in the snow. The youth of Japan has a wholesome dread of these bogies, and also fears a variety of *Oni*—demons and ogres—of whom blood-curdling stories are told. They have horns, but no tail, and their sole article of clothing is a loin-cloth of tiger skin. One of them produces the thunder by tapping on a set of tambourines, and sometimes he falls to the ground and hurts himself. Japanese ghosts do not walk the earth wound in sheets, for the simple reason that sheets form no part of Japanese sleeping arrangements. But their legs dwindle into nothingness, while the body is drawn out to an alarming height, and they hold their hands in front of them in a grabbling attitude. Sometimes the neck is of frightful length *(rokuro-kubi),* and twisted like a snake.

Of mythic beasts, the most important by far is that noble creature the Dragon,—Chinese by origin, but thoroughly

---

* The word *tengu* is written with the Chinese character 天 狗 lit. "heavenly dog." But in Japan this orthography is misleading, as the supernatural creature in question is entirely bird-like.

naturalised in Japan.* His affinities are with the watery element that rules in clouds and tempests. Sometimes he will ascend Fuji, borne thither on a cloud; at others he hides himself in the waters of some river or deep secluded lake, and will cause terrific commotion in heaven and earth if disturbed. The palace of the King of the Dragons is a marvellously rich abode lying far away, many leagues beneath the ocean waves. The Unicorn and the Phenix scarcely appear except in art, and the only function of the *Baku* (seemingly a large quadruped allied to the tapir) is to devour evil dreams. More popular is the giant *Namazu*,—an eel-like creature, but thicker and flat-headed and supplied with mustachios,—which dwells somewhere in the bowls of the earth, and whose occasional wrigglings are the cause of earthquakes. Another marine creature, the Octopus, which assumes semi-human form, inspires dread by coming ashore to steal potatoes, and by other pranks. The people also believe in Mermaids, but often confound with these imaginary beings the really existing seal, perhaps because of its almost pathetically human countenance. Among birds, a purely mythical being is the *Nue*. When the reader is informed that this so-called " bird " (for it flies, and sings in a voice at once " hoarse, guttural, loud, and very plaintive ") has " the head of a monkey, the body of a tiger, and the tail of a serpent," he will surely not scruple to admit, with the old commentator, that " it is a rare and peculiar creature."

For what is thought of magic foxes, badgers, and dogs, see page 115.

Book recommended. *Tales of Old Japan* by A. B. Mitford (Lord Redesdale).

Superstitions. Mention has been made in previous Articles of the popular Japanese belief in divination, in demonical possession, and in the efficacy of charms against fire, shipwreck, and disease. There exist also various superstitious notions

---

* Probably the dragon's real birthplace is still further west; but from the Japanese point of view, he is Chinese. A similar caveat applies to several other things called Chinese in Japan:—China was, if not the manufactory, at least the storehouse whence Japan drew them.

about numbers. For instance, 7 and all numbers into which 7 enters, as 17, 27, etc., are unlucky. Certain numerical proportions must be observed between the ages of man and woman in wedlock. By the rule known as *yo-me tō-me,* you should not marry a girl whose age differs by 4 years or by 10 years from your own. (But as Far-Eastern reckoning is always inclusive,—see page 12,—the real numbers are 3 and 9; thus a man of 21 must not marry a girl of 18, nor a man of 26 a girl of 17.) Ages also exercise an influence on certain occupations. Thus, trees must be grafted only by young men, because of the special need of vital energy in the graft. The notion that certain days are lucky, is still so firmly rooted that some newspapers which cater for the lower classes publish lists of them. For example, what are known as *tomo-biki no hi* are days exercising such irresistible influence on the future that if a funeral takes place on one of them, there will certainly soon be another funeral in the same family. The general idea that "misfortunes never come singly," is expressed by the adage *Ni-do aru koto wa, san-do aru,* " What happens twice will happen thrice."

Questions of place must be attended to no less carefully than proper times and seasons, if ill-luck is to be avoided. Thus, no Japanese would sleep with his head to the North (that is, facing South), for that is the direction in which corpses are laid out. The East is the luckiest side, the next being the South. There is always danger to be feared from the North-East, which quarter has received the name of the "demon's gate:"—no openings are left in a house on that side, and no well is ever dug there, but Buddhist temples are often built on the North-East of a city as a means of protection. Sometimes, in shifting house from one locality to another, it may be prudent not to go straight to the objective, but to make a circuit via some other point of the compass, and stop a night—maybe a longer period, according as the soothsayer shall indicate—on the way. Certain mountains and lakes must not be approached; for the inevitable result is a typhoon, especially if the intruder should disturb or carry off any of the water.

There are various superstitions connected with fire, that arch-enemy of a people whose cities are built of wood. Do not throw any nail-parings into the fire:—if you do, the fire will take vengeance by burning either you or your house. Do not throw persimmon-stones into the fire, or you will become a leper. Do not bring in any of those delicately beautiful Lent lilies (*higan-bana,* lit. equinox flowers) that bloom in scarlet profusion on the margins of the rice-fields at the time of the spring and autumn equinox. Your house may be burnt down. Perhaps this idea was suggested by the colour and shape of the flower resembling tongues of flame, besides which the word " equinox " is connected with the idea of death, it being at that festival that the departed spirits cross over the Buddhist Styx. In former days it was supposed that any one gazing on the Mikado would be struck blind, and accordingly that sacred personage's " dragon face " was always veiled by a fine bamboo mat from those to whom an audience was granted. Photography, when first introduced, was also considered dangerous, because likely to absorb some portion of the life or spirit of the person photographed.* Belonging to a different set of ideals, and not without a touch of quiet humour, is a charm in the shape of a short inscription which, at this very moment of writing (1904), is to be found pasted in every room of one of the best-known hotels in Japan. It keeps out ants, by informing them that " For every hundred cubic inches of ants, a charge of sixteen cash will be levied." The ant, being a thrifty creature, refuses to enter even on such moderate terms.

The above are samples merely, culled at haphazard. Of other superstitions concerning names, concerning clothes, concerning the weather, concerning sneezing, concerning words

---

* Photography is now dangerous in sober earnest to the photographer, if he falls into the clutches of the police for following his amusement in any of the " forbidden zones " that surround forts and other places under military ban.

to be avoided, etc., etc., etc., the tale is endless. A very fat volume could be filled, were a complete account of all Japanese superstitions, past and present, urban and rustic, to be brought together; for each province would contribute its quota. At the same time, all, or almost all, are now confined to the lower classes; or if they find any credence in the upper class, it is chiefly among the women-folk. The generation now at school is—both for good and for evil—distinctly Voltairian.

Books recommended. *A Japanese Miscellany* by Lafcadio Hearn; *Tales of Old Japan* by A. B. Mitford (Lord Redesdale).

Swords. The Japanese sword of ancient days (the *tsurugi*) was a straight, double-edged, heavy weapon some three feet long, intended to be brandished with both hands. That of mediæval and modern times (the *katana*) is lighter, shorter, has but a single edge, and is slightly curved towards the point. There is also the *wakizashi*, or dirk of about nine and a half inches, with which *harakiri* was committed. The four most famous Japanese sword-smiths are Munechika (10th century), Masamune and Yoshimitsu (latter part of the 13th century), and Muramasa (latter part of the 14th century). But Muramasa's blades had the reputation of being unlucky. Towards the close of the fifteenth century arose schools of artists in metal, who made it their business to adorn the hilt, the guard, the sheath, and other appurtenances in a manner which is still the delight of collectors. But to the Japanese connoisseur the great treasure is always the blade itself, which has been called " the living soul of the Samurai."

Japanese swords excel even the vaunted products of Damascus and Toledo. To cut through a pile of copper coins without nicking the blade is, or was, a common feat. History, tradition, and romance alike re-echo with the exploits of this wonderful weapon. The magic sword, and the sword handed down as an heirloom, figure as plentifully in the pages of Japanese novel-writers as magic rings and strawberry-marks used once upon a time to do in the West. The custom which obtained among the Samurai of wearing two swords, is believed to date from the beginning of the fourteenth century. It was abolished by an edict issued on the 28th March, 1876, and taking effect from the 1st January, 1877. The edict was obeyed by this strangely docile people without a blow being struck, and the curio-shops displayed heaps of swords which, a few months before, the owners would less willingly have parted with than with life itself. Shortly afterwards a second edict appeared, rescinding the first and leaving *any one* at liberty to wear what swords he pleased. But as the privilege of a class distinction was thus obliterated, none cared to take advantage of the permission, and the two-sworded Japanese gentleman is now extinct.

Excellent specimens of swords and scabbards may be seen at Tōkyō in the *Yūshū-kwan,* or Museum of Arms, situated in the ground of the Shōkonsha temple.

Japanese swords are made of soft, elastic, magnetic iron combined with hard steel. " The tempering of the edge," says Rein, " is carefully done in the charcoal furnace, the softer backs and the sides being surrounded up to a certain point with fire-clay, so that only the edge remains outside. The cooling takes place in cold water. It is in this way that the steeled edge may be distinguished clearly from the back, by its colour and lustre. The backs of knives, axes, and other weapons are united to the steel edge either by welding on one side, or by fitting the edge into a fluted groove of the back blade, and welding on both sides."

The most extraordinary circumstance connected with swords in this country is that ladders are made of them set edge up, which men climb, with the idea originally of propitiating the gods and gaining merit, though now the ordeal would seem to have sunk to the level of a mere acrobatic performance. On the occasion when the present writer witnessed one of these performances in the grounds of the temple of Asakusa at Tōkyō, he inspected the swords, could not detect any trace of deception, and is therefore unable to offer an explanation of the fact that several persons walked up this dreadful ladder barefoot without any untoward consequences.

Books recommended. *The Arts of the Japanese Sword* by B. W. Robinson; *Bushido: The Soul of Japan* by Inazo Nitobe; *Legend in Japanese Art* by Henri L. Joly; *The Samurai Sword: A Handbook* by John M. Yumoto.

Taste. Japanese taste in painting, in house decoration, in all matters depending on line and form, may be summed up in one word—sobriety. The bluster which mistakes bigness for greatness, the vulgarity which smothers beauty under ostentation and extravagance, have no place in the Japanese way of thinking. The alcove of a Tōkyō or Kyōto drawing-room holds one picture and one flower-vase, which are changed from time to time. To be sure, picture and vase are alike exquisite. The possessions of the master of the house are not sown broadcast, as much as to say, "Look what a lot of expensive articles I've got, and just think how jolly rich I must be !" He does not stick up plates on walls :—plates are meant to hold food. He would not, whatever might be his means, waste £1,000, or £100, or even £20, on the flowers for a single party :—flowers are simple things, perishable things; it is incongruous to lavish on them sums that would procure precious stones for heirlooms. And how this moderation makes for happiness ! The rich not being blatant, the poor are not abject; in fact, though poverty exists, pauperism does not. A genuine spirit of equality pervades society.

When will Europe learn afresh from Japan that lesson of proportion, of fitness, of sobriety, which Greece once knew so well ? When will America learn it,--the land our grandfathers used to credit with republican simplicity, but which we of the present age have come to connect with the

idea of a bombastic luxury, comparable only to the extrava-
gances of Rome when Rome's moral fibre was beginning to be
relaxed ? But it seems likely that instead of Japan's
converting us, we shall pervert Japan. Contact has already
tainted the dress, the houses, the pictures, the life generally,
of the upper class. It is to the common people that one must
now go for the old tradition of sober beauty and proportion.
You want flowers arranged ? Ask your house-coolie. There
is something wrong in the way the garden is laid out ? It
looks too formal, and yet your proposed alterations would
turn it into a formless maze ? Call in the cook or the
washerman as counsellor.

To tell the whole truth, however, the Japanese have not
escaped the defects of their equalities. Their sobriety tends
to degenerate into littleness. Grandeur in any shape, rugged
mountain ranges, the storm-tossed sea, wide sweeps of moor-
land, make no deep impression on them. They love to expatiate
on the natural beauties of their country. Nevertheless, with
so much to choose from, their taste in almost every instance
singles out views of limited extent and a kind of polished
loveliness partly dependent on human aid. In short, they
admire scenes, not scenery. He who has visited Matsushima,
the " Plains of Heaven " near Yokohama, or any other widely
celebrated spot, will appreciate what we mean. Again, they
do not set their houses on heights commanding distant
prospects. They build preferably on the flat or in a hollow,
where the fence of their dainty garden shuts off the outer world.

Tattooing. Long before Japan was sufficiently civilised to
possess any records of her own, Chinese travellers noted down
their impressions of this " mountainous island in the midst
of the ocean." One, writing early in the Christian era, gives
various interesting scraps of information,—among others that
" the men all tattoo their faces and ornament their bodies
with designs, differences of rank being indicated by the position
and size of the patterns." But from the dawn of regular

history far down into the Middle Ages, tattooing seems to have been confined to criminals. It was used as branding was formerly used in Europe, whence probably the contempt still felt for tattooing by the Japanese upper classes. From condemned desperadoes to bravoes at large is but a step. The swashbucklers of feudal times took to tattooing, apparently because some blood and thunder scene of adventure, engraven on their chest and limbs, helped to give them a terrific air when stripped for any reason of their clothes. Other classes whose avocations led them to baring their bodies in public followed suit,—the carpenters, for instance, and running grooms *(bettō);* and the tradition remained of ornamenting almost the entire body and limbs with a hunting, theatrical, or other showy scene. A poor artisan might end by spending as much as a hundred dollars on having himself completely decorated in this manner. Of course he could not afford to pay such a sum down at once; so he was operated on by degrees through a term of years, as money was forthcoming.

Soon after the revolution of 1868, a dire catastrophe occurred:—the Government made tattooing a penal offence! Some official, it would seem, had got hold of the idea that tattooing was a barbarous practice which would render Japan contemptible in the eyes of Europe; and so tattooing, like cremation, was summarily interdicted. Europe herself then came to the rescue, in the shape of two young English princes who visited Japan in 1881, and who, learning that globe-trotters had sometimes managed surreptitiously to engage a tattooer's services, did the like with excellent effect, Prince George (now Prince of Wales) being appropriately decorated on the arm with a dragon. From that time forward, no serious effort has been made to interfere with the tattooer's art, and in the hands of such men as Hori Chiyo and Hori Yasu* it has become an art indeed,—an art as vastly superior to the ordinary

* The name, or nickname, Hori is from *hori-mono,* "tattooing," itself derived from the verb *horu,* "to dig," hence "to engrave," and *mono,* "a thing." Hori Chiyo I. is no more, having killed himself for love in 1900: but Hori Chiyo II., quite a young man, reigns worthily in his stead.

British sailor's tattooing as Heidsieck Monopole is to small beer. Birds, flowers, landscapes of marvellous finish and beauty—thoroughly Japanese withal in style and conception —are now executed, some specimens being so minute as almost to render the aid of a microscope necessary in order properly to appreciate them.

The principal materials used are sepia and vermilion,—the former for the outline and ground, the latter for touching up and picking out special details, for instance, a cock's crest. A brown colour is occasionally produced by resorting to Indian red. Prussian blue, also yellow and green, may likewise be employed, but are considered dangerous. The needles are all of steel, the finest being used to prick in the outlines, the thicker ones for shading. There are six sizes in all. The most delicate work takes only three needles; but ordinary outlines require a row of from four to nine needles. Shading is done by means of superposed rows of needles tied together, as, for instance, five, four, and three, making twelve in all, and so on up to as many as sixty. In such cases the thickest needles are employed. The needles are always spliced to a bone handle by means of a silken thread; and this handle is held in the right hand leaning on the left, somewhat as a billiard cue is held. Though an appreciable fraction of the total length of the needles protrudes beyond the splicing, blood is rarely drawn, owing to the skill with which the instrument is manipulated.

The most recent refinement of the art is the use of cocaine, either as a wash or mixed with the sepia. But the pain, on an ordinarily fleshy arm, is not acute enough for most persons to care to avail themselves of it. Smooth arms are the best to operate on, hairiness being apt to make the colour run.

Tea is believed to have been introduced into Japan from China in A.D. 805 by the celebrated Buddhist saint, Dengyō Daishi. It had long been a favourite beverage of the Buddhists of the continent, whom it served to keep wakeful during their midnight devotions. A pious legend tells us that the origin of the tea-shrub was on this wise. Daruma (Dharma), an Indian saint of the sixth century, had spent many long years in ceaseless prayer and watching. At last, one night, his eyelids, unable to bear the fatigue any longer, closed, and he slept soundly until morning. When the saint awoke, he was so angry with his lazy eyelids that he cut them off and flung them on the ground. But lo ! each lid was suddenly transformed into a shrub, whose efficacious leaves, infused in water, minister to the vigils of holy men.

Though encouraged from the first by Imperial recommendations, tea culture made little or no progress in Japan till the close of the twelfth century, when another Buddhist, the abbot Myōe, having obtained new seeds from China, sowed them at Toga-no-o, near Kyōto, whence a number of shrubs were afterwards transplanted to Uji, which has ever since been the chief centre of Japanese tea growing. Thenceforward the love of tea-drinking was engrained in the Japanese court and aristocracy, and the *cha-no-yu,* or tea ceremonies, became a national institution. But it is doubtful whether the custom of drinking tea began to spread among the lower classes till the end of the seventeenth century, which was also the time when our own ancestors first took to it. Now, needless to say that the tea-house is one of the most widely spread, socially most important, and to wayfarers most agreeable of Japanese institutions. Not but what it is a blunder to dub inns and restaurants " tea-houses," as Europeans are apt to do. The tea-house *(chaya)* is a thing by itself,—in the country an open shed, in the towns often a pretty, but always open, house, sometimes with a garden, where people sit down and rest for a short time, and are served with tea and light refreshments only, while a few words of gossip or innocent banter are exchanged with mine hostess or her attendant smiling damsels. Of course, " *en tout bien, tout honneur.*"

The tea-plant belongs to the same family of evergreens as the camellia, and bears small white flowers slightly fragrant.

As a rule, the seeds are planted in terraces on gentle hill slopes; but level ground may also be availed of, provided it be kept thoroughly drained. The shrub is not allowed to attain a height of more than three or four feet. It is ready for picking in the third year, but is at its best from the fifth to the tenth year. The first picking takes place at the end of April or beginning of May, and lasts three or four weeks. There is a second in June or July, and sometimes a third.

As soon as possible after being picked, the leaves are placed in a round wooden tray with a brass wire bottom over boiling water. This process of steaming, which is complete in half a minute, brings the natural oil to the surface. The next and principal operation is the firing, which is done in a wooden frame with tough Japanese paper stretched across it, charcoal well-covered with ash being the fuel employed. This first firing is done at a temperature of about 120° Fahrenheit. Meanwhile the leaf is manipulated for hours by men who roll it into balls with the palms of their hands. The final result is that each leaf becomes separately twisted, and changes its colour to dark olive purple. Two more firings at lower temperatures ensue, after which the leaf is allowed to dry until it becomes quite brittle. Sometimes—and we believe this to have been the common practice in ancient days—the leaf is not fired at all, but only sun-dried.

All genuine Japanese tea is what we should term " green." It is partaken of, not only at meal-times, but also at intervals throughout the day. The cups are very small, and no milk or sugar is added. The tea drunk in respectable Japanese households generally costs 25 to 50 *sen* a lb., while from 1 to 3 *yen* will be paid for a better quality fit to set before an honoured guest. The choicest Uji tea costs 10 *yen* per lb. We have even heard of exceptionally fine samples being charged for at the rate of 25 *yen* per lb.; but the so-called " best qualities " sold at most shops are only from 5 to 7 *yen*. At the opposite end of the scale stands the so-called *bancha*, the tea of the lower classes, 10 to 15 *sen* per lb., made out of chopped leaves, stalks, and bits of wood taken from the trimmings of the tea-plant; for this beverage is tea, after all, little as its flavour has in common with that of Bohea or of Uji. Other tea-like infusions sometimes to be met with are *kōsen,* made by pouring hot water on a mixture of various fragrant substances, such as orange-peel, the seeds of the xanthoxylon, etc.; *sakura-yu,* an infusion of salted cherry-blossoms; *mugi-yu,* an infusion of parched barley; *mame-cha,* a similar preparation of beans. *Fuku-ja,* or "luck tea," is made of salted plums, seaweed, and xanthoxylon seeds, and is partaken of in every Japanese household on the last night of the year.

Japanese tea, unlike Chinese, must not be made with boiling water, or it will give an intolerably bitter decoction; and the finer the quality of the tea, the less hot must be the water employed. The Japanese tea equipage actually includes a small open jug called the "water-cooler" *(yu-zamashi),* to which the hot water is, if necessary, transferred before being poured on the tea-leaves. Even so, the first brew is often thrown away as too bitter to drink. The consequence of this is that Japanese servants, when they first come to an English house, always have to be taught how to treat our Chinese or Indian tea, and generally begin by giving practical proof of their incredulity on the subject of the indispensable virtue of boiling water.

Large quantities of Japanese tea—as much as 40,000,000 lbs. in a single season—are sent across the Pacific to the United States and Canada, and a large tea "trust" on American lines has even been suggested. What a change in the course of a single life-time! It is but fifty years since an enterprising widow of Nagasaki, named Ōura, made the first surreptitious shipment of 27 lbs.; for no intercourse was then permitted with the hated barbarian.

Books recommended. *The Book of Tea* by Kakuzo Okakura; *Cha-No-Yu: The Japanese Tea Ceremony* by A. L. Sadler.

Tea Ceremonies. Few things have excited more interest among collectors of Japanese curios than the *cha-no-yu,* or tea ceremonies, of which so many of the highly prized little "japanosities" in their collections are in one way or another the implements. And as quarrelling with other collectors is part of every true collector's nature, so also has the battle raged round the Japanese tea-table,—a veritable and literal storm in a tea-cup. One set disparages the tea ceremonies as essentially paltry and effeminate, and asserts that their influence has cramped the genius of Japanese art, by confusing beauty with archaism and making goals of characteristics worthy only to be starting-points. The opposite school sees in these same ceremonies a profoundly beneficial influence,— an influence which has kept Japanese art from leaving the narrow path of purity and simplicity for the broad road of a meretricious gaudiness.

What, then, are these tea ceremonies. And first of all, what is their history ? Have their votaries at all epochs been enamoured of simplicity and archaism to the degree which both friends and foes seem to take for granted ? If our own slight researches into the subject prove anything, they prove that these traits are comparatively modern.

The tea ceremonies have undergone three transformations during the six or seven hundred years of their existence. They have passed through a medico-religious stage, a luxurious stage, and lastly an esthetic stage. They originated in tea-drinking pure and simple on the part of certain Buddhist priests of the Zen sect, who found the infusion useful in keeping them awake during the performance of their midnight devotions. The first aristocrat whóse name is mentioned in connection with tea is Minamoto-no-Sanetomo, Shōgun of Japan from A.D. 1203 to 1218. He seems to have been a youthful debauchee, whom the Buddhist abbot Eisai endeavoured to save from the wine-cup by making him take tea instead. As is still the custom of propagandists, Eisai accompanied this recommendation by the gift of a tract on the subject. It was composed by himself, and bore the title of "The Salutary Influence of Tea-Drinking." In it was explained the manner in which tea " regulates the five viscera and expels evil spirits," and rules were given both for making the infusion and for drinking it. The ceremonial which Eisai introduced was religious. True, it comprised a simple dinner; but its main feature was a Buddhist service, at which the faithful worshipped their ancestors to the beating of drums and burning of incense. A tinge of the religious element has adhered to the tea ceremonies ever since. It is still considered proper for tea enthusiasts to join the Zen sect of Buddhism, and it is from the abbot of Daitokuji at Kyōto that diplomas of proficiency are obtained.

How long Japanese tea-drinking remained in this first religious stage is not clear. This we know, that by the year 1330, the second or luxurious stage had already been reached. The descriptions of the tea-parties of those days read like a chapter of romance. The Daimyōs who daily took part in them reclined on couches spread with tiger skins and leopard skins. The walls of the spacious apartments in which the guests assembled were hung, not only with Buddhist pictures, but with damask and brocade, with gold and silver vessels, and swords in splendid sheaths. Precious perfumes were burnt, rare fishes and strange birds were served up with sweetmeats and wine, and the point of the entertainment consisted in guessing where the material for each cup of tea had been produced; for as many brands as possible were brought in, to serve as a puzzle or *jeu de société*—some from the Toga-no-o plantations, some from Uji, some from other places. Every right guess procured for him who made it the gift of one of the treasures that were hung round the room. But he was not allowed to carry it away himself. The rules of the tea ceremonies, as then practised, ordained that all the things rich and rare that were exhibited must be given by their winners to the singing and dancing-girls, troupes of whom were present to help the company in their carousal. Vast fortunes were dissipated in this manner. On the other hand, the arts were benefited, more especially when, towards the close of the fifteenth century, the luxurious Yoshimasa, a sort

of Japanese Lorenzo de' Medici, abdicated the Shōgun's throne
in order to devote himself altogether to refined pleasures in his
gorgeous palace of Ginkakuji at Kyōto, in the company of his
favourites, the pleasure-loving Buddhist abbots Shukō and
Shinnō. From this trio of royal and religious voluptuaries are
derived several of the rules for tea-drinking that still hold
good. The tiny tea-room of only four and a half mats (nine
feet square) apparently dates from then. Shinnō was a great
connoisseur of antiquities and of what we now term curios.
He was also the first to manufacture a certain kind of teaspoon,
whence arose the custom of tea-fanciers manufacturing their
own spoons.

All through the fifteenth and sixteenth centuries, the tea
ceremonies continued to enjoy the unabated favour of the
Japanese upper classes. The gift of some portion of a
tea-service, such as a bowl or cup, was the most valued mark
of condescension which a superior could bestow. We read of
high-born warriors neglecting their sword for the sake of the
tea-pot, and of their being cashiered therefor, of others dying
bowl in hand when their castles were taken by the enemy, or
sending their tea-things away privately as their chiefest
treasure. Nobunaga and Hideyoshi, two of the greatest
military rulers of Japan, were both enthusiastic votaries of
the tea ceremonies. Hideyoshi probably gave the largest
tea-party on record, the card of invitation being in the form
of an official edict which is still preserved. All the lovers of
tea in the empire were, by this singular document, summoned
to assemble at a certain date under the pine grove of Kitano,
near Kyōto, and to bring with them whatever curios connected
with tea-drinking they possessed, it being further decreed that
all such as failed to respond to the summons should be debarred
from ever taking part in the tea ceremonies again. This was
in the autumn of 1587, the time when the Invincible Armada
was being equipped for the ceremonies of war. The tea-party
seems to have been successful. It lasted ten days, and
Hideyoshi fulfilled his promise of drinking tea at every booth.
The tenants of some of the booths were noblemen, of others

traders or peasants;—for all were invited regardless of birth, a proof that the custom had begun to filter down into the lower strata of society.

A few years later (1594) Hideyoshi called together at his palace of Fushimi the heads of all various schools into which, by this time, the art of tea-drinking had split up. Chief among these was Sen-no-Rikyū, a name which every Japanese enthusiast reveres,—for he it was, or least he principally, who collated, purified, and (so to say) codified the tea ceremonies, stamping them with the character which they have borne ever since. Simplicity had long been commanded by the poverty of the country, exhausted as it was by ages of warfare. He took this simplicity up, and raised it into a canon of taste as imperative as the respect for antiquity itself. The worship of simplicity and of the antique in objects of art, together with the observance of an elaborate code of etiquette—such are the doctrine and discipline of the tea ceremonies in their modern form, which has never varied since Sen-no-Rikyū's day. Though not the St. Paul of the tea cult, he was thus its Luther. Unfortunately he was not indifferent to money. He abused his unrivalled skill as a connoisseur of curios to enrich himself, and to curry favour with the great. Hideyoshi at last detected his venality and fraud, and caused him to be put to death.

The ceremonies themselves have often been described. They include a preliminary dinner, but tea-drinking is the chief thing. The tea used is in the form, not of tea-leaves, but of powder, so that the resulting beverage resembles pea-soup in colour and consistency.* There is a thicker kind called *koi-cha*, and a thinner kind *usu-cha*. The former is used in the earlier stage of the proceedings, the latter towards the end. The tea is made and drunk in a preternaturally slow and formal manner, each action, each gesture being fixed by an elaborate code of rules. Every article connected with the ceremony,

---

* Foreign *gourmets* resident in Japan have discovered that a delicious ice-cream can be made out of it.

such as the tea-canister, the incense-burner, the hanging scroll, and the bouquet of flowers in the alcove, is either handled, or else admired at a distance, in ways and with phrases which unalterable usage prescribes. Even the hands are washed, the room is swept, a little bell is rung, and the guests walk from the house to the garden and from the garden back into the house, at stated times and in a stated manner which never varies, except in so far as certain schools, as rigidly conservative as monkish confraternities, obey slightly varying rules of their own, handed down from their ancestors who interpreted Sen-no-Rikyū's ordinances according to slightly varying cannons of exegesis.

To a European the ceremony is lengthy and meaningless. When witnessed more than once, it becomes intolerably monotonous. Not being born with an Oriental fund of patience, he longs for something new, something lively, something with at least the semblance of logic and utility. But then it is not for him that the tea ceremonies were made. If they amuse those for whom they were made, they amuse them, and there is nothing more to be said. In any case, tea and ceremonies are perfectly harmless, which is more than can be affirmed of tea and tattle. No doubt, even the tea ceremonies have, if history libels them not, been sometimes misused for purposes of political conspiracy. But these cases are rare. If the tea ceremonies do not go the length of embodying a "philosophy," as fabled by some of their admirers, they have, at least in their latest form, assisted the cause of purity in art. Some may deem them pointless. None can stigmatise them as vulgar..

Books recommended. *The Book of Tea* by Kakuzo Okakura; *Cha-No-Yu: The Japanese Tea Ceremony* by A. L. Sadler.

Telegraphs. The first line of telegraphs in this country may be said to have been experimental; it was only 840 yards in length, and was opened for government business in 1869. During the following year Tōkyō and Yokohama, and Ōsaka and Kōbe, respectively, were connected by wire, and a general telegraphic system for the empire was decided on; but the necessary material and a staff of officers did not reach Japan until the end of 1871. The line from Tōkyō to Kōbe was completed and opened for traffic in the year 1872, and extended to Nagasaki in 1873.

On the introduction of telegraphy into Japan, a code was devised on the basis of the well-known "Morse code," which admitted of internal telegrams being written and transmitted in the vernacular. In that respect, as in so many others, Japan is unique among Eastern countries. In India and China, for instance, telegrams can be transmitted only when written in Roman letters or in Arabic figures. The new means of communication being thus placed within reach of the bulk of the people, it soon became familiar and popular. Telephone exchanges, too, have now been introduced in 24 of the larger towns. In Tōkyō there are upwards of 11,600 subscribers.

The first telegraph lines were surveyed, built, and worked under foreign superintendence, with fittings principally of English manufacture. But the rapid progress made by the Japanese in technical matters has enabled them to dispense with foreign experts. With the exception of submarine cables, iron and covered wires, and the most delicate measuring apparatus, all kinds of material and instruments are turned out of the Japanese workshops, while executively the system has been maintained solely by the native staff for several years past. Submarine cables connect all the principal islands of the empire, even recently acquired Formosa. Duplicate cables, belonging to the Great Northern Telegraph Company, connect Japan with Shanghai on the one hand, and with Vladivostock on the other. There is also one to Fusan in Korea, worked by the Japanese Government.

The tariff for native messages, which was framed on a very low basis, has met with excellent results. Though afterwards raised, it is still probably under that of any other country in the world. The rate for a single message of fifteen *Kana* characters to any part of the empire is 20 *sen* (fivepence), with 5 *sen* (a penny farthing) for every following five *Kana;*

for city local traffic it is only 10 *sen,* or twopence halfpenny,
with 3 *sen* for every following five *Kana.* The name and address
of the receiver go free. Telegrams in foreign languages within
the empire are charged at the rate of 5 *sen* per word, with a
minimum charge of 25 *sen* (sixpence farthing) for the first
five words or fraction of five words; but addresses count. For
city local traffic it is only 3 *sen* per word, with a minimum
charge of 15 *sen.*

The number of offices open for public business at the end of
1902 was 2,201. The length of wire open at the same date was
18,565 miles. The number of messages conveyed during that
year was over eighteen millions, the overwhelming majority
of them being in the native tongue. This, too, in a land where,
but a generation ago, the hatred of foreigners and all their
works was still so intense, especially in the South, that linemen
had to be kept constantly busy repairing the hacked poles !
In fact, many Japanese would not willingly pass under the
wires, and if compelled to do so, would screen their heads with
open fans to avert the diabolical influence.

Theatre. The Japanese theatre claims a peculiar importance,
as the only remaining place where the life of Old Japan can
be studied in these radical latter days. The Japanese drama,
too, has an interesting history. It can be traced back to
religious dances of immemorial antiquity, accompanied by
rude choric songs. An improvement was made in these dances
at the beginning of the fifteenth century, when some highly
cultivated Buddhist priests and the pleasure-loving Shōgun
Yoshimasa took the matter in hand, and inaugurated a new
departure by combining the religious dances with popular
tales whose themes were history and legend, and with snatches
of poetry culled from various sources. It had been the custom,
during the earlier Middle Ages, for a certain class of minstrels
to recite the tales in question to the accompaniment of the
lute. Thus, on a double basis, helped on too perhaps by some
echo from the China stage, yet independently developed, the
Japanese lyrical drama came into being. Edifices—half

dancing-stage, half theatre—were built for the special purpose
of representing these *Nō,* as the performances were called;
and though the chorus, which was at the same time an
orchestra, remained, new interest was added in the shape of
two individual personages, who moved about and recited
portions of the poem in a more dramatic manner. The result
was something strikingly similar to the old Greek drama.
The three unities, though never theorised about, were strictly
observed in practice. There was the same chorus, the same
stately demeanour of the actors, who were often masked;
there was the same sitting in the open air, there was the
same quasi-religious strain pervading the whole. We say
" was ; " but happily the *Nō* are not yet dead. Though shorn
of much of the formality and etiquette which surrounded them
in earlier days, representations are still given by families who
have handed down the art from father to son for four hundred
years. There is no scenery, but the dresses are magnificent.
Even the audience, composed chiefly of noblemen and ladies
of rank, is a study. They come, not merely to be amused,
but to learn, and they follow the play, book in hand ; for the
language used, though beautiful, is ancient and hard of
comprehension, especially when chanted. The music is—well,
it is Oriental. Nevertheless, when due allowance has been
made for Orientalism and for antiquity, it possesses a certain
weird charm. Each piece takes about an hour to act. But
the entire performance occupies the greater part of a day,
as five or six pieces are given, and the intervals between them
filled up by comediettas, whose broad fun, delivered in old-
fashioned colloquial, serves as a foil to the classic severity
of the chief plays.

From the *Nō* theatres of the high-born and learned to the
Shibai or *Kabuki* theatres of the common people is a great
descent, so far as taste and poetry are concerned, though the
interest of the more vulgar exhibitions, viewed as pictures
of manners—not in the world of gods and heroes, but in that
of ordinary Japanese men and women—will be of greater

interest to most foreign spectators. The plays given at these theatres originated partly in the comediettas just mentioned, partly in marionette dances accompanied by explanatory songs, called *jōruri* or *gidayū*. This explains the retention of the chorus, although in diminished numbers and exiled to a little cage separated from the stage, where they sit with the musicians. Hence, too, the peculiar poses of the actors, originally intended to imitate the stiffness of their prototypes, the marionettes. It was in the sixteenth century that this class of theatre took its rise. Oddly enough, though the founders of the Japanese stage were two women, named O-Kuni and O-Tsū, men alone have been allowed to act at the chief theatres, the female parts being taken by males, as in our own Shakespeare's age, while at a few inferior theatres the conditions are reversed, and only women appear. It would seem that immorality was feared from the joint appearance of the two sexes, and in sooth the reputation of O-Kuni and her companions was far from spotless.* Of late years the restriction has been relaxed, and performances by mixed troupes of actors and actresses may occasionally be witnessed.

From the beginning, plays were divided into two classes, called respectively *jidai-mono,* that is historical plays, and *sewa-mono,* or dramas of life and manners. Chikamatsu

---

* Mr. Lafcadio Hearn, writing to us to remonstrate on this reference to O-Kuni as needlessly severe, gives her story, which is, as he says, both picturesque and touching. It may be taken as typical of a whole class of Japanese love-tales:—

" She was a priestess in the great temple of Kitsuki, and fell in love with a swashbuckler named Nagoya Sanza, with whom she fled away to Kyoto. On the way thither, her extraordinary beauty caused a second swashbuckler to become enamoured of her. Sanza killed him, and the dead man's face never ceased to haunt the girl. At Kyoto she supported her lover by dancing the sacred dance in the dry bed of the river. Then the pair went to Yedo and began to act. Sanza himself became a famous actor. After her lover's death O-Kuni returned to Kitsuki, where, being an excellent poetess, she supported or at least occupied herself by giving lessons in the art. But afterwards she shaved off her hair and became a nun, and built a little temple in Kitsuki where she lived and taught. And the reason why she built the temple was that she might pray for the soul of the man whom the sight of her beauty had ruined. The temple stood until thirty years ago; but there is now nothing left of it but a broken statue of the compassionate god Jizo. The family still live at Kitsuki; and until the late revolution the head of the family was always entitled to a share in the profits of the local theatre, because his ancestress, the beautiful priestess, had founded the art."

Monzaemon and Takeda Izumo, the most celebrated of Japanese dramatists, divided their attention equally between the two styles. It may be worth mentioning that both these authors belonged to the eighteenth century, and that both of them dramatised the vendetta of the "Forty-seven Rōnins." But Chikamatsu's most famous piece is one founded on the piratical adventures of Kokusen-ya, who expelled the Dutch from Formosa in 1661. The Japanese *Kabuki* theatres are amply provided with scenery and stage properties of every description. One excellent arrangement is a revolving centre to the stage, which allows of a second scene being set up behind while the first is in course of acting. On the conclusion of the first, the stage revolves, carrrying away with it actors, scenery, and all; something entirely different greets the spectators' eyes without a moment's waiting.

The *Nō* actors were honoured under the old regime, whilst the *Kabuki* actors were despised. The very theatres in which they appeared were looked down on as places too vile for any gentleman to enter. Such outcasts were actors at that period that, when a census was taken, they were denoted by the numerals used in counting animals, thus *ip-piki, ni-hiki,* not *hitori, futari.* Those to whom Japanese is familiar will appreciate the terrible sting of the insult.* But these actors formed the delight of the shopkeeping and artisan classes, and they supplied to whole generations of artists their favourite objects of study. Most of the lovely old colour-prints representing frail beauties and other heroines were taken, not from the women themselves, but from the impersonation of them on the boards by actors of the male sex.

With the revolution of 1868, customs changed and class prejudices were much softened. Actors are ostracised no longer. Since 1886, there has been a movement among some of the leaders of Japanese thought towards the reform of the stage, Europe being of course looked to for models. No

---

* The reader who knows German will understand what is meant, when we say that it is as if, in speaking of their eating, the word *fressen* should have been used instead of *essen*.

tangible result seems, however, to have been produced as yet. For our own part, though favouring the admittance of actors into Japanese good society, if their manners fit them for such promotion, we trust that the stage may remain, in other respects, what it now is—a mirror, the only mirror, of Old Japan. When our fathers invented railways, they did not tear up the "School for Scandal," or pull down Covent Garden. Why should the Japanese do what amounts to the same thing ? The only reform called for is one which touches, not the theatre itself, but an adjunct, an excrescence. We mean the tea-houses which serve as ticket agencies, and practically prevent theatre-goers from dealing with the theatre direct. Engrossing, as these practical little establishments do, a large portion of the profits derived from the sale of tickets, they are probably the main cause of the frequent bankruptcy of the Tōkyō theatres.

Talking of reform and Europeanisation, it fell to our lot some years ago to witness an amusing scene in a Japanese theatre. The times were already ripe for change. A small Italian opera troupe having come to Yokohama, a wide-awake Japanese manager engaged them, and caused a play to be written for the special purpose of letting them appear in it. This play represented the adventures of a party of Japanese globe-trotters, who, after crossing the Pacific Ocean and landing at San Francisco where they naturally fall among the Red Indians who infest that remote and savage locality, at last reach Paris and attend a performance at the Grand Opéra. Thus were the Italian singers appropriately introduced. Hamlet-like, on a stage upon the main stage. But oh! the effect upon the Japanese audience! When once they had recovered from the first shock of surprise, they were seized with a wild fit of hilarity at the high notes of the *prima donna,* who really was not at all bad. The people laughed at the absurdities of European singing till their sides shook, and the tears rolled down their cheeks; and they stuffed their sleeves into their mouths, as we might our pocket-handkerchiefs, in the vain endeavour to contain themselves.

Needless to say that the experiment was not repeated. The Japanese stage betook itself to its wonted sights and sounds, and the play-going public was again happy and contented.

By a curious fatality, Japan has just (1903–4) lost all her greatest actors within a few months of each other,— Danjūrō, Kikugorō, and Sadanji. Among the lesser men, their survivors, Shikwan and Gatō perhaps rank highest. The actress of most repute is Kumehachi, a woman of over sixty, who excels in young men's roles. " Sada Yakko " was not locally known, except as a singing-girl, till the echoes of her success on the Parisian stage in 1900 reverberated on Japanese shores.

Of European authorities on the subject of the Japanese drama, there are few to mention. Aston's *History of Japanese Literature* will be found helpful, as usual, within the limits of a narrowly restricted space. Florenz's *Japanische Dramen* may be recommended to those who read German, together with the same author's versions of two dramas,—*Asagao* and *Terakoya.* The late T. R. McClatchie, the one European who made a speciality of the Japanese stage, produced nothing, in his *Japanese Plays Versified,* but some English pieces in " Ingoldsby Legend " style on four or five of the chief subjects treated by the native dramatists. Though extremely entertaining, they bear but the faintest resemblance to their so-called originals. Unfortunately, Japanese plays are apt to run to extreme length,—five, seven, twelve, even as many as sixteen acts. Adequately to translate them presupposes an intimate knowledge, not only of several phases of the language, but of innumerable historical and literary allusions, obsolete customs and superstitions, etc. Even to understand, or at any rate to relish, such translations when made, would demand considerable local knowledge on the part of the European reader. For all these reasons, doubtless, this field has been comparatively neglected hitherto. The *Nō,* though more ancient and to the Japanese themselves far more difficult, are in a way easier to bring before the foreign public, because of their concise, clear-cut character. The present writer, in the early days of his Japanese enthusiasm, tried his hand at several of them, which were published, along with other matter, in a volume entitled *The Classical Poetry of the Japanese,* long since out of print. He ventures to disinter from this limbo one of the versions then made, called *The Robe of Feathers,* which is founded on an ancient tradition localised at Mio, a lovely spot just off the Tōkaidō, near the base of Fuji.* The prose portions are rendered literally, the lyrical passages perforce very freely. It is hoped that the total result may succeed in conveying to the reader some idea of the delicate, statuesque grace of this species of composition. If he will keep in mind that music and dancing are of its very essence, he may perhaps be brought to see in it a far-off counterpart of the Elizabethan " masque."

THE ROBE OF FEATHERS.

(HA-GOROMO.)

Dramatis Personæ.

A Fairy.   A Fisherman.   The Chorus.

Scene.—The shore of Mio on the Gulf of Suruga.

[*The piece opens with a long recitative, in which the Fisherman and the Chorus describe the beauties of Mio's pine-clad shore at dawn in spring. The passage is a beautiful one; but after several efforts at reproducing it in an English form, the translator has had to abandon the task as impossible. At the conclusion of this recitative the Fisherman steps on shore, and the action of the piece commences as follows:†—*]

Fisherman. As I land on Mio's pine-clad shore and gaze around me, flowers come fluttering down from ethereal space, strains of music are

---

* See Murray's *Handbook for Japan,* 7th edit., p. 232.

† The end of the poetical opening of the piece is perhaps fairly rendered by the following lines:—

> But hark! methought I saw the storm-clouds flying,
>   And heard the tempest rave:
> Come, fishermen! come homeward plying!—
>   But no! no tempest frets the wave:
> 'Tis spring! 'tis spring! 'twas but the morning breeze,
>   That vocal grew th' eternal pines among;
> No murmur rises from th' unruffled seas,
>   No storm disturbs the thronging boatsmen's song!

re-echoing, and a more than earthly fragrance fills the air. Surely there is something strange in this. Yes! from one of the branches of yonder pine-tree hangs a beauteous robe, which, when I draw nigh and closely scan it, reveals itself more fair and fragrant than any common mortal's garb. Let me take it back to show to the old folks in the village, that it may be handed down in our house as an heirloom.

Fairy. Ah! mine is that apparel! Wherefore wouldst thou carry it away?

Fisherman. 'Twas found by me, forsooth, and I shall take it home with me.

Fairy. But 'tis a fairy's robe of feathers, a thing that may not lightly be bestowed on any mortal being. Prithee leave it on the branch from which it hung.

Fisherman. What, then, art thou thyself a fairy, that thou claimest possession of this feathery raiment? As a marvel for all ages will I keep it, and garner it up among the treasures of Japan. No, no! I cannot think of restoring it to thee.

Fairy. Alas! without my robe of feathers nevermore can I go soaring through the realms of air, nevermore can I return to my celestial home. I beg thee, I beseech thee, therefore, to give it back to me.

Fisherman. Nay! fairy, nay! the more I hear thee plead,
    The more my soul determines on the deed.
    My heartless breast but grows more cruel yet;
    Thou mayst not have thy feathers: 'tis too late.

Fairy. Speak, not, dear fisherman! speak not that word!
    Ah! know'st thou not that, like the hapless bird
    Whose wings are broke, I seek, but seek in vain,
    Reft of my wings, to soar to heav'n's blue plain?

Fisherman. Chain'd to dull earth, a fairy well may pine.

Fairy. Whichever way I turn, despair is mine;

Fisherman. For ne'er the fisher will her wings restore,

Fairy. And the frail fay sinks helpless evermore.

Chorus. Alas! poor maiden, in thy quiv'ring eyne
    Cluster the dews; the flow'rets thou didst twine
    Amidst thy tresses languish and decay,
    And the five woes* declare thy fatal day!

---

* Viz., the withering of the crown of flowers, the pollution by dust of the heavenly raiment, a deadly sweat, a feeling of dizzy blindness, and the loss of all joy.

Fairy.   Vainly my glance doth seek the heav'nly plain,
　　　　Where rising vapours all the air enshroud,
　　　　And veil the well-known paths from cloud to cloud.

Chorus.   Clouds! wand'ring clouds! she yearns, and yearns in vain,
　　　　Soaring like you, to tread the heav'ns again;
　　　　Vainly she sighs to hear, as erst she heard,
　　　　The melting strains of Paradise' sweet bird:*
　　　　That blessèd voice grows faint.   The heav'n in vain
　　　　Rings with the song of the returning crane;
　　　　In vain she lists, where ocean softly laves,
　　　　To the free seagull twitt'ring o'er the waves;
　　　　Vainly she harks where zephyr sweeps the plain;
　　　　These all may fly, but she'll ne'er fly again!

Fisherman.   I would fain speak a word unto thee.   Too strong is the pity that overcomes me, as I gaze upon thy face.   I will restore to thee thy robe of feathers.

Fairy.   Oh, joy! oh, joy,!   Give it back to me!

Fisherman.   One moment!   I restore it to thee on condition that thou do first dance to me now, at this very hour and in this very spot, one of those fairy dances whose fame has reached mine ears.

Fairy.   Oh, joy untold!   It is, then, granted to me once more to return to heaven!   And if this happiness be true, I will leave a dance behind me as a token to mortal men.   I will dance it here,—the dance that makes the Palace of the Moon turn round, so that even poor transitory man may learn its mysteries.   But I cannot dance without my feathers.   Give them back to me, I pray thee.

Fisherman.   No, No!   If I restore to thee thy feathers, thou wilt fly home to heaven without dancing to me at all.

Fairy.   Fie on thee!   The pledge of mortals may be doubted, but in heavenly beings there is no falsehood.

Fisherman.   Fairy maid! thou shamest me:
　　　　Take thy feathers and be free!

Fairy.   Now the maiden dons her wings
　　　　And rainbow robes, and blithely sings:—

Fisherman.   Wings that flutter in the wind!

Fairy.   Robes like flow'rs with raindrops lin'd!
　　　　[*The Fairy begins to dance.*]

---

* Literally, the *Karyobinga*, a corruption of the Sanskrit word *Kalaviṅgka*.

Fisherman. See her dance the roundelay!

Fairy. This the spot and this the day.

Chorus. To which our Eastern*· dancers trace
All their frolic art and grace.

I.

Chorus. Now list, ye mortals! while our songs declare
The cause that gave to the blue realms of air
The name of FIRMAMENT. All things below
From that Great God and that Great Goddess flow,
Who, first descending to this nether earth,
Ordain'd each part and gave each creature birth.
But older still, nor sway'd by their decree,
And FIRM as ADAMANT eternally,
Stand the wide heav'ns, that nought may change or shake,
And hence the name of FIRMAMENT did take.†

Fairy. And in this firmament a palace stands
Yclept the Moon, built up by magic hands;

Chorus. And o'er this palace thirty monarchs rule,
Whereof fifteen, until the moon be full,
Nightly do enter, clad in robes of white;
But who again, from the full sixteenth night,
One ev'ry night must vanish into space,
And fifteen black-rob'd monarchs take their place,
While, ever circling round each happy king,
Attendant fays celestial music sing..

Fairy. And one of these am I.

---

* The word "Eastern" does not refer to the position of Japan in Asia, but to that of the province of Suruga as compared with the then capital, Kyoto.

† The original Japanese word, whose derivation the Chorus thus quaintly begins by explaining, is not the firmament itself, but hisakata, the "pillow-word" (see p. 376) for the firmament, which lends itself to a similar rough-and-ready etymology. This passage has had to be paraphrased and somewhat amplified by help of the commentary in order to render it intelligible to English readers,—a remark which likewise applies to the description immediately below of the internal economy of the lunar government. The idea of the latter is taken from Buddhist sources. The Great God and Goddess here mentioned are the Shinto deities Izanagi and Izanami, the creators of Japan and progenitors of gods and men.

Chorus.   From those bright spheres,
            Lent for a moment, this sweet maid appears:
            Here in Japan she lights (heav'n left behind),
            To teach the art of dancing to mankind.

                              II.

Chorus.   Where'er we gaze, the circling mists are twining:
            Perchance e'en now the moon her tendrils fair*
            Celestial blossoms bear.
            Those flow'rets tell us that the spring is shining,—
            Those fresh-blown flow'rets in the maiden's hair.

Fairy.   Blest hour beyond compare!

Fisherman.† Heaven hath its joys, but there is beauty here.
            Blow, blow, ye winds! that the white cloud-belts driv'n
            Around my path may bar my homeward way.
            Not yet would I return to heav'n,
            But here on Mio's pine-clad shore I'd stray,
            Or where the moon in bright unclouded glory
            Shines on Kiyomi's lea,
            And where on Fujiyama's summit hoary
            The snows look on the sea,
            While breaks the morning merrily!
            But of these three, beyond compare,
            The wave-wash'd shore of Mio is most fair
            When through the pines the breath of spring is playing.—
            What barrier rises 'twixt the heav'n and earth?
            Here, too, on earth th' immortal gods came straying,
            And gave our monarchs birth,

Fairy.   Who, in this Empire of the Rising Sun,
            While myriad ages run,
            Shall ever rule their bright dominions,

---

* The inhabitants of the Far East see a cinnamon-tree in the moon, instead of our traditional " man." A Japanese poetess has gracefully suggested that the particular brilliancy of the autumn moon may come from the dying tints of its foliage.

† In the following song, as frequently elsewhere, the Chorus acts as the mouthpiece of the chief personage present on the scene. It should likewise be noted that the lyric passages contain a great number of allusions to, and more or less exact quotations from, the earlier poetry. It has not been thought necessary to embarrass the English reader with perpetual explanatory references. By an educated Japanese none would be required.

Chorus.   E'en when the feath'ry shock
            Of fairies flitting past with silv'ry pinions
            Shall wear away the granite rock!

III.

Chorus.   Oh, magic strains that fill our ravish'd ears!
            The fairy sings, and from the cloudy spheres,
            Chiming in unison, the angels' lutes,
            Tabrets, and cymbals, and sweet silv'ry flutes,
            Ring through the heav'n that glows with purple hues,
            As when Someiro's* western slope endues
            The tints of sunset, while the azure wave
            From isle to isle the pine-clad shores doth lave.
            From Ukishima's† slope—a beauteous storm—
            Whirl down the flow'rs: and still that magic form,
            Those snowy pinions, flutt'ring in the light,
            Ravish our souls with wonder and delight.

            [*The Fairy pauses in the dance to sing the next couplet,
            and then continues dancing till the end of the piece.*]

Fairy.   Hail to the Kings that o'er the Moon hold sway!
            Heav'n is their home, and Buddhas, too, are they.‡

Chorus.   The fairy robes the maiden' limbs endue

Fairy.   Are like the very heav'ns, of tend'rest blue:

Chorus.   Or, like the mists of spring, all silv'ry white,

Fairy.   Fragrant and fair,—too fair for mortal sight!

---

* The Sanskrit *Suméru*, an immense mountain formed of gold, silver, and precious stones, which, according to the Buddhist cosmogonists, forms the axis of every universe, and supports the various tiers of heavens.

† An alternative name for part of the shore of Mio. Mount Ashitaka, mentioned a little further on, is a mountain of singularly graceful shape rising to the south-east of Fuji, between it and the sea.

‡ Or rather Bôdhisattvas (Jap. *Bosatsu*). To be a Buddha is to have reached the highest degree of sanctity, "having thrown off the bondage of sense, perception, and self, knowing the utter unreality of all phenomena, and being ready to enter into Nirvana." A Bôdhisattva, on the other hand, has still to pass once more through human existence before attaining to Buddhahood. Readers will scarcely need to be told that "Buddha" was never the personal name of any one man. It is simply a common noun meaning "awake," "enlightened," whence its application to beings lit with the full beams of spiritual perfection.

Chorus. Dance on, sweet maiden, through the happy hours!
Dance on, sweet maiden, while the magic flow'rs
Crowning thy tresses flutter in the wind
Rais'd by thy waving pinions intertwin'd!
Dance on! for ne'er to mortal dance 'tis giv'n
To vie with that sweet dance thou bring'st from heav'n:
And when, cloud-soaring, thou shalt all too soon
Homeward return to the full-shining Moon,
Then hear our pray'rs, and from thy bounteous hand
Pour sev'nfold treasures on our happy land;
Bless ev'ry coast, refresh each panting field,
That earth may still her proper increase yield!

But ah! the hour, the hour of parting rings!
Caught by the breeze, the fairy's magic wings
Heav'nward uplift from the pine-clad shore,
Past Ukishima's widely-stretching moor,
Past Ashitaka's heights, and where are spread
The floating clouds on Fujiyama's head,—
Higher and higher to the azure skies,
Till wand'ring vapours shroud her from our eyes!

Book recommended. *The Kabuki Handbook* by A. S. Halford and G. M. Halford.

Time. Official and educated Japan is now entirely European and commonplace in her manner of reckoning time. Inquisitive persons may, however, like to take a peep at her earlier and more peculiar methods, which are still followed by the peasantry of certain remote districts. Old Japan had no minutes, her hours were equivalent to two European hours, and they were counted thus, crab-fashion:—

9 o'clock *(kokonotsu-doki)*, our 12 o'clock A.M. and P.M.
8 o'clock *(yatsu-doki)*   ,,   2   ,,   ,,   ,,   ,,
7 o'clock *(nanatsu-doki)*,   ,,   4   ,,   ,,   ,,   ,,
6 o'clock *(mutsu-doki)*,   ,,   6   ,,   ,,   ,,   ,,
5 o'clock *(itsutsu-doki)*,   ,,   8   ,,   ,,   ,,   ,,
4 o'clock *(yotsu-doki)*,   ,, 10   ,,   ,,   ,,   ,,

Half-past nine *(kokonotsu han)* was equivalent to our one o'clock, and similarly in the case of the other intermediate hours, down to half-past four which was equivalent to our eleven o'clock. But the hours were never all of exactly the same length, except at the equinoxes. In summer those of the night were shorter, in winter those of the day. This was because no method of obtaining an average was used, sunrise and sunset being always called six o'clock throughout the year. Why, it will be asked, did they count the hours backwards? A case of Japanese topsy-turvydom, we suppose. But then why, as there were six hours, not count from six to one, instead of beginning at so arbitrary a number as nine? The reason is this:—three preliminary strokes were always struck, in order to warn people that the hour was about to be sounded. Hence if the numbers one, two, and three had been used to denote any of the actual hours, confusion might have arisen between them and the preliminary strokes,—a confusion analogous to that which, in our own still imperfect method of striking the hour, leaves us in doubt whether the single stroke we hear be half-past twelve, one o'clock, half-past one, or any other of the numerous half-hours. Old-fashioned clocks, arranged on the system just described, are still sometimes exposed for sale in the curio-shops. They were imitated, with the necessary modifications, from Dutch models, but never passed into general use.

The week was not known to Old Japan, nor was there any popular division roughly corresponding to it. Early in the present reign, however, there was introduced what was called the *Ichi-Roku,* a holiday on all the ones and sixes of the month. But this arrangement did not last long. Itself imitated from our Sunday, the copy soon gave way to the original. Sunday is now kept as a day of rest from official work, and of recreation. Even the modern English Saturday half-holiday has made its way into Japan. Sunday being in vulgar parlance *Dontaku,** Saturday is called (in equally vulgar parlance) *Han-don,* that is, "half-Sunday," while Wednesday is *Naka-don,* or "mid[way between] Sunday[s]."

---

* A corruption of the Dutch *Zondag.*

But to return to Old Japan. Her months were real moons, not artificial periods of thirty or thirty-one days. They were numbered one, two, three, four, and so on. Only in poetry did they bear proper names, such as January, February, and the rest are in European languages. The year consisted of twelve such moons, with an intercalary one whenever New Year would otherwise have fallen a whole moon too early. This happened about once in three years. Japanese New Year took place late in our January or in the first half of February; and that, irrespective of the state of the temperature, was universally regarded as the beginning of spring. Snow or no snow, the people laid aside their wadded winter gowns. The plum-blossoms, at least, were always there to prove that spring had come; and if the nightingale was yet silent, that was not the Japanese poets' fault, but the nightingale's.

Besides the four great seasons of spring, summer, autumn, and winter, there were twenty-four minor periods *(setsu)* of some fifteen days each, obtained by dividing the real, or approximately real, solar year of three hundred and sixty-five days by twenty-four. These minor periods had names, such as *Risshun,* "Early Spring;" *Kanro,* "Cold Dew;" *Shōkan,* "Lesser Cold;" *Daikan,* "Greater Cold." In addition to this, years, days, and hours were all accounted as belonging to one of the signs of the zodiac (Jap. *jū-ni-shi*), whose order is as follows:—

1	*Ne,**	the Rat.	7	*Uma,*	the Horse.
2	*Ushi,*	„ Bull.	8	*Hitsuji,*	„ Goat.
3	*Tora,*	„ Tiger.	9	*Saru,*	„ Ape.
4	*U,*	„ Hare.	10	*Tori*	„ Cock.
5	*Tatsu,*	„ Dragon.	11	*Inu,*	„ Dog.
6	*Mi,*	„ Serpent.	12	*I,*	„ Boar.

---

* *Ne* is short for *nezumi,* the real word for "rat." In like manner, *u* stands for *usagi,* and *mi* for *hebi.* *I* is not an abbreviation of *inoshishi,* the modern popular name for a "boar," but the genuine ancient form of the word.

The Japanese have also borrowed from Chinese astrology what are termed the jik-kan, or "ten celestial stems,"—a series obtained by dividing each of the five elements into two parts, termed respectively the "elder" and the "younger brother" (*e* and *to*). The following series is thus obtained:—

1	*Ki no E,*	.. .. ..	Wood—Elder Brother.
2	*Ki no To,*	.. .. ..	Wood—Younger Brother.
3	*Hi no E,*	.. .. ..	Fire —Elder Brother
4	*Hi no To,*	.. .. ..	Fire —Younger Brother.
5	*Tsuchi no E,*	.. ..	Earth—Elder Brother.
6	*Tsuchi no To,*	.. ..	Earth—Younger Brother
7	*Ka* no E,*	.. .. ..	Metal —Elder Brother.
8	*Ka no To,*	.. .. ..	Metal —Younger Brother.
9	*Mizu no E,*	.. .. ..	Water—Elder Brother.
10	*Mizu no To,*	.. .. ..	Water—Younger Brother.

The two series—celestial stems and signs of the zodaic— being allowed to run on together, their combination produces the cycle of sixty days or sixty years, as sixty is the first number divisible both by ten and by twelve. The first day or year of the cycle is *Ki no E, Ne,* "Wood—Elder Brother, Rat;" the second is *Ki no To, Ushi,* "Wood—Younger Brother, Bull;" and so on, until the sixtieth, *Mizu no To, I,* "Water —Younger Brother, Boar," is reached, and the cycle begins again.

These things, especially the lunar calendar, still largely influence the daily actions of the people. The peasantry scrupulously observe the traditional times and seasons in all the operations of agriculture. For instance, they sow their rice on the eighty-eighth day *(Hachi-jū-hachi ya)* from the beginning of spring *(Risshun)*, and they plant it out in *Nyūbai*, the period fixed for the early summer rains. The 210th. and 220th. from the beginning of spring *(Ni-hyaku tōka* and *Ni-hyaku hatsuka*, generally coinciding with our 1st and 10th September respectively), and what is called Hassaku, that is, the first day of the eighth moon, Old Calendar, are looked on

---

* Short for *kane*, "metal."

as days of special importance to the crops, which are certain
to be injured if there is a storm, because the rice is then in
flower. They fall early in September, just in the middle of
the typhoon season. St. Swithin's day has its Japanese
counterpart in the *Ki no E Ne,* mentioned above as the first
day of the sexagesimal cycle, which comes round once in
every two months approximately. If it rains, it will rain for
that whole cycle, that is, for sixty days on end. Again, if it
rains on the first day of a certain period called *Hassen,* of
which there are six in every year, it will rain for the next
eight days. These periods, being movable, may come at any
season. Quite a number of festivals, pilgrimages to temples,
and other functions depend on the signs of the zodiac. Thus,
the *mayu-dama,* a sort of Christmas tree decorated with cakes
in honour of the silkworm, makes its appearance on whatever
date in January may happen to be the " First Day of the
Hare " *(Hatsu-U).*

We have said that official Japan has quite Europeanised
herself so far as methods of computing time are concerned.
The assertion was too sweeping. Although the Gregorian
calendar has been in force ever since the 1st January, 1873,
she has not yet been able to bring herself to adopt the
Christian era. Not only would the use of this era symbolise
to the Shintō Court of Japan the supremacy of a foreign
religion;—it would be derogatory from a political point of
view, the fixing of the calendar from time to time, together
with the appointing of "year-names," * having ever been
looked on in the Far East among the inviolable privileges and
signs of independent sovereignty, much as coining money is in
the West. China has its own year-names, which it proudly
imposes on such vassal states as Thibet. Japan has other year-
names. The names are chosen arbitrarily. In China the plan
was long ago introduced of making each year-name coincide
with the reign of an emperor. This has not hitherto been
the case in Japan, though an official notification has been

---

* In Japanese, *nengo.*

issued to the effect that the reigns and year-names shall so coincide in future. Either way, the confusion introduced into the study of history may be easily imagined. Hardly any Japanese knows all the year-names even of his own country. The most salient ones are, it is true, employed in conversation, much in the same way as we speak of the sixteenth century, or of the Georgian and Victorian eras. Such are Engi (A.D. 901–923), celebrated for the legislation then undertaken; Genroku (1688–1704), a period of great activity in various arts; Tempō (1830–1844), the last brilliant period of feudalism before its fall. But no one could say offhand how many years it is from one of these periods to another. In 1872 an attempt was made to introduce, as the Japanese era from which all dates should be counted, the supposed date of the accession of Jimmu Tennō, the mythical founder of the Imperial line; and this system still has followers. Jimmu's reign being held to have commenced in the year B.C. 660, all dates thus reckoned exceed by the number six hundred and sixty the European date for the same year. Thus, 1905 is 2565.

The following is a list of the year-names of the past century :—

Kyōwa,	1801—1804.*	Ansei,	1854—1860.
Bunkwa,	1804—1818.	Man-en,	1860—1861.
Bunsei,	1818—1830.	Bunkyū,	1861—1864.
Tempō,	1830—1844.	Genji,	1864—1865.
Kōkwa,	1844—1848.	Keio,	1865—1868.
Kaei,	1848—1854.	Meiji,	1868—

The present year, 1904, is the thirty-seventh year of Meiji. Astrologically speaking, it is *Ki no E Tatsu*, "Wood—Elder Brother, Dragon."

Books recommended. *A Daughter of the Samurai* by Etsu Inagaki Sugimoto; *The Five Sacred Festivals of Ancient Japan* by U. A. Casal; *Japan: An Attempt at Interpretation* by Lafcadio Hearn; *Japanese Clocks* by N. H. N. Mody; *The Japanese Fortune Calendar* by Reiko Chiba; *A Japanese Miscellany* by Lafcadio Hearn.

---

* It may be asked. Why not take *Kyowa* as equivalent to 1801–3, Bunkwa as equivalent to 1804–17, and so on in every case, instead of counting the final and initial years of each period twice ? The reason is that no new name ever came into force on the 1st January. In most cases the year was well-advanced before it was adopted.

Tobacco was introduced into Japan by the Portuguese towards the end of the sixteenth century, and was first planted in 1605. As in other countries, here too officialdom strove to impede its use; but by 1651 the law was so far relaxed as to permit smoking, though only out-of-doors. Now there is hardly a man or woman throughout the length and breadth of the land who does not enjoy the fragrant weed; for, as an anonymous author quoted by Sir Ernest Satow sarcastically remarks, " Women who do not smoke and priests who keep the prescribed rules of abstinence, are equally rare." Nevertheless, a reaction has begun to make itself felt,—a reaction grounded in the fear of national deterioration caused by the visibly deleterious effects of smoking on the physique of school-children. A law was accordingly passed in 1900, prohibiting this indulgence to minors, that is, to all persons under the age of twenty.

Tobacco has been a government monopoly for the last seven or eight years; but the total area of cultivation fixed for each year varies so widely as to render statistics on the subject practically useless. Of the numerous varieties of Japanese tobacco, the most esteemed is *Kokubu,* which is grown in the provinces of Satsuma and Ōsumi; but the plan commonly followed by dealers is to make blends of two or more sorts. Prices vary from 30 *sen* up to 1 *yen* for 100 *me,* that is, a little less than 1 lb., but are expected soon to double. All Japanese tobacco is light, and consequently well-suited for use in the form of cigarettes. One of the countless ways in which the nation is Europeanising itself is by the adoption of cigarette-smoking. But the tiny native pipe—it looks like a doll's pipe—holds its own side by side with the new importation. (See also Article on PIPES.)

Topsy-turvydom. It has often been remarked that the Japanese do many things in a way that runs directly counter to European ideas of what is natural and proper. To the Japanese themselves our ways appear equally unaccountable. It was only the other day that a Tōkyō lady asked the present writer why foreigners did so many things topsy-turvy, instead of doing them naturally, after the manner of her country-people. Here are a few instances of this contrariety:—

Japanese books begin at what we should call the end, the word *finis* (終) coming where we put the title-page. The foot-notes are printed at the top of the page, and the reader inserts his marker at the bottom. In newspaper paragraphs, a large full stop is put at the *beginning* of each.

Men make themselves merry with wine, not after dinner, but before. Sweets also come before the *pièces de résistance*.

The whole method of treating horses is the opposite of ours. A Japanese (of the old school) mounts his horse on the right side, all parts of the harness are fastened on the right side, the mane is made to hang on the left side; and when the horse is brought home, its head is placed where its tail ought to be, and the animal is fed from a tub at the stable door.

Boats are hauled up on the beach stern first.

On leaving an inn, you fee not the waiter, but the proprietor.

The Japanese do not say "north-east," "south-west," but "east-north," "west-south."

They carry babies, not in their arms, but on their backs.

In addressing a letter they employ the following order of words: "Japan, Tōkyō, Akasaka district, such-and-such a street, 19 Number, Smith John Mr."—thus putting the general first, and the particular afterwards, which is the exact reverse of our method.

Many tools and implements are used in a way which is contrary to ours. For example, Japanese keys turn in instead of out, and Japanese carpenters saw and plane towards, instead of away from, themselves.

The best rooms in a house are at the back; the garden, too, is at the back. When building a house, the Japanese construct the roof first; then, having numbered the pieces, they break it up again, and keep it until the substructure is finished.

In making up accounts, they write down the figures first, the corresponding items next.

Politeness prompts them to remove, not their head-gear, but their foot-gear.

Their needle-work sometimes curiously reverses European methods. Belonging as he does to the inferior sex, the present writer can only speak hesitatingly on such a point. But a lady of his acquaintance informs him that Japanese women needle their thread instead of threading their needle, and that instead of running the needle through the cloth, they hold it still and run the cloth upon it. Another lady, long resident in Tōkyō, says that the impulse of her Japanese maids is always to sew on cuffs, frills, and other similar things, topsy-turvy and inside out. If that is not the *ne plus ultra* of contrariety, what is ?

Men in Japan are most emphatically *not* the inferior sex. When (which does not often happen) a husband condescends to take his wife out with him, it is my lord's jinrikisha that bowls off first. The woman gets into hers as best she can, and trundles along behind. Still, women have some few consolations. In Europe, gay bachelors are apt to be captivated by the charms of actresses. In Japan, where there are no actresses to speak of, it is the women who fall in love with fashionable actors.

Strangest of all, after a bath the Japanese dry themselves with a damp towel !

Torii is the name of the peculiar gateway, formed of two upright and two horizontal beams, which stands in front of every Shintō temple. According to the orthodox account, it was originally a perch for the sacred fowls (*tori*="fowl; " *i*, from *iru*,="dwelling "), which gave warning of daybreak; but in later times—its origin being forgotten—it came to be regarded as a gateway or even as a merely symbolic ornament, so that whole avenues of *torii* were sometimes erected, while the Buddhists also adopted it, employing it to place tablets on with inscriptions, and ornamenting it in various newfangled ways, such as turning up the corners of the transverse beams, etc., etc. Accordingly, when the "purification" of the Shintō temples took place* after the restoration of the Mikado in 1868, one of the earliest official acts was the removal of these tablets. Ever since that time, too, the simplest form of *torii* has alone been set up, because alone considered ancient and national.

The present writer's opinion, founded partly on a comparison of the Japanese and Luchuan forms of the word (Jap. *torii*, Luch. *turi*), is that the orthodox etymology and the opinions derived from it are alike erroneous, that the origin both of the word and of the thing is obscure, but that indications deserving consideration point to the probability of both having been brought over from the Asiatic continent. The Koreans erect somewhat similar gateways at the approach to their royal palaces; the Chinese *p'ai lou,* serving to record the virtues of male or female worthies, seem related in shape as well as in use; and the occurrence of the word *turan* in Northern India and of the word *tori* in Central India, to denote gateways of strikingly cognate appearance, gives matter for reflection. Finally, we have the fundamental fact that almost every Japanese art and almost every Japanese idea can be traced back ultimately to the Asiatic mainland—an intellectual dependence so constant as to raise a strong presumption in favour of a Chinese or Buddhist (that is Indian) origin for any obscure individual item.

Mr. Aston, a great authority in such matters, agrees in believing that the thing—the torii itself—was imported from abroad (probably about A.D. 770), but holds that it was fitted with a pre-existing native name, which would have originally designated "a lintel" before it came to have its present sacred association.

Books recommended. *A Japanese Miscellany* by Lafcadio Hearn; *Shinto: The Kami Way* by Sokyo Ono in collaboration with Willaim P. Woodard.

* See p. 422.

Towels. The Japanese cotton towel, generally a yard long by a foot wide, serves various purposes besides that of drying the hands or the body. Both sexes occasionally employ it as a head-dress. Male artisans and coolies twist and then tie a towel across their foreheads to prevent the perspiration from running down into their eyes, while females of the same class make shift with one as a sort of light hood to cover the head. When doing the room of a morning, the maid of all work will save her hair in this way from the dust, and whole families may be seen thus protected on the occasion of the great annual house-cleaning. Holiday-makers sometimes protect their hair by the same device, and there is actually a special kind entitled *hana-mi-denugui,* or "flower-viewing towel," worn by festive bands who sally forth to admire the cherry-blossoms, and who —must it be owned ?—sacrifice not only to Flora, but to Bacchus, for which reason the wine-cup and the liquor-loving tortoise figure as the motives of ornamentation along with the pink blossom. For observe that towels afford a typical example of the national fondness for decorating even the most trivial articles of daily use. A study of them, as they flutter in the wind under the eaves of the shops devoted to their sale, would result in acquaintance with the whole gamut of popular art motives and symbolism. The vegetable world, the animal world both real and mythical, the stage and the wrestling ring, crests, riddles, Chinese ideographs congratulatory or otherwise characteristic,—all these and various other stores are drawn upon, the same subject being repeated in such a multiplicity of elaborated and abbreviated forms that not a little ingenuity is sometimes needed to discover the artist's intention. The latest source of inspiration has been the Russian war. Naval and military feats of arms may be seen represented or hinted at in every style,—realistic, picturesque, comic, allegorical.

Being thus variously useful as well as ornamental, towels make good presents, and thousands must be annually given away in every town. Inns often have towels of their own, specially inscribed or ornamented, one of which is presented to each departing guest if he has behaved liberally in the matter of "tea-money" to mine host. Shops sometimes do likewise. At New Year time, in particular, there is quite a shower of such civilities. When destined as a gift, the towel is generally folded in a piece of paper, which itself bears a suitable inscription, including the donor's address, with the occasional addition now-a-days of his telephone number; for even in such minutiæ, the Japanese of the lower middle class are up to date. Sometimes, instead of the host giving towels to his guests, the process is reversed. This happens notably in the case of pilgrim bands or clubs, who distribute to every inn at which they alight towels inscribed with the club's name, and perhaps a picture of the sacred mountain which is their goal. Towels are even offered to temples by the pious, appropriately inscribed.

Trade. Rarely has the fiat of a prince—a particular edict issued on a particular day—succeeded in deflecting the whole current of a nation's enterprise for over two centuries. This happened in Japan when the country was closed in A.D. 1624, foreigners being expelled, and foreign learning, foreign trade, and foreign travel alike prohibited. Till then the Japanese merchants and adventurers had been a power in Eastern seas. Nor was the commercial instinct theirs alone. The leaders of the nation had been nearly as keen. It is a mistake to suppose that aversion to intercourse with foreigners was an ingrained racial characteristic, or even an official tradition. On the contrary, when the Portuguese first came to Japan in the sixteenth century, both the local Daimyōs in Kyūshū and the central rulers,—notably Hideyoshi the Great, —hastened to welcome the new-comers and their trade. It was only when suspicions arose of nefarious designs upon Japanese national independence that a policy of exclusion was adopted, at first reluctantly and fitfully, then with systematic completeness. By the edict of 1624, all Japanese were forbidden to go abroad, and even the building of junks above a certain size was interdicted. From that instant, the movements of the native seafarers were curbed and their spirit was broken. A dribble of trade with the Dutch at Nagasaki, on the furthest confines of the empire, was all that remained. Internal trade itself, just springing into vigorous life after centuries of civil conflict, was hampered by the very perfection (along certain lines) and thoroughness of the feudal system. Not only did the central government at Yedo behave towards commerce as a stepmother; each Daimyō drew a cordon round his Daimiate. Sumptuary laws, rules, restrictions innumerable, monopolies, close guilds, an embargo on new inventions, the predominance of aristocratic militarism and of the artistic spirit,—all these things together formed an overwhelming obstacle to trade on a large scale. The Japanese merchant, relegated to a rank below that of the peasant, became a poor, timid creature with unbusinesslike methods, paltry aims, and a low moral standard.

Of course such an outline of a state of society, drawn with three or four rapid strokes, must not be accepted as a finished picture. Details would modify the impression. The Japan of the seventeenth and eighteenth centuries did possess some few important business houses, notably that of Mitsui, with whom the government formed a sort of left-handed alliance, borrowing money from it and employing it in sundry ways, much as our mediæval kings were wont to make use of the Jews and the goldsmiths. The memoirs of those times preserve also the names of a few individual speculators,—for instance, Kinokuni-ya Bunzaemon, who made a fortune in oranges and squandered it in riotous living. Some of our Western business expedients, or at least adumbrations of them, were known, such as clearing-houses, bills of lading, and bills of exchange. The two commercial centres were Ōsaka and Yedo. Here was conducted the sale of the government rice; for the peasants paid their taxes in kind, not in money, then a scarce commodity. Around these official rice transactions all other business revolved. It varied little from year to year, scarcely any scope being afforded for private enterprise.

When the country was thrown open some forty years ago, the few large commercial houses of old standing were looked to for the purpose of establishing relations with the strangers newly arrived. They declined to venture on what appeared a hazardous experiment. Such a new departure was also beyond the mental grasp of the lesser merchants, who worked together in guilds, along lines settled for them beforehand by time-honoured precedents. Thus it fell out that Yokohama and the other foreign settlements became resorts for unscrupulous and irresponsible men,—a calamity, truly, not only then but long afterwards. The Europeans at the ports naturally judged of the whole nation by the only specimens with whom they came in contact. The Japanese officials on the other hand, and to some extent the public at large, looked askance at the foreign mercantile community, because of its connection with a class indisputably contemptible. The average Japanese trader still has much to learn, especially in such matters as the punctual fulfilment of a contract and the meeting of an obligation; but he has become a keen man of business. Moreover, a new generation of merchants and bankers is coming to the fore,—men of good standing and liberal education. Though still comparatively few in number, these have taken up their calling in the spirit of earnestness and thoroughness which is characteristic of the modern Japanese in other walks of life. The oversea trade, built up and maintained by foreigners in the old " treaty port " days, tends gradually to pass into these new hands. It has made rapid strides, particularly since 1889, during which period of fifteen years the Japanese Government has taken an intelligently active interest in everything pertaining to the commercial and industrial welfare of the country.

The following figures may help to show Japan's rapid advance since the empire was thrown open to foreign trade in the second half of the nineteenth century:—

Total of Imports and Exports in 1868   ¥26,246,544.00
Total of Imports and Exports in 1904   606,637,960.00

The principal imports into Japan from abroad are:—boilers, engines and machinery of all kinds, iron ore, pig iron, manufactured iron and steel, lead, zinc, tin, kerosene oil, wheat, rice, beans, barley, flour, tinned provisions, alcohol, chemicals, dyes, paints, glass, paper, sugar both raw and refined, raw and manufactured cotton, raw and manufactured wool, flax, hemp, jute, China grass, tobacco, Cardiff coal, malt, manures of various descriptions, wood pulp, timber, and explosives.

The chief exports are:—tea, rice, dried fish, seaweed, gelatine, chillies, ginseng, ginger, pea-nuts, vegetables, *sake*, soy, beer, mineral waters, cotton manufactures, raw and manufactured silk, camphor, peppermint, coal, sulphur, copper, manganese, zinc, bronze, fish oil, vegetable wax, paper, cigarettes, matches, Portland cement, railway sleepers, timber, bamboos, brushes, straw braid, straw matting, wood chips, porcelain, curios, and works of art.

Books recommended. *Doing Business in Japan* edited by Robert J. Ballon; *Joint Ventures and Japan* edited by Robert J. Ballon; *Toward an Orderly Market: An Intensive Study of Japan's Voluntary Quota in Cotton Textile Exports* by John Lynch.

Treaties with Foreign Powers.   The subject of treaty revision was for so many years the hinge on which Japanese foreign policy turned, the working of the new treaties is still such a burning question to the foreign residents, that the new-comer desirous of peeping below the surface and learning something of the inner springs of local politics, will perhaps find an interest in details that might otherwise be condemned as "ancient history." In effect, is not the recent past our only trustworthy guide to the present and the near future ?

Japan's first treaty with the United States was that wrung from her, in 1854, by the terror which Commodore Perry's

" black ships " had inspired. Others, dating from 1858 to 1869 inclusive, followed with Russia, Great Britain, France, and the rest of the European powers great and small, the chief features in the documents, which were practically merged in one by the insertion of the most favoured nation clause, being (I) the opening of the ports of Yokohama, Kōbe, Ōsaka, Nagasaki, Niigata, and Hakodate to foreign trade and residence, with a radius of 10 *ri* (about 24½ miles) round each, termed " Treaty Limits," wherein foreigners might travel without passports; (II) the establishment of " exterritoriality," that is to say, the exemption of foreigners from the jurisdiction of the Japanese law-courts; (III) a very low scale of import dues, mostly five per cent *ad valorem*.

Such, in barest outline, were the old treaties, their tacitly assumed basis being the unequal status of the two contracting parties,—civilised white men on the one hand, Japan but just emerging from Asiatic semi-barbarism on the other. How to get them revised on more favourable terms, long formed the great crux of Japanese diplomacy. The matter was a complicated one, involving, as it did on the foreigner's part, the surrender of commercial and legal privileges that had been enjoyed for a long term of years,—involving, too, the extremely delicate question as to the fitness of Japan for admission into the family of Christian nations on equal terms. Legally, Japan had a claim to the revision of the treaties as far back as 1872; and the long tarrying of Prince Iwakura's embassy in the United States in 1872–3 was avowedly caused by the desire to conclude a new treaty then and there. But if Sir Francis Adams's account of the proceedings may be trusted, the Japanese authorities themselves ended by requesting a delay. Perhaps there had been gradually borne in upon them the consciousness that Japan was then in no position to offer suitable guarantees; nor indeed did her laws and usages approximate to the necessary standard for a whole decade more. A less radical, but equally thorny, obstacle in the way was the fact that the sixteen or seventeen foreign powers had pledged themselves to act conjointly in their negotiations, and that it was no easy matter to get England, France, Holland, and the rest to consent to any common basis on which a conference might be opened. Some held to the low import dues which favoured the operations of their merchants. Others —all perhaps—hesitated to place their nationals at the mercy of Japanese judges. Thus the *status quo* was preserved for years. One country, the United States, which had always been Japan's kindest patron, did, no doubt, show signs of breaking away from the league of the Western powers, and made a separate treaty in 1876, whereby all the chief points in dispute were surrendered. This treaty, however, contained one clause which invalidated all the rest,—a clause to the effect that the treaty was not to go into force until all the other powers should have concluded treaties of a similar purport. America's good-will on this occasion, though doubtless genuine, proved therefore to be of the Platonic order; and " the Bingham treaty," as it was called from the name of the minister who negotiated it, was consigned to the limbo of a pigeon-hole.

True, some declare that the paralysing little clause in this treaty was inserted, not by the American negotiator, but by the Japanese Government itself ! Impossible, it will be said. Improbable, assuredly. Still, when the reader calls to mind what has been mentioned concerning Prince Iwakura's alleged tergiversations, he will be led to hesitate before rejecting the possibility of such a thing. It will be seen immediately below that on two occasions more recent the Japanese negotiators did actually shift their basis at the eleventh hour; and if private individuals often tremble to see their heart's desire on the eve of accomplishment, and would give worlds to recall it at the last moment, why should not the same be sometimes true of governments ?

Meanwhile Japan's progress in Europeanisation had been such, above all her honest eagerness to reform her laws and legal procedure had been made so clearly manifest, that it began to be acknowledged on all sides, in diplomatic circles and in the home press, that the time had arrived for the admission of her claims, in return for granting which it was understood that she should throw open the whole empire to foreign trade and residence, instead of restricting these to the "Open Ports" of Yokohama, Kōbe, etc., as under the system of exterritoriality hitherto in vogue. A preliminary conference was held at Tōkyō in 1882, to settle the basis of negotiation. The Japanese proposals included the abolition of exterritoriality outside the foreign settlements as soon as an English version of the Civil Code should have been published, the abolition of exterritoriality even in the foreign settlements after a further period of three years, the appointment of no less than twenty-five foreign judges for a term of fifteen years, —the said judges to form a majority in all cases affecting foreigners,—and the use of English as the judicial language in such cases. Diplomacy, in Japan as elsewhere, talks much and moves slowly. To elaborate the scheme here outlined was the arduous work of four years, and 1886 was already half-spent when the great conference, intended to be final, met at Tōkyō. The English and German representatives led the way by making liberal concessions; and all was progressing to general satisfaction, when suddenly, in July, 1887, on the return from abroad of certain Japanese politicians holding radical views, the Japanese plenipotentiaries shifted the basis of their demands, and the negotiations were consequently brought to a standstill.

Nevertheless, as there remained a genuine desire on both sides to get the treaty revision question settled, the attempt to settle it was not given up. Some of the powers now allowed themselves to be approached singly. Mexico (absurd as it may sound) led the van. To be sure, she had no trade to be influenced, and no citizens in Japan to protect. Anyhow, she made her treaty, which was ratified early in 1889. In the summer of the same year several of the powers followed suit, —first the United States, next Russia, then Germany. France, too, was on the point of signing; and the other powers, though moving less quickly, were also moving in the same direction.

Suddenly again, Japanese public opinion—if that term may be employed, for want of a better, to denote the views of the comparatively small number of persons who in the Japan of those days thought and spoke on political subjects,—Japanese public opinion, we say, veered round. Among the new stipulations had been one to the effect that four foreign judges —not twenty-five—were to assist the native bench during the first few years following on treaty revision. This stipulation was denounced on all hands as contrary to the terms of the new Constitution, which had just been proclaimed. But the real objection lay elsewhere, and had its root in panic at the idea of Japan being thrown open to foreign trade and residence. For years the opening of the country had been prayed for as a blessing to trade, a means of attracting foreign capital to the mines and industries, a means of making Japanese manners and institutions conform to what were almost universally admitted to be the superior manners and customs of the West. The same anticipations remained, but the inferences drawn from them were reversed. Japan, it was now feverishly asserted, would be swamped by foreign immigration, her national customs would be destroyed, her mines, her industries would all come under foreign control, her very soil would, by lease or purchase, pass into foreign hands, her people would be practically enslaved, and independent Japan would exist no more. Such were the sentiments given voice to in every private conversation, re-echoed daily in the press. Nevertheless the Japanese Government, more enlightened than the Japanese public, endeavoured to continue the negotiations for treaty revision. Popular excitement then began to seek more violent vents. The Minister for Foreign Affairs, Count Ōkuma, had his leg blown off by a dynamite bomb. It became evident in October, 1889, that negotiations could no longer be carried on consistently with the public peace, and the Government once more drew back. Even those treaties which had already been concluded with America, Germany, and Russia were left unratified; and it was proved that the representatives of the other great powers had acted wisely in acting slowly, and had saved their respective governments from a humiliating rebuff.

A few months slipped by, and the tide once more began to flow. The native press—whether inspired from headquarters we cannot say—started a new watchword, which, being interpreted, signified " treaty revision on a footing of equality."* This was a fair phrase; but on examination, it turned out to mean simply that the foreign powers should concede everything, and Japan nothing at all. In fact, it was a case of

> " the fault of the Dutch,
> " That of giving too little, and taking too much."

The claim was preposterous; but—for the impossible does sometimes come to pass—it actually was granted ! Who knows ? Perhaps Great Britain thought thereby to obtain the Japanese alliance; perhaps it was only that she wanted to patch up, somehow and once for all, an old difference which had degenerated into a bore. Anyhow, in 1894, the Radical English ministry of the hour consented to a new treaty on the peculiar Dutch lines just mentioned. Hereby, either explicitly or else implicitly by the recognition of her legal codes (some of which had not even been published at that date !), Japan obtained the abolition of exterritoriality, full jurisdiction over British subjects, the right to fix her own import dues, the monopoly of the coasting trade, and the exclusion of British subjects from the purchase of land, or even from the leasing of land for agricultural or mining purposes. In exchange, Great Britain obtained—— ? The only items revealed by a microscopic scrutiny were that every one would be permitted to travel unmolested in the interior,—but in practice this privilege was enjoyed already, as would naturally be the case in any country ranking as civilised,—and that property might be leased in the interior for residential and commercial

---

* *Taito joyaku kaisei.*

purposes, a doubtful advantage, entailing, as it would, on merchants the expense of keeping up establishments in various cities for the same trade which had hitherto more economically centred in the Open Ports.

But all this was merely the beginning of the trouble. As the date for the enforcement of the treaty drew near, and men had to make arrangements accordingly, they found themselves confronted with obstacles which could never have arisen had the negotiators exercised ordinary foresight. The ambiguity of the document was not the least of its defects. A careful consideration of what was *not* stipulated for, as well as of what was, showed that, under the new treaty, British subjects might, if the Japanese Government so ordained, lose their privilege of publishing newspapers and holding public meetings, in a word, their birthright of free speech, and that it was doubtful whether their doctors and lawyers would be allowed to practise without a Japanese diploma. Even the period for which leases could be held was left uncertain; the conditions of the sale and re-purchase of leases in what had hitherto been the foreign " Concessions " were left uncertain; the right to employ labour and to start industries was left uncertain; the right of foreign insurance agencies to continue to do business was left uncertain. As for the question of taxation,—a matter of prime importance if ever there was one,—which almost immediately ramified into labyrinth, the negotiators had simply not troubled their heads about it. With things in this state, and with new duties of from thirty to forty per cent levied precisely on those articles which are prime necessities to us but not to the Japanese, could any one imagine such terms having ever been agreed to except as the result of a disastrous war ? The authorities in Downing Street apparently considered that a state of things endurable by British communities in certain other countries, should be good enough for the British community in Japan. But surely there is all the difference in the world between acquiescing in inconveniences of immemorial date, and running one's neck into a new noose.

The British treaty once concluded, other powers followed suit. To some of them the nature of the terms mattered little; for the preponderance of British commercial and residential interests has always been so great in Japan as almost to make it a case of " Eclipse first, and the rest nowhere." The United States—the only power which might have been expected to stand out for better terms—was precluded from so doing, partly by her traditional policy of exceptional condescension towards Japan, partly, as it would seem, by the fact of her government, like that of Great Britain, having failed to appreciate in all its practical details, the position which affairs would assume when the old order should have been abrogated and the new set up in its stead. Meanwhile the China war of 1894–5 took place, Japan's marvellous successes in which made resistance to any of her demands increasingly difficult. The German and French negotiators, however, kept their heads; and under the most favoured nation clause, resident Britishers and Americans—by a stroke of good luck, nowise thanks to the good management of their rulers—have come to share in certain ameliorations stipulated for by other powers: —their doctors, for instance, may practise, and their newspapers may continue to exist, though subject now to the Japanese censure, no longer independent as of old.

Such is the story of Japanese treaty revision, so far as it is publicly known. But we have access to no private sources of information, and we are (but for that we thank God) no politician. Diplomacy is not a game of chance. It is a game of skill, like chess, at which the better player always wins. The Japanese negotiators, who, to be sure, had more at stake than their opponents, entirely overmatched them in brains. By playing a waiting game, by letting loose Japanese public opinion when convenient, and then representing it as a much more potent factor than it actually is, by skilful management of the press, by adroitly causing the chief seat of the negotiations to be shifted from Tōkyō, where some of the local diplomats possessed an adequate knowledge of the subject, to the European chanceries which possessed little or none, by talent, perseverance, patience, tact, exercised year after year,—in a word, by first-rate diplomacy, they gained a complete victory over their adversaries, and at last avenged on the West the violence which it had committed in breaking open Japan a generation before.

From the point of view of patriotic Englishmen, the residents in Japan (that is, the class which possesses the best knowledge of the state of the case) almost unanimously regard the British Foreign Office with contempt, for having allowed itself to be so grossly misled and roundly beaten. But what avails that ? It is a hundred years since Nelson noted the humiliating fact that " England seldom gains anything by negotiation, except the being laughed at," and still the Foreign Office slumbers and blunders on as in Nelson's day. Diplomacy is not our talent. We must continue to endure British ineptitude in counsel, as we endure war, pestilence, and American journalism.

Sacrificed, as they have been, on the altar of *la haute politique,* the only sensible course for the foreign residents to pursue is to make the best of a bad bargain, and that is what they have set themselves to do by arranging for the execution of trustworthy English versions of the codes, such as may acquaint them with the details of their new position under Japanese laws, and by other endeavours to ensure the harmonious working of the new machinery. Down to 1899, their settlements in Japan had formed—as Shanghai still does to-day—a sort of little republic, without political rights, it is true, but also without duties. They paid few taxes, carried on their business free of police inquisition, printed what they liked in their newspapers, and, generally, did what was right in their own eyes. Now all that has been changed, and they must learn to jog along under less favourable conditions. Such miscarriages of justice as the " Kent case," the " Kōbe Water-works case," and the " Clifford Wilkinson case " * have not been calculated to reassure their minds as to the superiority

---

* We cannot here touch the very grave issues of the " Kent case " and the " Water-works case." But the " Clifford Wilkinson case " was so grotesquely amusing that not

of Japanese to English law; but they hope for the best. The heavy and complicated system of taxation,—especially the business tax, with its wheels within wheels—weighs their business down; but there again they hope for the best. Meantime lawyers, officials, and arbitrators can go on arguing and penning despatches to their hearts' content. The house-tax question alone has produced cumbrous volumes in several languages; but the day of settlement is not yet.

The conclusion would seem to be that neither the advocate of European official methods, nor those (and the present writer avows himself one of them) who love Japan but dislike jingoism, can find any source of edification in this page of modern history, on which so much pettiness and shiftiness are inscribed.

Books recommended. *A Brief Diplomatic History of Modern Japan* by Morinosuke Kajima; *The Complete Journal of Townsend Harris* edited by Mario Emilio Cosenza; *The Emergence of Japan as a World Power, 1895–1925* by Morinosuke Kajima; *Modern Japan's Foreign Policy* by Morinosuke Kajima.

Tycoon. The literal meaning of this title is "great prince" (大君). It was adopted by some of the Shōguns in their intercourse with foreign states,—Korea first in the seventeenth century, then the Western powers at the time of the opening of Japan. Their object apparently was to magnify their position, and they succeeded; for the European diplomats assumed that the Shōgun was a sort of Emperor, and dubbed him "His Majesty" accordingly.

Vegetable Wax. The vegetable wax-tree is closely allied to the lacquer-tree, both being sumachs of the genus *Rhus*. The berries of the wax-tree are crushed in a press; and the exuding matter, which is intermediate in appearance between wax and

---

to devote a word to it would be to defraud our readers of a good laugh. Mr. Wilkinson is the proprietor of the favourite Tansan mineral spring near Kobe, which he bottles for table use. A Japanese firm had imitated his label. He obtained a judgment against this firm, who thereupon appealed, and went on imitating the label. He then applied for an injunction to inhibit them from doing so, pending the result of the appeal. But the judge decided that the Japanese firm might continue to imitate the label in question, His Lordship opining that, as it was winter time probably very few bottles of Tansan water would be drunk, and Mr. Wilkinson's loss could therefore be but slight. (!!) By the way, we should apologise to Mr. Wilkinson for speaking of the case as amusing. It was amusing to the public, but doubtless appeared in quite a different light to him, as the butt of this Japanese juridical joke.

tallow, is warmed, purified, and made into candles. It is known in commerce as "Japan wax," and the tree producing it must not be confounded with the famous tallow-tree of China *(Stillingia sebicifera Euphorbiaceœ)*. The berries of the lacquer-tree are sometimes utilised in the same way as those of the vegetable wax-tree.

Volcanoes. See Earthquakes and Geography.

Weights and Measures. With a few notable exceptions, the Japanese weights and measures are decimal. The most useful are:—

		(Approximate Equivalent)	(Exact Equivalent)
Distance.	1 *bu*	line	1.4317 line.
10 *bu*	= 1 *sun*	inch	1.1931 inch.
10 *sun*	= 1 *shaku*	foot	11.9305 inches.
6 *shaku*	= 1 *ken*	double yard	1.9884 yard.
10 *shaku*	= 1 *jō*	10 feet	3.3140 yards.
60 *ken*	= 1 *chō*	120 yards	119.3040 "
36 *chō*	= 1 *ri*	$2\frac{1}{2}$ miles	2.4403 miles.

It may be of practical service to remember that 15 *chō* make almost exactly 1 English mile. The English mile and chain (80 chains = 1 mile) are the measure employed on all railways throughout the empire, and the sea mile (English Admiralty "knot") obtains for maritime distances. Otherwise the *ri* and *chō* are universally employed. The *hiro,* or "fathom," of about 6 feet, is identical with the *ken,* except that it is used more loosely for measuring such things as rope and depths at sea.

		(Approx.)	(Exact)
Cloth Measure.	1 *sun*	inch	1.4913 inch.
10 *sun*	= 1 *shaku*	foot	14.9130 inches.

1 *tan* (piece) varies from 25 to 30 *shaku.*
1 *hiki* (double piece) = 2 *tan.*

Notice how much longer the inch and foot of Cloth Measure are than the measures of Distance similarly named. In order

to distinguish the two kinds of foot, the Cloth Measure foot is
often called *kujira-jaku,* the Distance foot *kane-jaku.* In cheap
material the *tan* is apt to be short, in expensive stuffs long.

Superficies.

36 square *shaku*	= 1 *bu*	= 3.9538 square yards.		
30 *bu*	= 1 *se*	= 119(about) „	„	
10 *se*	= 1 *tan*	= 0.2451 acre.		
10 *tan*	= 1 *chō*	= 2.4507 acres.		

This is how agricultural land is measured. Town lots
and buildings go by *tsubo* only, whatever their size:—
1 *tsubo* = 1 *bu.* An English acre is nearly equivalent to
1,210 *tsubo,* or 4 *tan* and 10 *bu.* It may be useful to remember
that the *tsubo (bu)* is exactly the size of two Japanese mats
laid side by side. The area of rooms is computed in mats *(jō),*
which are always 6 *shaku* long by 3 *shaku* broad.

Capacity.

		(Approx. Equiv.)		(Exact Equiv.)	
10 *shaku* = 1 *gō*		⅓ pint		.3176 pint.	
10 *gō* = 1 *shō*		1½ quart		1.5881 quart.	
10 *shō* = 1 *to*		{4 gallons, or {1½ bushel		{3.9703 gallons. { .4962 bushel.	
4 *to* = 1 *hyō*		2 bushels		1.9852 bushel.	
10 *to* = 1 *koku*		{40 gallons, {or 5 bushels		{39.7033 gallons. { 4.9629 bushels.	

It was in *koku*—shall we translate it " bales ? "—of rice that
the incomes of Daimyōs and their retainers were formerly
computed, while the rations of the lower grade of Samurai
were computed in *hyō* or " bags." The *hyō* of charcoal is of
indeterminate size, as is also the *wa,* or " bundle," of fire-wood.

Weight.

10 *mō*	= 1 *rin*	= .5797 grain avoirdupois	
10 *rin*	= 1 *fun*	= 5.7972 grains	„
10 *fun*	= 1 *momme*	= 2.12 drachms	„
160 *momme*	= 1 *kin* (pound)	= 1.3227 lb.	„
1,000 *momme*	= 1 *kwan* or *kwamme*	= 8.2817 lbs.	„

It will be gathered from this table that the standard Japanese pound weight of 160 *momme* is approximately equivalent to 1⅓ lb. avoirdupois. Some commodities, however—such foreign foodstuffs as bread and meat—have a somewhat smaller pound of 120 *momme,* which is almost exactly the English pound, while tobacco is retailed in still smaller pounds of but 100 *momme (hyaku me).*

Woman (Status of). Japanese women are most womanly, —kind, gentle, faithful, pretty. But the way in which they are treated by the men has hitherto been such as might cause a pang to any generous European heart. No wonder that some of them are at last endeavouring to emancipate themselves. A woman's lot is summed up in what are termed " the three obediences,"—obedience, while yet unmarried, to a father; obedience, when married, to a husband and that husband's parents; obedience, when widowed, to a son. At the present moment, the greatest lady in the land may have to be her husband's drudge, to fetch and carry for him, to bow down humbly in the hall when my lord sallies forth on his walks abroad, to wait upon him at meals, to be divorced almost at his good pleasure. " Society," in our sense of the word, scarcely exists. Men do not call on ladies, can hardly even ask after them. Two grotesquely different influences are now at work to undermine this state of slavery—one, European theories concerning the relation of the sexes, the other, European clothes ! The same fellow who struts into a room before his wife when she is dressed *à la japonaise,* will let her go in first when she is dressed *à l'européenne.* Probably such acts of courtesy do not extend to the home, where there is no one by to see; for most Japanese men, even in this very year of grace 1904, make no secret of their disdain for the female sex. Still it is a first step that even on *some* occasions, consideration for women should at least be simulated.

Have we explained ourselves ? We would not have it thought that Japanese women are actually ill-used. There is probably very little wife-beating in Japan, neither is there any zenana system, any veiling of the face. Rather is it that women are all their lives treated more or less like babies, neither trusted with the independence which our modern manners allow, nor commanding the romantic homage which was woman's dower in mediæval Europe; for Japanese feudalism—despite its general similarity to the feudalism of the West—knew nothing of gallantry A Japanese knight performed his valiant deeds for no such fanciful reward as a lady's smile.* He performed them out of loyalty to his lord or filial piety towards the memory of his papa, taking up, maybe, the clan vendetta and perpetuating it. Our own sympathies, as will be sufficiently evident from the whole tenour of our remarks, are with those who wish to raise Japanese women to the position occupied by their sisters in Western lands. But many resident foreigners—male foreigners, of course—think differently, and the question forms a favourite subject of debate. The only point on which both parties agree is in their praise of Japanese woman. Says one side, "She is so charming that she deserves better treatment,"—to which the other side retorts that it is just because she is "kept in her place" that she is charming. The following quotation is from a letter to the present writer by a well-known author, who, like others, has fallen under the spell. "How sweet," says he, "Japanese woman is ! All the possibilities of the race for goodness seem to be concentrated in her. It shakes one's faith in some Occidental doctrines. If this be the result of suppression and oppression, then these are not altogether bad. On the other hand, how diamond-hard the character of the American woman becomes under the idolatry of which she is the object. In the eternal order of things, which is the higher being,—the childish, confiding, sweet Japanese girl, or the superb, calculating, penetrating, Occidental Circe of our more artificial society, with her enormous power for evil and her limited capacity for good ?"—That Japanese women are charming, either because or in spite of the disadvantages of

---

* Compare the Article on SAMURAI.

their position, is a fact which the admiration of foreign lady travellers proves more conclusively than aught else; for in their case such admiration cannot be suspected of any *arrière-pensée*. How many times have we not heard European ladies go into ecstasies over them, and marvel how they could be of the same race as the men ! And closer acquaintance does but confirm such views. Moreover, it reveals the existence of solid—we had almost said stern—qualities unsuspected by the casual observer. These delicate-looking women have Spartan hearts. Countless anecdotes attest their courage, physical as well as moral.

The following treatise by the celebrated moralist Kaibara so faithfully sums up the ideas hitherto prevalent in Japan concerning the relations between the sexes, that we shall give it in full, notwithstanding its length. The title, which is literally " The Greater Learning for Women " *(Onna Daigaku)*, might be more freely rendered by " The Whole Duty of Woman."*

THE GREATER LEARNING FOR WOMEN.

" Seeing that it is a girl's destiny, on reaching womanhood, to go to a new home, and live in submission to her father-in-law and mother-in-law, it is even more incumbent upon her than it is on a boy to receive with all reverence her parents' instructions. Should her parents, through excess of tenderness, allow her to grow up self-willed, she will infallibly show herself capricious in her husband's house, and thus alienate his affection, while, if her father-in-law be a man of correct principles, the girl will find the yoke of these principles intolerable. She will hate and decry her father-in-law, and the end of these domestic dissensions will be her dismissal from her husband's house, and the covering of herself with ignominy. Her parents, forgetting the faulty education they gave her, may indeed lay all the blame on the father-in-law. But they will be in error; for the whole disaster should rightly be attributed to the faulty education the girl received from her parents.

---

* This translation is reprinted from a paper by the present writer entitled *Educational Literature for Japanese Women,* contributed in July, 1878, to Vol. X. Part III. of the " Journal of the Royal Asiatic Society of Great Britain." An imitation of the original work, intended at the same time to serve as its refutation by preaching modern ideas to the Japanese " new woman," appeared in 1899 from the pen of the celebrated educationalist, Fukuzawa, but was not calculated to add to his reputation.

" More precious in a woman is a virtuous heart than a face of beauty. The vicious woman's heart is ever excited; she glares wildly around her, she vents her anger on others, her words are harsh and her accent vulgar. When she speaks, it is to set herself above others, to upbraid others, to envy others, to be puffed up with individual pride, to jeer at others, to outdo others,—all things at variance with the ' way ' in which a woman should walk. The only qualities that befit a woman are gentle obedience, chastity, mercy, and quietness.

" From her earliest youth, a girl should observe the line of demarcation separating women from men; and never, even for an instant, should she be allowed to see or hear the slightest impropriety. The customs of antiquity did not allow men and women to sit in the same apartment, to keep their wearing-apparel in the same place, to bathe in the same place or to transmit to each other anything directly from hand to hand. A woman going abroad at night must in all cases carry a lighted lantern; and (not to speak of strangers) she must observe a certain distance in her intercourse even with her husband and with her brothers. In our days, the woman of the lower classes, ignoring all rules of this nature, behave themselves disorderly; they contaminate their reputations, bring down reproach upon the heads of their parents and brothers, and spend their whole lives in an unprofitable manner. Is not this truly lamentable ? It is written likewise, in the ' Lesser Learning,' that a woman must form no friendship and no intimacy, except when ordered to do so by her parents or by the ' middleman.'* Even at the peril of her life, must she harden her heart like rock or metal, and observe the rules of propriety.

" In China, marriage is called *returning*, for the reason that a woman must consider her husband's home as her own, and that, when she marries, she is therefore returning to her own home. However humble and needy may be her husband's position, she must find no fault with him, but consider the poverty of the household which it has pleased Heaven to give her as the ordering of an unpropitious fate. The sage of old† taught that, once married, she must never leave her husband's house. Should she forsake the ' way,' and be divorced, shame shall cover her till her latest hour. With regard to this point, there are seven faults, which are termed ' the Seven Reasons for Divorce: ' (i) A woman shall be divorced for disobedience to her father-in-law or mother-in-law. (ii) A woman shall be divorced if she fail to bear children, the reason for this rule being that women are sought in marriage for the purpose of giving men posterity. A barren

---

* See page 310.
† Confucius.

woman should, however, be retained if her heart is virtuous and her conduct correct and free from jealousy, in which case a child of the same blood must be adopted; neither is there any just cause for a man to divorce a barren wife, if he have children by a concubine. (iii) Lewdness is a reason for divorce. (iv) Jealousy is a reason for divorce. (v) Leprosy, or any like foul disease, is a reason for divorce. (vi) A woman shall be divorced, who, by talking overmuch and prattling disrespectfully, disturbs the harmony of kinsmen and brings trouble on her household. (vii) A woman shall be divorced who is addicted to stealing.—All the 'Seven Reasons for Divorce' were taught by the Sage. A woman, once married and then divorced, has wandered from the 'way,' and is covered with the greatest shame, even if she should enter into a second union with a man of wealth and position.

"It is the chief duty of a girl living in the parental house to practise filial piety towards her father and mother. But after marriage, her chief duty is to honour her father-in-law and mother-in-law—to honour them beyond her own father and mother—to love and reverence them with all ardour, and to tend them with every practice of filial piety. While thou honourest thine own parents, think not lightly of thy father-in-law! Never should a woman fail, night and morning, to pay her respects to her father-in-law and mother-in-law. Never should she be remiss in performing any tasks they may require of her. With all reverence must she carry out, and never rebel aganst, her father-in-law's commands. On every point must she enquire of her father-in-law and mother-in-law, and abandon herself to their direction. Even if thy father-in-law and mother-in-law be pleased to hate and vilify thee, be not angry with them, and murmur not! If thou carry piety towards them to its utmost limits, and minister to them in all sincerity, it cannot be but that they will end by becoming friendly to thee.

"A woman has no particular lord. She must look to her husband as her lord, and must serve him with all worship and reverence, not despising or thinking lightly of him. The great life-long duty of a woman is obedience. In her dealings with her husband, both the expression of her countenance and the style of her address should be courteous, humble, and conciliatory, never peevish and intractable, never rude and arrogant:—that should be a woman's first and chiefest care. When the husband issues his instructions, the wife must never disobey them. In doubtful cases, she should enquire of her husband, and obediently follow his commands. If ever her husband should enquire of her, she should answer to the point;—to answer in a careless fashion were a mark of rudeness. Should her husband be roused at any time to anger, she must obey him with fear and trembling, and not set herself up against him in anger and frowardness. A woman should look on her husband as if he were Heaven itself, and never weary of thinking how she may yield to her husband, and thus escape celestial castigation.

" As brothers-in-law and sisters-in-law are the brothers and sisters of a woman's husband, they deserve all her reverence. Should she lay herself open to the ridicule and dislike of her husband's kindred, she would offend her parents-in-law, and do harm even to herself, whereas, if she lives on good terms with them, she will likewise rejoice the hearts of her parents-in-law. Again, she should cherish, and be intimate with, the wife of her husband's elder brother,—yea, with special warmth of affection should she reverence her husband's elder brother and her husband's elder brother's wife, esteeming them as she does her own elder brother and elder sister.

" Let her never even dream of jealousy. If her husband be dissolute, she must expostulate with him, but never either nurse or vent her anger. If her jealousy be extreme, it will render her countenance frightful and her accents repulsive, and can only result in completely alienating her husband from her, and making her intolerable in his eyes. Should her husband act ill and unreasonably, she must compose her countenance and soften her voice to remonstrate with him; and if he be angry and listen not to the remonstrance, she must wait over a season, and then expostulate with him again when his heart is softened. Never set thyself up against thy husband with harsh features and a boisterous voice !

" A woman should be circumspect and sparing in her use of words; and never, even for passing moment, should she slander others or be guilty of untruthfulness. Should she ever hear calumny, she should keep it to herself and and repeat it to none; for it is the retailing of calumny that disturbs the harmony of kinsmen and ruins the peace of families.

" A woman must be ever on the alert, and keep a strict watch over her own conduct. In the morning she must rise early, and at night go late to rest. Instead of sleeping in the middle of the day, she must be intent on the duties of her household, and must not weary of weaving, sewing, and spinning. Of tea and wine she must not drink overmuch, nor must she feed her eyes and ears with theatrical performances, ditties, and ballads. To temples (whether Shintō or Buddhist) and other like places, where there is a great concourse of people, she should go but sparingly till she has reached the age of forty.

" She must not let herself be led astray by mediums and divineresses and enter into an irreverent familiarity with the Gods, neither should she be constantly occupied in praying. If only she satisfactorily perform her duties as a human being, she may let prayer alone without ceasing to enjoy the divine protection.

"In her capacity of wife, she must keep her husband's household in proper order. If the wife be evil and profligate, the house is ruined. In everything she must avoid extravagance, and both with regard to food and raiment must act according to her station in life, and never give way to luxury and pride.

"While young, she must avoid the intimacy and familiarity of her husband's kinsmen, comrades, and retainers, ever strictly adhering to the rule of separation between the sexes; and on no account whatever should she enter into correspondence with a young man. Her personal adornments and the colour and pattern of her garments should be unobtrusive. It suffices for her to be neat and cleanly in her person and in her wearing-apparel. It is wrong in her, by an excess of care, to obtrude herself on the notice of others. Only that which is suitable should be practised.

"She must not selfishly think first of her own parents, and only secondly of her husband's relations. At New Year, on the Five Festivals,* and on other like occasions, she should first pay her respects to those of her husband's house, and then to her own parents. Without her husband's permission, she must go nowhere, neither should she make any gifts on her own responsibility.

"As a woman rears up posterity, not to her own parents, but to her father-in-law and mother-in-law, she must value the latter even more than the former, and tend them with all filial piety. Her visits, also, to the paternal house should be rare after marriage. Much more then, with regard to other friends, should it generally suffice for her to send a message to enquire after their health. Again, she must not be filled with pride at the recollection of the splendour of her parental house, and must not make it the subject of her conversations.

"However many servants she may have in her employ, it is a woman's duty not to shirk the trouble of attending to everything herself. She must sew her father-in-law's and mother-in-law's garments, and make ready their food. Ever attentive to the requirements of her husband, she must fold his clothes and dust his rug, rear his children, wash what is dirty, be constantly in the midst of her household, and never go abroad but of necessity.

"Her treatment of her handmaidens will require circumspection. These low and aggravating girls have had no proper education; they are stupid, obstinate, and vulgar in their speech. When anything in the conduct of their mistress's husband or parents-in-law crosses their wishes, they fill her ears with their invectives, thinking thereby to render her a service. But any woman who should listen to this

* See page 357.

gossip must beware of the heart-burnings it will be sure to breed. Easy is it by reproaches and disobedience to lose the love of those, who, like a woman's marriage connections, were all originally strangers; and it were surely folly, by believing the prattle of a serving-maid, to diminish the affection of a precious father-in-law and mother-in-law. If a serving-maid be altogether too loquacious and bad, she should speedily be dismissed; for it is by the gossip of such persons that occasion is given for the troubling of harmony of kinsmen and the disordering of a household. Again, in her dealings with these low people, a woman will find many things to disapprove of. But if she be forever reproving and scolding, and spend her time in bustle and anger, her household will be in a continual state of disturbance. When there is real wrong-doing, she should occasionally notice it, and point out the path of amendment, while lesser faults should be quietly endured without anger. While in her heart she compassionates her subordinates' weaknesses, she must outwardly admonish them with all strictness to walk in the paths of propriety, and never allow them to fall into idleness. If any is to be succoured, let her not be grudging of her money; but she must not foolishly shower down gifts on such as merely please her individual caprice, but are unprofitable servants.

" The five worst maladies that afflict the female mind are: indocility, discontent, slander, jealousy, and silliness. Without any doubt, these five maladies infest seven or eight out of every ten women, and it is from these that arises the inferiority of women to men. A woman should cure them by self-inspection and self-reproach. The worst of them all, and the parent of the other four, is silliness. Woman's nature is passive (lit, *shade*). This passiveness, being of the nature of the night, is dark. Hence, as viewed from the standard of man's nature, the foolishness of woman fails to understand the duties that lie before her very eyes, perceives not the actions that will bring down blame upon her head, and comprehends not even the things that will bring down calamities on the heads of her husband and children. Neither when she blames and accuses and curses innocent persons, nor when, in her jealousy of others, she thinks to set up herself alone, does she see that she is her own enemy, estranging others and incurring their hatred. Lamentable errors ! Again, in the education of her children, her blind affection induces an erroneous system. Such is the stupidity of her character that it is incumbent on her, in every particular, to distrust herself and to obey her husband.

" We are told that it was the custom of the ancients, on the birth of a female child, to let it lie on the floor for the space of three days. Even in this, may be seen the likening of the man to Heaven and of the woman to Earth; and the custom should teach a woman how necessary it is for her in everything to yield to her husband the first, and to be herself content with the second, place; to avoid pride, even if there be in her actions aught deserving praise; and on the other hand, if she transgress in aught and incur blame, to wend her way through the difficulty and amend the fault, and so conduct herself as not again to lay herself open to censure; to endure without anger and indignation the jeers of others, suffering such things with patience and humility. If a woman act thus, her conjugal relations cannot but be harmonious and lasting, and her household a scene of peace and concord.

"Parents! teach the foregoing maxims to your daughters from their tenderest years! Copy them out from time to time, that they may read and never forget them! Better than the garments and divers vessels which the fathers of the present day so lavishly bestow upon their daughters when giving them away in marriage, were it to teach them thoroughly these precepts which would guard them as a precious jewel throughout their lives. How true is that ancient saying: 'A man knoweth how to spend a million pieces of money in marrying off his daughter, but knoweth not how to spend an hundred thousand in bringing up his child! Such as have daughters must lay this well to heart."

*　　*　　*　　.*　　*　　*　　*　　*　　*　　*

Thus far our old Japanese moralist. For the sake of fairness and completeness, it should be added that the subjection of women has never been carried out in the lower classes of Japanese society to the same extent as in the middle and upper. Poverty makes for equality all the world over. Just as among ourselves woman-worship flourishes among the well-to-do, but is almost if not entirely, absent among the peasantry, so in Japan the contrary or rather complementary state of things may be observed. The peasant women, the wives of artisans and small traders, have more liberty and a relatively higher position than the great ladies of the land. In these lower classes the wife shares not only her husband's toil, but his counsels; and if she happen to have the better head of the two, she it is who will keep the purse and govern the family.

With the twentieth century, the "new woman" has begun to assert herself even in Japan. Her name figures on committees; she may be seen riding the "bike," and more usefully employed in some of the printing-offices and telephone exchanges. Such developments, however, affect but a small percentage of the nation.

Books recommended. *A Daughter of the Samurai* by Etsu Inagaki Sugimoto; *The Japanese Are Like That* by Ichiro Kawasaki; *Japanese Etiquette: An Introduction* by the World Fellowship Committee of the Tokyo Y.W.C.A.

Wood Engraving. A far-off Chinese origin followed by centuries in the chrysalis stage, a wakening from torpor soon after A.D. 1600 when peace had replaced continual civil tumults, then a gradual working up to perfection, a golden age from, say, 1730 to 1830, after which sudden decline and death,—such we have seen to be the life-history of many Japanese arts, such is the life-history of the lovely art of wood engraving.

In a country where printing is done, not with movable types, but from wooden blocks, and where consequently the same process would naturally serve for both letterpress and pictorial illustration, we may assume that if the former of these exists, the latter probably exists along with it. Now we know block-printing to have been practised in Japan in the eighth century, if not sooner. There is, therefore, no reason for discrediting the tradition that the printed Buddhist charms and paper slips of that period sometimes bore figures of divinities, though few, if any, of the surviving specimens can with certainty be dated back earlier than the year 1325. Even that date precedes by nearly a century the German block of St. Christopher. The earliest illustrated book at present known is the 1608 edition of a classical romance entitled *Ise Mono-gatari,*—a very crude production, to some copies of which a rough hand-colouring has been applied, not unlike that of the old English chap-books. But the father of really artistic xylography was Hishigawa Moronobu, who flourished between 1680 and 1701, and was the first to adopt that decorative use of masses of black which has lent such piquancy to the colour scheme of Japanese engravers since his time. And do not object, and tell us that this arbitrary prominence given to black in certain portions of the picture accords ill with nature. What came next, somewhere about 1710, from the first artists of the Torii School,—their broadsides in black and one tint, or black and two or three tints, without shadows, without perspective, of women with faces that neither Japan nor any other land has ever seen in real life,—these accord with nature equally little. But they display a tender harmony of colouring, a strength of touch, a power of composition, that elevate what at first strike a European as mere sketches to an ethereal form of art. When Hokusai and Hiroshige caught up the tradition, landscape was treated in an equally idealistic way. These colour-prints of the eighteenth and early part of the nineteenth century—the work of the Toriis, the Katsugawas, the Utagawas, and other schools—stand alone and unrivalled, resembling nothing so much as certain beautiful butterflies of fantastic yet harmonious hue.

The old coloured broadsides *(nishiki-e)* were published, as their degenerate modern representatives still are, sometimes in single sheets, very often in sets of three sheets to a picture, rarely in more than three. The first coloured book (copied from a Chinese one dated 1701) seems to have been issued about 1748, and the xylographic art as a whole may be said to have reached its culminating point about 1765, under Suzuki Harunobu and Torii Kiyonaga. Soon fans and other paper articles began to be adorned with engravings either black or coloured. In the last quarter of the eighteenth century what were called *Surimono* came into fashion,—dainty little works of art to which our Christmas cards are the nearest equivalent. Those by Hokusai (1760–1849) and his pupil Hokkei are particularly esteemed.

As happens to all arts, time brought with it greater complexity and a more florid taste. Instead of the two or three blocks of an earlier day, as many as thirty were now often employed; and the colours, after 1830, grew gaudy. The introduction of cheap European pigments, the troubles that attended the opening of the country, and the influence of debased European specimens hastened the downfall of the art.

Quite recently the broadsides of Gekkō and one or two other living artists have given hopes of revival, like those fine days which, in late autumn, sometimes make us think that summer is coming back.

The tools used by Japanese wood engravers and printers are few and simple. The picture, drawn upon thin translucent paper, is pasted face downwards upon a plank of wood, usually cherry or boxwood—sawn in the direction of the grain instead of across it, as in Europe—and scraped till every detail of the design becomes visible. The thin remaining layer is then slightly oiled, and the work of engraving begins, the borders of the outline being incised first with a knife, and the spaces between the lines of the drawing excavated by means of chisels and gouges. The block is then washed and is ready for use. The printer applies the ink or colour with a brush, and the impressions are taken upon specially prepared paper by rubbing with a flat padded disc, worked by hand pressure. Certain gradations of tone, and even polychromatic effects may be produced from a single block, and uninked blocks are often used for the purpose of embossing portions of the design. The effects of printing from two or more blocks was obtained in some cases by preparing a single block with ink of different colours, or with different shades of the same colour. At other times a lighter tint was obtained by simply wiping portions of the block. In the ordinary colourprints the effects are obtained by the use of a number of additional blocks engraved in series from copies of the impression taken from the first or outline block. Correctness of register is secured, simply but effectually, by means of a rectangular nick and guiding-line repeated at the corner and edge of each successive block.

The names of the following seven leaders in the development of Japanese wood engraving may be useful to collectors:—Hishigawa Moronobu (flourished 1680-1701), Torii Kiyonobu (1710–1730); Tachibana Morikuni (1670–1748); Nishigawa Sukenobu (1678–1750); Katsugawa Shunshō (1770–1790); Utagawa Toyokuni (1772–1828); Katsushika Hokusai (1760–1849).

Though it is a little aside from our subject, we may perhaps state here that Shiba Kōkan, an artist who flourished early in the nineteenth century, learnt from the Dutch a smattering of the principles of linear perspective, and is said to have introduced engraving on copper, in which, however, his countrymen have done little worthy of note. At the present day lithography and all the newest inventions in collotype, photogravure, etc., etc., etc., are availed of, and some slight reflex of the artistic spirit animating their forefathers in a more favoured age may be traced in the treatment, by such men as Ogawa, of these mechanical processes. See also Articles on ART and PRINTING.

Books recommended. *Chats on Japanese Prints* by Arthur Davison Ficke; *The Hokusai Sketchbooks: Selections from the Manga* by James A. Michener; *Japanese Prints: From the Early Masters to the Modern* by James A. Michener; *Japanese Woodblock Prints in Miniature: The Genre of Surimono* by Kurt Meissner; *Modern Japanese Prints: An Art Reborn* by Oliver Statler; introduction by James A. Michener; *The Modern Japanese Print: An Appreciation* by James A. Michener.

Wrestling. The wrestlers must be numbered among Japan's most characteristic sights, though they are neither small nor dainty, like the majority of things Japanese. They are enormous men,—mountains of fat and muscle, with low sensual faces and low sensual habits,—enormous eaters, enormous drinkers. But their feats of strength show plainly that the " training " which consists in picking and choosing among one's victuals is a vain superstition.

The wrestlers form a class apart, divided into grades, and having traditional rules for their guidance. The most important of these refer to the forty-eight falls which alone are permitted by the laws of the sport, namely, twelve throws, twelve lifts, twelve twists, and twelve throws over the back. The matches take place in a sanded ring, encircled by straw rice-bales and protected from the sun by an umbrella-like roof, supported on four posts. The wrestlers are naked, but for a gay-coloured apron. An umpire, who bears in his hand a fan, stays in the ring with them, to see that there be fair play and strict observance of the rules. The spectators are accommodated in the boxes of what resembles a temporary theatre surrounding the arena; but as the religious of Japan are nowise Puritanical, this theatre is sometimes erected in the grounds of a popular temple. The finest wrestling is to be witnessed twice yearly at the temple of Ekō-in in Tōkyō, during the months of January and May. Generally the combats are single, but occasionally sides are formed of as many as ten or twenty each. The plan then is for each side to choose a champion, it being incumbent on the victor to throw three adversaries in succession before he can gain a prize. As he himself is necessarily blown by the first or first two struggles, while his new adversary is quite fresh and springs upon him without a moment's interval, this is a great trial of endurance. To instance the popularity of the ring, it may be mentioned that a single ten days' season has been known to draw over 28,000 spectators. Devotees of the sport are sometimes carried away so far by their enthusiasm as to throw to a favourite champion articles of clothing or anything else that may be at hand. Not that the recipient retains any object thrown. One of his pupils brings it next day as a token to the owner, who then redeems it by a present of money.

The queerest historical episode connected with wrestling is that the Japanese throne was once wrestled for. This happened in the ninth century, when, the Mikado having died and left two sons, these wisely committed their rival claims to the issue, not of real, but of mimic warfare.

What is termed *Jūjutsu* is a separate art, and ranks higher in aristocratic esteem than the ordinary wrestling *(Sumō)* practised by the fat wrestlers. The police are officially instructed in *Jūjutsu,* and the Nobles' School and other academies have classes in it. Its principles, like those of so many Japanese arts, were formerly handed down as an esoteric secret from teacher to teacher; but the leading idea has always been clear enough,—not to match strength with strength, but to win by yielding to strength, in other words, by pliancy. Various ways of causing apparent death by pressure, and of recalling to life from such dead swoons, bone-setting, and also matters connected rather with moral than with physical training are included in the course.

Books recommended. *The Secrets of Judo: A Test for Instructors and Students* by Jiichi Watanabe and Lindy Avakian; *The Sport of Judo* by Kiyoshi Kobayashi and Harold E. Sharp; *Sumo: The Sport and the Tradition* by J. A. Sargeant; *The Techniques of Judo* by Shinzo Takagaki and Harold E. Sharp.

Writing. The Japanese, having obtained their civilisation from China and Korea, were inevitably led to adopt the ideographic system of writing practised in those countries. Its introduction into Japan seems to have taken place somewhere about A.D. 400, but the chronology of that early epoch is extremely obscure.

According to this ideographic system, each individual word has its separate sign, originally a kind of picture or hieroglyph. Thus, 人 is "a man," represented by his two legs; 月 is "the moon," with her horns still distinguishable; 馬 is "a horse,"—the head, mane, and legs, though hard to recognise in the abbreviated modern form of the character, having at first been clearly drawn. Few characters are so simple as these. Most are obtained by means of combination, the chief element being termed the "radical," because it gives a clue to the signification of the whole. The other part generally indicate more or less precisely the pronunciation of the word, and is therefore called the "phonetic." It is much as if, having in English special hieroglyphic signs for such easy, every-day words as "tree," "house," "hand," and "box" (a chest), we were to represent "box-wood" by a combination of the sign for "tree" and the sign for "box," a "box at the opera" by a combination of "house" and "box," a "boxing match" by a combination of "hand" and "box," and similarly in other cases. The Chinese language, being unusually full of homonymous words, lends itself naturally to such a method. Names of plants are obtained by combination of the character 艸 "herb," itself still to be recognised as a picture of herbs sprouting up from the soil. "The hand," 手 originally a rude picture of the outstretched fingers, helps to form hundreds of characters signifying actions. "The heart," 心 gives numerous abstract words denoting sentiments and passions. Similarly "the eye," "the mouth," "fire," "water," "silk," "rain," "metal," "fish," are parents of large families of characters. The study of this Chinese method of writing is most interesting,—so curious is the chapter of the human mind which it unrolls, so unexpected are the items of recondite history which it discloses. To give but one example, the character for "war," 軍 is formed partly from the character for "vehicle," 車 because the ancient Chinese, like the ancient Greeks, used to go forth to battle in chariots.

Unfortunately, the transfer of this system of ideographs from China to Japan was accompanied by inevitable complications. Even supposing Japanese organs to have been able (which they were not) to reproduce Chinese sounds exactly, all Chinese teachers of the language did not speak the same dialect. Hence the gradual establishment in Japan of two or three readings for each character,—one reading being preferred to another according to the context. Besides this, instead of always imitating the Chinese sound as far as possible, the Japanese also took, in many cases, to translating the meanings of the characters into their own language, thus adding yet another reading. For instance, the already-mentioned symbol 人 "man," has the two Chinese* reading *jin* and *nin,* and the Japanese translation *hito.* But these cannot be used indiscriminately. We say JIN-*riki-sha,* but NIN-*soku* ("a coolie"), and HITO when we mean simply a "person." In some cases there are Chinese readings only, and no Japanese. In some, a single character has several Japanese readings, while on the other

---

* *I.e.* Japanese-Chinese, or, as it is sometimes termed, Sinico-Japanese.

hand, the same Japanese word may be written with several different characters, just as in English each letter has various sounds and each sound may be represented by various letters.

In addition to the Chinese ideographs, there came into use in Japan during the eighth and ninth centuries another system of writing, called the *Kana,* derived from those Chinese characters which happened to be most commonly employed. There are two varieties of *Kana,*—the *Katakana* or "side *Kana,*" so called because the symbols composing it are "sides," that is, parts or fragments, of Chinese characters, as イ *i,* from the character 伊, ロ *ro,* from the character 呂, etc.; and the *Hiragana,* which consists of cursive forms of entire Chinese characters, as は *ha,* in which the outline of the original 波 may still be faintly traced. The invention of the former is popularly attributed to a worthy named Kibi-no-Mabi (died A.D. 776), and that of the latter to the Buddhist saint, Kōbō Daishi (A.D. 834). But it is more reasonable to suppose that the simplification—for such it really is, and not an invention at all—came about gradually, than to accept it as the work of two individuals.

Whereas a Chinese character directly represents a whole word—an idea—the *Kana* represents the sounds of which the word is composed, just as our Roman writing does. There is, however, this difference, that the *Kana* stands for syllables, not letters. The following tables of the *Katakana* and *Hiragana* will help to make this clear. We give the former in the order preferred by modern scholars, and termed *Go-jū-on,* or "Table of Fifty Sounds" (though there are in reality but forty-seven), the latter in the popular order, called *I-ro-ha,* which has been handed down from the ninth century :—

The *Katakana* Syllabary.

ア a	カ ka	サ sa	タ ta	ナ na	ハ ha	マ ma	ヤ ya	ラ ra	ワ wa
イ i	キ ki	シ shi	チ chi	ニ ni	ヒ hi	ミ mi		リ ri	キ (w)i
ウ u	ク ku	ス su	ツ tsu	ヌ nu	フ fu	ム mu	ユ yu	ル ru	
*	ケ ke	セ se	テ te	ネ ne	ヘ he	メ me	エ (y)e	レ re	エ (w)e
オ o	コ ko	ソ so	ト to	ノ no	ホ ho	モ mo	ヨ yo	ロ ro	ヲ wo

The *Hirakana* Syllabary.

い i	ろ ro	は ha	に ni	ほ ho	へ he	と to
ち chi	り ri	ぬ nu	る ru	を wo	わ wa	か ka
よ yo	た ta	れ re	そ so	つ tsu	ね ne	な na
ら ra	む mu	う u	ゐ w(i)	の no	お o	く ku
や ya	ま ma	け ke	ふ fu	こ ko	え y(e)	て te
あ a	さ sa	き ki	ゆ yu	め me	み mi	し shi
ゑ (w)e	ひ hi	も mo	せ se	す su		

The order of the *I-ro-ha* bears witness to the Buddhist belief of the fathers of Japanese writing. The syllabary is a verse of poetry, founded on one of the Sutras and so arranged that the same letter is never repeated twice. Transcribed according to the modern pronunciation, it runs thus:—

---

* The deficiency of a true *e* is supplied by エ *(y)e* or エ *(w)e*.

Iro wa nioedo,
Chirinu wo—
　　Waga yo tare zo
Tsune naran ?
　　Ui no oku-yama
Kyō koete,
　　Asaki yume miji,
Ei mo sezu.

Which is, being interpreted:

" Though gay in hue, [the blossoms] flutter down, alas!
Who then, in this world of ours, may continue forever ?
Crossing to-day the uttermost limits of phenomenal existence,
I shall see no more fleeting dreams, neither be any longer
intoxicated."* In other words, " All is transitory in this
fleeting world. Let me escape form its illusions and
vanities ! "

In both syllabaries, consonants can be softened† by placing
two dots to the rights of the letter. Thus カ is *ka,* but ガ is
ga; テ is *te,* but デ is *de,* and so on. In this way the
number of letters is raised considerably. There are various
other peculiarities, Japanese orthography almost rivalling
our own in eccentricity. Very few books are written in
Hiragana alone—none in *Katakana* alone. Almost all are
written in a mixture of Chinese characters and *Kana* of one
kind or another, the Chinese characters being employed for
the chief ideas, for nouns and the stems of verbs, while the
Kana serves to transcribe particle and terminations. It is
also often printed at the side of Chinese characters,
especially difficult ones, as a sort of running comment, which
indicates sometimes the pronunciation, sometimes the
meaning. Add to this that the Chinese characters are
commonly written and even printed in every sort of style—
from the standard, or so-called " square," to the most

---

* The present writer has been guided by Dr. K. Florenz to this revised rendering of a verse
by no means easy to translate.

† *I.e.,* technically speaking, surds can be changed into sonants.

sketchy cursive hand,—that each *Hiragana* syllabic letter has several alternative forms, that there is no means of indicating capitals or punctuation, that all the words are run together on a page without any mark to show where one leaves off and another begins,—and the result is the most complicated system of writing ever evolved upon this planet. An old Jesuit missionary declares it to be evidently "the invention of a conciliabule of the demons, to harass the faithful." At the same time, it must be owned that the individuals thus diabolically harassed are principally those foreigners who make their first attempt on the language when already of adult age. The often-repeated assertion that the ideographs waste years of school life is simply not true:— the Japanese lad of fifteen is abreast of his English contemporary in every way. The Japanese navvy makes as good a show at spelling out the newspaper or inditing a letter as the English navvy. After all, the average Englishman is not only abreast, but actually ahead, of the average Italian in reading and writing, notwithstanding that Italian orthography could be mastered in a day, whereas our own, in all its ramifications, might occupy a lifetime. The fact seems to be that, at a certain age, the mind will absorb any system of written symbols equally well. A large number can, practically, be learnt in the same time as a small number, just as a net with many meshes can be taken in by the eye as easily as a net with few. The same holds good of spoken symbols. Any language is assimilated equally well in early childhood,—a complex inflectional language in precisely the same time as a simple monosyllabic one. Nay more: place a child under favourable conditions, for instance, in an English family living in France and employing German governesses or tutors, and he will absorb all three languages in the same time, with the same ease, and with the same perfection as a single one would have taken had he remained in his native village. Evidently, there exists a whole educational domain to which arithmetical reasoning does not apply.

But to return. If Japanese writing is (to us) a mountain of difficulty, it is unapproachably beautiful. Japanese art has been called calligraphic. Japanese calligraphy is artistic. Above all, it is bold, because it comes from the shoulder instead of merely from the wrist. A little experience will convince any one that, in comparison with it, the freest, boldest English hand is little better than the cramped scribble of some rheumatic crone. One consequence of this exceeding difficulty and beauty is that calligraphy ranks high in Japan among the arts. Another is that the Japanese very easily acquire our simpler system. To copy the handwriting of a European is mere child's play to them. In fact, it is usual for clerks and students to imitate the handwriting of their employer or master so closely that he himself often cannot tell the difference. It seems odd, considering the high esteem in which writing is held in Japan, that the signature should not occupy the same important place in this country as it does in the West. The seal alone has legal force, the impression being made, not with sealing-wax, but with vermilion ink.

The influence of writing on speech—never entirely absent in any country possessing letters—is particularly strong under the Chinese system. We mean that the writing here does not merely serve to transcribe words:—it actually originates new ones, the slave in fact becoming the master. This is chiefly brought about through the exceptional amount of homophony in Chinese, that is, the existence of an extraordinarily large number of words sounding alike, but differing in signification. In the colloquial these are either not used, or are made intelligible by the context or by recourse to periphrasis. But the writer, possessing as he does a separate symbol for each, can wield them all at will, and create new compounds *ad infinitum*. Almost all the technical terms invented to designate objects, ideas, appliances, and institutions recently borrowed from Europe belong to this category. Some of these new compounds pass from books into common speech; but many remain exclusively attached to the written language, or are at least intelligible only by reference to the latter, while at the same time they endow it with a clearness and above all a terseness to which the colloquial can never attain.

This article may appropriately conclude by dispelling an illusion under which many intelligent persons labour, namely, that the Japanese nation is on the eve of dropping its own written system and taking up with ours instead. There is no longer the slightest chance of so sweeping a change. There once seemed to be—somewhere about 1885—and much time, money, and energy were devoted to the cause by an association called the *Rōmaji Kwai*, or Romanisation Society, which lingered on some eight or ten years and then perished. Besides the weight of custom, the most obvious of the causes that concerned to bring about this ill-success has been anticipated in the preceding paragraph, where mention was made of the superiority of the existing written language to the colloquial as a terse and precise instrument of thought. Supported by the Chinese character, Japanese writers can render every shade of meaning represented in the columns of a European newspaper or the pages of a technical European work, whether financial, diplomatic, administrative, commercial, legal, critical, theological, philosophical, or scientific. Who could wish them to throw away their intellectual weapons, and put themselves on a level with the men of the stone age? They could not do so if they would. But a third cause—a more general one—must be sought in the fact that the ideographic writing apparently possesses some inherent strength that makes it tend to triumph over (without entirely supplanting) phonetic writing, whenever the two are brought into competition in the same area. All the countries under Chinese influence exemplify this little known fact in a striking manner. Egypt, too, retained its hieroglyphics to the end. In Europe such competition has scarcely taken place, except in the case of the symbols for numbers and a few other ideas; but there, too, the general law has asserted itself. Which is the simpler, the more graphic, the more commonly used,—" three hundred and sixty-five " or " 365," " thirty-five degrees forty-one minutes twenty three seconds" or "35° 41′ 23″"," "pounds, shillings, and pence" or "£. s. d. ?" Doubtless an ideographic system of writing is infinitely more cumbrous as a whole than its rival; but it is easier in each particular case. Hence its victory. We commend these considerations—for additional proof or for disproof—to those who have always been taught to believe, not merely that an alphabet is the *ne plus ultra* of perfection, but that it is a thing needing only to be known in order to be adopted.

Books recommended. *A Guide to Reading & Writing Japanese* edited by Florence Sakade; *The Modern Reader's Japanese-English Character Dictionary* by Andrew N. Nelson; *Read Japanese Today* by Len Walsh.

Yezo, often incorrectly spelt Yesso, and officially styled the *Hokkaidō,* or "Northern Sea Circuit," is the northernmost of the large islands that form the Japanese archipelago. It lies, roughly speaking, between parallels 41½° and 45½° of north latitude—the latitude of that part of Italy which stretches from Rome to Venice;—but it is under snow and ice for nearly half the year, the native Ainos tracking the bear and deer across its frozen and pathless mountains, like the cave-men of the glacial age of Europe. It is asserted that Yoshitsune, the great Japanese hero, fled into Yezo and died there; but little attempt was made by the Japanese to colonise it until early in the seventeenth century, when the Shōgun Ieyasu granted it as a fief to one Matsumae Yoshihiro, who conquered the south-western corner of the island, establishing its capital at Matsumae, some sixty miles to the south-west of the modern port of Hakodate. His successors retained their sway over Yezo until the recent break-up of the feudal system. They treated the luckless Ainos with great cruelty, and actually rendered it penal to communicate to these poor barbarians the art of writing or any of the arts of civilised life. Frequent rebellions, suppressed by massacres, were the result. In the latter part of the eighteenth century, however, and in the first half the nineteenth, a few Japanese literati made their way into the island. It is to their efforts—to the efforts of such men as Mogami, Mamiya, and Matsura—that our first scientific information concerning the people, the language, and the productions of Yezo is due. The Imperial government has done all in its power to redress the wrongs of the hitherto down-trodden natives.

At one time, the Russians endeavoured to obtain a footing in Yezo; but the opening of Japan nipped this encroachment in the bud. Japanese statesmen eagerly plunged into the task of developing the resources of the island. With this end in view, they created a special executive department, entitled the *Kaitakushi,* and engaged the services of a party of American employés headed by General Capron. Large sums were expended on model farms and other public works, and a fictitious prosperity set in. The bubble burst in 1881, when the *Kaitakushi* was dissolved, since which time the government of the island has undergone repeated reorganisation.

Yezo is interesting from a scientific point of view. The great depth of the Straits of Tsugaru, which separate it from the Main Island, shows that it never—at least in recent geological epochs—formed part of Japan proper. The fauna of the two islands is accordingly marked by notable differences. Japan has monkeys and pheasants, which Yezo has not. Yezo has grouse, which Japan has not. Even the fossils differ on both sides of the straits, though occurring in similar cretaceous formations. Scientific, or rather unscientific, management played a queer trick with the city of Sapporo, if the local gossips are to be credited. The intention—so it is said—was to lay out the city *à l'américaine,* with streets running due north and south and due east and west. The person entrusted with the orientation of the plan was of course aware of the necessity of allowing for the deviation of the compass; but being under the influence of some misconception, he made the allowance the wrong way, and thus, instead of eliminating the error, doubled it. It is pleasant to be able to add that the result was a practical improvement undreamt of by the mathematicians. The houses, having no rooms either due north or due south, suffer less from the extremes of heat and cold than they would have done had they been built with some rooms on which the sun never shone, and others exposed to the sun all the year round.*

Book recommended. *The Wonderful World of Netsuke: With One Hundred Masterpieces of Miniature Sculpture in Color* by Raymond Bushell.

Yoshiwara. When Yedo suddenly rose into splendour at the beginning of the seventeenth century, people of all classes and from all parts of the country flocked thither to seek their fortune. The courtesans were not behindhand. From Kyōto, from Nara, from Fushimi, they arrived—so the native accounts inform us—in little parties of threes and fours. But a band of some twenty or thirty from the town of Moto-Yoshiwara on the Tōkaidō were either the most numerous or the most beautiful; and so the district of Yedo where they took up their abode came to be called the Yoshiwara.† At first there was no official supervision of these frail ladies. They were free to ply their trade wherever they chose. But in the year 1617, on the representations of a reformer named Shōji Jin-emon, the city in general was purified, and all the libertinism in it— permitted, but regulated—was banished to one special quarter near Nihonbashi, to which the name of Yoshiwara attached itself. This segregative system, which became general and permanent, has had at least one excellent result:—the Japanese streets at night exhibit none of those scenes of brazen-faced solicitation to vice which disgrace our Western cities. Later on, in A.D. 1656, when the metropolis had grown larger and Nihonbashi had become its centre, the authorities caused the houses in question to be removed to their present site on the northern limit of Yedo, whence the name of *Shin* (i.e. New) *Yoshiwara,* by which the place is currently known. Foreigners

---

* A specialist in such matters calls our attention to the fact that the story has, as the common phrase is, " not a leg to stand on," for the reason that the deviation of the compass is so slight in this part of the world as to be practically insignificant even when doubled. We leave the story, however, as an instance of modern myth-making.

† The weight of authority is in favour of this account of the origin of the name. According to others, the etymology is *yoshi*, " a reed," and *hara*, " a moor," and the designation of " reedy moor " would have been given to the locality on account of its aspect before it was built over. There is another Chinese character *yoshi* meaning " good," " lucky;" and with this the first two syllables of the name are now usually written 吉 原

often speak of "*a* Yoshiwara," as if the word were a generic
term. It is not so. The quarters of similar character in other
parts of Japan are never so called by the Japanese themselves.
Such words as *yūjoba* and *kuruwa* are used to designate them.

Japanese literature is full of romantic stories in which the
Yoshiwara plays a part. Generally the heroine has found her
way there in obedience to the dictates of filial piety in order to
support her aged parents, or else she is kidnapped by some
ruffian who basely sells her for his own profit. The story often
ends by the girl emerging from a life of shame with at least
her heart untainted, and by the good people living happily ever
after. It is to be feared that real life witnesses few such
fortunate cases, though it is probably true that the fallen
women of Japan are, as a class, much less vicious than their
representatives in Western lands, being neither drunken nor
foul-mouthed. On the other hand, a Japanese proverb says
that a truthful courtesan is as great a miracle as a square egg.

In former times, girls could be and were regularly and legally
sold into debauchery at the Yoshiwara in Yedo and at its
counterparts throughout the land,—a state of things which the
present enlightened government hastened to reform. Towards
the close of the nineteenth century, an agitation against the
whole system was begun by the missionaries, notably by the
Japan branch of the Salvation Army, supported by a section
of the Tōkyō press. It bore fruit in 1900, in the passing of a
new law enabling any girl to free herself at once from the
fetters of shame by a mere declaration of that intention to the
police. Over 400 in Tōkyō alone immediately had recourse to
the means of liberation thus unexpectedly provided, and before
the end of the year over 1,100 had left with or without the
consent of the keepers of the brothels. In fact, the rush became
so great that many houses had to close their doors. When we
add that a weekly medical inspection of the inmates of all
such places had been introduced as early as 1874 in imitation
of European ways, that each house and each separate inmate
of each house is heavily taxed, and that there is severe police

control over all,—we have mentioned all that need here be said on a subject which could only be adequately discussed in the pages of a medical work. Those interested in this particular department of sociology will find full and curious details in *The Nightless City*, published anonymously at Yokohama in 1899.

Zoology.   Japan is distinguished by the possession of some types elsewhere extinct—for example, the giant salamander— and also as being the most northerly country inhabited by the monkey, which here ranges as high as the 41st degree of latitude, in places where the snow often drifts to a depth of fifteen or twenty feet.   But in its main features the Japanese fauna resembles that of North China, Korea, and Manchuria, —one indication among many of the direction in which the ancient land connection of Japan with the Asiatic continent must be sought.   The Japanese fauna, both terrestrial and marine, is unusually rich.   Take a single instance:—there are already 137 species of butterflies known, as against some 60 in Great Britain, and over 4,000 species of moths, as against some 2,000 in Great Britain.

The chief mammals are the monkey *(Inuus speciosus Tem.)*, ten species of bats, six species of insectivorous animals, three species of bears, the badger, the marten, the mink *(itachi)*, the wolf, the fox, two species of squirrel, the rat, the hare, the wild-boar, the otter, a species of stag, and a species of antelope. Most of our domestic animals are also met with, but not the ass, the sheep, or the goat.   Other missing animals are the wild cat and the hedgehog.   No less than 359 species of birds have been enumerated.   We can only here call attention to the uguisu *(Cettia cantans* T. and Schl.)—a nightingale having a different note from ours—to the handsome copper pheasant, to the long-tailed fowls (see Article so entitled), and to the cranes and herons so beloved by the artists of Japan.

Of reptiles and batrachians there are but 30 species.   Of these, the already mentioned giant salamander is by far the

most remarkable, some specimens attaining to a length of over
5 ft., and a weight of over 14 lbs. There are also some large,
but harmless, snakes. The only poisonous snake is a small
species of adder *(Trigonocephalus Blomhoffi)*, known to the
Japanese under the name of *mamushi.* The country folk look
on its boiled flesh as a specific for most diseases. The peasants
of certain thickly wooded districts also harbour an inveterate
belief in the existence of a kind of boa, which they call
uwabami, and circumstantial accounts of the swallowing alive
of some child or woman by one of these monsters appear from
time to time in the vernacular press. Zoologists, however, have
not yet given the Japanese boa official permission to exist.
Another creature undoubtedly mythical is the bushy-tailed
tortoise so often depicted in Japanese art. The idea of it was
probably suggested by nothing more recondite than the
straggling water-weeds that sometimes adhere to the hinder
parts of a real tortoise's body.

With regard to fish, Dr. Rein remarks that the Chinese and
Japanese waters appear to be richer than any other part of
the ocean. The mackerel family *(Scomberoidæ)*, more
particularly, is represented in great force, the 40 species into
which it is divided constituting an important element of the
food of the people. But the fish which is esteemed the greatest
delicacy is the tai, a kind of gold-bream. The gold-fish, the
salmon, the eel, the shark, and many others would call for
mention, had we space to devote to them. Altogether, the
number of species of fish inhabiting or visiting Japan cannot
fall far short of 400.

Insects are extremely numerous, but, excepting the beetles,
moths, and butterflies, are not yet even fairly well-known, so
that a rich harvest here awaits some future naturalist. There
are two silk-producing moths, the *Bombyx mori* and the
Antheræa yamamai. Of dragon-flies the species are numerous
and beautiful. There are but few venomous insects. The
gadfly torments the traveller only in Yezo and in the northern
half of the Main Island; the house-fly is a much less common

plague than in Europe, except in the silk districts, and the bed-bug is entirely absent. On the other hand, the mosquito is a nightly plague during half the year in all places lying at an altitude of less than 1,500 feet above the sea, and in many even exceeding that height; the *buyu*—a diminutive kind of gnat—infests many mountainous districts during the summer months, and the flea is unpleasantly common in summer.

The chief crustacea are fresh-water and salt-water crabs, together with crayfishes, which here replace the lobsters of Europe and are often erroneously termed lobsters by the foreign residents. One species of crab (the *Macrocheirus Kœmpferi Sbd.*) is so gigantic that human beings have been killed and devoured by it. It legs are over a yard and a half in length. There is another species—a tiny, but ill-favoured one—which is the object of a singular superstition. The common folk call it *Heike-gani,* that is, the Heike crab. They believe these creatures to be the wraiths of the Heike or Taira partisans, whose fleet was annihilated at the battle of Dan-no-ura in A.D. 1185.

Of molluscs, nearly 1,200 species have been described by Dunker, the best authority on the subject; and his enumeration is stated by Dr. Rein to be far from exhaustive. Of sea-urchins 26 species are known, and of starfishes 12 species. The coral tribe is well represented, though not by the reef-forming species of warmer latitudes. There are also various kinds of sponges. Indeed, one of the most curious and beautiful of all the many curious and beautiful things in Japan is the Glass Rope Sponge *(Hyalonema Sieboldi),* whose silken coils adorn the shell-shops at Enoshima.

The rapid extinction of many living creatures in Japan is scarcely less matter for regret than the cutting down of the forests to furnish railway sleepers and materials for the manufacture of paper. The deer have been practically exterminated since the present writer came to live in the country, and so have the herons. As for the cranes, they seem to have been all either killed or frightened away during the late sixties, when they ceased to be preserved as a royal bird. The pheasants have sadly diminished in number, owing to wholesale slaughter with the object of exporting their feathers to grace ladies' bonnets in foreign lands; and various species of small birds are now sharing the same fate, as many as a hundred thousand at a time being, it is said, shipped off that the tiny feathers may be dyed various colours and set to various uses in female adornment or art manufacture. Such are some of the drawbacks of foreign intercourse and of cheap and rapid transport. Europeanisation is not all gain. The European tourists seeks distant lands with intent to admire nature and art. But nature is laid waste for his sake or for the sake of his friends at home, while art is degraded and ultimately destroyed by the mere fact of contact with alien influences.

APPENDIX

THE INVENTION OF A NEW RELIGION*

This was written by Prof. Chamberlain and first published by The Rationalist Press Association of London in the year 1912, and is here reprinted by their kind permission.

Voltaire and the other eighteenth-century philosophers, who held religions to be the invention of priests, have been scorned as superficial by later investigators. But was there not something in their view, after all. Have not we, of a later and more critical day, got into so inveterate a habit of digging deep that we sometimes fail to see what lies before our very noses. Modern Japan is there to furnish an example. The Japanese are, it is true, commonly said to be an irreligious people. They say so themselves. Writes one of them, the celebrated Fukuzawa, teacher and type of the modern educated Japanese man: "I lack a religious nature, and have never believed in any religion." A score of like pronouncements might be quoted from other leading men. The average, even educated, European strikes the average educated Japanese as strangely superstitious, unaccountably occupied with supra-mundane matters. The Japanese simply cannot be brought to comprehend how a "mere parson" such as the Pope, or even the Archbishop of Canterbury, occupies the place he does in politics and society. Yet this same agnostic Japan is teaching us at this very hour how religions are sometimes manufactured for a special end—to subserve practical worldly purposes.

Mikado-worship and Japan-worship—for that is the new Japanese religion—is, of course, no spontaneously generated

---

* The writer of this pamphlet could but skim over a wide subject. For full information see Volume I. of Mr. J. Murdoch's recently-published *History of Japan*, the only critical work on that subject existing in the English language.

phenomenon. Every manufacture presupposes a material out of which it is made, every present a past on which it rests. But the twentieth-century Japanese religion of loyalty and patriotism is quite new, for in it pre-existing ideas have been sifted, altered, freshly compounded, turned to new uses, and have found a new centre of gravity. Not only is it new, it is not yet completed; it is still in process of being consciously or semi-consciously put together by the official class, in order to serve the interests of that class, and, incidentally, the interests of the nation at large. The Japanese bureaucracy is a body greatly to be admired. It includes most of the foremost men of the nation. Like the priesthood in later Judæa, to some extent like the Egyptian and Indian priesthoods, it not only governs, but aspires, to lead in intellectual matters. It has before it a complex task. On the one hand, it must make good to the outer world the new claim that Japan differs in no essential way from the nations of the West, unless, indeed, it be by way of superiority. On the other hand, it has to manage restive steeds at home, where ancestral ideas and habits clash with new dangers arising from an alien material civilisation hastily absorbed.

Down to the year 1888, the line of cleavage between governors and governed was obscured by the joyful ardour with which all classes alike devoted themselves to the acquisition of European, not to say American, ideas. Everything foreign was then hailed as perfect—everything old and national was condemned. Sentiment grew democratic, in so far (perhaps it was not very far) as American democratic ideals were understood. Love of country seemed likely to yield to a humble bowing down before foreign models. Officialdom not unnaturally took fright at this abdication of national individualism. Evidently something must be done to turn the tide. Accordingly, patriotic sentiment was appealed to through the throne, whose hoary antiquity had ever been a source of pride to Japanese literati, who loved to dwell on the contrast between Japan's unique line of absolute monarchs and the short-lived dynasties of

China. Shintō, a primitive nature cult, which had fallen into discredit, was taken out of its cupboard and dusted. The common people, it is true, continued to place their affections on Buddhism, the popular festivals were Buddhist, Buddhist also the temples where they buried their dead. The governing class determined to change all this. They insisted on the Shintō doctrine that the Mikado descends in direct succession from the native Goddess of the Sun, and that he himself is a living God on earth who justly claims the absolute fealty of his subjects. Such things as laws and constitutions are but free gifts on His part, not in any sense popular rights. Of course, the ministers and officials, high and low, who carry on His government, are to be regarded not as public servants, but rather as executants of supreme—one might say supernatural—authority. Shintō, because connected with the Imperial Family, is to be alone honoured. Therefore, the important right of burial, never before possessed by it, was granted to its priests. Later on, the right of marriage was granted likewise—an entirely novel departure in a land where marriage had never been more than a civil contract. Thus the Shintō priesthood was encouraged to penetrate into the intimacy of family life, while in another direction it encroached on the field of ethics by borrowing bits here and there from Confucian and even from Christian sources. Under a *régime* of ostensible religious toleration, the attendance of officials at certain Shintō services was required, and the practice was established in all schools of bowing down several times yearly before the Emperor's picture. Meanwhile Japanese politics had prospered; her warriors had gained great victories. Enormous was the prestige thus accruing to Imperialism and to the rejuvenated Shintō cult. All military successes were ascribed to the miraculous influence of the Emperor's virtue, and to the virtues of His Imperial and divine ancestors—that is, of former Emperors and of Shintō deities. Imperial envoys were regularly sent after each great victory to carry the good tidings to the Sun Goddess at her great shrine at Ise. Not there alone, but at the other principal Shintō shrines throughout the land, the cannon captured from Chinese or Russian foes were officially installed, with a view to identifying Imperialism, Shintō, and national glory in the popular mind. The new legend is enforced wherever feasible—for instance, by means of a new set of festivals celebrating Imperial official events.

But the schools are the great strongholds of the new propaganda. History is so taught to the young as to focus everything upon Imperialism, and to diminish as far as possible the contrast between ancient and modern conditions. The same is true of the instruction given to army and navy recruits. Thus, though Shintō is put in the forefront, little stress is laid on its mythology, which would be apt to shock even the Japanese mind at the present day. To this extent, where a purpose useful to the ruling class is to be served, criticism is practised, though not avowedly. Far different is the case with so-called "historical facts," such as the alleged foundation of the Monarchy in 660 B.C. and similar statements paralleled only for absurdity by what passed for history in mediæval Europe, when King Lear, Brute, King of Britain, etc., were accepted as authentic personages. For the truth, known to all critical investigators, is that, instead of going back to a remote antiquity, the origins of Japanese history are recent as compared with that of European countries. The first glimmer of genuine Japanese history dates from the fifth century *after* Christ, and even the accounts of what happened in the sixth century must be received with caution. Japanese scholars know this as well as we do; it is one of the certain results of investigation. But the Japanese bureaucracy does not desire to have the light let in on this inconvenient circumstance. While granting a dispensation *re* the national mythology, properly so called, it exacts belief in every iota of the national historic legends. Woe to the native professor who strays from the path of orthodoxy. His wife and children (and in Japan every man, however young, has a wife and children) will starve. From the late Prince Ito's grossly misleading *Commentary on the Japanese Constitution* down to school compendiums, the absurd dates are everywhere insisted upon. This despite the fact that the mythology and the so-called early history are recorded in the same works, and are characterised by like miraculous impossibilities; that the chronology is palpably fraudulent; that the speeches put into the mouths of ancient Mikados are centos culled from the Chinese classics; that their names are in some cases derived from Chinese sources; and that the earliest Japanese historical narratives, the earliest known social usages, and even the centralised Imperial form of Government itself, are all stained through and through with a Chinese dye, so much so that it is no longer possible to determine what percentage of old native thought may still linger on in fragments here and there. In the face of all this, moral ideals, which were of common knowledge derived from the teaching of the Chinese sages, are now arbitrarily referred to the "Imperial Ancestors." Such, in particular, are loyalty and filial piety— the two virtues on which, in the Far-Eastern world, all the others rest. It is, furthermore, officially taught that, from the earliest ages, perfect concord has always subsisted in Japan between beneficient sovereigns on the one hand, and a gratefully loyal people on the other. Never, it is alleged, has Japan been soiled by the disobedient and rebellious acts common in other countries; while at the same time the Japanese nation, sharing to some extent in the supernatural virtues of its rulers, has been distinguished by a high-minded chivalry called *Bushido*, unknown in inferior lands.

Such is the fabric of ideas which the official class is busy building up by every means in its power, including the punishment of those who presume to stickle for historic truth.

* * * * *

The sober fact is that no nation probably has ever treated its sovereigns more cavalierly than the Japanese have done, from the beginning of authentic history down to within the memory of living men.

Emperors have been deposed, emperors have been assassinated; for centuries every succession to the throne was

the signal for intrigues and sanguinary broils. Emperors
have been exiled; some have been murdered in exile. From
the remote island to which he had been relegated one managed
to escape, hidden under a load of dried fish. In the fourteenth
century, things came to such a pass that two rival Imperial
lines defied each other for the space of fifty-eight years—the
so-called Northern and Southern Courts; and it was the
Northern Court, branded by later historians as usurping and
illegitimate, that ultimately won the day, and handed on the
Imperial regalia to its successors. After that, as indeed before
that, for long centuries the government was in the hands of
Mayors of the Palace, who substituted one infant Sovereign
for another, generally forcing each to abdicate as soon as
he approached man's estate. At one period, these Mayors of
the Palace left the Descendant of the Sun in such distress
that His Imperial Majesty and the Imperial Princes were
obliged to gain a livelihood by selling their autographs ! Nor
did any great party in the State protest against this condition
of affairs. Even in the present reign—the most glorious in
Japanese history—there have been two rebellions, during one
of which a rival Emperor was set up in one part of the
country, and a republic proclaimed in another.

As for Bushido, so modern a thing is it that neither
Kaempfer, Siebold, Satow, nor Rein—all men knowing their
Japan by heart—ever once allude to it in their voluminous
writings. The cause of their silence is not far to seek: Bushido
was unknown until a decade or two ago !

*The very word appears in no dictionary, native or foreign,
before the year 1900.* Chivalrous individuals of course existed
in Japan, as in all countries at every period; but Bushido,
as an institution or a code of rules, has never existed. The
accounts given of it have been fabricated out of whole cloth,
chiefly for foreign consumption. An analysis of medieval
Japanese history shows that the great feudal houses, so far
from displaying an excessive idealism in the matter of fealty
to one emperor, one lord, or one party, had evolved the
eminently practical plan of letting their different members

take different sides, so that the family as a whole might come out as winner in any event, and thus avoid the confiscation of its lands. Cases, no doubt, occurred of devotion to losing causes—for example, to Mikados in disgrace; but they were less common than in the more romantic West.

Thus, within the space of a short lifetime, the new Japanese religion of loyalty and patriotism has emerged into the light of day. The feats accomplished during the late war with Russia show that the simple ideal which it offers is capable of inspiring great deeds. From a certain point of view the nation may be congratulated on its new possession.

*   *   *   *   *

The new Japanese religion consists, in its present early stage, of worship of the sacrosanct Imperial Person and of His Divine Ancestors, of implicit obedience to Him as head of the army (a position, by the way, opposed to all former Japanese ideas, according to which the Court was essentially civilian) ; furthermore, of a corresponding belief that Japan is as far superior to the common ruck of nations as the Mikado is divinely superior to the common ruck of kings and emperors. Do not the early history-books record the fact that Japan was created first, while all other countries resulted merely from the drops that fell from the creator's spear when he had finished his main work. And do not the later annals prove that true valour belongs to the Japanese knight alone, whereas foreign countries—China and Europe alike—are sunk in a degrading commercialism. For the inhabitants of " the Land of the Gods " to take any notice of such creatures by adopting a few of their trifling mechanical inventions is an act of gracious condescension.

To quote but one official utterance out of a hundred, Baron Oura, minister of agriculture and commerce, writes thus in February of last year:—

> That the majesty of our Imperial House towers high above everything to be found in the world, and that it is as durable as heaven and earth, is too well known to need dwelling on here. . . . If it is considered that our country needs a religious

faith, then, I say, let it be converted to a belief in the religion of patriotism and loyalty, the religion of Imperialism—in other words, to Emperor-worship.

The Rev. Dr. Ebina,* one of the leading lights of the Protestant pastorate in Japan, plunges more deeply still into this doctrine, according to which, as already noted, the whole Japanese nation is, in a manner, apotheosised. Says he:—

> Though the encouragement of ancestor-worship cannot be regarded as part of the essential teaching of Christianity (!), it†
> is not opposed to the notion that, when the Japanese Empire was founded, its early rulers were in communication with the Great Spirit that rules the universe. Christians, according to this theory, without doing violence to their creed, may acknowledge that the Japanese nation has a divine origin. It is only when we realise that the Imperial Ancestors were in close communion with God (or the Gods), that we understand how sacred is the country in which we live. [Dr. Ebina ends by recommending the Imperial Rescript on Education as a text for Christian sermons.]

It needs no comment of ours to point out how thoroughly the nation must be saturated by the doctrines under discussion for such amazing utterances to be possible. If so-called Christians can think thus, the non-Christian majority must indeed be devout Emperor-worshippers and Japan-worshippers. Such the go-ahead portion of the nation undoubtedly is—the students, the army, the navy, the emigrants to Japan's new foreign possessions, all the more ardent spirits. The peasantry, as before noted, occupy themselves little with new thoughts, clinging rather to the Buddhist beliefs of their forefathers. But nothing could be further removed from even their minds than the ideas of offering any organised resistance to the propaganda going on around them.

As a matter of fact, the spread of the new ideas has been easy, because a large class derives power from their diffusion, while to oppose them is the business of no one in particular. Moreover, the distinterested love of truth for its own sake

---

* We quote from the translation given by Mr. Walter Dening in one of the invaluable *Summaries of Current Japanese Literature*, contributed by him from time to time to the columns of the *Japan Mail*, Yokohama.

† " It " means Christianity.

is rare; the patience to unearth it is rarer still, especially in the East. Patriotism, too, is a mighty engine working in the interests of credulity. How should men not believe in a system that produces such excellent practical results, a system which has united all the scattered elements of national feeling into one focus, and has thus created a powerful instrument for the attainment of national aims. Meanwhile a generation is growing up which does not so much as suspect that its cherished beliefs are inventions of yesterday.

The new religion, in its present stage, still lacks one important item—a sacred book. Certain indications show that this lacuna will be filled by the elevation of the more important Imperial Rescripts to that rank, accompanied doubtless by an authoritative commentary, as their style is too abstruse to be understanded of the people. To these Imperial Rescripts some of the poems composed by his present Majesty may be added. In fact, a volume on the whole duty of Japanese man, with selected Imperial poems as texts, has already appeared.*

*　　*　　*　　*　　*

One might have imagined that Japan's new religionists would have experienced some difficulty in persuading foreign nations of the truth of their dogmas. Things have fallen out otherwise. Europe and America evince a singular taste for the marvellous, and find a zest in self-depreciation. Our eighteenth-century ancestors imagined all perfections to be realised in China, thanks to the glowing descriptions then given of that country by the Jesuits. Twentieth-century Europe finds its moral and political Eldorado in distant Japan, a land of fabulous antiquity and incredible virtues. There is no lack of pleasant-mannered persons ready to guide trustful admirers in the right path. Official and semi-official Japanese, whether ambassadors and ministers-resident or

---

* For over a thousand years the composition of Japanese and Chinese verse has formed part of a liberal education, like the composition of Latin verse among ourselves. The Court has always devoted much time to the practice of this art. But the poems of former Emperors were little known, because the monarchs themselves remained shut up in their palace, and exercised no influence beyond its walls. With his present Majesty the case is entirely different. Moreover, some of his compositions breathe a patriotism formerly undreamt of.

peripatetic counts and barons, make it their business to spread a legend so pleasing to the national vanity, so useful as a diplomatic engine. Lectures are delivered, books are written in English, important periodicals are bought up, minute care is lavished on the concealment, the patching-up, and glossing-over of the deep gulf that nevertheless is fixed between East and West. The foreigner cannot refuse the bolus thus artfully forced down his throat. He is not suspicious by nature. How should he imagine that people who make such positive statements about their own country are merely exploiting his credulity ? *He* has reached a stage of culture where such mythopœia has become impossible. On the other hand, to control information by consulting original sources lies beyond his capacity.

For consider this peculiar circumstance: the position of European investigators *vis-à-vis* Japan differs entirely from that of Japanese *vis-à-vis* Europe. The Japanese possess every facility for studying and understanding Europe. Europeans are warded off by well-nigh insuperable obstacles from understanding Japan. Europe stands on a hill-top, in the sunlight, glittering afar. Her people court inspection. " Come and see how we live "—such was a typical invitation which the present writer recently received. A thousand English homes are open to any Japanese student or traveller who visits our shores. An alphabet of but six-and-twenty simple letters throws equally wide open to him a literature clearly revealing our thoughts, so that he who runs may read. Japan lies in the shadow, away on the rim of the world. Her houses are far more effectually closed to the stranger by their paper shutters than are ours by walls of brick or stones. What we call " society " does not exist there. Her people, though smiling and courteous, surround themselves by an atmosphere of reserve, centuries of despotic government having rendered them suspicious and reticent. True, when a foreigner of importance visits Japan—some British M.P., perhaps, whose name figures often in the newspapers, or an American editor, or the president of a great American college—this personage is charmingly received. But he is never left free to form his own opinion of things, even were he capable of so doing. Circumstances spin an invisible web around him, his hosts being keenly intent on making him a speaking-trumpet for the proclamation of their own views.

Again, Japan's non-Aryan speech, marvellously intricate, almost defies acquisition. Suppose this difficult vernacular mastered; the would-be student discovers that literary works, even newspapers and ordinary correspondence, are not composed in it, but in another dialect, partly antiquated, partly artificial, differing as widely from the colloquial speech as Latin does from Italian. Make a second hazardous supposition. Assume that the grammar and vocabulary of this second indispensable Japanese language have been learnt, in addition to the first. You are still but at the threshold of your task, Japanese thought having barricaded itself behind the fortress walls of an extraordinarily complicated system of writing, compared with which Egyptian hieroglyphics are child's play. Yet next to nothing can be found out by a foreigner unless he have this, too, at his fingers' end. As a matter of fact, scarcely anyone acquires it—only a missionary here and there, or a consular official with a life appointment.

The result of all this is that, whereas the Japanese know everything that it imports them to know about us, Europeans cannot know much about them, such information as they receive being always belated, necessarily meagre, and mostly adulterated to serve Japanese interests. International relations placed—and, we repeat it, inevitably placed—on this footing resemble a boxing match in which one of the contestants should have his hands tied. But the metaphor fails in an essential point, as metaphors are apt to do—the hand-tied man does not realise the disadvantage under which he labours. He thinks himself as free as his opponent.

Thus does it come about that the neo-Japanese myths concerning dates, and Emperors, and heroes, and astonishing national virtues already begin to find their way into popular English text-books, current literature, and even grave books of reference. The Japanese governing class has willed it so, and in such matters the Japanese governing class can enforce its will abroad as well as at home. The statement may sound paradoxical. Study the question carefully, and you will find that it is simply true.

*   *   *   *   *

What is happening in Japan to-day is evidently exceptional. Normal religious and political change does not proceed in that manner; it proceeds by imperceptible degrees. But exceptions to general rules occur from time to time in every field of activity. Are they really exceptions, using that term in its current sense—to denote something arbitrary, and therefore unaccountable ? Surely these so-called exceptions are but examples of rules of rarer application.

The classic instance of the invention of a new national religion is furnished by the Jews of the post-exilic period. The piecing together, then, of a brand-new system under an ancient name is now so well understood, and has produced consequences of such world-wide importance, that the briefest reference to it may suffice. Works which every critic can now see to be relatively modern were ascribed to Moses, David, or Daniel; intricate laws and ordinances that had never been practised—could never be practised—were represented as ancient institutions; a whole new way of thinking and acting was set in motion on the assumption that it was old. Yet, so far as is known, no one in or out of Palestine ever saw through the illusion for over two thousand years. It was reserved for nineteenth-century scholars to draw aside the veil hiding the real facts of the case.

Modern times supply another instance, less important than the first, but remarkable enough. Rousseau came in the middle of the eighteenth century, and preached a doctrine that took the world by storm, and soon precipitated that world in ruins. How did he discover his gospel. He tells us quite naïvely :—

All the rest of the day, buried in the forest, I sought, I found there the image of primitive ages, whose history I boldly traced. I made havoc of men's petty lies; I dared to unveil and strip naked man's true nature, to follow up the course of time and of the circumstances that have disfigured it, and, comparing man as men have made him with man as nature made him, to demonstrate that the so-called improvements [of civilisation] have been the source of all his woes, etc.*

In other words, he spun a pseudo-history from his own brain. What is stranger, he fanatically believed in this his pure invention, and, most extraordinary of all, persuaded other people to believe in it as fanatically. It was taken up as a religion, it inspired heroes, and enabled a barefoot rabble to beat the finest regular armies in the world. Even now, at a distance of a century and a half, its embers still glow.

Of course, it is not pretended that these various systems of religion were *arbitrary* inventions. No more were they so than the cloud palaces that we sometimes see swiftly form in the sky and as swiftly dissolve. The germ of Rousseau's ideas can be traced back to Fénelon and other seventeenth-century thinkers, weary of the pomp and periwigs around them. Rousseau himself did but fulfil the aspiration of a whole society for something simpler, juster, more true to nature, more logical. He gave exactly what was needed at that moment of history— what appeared self-evident; wherefore no one so much as thought of asking for detailed proofs. His deism, his statements concerning the " state of nature " and the " social contract," etc., were at once recognised by the people of his day as eternal verities. What need for discussion or investigation ?

The case of Judæa is obscure; but it would seem that something analogous must have happened there, when the continuity of national life had been snapped by the exile. A revolutionised and unhappy present involved a changed attitude towards the past. Oral tradition and the scraps of written records that had survived the shipwreck of the kingdom fell, as it were, naturally into another order. The kaleidoscope having been turned, the pattern changed to itself. A few gifted individuals voiced the enthusiasm of a whole community,

---

* *Confessions*, Book VIII, year 1753.

when they adopted literary methods which would now, in our comparatively stable days, be branded as fraudulent. They simply could not help themselves. The pressing need of constructing a national polity for the present on the only basis then possible—Yahwe worship—*forced* them into falsifying the past. The question was one of life and death for the Jewish nationality.

Europeans there are in Japan—Europeanised Japanese likewise—who feel outraged by the action of the Japanese bureaucracy in the matter of the new cult, with all the illiberal and obscurantist measures which it entails. That is natural. We modern Westerners love individual liberty, and the educated among us love to let the sunlight of criticism into every nook and cranny of every subject. Freedom and scientific accuracy are our gods. But Japanese officialdom acts quite naturally, after its kind, is not allowing the light to be let in, because the roots of the faith it has planted need darkness in which to grow and spread. No religion can live which is subjected to critical scrutiny.

Thus also are explained the rigours of the Japanese bureaucracy against the native liberals, who, in its eyes, appear, not simply as political opponents, but as traitors to the chosen people—sacrilegious heretics defying the authority of the One and Only True Church.

" But," you will say, " this indignation must be mere pretence. Not even officials can be so stupid as to believe in things which they have themselves invented." We venture to think that you are wrong here. People can always believe that which it is greatly to their interest to believe. Thousands of excellent persons in our own society cling to the doctrine of a future life on no stronger evidence. It is enormously important to the Japanese ruling class that the mental attitude sketched above should become universal among their countrymen. Accordingly, they achieve the apparently impossible. " We believe in it, although we know that it is not true." Tertullian said nearly the same thing, and no one has ever doubted *his* sincerity.

INDEX.

¶ When there are several references, the most important is given first.